Praise for *Theology of the Body Explained*

"In my biography of the Pope, I wrote that the theology of the body needed explication for those who weren't specialists in biblical studies, theology, or philosophy. I am delighted that Christopher West has taken up that challenge. With intellectual care, with the experience bred of long years of teaching this material in the classroom and the parish, and taking account of his own experiences as a husband and father, Christopher West has put us in his debt by making the 'theology of the body' available to a wide and, I hope, appreciative readership."

— From the foreword to the first edition by George Weigel,
Senior Fellow, Ethics and Public Policy Center, Washington, D.C.

"This book will be of enormous pastoral value to those seeking to put forth the Church's liberating teachings on sexuality. Reading John Paul's text directly can be quite daunting for those without a background in philosophy and theology. This is what makes this book so exciting—it succeeds in 'translating' the Holy Father's insights into a much more accessible language."

— Monsignor Lorenzo Albacete,
Founding Professor, John Paul II Institute for Studies on Marriage and Family, Washington, D.C.

"John Paul II's theology of the body offers a powerful resource for evangelization in an age which is beginning to count the cost of the sexual revolution. Christopher West's book makes this resource available for the first time to people at all levels within the Christian community. Love, sexuality, and human flourishing are inseparable. Those who have doubted this will find West's book a transforming experience, and those who have been wounded will find in it liberation, healing, and peace."

— George Cardinal Pell,
Archbishop of Sydney, Australia

Also by Christopher West

Good News About Sex and Marriage: Answers to Your Honest Questions About Catholic Teaching

Theology of the Body for Beginners: A Basic Introduction to John Paul II's Sexual Revolution

The Love That Satisfies: Reflections on Eros and Agape (based on Benedict XVI's *Deus Caritas Est*)

REVISED EDITION

Theology of the Body Explained

A Commentary on John Paul II's
Man and Woman He Created Them

Christopher West

With a Foreword by Michael Waldstein

Pauline
BOOKS & MEDIA
Boston

Nihil Obstat: Dr. William May, Ph.D.
Imprimatur: ✠ Seán Cardinal O'Malley, O.F.M. Cap.
Archbishop of Boston
August 6, 2007

Library of Congress Cataloging-in-Publication Data

West, Christopher, 1969–
   Theology of the body explained : a commentary on John Paul II's Man and woman He created them / Christopher West ; foreword by Michael Waldstein. — 2nd ed.
      p. cm.
   ISBN 0-8198-7425-6 (pbk.)
   1. John Paul II, Pope, 1920–2005. Theology of the body. 2. Body, Human—Religious aspects—Catholic Church. 3. Catholic Church—Doctrines. I. Title.
   BX1795.B63W47 2007
   233'.5—dc22

                                                2007026223

The Scripture quotations contained herein are from the *New Revised Standard Version Bible: Catholic Edition*, copyright © 1989, 1993, Division of Christian Education of the National Council of the Churches of Christ in the United States of America. Used by permission. All rights reserved.

Excerpts from the English translation of the *Catechism of the Catholic Church* for use in the United States of America, copyright © 1994, United States Catholic Conference, Inc. —Libreria Editrice Vaticana. Used with permission.

Unless otherwise noted, all the excerpts from John Paul II's writings and Benedict XVI's writings are Copyright © Libreria Editrice Vaticana and are used with permission.

Excerpts from the following are used with permission:

Dooley, David, ed. *The Collected Works of G. K. Chesterton.* Volume I. San Francisco: Ignatius, 1986. (Used with permission of the Royal Literary Fund, England.)

Derrick, Christopher. *Sex and Sacredness.* San Francisco: Ignatius Press, 1982.

John Paul II. *Crossing the Threshold of Hope.* New York: Alfred A. Knopf/ Random House, 1994.

John Paul II. *Memory and Identity.* New York: Rizzoli Books, 2005.

John Paul II. *Rise, Let Us Be on Our Way.* New York: Warner Books, 2004.

Kreeft, Peter. *Everything You Ever Wanted to Know about Heaven.* San Francisco: Ignatius Press, 1990.

Ratzinger, Joseph. *The Spirit of the Liturgy.* San Francisco, CA: Ignatius Press, 2000.

Springtime of Evangelization: The Complete Texts of the Holy Father's 1998 Ad Limina Addresses to the Bishops of the United States. San Diego, CA: Basilica Press, 1999.

Swiezawski, Stefan. *Person and Community: Selected Essays,* trans. Theresa Sandok. New York: Peter Lang, 1993.

Weigel, George. *Witness to Hope.* Copyright © 1999 by George Weigel. Reprinted by permission of HarperCollins Publishers.

Wojtyla, Karol. *Love and Responsibility.* San Francisco: Ignatius Press, 1993. (Used with permission of Farrar, Straus & Giroux.)

Wojtyla, Karol. *Sources of Renewal.* San Francisco: Harper & Row, 1979.

Cover design by Rosana Usselmann

Cover art: Michelangelo Buonarroti (1475–1564). The Sistine Chapel; ceiling frescoes after restoration. *The Creation of Adam.* Sistine Chapel, Vatican Palace, Vatican State. Photo credit: Erich Lessing / Art Resource, NY.

Published by Pauline Books & Media, 50 Saint Paul's Avenue, Boston, MA 02130-3491. www.pauline.org.
Printed in the U.S.A.

Pauline Books & Media is the publishing house of the Daughters of St. Paul, an international congregation of women religious serving the Church with the communications media.

2 3 4 5 6 7 8 9   15 14 13 12 11

For my brother, Nathan Paul Gardner West,
and with gratitude to God
for the life of Karol Josef Wojtyla

Contents

Acknowledgments xxiii

Acknowledgments to the First Edition xxv

Foreword by Michael Waldstein xxvii

Foreword to the First Edition by George Weigel xxxiii

Introduction 1
Need for a Revised Edition 3

PROLOGUE
The Human Body, Catholicism, and John Paul II 7
1. What Is the Theology of the Body? 9
    The Wednesday Catechesis 9
    The "Crisis of the Body"..................................... 11
    The Gospel of the Body 14

2. What Makes the Human Body "Theological"? 15
    The Sacramentality of the Body............................... 15
    Sign of the Mystery Hidden in God 17
    The Marriage of Theology and Anthropology 21
    The Scandal of the Body 22

3. The Great Spousal Analogy 23

God Wants to "Marry" Us 23

Understanding the Spousal Analogy Properly 28

The Particular Value of the Spousal Analogy 29

Influence of St. John of the Cross 31

Personalism and the Sincere Gift of Self. 34

4. The Spiritual Battle 36

Plagiarizing the Primordial Sacrament 36

The Symbolic and the Diabolic 38

"Angelism" and "Animalism". 39

Integrating Body and Spirit 40

5. The Deepest Substratum of Ethics and Culture 42

At the Origins of Evil. 43

The Wellspring of Culture 44

Christ Heals the Rift. 46

Need for a Paradigm Shift 48

Man Cannot Live Without Love. 49

6. Wojtyla's Philosophical and Theological Project 51

The Modern "Turn Toward the Subject" 51

"Thomistic Personalism". 54

What Is Phenomenology? 56

Loving and Interiorizing the "Splendor of the Truth" 57

Saving the "Subjective Turn" from Subjectivism 60

Other Steps in Wojtyla's Thought 63

7. A Response to the Humanae Vitae Crisis 67

The Need for a "Total Vision of Man" 67

The Need for a Personalistic Ethic 70

The Personalistic Norm. 72

Structure of the Catechesis. 73

PROLOGUE—IN REVIEW 78

Part I

THE WORDS OF CHRIST

Chapter 1

Christ Appeals to the "Beginning"

[Cycle 1—Original Man] 87

1. What Is Meant by "Beginning"? 88
  Unity and Indissolubility 89
  Two Creation Accounts 90
  Continuity in the "Redemption of the Body" 92
  Revelation and Experience 94

2. The Meaning of Original Solitude 96
  A Twofold Meaning 96
  Man in Search of His Own Identity 97
  Objective-Subjective Harmony 98
  Partner of the Absolute 99
  The Alternative Between Death and Immortality 100
  The Body Expresses the Person 102

3. The Meaning of Original Unity 103
  The Unity of the Two 103
    The Meaning of Adam's "Sleep" 104
    The Meaning of Adam's Rib 105
  Communion of Persons 106
    Communion Overcomes and Affirms Solitude 107
    A Dramatic Development of Catholic Thought 108
  Theology of Sex 109
  Man as a Subject in Relation 111
  The Original Conjugal Act? 114
    Man's "Original Virginal Value" 116
    The Vital Power of Communion 120

4. The Meaning of Original Nakedness 120
  The Key to Biblical Anthropology 121
  Penetrating Their Experience 123

Shame as a Phenomenon 124

The Peace of the Interior Gaze 126

5. Man in the Dimension of Gift 128

A. The Spousal Meaning of the Body 128

Hermeneutics of the Gift 128

The Original Way of Living the Gift 129

Discovery of the "Spousal" Meaning of the Body 130

Incarnate Love 131

Revelation and Discovery of the Meaning of Life 132

The Freedom of the Gift 133

"Own Sake" and "Self Gift" 135

Spousal Meaning of the Body and the
Affirmation of the Person 136

Spousal Meaning of the Body: Rooted in Love 138

B. The Mystery of Original Innocence 139

Grace as a Gift to the Human Heart 139

Innocence and the Exchange of the Gift 141

Giving and Receiving Interpenetrate 142

The Ethos of the Human Body 144

Ethos and the Subjectivity of Man 146

Subjectivity and Purity 147

The Primordial Sacrament and the Body as "Sign" 148

The First Feast of Humanity 148

John Paul's Thesis Statement 149

6. "Knowledge" and Procreation (Gen 4:1) 153

The Meaning of "Knowledge" 153

Knowledge Leads to "a Third": Fatherhood and Motherhood 156

Eulogy of Femininity 157

Attack on Creative Love and the Perspective of Redemption 158

The Knowledge-Generation Cycle: Life Refuses to Surrender 159

Conclusion of Chapter 1 161

Christ's Words Remain Pertinent Today 161

Questions of Human Life 162

CHRIST APPEALS TO THE "BEGINNING"—IN REVIEW 163

Chapter 2

Christ Appeals to the Human Heart

[Cycle 2—Historical Man] 169

  1. In the Light of the Sermon on the Mount 171
    Ethical Meaning: The New Ethos 171
      Fulfillment of the Law 173
    Anthropological Meaning: Penetrating the "Heart" 176

  2. The Man of Concupiscence 177

    A. The Meaning of Original Shame 178
    Casting Doubt on the Gift 178
    The Entrance of Shame 182
    The Dimensions of Shame 184
      Shame Shakes the Foundations of Existence 185
      Shame Is Immanent and Relative 187
      Shame Has a Twofold Meaning 189

    B. Insatiability of the Union 192
    Concupiscence Shatters the Original Communion of Persons 192
      The Second Discovery of Sex 193
      Sin's Effect on Woman 194
      Both Are Subject to Concupiscence 196

    C. The Corruption of the Spousal Meaning of the Body 197
    Living the Body Flows from the Heart 198
    Concupiscence Habitually Threatens Love 199
    Loss of the Freedom of the Gift 201
      Maintaining the Balance of the Gift 203
    The Personal Analogy of Belonging 205

  3. Commandment and Ethos 206

    A. It Was Said, "Do Not Commit Adultery" 207
    The Law 207
    The Prophets 209
      Anthropology and Ethics of the Sign 210

    B. "Whoever Looks with Lust..." 211
    The Wisdom Tradition and the New Ethos 212

The Inner State of the Man of Concupiscence 216

    External Modesty. 217

Penetrating the "Lustful Look" 217

Concupiscence as a Reduction. 219

    Psychological Interpretation of Lust 220

    "Eternal" Sexuality 221

C. "Has Committed Adultery in the Heart..." 222

A Key Change of Direction. 222

The Typical Interpretation Requires a Deepening. 222

    A Clarion Call to Uphold Woman's Dignity. 224

The Real Possibility of Purity of Heart 226

The Guiding Thread of Existence 228

4. The "Heart"—Accused or Called? 229

A. Condemnation of the Body? 230

Manichaeism. 230

Irreconcilable Difference in Mentality 231

Negation of the Body versus Victory over Lust 233

B. The "Heart" Under Suspicion? 236

"Masters of Suspicion" 236

The Meaning of Life Is at Stake. 238

Grace, Faith, and Man's Real Possibilities 239

    Grace Restored 240

    Christ's Call Wells Up from Within 242

C. Eros and Ethos 242

Is Eros Equated with Lust? 242

Longing for the True, Good, and Beautiful 243

The Problem of Erotic Spontaneity 244

    Mature Spontaneity and Noble Pleasure 246

5. The Ethos of the Redemption of the Body 248

The Whole Mission of Christ. 248

Growing in Holiness 250

Redemption, Not Repression 251

6. Purity as "Life According to the Spirit" 253

Blessed Are the Pure in Heart. 253

From Physical Purity to Moral Purity 254

"Flesh" and "Spirit" According to St. Paul 256

Justification by Faith 257

"Works of the Flesh" and "Fruit of the Spirit" 259

The Freedom for which Christ Has Set Us Free 261

  Freedom and Purity 262

  Authentic Freedom 265

Purity—Keeping the Body "in Holiness and Reverence" 266

The Pauline Description of the Body 268

  Restoring Harmony in the Body 269

  The Need for a Pure Purity 270

Purity as a Virtue and a Gift 272

  God's Glory Shining in the Body 275

Purity and Wisdom: To the Pure All Things Are Pure 276

7. The Gospel of Purity of Heart—Yesterday and Today 277

The Theology and Pedagogy of the Body 279

  Spirituality of the Body 280

  The Church Applies Christ's Words Today 281

Appendix: The Ethos of the Body in Art and Media 283

A Perennial Object of Culture 284

The Ethos of the Image and the Ethos of Seeing 285

True Art versus Pornography 287

Conclusion of Chapter 2 290

  Christ Appeals to the Human Heart—In Review 291

CHAPTER 3

Christ Appeals to the Resurrection

[Cycle 3—Eschatological Man and
Cycle 4—Continence for the Kingdom] 297

1. Resurrection of the Body as a Reality of the Future World 299

  *A. The Synoptics: "He Is Not the God
  of the Dead but of the Living"* 299

  The Third Part of the Triptych 299

  Witness to the Power of the Living God 300

  The New Meaning of the Body 302

The Fulfillment of Marriage 302
We Will Be "Like" Angels 303
Spiritualization of the Body. 307
Divinization of the Body 308
The Beatific Vision: Seeing God "Face to Face" 310
The Eschatological Experience 312
The Body: A Witness to Love 313
The Perfection of Subjectivity. 314
The Marriage of Divinity and Humanity. 315
A New Threshold for Understanding Man. 315
Divine-Human Communion. 316
Knowledge of God 318
Communion of Saints: Fulfillment of the
Spousal Meaning of the Body. 319
A Union of Communion. 319
A Virginal Communion 321
The Perfect Freedom of the Gift 322
A Development of the Truth about Man 324
Communion Is Fundamental 324
Icon or Idol? 326

B. Pauline Interpretation of the Resurrection
in 1 Corinthians 15:42–49 327
God's Reply to Death. 327
The First Adam Bears Potential for the New Adam. 329
The Spiritual Body 331

2. Continence for the Kingdom of Heaven [Cycle 4] 332

A. The Words of Christ in Matthew 19:11–12 334
Christ's Words Mark a Turning Point 334
Voluntary, Supernatural, Virginal Communion 335
Continence for the Kingdom and Spiritual Fruitfulness. 337
Joseph and Mary's Virginal Marriage 338
Marriage and Celibacy Both Flow
from the Ethos of Redemption. 339
Correct Understanding of the "Superiority" of Celibacy. 341
Solitude, Communion, and the Spousal Meaning of the Body 343

Marriage and Celibacy Explain and Complete Each Other........ 345

Marriage Reveals the Spousal Character of Celibacy 346

Celibacy Reveals the Sacramentality of Marriage................ 348

Celibacy Anticipates Man's Definitive Fulfillment 349

Liberation from Concupiscence............................ 351

B. Paul's Understanding of the Relation
Between Virginity and Marriage (1 Cor 7) 352

Christ's Statement and the Teaching of the Apostles 352

Paul's Argumentation....................................... 353

Does Paul View Marriage as an Outlet for Concupiscence? 355

Why Celibacy Is "Better" According to St. Paul................. 357

Both Vocations Are a Call to Holiness......................... 358

The Grace Operative in Married Life 359

Conclusion of Part I 361

The Redemption of the Body and the Hope of Every Day............. 361

Christ Fulfills the Proto-Evangelium 362

The Hope of Every Day 362

The Theology of the Body Is Fundamental..................... 364

CHRIST APPEALS TO THE RESURRECTION—IN REVIEW 365

PART II

THE SACRAMENT

CHAPTER 1

The Dimension of Covenant and of Grace

[Cycle 5—The Sacramentality of Marriage] 375

1. Ephesians 5:21–33 377

A. Introduction and Connection 377

The Text of Ephesians 5:21–23.............................. 377

The Crowning of the Themes of Scripture 377

The Incarnate Person: Body and Sacrament 378

B. Detailed Analysis 381

The Context of Ephesians 381

Modern Sensitivities and St. Paul's Interpretive Key 382

Mutual Submission "Out of Reverence for Christ" 383

The Spousal Analogy 386

Giving and Receiving the Gift 387

Two Directions of the Spousal Analogy 389

Head and Body Analogy 391

Sacredness of the Body 393

Baptism Expresses Christ's Spousal Love for the Church 394

Physical Beauty as an Image of Holiness 395

The Husband Must Desire His Wife's Beauty 397

True Love Recognizes Woman's True Beauty 400

Spousal Love and the Eucharist 403

This Is a Great Mystery-Sacrament 403

Recovering the Broader Meaning of "Sacrament" 404

Keystone of the Spousal Analogy 405

The Sacrament Proclaims and Accomplishes the Mystery 407

2. Sacrament and Mystery 408

Christ Reveals the Mystery Hidden for Ages in God 408

The Mode of Gift and the Veils of Faith 409

The Spousal Analogy: From the Old Testament to the New 410

Your Maker Is Your Husband 410

From Isaiah to Ephesians: New Aspects of Revelation 412

The Reality of the Gift, the Meaning of Grace 413

*The Single "Great Sign" Communicates
the Radical Character of Grace* 414

Conjugal Union in Light of the Incarnation 415

The Foundation of the Sacramental Order 416

Marriage as the Primordial Sacrament 417

The Body Pervaded by Grace 420

The Sacrament of Creation 421

Marriage: Platform for the Realization of God's Eternal Plans 423

Being Chosen and Being Able to Choose 424

Sin and the Loss of Supernatural Efficacy 425

Sacrament of Creation Fulfilled in Sacrament of Redemption 427

Signs of Creation and Redemption 428

Christ's Spousal Love Is Unitive and Life-Giving 430

Marriage: Prototype of All the Sacraments 431

Nature and Grace 431

Grace of the Primordial Sacrament Restored 432

Marriage Provides the Basic Structure of Salvation 433

3. Sacrament and "Redemption of the Body" 435

A. The Gospel 435

The Anthropology of Redemption 436

The Ethos of Redemption 437

Marriage Reveals God's Will to Save Us from Sin 439

Marriage Is a Call to "Life in the Spirit" 441

Overcoming Concupiscence 441

Better to Marry Than to Be Aflame with Passion 442

Marital Intercourse as "Life in the Holy Spirit" 443

Procreation: An Integral Part of Creation and Redemption 445

Marriage and the Eschatological Hope of Redemption 446

B. Ephesians 448

The Spousal and Redemptive Meaning of Love 448

Understanding Human Existence 450

Spousal Love Embraces the Universe 451

THE DIMENSION OF COVENANT AND OF GRACE—
IN REVIEW 452

CHAPTER 2

The Dimension of Sign
[Cycle 5—The Sacramentality of Marriage, cont'd.] 461

1. "Language of the Body" and the Reality of the Sign 463

Words "Made Flesh" 463

The Interplay of Form and Matter 465

The "Prophetism of the Body" 467

Man: The Author of His Own Language 468

"Language of the Body" Reread in the Truth 469

"Language of the Body" and Victory over Concupiscence 470

2. The Song of Songs 474

Interpreting the Song of Songs 475

Mutual Fascination with the Body 477

Experience of the Beautiful 478

    "Eyes of the Body" and "Eyes of the Heart" 480

"My Sister, My Bride" 481

    Common Belonging Brings Peace 483

"A Garden Closed, a Fountain Sealed" 484

    The Bride Remains "Inviolate": Reciprocal Belonging 488

Sensuality and Spirituality 490

Love Is "Strong as Death" 491

Eros and Agape 493

    Limitations in the Language of the Body 494

    Sign and Reality 497

3. When the "Language of the Body" Becomes
the Language of the Liturgy (Reflections on Tobit) 498

    Conjugal Life and Liturgical Life 499

    The Marriage of Tobias and Sarah 500

        Love as a Test of Life-or-Death 501

    The Prayer of Tobias and Sarah 503

    Love Is Victorious Because It Prays 505

        That Good May Conquer 506

    The Spouses' "Conjugal Creed" 507

    Ephesians 5: The Language of the Liturgy
    Becomes the "Language of the Body" 509

    The Sacramental Sign—Mystery and Ethos 512

        Spiritually Mature Sexual Attraction 514

        THE DIMENSION OF SIGN—IN REVIEW 516

CHAPTER 3

He Gave Them the Law of Life as Their Inheritance

[Cycle 6—Love and Fruitfulness:
Reflections on *Humanae Vitae*] 521

1. The Ethical Problem 524

    The Moral Norm and the Truth of the "Language of the Body" 524

    Signs and Countersigns 526

    The Rightness of the Norm and Its Practicability 530

        Development of the Council's Teaching 531

        True Pastoral Concern 533

    Responsible Parenthood 535

The Truth of the Language of the Body
and the Evil of Contraception. 537

The Ethical Regulation of Births 540

Two Irreconcilable Views of the Person 542

Self-Mastery and the Freedom of the Gift 544

The Integral Vision of Natural Fertility Regulation 547

Personalistic Interpretation of Natural Law 548

Having a Procreative Attitude. 549

2. Outline of Conjugal Spirituality 551

The Power that Flows from Sacramental "Consecration". 551

Christian Realism 552

Infallible Means of Conjugal Spirituality. 554

Holiness: Logic of the Sincere Gift of Self 556

The Role of Conjugal Love in the Life of Spouses 558

The Poles of the Debate. 558

Authentic Love Rejoices with the Truth 560

Conjugal Love Fulfills the Ends of Marriage. 561

Analysis of the Virtue of Continence 562

Continence Is a Permanent Moral Attitude 564

Continence Upholds the Incomparable Value of the Body. 566

Continence Purifies and Deepens Spousal Union 569

Continence: Arousal and Emotion 571

Balance Between Arousal and Emotion 573

The Gift of Reverence 574

Conjugal Spirituality from "the Beginning" 575

The Exceptional Meaning of the Conjugal Act. 577

The Inner Harmony of Marriage. 579

Antithesis of Authentic Conjugal Spirituality. 580

Ethical, Personal, and Religious Content of Sexual Union. 583

Conclusion 584

Humanae Vitae and the Authentic Progress of Civilization. 584

Biblical and Personalistic Aspects 585

Technology, Ethics, and Progress 586

Humanization and Evangelization. 588

He Gave Them the Law of Life
as Their Inheritance—In Review 589

EPILOGUE

The Gospel of the Body and the New Evangelization 595

1. The Antidote to the Culture of Death 597
   Ramifications for All of Theology. 597
      Mainstream Mysticism 599
   Incarnating the Gospel Message. 600
      Bringing Heavenly Mysteries Down to Earth 601
      The Human Question and the Divine Answer 602

2. The Church's Response to Modern Rationalism 606
   The Spousal Analogy and the "Analogy of Faith" 606
   Man as "Absolute" or "Partner of the Absolute". 607
   Turn to Christ. 610

3. In Conclusion... 613
      EPILOGUE—IN REVIEW. 614

Bibliography 617

Index 623

Acknowledgments

———— ∽ ————

I AM GRATEFUL to the following men and women who helped with the second edition of this work:

Dr. Michael Waldstein, for his new translation of the Pope's text, which inspired me to update my commentary, for his fine scholarship, which has added tremendously to my own understanding, for reviewing this commentary and offering many helpful suggestions, and for writing the foreword to the second edition;

Melanie Anderson, my personal assistant, for her research and other countless acts of selfless service without which my life would be unmanageable;

Dr. Peter Colosi, for reviewing the Prologue;

all the staff at Pauline Books & Media, for their commitment to this project;

my spiritual family—Father Jim Otto, Jennifer Simmons, Monsignor John Esseff, and Father John Horn—whose prayers and spiritual guidance have been invaluable to me;

my wife Wendy and my children John Paul, Thomas, Beth, and Isaac, without whose love and support I could not have completed this project.

Acknowledgments to the First Edition

———————— ∽ ————————

I AM GRATEFUL to the following men and women who have helped make this book a reality:

Pope John Paul II, for the tremendous gift of his theology of the body;

Mary Jane Rice, for first introducing me to the Pope's catechesis on the body;

Steve Habisohn, for his steadfast moral support and for helping finance the sabbatical that enabled me to write this book;

all the staff at Pauline Books & Media, especially Sister Marianne Lorraine, FSP, for her dedication to this project and for her expert editing;

Monsignor Lorenzo Albacete, for all the wisdom he has passed on to me, for his affirmation of my work, and for bringing his theological genius to bear in reviewing my manuscript;

George Weigel, for writing the foreword;

Archbishop Chaput, for his support and encouragement of my "mission";

Jeanne Monahan and Jay Wonacott, for critiquing early drafts;

Father Richard Hogan, for critiquing the prologue;

Eric Scheidler, for his extensive help in reviewing and restructuring the initial manuscript;

Nathan West and Jessica Wunsch, for their research;

and Wendy West, for proofing the original text, adding feminine insight, and for all her sacrifices during the three years it took me to complete this project.

Foreword

―――――∽―――――

IN JUNE 2005, WHEN I HAD completed the first draft of the new translation of John Paul II's theology of the body, I contacted Christopher West because I had learned about his many years of intensive experience in teaching the theology of the body to various audiences at universities, seminaries, parishes, etc. An intensive exchange of e-mails followed (more than a hundred) in which he helped me to hammer out formulations, to make them clearer and more communicable. In many instances he persuaded me to go back to the phrasing of the original English translation published in *L'Osservatore Romano*, substantial passages of which he had memorized and held dear; in other instances I persuaded him of new proposed formulations; in yet others we reached a third formulation that neither of us had originally thought of. It is a joy for me to express my gratitude for this fruitful collaboration.

An initially unexpected fruit of our collaboration was West's decision to revise his *Theology of the Body Explained* on the basis of the new English text. A further reason for the new edition is the discovery of the original chapter and section headings in Karol Wojtyla's manuscript, which would later (after his election) be delivered by John Paul II during the Wednesday audiences as the theology of the body. These headings allow a new level of insight into the text, as West shows in his revised commentary.

John Paul II conceived his theology of the body as an eminently practical work. To all human beings, he points out, the body and its power to express love is a matter of intense practical concern. How can men and women find true fulfillment in love? John Paul II answers that they can find it by realizing God's plan for human love, which Jesus reveals in his teaching about the body. "Those who seek fulfillment... are called first of all to make of this 'theology of the body' ...the content of their lives and behavior." At root, they are called to "a deepened consciousness of the meaning of the body in its masculinity and femininity ...an accurate consciousness of its spousal meaning, of its generative meaning" (TOB 23:5). We owe a debt of great gratitude to Christopher West for making John Paul II's often difficult account of Jesus' teaching about the body accessible in a pedagogically effective and practical way. The theology of the body movement has been gathering momentum, particularly in the United States, thanks in large measure to West.

According to St. Thomas Aquinas, a distinctive mark of theology—in contrast to all other sciences—is to be, at one and the same time, eminently practical and speculative. Still, he argues, theology is above all speculative rather than practical because it is above all the study of God, who is eternal and not subject to human action (*Summa Theol.* 1.1.4). In the theology of the body John Paul II opens up the divine core of theology with his great power of speculative penetration. He shows the deep connections between the divine communion of persons in the Trinity and the human communion of persons between man and woman, mediated by their male and female bodies. Contrary to contemporary natural science and its "flat" materialism, according to which the only real properties of bodies are those grasped by mathematical physics, he shows that the body has a great interior subjective and personal depth. It is sacramental.

> The sacrament, as a visible sign, is constituted with man, inasmuch as he is a "body," through his "visible" masculinity and femininity. The body, in fact, and only the body, is capable of making visible what is invisible: the spiritual and the divine. It has been created to transfer into the visible reality of the world the mystery hidden from eternity in God, and thus to be a sign of it. (TOB 19:4)

The mystery hidden in God is the eternal communion of persons in the Trinity. This Mystery of all mysteries comes to light and is communicated in God's plan for the spousal communion of man and woman. West is a reliable and effective guide also in this speculative dimension of John Paul II's work. He shows how all the parts of John Paul II's deep theological argument are connected with the key statement just quoted. In simple and clear language, often relying on the *Catechism of the Catholic Church*, West guides the reader through the complex text.

The two aspects of theology, its practical power and speculative depth, are intimately related. What gives to theology its practical power is the encounter with the glory and beauty of trinitarian love made visible in the person of Jesus (cf. Hans Urs von Balthasar's trilogy *Glory*, *Theodrama*, and *Theologic*). John Paul II embodies this intimate relation between the two aspects of theology as well as the order between them. His pastoral method is to show the great beauty of love between man and woman as a participation in the Mystery of all mysteries, trinitarian love. He shows it as a beauty that can be lived and in some degree experienced. West's commentary is helpful above all because it facilitates the encounter with this beauty and the reverence for the body that flows from it.

Since West first discovered the theology of the body in 1993, he has been a pioneer in the difficult task of seeking the right language with which to explain John Paul II's difficult theological and philosophical teaching in more accessible categories. It has been a process of trial and error, as he readily admits. Those who have followed his career over the years will recognize that this newly revised commentary is the fruit of West's own ever deepening understanding and integration of the material. His ever closer study of John Paul II and assimilation of John Paul's clarity of vision is evident throughout.

I have studied West's commentary personally and profited much from it. I find it faithful both to the letter and the spirit of John Paul II. During a two-day visit at his home, and in subsequent exchanges, West and I talked through various differences in interpretation among those who study John Paul II and Catholic teaching on sexuality in general. For example, there are some Catholic moralists who hold that the condition of interior battle and permanent opposition between erotic emotion and moral reason is the inevitable human condition, inevitable at least for the male sex. A particular understanding of marriage as a "remedy of concupiscence" tends to go with this assessment of male sexuality, apparently in accord with St. Paul's statement, "It is better to marry than to be aflame" (1 Cor 7:9). Men must repress sexual concupiscence in relation to all women except their own wives. It is only with their own wives that they can live out their concupiscence with some legitimacy and, in this way, tame it.

West shows how deeply John Paul II disagrees with this negative approach. Sexual concupiscence must and can be overcome, even between spouses. "Adultery 'in the heart' is not committed only because the man 'looks' in this way at a woman who is not his wife, but *precisely because he looks in this way at a woman. Even* if he were to look in this way at the woman who is his wife, he would commit the same adultery 'in the heart'" (TOB 43:2). Christ is the redeemer of the body. He enables men and women to live a life according to his Spirit, in which "looking" and erotic emotions are purified by a deep and powerful awareness of the spousal meaning of the body.

John Paul II has called the Sistine Chapel with its many nudes "a sanctuary of the theology of the body" that teaches men and women the right way of looking at each other—of *looking*, one should take note, not only of looking *away*.

> In the course of the various epochs from antiquity down—and especially in the great period of classical Greek art—there are works of art whose subject is the human body in its nakedness, the contemplation of which allows one to concentrate in some way on the whole truth of man, on the dignity and beauty—even "suprasensual" beauty—of his masculinity and femininity. These works *bear within themselves in a hidden way, as it were, an element of sublimation* that leads the viewer through the body to the whole personal mystery of man. In contact with such works we do not feel pushed by their content toward "looking to desire," as the Sermon on the Mount puts it; in some way we learn the spousal meaning of the body, which corresponds to and provides the measure for "purity of heart." (TOB 63:5)

West is to be commended for proposing this positive teaching forcefully and with clarity, even in the face of strong opposition. Those who do not believe concupiscence can be substantially overcome would do well to read John Paul II more closely, and this commentary can be of great service in such a reading. Faithful to John Paul II's clear teaching on the matter, West makes the necessary qualifications: absolute confidence in a supposedly complete victory over the effects of original sin in the sexual sphere is a sure recipe for disaster, a recipe for confidently entering situations of temptation and then being swept away by concupiscence. Still, West is absolutely right to uphold the positive side of John Paul II's teaching and to place the main emphasis there. A thorough transformation of the human heart by the Spirit of Christ is not only possible but also necessary for a Christian.

The Spirit of Christ does not destroy erotic emotion. In the section to which John Paul II gave the heading "The Problem of Erotic Spontaneity" (TOB 48), he writes:

> Man reaches that *deeper and more mature spontaneity* with which his "heart," by mastering drives, rediscovers the spiritual beauty of the sign constituted by the human body in its masculinity and femininity. Inasmuch as this discovery becomes firm in conscience as conviction and in the will as the orientation both of possible choices and of simple desires, the human heart comes to share, so to speak, in another spontaneity of which the "carnal man" knows nothing or very little. There is no doubt that by Christ's words according to Matthew 5:27–28, we are called precisely to such spontaneity. And perhaps the most important sphere of "praxis"—with respect to the most "interior" acts—is the one that traces the road step by step toward such spontaneity. (TOB 48:5)

It is clear that West has understood John Paul II's argument on a deep level and has allowed himself to be formed by John Paul II's own sensibility, particularly by his reverence for human sexuality as a sacred work of God, icon of the love of Christ for his Church. West is aware of the tendency in our culture to speak without tact or reverence about intimate details, often with an appetite for sensationalist impact. He realizes that reverence is a matter of truth and of truly discerning eyes, not a mere moral matter (see esp. TOB 56–57; 131–32).

I urge those who know and love John Paul II to welcome this commentary. They can certainly profit from a close study of West's insights, as I have. For those who are new to John Paul II's thought, West's work offers readers an excellent entry and much solid assistance in decoding John Paul II's difficult text. It will encourage them to read John Paul II himself with more open eyes and with clearer reflection. May God's blessing rest on this important work.

MICHAEL WALDSTEIN

Foreword to the First Edition

⎯⎯⎯⎯⎯∽⎯⎯⎯⎯⎯

FUTURE GENERATIONS WILL remember Pope John Paul II for many things: his great personal witness to the truths of Christian faith; his epic role in the collapse of communism; his ecumenical initiatives; his healing the wounds of centuries between Catholics and Jews. The list could go on and on.

While writing *Witness to Hope: The Biography of Pope John Paul II*, I came to the conclusion that John Paul's longest-lasting theological contribution to the Church and the world might well be something that very few people have ever encountered: his innovative "theology of the body," which he laid out in 129 general audience addresses between 1979 and 1984. In my biography of the Pope, I described the "theology of the body" as a bit of a theological time bomb, something that would explode within the Church at an indeterminate point in the future. His theology would have a tremendous effect, reshaping the way Catholics think about our embodiedness as male and female, our sexuality, our relationships with each other, our relationship with God—even God himself. I also wrote that the Pope's dense, compact addresses that make up the "theology of the body" needed explication for those who weren't specialists in biblical studies, theology, or philosophy.

I am delighted that Christopher West has taken up that challenge in *Theology of the Body Explained*. With intellectual care, with the experience bred of long years of teaching this material in the classroom and the parish, and taking account of his own experiences as a husband and father, he explains each of the Pope's 129 addresses, showing how the meaning of each address fits into a coherent whole. Christopher West also demonstrates how the "theology of the body" is readily applicable to the quotidian realities of marriage and family life. Teachers and students, priests and pastoral workers, couples preparing for marriage, couples looking to deepen their marriages, and couples reflecting back on the meaning of their venerable marriages will all find here much to think about and pray over.

In his great encyclical, *Veritatis Splendor*, John Paul II takes the story of Christ's dialogue with the rich young man (Mt 19:16–22) as the paradigm of the Christian moral life. What good must I do, the young man asks, in order to have eternal life? For that is the purpose of the moral life: to fit us for beatitude, to make us the kind of people who can live with God forever. It takes a special kind of people to do that—in a word, it takes saints. And saints are what we all must become if we are to realize our baptismal destiny. The "theology of the body" shows us how sexual love within the bonds of faithful and fruitful marriage is a path to sanctity—and thus a path to God and to eternal life.

A sex-saturated culture imagines that the sexual revolution has been liberating. The opposite is the truth: men and women chained to their appetites and passions are not free. What can liberate us from that kind of bondage? The "theology of the body" answers the question: loving truly, loving chastely, loving in ways that are radically life-giving and life-affirming rather than life-avoiding or life-denying. Some will, no doubt, find it odd that the Catholic Church takes human sexuality far more seriously than the editors of *Playboy* and *Cosmopolitan*. But that's the plain truth of the matter. And the "theology of the body" shows why and how that's the case.

Catholics should remember that the "theology of the body" is not *for-Catholics-only*. With his groundbreaking audience addresses, John Paul II has made a tremendous contribution to human thought and to the possibility for human happiness,. So I wish for Christopher West's book the widest possible audience. Catholics should share it with other Catholics, to be sure. But Catholics should also share it with Protestant, Orthodox, Jewish, Muslim, and even agnostic friends. The responses, especially among women, may be surprising—happily surprising.

The great struggle of the twenty-first century, like the twentieth, will be the struggle to defend and promote the dignity of the human person. John Paul II's "theology of the body" is a tremendous resource for all those who fight that good fight. Christopher West has put us in his debt by making the "theology of the body" available to a wide—and, I hope, appreciative—readership.

GEORGE WEIGEL

Introduction

———— ∽ ————

I REMEMBER OCTOBER 16, 1978, very clearly. I was in the third grade at Sacred Heart School in Lancaster, Pennsylvania. The bishop had given a holy card of the "smiling Pope" (John Paul I) to all the students in the diocese just two weeks earlier. Now, after the Pope's sudden death, we were sitting in class awaiting news of his successor.

The following scene is seared in my memory. Our teacher's aid, Sister Eugene—a quiet, elderly nun who must have had some Slavic blood in her—had been keeping vigil in front of the television across the hall. In a loud flurry, she burst into our classroom with eyes and hands raised to heaven screaming at the top of her lungs, *"He's Polish! He's Polish! He's Poooool-ish!"*

Little did I know then what an impact this Polish Pope would have on my life. Although I would not discover it for another decade and a half, a series of talks that John Paul II began within the first year of his pontificate would forever change the way I view the universe and my place within it.

During the same time John Paul II presented his catechesis on God's glorious plan for the body and sexuality, I was being groomed in the sexual lies promoted within our culture. After several years of unchaste living, I returned to my faith with multiple questions about God's plan for man and woman's relationship. Looking for answers, I began a prayerful study of the scriptural texts on marriage and sexuality. Over the course of about two years of intense study, a grand "nuptial

1

vision" began to emerge. The spousal imagery of the Scriptures brought my faith to life, shedding light on the entire mystery of man and woman's creation, fall, and redemption in Christ. Moreover, this "nuptial vision" was setting me *free* from the lies that had formed me as I grew up. I was on fire. Expecting an enthusiastic response, I began sharing this vision with others. Instead, Christians I considered more learned than I often responded with blank stares or worse.

In early fall of 1993, a committed Catholic woman who taught at my sister's high school came to dinner, and I hesitantly decided to test some of my "nuptial vision" on her. To my surprise, she immediately replied, "You must have read the Pope's theology of the body." "What's that?" I probed. "Gosh, I thought you'd already read it. What you're saying sounds like the Pope." I pressed her, "*What is this theology of the body? Where can I get it?*" She told me that the Daughters of St. Paul published it in four little volumes.[1]

I devoured the entire catechesis in a matter of weeks. Not only did I find abundant confirmation of what I had learned in my own study, the Pope's reflections took me to a new level altogether. I realized that these four little volumes contained an unmined treasure for the Church and a revolution for the world. Indeed, they contained the answer to the crisis of our times. I knew then I was going to spend the rest of my life studying the Pope's thought and sharing it with others. When I learned that the Pope had established a theological institute for the specific purpose of exploring this biblical "nuptial vision," there was no question where I would go for graduate studies.

Today more and more people are hearing *about* John Paul II's theology of the body (TOB). Still, for the vast majority of Christians, the actual content of the Pope's catechesis remains unknown. Why? As papal biographer George Weigel observes, "The density of John Paul's material is one factor; a secondary literature capable of 'translating' John Paul's [TOB] into more accessible categories and vocabulary is

---

1. *Original Unity of Man and Woman* (1981); *Blessed Are the Pure of Heart* (1983); *The Theology of Marriage and Celibacy* (1986); and *Reflections on Humanae Vitae* (1984). These texts, which reprinted the Vatican newspaper *L'Osservatore Romano's* translation of the catechesis, are no longer in print. Later, Pauline Books & Media published a one-volume, copyedited edition under the title *The Theology of the Body: Human Love in the Divine Plan* (1997). Finally, they replaced that edition in 2006 with a much-improved English translation upon which I will comment further.

badly needed."[2] This book attempts just that. However, as you can tell from its size, this is not a *Reader's Digest* version. While smaller-scale efforts are also needed,[3] my goal here is to unpack the entire catechesis from start to finish.

Need for a Revised Edition

The first edition of this commentary, which was released in 2003, was based on the English text of TOB published in the four volumes mentioned above. This newly revised edition is based on the much improved "critical edition" of TOB, translated by Dr. Michael Waldstein of the International Theological Institute and published by Pauline Books & Media under the Pope's original title, *Man and Woman He Created Them: A Theology of the Body*[4] (2006). In the preface to this new TOB translation, I described its many improvements as follows:

> John Paul II's original structure and system of headings, never before translated from Polish, have been retrieved. The Pope's trademark use of italics, much of which had been lacking in the first translation or removed by subsequent editors, has been fully restored. Inconsistencies caused by different translators have been corrected. Sentences have been properly reconstructed. John Paul II's own numbering of paragraphs has been restored. And perhaps most excitingly of all, undelivered sections of Wojtyla's original manuscript have been unearthed and translated into English for the very first time. In short, nearly twenty-two years after John Paul II delivered the final address of the series, the English-speaking world is finally able to appreciate—inasmuch as any translation can offer—the original splendor of the Pope's project.[5]

---

2. *Witness to Hope* (New York: Harper Collins, 1999), p. 343.

3. See Mary Healy, *Men and Women Are from Eden: A Study Guide to John Paul II's Theology of the Body* (Cincinnati, OH: Servant, 2005); Anthony Percy, *Theology of the Body Made Simple* (Boston, MA: Pauline Books & Media, 2006); Christopher West, *Theology of the Body for Beginners* (West Chester, PA: Ascension Press, 2004).

4. *Man and Woman He Created Them* is the title of the unpublished manuscript written by Cardinal Wojtyla prior to his election as pope, from which, as pope, he derived the series of catechesis commonly called "Theology of the Body." We might conceive of these two titles as follows. If we are speaking of the book itself, it is properly called *Man and Woman He Created Them*. If we are speaking of the book's content, or the kind of theology this book contains, it is properly called "theology of the body."

5. Preface, John Paul II, *Man and Woman He Created Them: A Theology of the Body* (Boston, MA: Pauline Books & Media, 2006), p. xxix. For a discussion of the need for this new translation by Waldstein himself, see his introduction, TOB, pp. 11–14.

If the undelivered material is initially the most exciting aspect of the new translation, the insertion of the Pope's original headings is without a doubt the most rewarding. Having worked closely with the text since 1993, I thought I had oriented myself fairly well within its vast landscape. However, I now see how I had been wandering through the promised land without a map. There were milk and honey to be had without the headings, but it took more effort to find one's way to it. The proper headings not only orient the reader, organize the argument, and reveal the rigor of John Paul's thought. Careful attention to the headings as one studies the text provides previously inaccessible vantage points over the landscape. New vistas open and familiar landmarks shine much more brilliantly. The reader realizes that the previous editions of the Pope's work presented his vision in a rather flat or two dimensional way. Now, with close study of the headings, the Pope's vision almost pops out in 3-D.

All this, of course, demonstrates the need for a revised edition of my commentary. Beyond the work of changing quotes according to the new translation, I have substantially reorganized the outline of the text to reflect what we now know about the structure of John Paul's original manuscript. After setting the stage in the Prologue, also thoroughly revised and updated, I follow the Pope's original outline very closely, explaining the Pope's method, his train of thought, his scholarly vocabulary, and his original ideas and concepts. Points of interest and application are set aside in gray boxes to distinguish them from my exposition of the actual catechesis. I also reference the *Catechism of the Catholic Church* extensively to demonstrate the organic relationship of the TOB with the whole of Catholic faith. As Waldstein observes, the TOB, in fact, can "serve as a John Pauline lens for reading the *Catechism*."[6] Furthermore, while I designed this book to stand alone, I encourage those who wish to read it in tandem with the Holy Father's addresses, weighing what I say against the actual text.

By design, and by necessity of my own limitations, this is not the work of a stellar, academic theologian. Rather, it is the work of a teacher and a catechist trained in theology, with an ardent desire not only to encourage the academic study of the Pope's catechesis, but also to extend its liberating message beyond the realms of academia. One

---

6. See Waldstein, Introduction, TOB, p. 15, n. 23.

might say I am attempting to do splits (always a difficult trick in gymnastics) between an academic exposition of the Pope's teaching and a more popular one. John Paul's text is at times so difficult that both audiences can benefit from explanations. Finding the best language, images, and anecdotes with which to accomplish these academic-popular "splits," however, remains a process of trial and error. Hence, I imagine the future will bring further editions of this commentary as I continue to grow in my own understanding and find ever better ways of presenting the material.

Readers should also know that, while deeply rooted in tradition, John Paul's TOB offers a bold development of thinking. Such developments always afford a creative tension in the Church as scholars, catechists, and laity alike seek to understand them and apply them in Christian life. Differences in interpretation and the debates they engender are a healthy part of this process. Like every interpreter of the Pope's thought, I bring my own personal perspectives, gifts, and shortcomings to the table. As St. Paul says, "test everything; hold fast to what is good" (1 Thess 5:21).

Ultimately, no human words can do justice to the sacred mystery revealed by the human body and by man and woman's communion in "one flesh." As St. Paul says, this is a "great mystery" that refers to Christ and the Church (see Eph 5:31–32). If the human words contained in this book provide only a glimmer of the "great mystery" of that one divine Word, they will have served their purpose. Glimmers are all we get on this side of eternity. But they are enough to light a burning fire of hope within us for the consummation of the "marriage of the Lamb." Let it be, Lord, according to your Word. Amen.

The Human Body, Catholicism, and John Paul II

―――――∽―――――

> The body, in fact, and only the body, is capable of making visible what is invisible: the spiritual and the divine. It has been created to transfer into the visible reality of the world the mystery hidden from eternity in God, and thus to be a sign of it. (TOB 19:4) [1]

THIS IS THE THESIS STATEMENT of John Paul II's TOB, the brush with which he paints his entire catechesis. Every word of this commentary starts from and returns to this basic point: the body, precisely in the mystery of sexual difference and the call to union, is *a sign* of the "great mystery" hidden in God from eternity. As we shall ponder at length, the body enables us in some way not only to *see* this invisible mystery but also to *enter into* it, *participate* in it, *experience* it. The body, then, is the antidote to theological abstraction. The God of biblical revelation is not merely a theological idea or a concept. The God of biblical revelation is an eternal union of three divine *Persons*, the second of whom has dwelt among us in the *flesh*, in order to take our flesh up with him into trinitarian bliss. If it seems strange to reflect on the body as a theology, as a "study of God," it shouldn't if we believe in the Incarnation.

―――――

1. All references to the TOB will be provided in the text, rather than in a footnote. The numbers refer to audience and paragraph as provided in *Man and Woman He Created Them: A Theology of the Body* (Pauline Books & Media, 2006). TOB 19:4 thus refers to general audience no. 19, par. 4.

For through "the fact that the Word of God became flesh, the body entered theology...through the main door" (TOB 23:4).

"The chief purpose of theology," as John Paul II wrote in his encyclical *Fides et Ratio*, "is to *provide an understanding of revelation and the content of faith.* The very heart of theological inquiry will thus be the contemplation of the mystery of the Triune God. The approach to this mystery begins with reflection upon the mystery of the Incarnation."[2] This is *precisely* what the Holy Father's TOB *is*. As I once heard it stated quite succinctly, if the language of Israel is Hebrew and the language of Islam is Arabic, the language of Christianity is *the body*. There is simply no other way to "do" theology in the Christian sense. It all begins with the Incarnation—with God's human *body*.

To ask questions about the meaning of the human body starts us on an exhilarating journey that—if we stay the course—leads us from the union of the sexes to the union of Christ and the Church and, from there, into the heart of the mystery of the Triune God. It seems that relatively few Christians, however, have "stayed the course." A great many obstacles, prejudices, taboos, and fears can easily derail us as we face the enigma of our own embodiment as male and female. The temptation to "spiritualize" Christ and Christianity is constant and fierce. The enemy incessantly denies Christ come in the flesh (see 1 Jn 4:2–3). Thus, it shouldn't surprise us that theological reflection on the human body has a checkered past. On the one hand, throughout history Christian thinkers have contributed extensively to an integral understanding of the goodness of the body and have valiantly fought heresies to the contrary. On the other hand, we can find what seem to be unflattering and even contemptuous treatments of the body and sexuality in the writings of various churchmen. John Paul II's TOB builds on the positive foundations of the past, especially of the mystical tradition, and definitively corrects the "suspicion toward the body" that has plagued many sons and daughters of the Church.

The fact that it has taken two thousand years of Christian reflection to arrive at such a penetrating and extensive theology of the human body attests to the difficulty of the task. Only now has history provided the right soil for such a theology to take root and blossom. The turbulence of the twentieth century itself marked the beginning of

---

2. *Fides et Ratio*, 93.

a "new passover" of sorts for the Church and humanity. Passover implies new life, but it also implies death. The century that began with the hope of unlimited progress ended as the bloodiest of all centuries. Its first half produced two world wars and the deadliest totalitarian regimes in history. Its second half spawned fears of global destruction by nuclear war and saw the West jettison the sexual mores that— by upholding marriage and the family—place society on its only firm foundation. Without doubt, the sexual revolution's subsequent "culture of death" has brought far more carnage than the warfare and death camps that reddened the landscape of the bloodiest century.

The "signs of the times" show that we stand at a critical moment in the human drama. The many negative factors of today's world can breed pessimism. But John Paul II insisted that "this feeling is unjustified: we have faith in God our Father and Lord and in his mercy.... God is preparing a great springtime for Christianity, and we can already see its first signs."[3] (The international groundswell of interest in this TOB is certainly one of those signs.) Humanity must now cross the "threshold of hope." We must now "passover" from a culture of death to a culture of life. Only in this context can we understand the full significance of John Paul II's TOB.

1. What Is the Theology of the Body?

The Wednesday Catechesis

Since Pope Pius IX began the custom in the 1870s, the Wednesday general audience has provided one of the main platforms for the pope to address his flock. John Paul II was the first pope, however, to use his Wednesday audiences to present a systematic catechesis spanning several years. His catechesis on the body began on September 5, 1979, and—after various interruptions, including the 1981 assassination attempt—concluded over five years later on November 28, 1984. The length of this catechesis and its place as the inaugural teaching project of John Paul II's pontificate point to its fundamental significance. And its content, as George Weigel famously expressed it, constitutes "a kind

---

3. *Redemptoris Missio*, 86.

of *theological time bomb* set to go off with dramatic consequences...perhaps in the twenty-first century."[4]

We now know that Karol Wojtyla had written the TOB to be published as a book entitled *Man and Woman He Created Them*.[5] Its publication was interrupted, however, by the election of its author to the Chair of Peter in October 1978. Providentially, this gave the text another destiny and a global audience. It also made it an official work of John Paul II's magisterium, rather than the private work of a Polish theologian. Sometime after his election, John Paul II personally adapted his manuscript for the Wednesday audience format, dividing it into 135 catechetical addresses,[6] but delivering only 129.[7]

Since "catechesis" is the proper literary genre in which to place the TOB,[8] we would do well to define this term. "Catechesis" comes from the Greek verb *katekhein,* meaning to resound or echo. In the New Testament this word refers to *instructing people in the way of the Lord*, in the "mystery" of Christ. As Waldstein observes, in some intellectual circles "catechesis" connotes a lack of sophistication, as if catechetical instruction were intended only for the immature. Not so! The goal of catechesis is intimacy with the person and mystery of Christ—an intimacy that must continually deepen throughout a person's life and at all possible levels of intellectual formation. Thus, catechesis is intended for everyone, "though academics," Waldstein observes, "may be less aware of their own need."[9]

This is why bishops, as Vatican II expressed it, "should be especially concerned about [providing] catechetical instruction." In fact, in the

---

4. *Witness to Hope*, p. 343.

5. Scholars knew that John Paul II had begun writing the TOB as a cardinal in Poland, but for many years it was generally presumed that he had completed the project as Pope. For a discussion of what Waldstein learned on this matter from his research in the John Paul II archives, see Introduction, TOB, pp. 4–11.

6. The most widely referenced Italian edition includes only 133 of the 135 addresses. In order to maintain the same numbering for ease in cross-referencing, the 2006 English edition numbers the two missing talks as 95b and 117b. For a discussion of this discrepancy, see Introduction, TOB, p. 5.

7. As mentioned in the Introduction, the undelivered material has been translated and published in English for the first time with the Waldstein translation of 2006. These six "missing" addresses contain additional material from the Song of Songs, the book of Tobit, and Ephesians (see TOB 108–17).

8. See Waldstein, Introduction, TOB, pp. 14, 18.

9. Ibid., p. 18.

life of a bishop, "preaching and catechetical instruction...always hold pride of place."[10] We can conclude, then, "that the Wednesday catecheses have a certain primacy of place in the ordinary magisterium of the Bishop of Rome as pastor of the universal Church."[11] Thus, John Paul II's Wednesday catechesis on the body is not a mere footnote in his teaching office. Among "the catecheses of John Paul II, TOB stands out as lonely Mount Everest among the hills." This "is John Paul II's masterwork," the "core of his great vision," his "catechesis par excellence."[12] Indeed, the compelling theological and anthropological vision detailed in these addresses informs all his subsequent papal teachings. We simply have not penetrated the vision of John Paul II if we have not penetrated his TOB.

Penetrating the TOB, however, is no easy task. These 135 addresses constitute a dense, scholarly tome. While this does not mean that only the elite can understand John Paul's teaching, it does mean that those who wish to understand it and those who present it must make a diligent effort if the Pope's teaching is to become bread broken for all.

The "Crisis of the Body"

Based on his extensive pastoral and ecclesial experience, John Paul II discerned that the most pressing catechetical need at the dawn of his pontificate was to reconnect men and women with the nature and meaning of human *bodiliness*. Many found this more than a bit odd. The general sense of many of the pilgrims attending John Paul's initial Wednesday talks on the body was puzzlement.[13] People expect religious instruction to emphasize the "spiritual" realm. What was all this talk about the body?

But such a distinctly un-Christian view of "spirituality" was the precise problem John Paul was targeting. Throughout the West, a disincarnate spirituality rooted in a Cartesian divorce between body and soul was posing "an immense threat to life: not only to the life of individuals but also to that of civilization itself."[14] In his 1994 *Letter to*

---

10. *Christus Dominus*, 13, 14.
11. Waldstein, Introduction, TOB, p. 14.
12. Ibid., pp. 4, 11, 15, 128.
13. See *Witness to Hope*, p. 333.
14. *Familiaris Consortio*, 21.

Families, John Paul II summarized this Cartesian "crisis of the body" as follows:

> Unfortunately, Western thought, with the development of *modern rationalism,* has been gradually moving away from [*the teaching about God and man* which was brought to fulfillment by Christ]. The philosopher who formulated the principle... "I think, therefore I am" [René Descartes], also gave the modern concept of man its distinctive dualistic character. It is typical of rationalism to make a radical contrast in man between spirit and body, between body and spirit. But man is a person in the unity of his body and his spirit.... The separation of spirit and body in man has led to a growing tendency to consider the human body, not in accordance with the categories of its specific likeness to God, but rather on the basis of its similarity to all the other bodies present in the world of nature, bodies which man uses as raw material in his efforts to produce goods for consumption. But everyone can immediately realize what enormous dangers lurk behind the application of such criteria to man. When the human body...comes to be used as *raw material...*we will inevitably arrive at a dreadful ethical defeat (no. 19).

In the modern "cult of the body," the problem is not that people overvalue the body—*they don't value it enough.* The ancient heresy of Manichaeism[15] has once again reared its ugly head, entering the modern mind (including that of many Christians) like a wolf in sheep's clothing. John Paul continues:

> Within a similar anthropological perspective, the human family is facing the challenge of a *new Manichaeism,* in which body and spirit are put in radical opposition; the body does not receive life from the spirit, and the spirit does not give life to the body. Man thus *ceases to live as a person and a subject.* Regardless of all intentions and declarations to the contrary, he becomes merely an *object.* This neo-Manichaean culture has led, for example, to human sexuality being regarded more as an area *for manipulation and exploitation* than as the basis of that *primordial wonder* which led Adam on the morning of creation to exclaim before Eve: "This at last is bone of my bones and flesh of my flesh" (Gen 2:23). This same wonder is echoed in the words of the Song of Solomon: "You have ravished my heart, my sister, my bride, you have ravished my heart with a glance of your eyes" (Song 4:9). How far

---

15. Mani, or Manichaeus, after whom this heresy is named, condemned the body and all things sexual because he saw the source of evil in the material world. While the entire TOB is a rebuttal to Manichaeism, John Paul addresses it directly in Part I, Chapter 2 (see TOB 44–45).

removed are some modern ideas from the profound understanding of masculinity and femininity found in divine revelation! Revelation leads us to discover in *human sexuality a treasure proper to the person*, who finds true fulfillment in [marriage and] the family but who can likewise express his profound calling in virginity and in celibacy for the sake of the kingdom of God.[16]

The above paragraphs offer both a precise diagnosis of what ails the modern world *and* a prescription for what alone can heal it. A Cartesian separation of body and spirit has led to a lost sense of human identity. Rather than discovering a sign of the divine image in our bodiliness, we see only our likeness to the animals. Thus, the ancient Manichaean devaluation of the body takes on a new face. We condemn the body to gross dehumanization. We objectify it, manipulate it, and— precisely because of such dualism—we fail to recognize that every "it," every human body we dominate and exploit is, in fact, a "he" or a "she," a human subject, a *person*. And since human bodiliness manifests itself mainly through sex (see TOB 44:5), the sexual relationship suffers a mortal wound. Marriage and the family dis-integrate. In turn, culture at large begins to break down, heading toward collapse.

In short, the reason the modern world is ailing "is that our society has broken away from the full truth about...what man and woman really are as persons. Thus it cannot adequately comprehend the real meaning of the gift of persons in marriage, responsible love at the service of fatherhood and motherhood, and the true grandeur of procreation."[17]

Working all of this in reverse, we discover the only cure for what ails the modern world. We must recover a sense of *primordial wonder* at the divinely inspired beauty of the human body. We must come to recognize in the human body the revelation of the human *person* whose dignity demands he never be used or manipulated. We must rediscover *the treasure* of human sexuality as a stupendous sign of the divine image in man and as an invitation to human freedom to live this divine image through the sincere gift of one's life in marriage or in celibacy for the kingdom. And we do all of the above precisely by pondering "the profound understanding of masculinity and femininity found in divine revelation." This is what John Paul II's TOB *is*.

---

16. *Letter to Families*, 19.
17. Ibid., 20.

The Gospel of the Body

John Paul II's TOB is most often cast as an extended catechesis on marriage and sexual love. It certainly is that, but it is also *so much more*. Through the mystery of the incarnate person and the biblical analogy of spousal love, John Paul II's catechesis illumines the entirety of God's plan for human life from origin to eschaton with a splendid supernatural light. As we are already seeing, the TOB is not only a response to the sexual revolution, it's a response to the Enlightenment. It's a response to modern rationalism, Cartesian dualism, and all the disembodied anthropologies infecting the modern world. In short, the TOB is one of the Catholic Church's most critical efforts in modern times to help the world become more "conscious of the mystery and reality of the Incarnation" (TOB 23:4)—and, through that, to become conscious of the *humanum*, of the very purpose and meaning of human life.[18]

God has revealed his mystery through the Word made flesh—theology *of the body*. This phrase is not only the title of a series of talks by the late and great John Paul II. It represents the very "logic" of Christianity. In its course, John Paul II's catechesis on the body will plunge us headfirst into "the perspective of the whole gospel, of the whole teaching, even more, of the whole mission of Christ" (TOB 49:3). The TOB, then, is nothing but an extended proclamation of and commentary on the Gospel of Jesus Christ, the Gospel of the incarnate Word—the "Gospel of the body." "The richest source for knowledge of the body is the Word made flesh."[19] Thus, from start to finish, John Paul's catechesis calls us to encounter the living, incarnate Christ and to ponder how *his* body reveals the meaning of *our* bodies.

Vatican II put it succinctly: "The truth is that only in the mystery of the incarnate Word does the mystery of man take on light. For Adam, the first man, was a figure of him who was to come, namely Christ the Lord. Christ, the final Adam, by the revelation of the mystery of the Father and his love, fully reveals man to himself and makes his supreme calling clear."[20] This bold declaration of the Council was John Paul II's anthem. In fact, he considered it "the reply, so long awaited, which the

---

18. See Christopher West, Preface, TOB, p. xxvii.
19. *Letter to Families*, 19.
20. *Gaudium et Spes*, 22.

Church has given to modern rationalism."[21] The epilogue will revisit this "reply to modern rationalism" in light of all that we learn from the Pope's TOB. For now it is enough to observe that the entirety of TOB is simply an extended commentary on this fundamental truth: Christ fully reveals man to himself through the revelation—*in his body*—of the mystery of the Father and his love.

Christ's body, above all, proclaims and reveals the "Gospel of the body." Christ's body conceived of a virgin, born in a stable in Bethlehem, circumcised on the eighth day, raised by Mary and Joseph, baptized in the Jordan River, transfigured on the mountain, "given up for us" in his passion and death, risen in glory, ascended to the Father, and participating eternally in the life of the Trinity—the story of this body and the spiritual mystery it reveals *is* the Gospel.[22] And every-*body* that comes into the world is destined to share in this Gospel by becoming "one body," one spirit with Christ. This is the deepest meaning of our creation as sexually embodied persons—we are destined for union with the God who has taken on flesh. For man and woman's union in one flesh is a "great mystery," which, right from the first pages of Genesis, signifies and foreshadows Christ's spousal union with the Church (see Eph 5:31–32). This is the good news, the "Gospel of the body."

2. What Makes the Human Body "Theological"?

The Sacramentality of the Body

When people hear the word "theology," they do not tend to associate it with the human body. Conversely, when people hear the word "body," they do not tend to associate it with the study of God. Indeed, the very phrase "theology of the body" usually strikes people as an artificial linking of two realms that have no business together. But this only serves to demonstrate how deep-seated the Cartesian worldview has become and how far we have drifted from an authentically Christian, incarnational, sacramental vision of the real. By pondering the Christian mystery—the mystery of the Incarnation—we discover

---

21. *Letter to Families*, 19.
22. See *Catechism of the Catholic Church* (*CCC*), no. 515.

that the *theological* and *bodily* realms not only belong together. They are, in fact, "destined" for each other. As St. Paul put it, the body is *meant* for the Lord, and the Lord is *meant* for the body (see 1 Cor 6:13).

It is quite *logical*, then, for Christians to recognize the body as theological. The human body reveals the "logic" of God, the *Logos* of God. For the divine *Logos*—the eternal "reason" behind all that is—became flesh and dwelt among us (see Jn 1:14). We cannot *see* God. As pure spirit, God is totally beyond our vision. But the stunning proposal of Christianity is that God "has made himself visible in the flesh."[23] Elsewhere, quoting from the Church's liturgy, the *Catechism* asserts that "in the body of Jesus 'we see our God made visible and so are caught up in love of the God we cannot see.'"[24] St. John can therefore proclaim, it is that "which we have seen with our eyes," that "which we have touched with our hands" that we proclaim to you concerning the *Logos*. And that divine *Logos* was made visible (see 1 Jn 1–3).

Making visible the invisible is what John Paul II means by speaking of the sacrament, or "sacramentality," of the body. This is obviously a broader meaning of the word than the sense in which we speak of the seven sacraments (we will clarify this important distinction later). The human body is the "sacrament" of the *human person* in the sense that it makes the invisible mystery of the person visible. Furthermore, in Jesus of Nazareth, his human body becomes the "sacrament" of his *divine Person*.[25] Christ's body "thus expresses humanly the divine ways of the Trinity."[26] Understanding the *sacramentality* of the body as such is the key that opens the door to understanding the body not only as something *biological* but also as something *theological*. Waldstein observes that the "main reason it is difficult for people in the modern age, and particularly for modern intellectuals, to understand the Catholic vision of sex...is—biology." Failing to see the sacramental-theological meaning of the body and reducing it instead to something merely biological "prevents us from understanding and living sex in its full meaning. The nature of sex has become invisible through our Cartesian glasses."[27]

23. *CCC*, no. 1159.
24. *CCC*, no. 477.
25. See *CCC*, no. 515.
26. *CCC*, no. 470; see also no. 477.
27. Waldstein, Introduction, TOB, p. 97.

Let us now return to the Pope's thesis statement, with which I began my commentary. The first part of his thesis states that the "body, in fact, and only the body, is capable of making visible what is invisible: the spiritual and the divine" (TOB 19:4). Contrary to widespread heretical belief, the human person is *not* a spirit trapped in a body. The body is not merely a "shell" or a "house" for the soul. The human being is a *profound unity of soul and body* and it is precisely this unity that constitutes human nature. Thus, "spirit and matter, in man, are not two natures united, but rather their union forms a single nature."[28] In other words, man does not have a "spiritual nature" and a "physical nature," but rather a *human nature* that is both spiritual and physical. Can one *see* the spiritual aspect of human nature? In a sense one can, but only *through the body*. For only the body "is capable of making visible what is invisible: the spiritual and divine." Obviously, to see a human person is to see that person's body. In fact, the human person does not so much "have" a body. Rather, the human person *is* a body.[29]

But there is more to see when we look at the human body—much more! As the Pope's thesis indicates, to look at a human body-person is to see not only the human spirit made visible, but also to see something of *the divine* made visible. In fact, to say "theology of the body" is another way of saying that the human person is made in *God's image and likeness*. This brings us to the second part of the Pope's thesis. The human body "has been created to transfer into the visible reality of the world the mystery hidden from eternity in God, and thus to be a sign of it" (TOB 19:4).

Sign of the Mystery Hidden in God

What is this "mystery hidden from eternity in God" (see Eph 3:9) of which the body is a sign? And in what way is the body a "sign" of it? Sublime questions. Lest we proceed too quickly or casually, we should remember that angels fear to tread where John Paul II humbly dares to take us. His entire catechesis offers patient, prayerful, and studied reflections on these two questions—always with profound reverence for

---

28. *CCC*, no. 365.
29. See Index, TOB, p. 681, for a list of twenty-five examples of John Paul II saying, in one way or another, that the human person *is* a body.

the transcendent "otherness" of the Mystery he is pondering. In due time, we will follow John Paul II "if possible 'to the very depths' " (TOB 87:6) of these mysteries (without, of course, claiming in any way to exhaust them—a metaphysical impossibility). For now we must content ourselves with some preliminary observations.

In the Christian sense, "mystery" does not indicate a divine puzzle to be solved. It indicates the hidden reality and plan of God, the "innermost secret" of God. Although man is forever seeking this mystery, he cannot discover it on his own. The divine mystery is invisible, intangible, incommunicable, ineffable. It is so vast, so far "beyond" man that the only way one can possibly encounter it is if the Mystery chooses to come down to our level and reveal itself. The Mystery *has*. This is the Church's astounding claim and proposal to the world. "By sending his only Son and the Spirit of Love in the fullness of time, God has revealed his innermost secret: God himself is an eternal exchange of love, Father, Son, and Holy Spirit, and he has destined us to share in that exchange."[30]

God is not a tyrant. God is not a slave driver. God is not an old man with a white beard sitting on a throne ready to strike us down whenever we fail him. Nor is God an impersonal "force" at the origins of the cosmos. God has revealed himself in Jesus Christ and through the Holy Spirit as *an eternal exchange of love*. And the sole reason God created us is to share his eternal bliss and beatitude with us. As the *Catechism* insists, "God has no other reason for creating than his love and goodness."[31] All then *is gift*. Human happiness and flourishing come *only by way of welcoming this gift*. Every human hunger, every "ache" and human longing is a cry of the heart for this *gift*—to participate in the eternal exchange of divine love for which we are created. If we listen carefully and prayerfully to what the body "says," we will come to hear it whispering to us this deepest secret hidden in God from all eternity: God is an eternal communion of love, and we are destined to share in this divine bliss! It is *this* theological reality that the human body signifies.

But what enables us to understand the body in this way? According to John Paul's catechesis, it is precisely the gratuitous beauty of sexual

---

30. *CCC*, no. 221.
31. *CCC*, no. 293.

difference and the call of man and woman to become "one flesh" (Gen 2:24). "The sacrament, as a visible sign, is constituted with man," the Pope says, "through his 'visible' masculinity and femininity" (TOB 19:4). In this sacramental context "we fully understand the words in Genesis 2:24: 'For this reason a man will leave his father and his mother and unite with his wife, and the two will be one flesh'" (TOB 19:5). In other words, spousal union in God's design is the original effective sign that communicates the "great mystery" of the inner life of the Trinity to the world. *Stunning.* The more we ponder this, the more the implications multiply. To begin with, the body—and more specifically, the union of man and woman in "one flesh"—*must* be essentially linked to the Incarnation of the Word. For Christ and *only Christ* can communicate divine life to the world. Indeed, as St. Paul says, the one flesh union is a "great mystery," a great foreshadowing that *refers to Christ and the Church* (see Eph 5:31–32). And it does so right from the beginning!

In short, what we will learn throughout our study of the TOB is that human sexuality "is an echo in the human creature," as Angelo Cardinal Scola expresses it, "of that unfathomable mystery from which Jesus Christ has lifted a corner of the veil: the difference in perfect unity that exists in the Trinity, the three persons who are the one God." Scola concludes that the "most appropriate word, coined by Christian thought, for indicating this impenetrable mystery is 'communion.'"[32] God himself is an eternal *Communion* of three Persons. This is the "theology" inscribed in the human body, in masculinity and femininity. A man's body does not make sense by itself, nor does a woman's body. Seen in light of each other, we discover the call to *communion.* And this communion of "two," in the normal course of events, leads to "a third" (see TOB 21:4).

Here we discover an earthly sign, a created or human version, so to speak, of the uncreated divine mystery of the Trinity. "In some way, therefore—even if in the most general way—the body enters into the definition of sacrament, which is 'a visible sign of an invisible reality,' namely, of the spiritual, transcendent, and divine reality. In this sign— and through this sign—God gives himself to man in his transcendent truth and in his love" (TOB 87:5). Of course, we cannot reduce the

---

32. *The Nuptial Mystery* (Grand Rapids, MI: Eerdmans, 2005), p. 131.

spiritual and divine mystery to its bodily sign. The Mystery itself *infinitely* transcends its bodily sign. Thus, the body never affords a total clearing of the mystery it signifies. Yet, as human beings, we need the sign of the body not only to speak about the spiritual mystery of God, but to encounter it. This is the very logic of the Incarnation. As the *Catechism* relates, "As a being at once body and spirit, man expresses and perceives spiritual realities through physical signs and symbols. As a social being, man needs signs and symbols to communicate with others.... The same holds true for his relationship with God."[33]

■ Because of sin we all have blurred vision when it comes to seeing the body as a "sign" of the divine mystery. We know the body says *something*, something we all have a deep hunger to know, understand, and experience. But we need an epiphany to realize that that "something" is the "great mystery" of the Trinity and of Christ's love for the Church. The following experience brought this home to me. I had always been drawn to a beautiful old chapel at the seminary in the Archdiocese of Denver where I teach. One day I overheard a tour guide explain the rich symbolism of the architecture. The chapel, built in the shape of a cross, has an elaborate chandelier representing Christ as "Light of the World." The chandelier hangs at the place of Jesus' head on this cross. Twelve pillars in the nave represent the twelve apostles, and seven arches between these pillars represent the seven sacraments. Every detail has a meaning. The architect had designed this chapel in the lines and curves of its bricks and mortar to proclaim the "great mystery" of Christ and the Church. Although the beauty of this chapel had always drawn me to it, I needed to have someone who understood the chapel's meaning explain it. When he did, it was like putting on a new pair of glasses. When he did—epiphany!

The analogy with the chapel is more pertinent than one might first think. The human body itself is a chapel of sorts—a "temple of the Holy Spirit." The divine Architect designed our male and female bodies (both externally and internally) to proclaim the mystery of Christ and his life-giving union with the Church. Ultimately, whether we realize it or not, this is why we are all

---

33. *CCC*, no. 1146.

drawn to the human body—why we are deeply stirred by the mystery of its masculine and feminine beauty, and why we all yearn for intimacy and communion. Sin has blurred our vision. We are dyslexic and sometimes even illiterate when it comes to reading this "language." We are even prone at times to desecrate this holy temple because of our blindness. In some sense, each one of us is the blind man in the Gospel who must cry out, "Jesus, son of David, have mercy on me! I want to see!" John Paul's TOB is like a pair of reading glasses that brings the Word proclaimed by the body into focus. With these glasses, we are able to see the body for what it is—a proclamation of the "great mystery" of Christ and the Church and an icon of the inner life of the Trinity.

The Marriage of Theology and Anthropology

John Paul II's theological vision of the body can seem almost too grand. How could something so "earthy" and human be meant to reveal something so heavenly and divine? As the phrase "theology of the body" indicates, John Paul wants to help us embrace the profound link or marriage between *theology* (the study of God) and *anthropology* (the study of man). John Paul observes in one of his early encyclicals that many currents of thought both in the past and present tend to separate theology and anthropology and even set them in opposition. The Church, however, "seeks to link them up in human history in a deep and organic way." In fact, the Holy Father states that an emphasis on this theology-anthropology link was "one of the basic principles, perhaps the most important one, of the teaching of the [Second Vatican] Council." Whatever our fears or reluctance, John Paul insists that "we must act upon this principle with faith, with an open mind and with all our heart."[34]

John Paul does precisely this throughout his TOB. By virtue of the Incarnation, *the human body is the link* between theology and anthropology. As the Holy Father says, Christ's body is "a tabernacle of glory... where the divine and the human meet in an embrace that can never be separated."[35] We are speaking here of a perfect marriage of the divine and human that does not blur the distinction. Christ is not a confused

---

34. *Dives in Misericordia*, 1.
35. *Orientale Lumen*, 15.

mixture of the divine and the human. He is true God and true man united in the mystery of his divine Person.[36] Jesus Christ is the God-Man, or as John Paul poetically expressed it, he is "the human face of God and the divine face of man."[37] Elsewhere the Pope writes: "The mystery of the Incarnation lays the foundations for an anthropology which, reaching beyond its own limitations and contradictions, moves toward God himself, indeed toward the goal of 'divinization.'"[38]

Christianity is often accused of "demonizing" the body. No! *Demons* demonize the body and then spitefully blame the Church for their dirty work. Christianity, in fact, *divinizes* the body! Quoting St. Athanasius, the *Catechism* teaches us that "the Son of God became man so that we might become God." In other words, the "Word became flesh to make us *'partakers of the divine nature.'*"[39] And we do so *bodily*. For in Christ "the whole fullness of deity dwells bodily" (Col 2:9).

The Scandal of the Body

The paradox and implications of an enfleshed God never fail to confound the human heart. A phantom deity is much more tenable and, let us be honest, much more becoming than a God with a human body—a male body which was, as the patristic saying goes, "complete in all the parts of a man." Christians are those who face squarely the implications and the scandal of an incarnate God and proclaim: "I believe" (*credo*). The Catholic Church remains forever immersed in wonder at this paradox, honoring and praising the womb that bore him and the breasts he sucked (see Lk 11:27).

A suspicion toward the physical world and discomfort with all things sexual is by no means a neurosis induced by Christianity. It hangs like a dark shadow over all human experience.[40] Like the rest of humanity, Christians have been and still are affected and even infected by it. Through the centuries the Church has defended the goodness of the physical world and the sacredness of the human body against many

---

36. See *CCC*, no. 464.
37. *Ecclesia in America*, 67.
38. *Novo Millennio Inuente*, 23.
39. *CCC*, no. 460.
40. For an excellent treatment of this, see the chapter entitled "Flight from Sex" in Christopher Derrick's book *Sex and Sacredness* (San Francisco: Ignatius Press, 1982).

heresies.[41] The Church still battles today to counter the heretical "spirit good-body bad" dichotomy that many people assume to be orthodox Christian belief. How can one stress it enough? *Christianity does not reject the body!* In a virtual "ode to the flesh," the *Catechism* proclaims: "'The *flesh* is the hinge of salvation.'[42] We believe in God who is creator of the *flesh*; we believe in the Word made *flesh* in order to redeem the *flesh*; we believe in the resurrection of the *flesh*, the fulfillment of both the creation and the redemption of the *flesh*."[43]

Suspicion toward the body, sexuality, and the material world is not only alien to authentic Christian belief, but is its very antithesis (see TOB 46:6). We encounter the spiritual mystery of God most intimately *through our bodies* and the elements of the material world: through bathing *the body* with water; anointing *the body* with oil; eating and drinking *the body* and *blood* of Christ; confessing with one's own *lips* to another *body*; the laying of *hands* on another *body*; and yes, through that reality by which a man and woman join their lives together so intimately as to be "*one body*."[44] In fact, marriage is not just one of the seven sacraments. Insofar as marriage points us "from the beginning" to the infinitely greater mystery of Christ's union with the Church, John Paul teaches that marriage is "*the foundation of the whole sacramental order*" (TOB 95b:7). This means that "all the sacraments of the New Covenant find their prototype in some way in marriage" (TOB 98:2). For each sacrament has as its aim to unite us with Christ our Bridegroom in a fruitful and indissoluble union of love. This earthy, spousal mysticism is deeply imbedded in the Catholic imagination and permeates John Paul's TOB.

3. The Great Spousal Analogy

God Wants to "Marry" Us

Scripture uses many images to describe the mystery of God's relationship with humanity: father and son, bridegroom and bride, king

---

41. See *CCC*, no. 299.
42. Tertullian, *De res.* 8, 2: PL 2, 852.
43. *CCC*, no. 1015, emphasis added.
44. See *CCC*, nos. 1084, 1113.

and subjects, shepherd and sheep, vine and branches, head and body. Christ even compares himself to a mother hen caring for her chicks. Each of these images has value. But one stands out among the others. One has influenced the whole history of Christian thought like no other. This image, in fact, is not merely an image but a *sacrament* that *efficaciously* communicates the mystery it signifies: the relationship of bridegroom and bride.[45] The Scriptures employ this image more than any other. The greatest mystics also favor it. John Paul, deeply imbued with Carmelite mysticism, shares this same preference. In keeping with the Carmelite tradition, John Paul uses the "great spousal analogy" as a lens through which to view the entirety of God's plan of salvation.[46]

We can observe that from beginning to end, the Bible tells a story about marriage.[47] It begins with the creation of man and woman and their call to become "one flesh." Throughout the Old Testament the prophets speak of God's love for his people as the love of a husband for his bride. The Song of Songs—that great biblical ode to erotic love at the pinnacle of the Old Testament—has given countless saints a language for describing their own mystical experiences of union with God. In the New Testament, Christ literally *embodies* the love of the eternal Bridegroom, becoming "one flesh" with all humanity through the Incarnation. Skip to the end of the Bible; the book of Revelation describes heaven as *the marriage of the Lamb.*

Penetrating further into this scriptural paradigm, we can observe that *the first* human words recorded in the Bible are the words of the bridegroom rejoicing at the sight of his naked bride: "At last, you are the one!" (see Gen 2:23). And *the final* human words recorded in the Bible are the words of the Bride longing for the gift of the Bridegroom: "The Spirit and the Bride say, 'Come'... Come, Lord Jesus!" (Rev 22:17, 20). The whole of biblical revelation unfolds between the marriage of *the first* Adam and Eve and the marriage of *the final* Adam and Eve, Christ and the Church. In turn, spousal theology looks to these nuptial

---

45. See *CCC*, nos. 757, 772, 796, 808, 823, 867, 1089.

46. It is important to realize that the spousal analogy is not the only lens through which to view the truths of the faith, even if it is fundamental. John Paul II's preference for the spousal analogy does not undermine other theological traditions in any way (they are all vital to the universality of the Church). A comparative study of the TOB with these other traditions would be helpful, but is beyond the scope of this project.

47. See *CCC*, no. 1602.

bookends as a key for interpreting all that lies between. From this perspective we see that God's mysterious and eternal plan is to espouse us to himself forever (see Hos 2:19)—to "marry" us. Respecting our freedom, the heavenly Bridegroom proposes this marital plan and awaits our *fiat*, our freely given "yes" to his invitation.

One of the critical illuminations of the TOB is that this eternal "marital plan" is not "out there" somewhere. It could not be any closer to us. It is *right here*, mysteriously recapitulated in our very being as male and female. The Gospel mystery is inscribed sacramentally in the theology of our bodies: "'For this reason a man shall leave his father and mother and be joined to his wife, and the two shall become one flesh.' This is a great mystery, and I mean in reference to Christ and the church" (Eph 5:31–32). Christ left his Father in heaven; he left the home of his mother on earth—to give up his body for his Bride, so that we might become "one flesh" with him.[48] Where do we consummate our marriage with Christ? Heaven is the ultimate answer. But here on earth we consummate it sacramentally in the Eucharist. "*The Eucharist*," as John Paul II describes it, "is *the Sacrament of the Bridegroom and of the Bride*." In fact, "Christ, in instituting the Eucharist...thereby wished to express the relationship between man and woman, between what is 'feminine' and what is 'masculine.' It is a relationship willed by God in both the mystery of creation and in the mystery of Redemption."[49]

Let us pause to ponder this astounding statement. The deepest truth of human sexuality, according to John Paul II, is revealed through the Eucharist. In fact, in giving us *his body* in the Eucharist—the gift of *himself* as Bridegroom—Christ wanted to reveal the deepest meaning of *our bodies* as male and female. It is in the Eucharist that Christ fully reveals man to himself and makes his supreme calling clear! Conversely, when all the confusion is cast out and all the distortions untwisted, we discover that the deepest meaning of human sexuality is its signification of the Eucharist. The holy communion of man and woman in "one flesh" is a great mystery that is meant to signify the holy communion of Christ and the Church consummated in the Eucharist.

---

48. See *CCC*, nos. 790, 791, 1396, 1621.
49. *Mulieris Dignitatem*, 26.

■   I never met my father-in-law; he died when my wife was a
girl. But I admire him tremendously because of this story. At Mass
the day after his wedding, having just consummated his marriage
the night before, he was in tears after receiving the Eucharist.
When his new bride inquired as to the reason, he said, "For the
first time in my life I understood the meaning of those words,
'This is my body given for you.'"

The spousal analogy, then, is not merely a happy coincidence. This
is the fundamental manner in which God chose to reveal his own
covenant of life and love to the world—by creating us in such a way (as
male and female) that we could image this covenant and participate in
it. Whenever God establishes a covenant with his people, whether it is
with Adam (Gen 1:28), Noah (Gen 9:1), Abraham (Gen 17:5–6),
Jacob (Gen 35:10–12), or Moses (Lev 26:9), we see the call of bridegroom and bride to *signify* this covenant in spousal union. The very
promise of the Old Covenant established with Abraham was fruitfulness in the marital embrace: "Behold my covenant is with you, and you
shall be the father of a multitude of nations.... I will make you exceed-
ingly fruitful" (Gen 17:4, 6). Then God commanded Abraham: "You
shall be circumcised in the flesh of your foreskins, and *it shall be a sign*
of the covenant between me and you.... So shall my covenant be *in your
flesh* an everlasting covenant" (Gen 17:11, 13).

■   Male circumcision is a central element of Old Testament revelation. Despite a common reluctance to do so, we must ponder
this oddity: Why would the Heavenly Father demand of his people
that the most intimate part of the male genitalia be perpetually
deprived of its natural covering? Why did the Lord of the Universe
institute *this* to set his chosen people apart and identify them as his
followers? How is *this* physical reality an effective sign of God's
spiritual, covenant love in the world? While scholars of Scripture
and Jewish history can answer these questions more fully—indeed,
the meaning of circumcision as actually practiced in the ancient
Near East is multiform—I will offer the following musings.

Who would most often see this sign and when? Every time a
male descendant of Abraham consummated his marriage, he and
his wife would be reminded of God's promise of fruitful love.

Circumcision "speaks" in some way of the mystery of fatherhood and of the price required of men if they are truly to image *God's* fatherhood in the world. By inflicting this wound upon the male, it appears as if the Heavenly Father is saying that men must come to learn something that women already seem to know. Namely, participation in God's generous love involves the shedding of blood and the sacrifice of one's own flesh (*right where it hurts*, if one might dare to acknowledge it). Is this not precisely what Christ the Bridegroom teaches us? Circumcision foreshadows his ultimate sacrifice of flesh and blood.[50] The promise of fruitful spousal union given to Abraham is definitively consummated in Christ's body "given up for us." The cross, in turn, John Paul tells us, becomes "a fresh manifestation of the eternal fatherhood of God."[51]

Here we gain insight into why it was the Father's will, as Wojtyla once reflected, for Christ to allow himself to be "stripped naked" in the hour of his passion.[52] What might the spectators have noticed about the man crucified in the middle? He was a son of Abraham, a Jew—a "chosen one." Yet this was not simply any Jew. This was the "King of the Jews." This was *the* Chosen One. Those persons gathered at the foot of the cross—Jews and Gentiles alike—were eyewitnesses to the definitive and most intimate revelation on earth of the mystery of the Father's love unveiled in Christ's (circumcised) flesh. As St. Cyril of Jerusalem triumphantly proclaims, Christ "was nailed naked to the Cross, and by his very nudity defeated the principalities and powers, dragging them into his triumphal cortege."[53] In the "naked Christ" and his body "given up for us," do we not see how the sign of the Old Covenant—circumcision—is fulfilled in the sign of the New—the Eucharist? The Eucharistic sacrifice, in fact, effects the most fruitful spousal union of the cosmos: "Woman, behold, your son!" (Jn 19:26). Based on the biblical context, we could put Christ's words from the cross this way: "Woman, behold, in these your spiritual labor pains, you are giving birth to offspring more numerous than the stars."

---

50. See *CCC*, no. 1150.
51. *Redemptor Hominis*, 9.
52. See *Sign of Contradiction* (New York: Seabury Press, 1979), p. 192.
53. *Mystagogical Catechesis*, 2:2.

If the Old Covenant was established on Abraham's fertility, we can recognize that the New Covenant was established on Mary's fertility. Her *fiat*—"Let it be done unto me"—marks a new *virginal* expression of spousal love and fruitfulness. In offering her "yes" to God's marriage proposal, she stands as "the archetype of humanity."[54] In turn, this biblical "woman" becomes the guarantor of realism in the life-giving communion of God and man. With her *fiat* Mary not only becomes God's virginal Bride (here Mary is a perfect symbol of the Church as Bride), she also conceives God's eternal Son (here Mary is a perfect symbol of the Church as Mother). Mary, having received the ineffable, invisible, eternal, immortal power and "seed" of the Most High God (see Lk 1:35), was impregnated with the fulfillment of all God's promises and the realization of man's eternal destiny. As the *Catechism* states, "The spousal character of the human vocation in relation to God is fulfilled perfectly in Mary's virginal motherhood."[55]

Understanding the Spousal Analogy Properly

In his fine and scholarly work *The Nuptial Mystery*, Angelo Cardinal Scola justly warns of two imbalances to be aware of in understanding the spousal analogy. One involves excess and the other deficiency.

An excessive or "maximalist" interpretation, Scola writes, "ultimately tends toward an anthropomorphic deformation of our understanding of God, and even into introducing sexuality into God himself.... Its underlying logic, whether its proponents intend it to or not, ultimately makes the claim that spousal categories are...the only categories fit to illuminate Christian dogma. To move in this direction is to engage in bad theology."[56] For all the value of the spousal analogy, it is critical (lest we end in heresy!) to recognize its limits. As John Paul II points out, "analogy" always indicates, at the same time, both similarity and substantial dissimilarity (see TOB 33:3). It should be obvious that the spousal analogy "cannot offer an adequate and complete understanding of that absolutely transcendent Reality." The divine mystery "remains *transcendent with respect to this analogy* as with

---

54. See *Mulieris Dignitatem*, 4.
55. *CCC*, no. 505.
56. *The Nuptial Mystery*, p. 394.

respect to any other analogy with which we try to express it in human language" (TOB 95b:1).

Perhaps in response to the "maximalist" imbalance, there are those who run the opposite risk of a "minimalist" interpretation. Scola observes that such thinkers "fight every attempt to give the nuptial mystery theological weight." For them, "spousal vocabulary could at most be likened to the language of the parables (and thus would not have even a symbolic value): nuptial images would be on par with many other biblical images, for example those of the shepherd and his sheep."[57] In response, one must certainly acknowledge that the spousal analogy, like all analogies, is woefully inadequate in its representation of the divine mystery. Yet, if all analogies are inadequate, the biblical evidence and the weight of the theological tradition indicate that the spousal analogy is the *least* inadequate. "In this entire world," John Paul says, "there is not a more perfect, more complete image of God, Unity and Community. There is no other human reality which corresponds more, humanly speaking, to that divine mystery."[58]

The Particular Value of the Spousal Analogy

Spousal love indicates a total self-giving, a total self-donation. This is the particular value of the spousal analogy, according to John Paul II: it emphasizes the aspect of God's "total" *gift of himself* to man (see TOB 95b:4). This is "a characteristic of the mystery that is not directly emphasized...by any other analogy used in the Bible" (TOB 95b:3). To recognize "theology" in the body is to recognize the body as a sign of this divine self-giving love. The body itself, as we will learn in great detail from John Paul, has a "spousal meaning."[59] For it is the body that reveals (makes visible) the call to self-giving love. It is the body that reveals the mystery of "gift." John Paul makes this point clearly when he states, "This is *the body: a witness* to creation as a fundamental gift, and therefore a witness *to Love as the source from which this same giving*

---

57. Ibid., p. 395.

58. Homily on the Feast of the Holy Family, December 30, 1988.

59. Most students of the TOB in the English-speaking world are more familiar with the expression "nuptial meaning of the body." This is how the Italian phrase "*significato sponsale del corpo*" was most often rendered in the first English translations of the Pope's catecheses. The new Waldstein translation uses "spousal meaning of the body," a more accurate translation.

springs. Masculinity-femininity—namely, sex—is the original sign of...[God's] creative donation.... This is the meaning with which sex enters into the theology of the body" (TOB 14:4).

Penetrating further, we can recognize the value of the spousal analogy across the breadth of human experience. Every genuine expression of love bears a threefold spousal imprint, so to speak. For spousal love rests on these three interrelated dynamisms:[60] the complementarity of sexual difference or "otherness";[61] the call to communion through the self-giving love to which this summons us; and the fecundity to which this leads.[62] We find the paradigmatic expression of this love obviously in Genesis 2:24—"the two shall become one flesh." But marriage is not the only way to express the call to love inscribed in the spousal meaning of the body. The spousal character is a permanent dimension of love since all love entails some sort of complementarity ("otherness"), mutual self-giving, and fruitfulness. "Every form of love will always bear this masculine and feminine character."[63]

This is true even of God's love. For the Scripture proclaims spousal love to be a "great mystery" that refers to Christ and the Church (see Eph 5:31–32). To take this spousal analogy seriously, then, is to recognize with John Paul II that the

> Church cannot therefore be understood as the mystical body of Christ, as the sign of man's covenant with God in Christ, or as the universal sacrament of salvation, unless we keep in mind the "great mystery" involved in the creation of man as male and female and the vocation of both to conjugal love, to fatherhood and to motherhood. The "great mystery," which is the Church and humanity in Christ, does not exist apart from the "great mystery" expressed in the "one flesh"...reality of marriage and the family.[64]

----

60. Angelo Scola presents this idea under the concept of "nuptiality" in his article "The Nuptial Mystery at the Heart of the Church," *Communio* (Winter 1998): 631–62. He expands on it at great length in his book *The Nuptial Mystery* (Eerdmans, 2005).

61. Since the body reveals the interior mystery of the person, sexual complementarity cannot be reduced to biological complementarity. It refers to the whole mystery of man and woman as incarnate persons.

62. John Paul II sometimes distinguishes the body's "generative" or "procreative meaning" from its "spousal meaning" (see TOB 21:2; 23:5), but he also states that the procreative meaning of the body is rooted in its spousal meaning and comes forth organically from it (see TOB 39:5).

63. Pontifical Council for the Family, *The Truth and Meaning of Human Sexuality*, 10.

64. *Letter to Families*, 19.

Here we see just how deeply John Paul's teaching thrusts its roots into Carmelite soil.

Influence of St. John of the Cross

While taking the Catholic sacramental imagination to new heights, John Paul II's TOB remains firmly grounded in the spousal and mystical theology of St. John of the Cross.[65] In studying the works of the Spanish mystic as a young man, Karol Wojtyla encountered a Doctor of the Church (he was named such by Pope Pius XI when Wojtyla was six years old) who saw the spousal analogy as something that illuminated the entirety of the Christian mystery. Christianity itself, as this humble Carmelite friar believed, is an invitation to enter into "mystical marriage" with God.

As John of the Cross wrote, this involves "a total transformation in the Beloved, in which [God and the soul] surrenders the entire possession of self to the other with a certain consummation of the union of love. The soul thereby becomes divine, God through participation, insofar as is possible in this life." He elaborates: "Just as in the consummation of carnal marriage there are two in one flesh, as Sacred Scripture points out (Gen 2:24), so also when the spiritual marriage between God and the soul is consummated, there are two natures in one spirit and love."[66] "A reciprocal love is thus actually formed between God and the soul," as the mystical Doctor wrote elsewhere, "*like the marriage union and surrender*, in which the goods of both...are possessed by both together. *They say to each other what the Son of God spoke to the Father....* All that is mine is yours and yours is mine [Jn 17:10]."[67]

The *Catechism* observes that the "personal relation of the Son to the Father is something that man cannot conceive of nor the angelic powers even dimly see." And yet, confirming precisely the above teaching of

---

65. In what follows, I am indebted to the research of Michael Waldstein from which I draw extensively. By demonstrating the organic connection between John Paul II's TOB and John of the Cross, Waldstein has provided a critical contribution to the entire TOB "cause." His research reveals more clearly how the various original insights of John Paul II represent an organic development of the Catholic theological tradition and not a departure from it.

66. John of the Cross, Commentary on st. 22:3 of the *Spiritual Canticle* (cited also in Introduction, TOB, p. 31).

67. John of the Cross, *The Living Flame of Love*, commentary on st. B3, pars. 78–80 (cited also in Introduction, TOB, pp. 27–28).

John of the Cross, the *Catechism* maintains that "the Spirit of the Son grants a participation in that very relation to us who believe that Jesus is the Christ and that we are born of God."[68] Here we see a certain "touchpoint" between the spousal image and the father-son image.

> Neither St. John of the Cross nor Wojtyla/John Paul II apply spousal language directly to the Trinity. It is the father-son relation, not the bride-bridegroom relation, that is the normative image for the Trinity, in agreement with the teaching of Jesus. Yet, it is clear to both that the archetype and source of spousal love lies in the Trinity: "All that is mine is yours, and yours is mine."[69]

For John of the Cross and his student, John Paul II, human participation in this intimate exchange of the Trinity is not merely a theological idea. It is meant to be a dynamic encounter *experienced through faith* and *lived in contemplative prayer*. As John Paul colorfully expressed in his apostolic letter on St. John of the Cross, through a "life of faith and Christian contemplation" we can gain an "intimate and savory knowledge...of God." Such "savory" knowledge of the divine "is something that goes much beyond theological or philosophical reflection. Many simple and unselfish souls receive it from God by means of the Spirit."[70]

This is *most* important. The common temptation of those with an aptitude for scholarly theology is that of getting "stuck in the head."[71] There are many "simple folk" who, while they couldn't make sense of John Paul II's theological scholarship, have an intimate mystical experience of precisely that which he writes about. These simple souls are actually far better off than those who, while having a gifted grasp of academic theology, have not made the painful and arduous journey "from the head to the heart." The heart is our "hidden center, beyond the grasp of our reason.... It is the place of encounter."[72] Fine-tuning the mind with rigorous academic study is fine and good, but it is not

---

68. *CCC*, no. 2780.

69. Waldstein, Introduction, TOB, p. 33.

70. *Master in the Faith*, 10.

71. I speak here from experience. I have learned (and continue to learn) only through much pain and suffering that studying, teaching, lecturing, and writing books *about* the TOB is one thing. *Living it* is another. If what follows, then, is an indictment of anyone, it is an indictment of myself.

72. *CCC*, no. 2563.

sufficient. In the end, the academic study of theology is for naught if the truths studied do not lead people to a living and transformative *encounter* with the "Mystery" in the depths of the heart.

If our study of John Paul II's TOB is to be more than an academic exercise, we must approach the mystery it explores "on our knees." If we are actually to live the "mystical marriage" with God and not just learn *about* it, we must not fear to allow reason to be "overwhelmed" by love's sweetness and all-embracing power. In short, the scholarly study of theology—if it is not only to *inform* us but also to *transform* us—must be deeply integrated and permeated with prayer. As John Paul II wrote:

> The great mystical tradition of the Church of both East and West... shows how prayer can progress, as a genuine dialogue of love, to the point of rendering the person wholly possessed by the divine Beloved, vibrating at the Spirit's touch, resting filially within the Father's heart. This is...a journey totally sustained by grace, which nonetheless demands an intense spiritual commitment and is no stranger to painful purifications (the "dark night"). But it leads, in various possible ways, to the ineffable joy experienced by the mystics as "nuptial union."

Then he asks, "How can we forget here, among the many shining examples, the teachings of St. John of the Cross...?"[73]

One must add that such intimate and "savory" experiences of prayerful union with God are not only intended for an elite few. Waldstein writes, "Against those who dismiss St. John of the Cross as preoccupied with extraordinary and miraculous mystical phenomena that are irrelevant for ordinary believers," at the core of John Paul II's vision is the belief "that St. John of the Cross's teachings concern the normal development of the supernatural life of faith and love."[74] What John of the Cross and John Paul II describe is none other than "the lived experience of Christ's promise: 'He who loves me will be loved by my Father, and I will love him and manifest myself to him' (Jn 14:21)."[75]

---

73. *Novo Millennio Inuente*, 33.
74. Waldstein, Introduction, TOB, p. 87.
75. *Novo Millennio Inuente*, 33.

Personalism and the Sincere Gift of Self

Waldstein observes that Wojtyla gained a threefold conviction about love from the Spanish mystic that "runs like a deeply embedded watermark through [all] the works of Wojtyla/John Paul II."[76]

(1)   Love involves the gift of self.
(2)   The relationship of spouses is the paradigm of self-giving love in human experience.
(3)   The relationship of Father, Son, and Holy Spirit is the source and model of all self-giving love.[77]

This threefold thesis represents the nexus of Wojtyla/John Paul II's philosophical and theological "personalism." Personalism offers an approach to the ethical life based on a keen awareness of the interior value and dignity of *the person* as a subject of his own acts. It is also based on an integral view of self-giving love as the path to the person's moral perfection. As we shall see, Wojtyla's personalistic approach was greatly enriched by his study of the modern philosophy of Max Scheler (phenomenology). Indeed, "personalism" as such is a modern philosophical movement. However, Wojtyla first encountered an emphasis on the inner world of the person in his study of John of the Cross.

We can recognize the influence of a certain young Polish bishop's personalism in the following teaching of the Second Vatican Council:

> Indeed, the Lord Jesus, when he prayed to the Father "that all may be one...as we are one" (Jn 17:21–22), opened up vistas closed to human reason, for he implied a certain likeness between the union of divine Persons, and the unity of God's sons in truth and love. It follows then, that if man is the only creature on earth that God willed for its own sake, man can only find himself through the sincere gift of self.[78]

Throughout our study we will unfold this key teaching of the Council in relation to the above threefold thesis about love. For now, we can observe that this call of the human person to become a "sincere gift" (point one of what John Paul learned from John of the Cross) is revealed precisely in and through the human body and its spousal meaning (see TOB 15:1). For the spousal relationship is the paradigm

---

76. Waldstein, Introduction, TOB, p. 23.
77. See ibid., pp. 23–24, 29–34, 78.
78. *Gaudium et Spes*, 24.

of all self-giving love (point two above). In turn, living according to
the spousal meaning of our bodies leads not only to the unity of spouses but also serves to build "the unity of all God's sons in truth and
love" (see TOB 100:1; 107:7). Finally, such unity—both the unity of
all God's people (the Church) and the unity of spouses—resounds
as an "echo" in the created world of the eternal unity of Father and Son
in the Holy Spirit: "that all may be one...*as* we are one" (point three
above).

For John Paul II, a great deal hinges on that "*as*" Jesus spoke in his
prayer to the Father. It demonstrates that viewing the Trinity as the
model of human unity and communion—including spousal communion—flows implicitly from the teaching of Christ himself. We can
relate this "as" to other similar instances: "*As* the Father has loved me, so
have I loved you" (Jn 15:9). "This is my commandment, that you love
one another *as* I have loved you" (Jn 15:12). "Husbands, love your wives
as Christ loved the church" (Eph 5:25). The whole of John Paul II's
theological and anthropological vision flows through these "as's"—from
the Father, through Christ's spousal love for the Church, and into the
lives and bodies of concrete men and women.[79]

Oh, that we might live in the "great mystery" of this irradiation of
love! Tragically, as the Pope observes, the deep-seated roots of this mystery "which *has Christ the bridegroom as its ultimate surety*, have been lost
in the modern way of looking at things. The 'great mystery' is threatened in us and all around us."[80] From where does this threat come? It is
no coincidence that St. Paul follows up his teaching on the "great mystery" of spousal union in Ephesians 5 with a call to spiritual battle in
Ephesians 6.

---

79. Waldstein concludes his Introduction to the TOB with a similar statement: "In
Man and Woman He Created Them, John Paul II left us the core of his great vision, deeply
rooted in St. John of the Cross, a vision focused on the mystery of love that reaches from
the Trinity through Christ's spousal relation with the Church to the concrete bodies of
men and women" (p. 128). As stated at the outset of this Prologue, we can also move in
the other direction—from the human body to the union of the sexes, from there to the
union of Christ and the Church, and from there to the union of the three Persons of the
Trinity. This is obviously not a "continuum." For an infinite abyss separates the creature
from the Creator. We can only cross that abyss from earth to heaven because Christ
himself first crossed it from heaven to earth. Once again, we see that everything in the
TOB hinges on the Incarnation.

80. *Letter to Families*, 19.

4. The Spiritual Battle

Human life involves a dramatic battle between good and evil. Indeed, as the Second Vatican Council observed, "a monumental struggle against the powers of darkness pervades the whole history of man. The battle was joined from the very origins of the world and will continue until the last day, as the Lord has attested."[81] It is a battle between truth and lies, between the Word and the anti-Word.

Plagiarizing the Primordial Sacrament

In the beginning, God created everything through his Word—the Word that is truth, love, and "gift." If all of creation involuntarily echoes this Word, God gave man and woman their own voices with which to recite it freely. This "freedom is an exceptional sign of the divine image within man. For God has willed that man remain 'under the control of his own decisions'" (see Sir 15:14).[82] If the human being is the only creature on earth that God created for "its own sake," he is not meant to live for his own sake. He can only find himself "through the sincere gift of himself."[83] This was the divine Word inscribed in the *spousal meaning of the human body*. In the beginning, at the sight of each other's nakedness, the truth of this Word welled up in the hearts of man and woman as a spontaneous love song, sung in the original harmony of what Genesis calls "one flesh." This is why they were naked without shame (see Gen 2:25)—because they lived the truth of "the gift," at least initially.

Between the experience of their original nakedness and the entrance of the fig leaves, man and woman would have their first encounter with "the father of lies." His goal was to get them to deny the gift of God's love, to deny the divine Word. Hence, Wojtyla/John Paul II describes Satan as the "anti-Word."[84] John Paul II's TOB does not emphasize the schemes of the anti-Word but rather the glory and goodness of the Word. Still, in a time such as ours, when even many

---

81. *Gaudium et Spes*, 37.
82. Ibid., 17.
83. Ibid., 24.
84. See *Sign of Contradiction*, pp. 29–34, and *Dominum et Vivificantem*, 37.

Christians consider Satan to be a mere symbol of evil, it is fitting to understand the ways in which this fallen angel actively seeks our ruin. We should ponder: If there is an enemy who wants to keep us from heaven (the marriage of the Lamb), and if the union of man and woman is the foundational way God reveals his plan, what is the enemy going to attack? Where is he going to aim all his arrows?

Tertullian, an early Christian writer, insightfully observed that Satan seeks to counter God's plan by plagiarizing the sacraments.[85] In the sacraments God accomplishes his plan for man, and in them we find the meaning of life and true happiness. By commandeering the sacraments for his purposes, the deceiver markets his counterfeit version of man's path to happiness. In the beginning, there was only one sacrament (see TOB 98:3), what John Paul calls the "primordial sacrament"—the union of man and woman in marriage. This is where Satan attacks. Thus, we can conclude with John Paul that sin and death "have entered into man's history *in some way through the very heart of that unity that had from the 'beginning' been formed by man and woman*, created and called to become 'one flesh' (Gen 2:24)" (TOB 20:1).

God revealed himself to the first man and woman as the God of love, the God of the covenant. This was the Word inscribed in the sacramentality of their bodies and their call to become "one flesh." Soon thereafter, however, the anti-Word entered the scene purveying his own counterfeit version of the story. In a retreat preached to Pope Paul VI in 1976, the future Pope John Paul II observed that if Satan's ultimate goal is to have man deny God's existence, such a denial was not possible "in the beginning." God's existence was all too obvious to the first man and woman. Hence, the first "lap" in the devil's scheme was to "aim straight at the God of the covenant."[86] In other words, Satan sets out to convince man that God is not to be trusted; that he is not a loving Father, but a tyrant, an enemy, against whom man has to defend himself. The Holy Father later emphasized in his international best-seller, *Crossing the Threshold of Hope*, that this "*is truly the key for interpreting reality.... Original sin attempts, then, to abolish fatherhood.*"[87]

---

85. *Prescription Against Heretics*, bk. 40, cited in Father Gabriele Amorth, *An Exorcist Tells His Story* (San Francisco: Ignatius Press, 1999), p. 182.

86. *Sign of Contradiction*, p. 30.

87. *Crossing the Threshold of Hope* (New York: Alfred A. Knopf, 1994), p. 228.

The truth and meaning of this gripping statement will come to light throughout our analysis of the TOB. For now, if we are to understand the nature of the weed which John Paul is trying to uproot in his catechesis, it is important to understand the method by which the deceiver constructs this counterfeit worldview. The devil cannot create out of nothing. As a creature himself, all he can do is take what God created to reveal the mystery of his own fatherhood and twist it, distort it—or, more aptly, tempt us to do so. So if we are looking for what is most sacred in this world, all we need do is look for that which is most often profaned. Is there any question at this moment of history what that is? The gift of the body and sexuality is under a violent, unrelenting attack.

The Symbolic and the Diabolic

In our culture's attack on God's plan for the body and sexuality, we see a great clash between the "symbolic" and the "diabolic." In the Greek, *symballein* means to bring together, gather up, unite. *Diaballein* means to scatter, break apart, rupture. God's eternal plan for man as *symbolized* through the body is union, communion, marriage—this brings life. The deceiver's counterplan for man as *diabolized* through the body is separation, fracture, divorce—this brings death. In a word, Satan aims to make the symbolic *diabolic*. God created the body and the mystery of sexuality with a sacramental language that speaks his own Word. The deceiver incessantly commandeers this holy ground in order to scramble the body's language so that it contradicts the divine Word.

Confronted by a culture that so gravely distorts the meaning of the body and sexuality, Christians can be tempted to eschew these divine gifts. Indeed, one of the main threats facing the Church today is a "spiritualism" in which people disembody their call to holiness. Yet if we respond to the lies in this way, we have not conquered those lies; we have inadvertently bought into them. The body proclaims the Word. The spirit that denies this "incarnational reality" is none other than that of the anti-Word (see 1 Jn 4:2–3).

How, then, do we conquer these lies and live an integrated life, an embodied spirituality? We must first reclaim what Satan has plagiarized. John Paul's entire catechesis on the body is a clarion call to do just that. The very title—*theology* of the *body*—calls us to the integration of the spiritual and the material. Without this integration we inevitably suffer from a kind of "split personality."

"Angelism" and "Animalism"

The spiritual has an ontological priority over the physical. Yet, without blurring the distinction, God united spirit and matter by creating man from the dust of the ground and from the breath of his own life (see Gen 2:7). In this way, man is similar to both angels and animals but also remarkably different. Angels are spiritual persons, but they are not bodies and, hence, are not sexually differentiated. Animals are bodies and are sexually differentiated, but they are not persons. Human beings, however, are a strange combination of the two. We are "angimals," so to speak; spiritual *and* physical creatures; we are sexually differentiated *body-persons*.[88] This means that man can be neither reduced to the material world, nor divorced from it. Although the "invisible" determines man more than the "visible," the visible expresses the invisible (see TOB 7:4).

This original harmony of body and soul, sexuality and spirituality was sustained by the harmony between God and man and was manifested most pointedly in the original harmony of man and woman. Like nothing else, the primordial sacrament—that indissoluble union of two persons in one flesh—speaks to the original alliance of spirit with flesh. Yet when man accepted the anti-Word, his sin shattered these harmonies, introducing a "great divorce" into the original order and unity of the cosmos. A fallen world, then, is a world of estranged spouses: estrangement between divinity and humanity, heaven and earth, soul and body, spirituality and sexuality, sacredness and sensuality, masculinity and femininity.[89] According to its own diabolic logic, such alienation leads to death. When such estrangement becomes

---

88. See *CCC*, nos. 327, 362–68.

89. This same estrangement carries over into a great many realities that belong together in a creative tension, in a creative unity-in-distinction: theology and anthropology, God and science, reason and faith, head and heart, truth and freedom, academia and prayer, objectivity and subjectivity, theology and philosophy, grace and nature, east and west, right and left, conservative and liberal, action and contemplation, virginity and marriage, joy and suffering. It is only a result of sin that distinction causes disunity. "In the beginning it was not so" (Mt 19:8).

embedded in the fabric of society, that society can be nothing but a "culture of death."

Those who perpetuate such a culture tend to live that "great divorce" within their spiritual/material nature as if it were completely normal. Lacking the reintegration of spirit and flesh to which we are called in Christ, they inevitably lean toward one side of the divide or the other, toward what we could call "angelism" and "animalism." One manifests a spiritual value deprived of earthiness while the other manifests an earthiness blind to spiritual value.[90] Both contribute equally to the disintegration of man and culture.

Angelism promotes a "spiritual life" divorced from the body. Failing to uphold the body's personal dignity, it tends toward prudishness and puritanism. Because it considers the body and all things sexual inherently tainted and "unspiritual," it leads to repression of sexual feelings and desire. The angelistic moral code is rigorism; it condemns even some of the most natural manifestations of sexuality as impure. Many Christians throughout history have fallen prey to this distortion. Even today people make the calamitous mistake of considering this "holiness."

Animalism, on the other hand, springs from a materialistic worldview and promotes a "carnal" life divorced from the spirit. Since in this outlook the body and sexual matters are not informed by man's spiritual dignity, animalism tends toward the indecent and the shameless. It encourages men and women to indulge their fallen sexual impulses without restraint and promotes bodily pleasure as man's ultimate fulfillment. The animalistic moral code is permissivism; it condemns any manifestation of temperance as a hindrance to freedom. All we need to do is turn on the television or walk through the check-out line at a grocery store to see how prevalent this distortion has become.

Integrating Body and Spirit

Cultural trends tend to oscillate between these two extremes. The twentieth century, for example (at least in much of the West), began with a widespread prudishness in which the mere sight of a woman's

---

90. See Rocco Buttiglione, *Karol Wojtyla: The Thought of the Man Who Became Pope John Paul II* (Grand Rapids, MI: Eerdman's Publishing, 1997), p. 25.

ankle could cause scandal. Yet it ended with a widespread shameless-ness that has "normalized" even the most base sexual perversions. In this way we see how angelism and animalism each contain the seeds of the other. There is no "pure" angelist just as there is no "pure" animalist. Each is trying unsuccessfully to suffocate an indomitable aspect of his own nature, which, resisting the weight of repression, will eventually explode with a force that propels the person (and the culture) to the other extreme. Pendulum swing is understandable, but the Incarnation teaches another way—the path of (re)integrating spirit and flesh.

The need for man to discover his true (integrated) self could not be any more pressing. The stakes are incredibly high. Wojtyla knew well that a dualistic anthropology coupled with the modern will to power lead us to the gas chamber, to the abortion mill, to the culture of death. According to Wojtyla's read on "the signs of the times," it seems the ancient clash between the "great mystery" and the "great divorce," between the "symbolic" and the "diabolic" is coming to a head. In the retreat given to the Roman Curia in 1976, Cardinal Wojtyla boldly stated that we may now be "experiencing the highest level of tension between the Word and the anti-Word in the whole of human history." He even went so far as to suggest that this may be "the last lap along that way of denial which started out from around the tree of the knowl-edge of good and evil."[91]

The attack on God's fatherhood—on the truth that "God is love"—was only the first lap in "a very long process that winds its devious way throughout history." The deceiver has worked in stages, patiently awaiting the opportune time to induce man toward the ultimate denial of God's very existence. In "the first stage of human history this temp-tation was not only not accepted, but also had not been fully formulat-ed. But the time has now come," Wojtyla tells us; "this aspect of the devil's temptation has found the historical context that suits it." Man is now prepared to deny the very existence of God. This is not the athe-ism of the skeptics or the despairing that has dotted history. This is a planned, systematic attempt at "liberation from the very idea of God in order to bolster man."[92] This is the idea that to believe in God—espe-cially the Christian God—is inherently dehumanizing. The French

91. *Sign of Contradiction*, pp. 34–35.
92. Ibid., pp. 31, 34.

Jesuit theologian Henri de Lubac described this as "atheistic human-ism."[93] In Karol Wojtyla he would find a voice of agreement that this radical denial of God is at the heart of all the man-made hells of the twentieth century.

5. The Deepest Substratum of Ethics and Culture

John Paul II did not reflect on the human condition through binoc-ulars. He was a man with calloused hands who was personally involved in the greatest tragedies and triumphs of the twentieth century. The rich and often pained texture of his life made Karol Wojtyla uniquely suited to press into life's hardest questions. Prior to becoming the 264th and third longest reigning-pope in history, he was an orphan (his mother and brother died when he was a boy, and his father when he was twenty), a quarryman, factory worker, athlete, avid outdoorsman, actor, mystic, poet, playwright, patriot, parish priest, confessor, spiritual director, philosopher, theologian, author, university professor, bishop, father of the Second Vatican Council, and cardinal.

He was such a champion of human life, dignity, and freedom pre-cisely because of the crucible of death, degradation, and tyranny in which he was formed. The Nazis invaded his beloved Poland when he was nineteen. Death and degradation surrounded him. The stench of burning bodies from nearby Auschwitz hovered in the air. He would have been sent there, too, or shot on the spot, had his role in the under-ground resistance or his clandestine seminary studies been discovered. Several brushes with death—and, at times, his inexplicable survival—seem to indicate that Providence had special plans for Karol.[94] The Nazis left Poland six years later, but another totalitarian power took control. As a young man, Wojtyla mounted a cultural resistance to Communism that would continue throughout his life as priest, bishop, cardinal, and pontiff, ultimately playing an essential role in the collapse of the Iron Curtain.

While many of his contemporaries concluded that life was absurd, Wojtyla wrestled with God, searching for answers to life's hardest ques-

---

93. See Henri de Lubac, *The Drama of Atheistic Humanism* (San Francisco: Ignatius Press, 1995). See also *CCC*, no. 2124.
94. See *Witness to Hope*, pp. 69–72.

tions. How? Why? What could lead man, who is bestowed with God-like dignity, to drink from the dregs of raw evil? Surface solutions did not interest Wojtyla. He wanted to go to the root of it all and find the first event in the chain reaction that led humanity to embrace the evils that flow from "atheistic humanism." What is that root?

At the Origins of Evil

Although the origin of sin and evil is shrouded in mystery, there are certain things we can know. At the root of man's sin is a failure to trust God, an abuse of freedom, and an act of disobedience.[95] In short, sin consists of a failure of love in man's heart. What John Paul II empha-sizes in his teaching is that the divine plan of love has been inscribed by God *in the body*—more specifically, in our creation *as male and female* and the call of the two to become "one flesh." "This is *the body*," he says, "a witness *to Love*" (TOB 14:4). At the origin of evil, then, is man's fail-ure to read and embrace the "witness of the body."

The Holy Father was convinced that the call to spousal love and communion inscribed in our masculine and feminine bodies is "the fundamental component of human existence in the world" (TOB 15:5), "the foundation of human life,"[96] and, hence, "the deepest sub-stratum of human ethics and culture" (TOB 45:3). John Paul's quest for answers to the enigma of human existence led him to the firm convic-tion, as he himself states, that the dignity and balance of human life depend always and everywhere on the proper ordering of love between the sexes. Who will woman be for man? Who will man be for woman? The human project stands or falls on the answer to these questions (see TOB 43:7). For if we live according to the true spousal meaning of our bodies, *we fulfill the very meaning of our being and existence* (see TOB 15:1). But if we reject the true meaning of our bodies, we forfeit the transcendent, spiritual truth of love, separate ourselves from God, and civilization ultimately implodes.

While this dynamic is played out primarily in marriage and family life, it applies to all men and women, whatever their state in life. Inasmuch as *human existence itself* is linked to the mystery of human

---

95. See *CCC*, no. 397.
96. *Ecclesia in America*, 46.

sexuality, answers to the most basic questions about human life pass by way of our understanding of maleness and femaleness and the call of the two to communion. "What does it mean to be a man?" is the most important question a man can ask himself. Likewise, "What does it mean to be a woman?" is the most important question a woman can ask herself. These are *inherently sexual* questions—or, rather, questions inherently about sexuality—because, created as male and female, we are inherently sexual beings. As John Paul affirms, "sexuality...is by no means something purely biological, but concerns the innermost being of the human person as such."[97] Thus, the way men and women answer the above questions determines whether the entire edifice of culture and society rests on solid rock or shifting sands.

The Wellspring of Culture

We can appreciate the vital role of the sexual relationship in shaping ethics and culture in the simple truth that the family is the fundamental cell of society. If society has a cancer, it must be treated at this cellular level.[98] But, pressing further, what is the nucleus of this cell? What is the origin of the family if not the sexual embrace? Wojtyla describes the conjugal union of man and woman, then, not only as "the *natural* foundation" but also as "the ontological core of the family."[99] In this sense, conjugal union is also the fountainhead of civilization, the wellspring of culture. Open to God's inspiration and ordered toward love and life, it builds families and, in turn, a culture of love and life. Closed to divine inspiration and ordered against love and life, sexual union not only disorients and disintegrates marriage and the family, but it also ultimately leads to a culture of utility and death. In short, the relationship of the sexes becomes the meeting place of God and man and the origin of a truly human civilization, or it becomes man's point of closure to God and the first step in the disintegration of civilization.

Is this not why fruitful spousal union was so strongly emphasized throughout salvation history, beginning with the Creator's first instruc-

---

97. *Familiaris Consortio*, 11; see *CCC*, no. 2332.

98. See *CCC*, no. 2207.

99. "Parenthood as a Community of Persons," in *Person and Community: Selected Essays*, trans. Theresa Sandok (New York: Peter Lang, 1993), p. 339.

tion to man and woman to "be fruitful and multiply" (Gen 1:28)? This is not merely an injunction to propagate; in some way it holds the key to human flourishing. For it calls us to live in the image in which we are made. It calls us to love as God loves, by first receiving that love and then sharing it in life-giving communion with the "other." This sums up the Gospel and is the key to human happiness. Hence, the "new" commandment Christ gives us to love as he loves (see Jn 15:12) is nothing but an echo and reformulation of the original human vocation outlined in Genesis—and, as we learn in a theology of the body, this vocation is stamped in our flesh. The family relationships founded on the union of the sexes provide the most basic school in which we learn the law of life that is God's self-giving love. The spousal meaning of the body proclaims the basic truth upheld by the Church's teaching on sexual morality, that man can only find himself through the sincere gift of himself.

Hence, confusion about sexual morality, as Karol Wojtyla wrote in his 1960 book *Love and Responsibility*, "involves a danger perhaps greater than is generally realized: the danger of confusing the basic and fundamental human tendencies, the main paths of human existence. Such confusion," he concluded, "must clearly affect the whole spiritual position of man."[100] Because human life itself passes by way of sexual union, the choices and actions of men and women "take on the whole weight of human existence in the union of the two" (TOB 115:3).

This is why John Paul II devoted the first major teaching project of his pontificate to presenting a theology of the body. If his goal is to show the world the path for building a culture of life, the only adequate starting point is to return to God's original plan for the body and sexuality. As the Holy Father states, it "is an illusion to think we can build a true culture of human life if we do not...accept and experience sexuality and love and the whole of life according to their true meaning and their close inter-connection."[101] Unless we regain an incarnate theological vision of man and woman and their call to communion, we will remain divided at the deepest level of the interaction of body and soul, and the "great divorce" will reign supreme over the "great mystery" of spousal union.

---

100. *Love and Responsibility*, p. 66.
101. *Evangelium Vitae*, 97.

Christ Heals the Rift

The first sentence of John Paul II's first encyclical serves as the lodestar for his entire pontificate: "The Redeemer of man, Jesus Christ, is the center of the universe and of history."[102] This radical "Christocentrism"—a specific rebuttal to modern atheistic ideologies—reveals John Paul II's deepest conviction: Only in the mystery of the Word made flesh does the enigma of the universe, of history, and of humanity come to light. "Christ fully reveals man to himself and makes his supreme calling clear" specifically by revealing the love of the Father, poured out to heal the rift in us caused by original sin.

The very dynamism of the Incarnation effects this healing. The Word made flesh *is* the reconciliation of the "great divorce" between God and man, heaven and earth, soul and body, sacredness and sensuality, spirituality and sexuality, man and woman. All is made one, all is summed up, all that had been fractured is brought back together in Christ (see Eph 1:10). Through the "redemption of the body" and the "life in the Spirit" afforded by Christ's death and resurrection, man is recreated in the unity of flesh and spirit (see Rom 8). Of course, talking about this reintegration in Christ is one thing. Experiencing it is another. The effects of original sin and the temptations of the fallen world weigh on man like the leverage of a crowbar continually trying to pry flesh and spirit apart. How, then, is one to experience this healing? Above all, it requires *faith*.

Faith, as John Paul learned from John of the Cross, is the means of "mystical marriage" with God. If original sin leads us to doubt the benevolent love of the Father and to close our hearts to the gift of his "marriage proposal," John Paul tells us that "*faith*, in its deepest essence, is *the openness* of the human heart to the gift: *to God's self-communication in the Holy Spirit*."[103] This life is poured out for us in Christ's self-gift to his Bride on the cross. In essence, Christ's self-gift says to us: "You don't believe in the Father's love? Let me make it real for you; let me incarnate it for you so that you can taste and see. You don't believe that God wants to give you life? I will bleed myself dry so that my life's blood can vivify you. You thought God was a tyrant, a slave driver? You

---

102. *Redemptor Hominis*, 1.
103. *Dominum et Vivificantem*, 51.

thought he would whip your back if you gave him the chance? I will take the form of a slave; I will let you whip my back and nail me to a tree; I will let you lord it over me to show you that the Father has no desire to lord it over you. I have not come to condemn you, but to save you. I have not come to enslave you, but to set you free. Turn from your disbelief. *Believe* and *receive* the gift of eternal life I offer you."

This is the divine "marriage proposal." Christ entrusts himself as a gift to our freedom. Faith, then, is the human heart's openness to the gift of divine love. It is man's freely given "yes" to heaven's marriage proposal.[104] Understood in this way, faith—as the only means of "mystical marriage"—is the *only* path to reconciling the "great divorce." It is the only path to that holiness which gradually heals man's internal split. John Paul tells us that "holiness is measured according to the 'great mystery' in which the Bride responds with the gift of love to the gift of the Bridegroom."[105] Holiness, in other words, is Love loved. Each time a human heart receives and reciprocates God's love, the reconciliation of divinity and humanity, body and soul, man and woman takes root. Bringing about this reconciliation is the meaning and purpose of the Incarnation and the Redemption. As the Holy Father says, the man who opens himself to Christ's gift

> finds again the greatness, dignity, and value that belong to his own humanity. In the mystery of the redemption, man becomes newly "expressed" and, in a way, is newly created. He is newly created! ... The man who wishes to understand himself thoroughly—and not just in accordance with immediate, partial, often superficial, and even illusory standards and measures of his being—must with his unrest, uncertainty and even his weakness and sinfulness, with his life and death, draw near to Christ. He must, so to speak, enter into him [Christ] with all his own self, he must "appropriate" and assimilate the whole reality of the Incarnation and Redemption in order to find himself. If that profound process takes place within him, he then bears fruit not only of adoration of God but also of deep wonder at himself.[106]

If atheistic humanism claims to be the "religion" that trumpets man's greatness, the Pope insists that "the name for that deep amazement at man's worth and dignity is the Gospel, that is to say: the Good

---

104. See *CCC*, nos. 14, 142, 166.
105. *Mulieris Dignitatem*, 27; see also *CCC*, no. 773.
106. *Redemptor Hominis*, 10.

News. It is also called Christianity."[107] Christianity is the religion that upholds man's dignity and calls him to embrace his own greatness. But there is a "catch" of sorts, a rub. For man to embrace his own greatness, Christianity teaches that he must also embrace his own death. The mystical marriage is consummated on the wood of the cross. Thus, we must follow Christ the whole way to Calvary if we are to be recreated (resurrected) in the unity of flesh and spirit.

Coping with the pains of our own disintegration (whether we tend toward angelism or animalism) can seem like a fine alternative to being nailed to a tree. Even for those who "take up their crosses and follow," the path to integrating body and soul remains arduous. The deceiver is always at work plagiarizing the Word and lying to us about the meaning of our bodies and our sexuality. Yet the "reason the Son of God appeared was to destroy the works of the devil" (1 Jn 3:8). Christ appeared bodily to restore the body's original symbolic meaning; to enable us once again to read the "language" of the body in truth and to enter into holy communion—within ourselves, with one another, and with God. This theological language of the body, as exemplified in Christ, proclaims that God is "gift," he is love, he is benevolent Father. This is the body, John Paul tells us, "a witness *to Love*" (TOB 14:4). It is this same divine love that our bodies invite us to participate in as male and female by becoming "one flesh."

Need for a Paradigm Shift

To reckon with the mystery of Christ crucified is to recognize the need for a radical reorientation of the basic premises with which most men and women view the universe. Contemplating the "naked Christ" and his body "given up for us" compels a radical paradigm shift both in the way we view God (theology) and in the way we view ourselves (anthropology), especially with regard to our own sexual embodiment. Christ crucified is the divine rebuttal to the deceiver's lies. Here the true Word inscribed in human flesh (self-donation) definitively trumps the anti-Word (self-gratification).

In the beginning, the evil one had placed in doubt the truth that God is love, leaving man with the sense of a master-slave relationship.

---

107. Ibid.

Ever since, as John Paul says, man has felt "goaded to do battle against God,"[108] even to the point of murdering his incarnate Son. Yet in this moment—when the Son of God allowed us to nail him to a tree—we realize, as the Holy Father states, that *"the paradigm of master-slave is foreign to the Gospel."*[109] It is a paradigm drawn from a world in which God is an absent father, not a loving father. It is a paradigm drawn from a lie, a paradigm constructed by the "father of lies."

This revelation changes *everything*. We live under friendly skies. We can put our defenses down and open to the heavens without fear. When we do, we find our posture straightening as the weight of a universal deception falls from our shoulders. When we "repent and believe in the good news" (Mk 1:15), we realize, perhaps for the first time, that life is "very good" (Gen 1:31) and that our existence is nothing but a sheer, gratuitous gift. Life, then, becomes thanksgiving offered to God (*eucharistia*) for so great a gift. In turn, we desire to become the same gift to others that life is to us. The real epiphany comes when we realize that these transcendent, spiritual truths—God is love; life is good; "the gift" of life and love is meant to be experienced and shared—have been stamped in our bodies all along. "Be fruitful and multiply." "Therefore a man leaves his father and his mother and cleaves to his wife, and they become one flesh." These texts of Genesis already contain in some way the fundamental truth of who God is and who we are made in his image and likeness. These texts reveal that Love—divine love, the Love of the life-giving Trinity—is the Word implanted in our souls and inscribed in our flesh. To read this Word in truth and to put it into practice is to discover "the very meaning of our being and existence."

Man Cannot Live Without Love

The truth that we are made in the image of life-giving love explains why the body and sexuality fascinate us and make us crave intimacy, touch, and union. Yes, in our fallen world this fascination expresses itself in gross distortions that destroy lives. But once we learn with Christ's help to "untwist" all our confusions and lusts, we discover in

---

108. *Crossing the Threshold of Hope*, p. 228.
109. Ibid., p. 226.

the mystery of human sexuality man's basic hunger for the God who is love. As John Paul so eloquently stated: "Man cannot live without love. He remains a being that is incomprehensible for himself, his life is senseless, if love is not revealed to him, if he does not encounter love, if he does not experience it and make it his own, if he does not participate intimately in it. This...is why Christ the Redeemer 'fully reveals man to himself'"[110]—because his body "given up for us" reveals the truth about incarnate love.

We need not be conformed to the lies that assail us. We can be transformed by the renewal of our minds if we, like Christ, offer our bodies as a living sacrifice to God. This *bodily* offering, St. Paul tells us, is our *spiritual* act of worship (see Rom 12:1–2). If we are truly willing to die with Christ, we too can live a new life, an incarnate life, an embodied spirituality. Only then do we feel at home in our own skin. Only then do the deepest desires of our hearts for intimacy and union make sense. Only then do we know who we are, why we exist, how we are to live, why there is evil in the world (and how to overcome it), and what our ultimate destiny is (and how to reach it). Christ does not cancel our humanity; he restores it to its original glory. Christ does not nullify our deepest desires and aspirations; he fulfills them superabundantly.

This is the Church's proposal to the world. Unfortunately, even in traditionally Christian nations, the vast majority of modern men and women have not yet heard the Christian proposal. People tend to think of Christianity as an oppressive list of rules to follow, with a particularly heavy emphasis on sexual prohibitions. What a tragic impoverishment of the "great mystery"! Hence, John Paul II incessantly spoke about the need for a "new evangelization." The epilogue of this book will seek to show how the TOB undergirds this new evangelization. Before we unpack the Pope's catechesis, however, we need to understand how it imbues Karol Wojtyla's lifelong philosophical and theological project and how, through this project, he attempts to engage the modern world with the truth about Jesus Christ.

---

110. *Redemptor Hominis*, 10.

6. Wojtyla's Philosophical and Theological Project

The Modern "Turn Toward the Subject"

Why does the modern world seem almost programmed to tune out the Church's proposal? Along with revolutions in economics, politics, science, and technology, the complex process of change in Western civilization called "modernization" has brought with it a critical shift of consciousness, a new rationalist mind-set that has no place for the "great mystery" of Christ and the Church. As John Paul II wrote:

> Modern rationalism *does not tolerate mystery*. It does not accept the mystery of man as male and female, nor is it willing to admit that the full truth about man has been revealed in Jesus Christ. In particular, it does not accept the "great mystery" proclaimed in the *Letter to the Ephesians*, but radically opposes it.... Rationalism provides a radically different way of looking at creation and the meaning of human existence.[111]

To understand this phenomenon, we must return to René Descartes's dictum: "*I think, therefore I am*." John Paul II described this as "the motto of modern rationalism."[112] Descartes turned his back on metaphysics and inaugurated the "anthropological" or "subjective turn" in philosophy. Modern philosophy *starts with man*. In other words, rather than starting with the objective realm of "being" and "existence," modern philosophy begins with man's *conscious* and *subjective* experience of being and existing—"I think, therefore I am." John Paul exclaims: "How different from the approach of St. Thomas, for whom it is not *thought which determines existence, but existence...which determines thought*!"[113]

A philosophy of being acknowledges that I think because there is an objective reality beyond me—an Uncreated Being that *is* existence—that created me as I am (to think). My subjective thoughts are therefore answerable to this objective reality. A philosophy of pure consciousness, on the other hand, reduces reality to what I can *think about it*, because only "that which corresponds to human thought makes sense. The

---

111. *Letter to Families,* 19.
112. *Crossing the Threshold of Hope,* p. 51.
113. Ibid., p. 38.

objective truth of this thought is not as important as the fact that something exists in human consciousness."[114] Man, then—not God—
becomes the measure of the real. We see here how the modern turn
toward the subject has ended in a *subjectivism*, a denial of the very concept of objective reality, of truth.

"There is no truth," people say. But, in response, one feels compelled to ask, "Is that *true*?" Many will retort, "Well, if truth exists, you
can't *know* it." Again, it prompts the question, "How do you *know*?"
"Well, you can't be *sure*," they will say. "Are you *sure*?" "Truth is simply
inescapable. It cannot be denied. The attempt to deny truth is always a
self-contradiction. It destroys itself in the very act of being asserted."[115]
If it is true that there is no truth, then it is *not true* that there is no
truth. In other words, *there is truth*.

Why do so many people chafe at the thought of truth, especially
that the body is answerable to truth? The modern mind views any claim
to truth as a threat to human freedom. But is truth really the enemy of
freedom? Christ taught that it was precisely the truth that set us free
(see Jn 8:32). From this perspective, you simply cannot have one without the other. As John Paul observed, "Truth and freedom either go
together hand in hand or together they perish in misery."[116] Thus, one
of the greatest challenges for the Church today is to recover the inherent link between *freedom* and *truth* taught by Christ.

Truth without freedom leads to tyranny. Conversion by the sword is
meaningless and disrespectful. This is obvious to us today. What is not
so obvious to the modern world, however, is that freedom without truth
also leads to tyranny. If there is no truth, no objective standard to which
we are all accountable, then all that exists is a power struggle between
opposing opinions. Objective reality does not settle disputes; power
does. Might makes right. Those with the most money, media influence,
or military muscle will impose their self-serving view of the world
on the weak. "In this way," as John Paul II wrote, "democracy, contra-
dicting its own principles, effectively moves towards a form of totalitar-
ianism."[117]

---

114. Ibid., p. 51.
115. Walter J. Schu, *The Splendor of Love: John Paul II's Vision for Marriage and Family*
(New Hope, KY: New Hope Publications, 2003), p. 201.
116. *Fides et Ratio*, 90.
117. *Evangelium Vitae*, 20.

Truth and freedom, objectivity and subjectivity, must be held together if man is to be himself and if human society—beginning with the relationship of man and woman—is to flourish. Herein lies Wojtyla's lifelong project. By focusing on subjectivity to the neglect of objectivity, modern philosophy erred grievously by divorcing *freedom from truth.* This has led to subjectivism and moral relativism. But modern sensitivities have also challenged men like Wojtyla to recognize that conventional formulations of the faith may well have focused on objectivity to the neglect of subjectivity, leading some in the Church to divorce *truth from freedom.* This has lead in various cases to an imposition of Christianity disrespectful of people's religious freedom. Hence, Wojtyla believed modern philosophy's desire to begin with the subjective themes of experience, consciousness, and freedom could enrich the faith, so long as one remains grounded in a philosophy of being and of objective truth. He believed that objective reality could be affirmed and reclaimed through a careful but nonetheless explicit appeal to subjective human experience. This would require a "personalism" sensitive to modern thought but rooted in the philosophy of St. Thomas.

■ If the objective truth of the matter is that it is raining outside, human experience can and should confirm this. Not only could we look outside and see it, but we could also step outside and *feel* it. Applying the image, if the Church's doctrine on faith and morals is true, our experience can and should confirm this. John Paul's goal is to get us to step into the rain, so to speak, to *experience* it, to get soaked, and to spend our lives joyfully playing in the rain like children. Taking this image a step further, we can recognize the need of childlikeness if we are to *experience* the objective truth as a liberating good ("unless you turn and become like children" —Mt 18:3). Some might have an objective knowledge of the rain but be at odds with it internally. If such a person fails to become like a child, he will either live in a state of continual resentment toward the rain, or he will deny its existence and create his own illusory world "unhindered" by "undesirable" weather. But herein lies the devil's perennial deception—reality (God) is not a hindrance, it is not undesirous. Submission to reality (God) is ultimate freedom and the fulfillment of every desire. But only a "child" can see this. Only children like to play in the rain.

"Thomistic Personalism"

Having been formed in the Thomistic school both in the underground seminary and in his doctoral studies, the Pope always considered himself a Thomist. But this does not mean he limited himself to scholastic terminology and formulations. As a Thomist, the Pope would certainly side with the traditional, objective philosophy of being over the modern, subjective philosophy of consciousness—if forced to choose between the two. But he does not see it as an either/or proposition. His philosophical project has been to find the both/and—to "make room" for subjectivity within a realist philosophy. This would demand from Wojtyla a creative engagement with modern thought without sacrificing his Thomistic principles. Thus, upon the foundations of St. Thomas's "objectivistic" understanding of man as a *person*, Wojtyla built what he called a "Thomistic personalism." In a 1961 essay of that title, Wojtyla wrote:

> St. Thomas was familiar with the concept of person and defined it very clearly. This is not to say, however, that he was equally familiar with the problem of personalism.... We would, however, be correct in thinking that, since he presented the problem of the person so clearly, he also provided at least a point of departure for personalism in general. And although the problem of personalism was formulated much later...in contemporary thought and life—still, Thomas's overall philosophy and theology allows us to speak of Thomistic personalism.
>
> For St. Thomas, the person is, of course, a subject...and this is what makes the person capable of consciousness and self-consciousness. On the other hand, when it comes to analyzing consciousness and self-consciousness—which is what chiefly interests modern philosophy and psychology—there seems to be no place for it in St. Thomas's objectivistic view of reality.... St. Thomas gives us an excellent view of the objective existence and activity of the person, but it would be difficult to speak in his view of the lived experiences of the person.[118]

As we observed earlier, Wojtyla first encountered an emphasis on the lived experiences of the person in the writings of John of the Cross. As a young priest, Wojtyla wrote his doctoral dissertation on faith according to St. John of the Cross under the direction of the well-known Thomist Garrigou-Lagrange at the *Angelicum* in Rome.[119]

---

118. *Person and Community*, pp. 165, 170, 171.
119. See *Faith According to St. John of the Cross* (San Francisco: Ignatius Press, 1981).

Faith, Wojtyla concluded, is not merely an intellectual assent to objective truths. The intellect cannot grasp God, for God is not merely a concept or an object. In the "dark night of the soul" the emotions are purified and the intellect opens itself to love's overwhelming sweetness. Through this love the believer *experiences* God in the mutual exchange of a personal self-donation. Faith, then, is the means of "mystical marriage" with God. Wojtyla wrote in his dissertation that this understanding of faith firmly places John of the Cross in the theological tradition of St. Thomas Aquinas. However, St. John's works are not only speculative treatises. They witness to a lived mystical experience of union with God, of personal participation in the intimate life of the Trinity.[120]

In this view, personal experience does not trump the objective content of faith but confirms and affirms it, enabling the person to *interiorize* it and make it his own. This insight into faith as an *experiential* reality also provided an important foundation for Wojtyla's habilitation thesis[121] on the thought of German philosopher Max Scheler.[122] He found in Scheler both a helpful confirmation of his Carmelite sensitivities and an unreconcilable departure.

Scheler was a disciple of Edmund Husserl (1859–1938), the founder of a modern philosophical method called "phenomenology." In an effort to counter Immanuel Kant's ethics of pure duty,[123] Scheler developed a rich ethical system based on the emotional experience of values. However, if Kant ignored the emotional life in favor of duty, according to Wojtyla, Scheler fell prey to the opposite problem. He ignored duty—even setting himself against it—in favor of emotionally perceived values. By doing so, while Scheler provided a valuable account of human experience, his system fails to remain grounded in objective reality. Thus, Wojtyla concluded that Scheler's phenomeno-

---

120. Ibid., pp. 21–22.

121. The habilitation thesis, as a postdoctoral work, gives one the right to teach at a university in the European system. It corresponds to the "first book" that is required of assistant professors in the U.S. to become associate professors.

122. *Evaluation of the Possibility of Constructing a Christian Ethics on the Assumptions of Max Scheler's System of Philosophy.* Unfortunately, this has not been published in English. The Spanish edition is *Max Scheler y la etica cristiana* (Madrid: Biblioteca de Autores Cristianos, 1982).

123. In Kant's ethics of pure duty, man must detach himself from any subjective or emotionally felt value. An ethical action is purely a willing of the law. The only relevant "feeling" is that which arises from duty for duty's sake.

logy could not be considered a self-sufficient basis for Christian ethics. Nonetheless, so long as one remains grounded in a realist philosophy, Wojtyla believed that the phenomenological method could provide a much-needed stamp of subjective experience to the normative science of ethics.

What Is Phenomenology?

Much attention is given to the role of phenomenology in the life and teaching of Wojtyla/John Paul II, and rightly so.[124] It is difficult, however, to define "phenomenology." As a philosophical method it has developed many variants, some of which are more compatible with Catholic faith than others. Wojtyla/John Paul II used this method to retrieve the ordinary experiences of everyday life and study these phenomena precisely *as we experience them*. Phenomenology in this sense involves a style of thought that humbly receives whatever is given by experience. It "lets the data speak" and listens attentively to what it says. With this approach, the intellect does not seek to dominate reality but rather receives it lovingly. In fact, "John Paul II emphasizes love as the animating principle of phenomenology."[125] By studying the phenomena of everyday life, Wojtyla discovers in the subjectivity of man's inner world a unity with the objectivity of man's outer world. By analyzing this unity he can confirm objective truths while avoiding "objectivizing" abstractions. He demonstrates that the Church's vision of man is not foisted upon him from "the outside" but corresponds to his self-experience as a person on "the inside."

With full knowledge that the Church's message "is in harmony with the most secret desires of the human heart,"[126] Wojtyla does not need and does not attempt to force assent to his proposals. Rather, he

---

124. For one account, see Richard Hogan, *The Theology of the Body in John Paul II: What It Means, Why It Matters* (Ijamsville, MD: Word Among Us Press, 2006), prologue. Hogan places great emphasis on John Paul II's study and use of phenomenology, seeing it as a new "moment" in the history of theological development similar to Augustine's integration of the faith with Plato, and Thomas's integration of the faith with Aristotle. Various schools of thought have arisen with varying points of view on these matters. Alas, a comparative analysis of their positions is not only beyond the scope of this project, but beyond the scope of my expertise.

125. Waldstein, Introduction, TOB, p. 65.

126. *CCC*, no. 2126.

invites men and women to reflect honestly on their self-experience to see if it confirms his proposals. In doing so, Wojtyla shows remarkable respect for and trust in the freedom of the person and a bold confidence in the ability of each person's conscience to recognize—and desire—the truth when it presents itself. His presentation of the faith, therefore, is never an imposition but always and only a proposition—an appeal to each person's freedom.[127] Wojtyla/John Paul II's vision of man and of the ethical life cannot be understood apart from his passion and respect for human freedom. There is no place for a tyranny of truth in the life of a personal subject created for "his own sake." Truth can only have meaning in a person's life if he freely embraces it. But if freedom for Wojtyla is inviolable within just limits, it also entails a particular responsibility to search for the truth and adhere to it once found.[128]

Loving and Interiorizing the "Splendor of the Truth"

Contrary to some criticisms, Wojtyla/John Paul II's respect for and use of modern philosophy in his presentation of the faith does not by any means imply a yielding of Catholicism to relativism. Rocco Buttiglione assures us that "John Paul II could repeat the words of his predecessor, Pius X, who refused to accept the errors of modern times. But the rejection of the errors of modern times does not mean that we should not correct the one-sidedness of the exposition of sound doctrine, which furnished the occasion for the rise of these errors."[129] How often is the Church's doctrine rejected because it is thought to be hopelessly removed from "real life" experience? How often have children educated in the faith rejected it as adults because their teachers—whether parents, pastors, or others—tended to impose religion upon them without respect for and education in authentic human freedom? Freedom must be challenged to submit itself to truth, but no one can be forced to accept the truth without doing violence to the dignity of the person. When truth is presented in its full splendor, it does not need to be imposed. It has its own appeal that naturally attracts us. When

---

127. As the Council teaches, "The truth cannot impose itself except by virtue of its own truth, as it makes its entrance into the mind at once quietly and with power" (*Dignitatis Humanae*, 1).

128. See *CCC*, no. 2467.

129. *Karol Wojtyla: The Thought of the Man Who Became Pope John Paul II*, p. 372.

Christians witness joyfully to the "splendor of the truth," others seek it out and embrace it freely.

Embracing the truth does not only mean accepting it intellectually. It also means *interiorizing* it, making it one's own. This is extremely important. For one can know reality but remain at odds with it by failing to interiorize it. In such cases the incongruity eventually becomes too painful, and the person will often deny reality in favor of a counterfeit that promises "relief." But such a person lives an illusion in which peace eludes him. For a person to be at peace with himself and the world, he must not only know the truth, he must interiorize it, feel it, experience it, and freely embrace it as his own. To do so, he must trust the truth wholeheartedly, have an impassioned love for the objective good, and abandon himself to it fearlessly. But he can only do this if truth is *perfect love*, which is only possible if truth itself is a *perfect person*. Truth is. Truth's name is Jesus Christ.

Here Wojtyla's philosophy opens itself to theology, to divine love. Wojtyla's Thomistic-Carmelite personalism (enriched by his use of the phenomenological method) ultimately calls us to an awareness of objective truth through the *experience* of divine love—through an experience of reality as the good, beatifying, gratuitous gift that it is. In *Crossing the Threshold of Hope*, John Paul observes that classical philosophy recognizes that "nothing is in the intellect that was not first in the senses." Nevertheless, he then emphasizes that "*the limits of these 'senses' are not exclusively sensory.*" Man can "sense" the transcendent. He has a "religious sense."[130] "It is therefore possible," the Pope affirms, "to speak from a solid foundation about *human experience, moral experience, or religious experience.* And if it is possible to speak about such experiences, it is difficult to deny that, in the realm of human experience, one also finds good and evil, truth and beauty, and God."[131]

This interior *experience* of God is gained not only by intelligent discernment and technical knowledge (although these are important) but also through the engagement of the deepest impulses of one's person— through the meeting of one's freedom with the God who gave us freedom as the capacity to meet him. In short, if the philosophy of being

---

130. For an in-depth study of this idea, see Luigi Giussani, *The Religious Sense* (Montreal: McGill-Queen's University Press, 1997).

131. *Crossing the Threshold of Hope*, pp. 33–34.

addresses the "God question" by providing rational proofs for his existence, Wojtyla addresses the same question by inviting each person to "taste and see"—engage your freedom in self-donation and *experience* God's love for yourself. In this way "proof" of God's existence is verified not only with one's reason but by faith as a lived *experience* of the heart. As John Paul wrote toward the end of his life, reflecting on his own philosophical and theological approach:

> I always tried to achieve a harmony between faith, reason, and the heart. These are profoundly connected, each giving life to the other. This coming together of faith, reason, and the heart is strongly influenced by our sense of wonder at the miracle of a human person— at man's likeness to the Triune God, at the immensely profound bond between love and truth, at the mystery of mutual self-giving and the life that it generates.[132]

The above quote offers not only a penetrating look into the Pope's philosophical/theological approach, but also a grand synthesis of his life's work, especially as related to TOB. It is precisely by looking with wonder at the human person that we come to see the trinitarian likeness revealed in spousal union and the life it generates. This sense of wonder, in turn, enables a person to *interiorize* "the immensely profound bond between love and truth" and enables him or her to experience the beautiful "harmony between faith, reason, and the heart." Faith then becomes a means of union ("mystical marriage") with God totally in keeping with reason and lived as an experience of the heart. "And we find ourselves by now," John Paul asserts, "very close to St. Thomas, but the path passes not so much through being and existence as through people and their meeting each other, through the 'I' and the 'Thou.'...In the *sphere of the everyday* man's entire life is one of 'coexistence'—'thou' and 'I'—and also in the *sphere of the absolute and definitive*: 'I' and 'THOU.'"[133] For God himself—the absolute and definitive basis of all that exists—is himself an eternal Mystery of "coexistence"—Father, Son, and Holy Spirit. And so John Paul concludes that in all its theological depth, our *"faith is profoundly anthropological,* rooted constitutively in coexistence, in the community of God's people, and *in communion with this eternal 'THOU.'"*[134]

---

132. *Rise, Let Us Be on Our Way* (New York: Warner Books, 2004), p. 97.
133. *Crossing the Threshold of Hope*, p. 36.
134. Ibid.

Saving the "Subjective Turn" from Subjectivism

By wedding theology and anthropology, objectivity and subjectivity, John Paul II provides a vision of the human person that avoids the pitfalls of abstraction *and* subjectivism. Here again we encounter the "great mystery" of spousal union. At the crux of the marriage of theology and anthropology, objectivity and subjectivity, is the marriage of God and man in the person of Christ. In Christ, our humanity—body and soul—embraces ultimate reality without any incongruity. From Wojtyla's perspective, the moral relativism that has resulted from the modern "turn to the subject" is only the product of an anthropological stagnation in the absence of faith. In other words, man turns to himself and "stays" there, failing to see that his own humanity points him beyond himself, failing to see that *anthropology* points to *theology*. Modern philosophy, John Paul wrote, "in its one sided concern to investigate human subjectivity, seems to have forgotten that men and women are always called to direct their steps toward a truth which transcends them."[135]

To use the spousal image, moral relativism results from the Bride (man) looking in a mirror without recognizing the spousal meaning of her own body that opens her to union with her Bridegroom (Christ). In the absence of this openness to the "Other"—that is, in the absence of faith (recall John Paul's definition of faith as "openness to the gift of God")—the Bride opts for a sterile, narcissistic self-focus. At this point the "subjective turn" erodes into *subjectivism*. But when the Bride recognizes the spousal meaning of her humanity and opens to Christ, human subjectivity encounters the possibility of becoming "objective to the very depths" (TOB 19:1). To the degree that the Bride opens herself to Christ the Bridegroom, human subjectivity becomes informed by Truth himself. In this way we "move from *phenomenon* to *foundation*, a step as necessary as it is urgent," John Paul wrote. "We cannot stop short at experience alone; even if experience does reveal the human being's interiority and spirituality, speculative thinking must penetrate to the spiritual core and the ground from which it rises."[136] That ground is Christ the Bridegroom.

---

135. *Fides et Ratio*, 5.
136. Ibid., 83.

■ We shall see more clearly in our study of Genesis how, prior to sin, the subjective experiences of Adam and Eve were "objective to the very depths" (TOB 19:1). The harmony of subjective experience with objective reality becomes tenuous only as a result of having lost "purity of heart." Redemption in Christ, however, offers us the possibility of gradually regaining the purity of our origins, albeit a difficult and lifelong journey. The harmony of subjective and objective reality solidifies in our *experience* of the efficacy of redemption—that is, in our experience of the real power of redemption to restore "purity of heart." Because of the strong tendency to impurity, people often hold the subjective experiences of the heart in suspicion, fearing they can never come in tune with objective reality. This is understandable. On the one hand, we must not underestimate the tenacity of the human inclination to sin (concupiscence). On the other hand, as John Paul stresses, *"Man cannot stop at casting the 'heart' into a state of* continual and irreversible *suspicion* due to the manifestations of the concupiscence of the flesh.... Redemption is a truth, a reality, in the name of which man must feel himself called, and 'called with effectiveness'"* (TOB 46:4).

John Paul's Christo-centric theological anthropology saves the modern desire to "start with man" from ending in subjectivism. If it is true, as faith teaches, that man is made in the image of God and is created for eternal union with him, then starting with man—if we stay the course and penetrate to his spiritual core—will ultimately lead to God. Starting with the subjective perspective will ultimately lead to objective reality *if* we follow John Paul and *press into that link between anthropology and theology* "with faith, an open mind, and all our heart."[137]

If modern rationalism makes man the measure of all things, theological anthropology discovers that *the God-man* is the measure of all things. Jesus Christ "is the center of the universe and of history." The Word made flesh "fully reveals man to himself"—not by tyrannically asserting his divine prerogatives (this would contradict the dignity of a creature made for "its own sake"), but by making the humble and sin-

---

137. *Dives et Misericordia*, 1.

cere *gift of himself* to man (this, as we discussed above, is precisely what the spousal analogy illuminates about God). Man, in turn, discovers his rightful place in the universe when he freely receives this gift (faith) and makes a "sincere gift" of himself back to God and to others.

The world, it seems, is poised and ready to "receive" the true purpose and logic of human existence—the true "Logos"—precisely because, as Cardinal Ratzinger put it, radical forms of subjectivism have lead to the "dissolution of the subject." Man is hurting and is crying out for answers to his pain. Perhaps this unfortunate situation "will help us to overcome the unbounded inflation of subjectivity and to recognize once more that a relationship with the Logos...brings salvation to the subject, that is, to the person. At the same time it puts us into a true relationship of communion that is ultimately grounded in trinitarian love."[138] As we shall see more clearly through our study of John Paul II's TOB, these profound truths are stamped in the "great mystery" of masculinity and femininity and in our call to become "one flesh."

Rationalism fails man right here. It "does not accept the mystery of man as male and female, nor is it willing to admit that...*Christ reveals man to himself.*"[139] This is why man is in such pain. As an extended commentary on this truth of *Gaudium et Spes*, 22, the TOB is John Paul's most important, provocative, and challenging engagement with modernity. It is his most compelling attempt to forge a link between objective reality and subjective human experience, between truth and freedom, theology and anthropology, God and man. The TOB echoes and contains the entire history of his thinking about man.

Having looked briefly at the foundations of his lifelong project in his dissertation on St. John of the Cross and his thesis on Max Scheler, there are still other stages along the development of Wojtyla's thought that inform the TOB. While it is beyond the scope of this book to trace these stages in detail, it is important at least to provide a short overview.[140]

---

138. Joseph Ratzinger, *The Spirit of the Liturgy* (San Francisco: Ignatius Press, 2000).

139. *Letter to Families*, 19.

140. Many books have been written on the history and development of Wojtyla's anthropology. For the serious student, I would especially recommend Kenneth Schmitz's *At the Center of the Human Drama: The Philosophical Anthropology of Karol Wojtyla/Pope John Paul II* (Washington, DC: Catholic University of America Press, 1993); Mary Shivanandan's *Crossing the Threshold of Love: A New Vision of Marriage in*

Other Steps in Wojtyla's Thought

Karol Wojtyla began to express his thoughts, questions, and yearnings in the poetry[141] and plays[142] he wrote as a young man. Already in these earliest works we see him reflecting on the questions that will mark his most developed anthropology. After his doctoral work and habilitation thesis (discussed above), Wojtyla would further develop the themes of experience and ethics, person and nature, freedom and law, value and duty, subjectivity and objectivity in the lectures and essays he delivered as a professor at the Catholic University of Lublin.[143]

During these years (beginning in 1954 and diminishing throughout the '60s and '70s as his ecclesial duties increased), Wojtyla would sharpen his ideas against the minds of other great scholars in the "Lublin School of Philosophy." By engaging in a bold philosophical initiative that sought to link the three great fields of *metaphysics, anthropology,* and *ethics,* the Lublin School believed their work—if given proper exposure—could redirect the entire course of modern philosophy. Stefan Swiezawski, one of Wojtyla's colleagues in the school, would later write: "In the work and discussions of our group...we were deeply convinced that our efforts...had crucial significance not just for our university, for Poland, and for Europe, but for the whole world." The exposure they needed came when one of their own was elected pope. Swiezawski comments that their work had "suddenly found a simply unprecedented opportunity to reach all parts of the world and influence the development of the spiritual face of the coming age in every corner of the globe."[144]

---

the *Light of John Paul II's Anthropology* (Washington, DC: Catholic University of America Press, 1999); Rocco Buttiglione's *Karol Wojtyla: The Thought of the Man Who Became Pope John Paul II* (Grand Rapids, MI: William B. Eerdmans Publishing Co., 1997); and Jaroslaw Kupczak's *Destined for Liberty* (Washington, DC: Catholic University of America Press, 2000). Waldstein's Introduction to *Man and Woman He Created Them* also provides a particularly excellent account of the development of Wojtyla's thought (see TOB, pp. 23–94).

141. A complete collection of Karol Wojtyla's poems can be found in *The Place Within: The Poetry of Pope John Paul II* (New York: Random House, 1982).

142. See Karol Wojtyla, *The Collected Plays and Writings on Theater* (Berkeley: University of California Press, 1987).

143. See *Person and Community: Selected Essays,* trans. Theresa Sandok (New York: Peter Lang, 1993). Other volumes of his essays are in production.

144. Ibid., pp. xiii, xvi.

Karol Wojtyla wrote his first book, *Love and Responsibility*,[145] in the late 1950s, based on years of intense pastoral work with young people and engaged and married couples. This largely philosophical treatise, steadfastly personalistic in approach, explores the way men and women experience the sexual urge, emotion, sensuality, shame, etc., and shows how these can and must be integrated with an "education in love." Wojtyla argues that failure to accept "responsibility for love" turns people into objects to be used. Furthermore, he convincingly demonstrates that Catholic moral teaching on sex and marriage corresponds perfectly with the dignity of the person and the desires of the heart for betrothed love.

The Second Vatican Council was the next major force to shape Wojtyla's thinking. The young bishop from Krakow would serve as one of the main protagonists at this preeminently "pastoral" Council, which sought to engage an ever changing modern world with the unchanging truth of Jesus Christ. George Weigel reports in his biography of the Pope that Wojtyla had prepared a prescient essay for the Ante-Preparatory Commission of the Council. In it Wojtyla stressed that the question of a humanism adequate to the aspirations of today's men and women should be the epicenter of the Council's concerns. The Church needed to furnish her twenty centuries-old answer to the human question in a way that would "ring true" in late modernity. With two thousand bishops from around the globe proposing and debating the best way to do so, the Council would become a kind of postdoctoral school of philosophy and theology for Wojtyla.[146] It would also spawn two more books from the Polish bishop before his ideas on implementing the Council would forever shape Church history as papal documents. The key teachings of the Council, which Wojtyla undoubtedly had a hand in shaping, confirmed and deepened the basic conviction he had gained early in his life from John of the Cross. The objective content of the Church's faith must become a subjective experience of the person through a dynamically lived *communion* with Christ ("mystical marriage"). In this encounter, Christ "fully

---

145. This was first published in English in 1981 (New York: Farrar, Straus, & Giroux) and reprinted in 1993 (San Francisco: Ignatius Press). Citations in this book from *Love and Responsibility* are taken from the Ignatius Press edition.

146. See *Witness to Hope*, pp. 158–60.

reveals man to himself" and man, in turn, "finds himself through the sincere gift of self."[147]

Wojtyla wrote *The Acting Person*[148] in his "spare time" following the Council to explore the philosophical foundations of the conciliar documents. This extremely dense work of philosophical personalism offers a rigorous attempt to rescue the modern turn to the subject from subjectivism. Wojtyla does so by linking all that is good in Scheler's subjective concept of "person" with the objective truth of the person found in St. Thomas. His thesis, as the title indicates, is that the irreducible core of the person is revealed through his *actions*. Experience confirms that, while some things passively happen to us, we are also free to *determine* our own actions. We are not only passive objects but also *acting subjects*. We experience our actions as "our own" and "no one else's." Here "action" is incorporated into subjectivity. In this experience of freedom and subjectivity (what Wojtyla calls "efficacy"), man begins to experience his own transcendence as a person. Wojtyla believes there is a law of self-giving that defines the person *objectively* (here, again, we see the Spanish mystic's spousal vision shining through). And in the experience of his own freedom, his own ability to act, man comes to experience this truth of his personhood *subjectively*.

As stated above, one of the main tasks of the Council was to make the objective truths of faith an experience of life, to bring about their subjective appropriation. If *The Acting Person* seeks to provide a philosophical basis for this task, Wojtyla's book *Sources of Renewal* seeks to facilitate its pastoral implementation. This concerns not so much "how" but "what" is to be implemented. According to Wojtyla, this is the more important question.[149] The sources of the Church's renewal are

---

147. These passages from *Gaudium et Spes*, 22 ("Christ fully reveals man to himself") and 24 (man is created for "his own sake" but can only find himself through "the sincere gift of self") summarize the essential theological and philosophical proposals of the Second Vatican Council regarding who man is and how he is to live. They are so pivotal in the work of John Paul II that one would be hard pressed to find any significant catechetical project of his that did not use these texts.

148. *The Acting Person* was first published in Polish in 1969. It was published in English in 1979 (*Analecta Husserliana*, 10; Dordrecht, Holland: Reidel). For a discussion of the controversy surrounding the English translation, see *Witness to Hope*, pp. 174–75. For an excellent summary of *The Acting Person*, see Gerard Beigel's *Faith and Social Justice in the Teaching of Pope John Paul II* (New York: Peter Lang, 1997), chap. 2.

149. See *Sources of Renewal* (San Francisco: Harper & Row, 1979), p. 420.

found in the Holy Spirit's work in the Council and its teachings. Renewal itself, however, comes only when the work of the Spirit is incarnated through a vibrantly lived and personally appropriated faith in Jesus Christ. The "proof of the realization of the Council," Cardinal Wojtyla wrote, will be manifested when "the doctrine of faith and morals" that the Council presented resounds in "the consciousness of Christians." The Council therefore afforded "an enrichment of faith in the objective sense, constituting a new stage in the Church's advance toward 'the fullness of divine truth.'" But what is more hoped for as a fruit of the Council—and what *Sources of Renewal* seeks to facilitate— "is an enrichment [of the faith] in the subjective, human, existential sense."[150] John Paul II's TOB—precisely because of its remarkable ability to allow doctrine to resound in the consciousness of Christians —may prove to be the most bountiful theological fruit of the Council itself.

The next milestone in our brief retracing of the development of Wojtyla's thought was the Lenten retreat he preached to Pope Paul VI and the Roman Curia in 1976. The full text of the twenty-two conferences he delivered is published under the title Wojtyla assigned: *Sign of Contradiction*.[151] Based on the words Simeon addressed to Mary (see Lk 2:34), Cardinal Wojtyla wove a broad tapestry of uplifting, sobering, and even daring reflections on what he considers to be the question of the day: "Who is man and how does Christ fully reveal man to himself?" Through his insightful reading of the "signs of the times," he envisioned "a new Advent for the Church and for humanity.... A time of great trial but also of great hope." He concluded, "For just such a time as this we have been given the sign: Christ, 'sign of contradiction' (Lk 2:34). And the woman clothed with the sun: 'A great sign in the heavens' (Rev 12:1)."[152] Here again we encounter the sacramentality of the body. For the signs Wojtyla spoke of are those of a man and a woman—the New Adam and the New Eve.

Nowhere is the Church, following her Bridegroom, more of a "sign of contradiction" than in her teaching on man and woman's relationship. Similarly, nowhere is there more of a disconnection between

---

150. Ibid., pp. 17–18.
151. This was published in English by Seabury Press in 1979.
152. *Sign of Contradiction*, p. 206.

Church doctrine and the consciousness of Christians than in the Church's sexual ethic. Wojtyla knew that if the renewal the Council envisaged was to take root, a bridge had to be built that would enable Christians to appropriate personally and live vibrantly God's plan for human sexuality. In a 1974 essay on marriage and the family, he emphasized the need for "a special theological synthesis" in this regard, "a special theology of the body, so to speak." [153] This seems to be the first mention of the phrase "theology of the body" in the writings of Wojtyla. The qualifier "so to speak" indicates the novelty, at the time, of the expression.

Thereafter, sometime between 1974 and 1978, Cardinal Wojtyla drafted his masterwork—a biblical reflection on the human body and sexuality founded upon and imbued with the mystical-spousal personalism he had developed and refined throughout his academic and pastoral career—and gave it the title *Man and Woman He Created Them*. Little did he know, however, that he would be elected pope before his manuscript could go to press. It seems God had bigger plans for his "special theology of the body, so to speak" than Wojtyla could ever have realized. Having only very recently completed his TOB (John Paul II told Weigel that he was still drafting the text in August 1978 during the conclave that elected John Paul I[154]), the Holy Spirit's choice of *this* man for pope—after the whirlwind of two conclaves within seven weeks—seems nothing short of a divine endorsement of the project. Indeed, the Holy Spirit tends to grant the Church what she needs when she needs it. God knows the Church needed to formulate a compelling, pastoral response to the sexual revolution. If the end result of a "culture of death" is death, nothing short of the survival of civilization was at stake.

7. *A Response to the* Humanae Vitae *Crisis*

The Need for a "Total Vision of Man"

Wise men and women throughout history, and certainly not just Christians, have recognized that respect for the procreative function of

---

153. *Person and Community*, p. 326.
154. See *Witness to Hope*, p. 336.

sexual union is the linchpin of sexual morality.[155] Hence, if the modern brand of sexual "liberation" was to flourish, this linchpin had to be removed. Here lies the main point of contention in the clash between the Church and the modern world—the Church's insistence that God established an inseparable link between sex and procreation, a link that man cannot break.

This clash is rooted in two irreconcilable *anthropologies*—two irreconcilable concepts of the *human body* and of human sexuality.[156] Rationalism sees the body only as a biological reference point while the Church has always taught that the body is an expression of the human *person*. If the person merely "has" a body, then he will conclude that he is free to dominate and manipulate that body at will, in the same way he exercises dominion over the rest of the material world. In this Cartesian way of thinking, people give no more thought to tinkering with their fertility than they do to tinkering with their hair color. But if, as the Church insists, man *is* a body,[157] then what we do to the human body—especially to something as existentially significant as fertility—will have an immediate impact on the *human person* and on the *communion of persons*.

These disparate anthropologies collided when Pope Paul VI's encyclical *Humanae Vitae*—which reaffirmed the Church's constant teaching on the immorality of contraception—fell like a bomb on the Church in 1968. If it was understandable that people outside the Church might dismiss the papal pronouncement as antiquated gibberish, the uproar the encyclical caused *within the Church* showed how far the Cartesian view of man had seeped into the minds of Catholics. Modern rationalism presents only "partial truths" about man and effectively divorces him from the "great mystery" of his body and of spousal love. Paul VI recognized this disconnection when he stated: "The problem of birth [regulation], like every other problem regarding human life, is to be considered *beyond partial perspectives*." It must be seen "in

---

155. Even Sigmund Freud observed in his *Introductory Lectures in Psychoanalysis* (New York: Norton, 1966) that the "abandonment of the reproductive function is the common feature of all perversions. We actually describe a sexual activity as perverse," he wrote, "if it has given up the aim of reproduction and pursues the attainment of pleasure as an aim independent of it" (p. 392).

156. See *Familiaris Consortio*, 32.

157. See the index, TOB, p. 681.

light of a *total vision of man* and of his vocation, not only his natural and earthly but also his supernatural and eternal vocation."[158] This was John Paul II's cue (see TOB 23, 133). Paul VI did not provide this "total vision of man and his vocation." John Paul II *does* and that, in large measure, is what his TOB *is*.

Waldstein observes that "the purpose of TOB as a whole is to defend the spousal meaning of the body against the alienation between person and body in the Cartesian vision of nature." Then he concludes, with a precise turn of phrase, that all "the fundamental questions of our age—questions about the meaning of the body, about the meaning of love, about nature, technology, and progress—come together in the issue of *Humanae Vitae* as in a tight knot."[159] John Paul himself sees his entire catechesis on the body as "*an extensive commentary* on the doctrine contained precisely in *Humanae Vitae*" (TOB 133:2). Questions come from this encyclical that "run in some way through the whole of our reflections" (TOB 133:4). In order to understand these questions, we need a "total vision of man," or what John Paul II calls an "adequate anthropology."

Here "adequate anthropology" does not mean a "merely sufficient" understanding of man, but one that is full, total, integral, complete. Embodiment is the basis of this *anthropology*, which is also *theological*, since man is made in God's image as male and female. By now we should recognize that the term "theology of the body" does not refer only to the physical "part" of a theological anthropology, as if we need-ed to add to this a "theology of the soul." This two-tiered notion smacks of the Cartesian view of the human being that the TOB is seeking to overcome. The body itself is the revelation of the soul. Thus, rediscovering the meaning of the human body leads to rediscov-ering the meaning of the whole human person. It leads, as John Paul says, to "the rediscovery of the meaning of the whole of existence, of the meaning of life" (TOB 46:6). By analyzing key biblical texts, we will "discover precisely the anthropology that can be called 'theology of the body.' And this *theology* of the body is the basis of the most appropriate method...of man's education (or rather, self-education)" (TOB 59:3).

---

158. *Humanae Vitae*, 7, emphasis added.
159. Waldstein, Introduction, TOB, p. 107.

This is exactly what is at stake in the teaching of *Humanae Vitae*—a proper education in what it means to be human. As the title of the encyclical indicates, Paul VI was charged, as all popes are, with upholding the integral truth *of human life*. On the tenth anniversary of *Humanae Vitae*, Cardinal Wojtyla described the issue of contraception as a "struggle for the value and meaning of humanity itself."[160] Just two and a half months later when he assumed the Chair of Peter, John Paul II knew he had to make a compelling case for *Humanae Vitae*. For he understood that widespread use of contraception was effectively disorienting "the deepest substratum of human ethics and culture" (TOB 45:3). It was thus altering humanity's course at its foundations—away from a culture of love and life and toward a culture of utility and death.[161]

Inadequate, legalistic formulations of moral theology coupled with disparaging treatments of sexual matters by some previous churchmen had led countless people to turn a deaf ear to Rome whenever she spoke on sexual matters. John Paul was confident, however, that he had something to say that could make a difference. He believed he could demonstrate that *Humanae Vitae* was not against man but unstintingly *for* him; that *Humanae Vitae* was not opposed to conjugal love and sexual pleasure but called men and women to the most spiritually intense experiences of them. To get there, however, questions surrounding sexual morality needed to be reframed. Instead of asking: "How far can I go before I break the law?" we need to ask, "What does it mean to be human?" "What is a person?" "What does it mean to love?" "Why did God make me male or female?" "Why did God create sex in the first place?"

The Need for a Personalistic Ethic

Prior to the mid-twentieth century, Church pronouncements on sexual matters had focused mainly on the exterior "duties" of spouses

---

160. Cited in *Crossing the Threshold of Love*, p. 113.

161. For a detailed discussion of the destructive sequellae of contraception, see Patrick Fagan, "A Culture of Inverted Sexuality," *Catholic World Report* (November 1998): p. 57. See also Christopher West, *Good News About Sex and Marriage: Answers to Your Honest Questions About Catholic Teaching*, rev. ed. (Cincinnati, OH: Servant Books 2004), pp. 121–28.

and the objective "ends" of the sexual act—formulated in a strict hierarchy as procreation, the mutual help of spouses, and the remedy for concupiscence. Attention seemed almost fixated on the "primary end" of procreation with little or no attention given to the meaning and experience of conjugal love.[162] Objectively speaking, the traditional formulation on the ends of marriage is true. But for most people today, focusing merely on the objective reality tends to create a "disconnect" with the interior experience of the persons involved. As John Paul says, "We cannot consider the body as an objective reality outside of man's personal subjectivity." Hence, questions of sexual morality are closely bound up "with the content and quality of [the] subjective *experience*" of the persons involved (TOB 60:1).

John Paul's "personalism"—deeply rooted, as we have seen, in the Gospel and the teachings of John of the Cross, and subsequently enriched by the phenomenology of Max Scheler—treats ethical questions from this "insider's" point of view. In *Love and Responsibility*, Wojtyla insists that the "personal order is the only proper plane for all debate on matters of sexual morality."[163] Accordingly, students of theology will recognize a new focus in the Pope's analysis. For example, John Paul speaks much more about the *interior meaning* of sexual union as self-donation for the sake of the communion of persons than about the *objective end* of sexual union as procreation. However, as the Pope himself asserts, "In this renewed orientation, the traditional teaching on the ends of marriage (and on their hierarchy)" is not done away with, but "is confirmed and at the same time deepened from the point of view of the interior life of the spouses" (TOB 127:3). John Paul's personalism, therefore, does not separate us from objective truth as some think. Rather, through his explicit appeal to personal experience, the Holy Father provides "subjective resonance" for objective norms.

The Pope recognizes that as a person, man is conscious of his acts. This means he can *experience* the objective good that fulfills him and the evil that harms him. When he does, the objective norm no longer

---

162. Some have tried to find a place for conjugal love among the traditional ends of marriage by equating it with the "mutual help of spouses." Love, however, is not an "end" of marriage at all. It is the governing form of marriage from which the ends flow. We will discuss this in more detail in Part II, Chapter 3 (see pp. 558–62).

163. *Love and Responsibility*, p. 18.

feels imposed from the outside but wells up from within. People no longer feel forced to conform to truth. They *want* to conform to truth. John Paul maintains that, despite sin, an "echo" of God's original plan remains deep within every human heart. In his TOB, the Pope aims to help people peel away the layers of debris that cover the true desires of their hearts so that this "echo" can resound. The more it does, the more our subjective experience harmonizes with objective reality. The more that echo resounds, the more we can read the "language of the body" and the desires of our hearts "in truth." People who come to understand the Pope's TOB cannot help but recognize the inner movements of their own hearts being laid bare. It rings true. "I can identify with this," they respond. "I experience life this way. *This* is what I desire."

The Personalistic Norm

This "insider's view" of the ethical life crystallizes in what Wojtyla calls the *personalistic norm*. In its negative form, it states that *a person must never be used as a means to an end*. We know from our experience that this violates our dignity. In its positive form, it states that *the only proper response to a person is love*.[164] We know also from experience that the deepest desire of our hearts is to love and be loved. The opposite of loving, then, for Wojtyla, is not hating but *using*. Such using often masquerades as love. Since the sexual revolution dawned, at least two generations of men and women have now been groomed in the "art" of sexual utility.

But the human heart cannot feign solace in a world of sexual utilitarianism for long. As more and more people *experience* the self-inflicted wounds of a counterfeit sexual liberation, the world is fast becoming a mission field ready to soak up John Paul's message. By relinking the desires of the human heart with the truth, the TOB offers true sexual liberation—the freedom for which Christ has set us free, the freedom to love in the image of God as male and female. In fact, the Pope's TOB has already sparked a new kind of "sexual revolution." It resembles the revolution that toppled the Iron Curtain—starting slowly and quietly in human hearts that welcome the truth that this Polish Pope proclaimed about the human person. Then it spreads from heart

---

164. See ibid., p. 41.

to heart, gathering a great multitude who glimpse their true dignity and will not rest until the shackles of dehumanizing ideologies (political, sexual, or otherwise) break.

Since Karol Wojtyla has taken modern philosophy's "turn to the subject" so seriously, George Weigel believes that when this "theological time bomb" explodes, "the *theology of the body* may well be seen as a critical moment not only in Catholic theology but also in the history of modern thought."[165] Looking at the subject alone turns us into navelgazers. In this environment, an idolatrous, self-indulgent cult of the body trumps the "abstractions" of theology. However, a theology *of the body*—which links the modern turn to the subject with objective and ultimate reality—provides the necessary bridge for the modern world to reconnect with Christ.

Christ—the *theological* Word made *flesh*—is the link between the human person and the ultimate reality. Christ himself *is* ultimate reality. In his body "given up for us," we come to see the ultimate meaning of our own bodies revealed. In this way, "Christ fully reveals man to himself." John Paul II's TOB, then, as we have already emphasized, is nothing but an incarnate meeting with the incarnate Christ. It is a gentle, whispering affirmation of the truth every person intuits—we are made as male and female for a love that never ends. The "revelation of the body" is that this love is God: Father, Son, and Holy Spirit.

Structure of the Catechesis

Michael Waldstein provides a thorough and very helpful presentation of the structure of John Paul's catechesis in his Introduction to TOB (see pp. 105–20). Here I will provide a simple overview in order to orient the reader with the basic outline. Understanding the basic structure is itself instructive and will prove very helpful as we venture into the Pope's teaching.

Many of the details of the Pope's own conception of the text have only come to light with Waldstein's discovery of the Pope's original chapter and section headings. As I wrote in the Introduction, spending time with these headings is most rewarding. It opens the text in marvelous ways. Prior to 2006, the 1986 Polish edition of TOB was the

---

165. *Witness to Hope*, p. 343.

only one that supplied these headings, thus retaining the Pope's intended structure. In this revised edition of my commentary, I follow the Pope's originally intended structure very closely. All the part, chapter, and numbered and lettered headings in this commentary are John Paul's. Some subheadings have been altered and others added to organize and facilitate my explanation of the text.[166] I have also supplied in brackets the major headings of the previous six-cycle structure I employed, which was based, in part, on the 1985 Italian edition. As Waldstein observed, "This way of reading the text...should not be rejected, but seen as an alternate and pedagogically effective way of organizing the argument."[167]

In short, one can observe that the TOB seeks to answer two of the most fundamental human questions: *What does it mean to be human?* and *How do I live in a way that will bring true happiness?* In order to answer the first question, the Pope looks at the three different phases or stages of the human drama: (1) our *origin* before sin, (2) our *history* affected by sin yet redeemed in Christ, and (3) our eschatological *destiny* when all things will be consummated in Christ. Then, in order to answer the second question, John Paul looks at questions of life vocation and specific questions of conjugal morality. In this light, a basic two-part, six-cycle structure emerges. This is the way I organized the first edition of my commentary:

PART I: Establishing an "Adequate Anthropology"

       Original Man (Cycle 1)
       Historical Man (Cycle 2)
       Eschatological Man (Cycle 3)

PART II: Applying an "Adequate Anthropology"

       Celibacy for the Kingdom (Cycle 4)
       The Sacramentality of Marriage (Cycle 5)
       Love and Fruitfulness—Reflections on *Humanae Vitae* (Cycle 6)

---

166. It would be a fruitful exercise to compare the table of contents of this commentary with John Paul II's table of contents in *Man and Woman He Created Them: A Theology of the Body.*

167. Waldstein, Introduction, TOB, p. 113.

Using a fitting image, John Paul calls the first three cycles the "triptych" of the TOB. A triptych is a religious piece of art consisting of three painted panels joined by hinges and traditionally placed above the high altar of a church. As with a triptych, there are clear boundaries between the different panels (original sin delineates *original man* from *historical man,* and Christ's second coming delineates *historical man* from *eschatological man*) yet there are also hinges. Christ is that hinge. In Christ we see a certain continuity between our origin, our history, and our eschatological destiny. For Christ—the eternal One at the center of the universe and of history—is "present" in all three states as in one eternal moment. We must separate this eternal moment into different stages within time, but they all refer to Christ and in him they are one.

John Paul paints the three "panels" of his triptych with the following key words of Christ:

CYCLE 1: "For your hardness of heart Moses allowed you to divorce your wives, but from the beginning it was not so" (Mt 19:8).

CYCLE 2: "You have heard that it was said, 'You shall not commit adultery.' But I say to you that everyone who looks at a woman lustfully has already committed adultery with her in his heart" (Mt 5:27–28).

CYCLE 3: "For in the resurrection they neither marry nor are given in marriage" (Mt 22:30).

We call these "key words," John Paul says, "because they open—like a key—the various dimensions of theological anthropology" (TOB 106:5). By basing the three cycles of his "adequate anthropology" on the words of the incarnate Word, the Pope makes a deliberate anthropological statement: *Christ fully reveals man to himself.* If John Paul's goal is to meditate on the human body in order to discover who man is as male and female, the "richest source for knowledge of the body is the Word made flesh."[168] There is no other suitable starting point for an adequate anthropology.

---

168. *Letter to Families,* 19.

Cycle 4 on celibacy is also based on Christ's words: "For there are eunuchs who have...made themselves eunuchs for the sake of the kingdom of heaven" (Mt 19:12). Cycle 5 is based on the "great mystery" of Ephesians 5, and in Cycle 6, the Pope reflects on key passages from *Humanae Vitae*. Along the way, John Paul II's *thoroughly biblical* vision draws from forty-six books, 233 chapters, and over 1,000 verses of Scripture.[169] But we can see that the primary "teacher" from whom John Paul draws is Christ himself. Secondarily he draws from St. Paul. And in the final cycle John Paul II draws from the magisterium of his predecessor Pope Paul VI.

While the above six-cycle structure is a theologically correct and pedagogically effective way to understand the Pope's argument, John Paul II's original manuscript divides the text in the following manner:

PART I: The Words of Christ

            Christ Appeals to the "Beginning" (Chapter 1)
            Christ Appeals to the Human Heart (Chapter 2)
            Christ Appeals to the Resurrection (Chapter 3)
              Continence for the Kingdom

PART II: The Sacrament

            The Dimension of Covenant and of Grace (Chapter 1)
            The Dimension of the Sign (Chapter 2)
            He Gave Them the Law of Life as Their Inheritance
            (Chapter 3)

The structures are similar but have important distinctions. First, the title of Part I, as well as the titles of Chapters 1–3, highlight the fact that Christ is the teacher of the TOB. Christ is the only adequate answer to the question: *What does it mean to be human?* Second, the Pope conceived of celibacy for the kingdom as a subsection of his reflections on the resurrection (Eschatological Man). This highlights the fact that Christian celibacy anticipates the final reality to which we are all destined—that state in which all human longing for spousal love and union will be fulfilled in the marriage of the Lamb. Third, the

---

169. These calculations are based on Waldstein's Scripture Index (see TOB, pp. 725–30). The breakdown by Testament is as follows: Old Testament: 26 books, 140 chapters, 554 verses; New Testament: 20 books, 93 chapters, 493 verses.

entirety of Part II falls under the heading "The Sacrament." This refers, of course, to marriage as a sacrament. But "The Sacrament" refers also in a broader sense to the manner in which the divine Mystery "has *become visible* and thereby *entered into the sphere of the Sign*" (TOB 95b:6). In the beginning, this Mystery was made visible through the primordial sign of spousal union. In the fullness of time, this same Mystery was made visible in the union of Christ and the Church. These two "great signs"—the union of husband-wife and the union of Christ-Church—express *one Mystery* and, thus, form one "great sacrament": *The* Sacrament[170] (see TOB 95b:7).

Like every sacrament, marriage has a divine dimension—the covenant and grace communicated—and a human dimension—the physical sign through which the divine reality is communicated. What the previous structure rendered as Cycle 5 is here divided into two different chapters according to these two dimensions. Chapter 2 offers previously omitted material from the Song of Songs, the Book of Tobit, and Ephesians (see TOB 108–17), all of which is extraordinarily rich and fills in some critical gaps in the previous editions of the Pope's work. (Immersing myself in this "new" content was a particular joy of revising my commentary.) Finally, the title for Cycle 6, "He Gave Them the Law of Life as Their Inheritance" (Chapter 3), speaks to the splendidly positive light in which the Pope views the teaching of *Humanae Vitae.* He sees it not "as a particular moral prohibition, but as a precious inheritance from the Creator that is closely connected with fostering life as a whole."[171]

WE ARE NOW PREPARED to begin the long journey of studying the catechesis itself. Like any venture worth taking, there are sure to be various challenges and obstacles to face along the way. Be not afraid to stay the journey! The TOB richly rewards the efforts of those who undertake the challenge of studying it. Indeed, if we study the TOB "on our knees," allowing its great treasures not only to *inform* us but also to *transform* us, the rewards are eternal. That is *the gift*—participation in

---

170. This is an extraordinarily profound insight of the TOB that John Paul painstakingly unfolds throughout the catechesis, but especially in Part II, Chapter 1.

171. Waldstein, Introduction, TOB, p. 109.

the eternal exchange of love between the Father, the Son, and the Holy Spirit. *Mary, Mother of God, pray for us that we, like you, might open ourselves to so great a gift and conceive eternity within.*

PROLOGUE—IN REVIEW

1. Christian theology begins with the Incarnation, with God's manifestation *in the human body.* Through the fact that the Word of God became flesh, the body entered theology through the main door. To ask questions about the meaning of the human body begins an exhilarating journey that leads us from the union of the sexes to the union of Christ and the Church and, from there, into the heart of the mystery of the Trinity.

2. The length of the TOB catechesis and its place as the inaugural teaching project of John Paul II's pontificate point to its fundamental significance. This is John Paul II's masterwork, the core of his great vision. We simply have not penetrated John Paul II's vision if we have not penetrated his TOB.

3. The only cure for *modern rationalism* and *neo-Manichaeism,* with their dualistic contrast between body and spirit, is to recover a sense of primordial wonder at the divinely inspired beauty of the human body. We must rediscover the *treasure* of human sexuality as a stupendous sign of the divine image in man and woman. We can only do so by pondering the profound understanding of masculinity and femininity found in divine revelation.

4. The phrase "theology of the body" represents the very logic of Christianity. Thus, the TOB is not merely an extended catechesis on marriage and sexual love. It is an extended commentary on the Gospel of the Incarnation, the Gospel of Jesus Christ—or, one might say, the "Gospel of the body." The TOB is an extended commentary on the truth that Christ fully reveals man to himself

through the revelation—*in his body*—of the mystery of the Father and his love.

5. We cannot *see* God. Yet God has made himself visible in the flesh. This making visible of what is invisible is what John Paul II means by the "sacramentality of the body." Only the body is capable of making visible what is invisible: the spiritual and divine. God created the human body to transfer into the visible reality of the world his own eternal Mystery—the mystery that God is an eternal exchange of love and that he has destined us to share in that exchange.

6. The union of the two in "one flesh" normally leads to a third. Here we encounter an echo in the created order of the uncreated mystery of trinitarian life and love. In fact, spousal union in God's design is the original effective sign that communicates the "great mystery" of the inner life of the Trinity to the world. We cannot reduce the infinitely transcendent mystery to its earthly sign. But man needs signs in order to encounter the Mystery.

7. As the phrase "theology of the body" indicates, John Paul wants to help us embrace the profound link or marriage between *theology* and *anthropology*. The human body *is the link* between the study of God and the study of man. Far from demonizing the body, Christianity divinizes the body. For in Christ "the whole fullness of deity dwells bodily" (Col 2:9).

8. The Church's sacraments—all physical, sensual, bodily realities—offer the most intimate encounter with the spiritual mystery of God. Marriage is not just one of the seven sacraments but is the foundation of the entire sacramental order. All of the sacraments find their prototype in some way in marriage as the primordial sacrament.

9. In keeping with the Carmelite tradition, John Paul uses the "great spousal analogy" as a lens through which to view the entirety of God's plan of salvation. The whole of biblical revelation unfolds between the marriage of *the first* Adam and Eve and the marriage of *the final* Adam and Eve, Christ and the Church. From this perspective we see that God's plan is to "marry" us. And this eternal

"marital plan" is mysteriously recapitulated in our very being as male and female.

10. We must avoid both excess and deficiency in understanding the spousal analogy. A "maximalist" interpretation deforms God by failing to recognize the substantial dissimilarity between the Creator and his creatures. A "minimalist" interpretation fights every attempt to give spousal imagery theological weight.

11. While taking the Catholic sacramental imagination to new heights, John Paul II's TOB remains firmly grounded in the spousal theology of St. John of the Cross. According to this revered Carmelite, all Christians are called to "mystical marriage" with God through a reciprocal love like the marriage union and surrender. This is not merely a theological idea to be reflected upon, but a mystical reality to be *experienced* by all who follow Christ.

12. John Paul II gained a rich view of the ethical life from John of the Cross. It is based on three interrelated theses: (1) Love involves the gift of self. (2) The relationship of spouses is the paradigm of self-giving love in human experience. (3) The relationship of Father, Son, and Holy Spirit is the source and model of all self-giving love.

13. Human life involves a dramatic battle between good and evil. It is a battle between truth and lies, between the Word and the anti-Word. If the primordial sacrament of spousal communion enabled the first man and woman to participate in God's life and love, the deceiver—intent on divorcing man from God's life and love—mounted his counterplan by attacking this sacrament. John Paul's TOB is a clarion call for Christians to reclaim what Satan has plagiarized.

14. The original temptation attacked God's benevolent love. *Original sin, then, attempts to abolish fatherhood.* In man and woman's heart, the primordial sign of God's covenant love became, in some way, a countersign. In other words, by accepting the devil's lie, the "symbolic" became "diabolic."

15. Man and woman must now contend with the "great divorce" that ruptured the original harmony of body and soul. Without reintegration in Christ, people either lean toward a "spiritual" life cut off from the body ("angelism") or a "carnal" life cut off from the spirit

("animalism"). This body-soul split lies at the root of the "culture of death."

16. The call to spousal love and communion revealed by our sexual bodies is the fundamental component of human existence in the world, the foundation of human life, and, hence, the deepest foundation of ethics and culture. Indeed, the human project stands or falls based on the proper ordering of love between the sexes. Thus, it is an illusion to think we can build a true culture of human life if we do not accept and experience sexuality and love and the whole of life according to their true meaning and their close interconnection.

17. Christ heals the "great divorce" and reunites us with the "great mystery" through the very dynamism of the Incarnation. If man is to find himself, he must appropriate and assimilate the whole reality of the Incarnation and the Redemption. He must be willing to die with Christ in order to be resurrected in the unity of flesh and spirit. Man cannot live without Christ because man cannot live without love. Christ's body—and every body—is a witness to Love.

18. In order to understand why the modern world seems almost programmed to tune out the Church, we must look at the "subjective turn" in modern philosophy. Descartes initiated this turn to the subject with his dictum, "I think, therefore I am." When human thought determines existence, man—not God—becomes the measure of reality. Here we see the roots of subjectivism and moral relativism.

19. To the modern mind, any claim to objective "truth" impinges on subjective human freedom. Truth and freedom, objectivity and subjectivity must be held together if man is to be himself and if human society is to flourish. Herein lies Wojtyla's lifelong philosophical project—to demonstrate the link between objective reality and subjective experience. This would require a personalistic approach sensitive to modern thought but rooted in Thomistic philosophy.

20. Wojtyla's sensitivity to "the person" was greatly enriched by the phenomenology of Max Scheler. Phenomenology involves a style

of thought that humbly receives what is given by experience. It "lets the data speak" and listens attentively to what it says. With this approach, the intellect does not seek to dominate reality, but rather receives it lovingly. In fact, John Paul II emphasizes love as the animating principle of phenomenology.

21. Wojtyla shows remarkable respect for and trust in the freedom of the person and a bold confidence in the ability of each person's conscience to recognize—and desire—the truth when it presents itself. There is no place for a tyranny of truth in the life of a personal subject. Freedom must be challenged to submit to truth, but no one can be forced to accept the truth without doing violence to the person. When truth is presented in its splendor, it does not need to be imposed.

22. By "making room" for subjectivity within an objective or realist philosophy, Wojtyla avoids the pitfalls of objectivizing rigorism and subjectivizing relativism. In this marriage of objectivity and subjectivity we encounter again the "great mystery" of God's spousal union with humanity in Christ. A theological anthropology prevents the "subjective turn" from stagnating on man. It enables man (the Bride) to remain open to Christ (the Bridegroom).

23. Other milestones in the development of Wojtyla's thought include his work in the Lublin School of Philosophy, his book *Love and Responsibility*, the Second Vatican Council, his books *The Acting Person* and *Sources of Renewal*, and the retreat he preached to the Roman Curia in 1976 entitled *Sign of Contradiction*.

24. Wojtyla took his cue in writing the TOB from Paul VI's statement in *Humanae Vitae* that in order to understand the Church's teaching on birth regulation, we needed a "total vision of man and of his vocation." This is precisely what the TOB provides. It offers an "adequate anthropology" on which to build an adequate understanding of *Humanae Vitae* and, in turn, all ethical questions.

25. In short, the TOB seeks to answer two of the most fundamental human questions: *What does it mean to be human?* and *How do I live my life in a way that will bring true happiness?* In light of these questions, a six-cycle structure emerges: Original Man, Historical

Man, Eschatological Man, Celibacy for the Kingdom, The Sacramentality of Marriage, Love and Fruitfulness.

26. John Paul's divided his original manuscript between "The Words of Christ" and "The Sacrament." It is further divided as follows: (Part I) Christ Appeals to the "Beginning"; Christ Appeals to the Human Heart; Christ Appeals to the Resurrection; (Part II) The Dimension of Covenant and of Grace; The Dimension of the Sign; He Gave Them the Law of Life as Their Inheritance.

Part I

THE WORDS OF CHRIST

CHAPTER 1

Christ Appeals to the "Beginning"

[Cycle 1—Original Man]

THIS FIRST CYCLE CONSISTS OF twenty-three general audiences delivered between September 5, 1979, and April 2, 1980 (TOB 1–23). John Paul II finds a source of great hope for all men and women in Christ's discussion with the Pharisees about marriage. If conflict, tension, jealousies, and divisions have tarnished the relationship of the sexes throughout history, Christ challenges his listeners to recognize that "from the beginning it was not so" (Mt 19:8). With these words, Christ calls all men and women burdened by the heritage of sin to realize a radical paradigm shift by reestablishing the original unity of the sexes as the norm for all who become "one flesh."

As the *Catechism* teaches, "According to faith the discord we notice so painfully [in the relationship of the sexes] does not stem from the *nature* of man and woman, nor from the nature of their relations, but from *sin*. As a break with God, the first sin had for its first consequence the rupture of the original communion between man and woman."[1] Yet the "good news" that Christ came to reconcile God and man means he also reconciles man and woman. "By coming to restore the original order of creation disturbed by sin, [Christ] himself gives the strength and grace to live marriage in the new dimension of the Reign of God." Therefore, "by following Christ, renouncing themselves, and taking up their crosses...spouses will be able to 'receive' the original meaning of

---

1. *CCC*, no. 1607.

marriage and live it with the help of Christ."[2] Even if the heritage of
sin carries with it the entire history of discord between the sexes, the
roots of man and woman's relationship go deeper, and Christ enables us
to tap into that deeper heritage.

The Church's teaching on marriage and sexuality can never be adequately understood apart from God's original plan, our fall from it, and
our redemption in Christ. Many modern men and women find the
Church's teaching on marriage and sexuality untenable because they
remain locked in a fallen view of themselves and the world. This narrow horizon makes it easy to "normalize" disordered patterns of thinking and relating. The pain and conflict that inevitably ensue may lead
people to yearn for something more, and such pain shows that we are
created for something more. But without any reference to God's original plan and the hope of its restoration in Christ, people tend to accept
the discord between the sexes as "just the way it is."

The following image may help frame our discussion. When we
normalize our fallen state, it is akin to thinking it normal to drive with
flat tires. We may intuit that something is amiss, but when everyone
drives around in the same state, we lack a point of reference for anything different. In Christ's discussion with the Pharisees, he points
them back to man and woman's "fully inflated" state. In turn, through
his penetrating exegesis of the Genesis texts, John Paul seeks to reconstruct the experience of "full inflation." Just as tires are meant to be
inflated, we know that we long for the original unity of man and
woman. Pushing the analogy, the good news is that Christ did not
come into the world to condemn those with flat tires. He came in love
to fill our tires once again with air. To the degree that we experience
this "re-inflation" (which is never perfect in this life), we no longer view
the Church's teaching on marriage and sexuality as a rigid ethic
imposed from "without." Rather, we experience it as a liberating ethos
welling up from "within."

1. What Is Meant by "Beginning"?

Men and women of all times and cultures have raised questions
about the nature and meaning of marriage. As John Paul observes, such

---

2. *CCC*, no. 1615.

questions are raised today "by single persons, by married and engaged couples, by young people, but also by writers, journalists, politicians, economists, demographers, in sum, by contemporary culture and civilization" (TOB 23:2). The questions of modern men and women are charged with problems unknown to the Pharisees who questioned Jesus about the lawfulness of divorce. Even so, Jesus' response to the Pharisees is timeless. In it John Paul finds the foundation for establishing an adequate vision of who men and women are, or—more so—who they are called to be and, thus, how they are called to live when they join in "one flesh."

According to the Gospel of Matthew, the dialogue between Christ and the Parisees took place as follows:

> And Pharisees came up to him and tested him by asking, "Is it lawful to divorce one's wife for any cause?" [Jesus] answered, "Have you not read that he who made them from the beginning made them male and female, and said, 'For this reason a man shall leave his father and mother and be joined to his wife and the two shall become one flesh'? So they are no longer two, but one flesh. What therefore God has joined together, let no man put asunder." They said to him, "Why then did Moses command one to give a certificate of divorce and to put her away?" He said to them, "For your hardness of heart Moses allowed you to divorce your wives, but from the beginning it was not so." (Mt 19:4–8; see also Mk 10:2–9)

Unity and Indissolubility

Moses allowed divorce as a concession to sin, but Christ can reestablish the original unity and indissolubility of marriage because he is "the Lamb of God who takes away the sin of the world" (Jn 1:29). Moses' reason for divorce, therefore, no longer holds sway. As the Holy Father says: "That phrase, 'let man not separate,' is decisive. In the light of this word of Christ, Genesis 2:24 [the two become one flesh] states the principle of the unity and indissolubility of marriage as the very content of the word of God expressed in the most ancient revelation" (TOB 1:3).[3] But Christ does not merely use his authority to reestablish an objective norm. He invites his questioners to reflect on the beauty of God's original plan in order to awaken their consciences. This original

---

3. *CCC*, no. 1644.

plan is stamped in them. "The hardness of their hearts"[4] has obscured it, but it is still within them. Christ knows that if they traced the "echoes" of their hearts back to "the beginning," this norm would well up *from within*. They would understand *subjectively* the reason for the *objective* indissolubility of marriage. And if they lived according to this deeper heritage of their hearts, they would desire nothing else.

The same holds true for the many people today who question the meaning of marriage. If we are to provide adequate answers to contemporary questions, we too must take Christ's invitation to reflect on God's plan "in the beginning." For the first pages of Genesis contain "the key to understanding the world of today, both its roots and its extremely radical—and therefore dramatic—affirmations and denials."[5]

Two Creation Accounts

Many have been surprised by John Paul's concern to show that his biblical interpretation harmonizes with contemporary methods. For example, he seems to take for granted the modern view that the two creation accounts in Genesis were written at different times by different authors (see TOB 2:2).[6] The so-called "Elohist" account of Genesis 1 derives from "Elohim," the term used for God in this account. The "Yahwist" account of Genesis 2 and 3 (believed to be a much older text) is so named because it uses the term "Yahweh" for God.

The Elohist account is loaded with a "powerful metaphysical content," defining man "in the dimensions of being and existing" (TOB 2:5). In fact, man is the only creature defined in relation to Being itself. He is the only creature defined *theologically*—not with a likeness to the other creatures, but with a likeness to God. "In the cycle of the seven days of creation...the Creator seems to halt before calling...[man] to existence, as if he entered back into himself to make a decision, 'Let us make man in our image, in our likeness' (Gen 1:27)" (TOB 2:3). The first phrases of the Bible make it clear that man cannot be reduced to

---

4. In the Hebrew, what we translate "hardness of heart" actually meant "non-circumcision of the heart." Since circumcision was the sign of the Old Covenant, John Paul notes later in his catechesis that non-circumcision meant "distance from the covenant with God" and "expressed indomitable obstinacy in opposing God" (TOB 34, n. 47).

5. Karol Wojtyla, *Sign of Contradiction*, p. 24.

6. See *CCC*, no. 289.

the elements of the world. He is certainly a physical creature, but he is also more than that; man is spiritual. The creative tension of the unity of body and soul defines him. This latter point is decisive for a theology *of the body.* "Man, whom God created 'male and female,' bears the divine image impressed in the body 'from the beginning'" (TOB 13:2). This establishes an "unassailable point of reference" in order to understand who we are (anthropology) and how we are to live (ethics).

Deeply imbedded in the truth of anthropology and ethics is man and woman's call to "be fruitful and multiply." This original divine blessing corresponds with their creation in God's image. As the Prologue noted, the capacity to "pro-create" (not as a response to biological instinct but by the free choice proper to persons) enables them to participate in the creative, covenant love of God. Precisely in this context it is necessary to understand the reality of the good or the aspect of value. With God's affirmation that everything he created is "very good" (Gen 1:31), we can conclude that "being and [the] good are convertible" (TOB 2:5). This means that everything that exists is good in itself. Nothing that exists is evil in itself. Evil, by definition, is always and only the deprivation of what is good. Therefore, to exist—just to *be*—is very good. More specifically, to exist *as male and female* and to bring more males and females into existence ("be fruitful and multiply") is very good. To think otherwise is unbiblical. This philosophy of value (axiology) lies at the foundation of every Christian discussion about creation and about human existence in particular.

In describing man's creation and his call to be fruitful and multiply, John Paul points out that the Elohist account contains only the objective facts and defines the objective reality. On the other hand, the Yahwist account seeks to penetrate man's psychology. In doing so it presents the creation of man especially in its subjective aspect. As the Pope states: "Chapter 2 of Genesis constitutes in some way the oldest description and record of man's self-understanding and, together with Chapter 3, it is the first witness of human conscience"[7] (TOB 3:1).

---

7. The first printing of the Waldstein translation of TOB rendered this "consciousness." The Italian, upon which Waldstein based his translation, according to John Paul II's expressed wish, does not distinguish consciousness and conscience. Further research of the original Polish manuscript led Waldstein to make some changes, which are reflected in the later printings of TOB.

With such explicit attention paid to man's "interiority," John Paul says that the Yahwist account provides "in nucleo" nearly all the elements of analysis of man to which contemporary philosophical anthropology is sensitive. Here the Holy Father is referring to the modern "turn to the subject" of which we previously spoke.

Significantly, Christ referred to *both* creation stories when he directed the Pharisees back to "the beginning." In this way Christ's words confirm that both the objective and the subjective elements of the "one flesh" union are indispensable in establishing a proper understanding of man and woman's relationship. As an exegete seeking to penetrate man's "interiority" in order to confirm objective truth, John Paul will spend most of his time examining the subjective experiences of Adam and Eve from the Yahwist text. By doing so, he brings a dramatic development of thinking to our understanding of the Elohist teaching that man is made in the divine image.

Continuity in the "Redemption of the Body"

The tree of the knowledge of good and evil marks the "boundary" between the state of original innocence (integral nature) and the state of historical sinfulness (fallen nature). Without any direct experience of it, "historical" men and women find it difficult to imagine what life was like on the other side of this boundary. Although we cannot actually cross this boundary, Christ orders us "in some sense to pass beyond the boundary" (TOB 4:1). John Paul emphasizes that there is *"an essential continuity in man and a link* between these two different states or dimensions of the human being." In "every man without exception, this state—the 'historical' state—plunges its roots deeply into his theological 'prehistory,' which is the state of original innocence" (TOB 4:1). Further along in the catechesis he explains that there is imprinted in the experience of fallen man "a certain 'echo' of the...original innocence of man: a photographic 'negative,' as it were, the 'positive' of which was precisely original innocence" (TOB 55:4). Although the negative of a photograph reveals something of the positive image, it needs to be "flipped over" for the colors to take on their true light. Thus even though we have no experience of original innocence, we can reconstruct it to a certain degree by "flipping over" our experience of innocence lost.

If we listen, we can still hear the original experience echoing in our hearts. In fact, John Paul describes this echo as a "co-inheritance" of sin. Sin is only intelligible in reference to original innocence. If sin means literally to "miss the mark," the word implicitly refers to the mark we are missing: original innocence.

When that echo of innocence resounds in us, we experience a deep awareness of our own fallenness, of grace lost. But this should not cause us to despair because it also opens us to the possibility of redemption, of grace restored. How tragic it would be if upon (re)discovering the beauty of God's original plan, we found no way to overcome sin in order to live it. Christ is the way! As we take up Christ's invitation to ponder our "beginning," we must keep in mind that there is *real power* in him to regain what was lost. Yes, we will always struggle with sin in this life because we have left the state of innocence irrevocably behind. Nonetheless, through "the redemption of the body" (Rom 8:23) won by Christ, we can come progressively to live as we were called to in the beginning. John Paul will continually return to this Pauline concept. By "redemption of the body" John Paul does not mean to single out one of the results of redemption. Rather, he intends to summarize the entire reality of Christ's Incarnation and paschal mystery. For John Paul, "the redemption of the body" is redemption itself. Man is always embodied man. Thus, just as a theological anthropology must be a theology of the body, so too must man's redemption be a redemption of the body.

"Precisely this *perspective of the redemption of the body guarantees the continuity and the unity* between man's hereditary state of sin and his original innocence" (TOB 4:3). In other words, if we could not begin reclaiming what was lost, the historical state would be hopelessly cut off from man's original vocation and destiny. The deepest longings of the heart would lead only to despair. But John Paul insists on this hopeful point: Historical man "participates not only *in the history of human sinfulness*, as a hereditary, and at the same time personal and unrepeatable, subject of this history." He "also participates *in the history of salvation*, here too as its subject and co-creator" (TOB 4:3). Herein lies the meeting point of the remarkable gift of God with the mystery of human freedom. In the face of grace lost, God presents us with the sheer gift of salvation, but it remains up to us to accept the gift. As free agents, that is, as persons, we must cooperate with God in our own salvation. Through faith ("openness to the gift") then, we become subjects and "co-creators" in salvation history.[8] From this perspective, historical man comes to view the "beginning" (original man) as his true fullness. The gift of salvation gives birth to the hope of returning in some way to the beginning at the end (eschatological man) as a sort of homecoming.

Revelation and Experience

John Paul observes in a footnote that many people see a line of complete antithesis between God's revelation and human experience. The Holy Father readily recognizes that human experience is inadequate for understanding revelation. But he still affirms it as a legitimate means of theological interpretation and a necessary reference point. "In the interpretation of the revelation about man, and above all about the body, we must, for understandable reasons," the Pope stresses, "appeal to experience, because bodily man is perceived by us above all in experience" (TOB 4:4). In the second footnote of this same address, John Paul asserts that we have a right to speak of the relationship between experience and revelation. Without this we "consider quite abstract concepts rather than the human person as a living subject." John Paul's own teaching is the fruit of a constant encounter between doctrine and life—objective truth and subjective experience.[9]

John Paul wants to unearth the "deep roots" of the Church's teaching on marriage and sexuality. Those deep roots are found in human subjectivity. Throughout his biblical exegesis, John Paul tries systematically to show how the dimension of man's personal subjectivity is an indispensable element in outlining a theology of the body. He says that "not only the objective reality of the body, but far more so, as it seems, the subjective consciousness as well as the subjective 'experience' of the body, enter at each step into the structure of the biblical texts and therefore require that one considers and reflects them in theology" (TOB 60:1). Here again John Paul seeks to justify his use of the phenomenological method in presenting the faith. We need not be suspicious of the philosophy of consciousness so long as we remain rooted in objective truth. Indeed, the original subjective experiences of man and

---

8. See *CCC*, nos. 306, 2008.
9. See *Love and Responsibility*, p. 15.

woman prior to sin completely accorded with objective truth. By penetrating their consciousness we find reality reflected there. We find reality *experienced* and given its proper subjective resonance. Following the Pope's lead, we need not fear to open ourselves "to every echo of experience, from whatever quarter it comes." The Pope's approach presents "a standing appeal to all to let experience, [our] own experience, make itself heard, to its full extent: in all its breadth, and all its depth."[10]

When John Paul speaks of "original human experiences," he has in mind not so much their distance in time but their basic significance. These original experiences did not take place in history as we understand it. As John Paul uses the word, "history" begins only with the "knowledge of good and evil," whereas the original experiences the Pope reflects on refer to a mysterious "prehistory." Furthermore, he attempts to reconstruct these experiences not so much to determine precisely who man and woman were "then," but to help us better understand *who we are now*—more so, who we are meant to be. In the final analysis, we cannot know the events and experiences of our "prehistory" with any "historical" certainty—that is, not as we understand history today. We know that the human race sprang from one man and one woman, and that through "a deed that took place *at the beginning of the history of man*,"[11] they disobeyed God and fell into sin. However, we approach these primeval events and experiences only by pondering "the symbolism of the biblical language."[12]

Explicitly appealing to the contemporary philosophy of religion and of language, the Holy Father states that this biblical language is mythical. He clarifies that the term "myth," however, "does not refer to fictitious-fabulous content, but simply to an archaic way of expressing a deeper content" (TOB 8:2). Thus, John Paul is not conceding to the idea that the biblical creation stories are merely human fabrications. By describing these divinely inspired stories as "mythical," he is simply acknowledging that our "theological prehistory" is shrouded in mystery. Myth, symbol, and metaphor are the only means at our disposal if we wish to enter into the mystery of our "beginning."

Mysterious as our prehistory is, the original experiences of man and woman remain at the root of every human experience. "Indeed, they are

---

10. Ibid., p. 10.
11. *CCC*, no. 390.
12. *CCC*, no. 375.

so interwoven with the ordinary things of life that we generally do not realize their extraordinary character" (TOB 11:1). John Paul focuses on three such experiences: *original solitude, original unity,* and *original nakedness.* His analysis takes us to the extraordinary side of the ordinary. The first extraordinary thing we recognize is the depth of original insight that John Paul extracts from one of the most familiar stories in the Bible. The Holy Father brings the Scriptures to life—to each and every human life. By penetrating these original human experiences, John Paul enables us to see that the story of Adam and Eve, far from being abstract, is a story about each of us. His insights resound in us. This is the gift afforded by John Paul's incorporation of the modern "turn to the subject."

2. The Meaning of Original Solitude

"It is not good that the man should be alone; I will make him a helper fit for him" (Gen 2:18). These words of God-Yahweh form the basis of the Pope's reflections on *original solitude.* As we shall see, original solitude will have an ample perspective in John Paul's reflections.

A Twofold Meaning

To begin with, "solitude" has two basic meanings. The most obvious meaning derives from the male-female relationship. Man is "alone" without woman. But John Paul insists that this solitude has a more fundamental meaning, one derived from man's nature. He is "alone" in the visible world as *a person.*

It is significant that the first man (ʾādām in Hebrew), is not defined as a male (ʾîš) until after the creation of woman (ʾiššāʰ). So Adam's solitude is not only proper to the male. It is proper to "man" as such, to every human person. As John Paul says, this solitude is "a fundamental anthropological issue that is in some way prior to the issue raised by the fact that man is male and female" (TOB 5:3). It is prior not so much in the chronological sense but "by its very nature," since it is man's first discovery of his own personhood. In this way, being a body—being some*body, a body-person—"belongs more deeply to the structure of the personal subject than the fact that in his somatic constitution he is also male or female"* (TOB 8:1).

In other words, the "first" human experience is one of simply "being a body," not of being as a body male or female. Experience of sexuality, of being male or female, is in some sense "secondary" to this primary experience. The essential point is that, although sexual difference is fundamental to the meaning of our humanity, each human being (each body-person) stands with his own dignity as a subject *prior* to his call to live in communion with an "other" person via the gift of sexual differ-ence. If one is to give himself away in an incarnate communion with an "other," he must first be the kind of creature capable of doing so; he must first be a "body-person." This is the essential significance and "pri-ority" of original solitude.

Man in Search of His Own Identity

Acknowledging Adam's need for a helper, God first creates the ani-mals and brings them to the man to see what he will call them. Naming the animals is certainly to be seen as preparation for the creation of woman; however, John Paul demonstrates that it has a profound significance in itself. By naming the animals, Adam realizes he funda-mentally differs from them. He looks for a "helper fit for him" but fails to find one among the animals. The experience only confirms his soli-tude. Adam's capacity to *name* the animals speaks of his fundamental difference from them. He has dominion over the earth and all its crea-tures. Adam's capacity to "till the earth" also reveals this. Tilling is a specifically human activity that seems to belong to the definition of man since no other living being is capable of it.

Adam realizes his unique capacity to "name" and to "till" through his experience of embodiment—through the unique relationship between his soul and body. In this psycho-somatic relationship, John Paul says "we touch the central problem of anthropology" (TOB 7:1). Through the experience of the body we penetrate man's self-conscious-ness, his experience and "discovery" of being a person. Adam is aware of himself; the animals are not. He has self-determination; the animals do not. He can consciously choose his acts; the animals cannot. He can consciously choose to *till* and *to name*; "and whatever the man called every living creature, that was its name" (Gen 2:19).

Thus, in naming or identifying the animals, he actually discovers his own "name," his own identity, his own freedom. For *"created man* finds himself from the first moment of his existence *before God* in search of his own being...in search of his own 'identity'" (TOB 5:5). And man's self-knowledge "goes hand in hand with knowledge...of all living beings to which man has given their names to affirm his own dissimilarity before them" (TOB 5:6). In other words, to the extent that Adam realizes he differs from the animals, he realizes who he is as a person. Solitude, therefore, signifies man's subjectivity.

John Paul observes that naming the animals is a "test" of sorts through which man gains self-awareness. "When we analyze the text of Genesis, we are in some way witnesses of how man, with the first act of self-consciousness, 'distinguishes himself' before God-Yahweh from the whole world of [animals]." This knowledge calls Adam "outside his own being." He "consequently reveals himself to himself and at the same time affirms himself in the visible world as a 'person'" (TOB 5:6). Here it seems we already find a foreshadowing of the new Adam, Jesus Christ, who, according to the familiar passage from Vatican II, will fully reveal man to man himself. Later John Paul will say that the first Adam already bore the capacity and readiness to receive all that would become the second Adam, Jesus Christ (see TOB 71:3). From the beginning man was created as a Bride for Christ. Adam is already discovering this in his solitude, that he is made for communion.

Thus, human "dominion" over creation is essential not only to man in solitude but also to man in the unity of male and female. In the Elohist account, man and woman's vocation to fruitful union is coupled with their call to "subdue the earth" and to have "dominion over the flesh of the sea, and over the birds of the air, and over every living thing that moves upon the earth" (Gen 1:28). In fact, man's experience of sexual difference and the call to communion will determine the way man exercises his dominion over creation. The loving communion of man and woman will facilitate a "loving" care of and for creation. But if love were denied in the male-female relationship, responsible dominion over creation would lead to abuse of the visible world.[13]

Objective-Subjective Harmony

In just a few sentences from the creation narrative in Genesis 2, we can perceive with great depth the subjectivity of the human being. The

---

13. See *CCC*, no. 373; see also *Evangelium Vitae*, 42.

Yahwist text makes it clear that man's creation as a person "reveals itself not on the basis of some primordial metaphysical analysis, but on the basis of man's sufficiently clear concrete subjectivity" (TOB 7:2). This demonstrates the objective-subjective complementarity of the two creation stories. Adam's experience of solitude in the Yahwist narrative is his *subjective* realization of being created in God's image, as *objectively* described in the first creation account. In other words, what the Elohist account only observes externally (man is a person made in God's image), the Yahwist account confirms by penetrating man's interiority—his consciousness, his psychology, his experience.

In fact, the Holy Father says that without understanding Adam's subjective experience of solitude, we cannot understand who man is as a creature made in God's image. Recognizing this objective-subjective harmony is crucial to John Paul's entire project. Through this harmony, the anthropological definition of the Yahwist text approaches the theological definition of man from the Elohist text. Here, right from the start, we are pressing into the link between theology and anthropology. If in the Yahwist text solitude is the frontier of communion, communion too will shed light on the image of God in man of which the Elohist text speaks.

Partner of the Absolute

From the beginning, man was created to be, as John Paul describes, a "partner of the Absolute." As a personal subject, he was called to enter a covenant with God, a relationship of eternal communion. Above all, as "subject of the covenant," man's solitude means that he, "*through his own humanity*, through what he is [i.e., a person], he is at the same time set into a *unique, exclusive, and unrepeatable relationship with God himself*" (TOB 6:2). We cannot understand who man is apart from his supreme call to enter a covenant of love with his Creator. Of course, this call to communion with God is not man's due. It is a sheer, gratuitous gift,[14] but a gift that reveals man's greatness. "The dignity of man rests above all on the fact that he is called to communion with God."[15] Our call to receive this gift explains who man is and why he aspires to

---

14. See *CCC*, no. 367.
15. *Gaudium et Spes*, 19; *CCC*, no. 27.

"something more." St. Augustine said it well: "You have made us for yourself, O God, and our heart is restless until it rests in you."[16]

This call to be "partner of the Absolute" hinges on man's freedom, his ability to determine his own actions. For John Paul, the term "self-determination" encapsulates a lifetime of philosophical reflection. It enables us to approach the core of the human person, of what distinguishes man from the other "bodies" in the world. God did not command the animals not to eat from the tree of the knowledge of good and evil, only Adam. Why? God's command presents a choice, and only *persons* have the free will necessary to choose. Human beings are the only creatures in the visible world that can disobey God. A squirrel cannot commit a sin. Nor can a squirrel choose to open itself to an eternal covenant of love with God. Love presupposes freedom. In other words, if God gives us as human beings the choice of entering an eternal covenant with him (and one another), we also have the choice of rejecting that covenant. If Adam chose to eat the forbidden fruit, he would die. This "death" differs from the possibility of death for the animals, because human death reveals human personhood.

The Holy Father says that based on man's experience of his own freedom, he should have understood that the forbidden tree had roots not only in the Garden of Eden but also in his own humanity. "In addition, he should have understood that this mysterious tree concealed within itself a dimension of solitude that was unknown to him up to this point" (TOB 7:3). This is not the solitude that confirmed man's personhood. This is the solitude of *alienation* from God that would be man's death.[17]

The Alternative Between Death and Immortality

John Paul poses an interesting question. Could Adam even have understood the words "you shall die," since he had no experience of death, only life? He concludes that man, "who had heard these words, had to find their truth in the inner structure of his own solitude" (TOB 7:3). In his solitude before God, Adam was totally aware of his depen-

---

16. See *CCC*, nos. 27, 30, 1024, 1718.

17. Mary Shivanandan describes this alienation as the third meaning of solitude. See *Crossing the Threshold of Love*, p. 101.

dence on God for his existence. In turn, he would have known that he was a limited being, by nature liable to nonexistence. Hence, he could have understood "death" in contrast to his original experience of having received life as a gift from his Creator. Here, just as historical man can envision original man's experience by contrasting it with his own, so too could original man envision the experience of "death" by contrasting it with his own experience of life.

In this way "the alternative between death and immortality has entered from the very beginning into the definition of man and... belongs 'from the beginning' to the meaning of his solitude before God himself" (TOB 7:4). One might say that man's solitude as a free creature suspends him, in some sense, between the tree of life and the tree of the knowledge of good and evil. He alone can choose his own destiny: death or immortality. No one can choose for him. And he *must* choose. Freedom, then, is man's capacity for eternity. It is his capacity for eternal life in communion with God *and* his capacity for eternal death in alienation from God.

In this way, original solitude enables us to understand that man is constituted in his very being by a relationship of *dependence* and *partnership* with God: dependence because man is a creature; partnership because man is a person created by a personal God who always extends to him a covenant of love. As we will learn, Satan's temptation to eat from the forbidden tree attacks this relationship of *partnership* and *dependence*. If God is not a God of love who extends a relationship of partnership to man, then dependence on this God comes to be seen as a threat to man's subjectivity. As a subject, man earnestly resists enslavement, and rightly so. Thus, the moment man perceives God as a domineering tyrant, he will shirk his dependence on him. And so Satan attacks God's benevolent Fatherhood, as noted in the Prologue.

John Paul tells us that this original meaning of solitude, permeated by the alternative between death and immortality, has a fundamental meaning for the whole theology of the body. It already sums up man's fundamental vocation: love of God and love of neighbor (see Lk 10:27). Furthermore, we shall see even more clearly in future reflections how original solitude already points man to his eschatological destiny of eternal communion with God. It already outlines the cosmic struggle involved if man is to claim that eternal destiny, a struggle that is always lived out in man's body.

The Body Expresses the Person

We might be tempted to think that man's knowledge of himself and his relationship to God was purely spiritual. But man was constituted as a specific unity of spirit and body. The Yahwist narrative expresses this by saying: "The LORD God formed man of dust from the ground, and breathed into his nostrils the breath of life; and man became a living being" (Gen 2:7). In the original language, the word "breath" is the same word for "spirit." It is through his body (his "dust"), then, that man lives "in the spirit"—his own spirit, and according to the Holy Spirit. It is through the experience of his own body that man comes to understand who he is and who God is.

The human body is so similar to animal bodies (especially other mammals) that, as John Paul observes, we might think that Adam would have reached the conclusion, based on the experience of his own body, that he was substantially similar to animals. However, while the animals were also created from the ground, the Yahwist text does not state that God breathed his Spirit into them. Hence, while in naming the animals, the man certainly realized that he was a "body among bodies," he also reached the conviction that he was alone.

The important point here is that everything we have been discussing about man's solitude—about his difference from the animals, his subjectivity as a person, his self-determination, his call to eternal communion with God, etc.—is revealed and experienced *through the body*. If it is true that the "invisible" determines man more than the "visible," it is also true that the visible expresses the invisible. John Paul insists that the "body expresses the person. It is thus, in all its materiality...penetrable and transparent, as it were, in such a way as to make it clear who man is (and who he ought to be)" (TOB 7:2).

This is a remarkable assertion since we tend to think of personhood as a merely spiritual reality, not a material one. *Human* personhood is always a materialized-spiritual reality. Man's original solitude (the first realization of personhood) is revealed through the body: The body reveals that it is "not good for the man to be alone." The body reveals man's call to communion with "a helper fit for him." This is the more familiar meaning of original solitude. In naming the animals, Adam found many other "bodies." But none of these bodies revealed a person, as did his own body. Here we can sense Adam's deep longing for an-*other* body that reveals an-*other* person who is called to communion with him.

Man's experience of original solitude,[18] then, paves the way for the creation of this "other" and already anticipates the experience of *original unity*. In John Paul's mind, all this has deep implications for the meaning of our being created in the image of God.

3. The Meaning of Original Unity

John Paul describes the biblical words about solitude—"It is not good that the man should be alone" (Gen 2:18)—as a kind of prelude to the creation of woman. Together with the crowning act of creating woman, "the meaning of original solitude enters and becomes part of the meaning of original unity" (TOB 8:1). In other words, all the truths about the human person revealed in original solitude "carry over" into the experience of original unity. In fact, original unity will be, in some sense, the definitive discovery of what it means to be a person.

The Unity of the Two

Original unity refers first to the fact that man and woman share a common humanity and second to the fact that they become "one flesh." They are "brother and sister" in the same humanity *before* they are "husband and wife." Still, the Holy Father says that the "key point" of original unity "seems to be precisely the words of Genesis 2:24... 'the two will be one flesh.' If Christ quotes these words when he appeals to the beginning, we should clarify the meaning of this original unity, which is rooted in the fact of the creation of man as male and female" (TOB 8:1).

Man is not fully human—his creation is not complete—until he emerges in what John Paul calls the "double unity" of male and female (see TOB 8:3). Double unity speaks of a "two-in-oneness," or a "unity-in-distinction." It is a oneness that does not blur their difference. Indeed, it is their difference that *affords* their unity, which is man's completeness. Everyone knows the experience of "incompleteness." It drives

---

18. *CCC* no. 357 offers a concise summary of original solitude.

us to seek communion with others. Not only do we want to be with others; we want to *know* another person and have our persons *known* by another person. Thus, we can all relate to the biblical expression that "it is not good to be alone." If man is to be fully himself, he needs a "helper."

Although only a few words describe woman's creation, John Paul shows that each one carries great weight. He remarks that the "mythical" language of the ancient narrative of Genesis leads us to that deep and mysterious content of woman's creation with ease. With the enthusiasm of a man in love with God's word, he adds that the text of woman's creation is "truly marvelous in the quality and the condensation of the truths contained there" (TOB 8:2).

The Meaning of Adam's "Sleep"

We read in Genesis 2, "So the Lord God caused a deep sleep [torpor] to fall upon the man, and while he slept took one of his ribs, and closed up its place with flesh; and the rib which the Lord God had taken from the man he made into a woman and brought her to the man." John Paul comments that contemporary men and women might immediately associate this "deep sleep" with a Freudian analysis of dreams and the subconscious, which, in Freud's mind, were always sexual. But "deep sleep" (tardēmāh in Hebrew) indicates not so much a passing from consciousness to subconsciousness, as a passing from consciousness to unconsciousness. For Adam, this deep sleep is "a specific return to non-being," since sleep almost annihilates man's conscious existence. As John Paul states in a footnote, this "underlines the *exclusiveness of God's action* in the creation of the woman. The man had no conscious part in it" (TOB 8:3).

▪ *Tardemah*, or "torpor" in English, John Paul notes, "is the term that appears in Sacred Scripture when, during the sleep or immediately after it, extraordinary events are to take place" (TOB 8:3). Interestingly, the Greek translation of the Hebrew Old Testament translates *tardemah* with *ekstasis*—"ecstasy" in English. While John Paul only makes passing reference to this, it is worth posing a possible meaning of Adam's sleep understood as a state of "ecstasy." Not only can we infer that Adam was "ecstatic" upon discovering the woman, but ecstasy literally means "to be outside oneself." And what is it that comes "outside" of the man? Woman. To go "outside oneself" also seems to connote the "sincere gift of oneself."

If by way of the analogy with sleep we can speak also of a dream, the content of Adam's dream, according to John Paul, is certainly that of finding a "second self" (in other words, someone who experiences solitude as a person and longs for communion). Yes, John Paul muses that Adam fell asleep dreaming of the perfect lover, you might say. Of course, we must not project onto Adam the way a fallen man might dream about an idealized and depersonalized body to suit his enjoyment. No, Adam dreamed in the purity of original innocence. He dreamed of an "other" body that revealed an "other" person, a person he could love as God loves. When he awoke, his dream had came true.

There "is no doubt," says the Holy Father, "that man falls into this 'torpor' with the desire of finding a being similar to himself.... In this way, the circle of the human person's solitude is broken, because the first 'man' reawakens from his sleep as 'male and female'" (TOB 8:3). In this "sleep" the generic man is "recreated" to be sexually differentiated as a unity in two ("double unity"). Even if it is fraught with difficulties and confusion now due to sin, does not everyone come, in some sense, to a stage of sexual "awakening"?

The Meaning of Adam's Rib

The Holy Father observes that being fashioned from Adam's rib is an "archaic, metaphorical, and figurative way" of expressing woman's creation (TOB 8:4). While some have thought this demeans women, John Paul stresses that the biblical author intends to affirm the indispensable equality of the sexes and place it on a sure foundation. As the Pope expresses it, Eve's creation from Adam's rib indicates "the homogeneity of the whole being of both" (TOB 8:4). "Homogeneity" means they share the same nature, they are of the same "genus." In other words, man and woman are made from the same "stuff." They share a common humanity. Later in his catechesis, John Paul states that "rib" also seems to indicate the heart—yet another affirmation that man and woman share the same humanity and the same dignity (see TOB 108:4).

Masculinity and femininity, then, are two "incarnations" of the same solitude before God and the world—two ways, in other words, of being a body-person made in God's image. Masculinity and femininity "complete each other." They are "two complementary dimensions of self-knowledge and self-determination and, at the same time, *two complementary ways of being conscious of the meaning of the body*" (TOB 10:1).

Recall that in naming the animal-bodies Adam realized he was "alone" in the world as a person. But upon sight of the woman-body, he proclaims ecstatically, "This at last is bone of my bones and flesh of my flesh." With this exclamation the Holy Father explains that he "seems to say, *Look, a body that expresses the 'person'!*" (TOB 14:4). For the Jews, bones meant simply "the human being."[19] "Bone from my bones," John Paul states in a footnote, "can thus be understood in the relational sense, like 'being from being.' 'Flesh from flesh' signifies that, although she has different physical characteristics, the woman has the same personhood that the man has" (TOB 8:4).

John Paul considers Adam's declaration the biblical prototype of the Song of Songs. The words of Genesis 2:23 are the original love song. They express "for the first time...joy and even exultation" (TOB 8:4). Later in his catechesis the Pope says that Adam's words "express wonder and admiration, or even better, the sense of fascination" (TOB 108:5). And "if it is possible to read impressions and emotions through such remote words, one could even venture to say that the depth and power of this first and 'original' emotion of the man before the humanity of the woman...seems something unique and unrepeatable" (TOB 9:1). In short, the gift of woman enthralls Adam. At last, having named animal after animal only to remain "alone," he has found one who is *like himself* (yet also different in very important ways). He has found another person whom he can *know* as a person and be *known* by as a person. He has found another person with whom he can live in *communion*.

Communion of Persons

In its primary meaning, the word "sex" refers to the differentiation of male and female, not to what they do together in becoming "one flesh." Thus, in the Yahwist account, prior to man's sexual "awakening"

---

19. See Psalm 139:15, for example.

as male and female, man is "sexless" in the sense that he is without ("less") the other sex. Without the "other," masculinity and femininity make no sense. According to God's words, this "is not good." Sexual difference, therefore, has an axiological meaning. In other words, masculinity and femininity have a *specific value* both before God and for each other. If it is "not good for man to be alone," it is good—*very good*—to exist as male and female, one *for* the other, and to join in the original unity of "one flesh."

Communion Overcomes and Affirms Solitude

The beauty and mystery of sexual difference specifically reveals man and woman's call to communion. And sexual difference specifically allows that communion to pass from an objective calling to an incarnate, subjective reality. "In this way, the meaning of man's original unity...expresses itself as an overcoming of the frontier of solitude and at the same time as an affirmation—for both human beings—of everything in solitude that constitutes 'man'" (TOB 9:2).

What does the Pope mean by this? Recall that original solitude has two meanings. Original unity overcomes man's solitude without woman (and we can also speak of woman's solitude without man). But the experience of original unity *affirms* their solitude in the sense that they differ from the animals because their union also differs essentially from that of animals. As persons, both man and woman have self-knowledge and self-determination. They are both subjects in the world and are conscious of the meaning of their bodies. This is the heart of the experience of man's solitude as a person in the visible world. Because this is common to man *and* woman, John Paul speaks not only of a "double unity" but also of a "double solitude." Only two *persons* are capable of rendering to each other that biblical "help." Only two *persons* are capable of love. "Double solitude," then, is the indispensable foundation of original unity. It is also the sure foundation of the true equality of man and woman.

In keeping with the Second Vatican Council, the Pope defines this unity as *communion personarum*—a "communion of persons."[20] John Paul says that the term "community" could also be used here if it were

---

20. See *Gaudium et Spes*, 12.

not generic and did not have so many meanings. "*Communio*" expresses more and describes their unity with greater precision, he says, "because *it indicates precisely that 'help' that derives in some way from the very fact of existing as a person 'beside' a person*" (TOB 9:2). "In this communion of persons, the whole depth of the original solitude of man...is perfectly ensured and, at the same time, this solitude is permeated and enlarged in a marvelous way by the gift of the 'other'" (TOB 18:5). In other words, their uniqueness as persons is not diminished in becoming "one" with the other. Instead, through communion man and woman live *together, with*, and *for* each other in such a way that they rediscover themselves, affirming all that it means to be a person, affirming "everything in solitude that constitutes 'man.'" John Paul says that this opening up to the other person (original unity) is perhaps even more decisive for the definition of man than his realization that he differed from the animals (original solitude).[21]

A Dramatic Development of Catholic Thought

Here we find ourselves at the threshold of a dramatic and long-needed development of Catholic thought in regard to how we image God. "The function of the image," according to John Paul, "is that of mirroring the one who is the model, of reproducing its own prototype" (TOB 9:3). The model of course is the Trinity. Hence, traditional formulations posited man's imaging of God in various trinitarian breakdowns of an individual's soul (e.g., memory, understanding, and will). The divine model, however, is not one person divided in three. The prototype of the image is, as John Paul describes it, "an inscrutable divine communion of Persons" (TOB 9:3).

Notice that God even refers to himself in the plural: "Let *us* make man in *our* image, after our likeness" (Gen 1:26). Hence "we can deduce that *man became the image of God not only through his own humanity, but also through the communion of persons*, which man and woman form from the very beginning" (TOB 9:3). In other words, not only as a rational individual does the human person image God (not only in the experience of original solitude), but also in the communion formed by man and woman (the experience of original unity).

---

21. See *CCC*, nos. 371–72, for a concise summary of the themes of original solitude and unity.

This marks a bold theological development on the Pope's part. Positing the divine image in the male-female communion—although it can be found under the surface of various texts in the theological tradition—has not been the explicitly held perspective. Following the trinitarian anthropology of Vatican II—which bases itself on the text of John "that they may all be one...*as* we are one" (Jn 17:21–22)—John Paul II clearly affirms that man "becomes an image of God not so much in the moment of solitude as in the moment of communion." He even states that this "trinitarian concept of the 'image of God'...constitutes, perhaps, the deepest theological aspect of everything one can say about man." Furthermore, the Pope makes the deliberate point of stating that on "all this, right from the beginning, the blessing of fruitfulness descended, linked with human procreation" (TOB 9:3). This will forever mark a critical development in Christian anthropology. Through his Wednesday audiences, and even more authoritatively in later statements,[22] John Paul brings the once dismissed idea[23] that man and woman image God *in and through their communion* into the realm of official magisterial teaching.

Theology of Sex

With this understanding of the divine image "we find ourselves within the very bone marrow" of the anthropological significance of the body. The body reveals the mystery of man. But because man, even in his corporeality as male and female, is "similar to God," the body also reveals something of the mystery of God. Thus, the Pope explains that this "marrow" or core of the meaning of the body is not only anthropo-

---

22. See, for example, *Mulieris Dignitatem*, 6–7. See also *CCC*, nos. 357, 1702, 2205.

23. Although they framed the question somewhat differently, both Augustine and Aquinas (among others) rejected the idea that male-female unity and fruitfulness imaged the Trinity. See St. Augustine, *On the Trinity*, bk. 12, chap. 5, and St. Thomas Aquinas, *Summa Theologica*, q. 93, a. 6. However, Michael Waldstein argues that, when read carefully, St. Thomas's and John Paul II's positions are not irreconcilable. He states that "according to both St. Augustine and St. Thomas one can speak, and speak properly, of a union of love between the divine Persons in terms that are drawn from interpersonal love between human beings. This conclusion shows that the teaching of John Paul II about the image of God is implicitly contained in St. Augustine and St. Thomas, even though they do not state it explicitly." "Pope John Paul II's Personalist Teaching and St. Thomas Aquinas: Disagreement or Development of Doctrine?" lecture presented at Thomas Aquinas College, January 12, 2001.

logical but also essentially theological. This is why he speaks of a theology *of the body*. The body reveals man and woman's call to communion and enables them to enter into it, thus imaging in some way the communion in God.

As John Paul stresses, this is an "incarnate communion"; it is from the beginning a communion in "one flesh" (Gen 2:24). Therefore, the "theology of the body, which is linked from the beginning with the creation of man in the image of God, becomes in some way also a theology of sex, or rather a theology of masculinity and femininity" (TOB 9:5). A "deep consciousness of human bodiliness and sexuality," the Pope even says, "establishes an inalienable norm for the understanding of man on the theological plane" (TOB 9:5). In other words, we cannot understand man theologically without understanding the meaning of sexual difference and our call to sexual communion. This call touches upon the core anthropological reality. As already stated, this core is also theological. From this perspective, sexual communion is an icon in some sense of the inner life of the Trinity. Of course, this does not mean that God is sexual. When using this analogy we must always recall the infinite dissimilarity between God and his creature. But this does not mean the analogy is extrinsic. Sexual difference and the call to union intrinsically reveal something of the perfect distinction, unity, and fruitfulness within the Trinity.[24]

As such, John Paul says that Genesis 2:24 (the two shall become one flesh) "was to have a broad and far-reaching perspective in God's revelation" (TOB 9:5). In fact, we can even recognize that in some sense the original unity of the sexes contains "in nucleo" all that God has to reveal to man about who God is (an eternal communion of Persons), who we are (male and female in the divine image), and how we are to live (in a similar communion of persons). It even provides a glimpse into the nature of our ultimate destiny (the communion of saints in communion with the Trinity). We will learn that man and woman's incarnate communion right from the beginning foreshadows God's definitive revelation in Christ and his incarnate communion with the Church. *This* is why God created us as sexual beings—to prepare us as an eternal Bride for Christ.

---

24. See *CCC*, nos. 42, 239, 370.

Indicating the course of his future reflections, John Paul mentions two of the dimensions of the "one flesh" union that will demand attention: the *ethical* dimension and the *sacramental* dimension. These two dimensions are also interrelated. For we cannot understand the Christian sexual *ethic* unless we understand what the union of the sexes means as a *sacramental sign* of Christ's union with the Church (see Eph 5:31–32).

> ■ The whole reality of married life is, of course, a sacrament of sexual unity—the unity of male and female in a lifelong bond. But as John Paul states, the "one flesh" union "is the regular *sign* of the communion of persons" in the sacrament of marriage (TOB 37:4). It serves as the sign that summarizes (or consummates) the whole reality of the giving of husband and wife to each other. As the Pope also says, "All married life is a gift; but this becomes most evident when the spouses, in giving themselves to each other in love, bring about that encounter which makes them 'one flesh.'"[25] Thus, John Paul affirms that by means of the "one flesh" union, the body "takes on the value of a sign, in a certain sense a sacramental sign" (TOB 45:2). Part 2, Chapter 2 will further explore the multiform reality of the "sacramental sign" of marriage.

Man as a Subject in Relation

We are trying to understand man, as John Paul says, "in the whole endowment of his being, that is, in the whole wealth of that mystery of creation standing at the basis of theological anthropology" (TOB 10:1). In this quest, the Pope affirms that the laws of knowing man correspond to those of his being (see TOB 4:2). We can only know who we are as human beings (and, more, who we are meant to be) to the degree that we are in touch with the original truth of our being male and female. This knowledge begins with original solitude and, from there, passes to original unity.

Man is not fully himself when he is "alone." He can only find himself in relation. Thus, for John Paul, *relationality* enters the definition of the human person. As he says, "'being a person' means both 'being a

---

25. *Letter to Families*, 12.

subject,' but also 'being in relation'" (TOB 109:4). As the *Catechism* expresses it, it is precisely "as image of God [that] we live in relation."[26] This starkly contrasts with the radical individualism promoted in the West today.

Philosophical anthropology cannot ascertain the divine explanation of man's call to exist "in relation." John Paul bases his teaching on the following statement of the Second Vatican Council:

> the Lord Jesus, when praying to the Father "that they may all be one...even as we are one" (Jn 17:21–22), *opened up new horizons closed to human reason* by implying that there is a certain parallel between the union existing among the divine persons and the union of the sons of God in truth and love. It follows, then, that if man is the only creature on earth that God has wanted for its own sake, man can fully discover his true self only in a sincere giving of himself.[27]

This teaching brings us to the heart of the mystery of what it means to be a human *person*. We are created for God's sake in the sense that God is the ultimate end of our existence. But we are not created for God's sake in the sense that God *needs* us for himself. God is totally complete in his own trinitarian communion. Nonetheless, love diffuses itself; it wants to share and give its own goodness, ever enlarging the circle of participation and communion. Hence, God creates us for *our own sake*, out of the sheer gratuitousness of his love. He creates us so that we might have the opportunity to participate in his own eternal goodness, in his own mystery of communion. It is true that the world was made for the glory of God. However, as the *Catechism* (quoting St. Bonaventure) explains, this means that "God created all things 'not to increase his glory, but to show it forth and communicate it,' for God has no other reason for creating than his love and goodness."[28]

This is God's gift to us—his own love and goodness. But he does not force it on us. To do so would contradict the reality of "gift." It would contradict the reality of our being created for *our own* sake. Respecting us as persons, God leaves us in the freedom and power of our own counsel. We can participate in the gift of love and communion only by opening ourselves to receiving it *as a gift* (faith) and by making

---

26. *CCC*, no. 2563.
27. *Gaudium et Spes*, 24, emphasis added.
28. *CCC*, no. 293.

a sincere gift of ourselves in return. And even this openness, even our free decision to respond to God's grace is, itself, a divine gift.[29] When we engage our freedom to open to "the gift," life itself becomes thanksgiving (*eucharistia*) for having been given so great a gift.

This clarifies the logic of the Council's teaching. Created for his "own sake," man can only fulfill himself through the "sincere gift" of self. In other words, man can only fulfill himself in authentic relation *to* and *with* other persons. A theology of the body shows us that this "relationality" is fundamentally revealed by sexual differentiation. Every human being—"with all his spiritual solitude, with the uniqueness and unrepeatability proper to the person"—is either a "he" or a "she." Sex, then, and thus the call to communion, is not only "an attribute of the person" but is also in this sense "constitutive for the person" (see TOB 10:1).

If men and women are to "find themselves," the solitude of every "he" or "she" must lead to the communion of a human "we" through the self-giving of one to the other. The original unity and reciprocal enrichment of the sexes, therefore, marks "the whole perspective of...[man's] history, including the history of salvation" (TOB 10:1). This, however, does not mean that everyone is called to the married state, but it does mean that we are all called to live in communion with others through the sincere gift of self. According to God's original plan, marriage is the most fundamental expression of that call to communion, the paradigm or model in some sense of all human communion and self-giving. But in the context of his discussion about marriage with the Pharisees, Christ will reveal another way to live the fullness of the call to incarnate self-giving as male and female (see Mt 19:12).

In its course, John Paul's TOB will profoundly enrich our understanding of the celibate vocation, the basis of which we find already in man's solitude before God and in his call to be "partner of the Absolute." In the final analysis, the human desire for communion with an "other" can only be satisfied in union with *the* "Other" (God). Sexual

---

29. If it is easy to recognize and refute the Pelagian position that one can follow God's law without divine grace, we must also recognize and refute the semi-Pelagian position. The semi-Pelagian position admits that we need grace to follow God's law, but holds that the decision to accept that grace is ours and ours alone. The truth upheld by the Church is that *all is grace, all is gift*—even the free decision to open oneself to God's grace. This, too, comes from God as a gift.

love and communion is only a *temporal* response to man's yearning for an *eternal* love and communion. Wojtyla places all of this in its proper perspective in the following passage from *Love and Responsibility*:

> It is not sexuality which creates in a man and a woman the need to give themselves to each other, but, on the contrary, it is the need to give oneself, latent in every human person, which finds its outlet...in physical and sexual union, in matrimony. But the need...to give oneself to and unite with another person is deeper and connected with the spiritual existence of the person. It is not finally and completely satisfied simply by union with another human being. Considered in the perspective of the person's eternal existence, marriage is only a tentative solution of the problem of a union of persons through love.[30]

The Original Conjugal Act?

We find this "tentative solution" to man's yearning for communion revealed from the beginning in Genesis 2:24, in the two becoming "one flesh." According to John Paul, this unity "is without doubt the unity that is expressed and realized in the conjugal act" (TOB 10:2). But, contrary to what some might imagine, this phrase is not a euphemism due to the biblical author's discomfort with sex. "One flesh" is an expression infused with meaning. It goes far deeper than any surface understanding of sex, leading us into the depths of the "great mystery" (see Eph 5:32) of interpersonal communion.

Several Greek Fathers (e.g., Gregory of Nyssa, John Chrysostom, Theodoret, and later John Damascene[31]) advanced the idea that in paradise man and woman would not have joined in "one flesh." Following this line of thinking, the bodily union of the sexes almost seems to have resulted from sin. Whatever the intention of these Greek Fathers (and we should not be too quick to assume an anti-sex prejudice), John Paul II stresses repeatedly throughout his catechesis that the "one flesh" union spoken of in Genesis 2:24 was instituted by the Creator *in the beginning*. The "words of Genesis 2:24 bear witness," the Holy Father says, to the "original meaning of unity." This unity, he continues, "is

30. *Love and Responsibility*, pp. 253–54.
31. See (as cited in Lawler, Boyle, and May, *Catholic Sexual Ethics*, 2nd ed. [Huntington, IN: Our Sunday Visitor, 1998], p. 266) Gregory of Nyssa, *De Opificio Hominis*, 17 (PG 44.187); John Chrysostom, *De Virginitate*, 17 (PG 48.546); *Homilia in Genesi*, 18 (PG 80.136); Damascene, *De Fide Orthodoxa*, 2.30 (PG 94.976).

realized through the body [and] indicates from the beginning...the 'incarnate' communion of persons—*communio personarum*—and requires this communion right from the beginning" (TOB 9:5).

Of course this "beginning" refers to our "prehistory," which remains shrouded in mystery. Therefore, as John Paul's carefully nuanced statements indicate, the precise manner or mode of their original "incarnate communion" is inaccessible to us. We must avoid projecting our historical experience of bodily union onto the beginning. Even so, the Holy Father affirms that man and woman were "created in the state of original innocence and called in this state to conjugal union" (TOB 97:5).

■   If John Paul's statements on the original unity of the sexes leave room for interpretation, one could argue that he only affirms that conjugal union was part of the original plan and not that man and woman actually engaged in it prior to their knowledge of good and evil. In fact, John Paul states at one point that the man knows the woman for the first time in the act of conjugal union only in Genesis 4:1 (see TOB 21:1). This is, of course, the first time they join together "in history" as we know it. John Paul always carefully distinguishes man's history from his theological prehistory. Again, original innocence would have afforded a manner of union beyond our comprehension. Whatever the "mode" of that union, John Paul wants to affirm that the experience of original unity was an incarnate, bodily experience and not merely a "spiritual" experience. Of course, in properly distinguishing between the spiritual and the physical, we must affirm that a spiritual unity takes precedence. A bodily union that was not preceded and informed by a spiritual union would be "animalistic." But, for the human person, spiritual love cannot (and must not) be divorced from the body. "In marriage, the physical intimacy of the spouses becomes a sign and pledge of spiritual communion."[32] John Paul speaks to this when he observes that man "is constituted in such a way from the 'beginning' that the deepest words of the spirit—words of love, gift, and faithfulness—call for an appropriate 'language of the body.' And without this language, they cannot be fully expressed." Man "is *in*

---

32. *CCC*, no. 2360.

some sense unable to express this singular language of his personal existence and vocation *without the body*" (TOB 104:7).

By balancing the proper relationship of prehistory and history and of spiritual and physical unity, we approach the original, incarnate union of the sexes, which John Paul affirms is witnessed to by Genesis 2:24 (the two become "one flesh"). For John Paul it seems important to affirm the prehistorical existence of such bodily communion if only to shed light on that from which historical man has fallen and, therefore, to provide a measure for that to which Christ calls him. Remember that John Paul seeks to reconstruct what may have happened "then" specifically for our benefit now.

Man's "Original Virginal Value"

Despite John Paul's repeated affirmation that God instituted the union of the two in "one flesh" from the beginning, an important truth must be upheld in the thought of those who insisted on Adam and Eve's virginity prior to sin. Since virginity, in its most basic meaning, refers to the absence of genital union, John Paul must have something different in mind when he states that a couple uniting in the conjugal act are meant to be "reliving in some way man's original virginal value" (TOB 10:2). What could this possibly mean? The Holy Father does not elaborate, so I offer the following interpretation.[33]

If the absence of genital intercourse most formally defines the term "virginity," it seems John Paul's carefully nuanced phrase "original virginal value" refers not to the absence of a bodily union but to the original integrity of body and soul. In the state of original innocence, man and woman experienced a perfect psychosomatic (soul-body) integration. They were "untouched" by the rupture of body and soul that would defile them as a result of original sin. In this sense, the experience of original unity did not impinge upon their "original virginal

---

33. In what follows, I am trying to strike a balance between the insights I have gained in private correspondence from Monsignor Lorenzo Albacete and Dr. Michael Waldstein. Without discarding the "old" understanding of virginity, Albacete mines new wealth from John Paul's idea of "virginal value." Without closing himself to new ideas, Waldstein safeguards the traditional and more obvious meaning of virginity. It is my opinion that these different emphases in interpretation can and should be held together in creative tension.

value." Whatever manner of union they enjoyed remained "virginal"—or, more specifically, retained its "virginal value"—since the spouses were untouched by the disintegration of sin. Not only was this unity not a loss of their personal integrity ("virginal value"), it was the deepest possible affirmation of it. Sin, however, marks the loss of man's virginal value (body-soul integrity) in the sense that it ruptured his psychosomatic unity. Thereafter, the lust that attends sexual union serves to accent and even exacerbate this body-soul rift. Lustful sexual union is always a dis-integrating experience, and, thus, an attack on the human being's virginal value.

■ This notion of virginity ("virginal value") seems to shine a bright light on the "blessedness" of the New Eve. In the formal sense of "virginity," Mary's title as the "Blessed Virgin" reminds us of her choice to refrain from sexual intercourse throughout the whole of her life (see Lk 1:34).[34] However, her particular blessing lies not in this fact per se, but in that she never experienced the rupture of body and soul. If the "virginal value" of the human being refers to the original integrity of body and soul, the title "Blessed Virgin" also calls to mind her Immaculate Conception. Being spared of all taint of original and personal sin, she is *perfectly integrated* in body and soul.

If lustful union attacks man's "virginal value," are men and women now bound to lust? Even the holiest men and women must still contend with concupiscence, that disordering of the passions which resulted from original sin. Yet even if Baptism does not remove concupiscence, Christ "came to restore creation to the purity of its origins."[35] Through the gift of redemption, it is possible for husbands and wives progressively to overcome lust and to love as Christ loves. To the degree that they do, they relive in a real sense that original "virginal" experience of love and unity. For, as Angelo Cardinal Scola expresses it, "virginity can be understood neither as only a specific vocation within the Church, nor primarily as a renunciation of something. It is rather the

---

34. See John Paul II, *Theotokos: A Catechesis on Mary, Mother of God* (Boston, MA: Pauline Books & Media, 2000), pp. 112–32.

35. *CCC*, no. 2336.

manner of love characteristic of Jesus Christ, which all Christians, even spouses, are therefore called to live."[36] "Husbands, love your wives *as* Christ loved the Church" (Eph 5:25).

This is one way to understand the goal of Christian marriage: it is for spouses to recover their "virginal value." They do so not by forego-ing sexual union but by allowing it to be taken up and "recreated" in Christ's redeeming sacrifice. Quoting John Paul: "When they unite with each other (in the conjugal act) so closely so as to become 'one flesh,' man and woman rediscover every time and in a special way the mystery of creation, thus returning to the union in humanity ('flesh from my flesh and bone from my bones') that allows them to recognize each other reciprocally and to call each other by name, as they did the first time." The Pope concludes that this "means reliving in some way man's original virginal value, which emerges from the mystery of his solitude before God and in the midst of the world" (TOB 10:2).

Thus, for spouses who—by continually surrendering their sexuality to Christ—experience a "real and deep victory" over lust,[37] sexual union becomes not a "loss" but a tremendous gain. They come to discover their true selves through the sincere gift of themselves to each other. Their communion confirms each of them in their virginal uniqueness, in the unrepeatability of their persons. Hence, to become "one flesh" returns them in some sense to the "one reality" of the *humanum*—the "one reality" of man, which is the mystery of human solitude before God. Solitude emphasizes man's fulfillment in spousal relation to God, the completeness of belonging to God and God alone. In the begin-ning, the spousal relation of man and woman did not detract from the human person's spousal relation to God but facilitated it. As a result of sin, however, men and women are now tempted to seek in sexual union what only union with God can offer—ultimate fulfillment. So long as sexual union is so idolized, it cannot positively facilitate union with God. In fact, when idolized as such, sexual union obscures man's union with God and with it man's "original virginal value."

But here is the good news for historical men and women: In and through the redemption Christ won for us, the sacramental power of

---

36. *The Nuptial Mystery* (Grand Rapids, MI: Eerdmans, 2005) p. 270.

37. Part I, Chapter 2 is devoted to discussing how Christ empowers us in just such a "real and deep victory" over lust. This phrase is taken from TOB 45:4.

marriage has been restored. Inasmuch as marital union continues, through the grace of the sacrament, to facilitate union with God—a union much greater and more fundamental than the union of the sexes—it enables spouses to rediscover their "original virginal value, which emerges from the mystery of [their] solitude before God." Through "sex" (it seems we can take this to mean both sexual difference and sexual union), John Paul says that man and woman not only "surpass" their own solitude, but they also assume the solitude of the other (the personhood of the other) as their own. If the body reveals the person, by becoming "one body" male and female become in some sense "one man" (almost "one human person") before God as in original solitude. In this way—in the sense that the experience of original unity also returns us to the experience of original solitude, to an exclusive union with God—we can speak of the sexual act as an expression of or even a reliving of "man's original virginal value."

To speak of male and female becoming in some way "one man," of course, implies a unity-in-distinction through which neither person is blurred as an individual, but each becomes more fully himself or herself. As John Paul observes: "The fact that they become 'one flesh' is a powerful bond established by the Creator through which they discover their own humanity, both in its original unity and in the duality of a mysterious reciprocal attraction" (TOB 10:2). Unity-in-duality, a two-in-oneness, is the key. This real unity and this real distinction is maintained in proper balance, however, only when man and woman's "reciprocal attraction" is integrated first with one's own subjectivity as a person and, in turn, is informed by an unwavering respect for the subjectivity of the other as a person.

Sexual attraction "in the beginning" summoned them to become a sincere gift for each other. It did not operate on its own, compelling a selfish indulgence at the expense of the other. Sexual attraction and desire was intimately bound up with choice and, therefore, with human subjectivity. Their ability to *choose* distinguished them from the animals. Human sexual activity, therefore, radically differs from the copulation of animals. If joining in "one flesh" was only a response to instinct and not the result of self-determination, their experience of unity would have indicated that they were similar to the animals rather than affirming their solitude. If historical man experiences sexual desire merely as an "instinct," this is the result of original sin. Therefore, if men and women of history are to become a "sincere gift" to one another, they *must* regain the integrity of self-mastery. The freely chosen, personhood-affirming communion of the first man and woman "must constitute the beginning and model of that communion for all men and women who in any period unite with each other so intimately that they are 'one flesh'" (TOB 10:3). This is what Christ confirms in his challenge to the Pharisees. Anything less does not correspond to our dignity as men and women made in the divine image. Anything less substitutes a counterfeit for the love and intimacy for which we long.

The Vital Power of Communion

One of John Paul's goals in his TOB is to place the teaching of *Humanae Vitae* within the context of biblical anthropology. Man and woman's communion is not closed in on itself. When they become "one flesh," men and women submit their whole humanity to the original blessing of fertility.

As stated above, love diffuses itself. It seeks to increase its own circle of communion. God, who is love, is a *life-giving* communion of Persons. We are made in this image as male and female. Thus, the original call to "be fruitful and multiply" is a call to live in the divine image. "Procreation," as John Paul expresses it, "is rooted in creation, and every time it reproduces in some way its mystery" (TOB 10:4). The mystery of creation is the mystery of God's overflowing trinitarian love, which shot us and the whole universe into being. When a man and woman become "one flesh," they renew this mystery "in all its original depth and vital power" (TOB 10:4). Or, at least, they are meant to do so. What might contraception, the deliberate sterilization of sexual union, do to this picture? In due time, John Paul will unfold the logical answer.

4. The Meaning of Original Nakedness

The human experiences that the Yahwist text speaks of have a basic significance for every man and woman in every age. Yet John Paul observes that these experiences so intermingle with the ordinary things of life that we tend to take them entirely for granted. Penetrating God's "revelation of the body" helps us discover the extraordinary side of the ordinary. We discover that these experiences provide an interpretive key for understanding human existence.

The Key to Biblical Anthropology

Having examined the experiences of *original solitude* and *original unity*, we turn now to the third "fundamental human experience": *original nakedness*. As we read in Genesis 2:25, "the man and his wife were both naked and were not ashamed." In light of the biblical text analyzed so far, John Paul recognizes that, at first glance, this verse may seem misplaced, adding nothing more than a cursory detail. Of course, based on the riches he has already mined from the Yahwist narrative, we would not expect John Paul to stop at first glance. Far from being peripheral, John Paul shows us that the meaning of original nakedness "is precisely the key for understanding...fully and completely" the first sketch of biblical anthropology (TOB 11:2). In other words, if we do not understand what it meant for the first man and woman to be naked without shame, we do not understand the original biblical meaning of our humanity.

Some might consider man's creation in the image of God as the more appropriate key to biblical anthropology. John Paul, in fact, calls the *imago Dei* the "root" of the biblical truth about man (see TOB 13:2). Original nakedness is nothing but the subjective reverberation and conscious reflection of this objective truth. As John Paul says, nakedness without shame "describes their state of consciousness, or even better, their reciprocal experience of the body...*with the greatest precision possible.*" Thus, Genesis 2:25 "makes a specific contribution to the theology of the body...that absolutely cannot be left out of consideration" (TOB 11:3).

The Pope observes that it is first necessary to establish that the experience of original nakedness involves a real non-presence of shame, and not a lack or underdevelopment of it. Original nakedness cannot be compared to the experience of young children, for example, who have yet to develop a sense of shame. Much less can nakedness *without* shame be compared to *shamelessness*. These are polar opposites. A shameless nakedness is immodest. It involves a lack or suppression of shame when shame is rightly called for (see Jer 3:2–3). Shame in one's nakedness is called for when nakedness poses a threat to the dignity of the person. The original experience of nakedness completely lacked shame because being naked posed no threat to the first couple's dignity. They *saw* the body as the revelation of the person and his (her) dignity. "Only the nakedness that turns the woman into an 'object' for the man, or vice versa, is a source of shame. The fact that 'they did not feel shame' means that the woman was not an 'object' for the man, nor he for her" (TOB 19:1).

On this side of the fig leaves, we can hardly imagine the experience of original nakedness. Original sin radically changed our experience of nakedness. Shame entered with sin, the shame that marks the "boundary" between original man and historical man. So how can we reconstruct the experience of original nakedness?

■ Karol Wojtyla provides a detailed, extremely rich, and well-balanced presentation of the problems of nakedness, shame, shamelessness, modesty, etc., in *Love and Responsibility*. Of particular interest is Wojtyla's discussion of "the law of the absorption of shame by love." He writes: "Shame is, as it were, swallowed up by love, dissolved in it, so that the man and the woman are no longer ashamed to be sharing their experience of sexual values. This process is enormously important to sexual morality."[38] He clarifies that this does not mean shame is eliminated or destroyed as in the case of shamelessness. Shame also has a positive role that is essential to love, for it protects the dignity of the person. Thus, the "swallowing of shame by love" does not mean removing the reserve or reverence that the inner mystery of the other person calls for. Still, Wojtyla writes that where there is genuine love, shame (in the negative sense) "as the natural way of avoiding the utilitarian attitude [toward the body] loses its *raison d'être* and gives ground. But only to the extent that a person loved in this way—and this is most important—is equally ready to give herself or himself in love."[39] In other words, nakedness does not offend nor elicit shame in relationships in which the persons are "aware of the gift" given and have "decided to respond to it in an equally personal way." Instead, in this situation, as John Paul says, "the human body in its naked-

---

38. *Love and Responsibility*, p. 181.
39. Ibid., p. 183.

ness...becomes the source of a particular interpersonal 'communication'" (TOB 62:3).

Penetrating Their Experience

Some would claim we cannot know much about the interior experience of original nakedness. They say we can only use an objective approach (via traditional metaphysics) to arrive at an "exterior" understanding. An exterior perception of the world certainly gives us crucial insight. Thus, the Pope agrees that this dimension cannot be ignored. But he maintains that the "biblical expression 'did not feel [shame]' directly points to 'experience' as a subjective dimension" (TOB 15:4). Hence, we cannot arrive at the full meaning of original nakedness "without going down into man's innermost [being]. Genesis 2:25 introduces us precisely to this level and wants us to look there for the original innocence of knowing" (TOB 12:4).

Here we see John Paul discussing the relationship between the traditional philosophy of being and the modern turn to the subject (philosophy of consciousness). Original nakedness can and should be examined using metaphysical categories. In other words, it can and should be looked at from the perspective of "the truth of being or reality," as the Pope puts it. This is indispensable and comes prior to any subjective investigation. However, if we stop at this level, we face the danger of abstraction. John Paul's analysis—based on a turn to the subject found not only in modernity but also in the Catholic mystical tradition—allows us to penetrate the conscious, experiential reality of original nakedness, not in opposition to an objective view but in tandem with it. For those who are skeptical of this approach, John Paul wants to insist that "the text of Genesis 2:25 expressly demands that we link the reflections on the theology of the body with the dimension of man's personal subjectivity" (TOB 11:3).

Despite our state of hereditary sinfulness, our roots still lie in the garden of innocence. As John Paul states, by referring historical man to the beginning, "Christ indirectly establishes the idea of continuity and connection between the two states, thereby allowing us to go back, as it were, from the threshold of man's 'historical' sinfulness to his original innocence" (TOB 11:4). Our experience of shame connected with nakedness is the "flip side" of original nakedness. We have lost the full consciousness of the meaning of the body afforded by the state of original holiness. But by examining our own experience of shame and "flipping it over," we can see the shape of that fullness we lack. In this way we can reconstruct, at least to some degree, the interior content of the experience of original nakedness.

Shame as a Phenomenon

John Paul begins his audience of December 19, 1979 (TOB 12), with an important question: "What is shame and how can one explain its absence in the state of original innocence, in the very depth of the mystery of the creation of man as male and female?" First, we must recognize that shame is an interpersonal reality. Although John Paul will eventually demonstrate that shame has a meaning within each person (he will call this "immanent shame"; see p. 187ff.), shame is generally experienced in relation to and with other persons. A person has no reason to be ashamed of his own nakedness when he is alone (so long as he is doing nothing shameful with his nakedness). But suppose a stranger were to walk in on you while you were getting out of the shower. Most people would instinctively feel a need to cover their nakedness. The phenomenologist cannot help but ask: Why?

According to John Paul, this "instinct" manifests a deep need of affirmation and acceptance as a person, and, at the same time, a fear that the "other" will not recognize and affirm the full truth of my person revealed by my nakedness (remember that the *body* reveals the person). We cover up to protect ourselves for fear that our dignity as "selves" (i.e., as persons) will not be upheld otherwise. Everyone, it seems, can attest to this phenomenon. If we can manage to take this fear of not being affirmed in the presence of another and "flip it over," we find ourselves at the threshold of the experience of original nakedness. We can almost enter in. We can almost "taste" it.

Original nakedness is precisely the experience of full consciousness of the meaning and dignity of the body. Based on this, there is no fear of standing naked before the other because, in doing so, both the man and the woman receive from the other the affirmation and acceptance they long for—the affirmation and acceptance that correspond perfectly with their dignity as persons. The Pope calls this experience the "original innocence of 'knowledge'" (TOB 12:3). Such knowledge is based on a profound experience of intimacy and interpersonal "communication." John Paul notes that we have lost the deeper meaning of this word. True "communication," according to the Holy Father, is the experience of a "common union." Hence, to "communicate" means to establish a *communion* through the reciprocal and sincere gift of persons to each other.

> ■ Surveys of married couples and even clinical studies consistently report "poor communication" as a leading cause of marital breakdown. Most marriage preparation and/or enrichment programs, therefore, place heavy emphasis on teaching "communication skills." Typically these consist of various speaking and listening techniques that enable spouses to converse more effectively. They are certainly beneficial. However, the countless marriage preparation and enrichment programs I have surveyed pay little if any attention to teaching the skills necessary for this deeper and more essential meaning of communication. The essence of marriage consists in establishing a "common union" through the free and sincere gift of self. Lust is the prime enemy of the self-giving that affords authentic marital communication. Hence, among the many important "communication skills" in married life (and life in general), learning to overcome lust is most important. Without this liberation from lust we cannot express the "freedom of the gift," which is "the condition of all life together in the truth" (TOB 43:6).

The experience of original nakedness testifies to their authentic "communication," to the purity of their reciprocal self-giving. Such purity allows them to know one another via their nakedness, since their nakedness itself "communicates" an intimate knowledge of the person. And it is a knowledge of each other's great dignity and goodness as male and female created in the image of God. As John Paul affirms: "'Nakedness' signifies the original good of the divine vision. It signifies the whole simplicity and fullness of this vision, which shows the 'pure' value of man as male and female, the 'pure' value of the body and of [its] sex" (TOB 13:1). The more we ponder the meaning of this original vision of nakedness—this "original innocence of knowledge"—the more the reality of sin and lust will make us want to weep. Those "garments of our misery" (Gregory of Nyssa's description of the fig leaves) constantly remind us of the tragedy of having lost sight of what God created our bodies to reveal—the spiritual mystery of our humanity and also, in some way, the mystery of his divinity.

When we realize the scandal of our blindness, we are led to our knees to beg God's mercy. And mercy *has* been revealed through the *body* of Christ. From the pulpit of the cross, Christ's naked body proclaims redemption to every man and woman who has ever lived under the inheritance of shame. "Fig leaves" will always be necessary in a fallen world. But as John Paul will demonstrate, even now we can regain something of the original good of God's vision.[40] Christ calls us, and calls us with *power*, to reclaim the original ethos of "seeing."

The Peace of the Interior Gaze

According to St. Augustine, the deepest desire of the human heart is to *see* another and *be seen* by that other's loving look.[41] This sums up well the experience of original nakedness. Of course we are talking about more than the mere sensory experience of seeing a naked body with the eyes. We are talking about an interior "gaze" manifested through the eyes that knows and affirms the other as a person. As John Paul expresses it, in the experience of original nakedness "the man and the woman *see each other still more fully and clearly* than through the sense of sight itself, that is, through the eyes of the body. They see and know each other, in fact, with all the peace of the interior gaze, which creates precisely the fullness of the intimacy of persons" (TOB 13:1). Original nakedness, then, indicates a total defenselessness before the other, a total absence of barriers, because of a total trust in the sincerity of their reciprocal exchange.

Total peace suffused the first man and woman's intimacy—their reciprocated interior gaze—precisely because, prior to sin, there was no rupture between the spiritual and the sensible. Gender difference and unity highlighted the spiritual-sensible difference and unity; it was where the spiritual-sensible difference and unity was most keenly "felt" and experienced. In this experience, it was as if the body was transpar-

---

40. See *CCC*, nos. 1264, 1426, 2519, 2715.
41. See St. Augustine, *Sermon* 69, c. 2, 3.

ent. Exterior nakedness revealed an interior nakedness. As John Paul observes: "To this fullness of *'exterior' perception*, expressed by physical nakedness, *corresponds the 'interior' fullness of the vision of man in God*, that is, *according to the measure of the 'image of God'* (see Gen 1:27)" (TOB 12:5). Man's perception of the world was in perfect harmony with God's. In beholding each other's nakedness, they saw not just *a* body but *some*body—another *person* who radiated God's glory through his masculinity and her femininity. Seeing this and knowing this, they experienced no shame, only a deep peace and a profound awareness of their own goodness. In this way John Paul says that the human body acquires a completely new meaning that cannot remain "external." The body expresses the person, which is something more than the "individual." The body expresses the personal human "self" through an *exterior* reality perceived from *within*.

To look at a body and see only an "individual" is to perceive merely the exterior reality. The seeing of original nakedness is very different. It "is not only a share in the 'exterior' perception of the world." It "also has an inner dimension of a share in the vision of the Creator himself—in that vision...[in] which... 'God saw everything that he had made, and indeed, it was very good' (Gen 1:31)" (TOB 13:1). The experience of the body, then, follows and indicates the experience of the heart.

▬ I once heard the word "intimacy" defined as "into-me-see." This explains well that experience of original nakedness. There is no fear in being seen externally because there is no fear of being seen internally. In lectures when I discuss how the nakedness of Adam and Eve reveals the original good of God's vision, I often ask: "How many of you can stand naked in front of a mirror and say, 'behold, it is very good'?" The laughs and bewildered looks point clearly to how far we have fallen from that original vision and experience of the human body. In some way, this reaction seems to indicate the extent to which we have normalized our "flat tires." Of course, our bodies do not look entirely the same as Adam and Eve's. Every grey hair, every blemish, every wrinkle reminds us that our bodies are on the road to decay. Prior to sin, Adam and Eve's bodies were not. They shone transparently with the glory of God. Even so, the corruption of sin has not triumphed; our bodies remain "very good." We cannot live an authentic human life if we do not overcome those obstacles that keep us from embracing this fundamental truth of our own goodness.

5. Man in the Dimension of Gift

A. THE SPOUSAL MEANING OF THE BODY

Hermeneutics of the Gift

In these words of Genesis, "God saw everything that he had made, and behold, it was very good," we glimpse not only the character of man and woman's interior gaze but also the divine motive behind creation itself, and behind our creation as male and female in particular— love. As the Pope points out, "only love, in fact, gives rise to the good and is well pleased with the good (see 1 Cor 13). As an action of God, creation thus means not only calling from nothing to existence." It "also signifies *gift*; a fundamental and radical gift" (TOB 13:3).

Self-giving and love are synonymous in the mind of the Holy Father. Of course, "the concept of 'giving' cannot refer to nothing. It indicates the one who gives and the one who receives the gift, as well as the relation established between them" (TOB 13:4). God gives the gift of creation, and man receives it. This establishes a "spousal" relationship between them. In fact, "spousal" donation, according to the Holy Father, "definitively shows the whole reality of the act of giving about which the first pages of Genesis speak to us" (TOB 15:5). All creation has a spousal character because creation itself constitutes the original and fundamental gift. But in the visible world this gift can only be fully realized in and received by man because man alone is made in God's image. Only a person endowed with freedom and self-determination can receive "the gift" of God, which is love, and reciprocate that gift (i.e., loving God in return). This is the original covenant God establishes with man in creation.

How did man realize this gift? How did he experience this call to "spousal" relationship with God (covenant) and enter into it? God placed a deep spiritual yearning for it in the human experience of solitude and, in turn, stamped it in his *body* by creating man as male and female and calling them to be an incarnate gift to one another. John

Paul says that the human body in all the original truth of its masculinity and femininity expresses the gift of creation. "This is *the body: a witness* to creation as a fundamental gift, and therefore a witness *to Love as the source from which this same giving springs.* Masculinity-femininity—namely, sex—is the original sign of...[God's] creative donation" (TOB 14:4).

We cannot understand human existence if we do not understand this reality of "gift." *All is gift.* God initiates the gift and creates man to receive the gift, which is God's divine life and love. This understanding of gift provides the interpretive key (or hermeneutic) of the Pope's anthropology. Through a *"hermeneutics of the gift"* (TOB 13:2) we approach "the very essence of the person" (TOB 14:2). Man is created as a person first to receive the gift of God's gratuitous love, and then to recapitulate that love by being gift to others. In fact, this call to be gift "constitutes the fundamental component of human existence in the world" (TOB 15:5). And God inscribed this call to be gift in the mystery of human sexuality. The complementarity of the body itself as male and female, as the revelation of the innermost being of man, of his subjectivity and freedom, summons man and woman freely to recapitulate the giving and receiving of the divine gift.

Now the words of Genesis 2:24 take on their meaning: *For this reason*—to recapitulate the divine gift—"a man leaves his father and his mother and cleaves to his wife and they become one flesh." This, as John Paul says, is "the meaning with which sex enters into the theology of the body" (TOB 14:5).

The Original Way of Living the Gift

We are learning that man, male and female, becomes aware of the reality of "gift" *through his body*—more specifically, through the mystery of sexual difference. Sex is "the sign of a gift that man, male-female, becomes aware of as a gift lived so to speak in an original way" (TOB 14:4). When John Paul speaks of the "original way" of living the gift, he means precisely what we have been discussing regarding the experiences of original solitude, unity, and nakedness. In fact, "the dimension of gift," according to John Paul, "is decisive for the essential truth and depth of the meaning of original solitude-unity-nakedness" (TOB 13:2).

In its first meaning—that man is "alone" in the world as a person—
original solitude reveals that man is a being capable of *receiving creation
as a gift* of God's life and love. In its second meaning, original solitude
reveals the need for a "helper," someone with whom the man can live in
a relationship of reciprocal gift. Original unity reveals that this relationship of *reciprocal gift has been established*. And original nakedness reveals
the *genuineness of the gift given*—that they are living with a full consciousness of the meaning of the body *as gift*. In this way, John Paul says
that the two words "alone" and "helper" hold the key to understanding
the essence of "the gift" as it manifests itself in man. The gift is first the
human being's own creation as a person (original solitude; "alone").
Then, in receiving his own life as a gift, the person desires to become
the same gift to an "other" that life is to him (original unity; "helper").
In turn, those two words reveal the essential content of man's existence
as a creature made in the divine image. For man images God both as an
individual ("alone") and in the male-female communion ("helper").

Hence, the words "alone" and "helper" summarize and reveal "the
norm of existence as a person" by showing that the relationship of
reciprocal gift fulfills man's original solitude. Not only that, but John
Paul will say that the relationship of reciprocal gift fulfills the deepest
meaning of man's being and existence. All of this is revealed through
awareness of the meaning of the body and of sex, a meaning that John
Paul calls "spousal."

Discovery of the "Spousal" Meaning of the Body

The verses of Genesis 2:23–25 overflow with anthropological
meaning. They express the joy of man's coming to be as male and
female (v. 23), establish their conjugal unity (v. 24), and finally testify to
the nakedness of both without shame (v. 25). This significant confrontation of man and woman in their nakedness "allows us to speak *of
revelation together with the discovery of the 'spousal' meaning of the body in
the mystery of creation*" (TOB 14:5).

The *spousal meaning of the body* is one of the most important and
synoptic concepts of the Pope's entire catechesis. From this point forward he will weave it throughout his addresses. But it is not simply a
"concept" or intellectual idea. The spousal meaning of the body speaks
of man and woman's *conscious experience* of their bodies as a gift and

sign of God's love—and, in turn, their sharing this love with one another in and through their bodies, their masculinity and femininity.

Incarnate Love

This *incarnate* concept of love points to the original integration and harmony of the interior and exterior dimensions of the human person. Man experiences his call to love from *within*. But the spousal meaning of the body also confirms this *exteriorly* precisely because man is a unity of body and soul. Based on this anthropological truth of body-soul integration, speaking of the human person means simultaneously speaking of the human body and sexuality. "This simultaneity is essential," the Pope says. For "if we dealt with sex without the person"—and we could also say if we dealt with the person without sex—"this would destroy the whole adequacy of the anthropology that we find in Genesis" (TOB 14:3).

The whole truth of the body and of sex, John Paul affirms, "is the simple and pure truth of communion between persons" (TOB 14:4). This communion is established through an integrated, incarnate love. Hence, John Paul defines the spousal meaning of the body as the body's *"power to express love: precisely that love in which the human person becomes a gift* and—through this gift—fulfills the very meaning of his being and existence" (TOB 15:1).[42] Here John Paul echoes that key text from the Second Vatican Council: "It follows then, that if man is the only creature on earth that God willed for its own sake, man can fully discover his true self only in a sincere giving of himself."[43] John Paul establishes here that this teaching of the Council is rooted not only in the spiritual aspect of man's nature but also in *his body*, in the complementary difference of the sexes and their call to become "one flesh."

> ■ Of course, this does not mean that everyone is called to marriage and the "one flesh" union. Nor could it possibly mean that sexual union is required in order to understand and live the meaning of life. It does mean, however, that we are all called to some expression of "spousal love"—to an incarnate self-giving. As Chapter 3 will

---

42. See *CCC*, no. 2331.
43. *Gaudium et Spes*, 24.

explain, everyone, regardless of their earthly vocation, finds the ultimate fulfillment of the spousal meaning of the body in the "marriage of the Lamb," that is, in union with Christ. And everyone's journey toward this heavenly reality, regardless of their earthly vocation, passes by way of our experience of sexual embodiment.

This interior law of the gift manifested in the exterior truth of the body is missed altogether by a purely naturalistic (or cosmological) view of man and his body. Since it does not penetrate the personal dimension, such an evaluation can only conclude that procreation is the primary end of sexual union. Without denying this truth, John Paul insists that the human body "is not only a source of fruitfulness and procreation, as in the whole natural order, but also contains 'from the beginning'...*the power to express love*" (TOB 15:1). But love is not to be considered another "end" of marriage. Rather, love must be the inner animating principle of marriage from which the ends of marriage flow. Procreation is the primary end flowing from authentic spousal love. If traditional formulations have stressed procreation to the neglect of spousal love, many modern theories stress spousal love to the neglect of procreation. If we seek to have an integral view of man, the two cannot be separated. Man loves *through his body*, which God blessed with the gift of fertility.

Revelation and Discovery of the Meaning of Life

Let us reflect for a moment on a particular aspect of the Pope's above quoted words. He says that if we live according to the true meaning of our bodies, *we fulfill the very meaning of our existence*. How? God is man's origin and end. And God *is love*. The meaning of life, then, is to love as God loves so as to reach our final end. This call to love is stamped in our sexuality. Anyone looking for the meaning of life has nowhere else to go. It is revealed in the spousal meaning of everyone's body—in masculinity and femininity. There lies the answer to the universal question: "What does it mean to be human?" There we find the law of the gift inscribed in our humanity. This is why misunderstanding and misuse of sexuality have such dire consequences for man and for society. A "culture of death" grows out of a world of people estranged from the spousal meaning of their bodies. In fact, original sin marks precisely the subjective loss or obscuring of the spousal meaning of the body.

As a result, for many people the experience of their body and sexuality—far from revealing life's meaning—seems inseparable from a gnawing sense of life's *meaninglessness*. Even many Christians who claim to have discovered life's meaning in a "spiritual" sense do not realize that that meaning is inscribed in *their bodies* as male and female, in their sexuality. Such persons may see the body as an annoying distraction, or even an inherent obstacle to living a Christian life. Not so! We cannot live an authentic Christian life apart from *the body*. This is what God's revelation teaches us. But we can also discover (or *re*discover) it in our own experience if we surrender our bodies to the grace poured out in the death and resurrection of Christ's body.

In his exegesis of Genesis 2, John Paul speaks repeatedly of the *revelation* and *discovery* of the spousal meaning of the body. He does this to emphasize that the theological thread of the Yahwist text is also anthropological. In other words, prior to sin complete harmony reigned between God's revelation and human experience. God revealed the body's spousal meaning, and man and woman discovered it and *consciously lived* it. Genesis 2:25 highlights this: "And the man and his wife were both naked and were not ashamed." As the inspired word of God, this is not only divine *revelation*. It speaks directly and specifically of man and woman's full and *conscious experience* of the spousal meaning of their bodies. Even though we have lost this conscious experience of the original meaning of our bodies through sin, by taking on flesh, the eternal Word *reveals* this meaning to us again. In his body given up for us, Christ offers us the redemption of our bodies, and with it the possibility of (re)*discovering* the body's spousal meaning. The conscious experience of redemption in Christ leads precisely to this (re)discovery of life's meaning through the revelation of the spousal meaning of the body of Christ.

The Freedom of the Gift

In the general audience of January 16, 1980 (TOB 15), particularly rich in content, John Paul introduces another key concept: the *freedom of the gift*. This freedom is inseparably linked to the spousal meaning of the body.

If men and women are created for their "own sake," they cannot be possessed by another. They cannot be owned or taken hold of by another. They are "incommunicable." Thus, a problem arises: How can men and women communicate themselves to each other without violating the other's dignity as an incommunicable person? The answer lies in the freedom of the gift. Adam was under no compulsion to satisfy mere "instinct" at the sight of woman's naked beauty. As the Pope points out, such a concept implies an interior constraint, similar to the instinct that stimulates copulation in animals. Instead, Adam was free with the freedom of the gift. This means the sight of Eve's nakedness inspired nothing but the desire to make a "sincere gift" of himself to her. He could freely *choose* her for who she was. This is an experience far from merely succumbing to an instinctual attraction toward a generic nakedness. This is a desire and love for another person inspired by the genuine recognition of that person's authentic value—that person's unrepeatability.

Furthermore, recognizing that she is a person made for "her own sake," Adam knew he could not "take" Eve or "grasp" her. He had to trust that she—in her freedom—would desire to open herself to the gift he initiated and would respond freely with the gift of herself to him, which she did. In doing so, she also *chose* him. This is how incommunicable persons communicate their persons—by freely bestowing the reciprocal and sincere gift of self. In this way, John Paul says that the human body and sex are raised "to the level of 'image of God' and to the level of the person and communion among persons" (TOB 14:6).

Freedom lies at the very basis of the spousal meaning of the body and the experience of original nakedness. Man and woman can only be naked without shame, according to the Holy Father, when "they are *free with the very freedom of the gift.*" The entrance of shame, therefore, indicates the loss of the freedom of the gift. Here John Paul means freedom as self-mastery or self-control. Such freedom "is indispensable *in order for man to be able to 'give himself,'*...in order for him (referring to the words of the Council) to be able to 'find himself fully' through 'a sincere gift of self'" (TOB 15:2). For man cannot give himself away if he does not first possess himself, if he is not in "control" of himself and his desires.

Self-control for original man, however, did not mean dominating unruly desires in order to keep them "in check." Such a concept can only stem from the projections of fallen man. In the beginning, man and woman experienced sexual desire as God created it, as the power and desire to love as God loves. Thus, they had no unruly desires to control. Free with the freedom of the gift, man and woman reveled in each other's goodness, in each other's beauty, according to the whole truth of their being as God revealed it to them in the mystery of creation. *This* reveling in each other's goodness enabled them to be naked without shame. This experience "can and should be understood as the revelation—together with the discovery—of the freedom that makes possible...the 'spousal' meaning of the body" (TOB 15:2). Hence, historical man's task will be to recover the truth of the body that sets him free. It is precisely for this freedom that Christ has set us free (see Gal 5:1).

"Own Sake" and "Self Gift"

That key anthropological statement of the Council (taken from *Gaudium et Spes*, no. 24) which we have been discussing has two main emphases. First, man is the only creature created "for his own sake." Second, man can only find himself "through the sincere giving of self."

God created the rest of creation for *our* sake. We are free to use (but not *ab*-use) creation for our benefit. The human person, however, since he exists "for his own sake," must *never* be used merely as a means to our own end. In our relations with others, we must always respect the fact that every person has, or at least should have, distinct personal ends.[44] Nonetheless, having been created for our own sakes, we are not meant to live for own sakes, but to live for others. The human heart cannot find happiness in self-indulgent isolation. Hence, the second emphasis of the Council's statement: Man, if he is to find himself, must become a "sincere gift" to others. As Christ said, if you lose your life, you will find it (see Mk 8:35).

■ Secular humanism may seem to promote the idea that man is made for his own sake. However—and here it makes its tragic error—it concludes that he is meant to live for his own sake. This

---

44. *Love and Responsibility*, p. 28.

results in a radical individualism that actually denies the initial premise. Individualism inevitably treats others not as persons in their own right, but as a means or as an obstacle in the every-man-for-himself quest for fulfillment. Secular humanism does not believe in the reality of gift because it denies God who *is* Gift. But the selfless call to be gift to others is the only path to true communion and solidarity among persons, starting with the most fundamental communion of all, that of man and woman in marriage. As we shall learn, the denial of the gift is the essence of original sin. Hence, as George Weigel keenly observes, through the original temptation the serpent "is the first and most lethal purveyor of a false humanism."[45]

The two emphases of the Council's statement ("own sake" and "self-gift") contain all the concepts that shed light on man's "beginning"—communion of persons; original solitude, unity, and nakedness; the gift; the spousal meaning of the body; and the freedom of the gift. In the first meaning of *solitude* (i.e., man differs from the animals), Adam discovers that he is the only creature willed "for his own sake." In the second meaning of solitude (i.e., man is alone without the opposite sex), he realizes that he can only fulfill himself by giving himself away to another creature also willed "for his own sake" (or shall we say *her* own sake?). *Original unity* is the "sincere giving" of man and woman to each other that forms the *communion of persons*. This call to be *gift* is revealed through their experience of *nakedness*. Our anatomy as male and female persons reveals the *body's spousal meaning*, which is fulfilled in the *freedom of the gift* of man and woman to each other.

Spousal Meaning of the Body and the Affirmation of the Person

In their first "beatifying meeting," man and woman discover their own selves in the gift of the other. In the purity of his love—in the purity of his sexual desire—man accepted woman as God willed her "for her own sake" in the mystery of her femininity. And in the purity of her love and desire, woman accepted man as God willed him "for his

---

45. *Witness to Hope*, p. 338.

own sake" in the mystery of his masculinity. This purity affords the perfect integration of the interior and exterior dimensions of the person. The pure of heart see that the exterior beauty of the human body is "oriented from within by the 'sincere gift' of the person." They see "such a *value* and such *a beauty that it goes beyond the simply physical level of 'sexuality'*" (TOB 15:4). The body becomes the threshold to the transcendent reality of the spirit and even in some way to the ultimate mystery of the divine.

John Paul says that in this manner, awareness of the spousal meaning of the body is in a way completed. Not only do the man and woman each become a sincere gift for the other, but the gift is also completed when each *receives* the gift of self made by the other. The spousal meaning of the body reveals both the call to become a gift and "the power and deep availability for the 'affirmation of the person'" which "is nothing other than welcoming the gift" (TOB 15:4). It is precisely this reciprocal giving and accepting of the gift that creates the communion of persons. This communion is constructed from within, from man's "interiority." But John Paul affirms that it also comprises "man's whole 'exteriority,' that is, all that constitutes the pure and simple nakedness of the body in its masculinity and femininity" (TOB 15:4).

John Paul also explains that this "affirmation of the person" concerns "the power to live the fact that the other—the woman for the man and the man for the woman—is through the body someone willed by the Creator for his own sake." This someone is "unique and unrepeatable, someone chosen by eternal Love" (TOB 15:4). Is there any man or woman who does not ache in the depths of his or her being for such affirmation? And, according to John Paul, in God's plan this is all revealed and lived "through the body." This does not mean that everyone must experience sexual union to be affirmed as a person. But it does mean that sexual union is supposed to be *this*: the deep affirmation of our goodness as persons through the sincere giving and receiving of the gift of selves.

This is the language of the sexual embrace: "I give myself totally to you, *all* that I am without reservation. Sincerely. Freely. Forever. And I receive the gift of yourself that you give to me. I bless you. I affirm you. *All* that you are, without reservation. Forever." This is an experience of being *chosen by eternal Love*. If sexual union does not say this, it does not correspond to the spousal meaning of the body. It does not correspond to the dignity of the person and can never satisfy the longings of the heart. If sexual union does not say this, it is not an expression of divine love but only a cheapened version of it.

Spousal Meaning of the Body: Rooted in Love

John Paul says that man can never avoid this indispensable "theme" of his own existence. Man is made for spousal love. It is stamped in his (and her) being, interiorly and exteriorly. Therefore, John Paul affirms that the spousal meaning of the body is "the fundamental component of human existence in the world" (TOB 15:5). This means we can only find the happiness we seek if we discover this love, if we discover (or *re*discover) the spousal meaning of the body. In the human quest for happiness, John Paul says that man will not fail to confer a spousal meaning on his own body. Even if many things distort our experience of sexuality, the desire for spousal union will always remain at the deepest level of *the person*. John Paul cannot emphasize this point enough: "One can understand this 'spousal' meaning of the human body only in the context of the person" (TOB 15:5).

Animals can copulate and reproduce, but their bodies do not have a spousal meaning because they are not persons and they cannot love. We can also observe in this context that animals also cannot experience shame. We are the only "bodies" in the world that wear clothing. Why? Because our capacity for shame is the "flip side" of our capacity for love. Animals have neither capacity. Thus, what may seem somewhat similar in the copulation of animals and the copulation of humans is seen to be worlds apart when we consider the interior dimension of the person. This is why the spousal meaning of the body "demands that it be revealed in all its simplicity and purity and manifested in its whole truth as a sign of the 'image of God'" (TOB 15:5).

Because of sin, we may feel far removed from experiencing the body as our first parents did in the state of original innocence. But only through that revelation of the original experience of the body can we understand that from which we have fallen *and* that to which we are called. In the fullness of time Christ took on flesh and was born of a woman so that we might experience the redemption of our bodies. In Christ we are called—and called *with power*—to recover the happiness that comes from living according to the full truth of our bodies, that comes from being rooted in Love. "Original happiness, the beatifying 'beginning' of man, whom God created 'male and female,' the spousal meaning of the body in its original nakedness: all of this expresses root-edness in Love" (TOB 16:1).

John Paul II's "hermeneutics of the gift" leads us precisely to Love as the origin, vocation, and destiny of the human person. The reality of "gift" confirms that the "irradiation of Love"—of God's own Spirit—is an integral part of the mystery of creation. "The first verses of the Bible...speak not only about the creation of the world and about man in the world, but also about grace, that is, about the self-communication of holiness, of the irradiation of the Holy Spirit, which produces a special state of 'spiritualization' in that first man" (TOB 16:1). Of course, this state of "spiritualization" does not imply a distancing from the body. It means the "*in*-spiration" of the body with the gift of the Holy Spirit. It means the complete integration and unity of soul and body, spirituality and sexuality, which man and woman enjoyed in the state of original innocence.

B. THE MYSTERY OF ORIGINAL INNOCENCE

Grace as a Gift to the Human Heart

We have been trying to "reconstruct" the first man and woman's experience of the body in the state of original innocence before shame. As "historical man" we do this almost by means of a contrast with our own experience of shame. John Paul defines original innocence as that which "*at its very roots, excludes the shame of the body* in the relation between man and woman, that which eliminates the necessity of this shame in man, in his *heart* or his *conscience*" (TOB 16:4). This prompts a question: What in original man radically eliminates any experience of shame? John Paul has a one-word answer: *grace*.

John Paul states that if creation is a gift to man, then grace determines man's fullness and deepest dimension as a creature. Grace is God's self-gift to man; it is God's Spirit breathed into the dust of our humanity. The state of original innocence speaks above all of this gift of grace that God gives and man receives. This grace made it possible for human persons to experience the meaning of the world as God's primary gift or donation, and this grace enabled them to experience the reciprocal donation of masculinity and femininity as a recapitulation of this gift. Their original communion of persons, then, was a participation in grace. And grace, John Paul tells us, is "participation in the inner life of God himself, in his holiness." It is "that mysterious *gift made to man's innermost [being]—to the human heart—that allows* both the man and the woman *to exist* from the 'beginning' *in the reciprocal relationship of the disinterested gift of self*" (TOB 16:3).

"Disinterested" obviously does not mean that man and woman lacked interest in each other. They were deeply interested in each other, but not selfishly so. Their experience of "the irradiation of God's love" (i.e., grace) enabled them to love one another sincerely, as God loves. In this we can understand the beatifying experience of the beginning connected with the awareness of the spousal meaning of the body. This blissful awareness of the body's meaning speaks of their conscious experience of God with them and *within* them—of God's Spirit (i.e., his love) radiating *through their bodies*. "Happiness," John Paul says, "is being rooted in Love. Original happiness speaks to us about the 'beginning' of man, who emerged from love and initiated love.... One can define this 'beginning' also as the original and beatifying immunity from shame as the result of love" (TOB 16:2).

If we allowed our hearts to enter into this "beatifying experience," we would taste the love for which we all long and the interior peace it brings. Perhaps we hesitate to imagine the experience of original happiness for fear of discovering that we cannot attain what we so earnestly long for. Why tantalize ourselves with false hopes? Is it not more realistic just to "make do" with the inheritance of our sinfulness?

Although we have left our original innocence irretrievably behind, John Paul stresses that the love God gave to man in the mystery of creation and in the grace of original innocence *he gave irrevocably*. In the fullness of time, Christ will bear witness to this irreversible love of the Father. His mission will be to proclaim that the grace of the mystery of creation was not lost forever, but becomes, for anyone open to receiving it, the grace of the mystery of redemption (see TOB 46:5). "Where sin increased, grace abounded all the more" (Rom 5:20). This means that in Jesus Christ we can attain the happiness for which we long. Even if we will always know suffering and tears in this life, we are alive with hope that in the end God will wipe away every tear from our eyes (see Rev 7:17). This is why we call the Gospel *good* news!

Innocence and the Exchange of the Gift

John Paul closes his address of January 30, 1980 (TOB 16), by stating that original innocence can be understood as "purity of heart." Purity of heart manifests "a tranquil witness of conscience" precisely by "preserving interior faithfulness to the gift according to the spousal meaning of the body" (TOB 16:5). Preserving this "faithfulness to the gift," is the key to man and woman's happiness (beatitude).

In his following address, John Paul explains what original man's experience of fidelity to the gift looked like. Once again, he does it by way of contrast with historical man's experience of shame. He says that shame corresponds to a threat inflicted on the personal intimacy of man and woman's relationship and thus bears witness to the interior collapse of innocence. This "threat to the gift" results from a radical interior alteration of the content of sexual desire. To the degree that it is lacking in God's love, sexual desire seeks to appropriate the other rather than be a gift to the other. John Paul describes this appropriation as the "antithesis of the gift" and "the extortion of the gift" (TOB 17:3). These vivid images *ex*-press the *in*-terior "content" of lust with pointed accuracy. To "extort" literally means "to twist" or to "turn out." Sexual desire "twisted" by sin does not trust in the freedom of the gift and refuses to risk becoming a gift. Instead, it grasps at the gift and even seeks to snatch it by force or manipulation. This effectively and utterly drains the gift of its meaning. It is the antithesis of the gift and the antithesis of the spousal meaning of the body.

But if we "untwist" this experience or "flip it over," we rediscover the content of the original experience of sexual desire. If shame expresses the above lack of fidelity to the gift and the spousal meaning of the body, then we can conclude that nakedness without shame expresses an experience of total fidelity to the gift and the spousal meaning of the body. If shame indicates "the extortion of the gift," nakedness *without* shame indicates *total freedom* in man and woman's self-giving. We have already described this as "the freedom of the gift."

Therefore, according to John Paul, fidelity to the gift consists in a moral participation in the eternal and permanent act of God's will that each should be loved and received for his or her own sake, and never reduced interiorly to a mere "object for me." This means that if man and woman are to find the happiness they desire in their relationship, they must freely give themselves to each other in the whole truth of their masculinity and femininity as the Creator wished them to be. Furthermore, at the same time they must fully accept and "welcome" each other, receiving each other precisely in the whole truth of their masculinity and femininity—body and soul—as the Creator wished them to be. In other words, sincere self-giving has no conditions or reservations. Since it participates in the love of God, the giving and receiving of spousal love is *total* and *irreversible*.

Giving and Receiving Interpenetrate

John Paul adds: "These two functions of the mutual exchange are deeply connected in the whole process of 'the gift of self': giving and accepting the gift interpenetrate in such a way that the very act of giving becomes acceptance, and acceptance transforms itself into giving" (TOB 17:4). This observation provides an important window into the dynamism of sexual complementarity.[46] We previously quoted John Paul saying that the reality of "gift" implies that there is one who gives and one who receives, and a reciprocal relationship is established between them. This giving and receiving, which established the original covenant between God and man, finds a symbolic reflection in the covenant relationship of man and woman. The male, by virtue of the specific spousal dynamism of his body, is disposed toward giving or initiating the gift. The female, by virtue of the specific spousal dynamism of her body, is disposed toward accepting or receiving the gift. Nonetheless, "giving" does not belong exclusively to the male, nor "receiving" exclusively to the female. They interpenetrate so that in giving the male receives and in receiving the female gives.

In fact, in the order of creation, it seems to John Paul that the man, before giving himself to the woman, first *receives* her from the hand of God. This seems to indicate that every human being's first posture as a

---

46. The work of Sister Prudence Allen, RSM, on sexual complementarity is of special import. See "Integral Sex Complementarity and the Theology of Communion," *Communio* (Winter 1990): 523–44. For greater depth of philosophical foundations on the issue of sexual complementarity, see the introduction to her books *The Concept of Woman: The Aristotelian Revolution (750 B.C.–A D. 1250)* (Grand Rapids, MI: Eerdmans, 1997), and *The Concept of Woman: The Humanist Reformation (1250–1500)* (Grand Rapids, MI: Eerdmans, 2002).

creature is one of *receptivity* to the gift of God. Indeed, it is impossible for a creature to give anything if he has not first received. Hence, only by receiving woman as a gift from God can the man then initiate the gift of himself to her. As John Paul says, "The woman has 'from the beginning' been entrusted to his eyes, to his consciousness, to his sensibility, to his 'heart'; he, by contrast, must in some way ensure the very process of the exchange of the gift, the reciprocal interpenetration of giving and receiving the gift, which, precisely through its reciprocity, creates an authentic communion of persons" (TOB 17:6).

In this intimate communion, man and woman discover their true selves *in the other* through the sincere gift of themselves *to each other* and in the sincere acceptance of each other's gift. When the whole dignity of the giving and receiving is ensured, both man and woman experience the "specific essence" of their masculinity and femininity. At the same time, the Pope says they reach the deep recesses of the "possession of self." This authentic self-possession enables them to give and receive each other in a way that corresponds to the essence of the gift. Furthermore, the Pope observes that this giving and receiving grows ever deeper and more intense. It grows as the finding of oneself in giving oneself bears fruit in a new and more profound giving of oneself. Here we approach the manner in which the sincere giving of male and female to each other reproduces in created form the Uncreated and Eternal spirating exchange of the Persons of the Trinity (keeping in mind, of course, the infinite difference between Creator and creature).

By living in the trinitarian image, man and woman fulfill the meaning of their being and existence; they reach beatitude. As we shall see, this "beatifying communion" points us right from the beginning to the beatific communion of heaven. There the created sign of trinitarian life will give way to its divine prototype, and man will participate in trinitarian life itself. Here we see the continuity between the experiences of original man and eschatological man. The experience of incarnate communion in the resurrection will be completely new. Yet John Paul also affirms that "at the same time, it will not be alienated in any way from the experience man shared 'from the beginning'" (TOB 69:5). In this way we see that our origin foreshadows our destiny. Even if historical man will lose sight of this vision, the Anointed One will come preaching "recovery of sight to the blind" (Lk 4:18).

The Ethos of the Human Body

In the audience of February 13, 1980 (TOB 18), John Paul offers a review of some of the concepts he has outlined thus far. He points to the novelty of his project when he states that theology has traditionally "built *the overall image of man's original innocence and justice before original sin* by applying the method of objectivization specific to metaphysics and metaphysical anthropology. In the present analysis," he continues, "we are trying rather to take into account the aspect of human subjectivity" (TOB 18:1).

John Paul knows that much of the Church's moral teaching (about sexuality in particular) seems "abstract" to modern man. People today do not think of the world in objective, metaphysical categories. They understand the world primarily through their own experiences. By penetrating the *experiences* of the first man and woman, John Paul wants to demonstrate that the Church's objective norms (ethics) actually correspond to the deepest subjective desires of the human heart (ethos). He wants to demonstrate that the Church's teachings are not hopelessly removed from real life experience. Nor are they imposed from "outside" of man, but, when properly understood, they actually well up from "within" him. John Paul believes that this approach to the Scriptures is actually more in keeping with the original texts.

Man and woman entered the world with complete knowledge of the spousal meaning of their bodies and what that called them to ethically—that is, to participate in God's mystery by loving each other as God loves. They did not need an objective norm commanding them to love. Filled with the grace of creation, they desired nothing else. This was the *ethos* (the interior experience of the good) by which they freely lived. In fact, the Holy Father says that original innocence manifests and at the same time constitutes the perfect *ethos* of the gift—the perfect ethos of love.

Having lost the original grace of creation, historical man also lost this original experience of the good. Deceived by a lie, he has become "disconnected" in his heart from what will make him truly happy. This is why John Paul insists that we must construct this theology of the body "from the beginning," carefully following Christ's words. Historical man must follow the trail of his heart back to the beginning in order to "reconnect" with God's original plan for his happiness—and this means reconnecting with the *ethos* of the gift inscribed in his body and in his heart. As we have stressed throughout, rediscovering the truth about the body and sexuality is no side issue. John Paul observes that man and woman were given to each other as a gift in the whole perspective of the existence of mankind and of the human family. He says that the "fundamental fact of...[the] existence of man in every stage of his history is that God 'created them male and female.'... In this way, a great creative perspective is opened up, which is precisely the perspective of man's existence, which continually renews itself by means of 'procreation'" (TOB 18:4–5). Man's existence and future obviously *depend* on the call of man and woman to become "one flesh."

This call is deeply rooted in the consciousness of humanity. Although "man and the woman *come forth from the mystery of creation* first of all *as brother and sister in the same humanity*," John Paul also remarks that, according to Genesis 2:24, "man and woman were created for marriage" (TOB 18:5).[47] Hence, understanding of "the spousal meaning of the body (and of the fundamental conditioning of this meaning) is important and indispensable for knowing who man is and who he ought to be, and therefore how he should shape his own activity. It is something essential and important for the future of human ethos" (TOB 18:4). Stated simply: If we do not understand the spousal meaning of our bodies, we do not know who we are and, therefore, we do not know how to live. Ethics is rooted in anthropology. How we are to live is rooted in *who we are* as God created us to be. When we interiorize the truth of who we are, we (re)experience "the ethos of the gift," that is, we come more and more to desire subjectively only that which is objectively good.

If we fail to realize this, living a moral life will inevitably become an attempt to follow what seem like arbitrary and imposed "rules." Without a deep interior knowledge and understanding of the "why" behind the "ought," we become unconvinced of the "ought" and sooner or later abandon it. A morality that fails to recognize and respect man as a living subject inevitably leads to this crisis.

---

47. In his catecheses on the Song of Songs (TOB 108–13), John Paul will provide a profound reflection on what it means that man and woman are first brother and sister in the same humanity (see TOB 109–10). He will also clarify in his catechesis on celibacy for the kingdom that our creation "for" marriage does not mean marriage is the only path to fulfill the spousal meaning of the body (see TOB 80).

Ethos and the Subjectivity of Man

Through the ethos of the gift we can outline the "subjectivity" of man. "Subjectivity" refers to the self-experience of personhood. A person knows that he is not some*thing* but some*one*. In other words, a subject knows he cannot be reduced to an object. Man is a subject precisely because he is made in the image of the divine Subject, God.

> ■ Traditional theological formulations often referred to God as "the divine object." There is nothing inaccurate about this formulation, but John Paul often balances this with the phrase "divine Subject." As George Weigel reports in *Witness to Hope*, the young Father Wojtyla preferred this phrase in his doctoral dissertation on John of the Cross. The renowned Father Garrigou-Lagrange, who directed young Wojtyla's dissertation, criticized him for not conforming to the more traditional language of "divine object," but Wojtyla insisted that there was a need for balance. Persons are certainly objects as well as subjects,[48] but as Weigel writes, "We do not come to know God as we come to know an object (a tree, a baseball, an automobile). Rather, we come to know God as we come to know another person, through mutual self-giving."[49]

A subject has the richness of an interior life that affords the freedom to act, to choose this or that—in a word, to love. A person feels stripped of his dignity when his freedom as a subject is denied and he is forced to act in a given way. Even if he is forced to act in a way that is objectively good, he will not experience it as good unless he makes that good *his own* by choosing it freely as a subject. Here we encounter the creative interplay of divine and human subjectivity. God does not force his will on us; we are not pawns in a cosmic scheme. God respects us entirely as the subjects he created us to be. He wants us to want *for ourselves* to participate in his plan. God initiates the gift—he proposes his loving plan—and invites us to participate. Then we, as subjects, must choose, recognizing that even a right choice is itself a gift, a grace. This divine "respect" God shows toward his own creature defines man as "partner of the Absolute."

---

48. See *Love and Responsibility*, p. 21.
49. *Witness to Hope*, p. 86.

Because the first man and woman interiorized the objective good by making God's will their own, they experienced the objective *ethic* as a liberating *ethos*. This is how the original ethos of the gift is to be understood. The first man and woman *experienced* the objective good as good precisely because they freely chose it in accord with their dignity as subjects. They desired nothing else. In this way John Paul says that "the subjective profile of...[their] love" was "objective to the very depths" (TOB 19:1) because man's subjective desires were nourished by the objective truth of the spousal meaning of the body. And this interior orientation toward the good is precisely purity of heart.

Subjectivity and Purity

At this point we can recall what we stated previously: When it is pure, subjectivity is completely objective. Purity of heart connects a person's subjective desires (ethos) with the objective order of love (ethics). We know this link was established in the hearts of the first man and woman—in other words, we know they were pure—because of the experience of original nakedness. "If 'they did not feel shame,' this means that they were united by the consciousness of the gift, that they had reciprocal *awareness of the spousal meaning of their bodies*, in which the freedom of the gift is expressed and *the whole inner richness of the person as subject is shown*" (TOB 19:1).

The Holy Father explains that in a way purity of heart made it impossible for them to reduce each other to the level of a mere object. Shame enters precisely when man and woman lose purity of heart. Because of this loss, they fail to respect "*the inner riches of the person as subject*" and come to look upon the person as an object to be used. Because of this loss of purity, the demands of love no longer spontaneously well up from "within" man. In fact, they often appear now as a burden imposed from "without." To use our previous image, when man is deceived by the "great lie," he actually prefers his flat tires and views any norm that calls him to inflate them as a burdensome imposition.

For historical man the discovery of the spousal meaning of the body will cease to be a simple reality of revelation and grace. Nonetheless, the Holy Father maintains that the original spousal meaning of the body "was to *remain as a task given to man by the ethos of the gift*, inscribed in the depth of the human heart as a distant echo, as it were, of original innocence" (TOB 19:2). Even though he must now look through "the veil of shame," historical man must continually rediscover himself as "the guardian of the mystery of the subject" so as to defend every subject from being reduced in any way to a mere object.

This flows from "purity of heart," which is the fruit of being filled with grace. So if we are to live and love as we are called and thus fulfill the meaning of our being and existence, our only hope is to be filled again with grace. And grace has been poured out. When we open our hearts to it, we come gradually to (re)experience the ethos of the gift. Then, to the extent that we (re)experience this ethos, living according to the full truth of the spousal meaning of the body becomes our deepest desire and longing—not imposed from the "outside" but welling up from "within." Then we recognize that our "tires" are made for air, we repent of ever thinking otherwise, and we allow Christ to inflate us.

The Primordial Sacrament and the Body as "Sign"

Prior to their "knowledge of good and evil," man and woman "are immersed in the very mystery of creation, and the depth of this mystery hidden in their heart is innocence, grace, love, and justice" (TOB 19:3). They *experience* innocence, grace, love, and justice precisely through the awareness of the meaning of their bodies, their masculinity and femininity and their call to become "one flesh." Seeing themselves with God's own vision, they know they are good, very good (see Gen 1:31). With this lived awareness of the meaning of their bodies, John Paul says that both man and woman enter the world as subjects of truth and love. This means that, prior to sin, the first man and woman freely chose to act with their bodies only in truth and in love.

The First Feast of Humanity

It is hard to imagine the freedom and *pure* delight taken in the experience of original nakedness and unity. John Paul, poet that he is, seeks to fire our imagination when he describes the original fullness of the experience of the spousal meaning of the body as *"the first feast of humanity"* (TOB 19:6). It is a feast of pure love, of God's and man's goodness. It is a feast of delight in the fact that "being and the good are convertible." To be alive is good. To be created male and female is good.

To become "one flesh" is very good. Even if historical man will find this "original feast" largely spoiled by sin and death, "nevertheless, we draw a first hope already from the mystery of creation: namely, that the fruit of the divine economy of truth and love, which revealed itself 'at the beginning,' is not Death, but Life, and not so much the destruction of the body of man made 'in the image of God,' but rather the 'call to glory' (Rom 8:30)" (TOB 19:6). "Glory," Wojtyla tells us, "is the irradiation of good, the reflecting of all perfection. And in one way it is also the inner atmosphere of the deity, the godhead.... In a very special way God transmits this glory to man. The glory of God is living man; the glory of God is man alive."[50]

This "call to glory" is stamped in our body-persons as male and female. Sin and death *cannot* overcome it. God extends to man *forever* this divine gift of life and love. We can reject the gift, but God will never withdraw it. Even if we have rejected the gift, we can still "repent and believe in the good news" (Mk 1:15). We can always rediscover the divine gift. Despite sin, a "spark" of the divine gift always remains within man. As the Holy Father says, "Man appears in the visible world as the highest expression of the divine gift, because he bears within himself the inner dimension of the gift" (TOB 19:3). With this statement, we approach the heart and essence of what John Paul means when he speaks of a "theology of the body." Man bears within himself the call to "be gift," that is, to love as God loves. This call to be gift is made *visible* through his body as male and female and through the call to life-giving communion in marriage.

John Paul's Thesis Statement

"Thus, in this dimension, a primordial *sacrament* is constituted, understood as a *sign that* efficaciously *transmits in the visible world the invisible mystery hidden in God from eternity*. And this is the mystery of Truth and Love, the mystery of divine life, in which man really participates" (TOB 19:4). This statement requires a careful explanation because it can be misunderstood. The Holy Father is speaking of marriage as a "sacrament"—a theological term that refers to the mediation of grace—in the context of the state of original innocence. Is there such

---

50. *Sign of Contradiction*, p. 181.

a thing? Do not the sacraments as such begin with Christ and the Church? In what way can we speak of a "primordial sacrament"—a sacramental mediation of grace from the "beginning" before the Incarnation and before the seven sacraments Christ instituted?

Let us jump ahead for a moment to where John Paul's ever deepening spiral of reflections will eventually take us. In his analysis of Ephesians (Part 2, Chapter 1), the Holy Father takes St. Paul's words seriously that we are chosen in Christ "before the foundation of the world" (Eph 1:4). Based on this, John Paul says that "we must deduce that *the reality of the creation of man* was already *permeated* by the perennial election of man in Christ." The primordial sacrament can only be properly understood in reference to Christ. The grace in which original man participated "was brought about precisely *out of regard for... [Christ]*...while chronologically anticipating his coming in the body" (TOB 96:5).

Therefore, the primordial sacrament, one might say, is a primordial preview of "the plan of the mystery hidden for ages in God" (Eph 3:9), which comes to fruition and is definitively revealed in Christ. St. Paul makes this explicit when he links the "one flesh" union of Genesis with the union of Christ and the Church. This is a "great mystery," he says (other translations say this is a "great sacrament"), and it refers to Christ and the Church (see Eph 5:31–32). John Paul says that Ephesians 5, in particular, authorizes us to speak of "sacrament" in the wider and perhaps also more ancient and fundamental meaning of the term.[51] If sacrament in its restricted meaning refers to the seven signs of grace instituted by Christ, in this broader meaning, sacrament "means the very mystery of God, which is hidden from eternity, yet not in an eternal concealment, but first in its very revelation and realization" (TOB 98:8).

But what is this "great mystery" hidden in God? As the *Catechism* says, the "innermost secret" of God is that "God himself is an eternal exchange of love, Father, Son, and Holy Spirit, and he has destined us to share in that exchange."[52] This eternal plan is already set in motion through the primordial sacrament, which John Paul understands as a sign that transmits effectively in the visible world that innermost secret

---

51. See TOB 93, n. 88, for a detailed discussion of the term "sacrament."
52. *CCC*, no. 221.

of God. How is the divine mystery made visible and effective in man's life? "The sacrament, as a visible sign, is constituted with man, inasmuch as he is a 'body,' through his 'visible' masculinity and femininity" (TOB 19:4). Through their bodies—and through their call to become "one body"—man and woman in some way *participate* in the divine exchange of trinitarian life and love.

> ■ "Participation" was an important theme in Wojtyla's book *The Acting Person* and was also developed in various essays published in *Person and Community*. By "participation" Wojtyla means "acting together with others."[53] But this does not simply mean "doing things" in conjunction with others. For Wojtyla, the essence of the *person* is revealed in the freedom of truly human action. Thus, when we truly act with others we participate in *"the very humanness of others."*[54] Participation takes place when subjects, acting together, experience "inter-subjectivity." This means living in communion with others (*communio personarum*) and in the broader sense building community. When John Paul speaks about "participating in the mystery of divine life," he is talking about sharing in the *very divinity of God.* He means participation in the divine nature (see 2 Pt 1:4); participation in the eternal *Communio Personarum.*[55] In fact, John Paul will eventually describe the communion of saints as the experience of the "perfect intersubjectivity of all" (TOB 68:4). In this way we can understand why Wojtyla concludes one of his essays with this striking statement: "The central problem of life for humanity in our times, perhaps in all times, is this: *participation or alienation?*"[56]

Here we encounter John Paul's thesis statement that the "body, in fact, and only the body, is capable of making visible what is invisible: the spiritual and the divine. It has been created to transfer into the visible reality of the world the mystery hidden from eternity in God, and thus to be a sign of it" (TOB 19:4). *This* is why the Pope speaks of a

---

53. *The Acting Person*, p. 261.
54. Ibid., p. 294.
55. *CCC*, no. 2780.
56. *Person and Community*, p. 206.

theology *of the body*. Recalling all that we said earlier about the proper understanding of "sign," (see pp. 17–21) the body, in the full beauty and mystery of sexual difference and the call to communion, is a sign—the primordial sign—of God's very own mystery. As the *Catechism* teaches, God "impressed his own form on the flesh...in such a way that even what was visible might bear the divine form."[57] Upon this incarnational mystery hinges the deepest essence of the *humanum*—of what is human. Upon this incarnational mystery hinges the incomparable dignity of every human being. Upon this incarnational mystery hinges everything that John Paul II proposes to the Church and the world about who man is and who he is called to be.

All of creation is sacramental in that it reveals something of the mystery of its Creator. But John Paul tells us that this "sacramentality of the world" reaches its fulfillment in man created in the image of God as male and female.[58] Man, in turn, reaches his fulfillment through the sincere gift of self, which was realized in an original way through the incarnate union of Genesis 2:24. According to John Paul, in view of the sacramentality of the human body we fully understand those words of Genesis 2:24, "For this reason a man leaves his father and his mother and cleaves to his wife and the two become one flesh." The Pope says that these words "are constitutive of the sacrament of Marriage" (TOB 19:5). John Paul later states more explicitly that the "Mystery hidden from all eternity in God...became *a visible reality through the union* of the first man and the first woman in the perspective of marriage" (TOB 97:4). *The union* of man and woman, consummated according to the words of Genesis 2:24, in some way sums up or consummates the "sacramentality of creation."

The Holy Father explains that against this vast background we come to understand the rich significance of original nakedness. The words of Genesis 2:25 ("they were both naked and not ashamed") "express the fact that, *together with man, holiness has entered the visible world*" (TOB 19:5). Holiness enabled man and woman *to see* the mystery of God revealed in and through each other's naked body. Through the original experience of the spousal meaning of their bodies, man and woman gained awareness of the "sacrament of the body" (TOB 19:5).

---

57. *CCC*, no. 704.
58. See *CCC*, nos. 41, 288, 315.

They were immune from shame because they were full of grace; that is, they were holy. It is "in his body as man or woman," John Paul says, that "man senses himself as a subject of holiness." He further explains that holiness "permits man to express himself deeply with his own body, precisely through the 'sincere gift' of self" (TOB 19:5). In other words, holiness enables us to love with our bodies as God loves. It enables us to realize that our bodies bear the stamp of God's mystery of love. Holiness enables us to see, live, and experience God's plan of love and communion *in our bodies.*

6. *"Knowledge" and Procreation (Gen 4:1)*

In his closing remarks on original man, John Paul shifts gears in order to reflect on Genesis 4:1, "Adam knew Eve his wife, and she conceived and bore Cain, saying, 'I have gotten a man with the help of the LORD.'" Having focused our attention on the unitive meaning of sexual difference, John Paul wants also to examine the procreative meaning. Even though this takes place *after* original sin in the chronology of the Yahwist account, John Paul includes this in his reflections on original man. He does so because "the term 'knew'...synthesizes the whole density of the biblical text analyzed so far" (TOB 21:1). Furthermore, he wants to stress the continuity and connection between original man and historical man. Finally, in closing his reflections on original man, John Paul wants to emphasize that sexual union, procreation, and moral choosing are intimately linked with man's creation in the image of God.

The Meaning of "Knowledge"

As John Paul notes, our contemporary language, although precise, often deprives us of the opportunity to reflect on the deeper meaning of things. The biblical word "knew," on the contrary, takes us beyond the surface of the sexual act to penetrate the rich experience of interpersonal unity. John Paul goes so far as to say that by speaking here of knowledge, "the Bible indicates the deepest essence of the reality of shared married life" (TOB 20:4).

"Knowledge" clearly distinguishes the sexual union of man and woman as persons from the copulation of animals. Animals do not "know" each other. Animals cannot "know" each other. Their mating and reproducing are determined by biological instinct, "by nature." For man, sexuality is not a passive biological determinant, "but reaches a level and content specific to self-conscious and self-determining persons" (TOB 21:4). The term "knowledge" indicates that human sexuality decides man's concrete personal identity. Biblical knowledge "reaches the innermost roots of this identity and concreteness, which man and woman owe to their sex. Such concreteness means both the uniqueness and unrepeatability of the person" (TOB 20:5).

■ A word on this "unrepeatability" of the person: A husband and wife who truly "know" each other have arrived at the irreducible core of the person, and each loves this *person*—not merely physical or spiritual attributes of the person, but the person himself (herself). At this level, they continually recognize and affirm the unrepeatability of the other; he (she) is utterly unique and cannot be repeated or replaced. When the "one flesh" union expresses a love at this level—and it is always meant to do so—it becomes impossible to imagine replacing one's spouse with someone else, whether in thought or in deed. To do so would be adultery committed in action or in "the heart." However, if becoming "one flesh" only expresses a love for certain pleasing attributes or characteristics of the other, these can be easily recognized and desired in someone else, and often to a "more pleasing" degree. Thus, the intuition that one is only valued at the level of certain pleasing characteristics casts a permanent shadow of doubt over the relationship. Only when love reaches the level of the unrepeatability of the person is it built on a stable foundation. This foundation lasts "forever" because the value of the person points to the infinite. This is why marriage is indissoluble and why adultery is such a grave violation, because marriage is meant to be a relationship based on a love that reaches the unrepeatability of the person.

Although the text speaks only of the man's knowledge of the woman, it is clear that in becoming "one flesh" man and woman share a reciprocal knowledge of each other through the reciprocal gift of themselves. Man and woman are *given* to each other in order to be *known* by each other. They "reveal themselves to one another with *that specific depth of their own human 'I,' which precisely reveals itself also through their sex*, their masculinity and femininity" (TOB 20:4).

This reciprocal "knowledge" (which can only be freely given and received, never grasped) is so intimate and unifying that man and woman "become one single subject, as it were, of that act and that experience, although they remain two really distinct subjects in this unity" (TOB 20:4). Biblical knowledge, then, speaks of unity-in-distinction, a two in oneness, or, in John Paul's personalist language, an "inter-subjectivity." In this unity neither person is lost or absorbed in the other, but discovers his or her true self through the sincere gift of self, that is, through the experience of *knowing* the other and *being known* by the other.

> ■   This gives us an accurate test of authentic love: In giving yourself to another, do you become more yourself or less yourself? Do you discover your true self, or do you feel absorbed by the other, lost in the other? True love always leads to self-discovery, never self-abasement. We see this reality of perfect unity and perfect distinction preeminently in the Trinity, the ultimate model of all love. Each Person of the Trinity is unique, unrepeatable, and distinct from the others. Yet each "is" himself in virtue of his relation to the others, that is, in virtue of the eternal mystery of self-giving and communion at the heart of the trinitarian life.[59]

In view of this "knowledge," the Pope says that their conjugal union contains a new, and in a way, a definitive discovery of the meaning of the human body. The knowledge man gained of himself through naming the animals (i.e., he differed from the animals, he was a person called to love, he had self-awareness and self-determination), comes to its fulfillment in his knowledge of woman. "The knowledge that stood at the basis of man's original solitude stands now at the basis of this unity" (TOB 21:1). Since everyone must pass from solitude to unity through the sincere gift of self, John Paul can say: "All human beings find themselves in their own way in that biblical 'knowledge'" (TOB 21:3). He adds "in their own way," because even if the one flesh union of marriage is the primary way, it is not the only way to enter into that

---

59. See *CCC*, nos. 254–55, 689.

biblical knowledge. Christ will call some men and women to forego sexual union "for the sake of the kingdom" (Mt 19:12).

Knowledge Leads to "a Third": Fatherhood and Motherhood

As we read in Genesis 4:1, man and woman also come to know each other in the "third," which springs from them both. Eve conceived and bore a son "with the help of the LORD." John Paul observes that fatherhood and motherhood manifest and completely reveal the mystery of human sexuality. Joining in "one flesh" always involves a particular consciousness of the meaning of the human body, bound up with fertility and procreation. In turn, the human power to generate new life—even if human generation remains radically "other"—is indissolubly bound up with the mystery of eternal generation in the Trinity. Through the mystery of procreation the embrace of man and woman is most clearly seen also as the embrace of God and man. John Paul says elsewhere that through their biblical "knowledge" man and woman share "in the great mystery of eternal generation. The spouses share in the creative power of God!"[60]

Fatherhood and motherhood point in some sense to the crowning of all that John Paul has said about the mystery of man and woman as persons made in the divine image. Recall that in discussing how man and woman image God in and through their communion, John Paul specifically stated that on "all this, right from the beginning, the blessing of fruitfulness descended, linked with human procreation" (TOB 9:3). Now the Pope says that every time a man and a woman join in that communion of persons that makes them "one flesh," thereby opening themselves to the "blessing of fertility," it "confirms and renews the existence of man as image of God" (TOB 21:7).

◼ With good reason, John Paul never defines *how* the fruitful communion of man and woman images the Trinity in terms of who might represent whom. While it may be a legitimate question for speculative theology, lining up spouses and their offspring with specific persons of the Trinity must be approached cautiously lest

---

60. *Mulieris Dignitatem*, 18 (see also 8).

we move too continuously from the gendered creature to the Uncreated (and un-gendered) God. Furthermore, the Trinity has not revealed itself as Husband, Wife, and Child, but as Father, Son, and Holy Spirit. This obviously has great import.[61]

Although hereditary sinfulness deprives man of God's likeness, he remains in God's image.[62] Thus, every time man and woman conceive a child "with the help of the LORD," they reproduce another image of God. The divine image constitutes a basis of "continuity and unity" between original man and historical man. Furthermore, man and woman not only reproduce another image of God, they also reproduce their own living image. They again recognize themselves, their own humanity, in the birth of "the third." With these profound reflections, John Paul concludes that the "words of Genesis that bear witness to the first birth of man on earth contain, at the same time, everything that one can and should say about the dignity of human generation" (TOB 21:7). As the Pope observes, within this mystery the Creator accords a particular dignity to the woman.

Eulogy of Femininity

John Paul was a man who loved woman with a purity as close to the beginning as it seems possible to reach in this life. It can even be said in light of the above analysis that he was a man who *knew* woman (in a celibate way, of course). He knew her distinctive beauty and dignity, and he stood in awe of the mystery of God's creative love revealed in her.

The Holy Father does not intend merely to state the obvious when he writes, "Woman's constitution differs from that of man" (TOB 21:3). He believes it is of great significance, and of particular credit to woman, that God has chosen her body to be the place of conception, the shrine of new life. "The whole exterior constitution of woman's body, its particular look," the Pope says, having "the power of a perennial attraction" that leads man to desire to unite with her, *"are in strict union with motherhood"* (TOB 21:5). Since the body reveals the person, John Paul believes that

---

61. See *CCC*, nos. 42, 239, 370, 2779.
62. See *CCC*, nos. 705, 2566.

this speaks volumes, not only about feminine biology but also about the dignity and nature of woman as a person. This is why he takes special care to note that "the Bible (and the liturgy following it) honors and praises throughout the centuries 'the womb that bore you and the breasts from which you sucked milk' (Lk 11:27). These words," he continues, "are a eulogy of motherhood, of femininity, of the feminine body in its typical expression of creative love" (TOB 21:5).

In her joyous proclamation, "I have gotten a man with the help of the LORD," woman expresses the whole theological depth of the function of begetting and procreating. Furthermore, in giving birth the first woman is fully aware of the mystery of creation—of everything we have been discussing about man's "beginning"—which is renewed in human generation. Yes, according to the Holy Father, the entire mystery, dignity, goodness, vocation, and destiny of man as revealed in Genesis is reproduced in some sense every time a child is conceived under the heart of a woman.

Attack on Creative Love and the Perspective of Redemption

This sheds a bright light on why, from the very beginning, Satan's enmity is aimed at "the woman" and her "offspring"—that is, her ability to bear new life: "The LORD God said to the serpent, '...I will put enmity between you and the woman, and between your offspring and hers; he shall crush your head, and you shall bruise his heel'" (Gen 3:14–15). John Paul reminded us of these words—the "Protoevangelium," or first announcement of the Gospel—right at the beginning of his catechesis. He said with these words "we witness the moment in which man, male and female...begins to live *in the theological perspective of redemption*.... We cannot forget this perspective as we follow the words of Christ...[back] to the 'beginning'" (TOB 4:3).

It is profoundly significant that both the reality of Satan's "enmity" and the reality of redemption focus on human fertility, more specifically, on woman's ability to bear offspring. Put another way, both man's sin and man's redemption focus on "*matri*mony," which literally means "the state of motherhood." As John Paul says, "Sin and death have entered into man's history *in some way through the very heart of that unity that had from the 'beginning' been formed by man and woman, created and called to become 'one flesh' (Gen 2:24)*" (TOB 20:1). We quoted this statement previously in the context of discussing the serpent's scheme to make the symbolic diabolic. Satan aims to alienate man from the life-giving communion of the Trinity. As we have learned, the original unity of the sexes was to be a sign that would "effectively transmit" the Trinity's inner life to them. So Satan attacks *"through the very heart of that unity that had from the 'beginning' been formed by man and woman,* created and called to become 'one flesh.'"

If Satan can convince man to distort this "primordial sacrament" (i.e., matrimony), it will no longer effectively communicate God's life and love. The union of man and woman, if distorted, could even become a *countersign* mocking God's life and love. In such a case the symbolic would become diabolic. In other words, what was meant to unite God and man (and man and woman) would instead divide them. We already see the importance of the first chapters of Genesis for a proper understanding of the encyclical *Humanae Vitae.* For contraception is a specific attempt to defraud that biblical knowledge of its potential to generate a "third." As such, contraception falsifies creative love and attacks the authentic meaning of matrimony.

The fact that after sin, spousal "knowledge" leads to "generation" demonstrates, already, that the promised redemption is unfolding. It is precisely the woman's "offspring" who will "crush the serpent's head," bringing victory over sin and death.

The Knowledge-Generation Cycle: Life Refuses to Surrender

Knowledge always precedes generation and remains intimately linked with it. The rich significance of the word "knowledge" indicates that "the third" who springs from their union is also "known" as a person who shares the same humanity as his parents. Bestowing the name "man" on the child ("I have gotten a man"), then, greatly differs from the experience of naming the animals. They *know* what the name "man" expresses: this "third" is "bone of their bones and flesh of their flesh" (see TOB 22:3). He is a body that expresses a *person.* In this way John Paul says that the biblical cycle of "knowledge-generation" comes to a close.

In the experience of this *knowledge* in which they give rise to another person, man and woman "are 'carried off' together," the Pope says, by "the very humanity which they...want to express anew" (TOB 22:3). They wish to express their humanity again (in "the third") in order to affirm the goodness of life and to overcome, in some sense, the inevitable prospect of death that now is part of their horizon due to sin. Man's awareness of the spousal and generative meanings of his body comes into contact right from the beginning with awareness of death. Yet John Paul says that the fact that "Adam knew his wife and she conceived and bore" (Gen 4:1) is like "a seal impressed in the original revelation of the body at the very 'beginning' of man's history on the earth" (TOB 22:5). This seal ensures that original sin has not destroyed God's original plan of life-giving communion.

In fact, as John Paul proclaims, "there always returns the 'knowledge-generation' cycle, in which life struggles always anew with the inexorable prospect of death, and always overcomes it" (TOB 22:7). What words of hope! We must all reckon with the reality of death. But man and woman's "knowledge" manifests the good news that life *refuses to surrender.* "*It is as if the reason for this unyielding strength of life, which shows itself in 'generation,' were always the same 'knowledge,'* with which man passes beyond the solitude of his own being, and even more, decides anew to affirm this being in an 'other'" (TOB 22:7). Man and woman affirm the goodness of life in their openness and readiness to beget a man with the help of the Lord (see Gen 4:1). John Paul continues:

> Despite all the experiences of his own life, despite the sufferings, the disappointments in himself, his sinfulness, and, finally, despite the inevitable prospect of death, man always continues, however, to place "knowledge" at the "beginning" of "generation"; in this way he seems to participate in that first "vision" of God himself: God, the Creator, "saw everything...and indeed, it was good." And always anew he confirms the truth of these words. (TOB 22:7)

Historical man will find it difficult to confirm the truth of these words. Due to sin and the difficulties now inherent in human life, men and women often teeter between hope and despondency, between the "risk" of communion and the "safety" of solitude, between affirming life's goodness and cursing existence. This can bring them to prefer not to bring an "other" into the world. It can even lead to them to consider the original blessing of fertility (see Gen 1:28) as a curse.

Yet the man and woman who take that risk of love, surrendering their bodies to each other in *knowledge* and potential *generation*, stare death in the face and boldly proclaim: "*Life is good.* Communion is better than solitude. Life is better than death. Life, in fact, conquers death. Where, O death, is your victory? Where, O death, is your sting?" (see 1 Cor 15:55). Everyone must take his stand. Everyone must choose his posture. This will have far-reaching implications, particularly for John Paul's reflections on *Humanae Vitae.*

Conclusion of Chapter 1

Christ's Words Remain Pertinent Today

Modern men and women have many pressing questions about the nature of marriage, much like the Pharisees who approached Jesus to ask him about divorce. Although many current problems were unknown to Christ's contemporaries, John Paul believes that Christ's response remains just as pertinent today as it was two thousand years ago. In the last century, man has gained tremendous knowledge about his body from a scientific point of view. However, such knowledge has led man in many cases to reduce the human body to the level of an "object" to be manipulated. This greatly differs from the biblical "knowledge" that recognizes the human body as the revelation of a personal subject with inviolable dignity.

By pointing to the beginning, Christ wishes that "man, male and female, be such a subject, that is, a subject who decides his own actions in the light of the integral truth about himself" (TOB 23:3). John Paul seeks to help modern man do this through the TOB—to help us understand fully who we are so that we can decide on our actions in that light. To move beyond partial perspectives of man's being and construct a "total vision of man," we *must* return to the "beginning." There we find the first inheritance of every human being in the world. There we find the first proclamation "of human identity according to the revealed word, the first source of the certainty of...[man's] vocation as a person created in the image of God himself" (TOB 23:1).

The archaic text of Genesis is completely "pre-scientific." Yet in the simplest and fullest way it reveals the truth so important for the "total vision of man." It is the truth of human subjectivity and "inter-subjectivity," that is, the communion between persons. The objective science of human sexuality is not inherently bad, and, as John Paul notes, we need not deprive ourselves of its results. Nonetheless, if a "science of the body" is to serve man, it must be informed by a "theology of the body." Without this, John Paul insists that no adequate answer can be given to contemporary questions connected with marriage and procreation.

Modern man may find the idea of constructing a theology of the body inappropriate. However, as John Paul points out, it should not surprise anyone familiar with the Incarnation. "Through the fact that the Word of God become flesh, the body entered theology," the Pope muses, "through the main door" (TOB 23:4). John Paul also adds that the Incarnation became the definitive source of the sacramentality of marriage.

Questions of Human Life

Questions about the body, marriage, and human sexuality, therefore, have a distinct religious and theological quality. They "are not only the questions of the sciences, but even more so the questions of human life" (TOB 23:5). We can observe here the title of Pope Paul VI's watershed encyclical, *Of Human Life* (*Humanae Vitae*). The problems of marriage and procreation that Paul VI addressed in this encyclical take us to the heart of the mystery *of human life*. Here John Paul II recalls that Paul VI himself spoke of the need for a "total vision of man" if we are to understand the teaching of *Humanae Vitae*. Herein lies one of John Paul's main inspirations for developing the TOB.

So many men and women seek in marriage the way to salvation and holiness. If they are to find the fulfillment for which they are looking, John Paul maintains that they "are called first of all to make of this 'theology of the body,'...the content of their lives and behavior. In fact, on the road of this vocation, how indispensable is a deepened consciousness of the meaning of the body in its masculinity and femininity!" This is so, the Holy Father continues, "given that all that forms the content of the life of the spouses must always find its full and personal dimension in shared life, in behavior, in feelings! And this all the more against the background of a civilization that remains under the pressure of a materialistic and utilitarian way of thinking" (TOB 23:5).

By pointing back to "the beginning," Christ wishes to tell men and women of every age that true fulfillment in the relationship of the sexes comes only through the "redemption of the body." This means regaining *the true meaning of the human body* that reveals both the dignity of the person and the call to communion. Only by understanding this personal and communal meaning of the body revealed "in the beginning" can we even begin to see the serious privation of a materialistic and utilitarian view. However, to give an exhaustive answer to our questions about marriage and sexuality, we must not stop only at man's beginning. We must also look at his history and ultimate destiny. We must look to Christ's words about lust in the "heart" (Mt 5:8) and about marriage in the resurrection (Mt 22:24–30). These words will form the basis of John Paul's subsequent reflections, first on historical man and then on eschatological man.

CHRIST APPEALS TO THE "BEGINNING"—IN REVIEW

1. Christ's discussion with the Pharisees about marriage is John Paul's point of departure. Moses allowed divorce because of men and women's "hardness of heart." But in the beginning "it was not so." Thus, we must look to God's original plan for marriage as the model and norm of every relationship in which man and woman become "one flesh."

2. The Elohist account presents the seven-day story of creation. It defines man objectively in the dimensions of being and existence as the only creature of the visible world made in God's image and likeness. The Yahwist account presents the subjective complement to the Elohist account. It penetrates man's psychology and defines him in the subjective dimensions of consciousness and experience.

3. The "redemption of the body" won for us by Christ guarantees the continuity between original man and historical man. The man who lives with the inheritance of sin cannot return to innocence, but neither is he entirely cut off from his origins. Each person, in fact, experiences a certain "echo" of original innocence. Christ calls us back to "the beginning" with the living hope that his gift of redemption has the power to restore what was lost.

4. Human experience is an indispensable element in constructing a theology of the body. John Paul examines three fundamental human experiences: *original solitude, original unity*, and *original nakedness*. He attempts to "reconstruct" these experiences of man's "prehistory" not so much to determine precisely who man and woman were "then," but to help us better understand who we are now—more so, who we are meant to be.

5. Original solitude is based on the words of Genesis: "It is not good that the man should be alone." This solitude means not only that man is "alone" without woman (and woman without man) but also that man is "alone" in the visible world as a *person*. Adam discovers in naming the animals that he alone is aware of himself and is able to determine his own actions.

6. In his solitude man discovers that he is a "partner of the Absolute" and a "subject of the covenant" with God. This realization hinges on man's freedom, which is most fully revealed in the alternative between death and immortality. In short, solitude determines that man stands alone in the visible world as a creature made in God's image.

7. Man's spiritual solitude is discovered through the experience of his body. The body expresses the person. The body expresses man's difference from the animals, his subjectivity, and his call to communion with God and with an "other" like himself.

8. Genesis describes the creation of woman in archaic, metaphorical, and "mythical" language. Adam's deep sleep indicates his return to non-being and God's "re-creation" of man as male and female. Woman's creation from Adam's rib indicates that male and female share the same humanity. They are "bone of the same bone and flesh of the same flesh."

9. The experience of original unity is based primarily on the key text of Genesis 2:24—the two become "one flesh." Original unity overcomes original solitude (in the sense of being alone without the opposite sex) and affirms everything about man's solitude (in the sense that he is a personal subject made in the divine image). The union of the sexes in "one flesh," then, is worlds apart from the copulation of animals.

10. John Paul defines the original unity as a "communion of persons" (*communio personarum*). He brings a dramatic development of thinking to the Church by positing the divine image not only in man's humanity as an individual but also in the communion of persons that man and woman form right from the beginning. The marital embrace itself is an icon in some sense of the inner life of the Trinity.

11. For John Paul, relationality enters the definition of the person. To be a person means "being subject" and "being in relationship." The beauty and mystery of sexual difference fundamentally reveals this relationality.

12. By joining in "one flesh" according to God's original plan, man and woman rediscover their "original virginal value." The virginity of "the beginning" cannot simply be equated with an absence of sexual union but is more properly understood as the original integrity of body and soul. The grace of the sacrament of marriage allows husbands and wives progressively to rediscover the original integrity of the "one flesh" union.

13. Original nakedness is the experience of nakedness without shame. As the clearest subjective indication of their creation in the divine image, it is the key to understanding biblical anthropology. Original nakedness indicates a full consciousness of the original meaning of the body as the revelation of the person. It indicates a pure and transparent spiritual communication between the man and the woman "prior" to communication in the flesh.

14. The tranquility of original nakedness derives from "the peace of the interior gaze," which apprehends "the original good of God's vision" in the nakedness of the other. In God's declaration of the goodness of creation, we recognize that the motive of creation itself is love. Love and self-giving are synonymous. God initiates his own self-gift by creating us in his image. Man receives this gift and reciprocates it. In this way, the covenant of love between God and man is itself a relationship akin to spousal self-giving and communion.

15. Man and woman recapitulate the gift of God in creation by becoming a gift to each other. This call to be gift is inscribed in the

spousal meaning of their bodies. The spousal meaning of the body is the body's capacity to express love, that love in which the person becomes a gift and thus fulfills the very meaning of his being and existence.

16. Before sin, man and woman did not experience sexual desire as something with a selfish will of its own. Rather, they experienced it as the desire to make a sincere gift of self—to love as God loves. The freedom of the gift indicates that man and woman respected one another as persons who were created for their "own sakes." They could not grasp or possess one another. If they were to live in communion, they had to bestow the gift of self freely.

17. The spousal meaning of the body reveals both the capacity to become a gift to the other and the capacity for the deep affirmation of the other. Affirmation of the person means receiving the gift the other offers and respecting the other as a person created for his (her) own sake.

18. Man can never avoid the spousal meaning of his body. It is the fundamental element of his existence in the world. Even if the spousal meaning of the body undergoes many distortions because of sin, it will always remain at the deepest level of the person.

19. Man's fullest and deepest dimension is determined by the irradiation of grace, that is, by God's gratuitous love poured into the human heart. Grace is participation in the interior life of God himself, in his holiness. The original unity of the sexes was itself a participation in God's life and holiness. Grace enabled them to be naked without shame, which attests to the sincerity of the reciprocal gift of self.

20. Original happiness refers to the original beatifying experience of man and woman's communion with God and with each other. Original happiness is being rooted in love. It speaks of man's emergence from love and his participation in love. It is manifested by the experience of original nakedness.

21. Sexual complementarity allows man and woman to live as "gift." Man, having first received woman as a gift from God, is disposed to initiate the gift of himself to the woman. In turn, the woman is disposed to receive his gift. But the giving and receiving interpene-

trate so that the giving becomes receiving and the receiving becomes giving. This is an ever deepening exchange that in some way reflects the eternal exchange within the Trinity.

22. The ethos of the gift enables us to penetrate the subjectivity of man. It refers to the inner orientation of the first man and woman toward the objective good. They did not need an external ethic enforcing the law of the gift. They desired nothing else. God's law was not imposed from "outside" but welled up from "within" each of them.

23. Through the visibility of masculinity and femininity and their call to communion, the invisibility of the divine mystery of love and communion is made visible. In this way we understand marriage as the "primordial sacrament." The body, in fact, and it alone is capable of making visible the invisible mystery of God. This is the mystery of truth and love in which man, male and female, really participates.

24. Original nakedness helps us understand that the primordial sacrament was efficacious; it truly communicated God's grace, his holiness, to man and woman. Holiness enabled them to be naked without shame. Holiness enabled man and woman to express themselves deeply with their bodies through the sincere gift of self.

25. "Knowledge" indicates the deepest essence of married life and synthesizes the whole depth of the original experiences of solitude, unity, and nakedness. Knowledge brings such a unity that spouses almost become the one subject of that act, while remaining two different subjects. Hence, knowledge speaks of a unity-in-plurality. Everyone finds himself, in his own way, through this biblical knowledge.

26. Knowledge leads to a "third." In her exaltation, "I have gotten a man with the help of the LORD," woman expresses the whole theological depth of procreation and begetting. The Bible and the liturgy express a eulogy of femininity by honoring and praising the womb that bore Christ and the breasts he sucked.

27. The "knowledge-generation cycle" speaks to the goodness of human life that persists and continues to assert itself despite the tragedy of sin and death. Through knowledge and procreation, life struggles with the prospect of death and always overcomes it.

28. Questions about the body, marriage, and sexuality have a distinctive religious quality. They are not only questions of science but more so they are the questions about the meaning of human life. This is why we must reconstruct God's original plan for the body according to the words of Christ.

CHAPTER 2

Christ Appeals to the Human Heart

[Cycle 2—Historical Man]

HISTORICAL MAN IS THE SECOND of the three cycles that establish John Paul's "adequate anthropology." In forty general audiences delivered between April 16, 1980, and May 6, 1981 (TOB 24–63), John Paul reflects on the reality of embodiment and erotic desire as man and woman experience them in history affected by sin. As we venture into these reflections, let us "be not afraid" to face honestly how far we have fallen from God's original plan. For only if we first realize how bad the "bad news" is, do we then realize how good the "good news" is. The "good news" is that historical man is not merely the man influenced by sin. He is also redeemed in Christ, who gives us *real power* to regain progressively—if arduously—what was lost. We must keep this in the forefront of our minds as we reflect on the effects of sin on our experience of the body and sexuality. Without this hope, we will be tempted to despair, or to minimize and even normalize sin.

Once again the Pope bases his reflection on Christ's own words, this time from the Sermon on the Mount regarding lust and adultery committed "in the heart." Many throughout history have seen in Christ's admonition a universal prohibition against eros. Yet John Paul demonstrates that Christ's words do not condemn the heart. Instead, they call us to reflect on the original meaning of sexual desire, our fall from it, and how Christ restores God's original plan through the "redemption of the body." If men and women have been driving with flat tires, Christ's words invite them to open their hearts to life "according to the Holy Spirit" so that they might come to experience eros according to its original "inflated" meaning.

Christ's words appeal to that "echo" in each of us of God's original plan. The more we tap into that echo, the more we realize that lust not only radically betrays authentic eros; it also radically betrays our authentic humanity. As the primordial plagiarization of love, lust can never satisfy our desire for communion with an "other." Love and all life together in truth requires liberation from lust. Faced with the incessant and alluring pull of lust, man seems helpless to overcome it. With only his own resources, he is helpless. But the good news of the Gospel is that "Jesus came to restore creation to the purity of its origins." "His grace restores what sin had damaged in us."[1]

Man cannot return to the state of original innocence. The redemption he experiences in Christ is more aptly a kind of participation in the future resurrection. Historical man—that is, fallen and redeemed man—lives in the constant tension of "already, but not yet."[2] Regarding the "not yet," historical man will always battle with concupiscence. Regarding the "already," John Paul insists that historical man can experience a "real and deep victory" in this battle. Since Christ rose from the dead *within history*, we can affirm with Wojtyla that

> the "redemption of the body" is already an aspect of human life on earth. This redemption is not just an eschatological reality but a historical one as well. It shapes the history of the salvation of concrete living people, and, in a special way, of those people who in the sacrament of matrimony are called as spouses and parents to become "one flesh" (Gen 2:24), in keeping with the intent of the Creator announced to the first parents before the fall.[3]

This is the "good news" of Christ's words in the Sermon on the Mount. They announce that Christ came to liberate eros from the distortion of lust. As the Pope says in *Veritatis Splendor*, Christ's words are "an invitation to a pure way of looking at others, capable of respecting the spousal meaning of the body."[4] So John Paul asks: "Should we *fear* the severity of these words or rather *have confidence* in their salvific content, in their power?" (TOB 43:7).

---

1. *CCC*, nos. 1708, 2336.
2. See *CCC*, nos. 1002–4.
3. "The Family as a Community of Persons," *Person and Community*, p. 326.
4. *Veritatis Splendor*, 15.

1. In the Light of the Sermon on the Mount

In the Sermon on the Mount, Christ says, "You have heard that it was said, 'You shall not commit adultery.' But I say to you that everyone who looks at a woman lustfully has already committed adultery with her in his heart" (Mt 5:27–28). John Paul points out that this is one of those passages that *fundamentally revises the way of understanding and of carrying out the moral law of the Old Covenant.* Like Christ's words that pointed us to the "beginning," John Paul says that the Lord's words about lust are pregnant with theological, anthropological, and ethical content (see TOB 44:1). They have "a key significance for the theology of the body" (TOB 24:1) and an "explicitly normative character" (TOB 24:2). These words, then, are not only directed toward those who heard the Sermon on the Mount with their own ears. They are also directed toward every human being (male and female) of the past and of the future.

John Paul observes that adultery "in the heart" concerns a desire for sexual knowledge of someone who is not one's spouse. Although Christ's words apply just as much to women as they do to men, for the sake of example Christ speaks of the lust of a man toward a woman and describes it as adultery committed "in the heart." As an interior act, this desire is expressed through the sense of sight, with mere looks. John Paul cites the case of David looking at Bathsheba as a prime example (see 2 Sam 11:2). How are we to understand this "new level" of the traditional commandment against adultery? In other words, why does Christ posit the immorality of adultery first "in the heart" before and even without an act of adultery being physically committed?

Ethical Meaning: The New Ethos

Christ summarizes his teaching in the Sermon on the Mount by saying, "You, therefore, must be perfect, as your heavenly Father is perfect" (Mt 5:48). As the *Catechism* observes, "It is impossible to keep the Lord's commandment by imitating the divine model from outside; there has to be a vital participation, coming from the depths of the heart, in the holiness and the mercy and the love of our God."[5] Christ's

---

5. *CCC*, no. 2842.

words about committing sin "in the heart" call us to enter this "vital participation" in God's holiness, in his mystery of love and self-giving. They inaugurate the fulfillment of God's promise to Israel: "I will make a new covenant with the house of Israel.... I will put my law within them, and I will write it upon their hearts" (Jer 31:31–33). [6]

Living a mature moral life as a Christian does not mean begrudgingly submitting oneself to an external code of ethics. Scripture and our own experience attest that it is possible to live in strict accordance with laws yet never grow in holiness. It is called "legalism" or "moralism." In such cases, people keep to legalistic observance of the formula, but the spirit of the law does not abound in their hearts. Christ calls us to something *very* different. He appeals to the *interior* man.[7] "First cleanse the inside of the cup and of the plate, that the outside also may be clean" (Mt 23:26). With these words Christ proclaims the "new ethos" of redemption. *Ethos* refers to a person's inner world of values—what attracts and what repulses him. It "embraces in its content the complex spheres of good and evil that depend on the human will and are subject to the laws of conscience and of the sensibility of the human 'heart'" (TOB 47:1). *Ethos*, therefore, can be defined as "the inner form, the soul, as it were, of human morality.... To reach it, it is not enough to stop 'on the surface' of human actions, but one must penetrate precisely the interior" (TOB 24:3). We must penetrate the human "heart" where moral value is connected with the dynamic process of man's *interior* life.

In the Sermon on the Mount, Christ speaks "about a human interpretation of the law that cancels...*the right meaning of good and evil specifically* willed by the Divine Legislator" (TOB 35:1). The typical interpretation of the law came to be "*marked by an objectivism*" that was "not concerned directly with the order of the 'heart'" (TOB 36:3). In fact, a faulty interpretation of the law had led the Israelites, in many cases, to compromise with lust (see TOB 36:2). Christ appeals to the interior man (ethos) in order to recover the original meaning of the law (ethic). In effect, Christ's teaching in the Sermon on the Mount expresses this: "You have heard the objective law and interpreted it *externally*. Now I tell you the subjective meaning of the law—what it

---

6. See *CCC*, no. 1965.
7. See *CCC*, nos. 1430–32.

calls you to *internally.*" In other words, "You have heard the *ethic.* Now I speak to you of its proper *ethos.*"[8]

■ Here we clearly see John Paul, as he himself states, drawing from the phenomenology of Max Scheler. For morality to be "real" to man, it must be connected with an experienced value. In emphasizing (or perhaps overemphasizing) this valid point, however, Scheler failed to recognize man's responsibility toward objective moral values when his perceptions of value are misguided. In Christ's words in the Sermon on the Mount, we see the call to *purity* in one's subjective values. For when man's heart is purified, his subjective values correspond to what is objectively true, good, and beautiful. But even the impure man has a duty toward the objective good. If Kant's ethical system was based on man's duty to the moral norm and Scheler's was based on man's experience of value, Wojtyla/John Paul II wants to draw the proper balance between duty and the experience of value. This proper balance is already visible in the first precept of the natural law: "the good is to be pursued and done." This precept contains both man's duty to the moral norm and motivates man by the good, by the experience of value.[9]

Fulfillment of the Law

This emphasis on the subjective dimension of "ethos" does not do away with objective norms. On the contrary, the *new ethos* "makes us, at one and the same time, enter the depth *of the norm itself*" (TOB 24:3) from the perspective of the personal subject and his *experience* of morality. As Christ himself said, "Think not that I have come to abolish the law and the prophets. I have come not to abolish them, *but to fulfill*

---

8. An organic relationship remains between the Law and the teaching of Christ that must be maintained, while any sharp contrast between them is to be avoided. The Christian ethos is certainly "new," but there is also a continuity with the Old Testament understood as "fulfillment." See Vatican Commission for Religious Relations with the Jews, *Notes on the Correct Way to Present the Jews and Judaism in Preaching and Catechesis in the Roman Catholic Church.* See also Pontifical Biblical Commission, *The Jewish People and Their Sacred Scriptures in the Christian Bible* (Boston: Pauline Books & Media, 2002).

9. My thanks to Dr. Michael Waldstein for helping me recognize and articulate this final point.

them" (Mt 5:17). "According to Christian tradition, the Law is holy, spiritual, and good, yet still imperfect. Like a tutor, it shows what must be done, but does not of itself give the strength, the grace of the Spirit, to fulfill it."[10] In this sense, the law is sterile. By itself it cannot give man life. But Christ came that we might have life and have it *to the full* (see Jn 10:10). He came to fill-us-full with the Spirit of life and love that enables us not only to meet the law's demands but also to *fulfill* the law. Thus, Jesus' "message is new but it does not destroy what went before; it leads what went before to its fullest potential."[11]

Man fulfills the law through "the 'superabounding' of justice" in the human heart that reorients the person's "interior perception of values" (TOB 24:3). This interior conversion creates a "subjective vitality"—that is, a heart *alive* (through the indwelling of the Holy Spirit) with the truth about what is good, what is just, what is holy. In effect, Christ is saying in the Sermon on the Mount: "You have heard the commandment not to commit adultery, but the problem is you *desire* to commit adultery." In turn, "Christ's faithful [are those who] 'have crucified the flesh with its passions and desires' (Gal 5:24); they are led by the Spirit and follow his desires."[12] When a person is led by the Spirit in this way, the law plays a different role in his life. It no longer constrains him but liberates him. In other words, such a person no longer needs an objective norm constraining him (or her) from committing adultery. Led by the Spirit, he *does not desire* to commit adultery. Lust, even if he is still capable of it, no longer holds sway in his heart.

When a person experiences this "subjective vitality," not only is his will set on what is true, good, and beautiful, but his "upright will orders the movements of the senses...to the good and to beatitude"[13] as well. For such a person, avoiding adultery no longer means that the will has to overpower the desires of the heart. The very idea of committing adultery repels the senses and the inner movements of the heart. Such a person understands, as the *Catechism* teaches, that the "perfection of the moral good consists in man's being moved to the good not only by his will but also by his 'heart.'"[14]

---

10. *CCC*, no. 1963.
11. John Paul II, "Homily on the Mount of Beatitudes, Galilee," March 24, 2000.
12. *CCC*, no. 2555.
13. *CCC*, no. 1768.
14. *CCC*, no. 1775.

Certainly the road to such perfection is long and arduous. Even the holiest of men and women will always retain a remnant of their disordered passions (concupiscence[15]) on this side of the resurrection. Nonetheless a person *alive* with the truth about good is not fooled by the devil's plagiarizations. He sees them for what they are—the twisting of what God created to be true, good, and beautiful. And when we see the true, good, and beautiful with our own eyes, the counterfeits lose their allure. At this point the moral norm is not external. It is not "imposed" from without but wells up from within. This is "a living morality," the Pope says (TOB 24:3). It is a *new ethos* in which the subjective desires of the heart come into harmony with the objective norm. Such a lived understanding of morality is essential if man is to discover himself. As John Paul affirms, this is the "morality in which the very meaning of being human is realized" (TOB 24:3).

■   John Paul repeatedly stresses that this is a "new" ethos with regard to the Old Testament (see TOB 49:1). Of course this "living morality" that abounds in man's heart through the Holy Spirit was not entirely inaccessible to the people of the Old Covenant. Nor, as one can plainly recognize, is it "automatic" for those baptized into the New Covenant. As St. Thomas observed, "There were...under the regime of the Old Covenant, people who possessed the...grace of the Holy Spirit.... Conversely, there exist carnal men under the New Covenant, still distanced from the perfection of the New Law."[16] When Christians remain distanced from the "new ethos," they tend either toward rigoristic "angelism" or permissive "animalism." While the "animalist" in particular might deny it, both poles, in fact, are working from the same faulty, rule-obsessed morality. For rigorously adhering to the law and rebelliously breaking it are two sides of the same legalistic coin. The "new ethos" that Christ establishes—when it is truly lived—contains the truths that both of these poles are seeking to protect: freedom from the law on the one hand and the fulfillment of the law on the other. If you are led by the Holy Spirit, you are not under the law. You are free with the freedom for which Christ has set you free. But this freedom is

15. See *CCC*, no. 2515.
16. Cited in *CCC*, no. 1964.

not license. This freedom desires the good, only chooses the good, and thus fulfills the law (see Gal 5).

Anthropological Meaning: Penetrating the "Heart"

Christ's words about adultery committed "in the heart" indicate something much more profound than one might first think. They certainly have an ethical meaning inviting us to the "living morality" of a new ethos. But even more, through this ethical meaning, Christ's words also have a profound *anthropological meaning* and invite us to reclaim the full truth of our humanity.

If we "follow the footsteps" of Christ's statement, so to speak, we will arrive again at the beginning—at that "very good" beginning when man and woman experienced an erotic desire permeated with divine love. Here we rediscover those "perennial meanings" of our humanity "that constitute an 'adequate' anthropology" (TOB 25:2). In turn, we will realize how far we have fallen from God's original design. In this way we learn who historical man is, or, rather, who he has become as a result of original sin. Christ's words call us back to who man was *before* sin. They "demand, so to speak, that man enters into his full image" (TOB 25:2). Hence we can understand why the ethical and anthropological meaning of Christ's words remain in a reciprocal relationship. By understanding how we are to live (ethics), we learn who we are (anthropology). Conversely, by understanding who we are, we learn how we are to live.

We discover both the ethical meaning and the anthropological meaning of Christ's words in his appeal to the inner man, to the "heart." The heart is not only "the seat of moral personality."[17] John Paul says that the "heart" is "in some way the equivalent of personal subjectivity" (TOB 49:7). "*With the category of 'heart,' everyone is identified in a singular manner, even more than by name.*" Each person "is reached in that which determines him in a unique and unrepeatable way." Through the "heart," man "is defined in his humanity 'from within'" (TOB 34:4). Emotions, thoughts, and affections originate in the heart. The heart, then, is where we know and experience the true meaning of the body, or, because of the hardness of our hearts, fail to do

---

17. *CCC*, no. 2517.

so. As John Paul says, "The 'heart' has become a battlefield between love and concupiscence. The more concupiscence dominates the heart, the less the heart experiences the spousal meaning of the body" (TOB 32:3).

2. The Man of Concupiscence

The truth about "historical man" is revealed, according to John Paul, by this concise statement from the Apostle John: "For all that is in the world, the lust [or concupiscence] of the flesh and the lust of the eyes and the pride of life, is not of the Father, but is of the world. And the world passes away, and the lust of it; but he who does the will of God abides forever" (1 Jn 2:16–17). This is a key statement for the entire theology of the body. St. John does not actually define concupiscence, but he does speak of its origin. The threefold concupiscence comes not "from the Father" but "from the world." John Paul II carefully points out that "the world" the apostle speaks of is not the world the Father created, which is always "very good" (Gen 1:31). It is rather the world man deformed by casting the love of the Father from his heart.

John Paul observes that there are a great many stories, sentences, and words in the Bible that confirm the truth

> that "historical" man carries in himself the inheritance of original sin; nevertheless the words of Christ spoken in the Sermon on the Mount seem to have—in all their concise formulation—a particularly rich eloquence.... To clarify the statements about concupiscence, one must grasp the biblical meaning of concupiscence itself—of the threefold concupiscence—and mainly of that of the flesh. One then comes to understand little by little why Jesus defines that concupiscence (precisely, "looking...[with lust]") as "adultery committed in the heart." (TOB 58:3)

In order to understand what concupiscence is, or rather, who the "man of concupiscence" is, "we must return once more to Genesis [and] *linger once more 'on the threshold'* of the revelation of 'historical' man." The mystery of sin marks the beginnings of human history. But this also marks the beginning of salvation history. Returning to Genesis "is all the more necessary, inasmuch as this threshold of the history of salvation proves to be at the same time a threshold of authentic human experiences" (TOB 26:2). Through these experiences we establish an "adequate anthropology," including the experience of original sin. Original sin is certainly a mystery, but this does not mean it is abstract. There is perhaps no mystery of our faith confirmed more by human experience than the reality of sin. And, as John Paul will masterfully demonstrate, we can even reconstruct Adam and Eve's experience of original sin through a phenomenological examination of the Yahwist text.

A. THE MEANING OF ORIGINAL SHAME

Casting Doubt on the Gift

How did the "man of concupiscence" take the place of the "man of original innocence"? Without completely analyzing the temptation and sin,[18] John Paul points to the "*key moment*" of the serpent's dialogue with the woman: "You will not die. For God knows that when you eat of it your eyes will be opened, and you will be like God, knowing good and evil" (Gen 3:4–5).

According to John Paul, this key moment "clearly implies casting doubt on the Gift and on Love, from which creation takes its origin as gift" (TOB 26:4). Man's existence, along with all of creation, was a gift of gratuitous love God gave to man. Created in the divine image and likeness, man could receive creation as a gift and reciprocate the gift of himself to God. Through this original covenant, God granted man the opportunity to participate in his very life, to be "like God" as a free gift (see pp. 99–100). This is the deepest yearning of the human heart, to be "like God," to participate in his happiness (beatitude), in God's life. But Satan wants to keep this from us. One could read the serpent's temptation like this: "God does not love you. He does not want you to be like him, nor does he intend to make a *gift* of his life to you. In fact, he is specifically withholding it from you by forbidding you to eat from this tree. If you want life (happiness), if you want to be 'like God,' then you have to reach out and grasp it for yourself because God won't give it to you."

---

18. See *CCC*, nos. 396–401.

Man determines his fundamental disposition in life with one of two irreconcilable postures: *receptivity* or *grasping*.[19] The posture each person assumes depends upon his concept of God. If God is love and the giver of all good things, then to attain the happiness we long for, we only need to *receive*. If God is a tyrant, then we will see him as a threat to our happiness, turn from our natural posture of receptivity, and seek to *grasp* life for ourselves. Certainly man also has the task of imaging God by taking the initiative and developing the world ("till [the earth] and keep it," Gen 2:15). But, as a creature, man becomes "like God" only by first *receiving* this likeness *from* God. In other words, as a creature, man's proper initiative always proceeds from his receptivity to the gift.

As the *Catechism* explains, "Constituted in a state of holiness, man was destined to be fully 'divinized' by God in glory." Man need only open himself to receive this as a gift. "Seduced by the devil, he wanted to 'be like God,' but 'without God, before God, and not in accordance with God.'"[20] Herein lies the denial of the gift and, in turn, the denial of man's receptivity before God. Man sets himself up as the initiator of his own existence and grasps at what God desired to give him freely.

■ The tendency to question the gift and "grasp" seems built into our fallen nature, as we can observe even in little children. For example, when my son asks for a cookie for dessert, before I can even get the cookie out of the box to present it to him as a gift, what does he do? He grasps at it. So I say to him, "Thomas, you're denying the gift. If you believed in the gift, all you would need to do is hold your hands out in confidence and *receive* the cookie as a gift." When we believe in the gift and receive it as such, the natural response is to say "thank you" for the gift. The problem with man in his relationship with God is that he does not believe in the gift. So he grasps at it. "If you knew the gift of God...you would have asked him and he would have given you living water" (Jn 4:10). Not only is Christ the gift given but he is also our example: "Have

---

19. For an excellent article on the nature of sin in relation to receptivity and grasping see Jean-Pierre Baput's "The Chastity of Jesus and the Refusal to Grasp," *Communio* (Spring 1997): pp. 5–13.

20. *CCC*, no. 398.

this mind among yourselves, which was in Christ Jesus, who, though he was in the form of God, did not count equality with God a thing to be grasped" (Phil 2:5–6).

Going further, the spousal imagery of the Scriptures provides particular insight into this dynamic of original sin. It is of the bridegroom's masculine constitution to *initiate* the gift and of the bride's feminine constitution to *receive* the gift. Hence, in the spousal analogy, God is symbolically "masculine" as the Heavenly Bridegroom, and man (male and female) is symbolically "feminine" as the Bride (this spousal analogy will come to fulfillment, of course, in the relationship of Christ and the Church). Using this spousal imagery, it can be said that original sin consists in the Bride's (man's) rejection of receptivity with relation to the Bridegroom (God). Do we not perhaps see in this reality why, according to the author of Genesis, the serpent approached the woman? He wanted man to reject his receptivity to the gift. As the one who embodies the "receptivity of the gift," woman stands as the archetype of all humanity.[21]

In succumbing to Satan's grievous lie, we detect the mystery of man who turns his back on "the Father." Man questions in his heart the deepest meaning of his existence as a gift from God; he doubts that Love was the origin of creation and the covenant. Conceiving God instead as a jealous tyrant goads man to do battle against him so as not to be enslaved. Thus, man turns his back on Love, casting "the Father" out of his heart.

At this point we penetrate the meaning of that gripping statement of John Paul's quoted earlier: "*This is truly the key for interpreting reality.... Original sin, then, attempts to abolish fatherhood.*"[22] In its essence, original sin denies the Fatherhood of God, God's benevolent love that originates (i.e., "fathers") all of creation. We cannot understand who man is in creation, who he has become in history, and who he is destined to be in the eschaton—we cannot understand reality—unless we understand the mystery of God's Fatherhood *and* its denial. This is why

---

21. See *Mulieris Dignitatem*, nos. 4, 27, 30. See also Edith Stein, *Essays on Woman* (Washington, DC: ICS Publications, 1987), pp. 62–63.

22. *Crossing the Threshold of Hope*, p. 228, emphasis in original.

"Christ, *through the revelation of the mystery of the Father and his love,* fully reveals man to himself and makes his supreme calling clear."[23]

■ This "key" for interpreting reality—that original sin attempts to abolish fatherhood—gives us the "key" for understanding the importance of the prayer Christ taught us. Is not the "Our Father" the specific antidote to the original lie of the deceiver? Does it not restore the truth about God and man denied by original sin? In the face of the devil's attack on God and his love, the first man and woman should have proclaimed that God is "our Father—hallowed be his name!"[24] In the face of Satan's temptation to break away from God's reign and set their will in opposition to God's, the first man and woman should have proclaimed: "God's kingdom come. *His* will be done on earth as it is in heaven!"[25] In the face of Satan's temptation to deny the gift, they should have proclaimed: "Our Father will *give* us our daily bread. We need not grasp at it!"[26] Finally, in this intense battle with the anti-Word, had the first man and woman only cried out in faith to the Father, "Spare us from yielding to temptation and deliver us from the evil one!"[27] God would surely have saved them. Perhaps we now understand more clearly why the *Catechism* asserts that the "Lord's Prayer 'is truly the summary of the whole gospel.'"[28] By denying the Fatherhood of God through original sin, man cut himself off from the original covenant and lost sight of his own dignity and calling. Yet the "Lord's Prayer brings us into communion with the Father and with his Son, Jesus Christ. At the same time it reveals us to ourselves."[29]

By resisting the "rays of fatherhood," man almost cuts his heart off from what is "of the Father" so that all that remains in him is what is "of the world." In this moment John Paul says we are witnesses in a sense of the birth of human lust and the subsequent deconstruction of man

---

23. *Gaudium et Spes*, 22, emphasis added.
24. See *CCC*, nos. 2779–2815.
25. See *CCC*, nos. 2816–27.
26. See *CCC*, nos. 2828–37.
27. See *CCC*, nos. 2846–54.
28. *CCC*, no. 2671.
29. *CCC*, no. 2799.

and woman's humanity. Recall that man and woman realized the gift of God's love precisely through the body and the experience of original nakedness. "This is *the body: a witness* to creation as a fundamental gift, and therefore a witness *to Love as the source from which this same giving springs*" (TOB 14:4). In this experience John Paul says that the human body bore in itself an unquestionable sign of the image of God. In fact, the original experience of the body provided the certainty that the whole human being was created in the divine image. In turn, the original acceptance of the body provided the basis for the acceptance of the whole visible world as a gift of God's love. What, then, would happen to their experience of the body if they questioned the gift and cast God's love from their hearts? Would they—could they—still experience the body as a "witness to Love"?

The Entrance of Shame

Lucifer promised Adam and Eve sight: "your eyes will be opened" (Gen 3:5). Yet all along that fallen "angel of light" desired to darken their vision. God had already freely given them not only sight but also the original good of his own vision. Satan dupes man into believing that God had created them blind and did not want them to see. Far from gaining anything by eating the forbidden fruit, man and woman lose what they had already been freely given. The Holy Father observes that, due to sin, man in some way loses the original certainty of the "image of God" expressed in his body. In fact, the body as a sign of the person and of the mystery of God's love "collapses," as the following words attest: "Then the eyes of both were opened, and they knew that they were naked; and they sewed fig leaves together and made themselves aprons" (Gen 3:7).

These words express the "frontier" between the man of original innocence and the man of concupiscence. Shame is the boundary experience. Nakedness originally revealed the gift of God's love and enabled them to participate in it. It "represented the full acceptance of the body in its whole human and thus personal truth" (TOB 27:3). Now nakedness reveals that they have been deprived of God's gift and are alienated from God's love. It reveals that they have lost sight of the body as the revelation of the person and of the divine mystery. A rupture and opposition now divide the spiritual and the sensible. This is what spawns shame. As John Paul expresses, shame enters when man "realizes for the first time that his body has ceased drawing on the power of the spirit, which raised him to the level of the image of God" (TOB 28:2).

Since gender difference highlights man's spiritual-sensible (soul-body) polarity in a particular way, gender difference itself is now "blamed" in a sense for the rupture sin caused. This is where the rupture of sin is immediately "felt" and experienced. John Paul observes that man is ashamed of his body because of concupiscence. Then he clarifies that man is ashamed not so much of his body as precisely of concupiscence (see TOB 28:5). In other words, man may attribute shame to the body and to gender difference, but this is almost always an excuse not to contend with the disorder of his own lustful heart.

The Pope explains that concupiscence indicates the state of the human spirit removed from "the original fullness of values" that man possessed in the dimensions of God. Thus concupiscence is to be understood as a lack—the lack of God's love in the human heart. In the sexual realm (what St. John calls the concupiscence or lust "of the flesh"), concupiscence refers to *un*-inspired sexual desire: sexual desire no longer informed by the Spirit, by God's love and grace.[30] In the Genesis text, shame rises because even after sin man and woman still know they are called to love—to be a sincere gift for each other. They have not forgotten what they experienced before sin. But their ability to bring about that love has been shaken at its very foundations. Love no longer spontaneously wells up through their bodies as the expression of the heart. The heart, lacking the *in*-spiration of God's love, now tends to lust—to treating the other as an object created for "my sake" (i.e., for the sake of my own self-gratification), rather than as a subject created for his or her "own sake." Shame announces the uneasiness of conscience connected with this "new" experience.

Historical man experiences the concupiscence of the flesh in two related ways. First, it asserts itself almost as a predisposition resulting from original sin. When left to itself, man's fallen nature inclines him to treat others as objects of enjoyment rather than as subjects to love. This basic disorder—while it comes from sin (original sin) and inclines man to sin—is not itself a sin. Sin, in the proper sense, demands the engagement of the will. This is the second "experience" of concupiscence.

---

30. *CCC*, no. 2351.

Only when a person engages his or her will to foster and follow that internal concupiscent impulse can one speak of lust as an "interior act," and therefore as a sin.

If concupiscent desire is a "given" of man's fallen nature, does this mean that historical man is bound by his lusts? No! As John Paul boldly proclaims, *"Christ has redeemed us!* This means he has...set our freedom free from the *domination* of concupiscence. And if redeemed man still sins, this is not due to an imperfection of Christ's redemptive act, but to man's will not to avail himself of the grace which flows from that act."[31]

The Dimensions of Shame

As he continues his analysis, the Holy Father wants to penetrate the phenomenon of lust by examining the first man and woman's experience and their state of consciousness. The "Yahwist text," he says, "expressly enables us to do so" (TOB 27:2). The revelation of man and woman's first experience of shame takes us to the depths of man's "new" discovery of himself as a body in the world. Yet this time the Pope states that it is as if the man of concupiscence felt that he had just stopped being above the animals. It is as if his experience of the body and sex was "driven back to another level" (TOB 32:2).

What distinguished man from the animals? Man could freely determine his own actions. He was not led by instinct but was master of himself. For the person to live according to his own dignity requires such mastery. Because of sin, however, John Paul says that the structure of self-mastery is, in a way, "shaken...to its very foundations" (TOB 28:3). Man suddenly realized that he had lost control of his body and its impulses. "It is as if he had experienced a specific *fracture of the personal integrity of his own body, particularly in that which determines its sexuality"* (TOB 28:4).

Because of the rupture of the original covenant with God, man experiences almost a rupture of his original spiritual and material unity. Here we touch upon that "great divorce" spoken of previously. The perfect integration between the "breath" of the spirit and the "dust" of their bodies was now lost. Hence, the Pope observes that man not only lost

---

31. *Veritatis Splendor,* 103.

the supernatural (and preternatural) gifts of grace that were part of his endowment before sin. He also "suffered damage in what belongs to nature itself, to humanity in the original fullness 'of the image of God'" (TOB 27:2). That "original fullness" is man's "natural" state.[32]

Shame Shakes the Foundations of Existence

The perfect integration of body and soul enabled the first man and woman to live in the perfect freedom of the gift. Since we tend to normalize our experience of disintegration, we can hardly imagine the "shock" of their new experience of having lost that freedom. Returning to our image, this would be akin to the shock of having driven with inflated tires and then having all four tires blow at the same time. Driving would be a totally different experience. As the Pope intuits, at the moment the first man and woman eat from the tree and fall from the original state of grace, shame touches "the deepest level and seems to shake the very foundations of their existence" (TOB 27:1). So the man and his wife hide themselves from the presence of the Lord when they hear him walking in the garden (see Gen 3:8). The precision of the dialogue that then ensues between God and man, along with the whole narrative of the fall, is "overwhelming," the Pope says. "It shows the surface of man's emotions in living the events, in such a way that, at the same time, it reveals their depth" (TOB 27:2).

The "LORD God called to the man and said to him, 'Where are you?' And he said, 'I heard the sound of you in the garden, and I was afraid because I was naked; and I hid myself'" (Gen 3:9–10). A certain fear always belongs to the essence of shame, but this is more than a fear of being physically naked. The experience of nakedness speaks of the interior movements of the heart. Nakedness before the Lord first indicated the unity established between God and man by the original covenant. Now, having eaten from the tree, man's own heart condemns him. He *knows* that he has broken the original covenant with God. He already feels the consequences *in his body*. In his state of fear and confusion, he can only "hide" in a fruitless attempt to escape the consequences of his actions. Here we have history's first "cover-up." As John

---

32. See John Paul's footnote 44 in TOB 27 for a summary of the magisterium's treatment of various issues regarding nature and grace.

Paul states, "With his shame about his own nakedness, the man seeks to cover the true origin of fear by indicating the effect so as not to name the cause" (TOB 27:1). The real origin of man's fear is his "closing of his heart" to God's gift. Shame, therefore, keenly manifests the betrayal of the trust that God extended to man in the original covenant. But Adam refuses to admit this to himself or to God.

This new experience of his body not only indicates that sin shattered his original relationship with God and with the woman. It also reveals that sin ruptured his original and harmonious relationship with the rest of creation. "The original acceptance of the body was in some sense the basis of the acceptance of the whole visible world" (TOB 27:3). Now, however, even the earth resists man and his task of "tilling the soil." The ground itself is "cursed" because of him (see Gen 3:17). Here we see that man's experience of his own gendered embodiment affects questions of ecology and questions of a society's work and economic structures. These issues are inseparable from sexuality, marriage, and family life. We must first reclaim the true meaning of these if we are to establish harmonious relationships with the environment, within the workplace, within culture at large, and between nations.

> ■ We see here the false dichotomy between the typically labeled "liberal" concern for social justice and the "conservative" concern for Church doctrine on sexual morality. John Paul was viewed as a man of contradiction because of his staunch support for both. Yet the contradiction did not lie in him. Social justice and sexual morality flow from the very same vision of the human person's dignity as a subject made in God's image and called to live in a communion of persons.[33] Furthermore, since man and woman's relationship is the deepest substratum of the social structure, there can be no social justice without a return to the full truth of the Christian sexual ethic.

Indeed, sin, injustice, and death entered the scene upon the denial of the gift revealed through masculinity and femininity: "You are dust and to dust you shall return" (Gen 3:19). Hence, the first man's fear also expresses "the sense of *insecurity* about his somatic structure *in the face*

---

33. See *CCC*, no. 2419.

of the processes of nature that operate with an inevitable determinism"
(TOB 27:4). In this way, John Paul suggests that man's fear in his
nakedness implies a "cosmic shame." Man's sin disrupted the whole
world order (see Rom 8:20–21). Man was created in God's own image
as the crown of creation. He was called to have dominion over the earth
and subdue it. Yet rather than the earth being subject to him, he is now
subject to the earth. And all of this is felt *in his body.* The body represents man's "transcendent constitution" (TOB 27:4). Man's body, which
once shone with the glory of God, must now return to the earth. Man
will either maintain hope and strive in his body to reclaim his transcendence, or he will surrender his body to decadence and decay. This is the
battle that has raged in man and all around him since "the beginning."

Shame Is Immanent and Relative

Shame in relation to the cosmos makes way for the shame that is
produced in humanity itself. Lust threatens man's dignity as a person
made in God's image. John Paul affirms again that man was God's
image both in his own person (original solitude) and in the interpersonal relationship of man and woman together (original unity/
communio personarum). The shame that results from lust, then, is both
immanent and *relative.*

Here we venture into the finer points of John Paul's analysis.
Immanent shame refers to the shame experienced *within oneself* due to
the loss of freedom (self-mastery) that resulted from the rupture of
body and soul. This is the "flip side" of the experience of original solitude, in which man discovered his unique dignity as an integrated
body-person. Immanent shame seems to indicate that man knew that
the disintegration of body and soul threatened the value and dignity of
his own personhood. The Pope remarks that this self-shame reveals a
"specific humiliation mediated by the body" (TOB 28:2). The person
now finds it very difficult to embrace his own body, and he fails to
perceive how essential his body is in understanding and embracing
his own humanity. John Paul concludes that this shame is so acute as to
create "a fundamental disquiet in the whole of human existence" (TOB
28:3).

Relative shame refers to the shame experienced *in relation* to the
other. This is the "flip side" of the experiences of original unity and

nakedness. Relative shame manifests a fear for one's own self in the presence of the other. This fear "compels them to cover their nakedness, to hide their own bodies, to withdraw from man's sight what constitutes the visible sign of femininity, and from woman's sight what constitutes the visible sign of masculinity" (TOB 28:1). Of course, this "visible sign" of masculinity and femininity refers most specifically to the genitals.

> ■ From all this we see that lust shatters the peace of the three original experiences of solitude, unity, and nakedness. Void of the gift, each experience is twisted into its negative form. Solitude becomes an experience of alienation. When the freedom of the gift is removed from communion, "commun-*ism*" is the only possibility—a coerced and, therefore, false unity that does not respect the dignity of the person as a self-determining subject. Finally, when lust is full-blown, nakedness without shame is twisted into shamelessness.
>
> The negative form of the original experiences of solitude-unity-nakedness can also be understood in the following way. The person still desires to express his own "self" (original solitude), but void of the gift deforms this into an egotistical and alienating self-assertion (radical individualism). The person still desires others (original unity), but void of the gift deforms this into a "using" of others (radical exploitation). The person still desires to see and be seen by another (original nakedness), but void of the gift deforms this into voyeurism and exhibitionism (radical perversion). If the original experiences led to thanksgiving, worship, and beatitude, the deformed experiences lead to self-gratitude, idolatry, and despair. As we shall see, by the revelation of "the Gift" (of the mystery of the Father and his love), Christ will fully restore man to himself by restoring the grace that afforded the original experiences. This will be fulfilled definitively in the eschaton, but we also can begin to reclaim this restoration in the here and now.

Both immanent and relative shame have a sexual character. John Paul observes that the sphere of sexuality seems to highlight the interior imbalance connected with immanent shame. In a way, man feels lust *within himself* even before he experiences it *in relation* to the "other." When he actually directs this lust toward the other, we see the sexual character of relative shame. In this way, as John Paul observes, immanent and relative shame overlap. Just as the experience of solitude leads to unity, on the "flip side," lust does not merely stay *within*, but is always directed toward an "other." When this happens, even if it is only a lustful look as Christ indicates, the other feels threatened and instinctively wants to hide. This is why we cover our bodies—specifically those parts of our bodies that distinguish us from the opposite sex: to protect ourselves from the threat of lust. This is the "experience" of shame.

As John Paul indicates, we see here that shame and lust explain one another. Lust "explains" shame because lust gives rise to shame. Shame "explains" lust by revealing the injury caused by lust, both within the person lusting (immanent) and in regard to the person toward whom that lust is directed (relative). In this way, as the Pope tells us, we understand better why—and in what sense—Christ speaks of lust as adultery committed in the heart. Adultery is inherently nonmarital. So is lust. Adultery is contrary to the dignity and value of the person. So is lust. Adultery is a countersign of the communion of love within the Trinity. So is lust.

Shame Has a Twofold Meaning

The need to cover the body in the presence of the other indicates that man and woman have lost "the peace of the interior gaze." In a word, they have lost purity. They no longer see the other's body as a revelation of God's mystery. They no longer see the other's body as the revelation of the person. Instead, they see the other's body more as a "thing" to be used for their own selfish gratification. With the ex-spiration of divine love from the human heart, sexual desire has become inverted, self-seeking.

■ It seems true, generally speaking, that men tend to experience their fallen sexual desires as geared toward physical gratification at the expense of a woman, while women tend to experience their fallen sexual desires as geared more toward emotional gratification at the expense of a man. We have all heard the expression that men will use love to get sex and women will use sex to get love (Wojtyla's book *Love and Responsibility* offers an in-depth analysis of these dynamics). Of course, women also have physical desires as men have emotional ones.

It should also be mentioned here that some men and women experience sexual desires toward members of the same sex. While same-sex attractions—since they are almost never freely chosen—are not in themselves sinful, they are part of the disorder of the sexual appetite caused by original sin. In other words, if the men and women of history sometimes experience erotic desire toward their own sex, we can certainly say that "in the beginning it was not so."[34] The good news is that, whatever our individual distortions, we are all called to experience the ethos of redemption, which has *real power* to restore God's original plan for sexuality in our hearts. This does not come easily nor completely in this life. Furthermore, the more deeply wounded a person is in his or her sexuality, the more time and effort it usually requires to experience healing. Indeed, some, like St. Paul, may experience a particular "thorn in the flesh" that, despite every sincere effort, is not removed in this life (see 2 Cor 12:7–10). On this point, we can observe that, through humble acceptance of one's cross, holiness can be compatible even with deep woundedness. That being said, we must also affirm that no one is exempt from what John Paul describes as the "task" Christ gives us of reclaiming God's original plan for the body and sexuality. As the *Catechism* states, "All Christ's faithful are to 'direct their affections rightly, lest they be hindered in their pursuit of perfect charity.'"[35] John Paul affirms that this task "*can* be carried out and that it is truly worthy of man" (TOB 48:4). As we take up this task, our hope lies in knowing that "he who began a good work in [us] will bring it to completion at the day of Jesus Christ" (Phil 1:6).

Despite their "shock" at having lost their original purity, they did not completely lose a sense of their own dignity. They still realized that

---

34. For a more thorough discussion of homosexuality in light of John Paul's TOB, see Christopher West, *Good News About Sex and Marriage: Answers to Your Honest Questions about Catholic Teaching*, chap. 8.

35. *CCC*, no. 2545.

they were created "for their own sakes," and were never meant to be used. Contrary to the idea of the early Protestant reformers, men and women are not "utterly depraved" as a result of original sin.[36] If they were, we could expect that they would have reveled shamelessly in their lusts. Instead, they clearly experienced lust as a threat. Thus, the Holy Father observes that shame has a twofold meaning, negative and positive. It indicates a threat to the value of the person (negative) and at the same time seeks to preserve this value interiorly (positive). In other words, shame indicates that man and woman have lost sight of the spousal meaning of the body. But it also indicates an innate need to protect the spousal meaning of the body from the threat of concupiscence. This is precisely why they cover those parts of the body that reveal its spousal meaning. The visibility of the sexual values of the body once revealed the truth of the person. In this new state of affairs, the sexual values of the body, ironically, are covered to ensure the value of the person.

This deeper penetration of shame as something positive and "protective" (this could also be called modesty) indicates a proper reverence for the mystery of the person in his or her "otherness." In this way, although the experience greatly differs, the Pope suggests that shame enables man and woman almost to remain in the state of original innocence (see TOB 31:1). This positive sense of shame, then, must always inform the relationship of the sexes. Even in marriage, when the body is unveiled, a couple must maintain a proper reverence and respect for the value of the person, otherwise such unveiling would involve a certain shamelessness. The grace of marriage empowers couples to rediscover something of the original experience of nakedness without shame—a nakedness that does not elicit shame (in the negative sense) because the couple trusts in each other's pure intentions of love. But marriage in no way justifies shamelessness. That would involve degrading one's spouse without a corresponding sense of shame for having done so.

Understanding the positive sense of shame also helps us realize that lust is not of the essence of the human heart. It is not of the essence of the sexual relationship and sexual desire. Lust, rather, involves a grave distortion of all these things. The heart goes deeper than these distortions, and still desires what is deeper. Shame indicates that the heart

---

36. See *CCC*, nos. 405, 406.

still senses an "echo" of God's original plan for sexuality and longs for it. Indeed, this distant memory of "the beginning" keeps shame (in the positive sense) alive in man's heart.

Hence, even though man's capacity for self-mastery has been "shaken to the very foundations," John Paul says that man still identifies himself with self-mastery and is always ready to "win" it (see TOB 28:2). He is always ready to fight the distortions of lust in order to regain the freedom that was lost. Of course, lust fights back and, at times, man can be easily lured away from the truth (see Rom 7:22–23). But in the deeper part of his heart, *man still desires the truth.*[37] If we keep this in mind, the Pope tells us that we can understand better why Christ, speaking of lust, appeals to the human heart. Lust, no matter how base, can never snuff out the spark of goodness that always remains deeply imbedded in the human heart. In the Sermon on the Mount, Christ appeals to that spark and, through the gentle "breath" of the Holy Spirit, seeks to fan that spark into flame.

B. INSATIABILITY OF THE UNION

Concupiscence Shatters the Original Communion of Persons

John Paul continues his analysis by taking us to the further stage of the study of lust, which he calls the "insatiability of the union" (TOB 29:1). The original unity the first couple experienced brought with it an explicit peace. But in man's heart, concupiscence distorted that original beatifying conjugal union of persons. After sin, the original capacity of communicating themselves to each other has been "shattered." Man and woman's relationship undergoes "a radical transformation." It no longer satisfies the longings of the heart as it once did, because they are crippled in their ability to love each other as they once did.

John Paul says that, as persons, man and woman are "called from eternity to exist 'in communion'" (TOB 30:5). This call defines us and reveals the deep meaning of our sexuality. We still desire communion even after sin. Yet we experience a "failure to satisfy the aspiration to realize in the 'conjugal union of the body'...the reciprocal communion

---

37. See *CCC*, no. 1707.

of persons" (TOB 30:5). This is what John Paul means by the "insatiability of the union": lust *never* satisfies our yearning for love.

The Second Discovery of Sex

The radical change in their experience of nakedness leads us to presume negative changes in the whole interpersonal man-woman relationship. Once again, the experience of the body gives us a window into the human heart. The role of the body, which was once the trustworthy foundation of their communion, is now "called into doubt" in man and woman's consciousness. Sexual difference, which had proclaimed and enabled the original communion of persons, "was abruptly sensed and understood as an element of the mutual opposition of persons" (TOB 29:2). The Pope points out that they obviously did not stop communicating with each other through the body and its movements, gestures, and expressions. However, the simple and direct communion that flowed from the purity of original nakedness "disappeared."

The Pope calls this new experience "the 'second' discovery of sex" and emphasizes that it differs radically from the first one (see TOB 29:4). In this new situation, rather than finding themselves united by their sexual differences, the man and the woman are divided and even opposed because of their masculinity and femininity. In short, what was once the experience of male *and* female is now the experience of male *or* female. The Pope contends that in this new situation sexuality almost impedes their true interpersonal communion. Sexuality had once made visible the other's subjectivity and enabled a full communion of persons. Now, as a result of man's "detachment from love" (TOB 29:4), sexuality has become objectified. As the Pope expresses it, "The subjectivity of the person gives way in some sense to the objectivity of the body" (TOB 32:5). This means the body ceases to be readily incorporated into subjectivity. Concupiscence "brings with it an almost constitutive *difficulty in identifying oneself with one's own body*"[38] (TOB 29:4). Now, if the man bound by concupiscence is to retain a regard for the subjectivity of the other—and at the same time for his own subjec-

---

38. This difficulty is exemplified not only in the widespread "animalistic" behavior of our culture but also in a widespread "spiritualism" that passes for Christianity. I was once trying to explain the TOB to a very kind and fervent Baptist woman. In talking about the body as the revelation of the person, she interjected with this objection: "I ain't *my*

tivity—he must cover the body; he must hide his nakedness to avoid being objectified by the other. This results from a new and fundamental lack of trust, which indicates the collapse of the original relationship of man and woman's communion.

This objectification leads men and women to seek "the mere sensation of sexuality" apart from a true communion of persons (see TOB 29:3). This happens precisely because sexuality is now detached from the person and his call to image God through communion. This is the tragedy of concupiscence: It exchanges a self-seeking gratification for the sincere gift of self; it *uses* the other as an object made for *my sake*, rather than loving the other as a subject made for his or her *own sake*. Yet, historical man often views this way of thinking and behaving as "normal."

Sin's Effect on Woman

At this point John Paul shifts his reflection to the words of Genesis 3:16 in which God says to the woman: "I will greatly multiply your pain in childbearing; in pain you shall bring forth children, yet your desire shall be for your husband and he shall rule over you." These words, like previous ones already analyzed, are loaded with content that can be mined through phenomenological analysis. The Pope says in typical form that these words reveal to us not only the exterior situation of man and woman, but they also enable us to penetrate the deep mysteries of their hearts.

These words also have a "future-oriented character" that impacts all human history. As John Paul expresses, "The history of human consciousness and human hearts was to confirm repeatedly the words contained in Genesis 3:16" (TOB 30:2).[39] Because of sin, woman now

---

body, honey. I'm gonna shed this tired skin when I go to see *my* Lord. My spirit's gonna be free, free at last." Here is a classic example of the "*difficulty in identifying oneself with one's own body*" of which the Pope speaks. Tragically, what stems precisely from concupiscence was masquerading in this good-hearted woman as a sort of virtue. She believed that by focusing attention on the body, I was "stuck" in the world, stuck on the things of the earth, whereas she had her mind set on "heavenly things." By virtue of Christ's Incarnation and Ascension, the body *is* a "heavenly thing."

39. For further development of these themes, see *Mulieris Dignitatem*, nos. 10 and 24, and *Letter to Women*.

experiences a particular "reduction" in comparison with man. Her special giftedness as woman—the fact that she embodies receptivity in relation to God, the man, and the gift of new life—will no longer be experienced as a gift but more as a burden, at times even a curse. The Pope clarifies that "there is no reason why one should understand this reduction as social inequality. Rather, the expression, 'Your desire shall be for your husband, but he will dominate you,' immediately indicates another form of inequality that *woman was to feel as a lack of full unity precisely in the vast context of union with man* to which both were called according to Genesis 2:24" (TOB 30:2).

Has history not told an ongoing tale of male domination and prejudice against women? To varying degrees this has even manifested itself in some cultures as an explicit *hatred of woman*, a hatred of what is "feminine" (misogyny). It must be stated emphatically—if Genesis did not make it obvious enough—that male domination seriously violates God's plan and is the specific result of sin.

■   It seems misogyny stems from the way woman constantly reminds the whole human race of what we have all rejected about ourselves through original sin—our *receptivity* in relation to God. Woman's particular receptivity to love and to life is her special "genius." Tragically, as a result of sin, woman's great blessing has come to be seen as a curse. Once again, spousal imagery helps reveal the mystery. Because of Satan's deception, we have come to see God's "masculine-bridegroom" initiative as that of a tyrant with a will to rule over us. Hence, we reject our posture of receptivity as "feminine-bride" in favor of being our own "masculine" lords. We want to be "like God" but without God.[40] In this situation, we come to see the "feminine"—which symbolizes our true humanity—as a weakness to be dominated and controlled, even snuffed out. Does this not explain, perhaps, why there has been a tendency to favor "masculinity" over "femininity" throughout history? But this conception of God as tyrant-ruler—and in turn, this symbol of what is "masculine"—is a gross distortion. Where is this distortion lived out? Primarily in the relationship of the sexes. The man,

40. See *CCC*, no. 398.

rather than imaging the true initiative of God—rather than loving his wife "as Christ loved the Church" (Eph 5:25)—comes to image the gross distortion of the tyrant-ruler: "He shall rule over you" (Gen 3:16). In turn, the woman, under the weight of male domination and history's discrimination against her, is tempted to reject her own femininity and take to herself the distorted "masculine" will-to-power simply in order to survive. Are these not some of the deepest reasons behind the women's liberation movement and the gender confusion so prevalent in our world today? John Paul shows implicit respect for all that is good and just in the feminist movement. But he also calls women "to promote a 'new feminism' which rejects the temptation of imitating models of 'male domination,' in order to acknowledge and affirm the true genius of women in every aspect of the life of society, and overcome all discrimination, violence, and exploitation."[41]

Both Are Subject to Concupiscence

The man's "domination" over the woman changes the whole dynamic of the original communion of persons. It indicates that lust has distorted the original masculine initiation of love. The man of concupiscence seeks not to make a gift of himself to woman, but he seeks to dominate and control her, to possess her and use her for his own ends. As John Paul expresses it, "*The relationship of the gift changes into a relationship of appropriation*" (TOB 32:6). Love "gifts." Lust "appropriates."

Yet woman still "desires her husband." If the distortions of a man's heart lead him to disregard woman's dignity and *use her*, the distortions of a woman's heart can lead her, at times, to disregard her own dignity and *allow herself to be used*. Yet at other times the Pope notes that the instincts that the woman directs to the man precede his desire or even aim at arousing it and giving it impetus (see TOB 31:3). In this way, woman also uses man for her own ends, treating him as an object and not as a person.

---

41. *Evangelium Vitae*, 99.

■ This dynamic in women is often lived out in an understandable retaliation against men and their lustful domination. A dramatic example of this was told to me by a counselor who had been working with a woman who was once a stripper in a "men's club." When the counselor asked her why she did it, she responded without hesitation: "Control." This woman, like the majority of women who compromise themselves in similar ways, had been sexually abused by older men as a child. Causing men to "lose control" by inciting their lusts was her way of "gaining control" over them. As she described it, "Every night I was able to put hundreds of desperate men at my mercy, begging for more. And I'd very easily walk away each night with over one thousand of their hard-earned dollars."

Although the biblical texts seem to indicate the man's lust more specifically, John Paul clearly states that both the man and woman have become subject to concupiscence. Shame, therefore, "touches the innermost [being] of both the male and the female personality, even though in a different way" (TOB 31:4). It is precisely this mutual experience of concupiscence that causes the opposition between the sexes. Obviously this opposition "neither destroys nor excludes the conjugal union willed by the Creator (see Gen 2:24), nor its procreative effects; but it confers on the realization of this union another direction" (TOB 30:5). This direction is very different from that of "the beatifying beginning." Hence, if men and women are to rediscover what it means to be a sincere gift for each other and thus fulfill the very meaning of their being and existence (see TOB 15:1), they *must* overcome the domination of concupiscence. Civilization itself depends on it.

C. THE CORRUPTION OF THE SPOUSAL MEANING OF THE BODY

John Paul has been trying to reconstruct the original experience of shame and lust, the experience that clearly indicates the crossing over from the state of original innocence to the state of historical sinfulness. We can penetrate the experience of both "states" by contrasting them with each other.

The Holy Father says that Genesis 2:24 speaks of the "union of bodies" in the sense of the authentic "union of persons." Becoming "one flesh," then, does not merely express the joining of two bodies. According to the Pope, this is a "sacramental expression" that corresponds to the communion of persons (see TOB 31:2). "Where the flesh is one, one also is the spirit."[42] Living this, experiencing this, left no need for shame in their nakedness. The entrance of shame, therefore, indicates the loss of the original communion of persons in the image of God. Fear and shame replaced the absolute trust that man and woman had in each other in the state of original innocence. Fear and shame indicate the beginning of concupiscence in man's heart, which John Paul describes as a "limitation, violation, or complete deformation of the spousal meaning of the body" (TOB 31:6).

Living the Body Flows from the Heart

When the Holy Father speaks of the meaning of the body, he is referring in the first place to "the full consciousness of the human being" (TOB 31:5)—or, we could say, the full awareness of what it means to be human. The body reveals the person. The body reveals, as in a "sacrament," the meaning and mystery of human life itself. But as John Paul stresses, the meaning of the body is not just something conceptual; it is not abstract. In gaining a full awareness of the human being through the body, we must include the actual lived experience of the body in its masculinity and femininity.

John Paul says that the meaning one attributes to his body determines that person's attitude in his way of *"living the body."* In other words, how we live as bodies—in particular, how we live out our sexuality—will flow from the attitude of our hearts regarding the meaning of our bodies, the meaning of our sexuality, the meaning of life itself. The body has an objective meaning, of course, which does not change based on subjective feelings. However, the Pope observes that this purely objective significance of the body and of sex is in a certain sense "a-historical." In other words, because of sin, historical man's subjective experience of the body and sexuality is different from their original, objective purpose and meaning. To the degree that historical man nor-

---

42. *CCC*, no. 1642.

malizes his fallen experience of the body and sex, the Church's teaching comes to be seen as abstract and disconnected from "real life" experience.

In Christ's words in the Sermon on the Mount, he appeals specifically to the *experience* of historical man. There is nothing abstract about "looking with lust." We all know immediately what that means in our own experience, in our own "hearts." This is why Christ's words sting so much. We *know* we are guilty. But Christ wants us to penetrate more deeply into our hearts where that "echo" of God's original plan still resounds. Tapping into that deeper heritage gives us the key to reconnecting the objective meaning of the body and sex with how we experience the body and sex subjectively. It gives us the key to "living the body" according to its true meaning and thus fulfilling the very meaning of existence.

Through the previous analysis of man and woman's experience before sin, we have discerned the body's spousal meaning and rediscovered what it consists of as "a measure of the human heart." The heart is still measured by this objective meaning of the body, that is, by the call to sincere self-giving. Lust, however, attacks this sincere giving, depriving man and woman of the dignity of the gift inscribed in the beauty and mystery of sexual difference. So when the man of concupiscence "measures" his heart by the spousal meaning of the body, he condemns himself. At this point he has three choices: normalize sin; fall into despair; or turn to Christ who came not to condemn, but to save (see Jn 3:17). As the Pope will repeatedly stress, Christ's words about lust do not so much condemn us but call us. They call us not just to force a subjectively lustful heart to submit to an objective ethic. They call us efficaciously to let the new *ethos* of redemption inform and transform our lustful hearts.

Concupiscence Habitually Threatens Love

Due to concupiscence, the human body "has almost lost the power of expressing this love in which the human person becomes a gift" (TOB 32:3). The Pope adds the word "almost" because a spark of God's plan remains in us. The spousal meaning of the body "*has not been totally suffocated...by concupiscence, but only habitually threatened*" (TOB 32:3). The Pope carefully maintains this essential point. Without this "almost" we would fall into the erroneous belief of the first Protestant reformers that man is "utterly depraved" due to sin.

■ The idea of "utter depravity" introduced by the Protestant reformers may seem to diverge only slightly from the Catholic belief that man is tragically fallen, yet in some way retains his basic goodness. However, a notion of utter depravity has dangerous and far-reaching implications. For example, "dying to self" does not mean rooting out the weeds in one's soul so that the wheat can flourish. If we are utterly depraved, we are all weeds. This means all of our aspirations and desires are suspect. One who "dies to himself" in such a fashion will end up nullifying the unique mystery and giftedness of his own personhood. He will end up "dying" not only to sin but also to the person God created him or her to be. Furthermore, if the human heart goes no deeper than its distortions, how can we hope to desire, let alone come progressively to experience, the restoration of God's original plan? In this view, the heart only desires corruption and "the tendency to sin (concupiscentia)...would be insurmountable."[43] Without the Pope's "almost," we come to see ourselves, to use one of Luther's images, as a "dung heap." Christ may cover us with a blanket of white snow. But even so, according to Luther's logic, we remain impure internally. Catholic anthropology insists that sin did not trump our "very good" creation. Hence John Paul maintains that the heritage of the human heart "is deeper than the sinfulness inherited" (TOB 46:6). Christ appeals to that deeper heritage of our hearts in order to revive it. Through the power of the Holy Spirit, he transforms us from within. Historical man has this lifelong task: to give voice to the deepest aspirations of his heart by accepting the grace of ongoing conversion.

We must now battle against concupiscence if we are to reclaim the freedom that enables us to make the sincere gift of self. This is difficult enough when lust manifests itself clearly. It is all the more difficult since lust "is not always plain and obvious; sometimes it is concealed, so that it passes itself off as 'love'" (TOB 32:3). Note John Paul's realism

43. *CCC*, no. 406.

here. At times only a fine line divides authentic love and lust. When fooled by lust, the heart can even mistake it for love. John Paul asks: "Does this mean that we should distrust the human heart?" Then he responds without hesitation: "No! It is only to say that we must remain in control of it" (TOB 32:3).

Far too many people, upon recognizing the distortions of their own hearts, succumb to the devil's trap by throwing out the baby with the bath water. We must certainly reckon with the forces of concupiscence within us. But concupiscence does not define the human heart. The heart goes deeper than its distortions. What, then, does the Pope mean by saying we must remain in control of our hearts? We need to penetrate the dynamics of concupiscence more deeply to answer that question.

Loss of the Freedom of the Gift

In short, John Paul tells us that concupiscence entails the loss of the interior freedom of the gift. Sexual desire is now manifested "as a quasi self-generating force...operating according to its own dynamics" (TOB 32:2). In other words, libido tends to have a mind of its own that pushes the body toward indulgence. In this way we have lost "control" of our own bodies and of the desires of our hearts. In a certain sense, this makes the interior freedom of self-giving impossible. "Concupiscence as such is not able to promote union as a communion of persons. By itself, it does not unite, but appropriates to itself" (TOB 32:6). Thus, concupiscent desire draws us away from affirming the person "for his or her own sake" and makes of that person an object of selfish gratification.

This also obscures our perception of the beauty that the human body possesses as an expression of the spirit. For the man of concupiscence, "beauty" is now determined not by the visibility of *the person* in and through his or her body, but by what type or kind of body satisfies or appeals to concupiscence. This concept of beauty is often totally divorced from the person.[44]

For John Paul, remaining in control of our hearts means regaining self-determination. It means controlling sexual impulses instead of being controlled by them. We should not conceive of this control, how-

---

44. John Paul II will provide an intriguing and redeeming analysis of physical beauty in his cycle of reflections on Ephesians 5 (Part II, Chapter 1).

ever, merely as the caging or corralling of a wild horse. While this approach may control the horse, it does not change it. If you opened the corral even for a moment, the horse would run wild. Corralling the horse may be a necessary first step, but the ultimate goal is to tame (transform) the horse so that it no longer requires a corral. Applying this image, in regaining self-mastery it may well be necessary at first to "cage" concupiscent desire by force of will. But *this is only a first step*. If we remain here, the moral norm still operates as a constraint. Christ calls us to progress from constraint to freedom—from merely meeting the demands of the law to *ful*-filling those demands. As John Paul says, "This is a still uncertain and fragile journey as long as we are on earth, but it is one made possible by grace, which enables us to possess the full freedom of the children of God (see Rom 8:21)."[45]

The ultimate role of the will is not to tyrannize or repress the passions, but to direct them with the transforming power of grace toward the truth of self-giving love. "The upright will orders the movements of the senses it appropriates to the good and to beatitude." Within the ethos of redemption, "emotions and feelings can be taken up into the *virtues*."[46] In other words, Christ calls us to experience a real and deep victory over concupiscence so that what we desire subjectively becomes progressively more in tune with the objective meaning of the body and sex. To the degree that we experience this transformation, we no longer need the "cage"; we come freely to desire the good. This is the freedom for which Christ has set us free (see Gal 5). This freedom enables us to live our bodies in holiness and reverence, liberated from lust's domination (see 1 Thess 4:4).

John Paul II's proclamation that the redemption of the body truly affords such freedom is one of the most important contributions of his entire catechesis, the "pearl," so to speak, of the TOB. It also seems to cause the most contention. An impulse-oriented view of the sexual appetite seems to dominate many evaluations of sexuality. Without a personalistic understanding of human (and Christian) freedom, virtually all one can do is "manage" his sexual appetite by "caging" it. Christians who take on this view almost inevitably view marriage as a legitimate opportunity to allow the "corralled horse" an occasional run.

---

45. *Veritatis Splendor*, 18.
46. *CCC*, no. 1768.

In turn, if a person thinks this way and constructs his or her life of "holiness" accordingly, it becomes almost impossible to imagine true freedom from the domination of concupiscence.

As Wojtyla observed in a pre-papal essay, the "very manner in which marriage [and the relationship of the sexes in general] is conceived must be from the start, to the greatest extent possible, freed from purely impulse-oriented, naturalistic presuppositions and shaped personalistically."[47] Within this deterministic, impulse-oriented view of sexuality, Wojtyla wrote, "There seems to be a tendency to limit the possibility of virtue and magnify the 'necessity of sin' in this sphere. Personalism, with its emphasis on self-determination, would entail the opposite tendency." It "would perceive the possibility of virtue, based on self-control and sublimation."[48] Sublimation is not repression of sexual desire but its transformation into something sublime, glorious. This is the real possibility afforded by the redemption of our bodies in Christ.

Maintaining the Balance of the Gift

We have already observed that the difference between authentic love and lust, although at times subtle, can be understood as the difference between "gift" and "appropriation." We see precisely this contrast in the Yahwist texts that describe man and woman's experience before and after original sin. Genesis 2:23–25 expresses their experience of living the body as gift. Genesis 3:7 and 16 express their experience of living the body as appropriation.

John Paul points out that the words of Genesis 3:16 ("he shall rule over you") "seem to suggest that this happens more at the woman's expense and that in any case she feels it more than the man" (TOB 33:1). Experience seems to confirm this. Even so, it is a two-way street. As John Paul states, "If a man relates to a woman in such a way that he considers her only as an object to appropriate and not as a gift, he condemns himself at the same time to become, on his part too, only an object of appropriation for her and not a gift" (TOB 33:1). Yet even this statement seems to indicate a priority of action on the man's part. This does not mean woman is merely passive; she too acts. The mascu-

---

47. "Parenthood as a Community of Persons," *Person and Community*, p. 330.
48. "The Problem of Catholic Sexual Ethics," *Person and Community*, p. 286.

line "priority of action," as we have described it, simply means that the man typically acts first. If woman embodies the "receptivity of the gift," it seems man embodies the "initiation of the gift."[49]

This is why John Paul believes that, right from the beginning, man was charged with the particular responsibility of being *"the guardian of the reciprocity of the gift and of its true balance"* (TOB 33:2). As we discovered in the Yahwist text, "The woman has...been entrusted to his eyes, to his consciousness, to his sensibility, to his 'heart'; he, by contrast," the Pope continues, "must in some way ensure...the reciprocal interpenetration of giving and receiving the gift, which, precisely through its reciprocity, creates an authentic communion of persons" (TOB 17:6).

All the man can do is "receive" femininity as a gift, and only when the woman freely gives it. He cannot take hold of woman as his own possession. He can only take the "risk" of initiating the gift of himself. It is a risk because he puts his gift of self in the hands of her freedom without fully knowing how she will respond. To be true to the gift, he can only wait and trust that the woman, sensing the genuineness of the gift he initiated, will receive his gift and respond freely with the gift of herself to him.

Concupiscence wreaks havoc on this mutual exchange. Tainted by lust, what the man initiates is often not the "sincere gift of self," but the desire to appropriate the woman and gratify himself. Sensing this, the woman frequently recoils, and rightly so since she knows she is never meant to be used. The man, then, will often be tempted to extort from woman her own gift. But this openly contrasts with the truth of love. Hence, although "maintaining the balance of the gift seems to be something entrusted to both, the man has a special responsibility, as if it depended more on him whether the balance is kept or violated or even—if it has already been violated—reestablished" (TOB 33:2). In other words, because the man embodies the "initiation of the gift," he has a particular responsibility to ensure that he initiates a genuine gift. He must first ensure this within his own heart. Then he must demonstrate that he desires to give himself to the woman sincerely and not appropriate her. In other words, he must demonstrate that he has acquired an integral self-mastery. For if a man cannot control himself,

---

49. Note: These phrases are not found in the Pope's catechesis, although he does speak of the husband as *the one who loves* and the woman as *the one who is loved* (see TOB 92:6).

he will inevitably seek to control woman in order to satisfy his own impulses and desires (we could also speak of a similar dynamic in women toward men).

John Paul recognizes that when discussing the diversity of men and women's roles, one has to realize that these have been conditioned to some degree by the social emargination of woman. He even says that the Old and the New Testaments give us sufficient proofs of such emargination. Nevertheless, the diversity of roles in man and woman's relationship is not merely the result of historical conditionings. Even when all exaggerations are purified (and we *must* seek to purify these), a fundamental and indispensable diversity of roles remains in the male-female relationship. One is not better than the other. They are merely different: different in a way that enables a true communion. Without *the difference* of the sexes, an incarnate, life-giving communion would be impossible.

The Personal Analogy of Belonging

If a person can never be appropriated or possessed without offending human dignity, is it wrong, then, for lovers to speak of "belonging" to one another? Not if they understand the proper limits of using such language. In fact, John Paul recognizes that the possessive pronoun "my" has always belonged to the language of human love and cites nearly thirty examples of it in the Song of Songs. But when true lovers, such as in the Song of Songs, refer to each other as "mine," this certainly does not denote possession in the sense of appropriating and using. Rather, John Paul says that in the eternal language of human love, the term "my" indicates the reciprocity and equal balance of the gift through which man and woman establish a true communion of persons.

Thus, man and woman can speak of belonging to each other only by way of analogy. When the man or the woman seeks to "possess" the other in the sense in which an object belongs to a person, the analogy of belonging breaks down and the communion of persons is impossible. Concupiscence leads precisely toward this demeaning sense of possession. "From possessing, the next step is 'enjoyment': the object I possess gains a certain significance for me inasmuch as it is at my disposal and I put it to my service, I use it" (TOB 33:5). This radically violates the other's creation for his or her "own sake." In this case, the "other" only has value so far as she (from the male perspective) is "useful" to me. As soon as she is not, she is no longer "loved." At this point another more "useful" person will be sought—that is, another person from whom I can more easily get the enjoyment I seek.

In short, this is the underlying sickness of a divorce culture. John Paul states that because of concupiscence, this way of seeing, evaluating, and "loving" almost constantly threatens us. But this way of "loving" is not really loving at all, since selfish enjoyment excludes disinterested giving. Generally speaking, a divorce mentality results from a counterfeit love that never reaches the great dignity and unrepeatability of the person, but only values those diminishable and repeatable attributes that bring self-gratification.

From John Paul's analysis we learn that if men and women are to "belong" to each other in the full expression of the communion of persons, they must first belong to Christ. They must first be in communion with him. The road to restored communion between the sexes passes by way of the death and resurrection of Jesus Christ. And there is no detour.

3. Commandment and Ethos

Christ's words about committing adultery in the heart have both an anthropological foundation and a directly ethical character. In section 2, *The Man of Concupiscence*, we sketched the anthropological foundation of Christ's words. In section 3, we will explore their ethical meaning.

To that end, John Paul will analyze the key text from Matthew 5 in "its *single parts*, with the goal of reaching afterwards a deeper *overall view*" (TOB 34:5). He divides the text as follows: (A) "It was said, 'Do not commit adultery'"; (B) "Whoever looks with lust"; and (C) "Has committed adultery in the heart." John Paul admits that the "method used here, that...*of breaking Christ's statement into three parts* that follow each other, may seem artificial. Yet, when we seek the ethical meaning of the whole statement, in its totality, the division of the text...can be helpful, as long as we do not merely set the pieces apart but bring them together. And this is what we intend to do" (TOB 42:1). The result is a rich and sustained argument that masterfully demonstrates "how deep down it is necessary to go, how the innermost recesses of the human heart must be thoroughly revealed, so that this heart might become a place in which the law is 'fulfilled'" (TOB 43:5).

The Pope devotes the first five audiences of this section (TOB 34–38) to placing Christ's words from the Sermon on the Mount in the context of "the Old Testament ethos." The ethos of the Israelites was, of course, drawn from the Law and the prophets. These provide the necessary frame of reference for understanding the nature of "*the new ethos*" Christ announced in the Sermon on the Mount, since this "new ethos" is nothing other than the *fulfillment* of the Law and the prophets. The interpretation of the law had become influenced by that "hardness of heart" Christ spoke of to the Pharisees. This flawed interpretation of the law brought about a situation contrary to God's original plan for the "one flesh" union. As John Paul says, the break from the ethos of creation alone provides the key to interpret the legislation of Israel regarding marriage and male-female relations in general. In the Sermon on the Mount, Christ also refers to the heart—to the "interior subject"—precisely because of man and woman's "hardness of heart."

A. IT WAS SAID, "DO NOT COMMIT ADULTERY"

The Law

Christ begins his teaching about lust with a reference to the Law of Moses: "You have heard that it was said, 'You shall not commit adultery.'" As Christ indicates, all those gathered on the mount to hear his words were certainly familiar with this norm. However, Christ's further words, "But I say to you...," show that the norm alone was not enough. The norm itself could not change the lustful heart.[50]

John Paul points out with various examples that in the interpretation of the Old Testament, the prohibition of adultery was balanced by compromising with concupiscence. For example, while most people were expected to be monogamous, the lives of men like David and Solomon show the establishing of real polygamy, which, the Pope says, "was undoubtedly for reasons of concupiscence." In fact, "the whole tradition of the Old Covenant indicates that the effective necessity of

---

50. See *CCC*, no. 1963.

monogamy as an essential and indispensable implication *of the commandment 'You shall not commit adultery'* never reached the consciousness and ethos of the later generations of the Chosen People" (TOB 35:3).[51]

Of course, the historical failures of the Jewish people in this regard are more of a commentary on fallen human nature than on the Jewish religion as such. God's revelation to Israel "endures forever."[52] Christ, however, as John Paul observes, does not accept the flawed interpretation of the law that became common in Israel. Men had subjected the law to human weakness and the limits of human willpower deriving precisely from the distortions of concupiscence. Hence, a compromised version of the law became superimposed on the original teaching of right and wrong connected with the Law of the Decalogue.

When men compromise with concupiscence, a basic principle comes into play. Stated simply, the less the heart conforms to truth, the more the need arises for laws that must corral the people into maintaining some semblance of order. So we find numerous and detailed precepts in the Old Testament that evaluate sexual conduct in a particular and even peculiar way.[53] John Paul admits that it is "difficult to avoid the impression that this evaluation has a negative character," and often "judges the woman...with greater severity" (TOB 36:3, 2). These laws were "not concerned directly with the order of the 'heart' but with the order of social life as a whole, at the basis of which stands, as always, marriage and the family" (TOB 36:3). However, some of these laws, while intending to maintain social order, actually protected the social dimension of sin.

Christ wants to rectify this situation. By appealing to men's hearts in the Sermon on the Mount, Christ indicates that the "discernment of good and evil inscribed in human conscience can turn out to be deeper and more correct than the content of a legal norm" (TOB 35:5). The way to the "new ethos" passes through the rediscovery of the ethos of creation, which had been lost in the general Old Testament understanding and in the application of the commandment against adultery (see TOB 42:2).

---

51. See *CCC*, no. 1610.
52. *CCC*, no. 1963.
53. For example, see Leviticus 18 and Deuteronomy 22:13–30; 25:11–12.

The Prophets

If Israel's legislation at times obscured the correct content of the commandment against adultery, the prophets point to the true content of the norm when they denounce Israel's unfaithfulness to Yahweh by comparing it with adultery.[54] The legislative texts describe adultery as the violation of the right of ownership. Moreover, in keeping with the mentality of the time, this referred primarily to the man's legal "ownership" of his wife—often one of many—and the "right" he had to her body. However, John Paul demonstrates that in the text of the prophets, the background of real and legalized polygamy does not alter the ethical meaning of adultery. Nor do the prophets speak of adultery as a violation of rights over the body. For the prophets, adultery is a sin because it constitutes the breakdown of man and woman's covenant.[55]

The prophets recognize that monogamy is the only correct analogy or sign of the "marital" covenant between God and the Chosen People. Adultery then becomes "the antithesis of this spousal relation" and "the opposite of marriage" (TOB 37:4). In this way, the prophets paved the way for Christ and what he would teach about the foundations of sexual morality.

It is true that a man and woman who have established a marital covenant have a legal "right" to sexual union, and adultery violates this right. But sexual union in marriage is not merely a legal "right." John Paul's rich personalism will not allow him to stop at this juridical description. This "bodily unity," he says, is "above all...the regular *sign* of the communion of persons" (TOB 37:4). It is the bodily expression of a covenant "born from love." Only such love establishes the proper foundation of that union in which man and woman become "one flesh." The Pope adds that it is precisely this spousal love that gives a fundamental significance to the truth of "covenant"—both in the man-woman relationship, and, analogously, in the Yahweh-Israel (God-man) relationship. Adultery not only violates a legal right; John Paul describes it as a radical *"falsification of the sign"* of man and woman's covenant love (see TOB 37:4). The prophets express precisely this

---

54. See Hosea 1–3, and Ezekiel 16, for example. In the text of the Pope's catechesis, he quotes Ezekiel 16 almost in its entirety because, as he says, "It expresses *the analogy between adultery and idolatry* in a particularly strong and comprehensive way" (TOB 37:3).

55. See *CCC*, no. 1611.

aspect of adultery in describing the infidelity of the Israelites to their covenant with Yahweh.

Anthropology and Ethics of the Sign

John Paul bases his understanding of the bodily union as "the regular sign" of the communion of persons in marriage on his previous reflections from Genesis. He will also develop this idea more fully in Part II when he reflects on Ephesians 5:31–32. For now he simply adds that this understanding of bodily union as the "sign" of married love is essential and important for the theology of the body, both from an ethical and an anthropological point of view (see TOB 37:5).

From an anthropological point of view, understanding the one flesh union as the regular sign of the marital covenant helps us understand who man and woman are as incarnate persons "called, in the very mystery of creation, to exist in the communion of persons 'in the image of God'" (TOB 32:1). From an ethical point of view, John Paul asserts that we "can speak of moral good and evil according to whether this relationship makes such a 'unity of the body' true and whether or not *it gives to that unity the character of a truthful sign*" (TOB 37:6). This key statement gives shape to the Holy Father's renewed context for understanding marriage and sexual morality. We will return to this statement several times.

The Pope is trying to help us see that Catholic teaching on sexuality is not rooted in arbitrary legislation. It is not based merely on the maintenance of juridical rights and duties, as has been emphasized by various treatises in the past.[56] Catholic sexual ethics rest on the firm foundation of anthropology. They rest on *who we are* and *who we are called to be* as men and women created in God's image. For John Paul, sexual morality is most clearly understood through the logic of "the truthful sign." In other words, in order to determine what is good, we

---

56. One can note the difference in language between the 1917 Code of Canon Law and the new Code of 1983. Canon 1081 in the 1917 Code speaks of marriage as a contract of yielding rights, first among them the *right to the body* (the *ius ad corpus*). Canon 1055 of the 1983 Code speaks of marriage in more personalist terms. It does not avoid the word "contract," but it views marriage also as a "covenant" and "partnership of the whole of life," which is "ordered to the good of spouses and the procreation and education of children."

only need to ask a simple question: Does this sexual attitude, thought, or action truly image God's free, total, faithful, and fruitful love? If it does not, it can never bring beatitude. It can never fulfill us. It is contrary to who we are and who we are called to be. This question transfers the discussion from legalism to liberty, from the prohibition and restriction of legislation to the empowerment and freedom of love. The question then shifts from "How far can I go before I violate the law?" to "What is the truth that sets me free and empowers me to love in God's image as male and female?" To this latter question John Paul could summarize his answer with one word: Christ!

B. "WHOEVER LOOKS WITH LUST..."

We have been analyzing the first part of Christ's statement in the Sermon on the Mount: "You have heard that it was said, 'You shall not commit adultery.'" When, in the second part of Christ's statement, he says, "But I say to you," we encounter "a direct transition to the new ethos" (TOB 38:1). Christ establishes this "new ethos" by transferring the meaning of adultery from the "body" to the "heart." Christ *knows* man's heart; "for he himself knew what was in man" (Jn 2:25). Although cultural conditions affect men and women of different times and places, the condition of man's heart—the "echo" of his original holiness and the tragedy of sin—remains the same in every time and place. As the Pope points out, the man of our time feels called by Christ's words about lust no less than the man of that time, whom the Teacher addressed directly (see TOB 34:3).

Even so, John Paul believes it is important to understand the context in which Christ's actual listeners received his revolutionary words. Thus, having looked briefly at the Law and the prophets, John Paul points us now to the Wisdom literature of the Old Testament. Presumably Christ's listeners, upon hearing his words, would have related them to these books since they contain repeated admonitions about lust and also advice as to how to preserve oneself from it.[57] John Paul logically concludes that these books paved the way for Christ's words.

---

57. See TOB 38:4 for a list of examples from Proverbs, Sirach, and Ecclesiastes.

The Wisdom Tradition and the New Ethos

True to their name, these books contain great wisdom. They reveal an intimate knowledge of the human heart and even develop a specific moral psychology. In this way, the Wisdom books "are in some way close to Christ's appeal to the 'heart' reported by Matthew" (TOB 38:5). Even so, John Paul says that with "one-sided" admonitions that often make woman out to be "a downright seducer of whom to beware," the Wisdom texts do not change man's ethos in any fundamental way. "Such a transformation of ethos had to await the Sermon on the Mount" (TOB 38:6). For example, whereas the Wisdom texts offer understandable admonitions such as "Turn away your eyes from a shapely woman" (Sir 9:8), John Paul says that in the Sermon on the Mount, Christ invites us "to a pure way of looking at others, capable of respecting the spousal meaning of the body."[58]

As experience attests, the battle with lust remains fierce. For the man bound by lust, "Turn away your eyes" retains all its wisdom. Christ, however, "speaks in the context of human experience and at the same time in the context of the work of salvation." In the new ethos, these "two contexts in some way superimpose themselves on each other and interpenetrate" (TOB 38:2). This means that, although we all *experience* lust, we can also *experience* a real transformation of our hearts through the *salvation* Christ offers us. As the *Catechism* teaches, in the "Sermon on the Mount...the spirit of the Lord gives new form to our desires, those inner movements that animate our lives."[59]

Christ did not die on a cross and rise from the dead merely to give us coping mechanisms for sin (we already had plenty of those without a savior). Christ died and rose again *to set us free from sin*. To the degree that a man's heart has been transformed and *vivified* by the Spirit of the Lord, he need not merely "cope" with lust by turning his eyes away from a woman (or a woman from a man). Through continual death and resurrection, our desires take on "new form." The more we grow in mastery of ourselves, the more we experience a proper "*ethos of seeing*" (TOB 63:6). We become empowered to look at others purely—and not only to "look" but also *to see* others purely, to *see* the true beauty of *the person* revealed—not despite the body but *in and through the body*.

---

58. *Veritatis Splendor*, 15.
59. *CCC*, no. 2764.

This is a "new" ethos in relation to that of the Wisdom texts, which seem to presuppose bondage to concupiscence. In this new ethos, the Pope tells us elsewhere,

> we come to an ever greater awareness of *the gratuitous beauty of the human body*, of masculinity and femininity.... With the passage of time, if we persevere in following Christ our Teacher, we feel less and less burdened by the struggle against sin, and we enjoy more and more the divine light which pervades all creation. This is most important, because it allows us to escape from a situation of constant inner exposure to the risk of sin—even though, on this earth, the risk always remains present to some degree—so as to move with ever greater freedom within the whole created world. This same freedom and simplicity characterizes our relations with other human beings, including those of the opposite sex.[60]

As we experience "the new ethos of seeing," we come to an ever deeper appreciation for the sacramentality of the human body. We come to see others with eyes of love and as signs of divine love. When we live from what the Pope calls "the deeper heritage of our hearts" (see TOB 46:6), we do not desire to lust. This deeper place in our "hearts" will not let us lust. Lust itself, although we may still experience its "pull," becomes distasteful in the measure that we experience a mature level of the virtue of chastity. Chastity, as Karol Wojtyla says, "is not a matter of summarily 'annihilating' the value 'body and sex' in the conscious mind by pushing reactions to them into the subconscious." If chastity "is practiced only in this way, [it creates] the danger of...'explosions.'" Rather, the "essence of chastity consists in quickness to affirm the value of the person in every situation, and in raising to the personal level all reactions to the value of 'the body and sex.'"[61]

The truly pure person experiences a profound *integration* of sexuality and personality. From the male perspective, what he is attracted to and what *he sees* in a woman's feminine beauty is the dignity of her person. Her femininity becomes a sign that makes visible the invisible mystery hidden in God from time immemorial. He sees her body as a theology, a "theophany" of sorts—a revelation of the mystery of God. Such a man has "passed over" from the Old Testament ethos to the

---

60. John Paul II, *Memory and Identity* (New York: Rizzoli Books, 2005), p. 29.
61. *Love and Responsibility*, pp. 170–71.

New Testament ethos. He is empowered not only to meet the law's demands but also to *fulfill the law.*

Attaining this level of purity is a task given to every man and woman.[62] It is certainly a fragile journey demanding a lifetime of diligent effort and arduous struggle. Victory does not come overnight, nor can one ever claim to have accomplished a permanent victory in this life.[63] Because lust will always be a reality in a fallen world, we will always need God's mercy. But the grace of his mercy *enables* us to attain a mature level of purity. No matter how deep our wounds and distortions go, the cross of Christ goes deeper, and John Paul continually insists that *real power* flows from Christ's death and resurrection to restore in us the purity that was lost through sin. Our struggle with concupiscence will only cease in the eschaton, but as the *Catechism* teaches: "Even now [purity of heart] enables us to see *according to* God." It "lets us perceive the human body—ours and our neighbor's—as a temple of the Holy Spirit, a manifestation of divine beauty."[64] The more we gaze with faith upon Christ, the more "his gaze purifies our heart." In turn, "the light of the countenance of Jesus illumines the eyes of our heart and teaches us to see everything in light of his truth."[65]

> ▰ Although Christ did not come to give us coping mechanisms for sin, so long as we live in the historical tension of the "already, but not yet" of redemption, we still need them. But if many spiritual advisors seem to focus on the "not yet," John Paul is at pains to balance this with the "already." The more we tap into this "already," the more the beauty of the body rouses praise of God, not lust. As John Climacus wrote in *The Ladder of Divine Ascent*, "Someone, I was told, at the sight of a very beautiful body, felt impelled to glorify the Creator. The sight of it increased his love for God to the point of tears. Anyone who entertains such feelings in such circumstances is already risen...before the general resurrection."[66]

---

62. See *CCC*, nos. 2013, 2545; see also *Veritatis Splendor*, 18.
63. See *CCC*, no. 2342.
64. *CCC*, no. 2519.
65. *CCC*, no. 2715.
66. *The Ladder of Divine Ascent*, step 15, 58, p. 168.

The following story illustrates what mature Christian purity looks like. Two bishops walked out of a cathedral just as a scantily clad prostitute passed by. One bishop immediately turned away. The other bishop looked at her intently. The bishop who turned away exclaimed, "Brother bishop, what are you doing? Turn your eyes!" When the bishop turned around, he lamented with tears streaming down his face, "How tragic that such beauty is being sold to the lusts of men." Which one of these bishops was *vivified* with the ethos of redemption? Which one had passed over from merely meeting the demands of the law to a superabounding fulfillment of the law?

As an important clarification, the bishop who turned his eyes *did the right thing*, since he knew that if he had not done so he would have lusted. We classically call this "avoiding the occasion of sin" by "gaining custody of the eyes." This is a commendable and necessary first step on the road to a mature purity. But it is only a first step. We are called to more. The bishop who turned away desired the good with his will, but his need to turn away in order to avoid lusting demonstrates that concupiscence still dominated his heart. As the *Catechism* teaches, the "perfection of the moral good consists in man's being moved to the good not only by his will but also by his 'heart.'"[67] To the degree that our hearts are transformed through ongoing conversion to Christ, our purity matures, enabling us to see the body for what it is: a sign that makes visible the invisible mystery hidden in God from time immemorial. To the degree that we cannot see this, the distortions of sin still blind us.

I am not suggesting the average man should look for opportunities to "test" his purity by gazing upon scantily clad women. Indeed, the large majority of men must heed the Old Testament admonition to "turn away your eyes." But for anyone who doubts that the purity of the "bishop who looked" is possible, I must add that the above example is adapted from the story of Bishop St. Nonnus of Edessa and the harlot Pelagia. Stories of their encounter differ and the details are sketchy. But it is generally reported that upon seeing the half-naked Pelagia parading through

67. *CCC*, no. 1775.

the streets of Antioch while his brother bishops turned away, Bishop Nonnus looked upon her with love and great delight. She noticed his look of love and was eventually converted through his counsel and preaching. She is known as St. Pelagia of Antioch.[68]

The Inner State of the Man of Concupiscence

The Pope points out that the Wisdom literature offers some "classic" descriptions of carnal concupiscence. Sirach 23, for example, describes concupiscence as a "burning fire" that heats the soul and "will not be quenched until it is consumed." The man of concupiscence "will never cease until the fire burns him up." John Paul develops this description with a remarkably keen phenomenological analysis of lust. This "flaring up in man," the Pope says, "invades his senses, arouses his body, draws the feelings along with itself, and in some way takes possession of the 'heart'" (TOB 39:2). It also causes the "outer man" to reduce the "inner man" to silence. In other words, because passion aims at satisfaction, "it blunts reflective activity and disregards the voice of conscience" (TOB 39:2).

Once the "outer man" has suffocated the voice of conscience and given his passions license, he remains restless until he satisfies the insistent need of the body and the senses for gratification. One might think that this gratification should put out the fire, but on the contrary, as experience attests, it does not reach the source of inner peace. Since it only touches "the most external levels" of the person, the man who commits his will to satisfying concupiscence finds neither peace nor himself. On the contrary, as Sirach points out, he "*is consumed.*"

John Paul can describe the phenomenon of lust with such vivid precision because he himself, no doubt, battled it in his own heart. Lest anyone think that popes are exempt, this Pope would have been the first to admit that, like the rest of us, he experienced concupiscence. But unlike so many of us, he was also a tremendous witness to the fact that "when passion is set into the whole of the spirit's deepest energies, it can also become a creative force" (TOB 39:2). If we allow our passions to "undergo a radical transformation," they can become, once again, the desire to love as God loves.

---

68. For an account of Nonnus and Pelagia, see Helen Waddell, *The Desert Fathers* (Ann Arbor: University of Michigan Press, 1957), pp. 181–96.

External Modesty

Without this radical transformation of our passions we can only exhibit an "external modesty." The Holy Father relates that a merely external modesty provides an appearance of decency, but is really more a fear of the consequences of indecency rather than a fear of the evil in itself. In other words, the heart is not changed. The externally modest person still desires to gratify his (or her) disordered passions without regard for conscience. However, he might manage to refrain from acting on his disordered desires when he fears the consequences of doing so.

Here is a common example from the male point of view. Men of lust often seek to gratify their passions by looking lustfully at women. However, a man speaking to a woman at whom he would like to look lustfully will usually muster up the willpower to refrain from doing so in order to avoid getting caught. However, he will immediately shed this veneer of modesty as soon as she turns around and can no longer see the manner of his look. He will then allow lust to "flare up" in his heart, since he is no longer in danger of being caught. In doing so, even though he does not commit adultery in the body, he commits adultery in his heart. Furthermore, according to a different translation, he makes that woman an adulteress in his heart.[69] He does not change her actual being into that of an adulteress, but he changes her in his mind, through imagining scenes of adultery with her. Such an external modesty points all the more to the importance of allowing Christ's words in the Sermon on the Mount to penetrate our hearts and transform us.

Penetrating the "Lustful Look"

Christ does not explain the meaning of lust in the Sermon on the Mount. He seems to presuppose knowledge of it in his listeners. John Paul says that if a person really does not know what lust is, then Christ's words do not apply to him. Yet everyone (male and female) *knows* these words apply to him, because everyone experiences lust in his heart. We know it as an interior act that can express itself in a "look" even without expressing itself in a bodily act. Christ appeals to this common experience. John Paul wants to penetrate more deeply into this phenomenon of looking lustfully.

---

69. John Paul seems to favor this more ancient translation (see TOB 24:4 and 38:1).

In a fallen world, and particularly today in our media culture, temptations to "look lustfully" besiege us. Christ is not saying that a mere glance or momentary thought makes one guilty of adultery. Only when lust "drags the will into its narrow horizon" (TOB 41:2) can we speak of committing adultery in the heart. Concupiscence itself is not a sin. It comes from sin (original sin) and inclines us to sin, but merely recognizing its tug within us does not mean we have sinned. On this side of heaven, we will always be able to recognize the pull of concupiscence. It is what we do when we recognize it that matters. If we choose with Christ's help to struggle against concupiscence, we enter into the paschal mystery and grow in virtue and holiness. If, on the other hand, we choose to indulge concupiscent impulse, we choose to sin. Sin requires that man *acts* and is not merely acted upon. In other words, sin involves the subjective dimension of self-determination. "Only then— that is, from this subjective moment and its subjective prolongation" (TOB 41:3)—can we say that a person has "looked lustfully" and, thus, committed adultery "in his heart."

When a man, having experienced the inclination to lust, activates his will (self-determination) to "look" at another in this way, he expresses what is in his heart; he expresses *who he is*. "Christ wants to show that the man 'looks' in conformity with what he is" (TOB 39:4). These are powerful words. In his TOB, John Paul wants to outline *who man is*. We gain crucial insight into this question by understanding how man looks at his own body and, even more so, how he looks at the bodies of others. The character of his look determines the way he formats or understands reality itself. According to John Paul, "Christ teaches us thus to see the look as the threshold, as it were, of the interior truth" (TOB 39:5).

"In the beginning" man looked at the world as the gift that it was. He looked with respect toward all of creation and gratitude toward the Creator. Having distinguished himself from the animals, man looked at himself with deep awe and wonder, knowing that as a "partner of the Absolute" he was the crown of creation and was called to love (see p. 99ff.). Man's respect for creation and deep wonder at himself crystallize, finally, in the peace of the original naked gaze of man and woman at each other. This gaze, this look, not only reveals that they know each other's worth, dignity, and goodness. It also reveals the deepest intention of their hearts with regard to existence. Their naked bodies witnessed to the truth that all of creation was a gift, and that Love was the source of that giving (see p. 128ff.). This is what they saw when they "looked" at each other. Life, then, meant offering themselves—their bodies—to God and to each other in thanksgiving for so great a gift.

The entrance of the threefold concupiscence affects *everything*. It changes, as John Paul says, "the intentionality of man's very existence" (TOB 41:1). "Intentionality," in John Paul II's phenomenological use of the term, means to be "about something." Concupiscence effects a profound shift in the direction of the self—in what the person is "about"— and this deep shift is manifested whenever a person "looks lustfully." If looking in this manner did not concern such a deep change of intentionality, Christ's words about the possibility of committing grave sin "in the heart" would have no meaning (see TOB 41:1). The person who lives from the threefold concupiscence no longer sees life as a gift to receive in thanksgiving from the hands of the Creator. Instead, concupiscence indicates the denial of the gift of God. From this perspective, life—if one is to attain it—must be *grasped*.

Concupiscence as a Reduction

The grave evil committed by the lustful look is precisely this: the denial of the gift expressed in the dignity of sexual difference. The man (male) who lives "the gift" recognizes woman as a gift to be received both from the hands of the Creator and through the freedom of her own self-determination as a personal subject. But the man who denies the gift does not wait to receive woman as a gift. Instead, he extorts her gift; he *grasps* at her instead of *receiving* her. By doing so, John Paul tells us that the man deprives the woman of her attraction as a person. By focusing merely on the attraction of her body, he reduces the woman to an object to satisfy the sexual "need" inherent in his fallen masculinity (we could say something similar with regard to the way a woman under lust's influence treats a man).

This "intentional 'reduction' is," the Pope tells us, "above all of an axiological nature" (TOB 40:3). In other words, it indicates a fundamental change in *the value* that man (male and female) assigns to the body, to sexuality, and also to the whole universe. The man absorbed by concupiscence no longer views creation with a sense of awe and wonder nor respects it as a gift from the Creator. Rather, creation and its goods are exploited and abused for selfish gain. They are grasped at rather than received with thanksgiving. In this way concupiscence alters the intentionality of man's entire existence at its roots. We can recall here our previous discussion regarding the effects of man's new attitude toward his body on ecology and societal structures of labor and the economy (see p. 186ff.).

Psychological Interpretation of Lust

The Holy Father points out that the biblical/theological meaning of lust differs from the psychological meaning. The science of psychology speaks of lust as a desire for or intense attraction toward the sexual value of another person. It places no ethical meaning on the word. The biblical use of the word, however, has great ethical significance, since it means a value is being impaired. This "value" is the value of the person revealed by the spousal meaning of the body. Lust is sexual desire divorced from the spousal (and procreative) meaning of the body. Lust has the internal effect of obscuring the true significance of the body, and hence, of the person itself. But the full value of the body-person can only be understood in light of the original call of man and woman as revealed in Genesis. Psychology by itself, then, does not have the context to understand lust as an impairment. It just seems "normal." Even if men and women can intuit that lust is contrary to their dignity, they cannot fully know why without the aid of revelation.

When we compare lust with what revelation tells us about the original mutual attraction of the sexes, we realize that lust is actually a rejection of true sexual desire. It involves, as we have already seen, an intentional "reduction" of God's original plan. The person who looks lustfully reduces both himself and the person at whom he looks lustfully. Each becomes less, not less in himself or herself, but less in the intentional order inasmuch as the person who looks lustfully abstracts sexual values from the whole mystery of the person. His look is not "about" seeing the beauty of the person revealed through the body. Rather, his look is "about" gratifying himself by reducing the other to an object of consumption. Lust entails a restriction or "closure of the horizon of the mind and the heart" (TOB 40:3) to the full truth of the person and the perennial call to communion. Sex "is part of all the whole richness of values" with which man and woman relate to one another. In fact, the body in its sexuality is meant to reveal all this "richness of values." It is one thing to recognize this, and we *must* come to recognize this through the integration of sexuality and personality. But it is quite another thing, the Pope points out, to reduce all the personal richness of the other's sexuality to an object of selfish enjoyment.

"Eternal" Sexuality

Sexuality provides an "invitation" and issues a "calling" to communion through reciprocal self-giving. John Paul states that this dimension and orientation of human thoughts and hearts is so fundamental to humanity that it "constitutes one of the main guiding threads of universal human culture" (TOB 40:2). In this universal sense John Paul speaks of the "eternal masculine," the "eternal feminine," and the "perennial attraction" between them. When man taps into this "eternal" dimension of sexuality, John Paul proclaims that it can free in him an entire gamut of spiritual-physical desires of an especially *personal* and *communal* nature—all of which correspond to a proportionate hierarchy of values regarding the person (see TOB 40:3). This is a spiritually mature sexual attraction. Concupiscence, on the other hand, does not have its sights on this "eternal" dimension. It seeks immediate gratification and thereby obscures the rich hierarchy of values that marks the perennial attraction of the sexes. Lust turns from the man and woman's personal-sexual call to communion and pushes sexual attraction toward utilitarian dimensions, within which men and women use one another merely to satisfy their own felt needs.

In this utilitarian mode, sexuality "ceases to be a specific language of the spirit; it loses its character as a sign. It ceases," John Paul continues, "to bear on itself the stupendous spousal meaning of the body...in the context of the consciousness and experience of this meaning" (TOB 40:4). In other words, while the body retains its spousal meaning objectively speaking, man no longer readily feels or experiences it. His conscience has become dulled to it. Using a precise, vivid image, John Paul says that lust "tramples on the ruins of the spousal meaning of the body" and "aims directly toward one and only one end as its precise object: *to satisfy only the body's sexual urge*" (TOB 40:4). The man of concupiscence is not concerned with the body's spousal/procreative meaning. In fact, he often sees it as a nuisance, since it impedes him from satisfying concupiscence. To his own demise, the man of concupiscence will continually seek ways of eliminating this obstacle in his insatiable desire for gratification. John Paul stresses again that such an intentional and axiological reduction is completely contained in the way man "looks" (see TOB 40:5).

C. "HAS COMMITTED ADULTERY IN THE HEART..."

A Key Change of Direction

Recall that in this section of our study—*Commandment and Ethos*—we are looking for the true ethical meaning of Christ's words about lust from the Sermon on the Mount. Christ first reminds his listeners of the commandment, "You shall not commit adultery"; then he adds, "But I say to you." Here Christ wants to demonstrate how this commandment "is to be understood and put into practice so that 'the justice' willed by God-Yahweh as Legislator might abound...in a measure greater than the one resulting from the [common] interpretation...of the Old Testament" (TOB 42:2).

It is within this perspective that John Paul turns his attention to the final part of Christ's statement: "has committed adultery in the heart." The Pope considers this "*the key expression*" for understanding the correct ethical meaning of Christ's words. "This expression is at the same time *the main source for revealing the essential values of the new ethos*" (TOB 42:4). What does this new ethos demand of us? It is obvious, according to Christ's teaching, that a man commits adultery in his heart when he looks lustfully at a woman other than his wife. However, the Pope says we can and even *must* ask whether Christ approves of a man looking lustfully at his own wife. John Paul's answer to this question immediately caught the attention of the international media.

The Typical Interpretation Requires a Deepening

Basic logic, when initially applied to this question, finds no problem with a man looking lustfully at his own wife. John Paul even stated early on in this cycle of reflections that "such a look of desire directed toward one's own wife is not adultery 'in the heart,' precisely because the man's relevant interior act refers to the woman who is his wife, in relation to whom adultery cannot take place" (TOB 25:4). If we stop at the surface, this reasoning seems entirely sound. However, as we have learned by now, John Paul II never stops at the surface. A deeper look at Christ's words indicates that there remain good grounds for doubt "whether this reasoning takes into account all the aspects of revelation and of the theology of the body" (TOB 42:7).

As John Paul will explain, this interpretation of Christ's words (i.e., that it is acceptable to lust after one's own wife) fails to take into account the subjective dignity of the persons involved. John Paul's personalist understanding of ethics will not allow him to reduce the illicit to the illegal. As Christ insists, we must penetrate the heart. Hence, John Paul believes this typical interpretation requires "a deepening" in light of the anthropological and theological insights gained from his study of Christ's words. In classic personalist form, John Paul states that Christ not only considers the legal status of the man and woman in question. He also makes the moral evaluation of sexual desire depend above all on *the personal dignity of the man and the woman*. The Holy Father concludes, therefore, that the moral evaluation of sexual desire "is important both in the case of unmarried persons and—perhaps even more so—in the case of spouses" (TOB 42:7).

When Christ speaks of committing adultery in the heart, it is significant that he does not refer to a woman who is not the man's wife. He simply refers to woman generically. As John Paul states, "Adultery 'in the heart' is not committed only because the man 'looks' in this way at a woman who is not his wife, but *precisely because he looks in this way at a woman*." He thus concludes: "*Even* if he were to look in this way at the woman who is his wife, he would commit the same adultery 'in the heart'" (TOB 43:2).

This statement evoked a firestorm of criticism from the international media. Accusations flew that John Paul had such a negative evaluation of sex that he was condemning it even within marriage. The reaction was so widespread and severe that it prompted the Vatican newspaper *L'Osservatore Romano* to publish a response.[70]

Claudio Sorgi, the author of the Vatican response, suggested that certain media reports reflected "superficiality, lack of respect, and

---

70. See *L'Osservatore Romano*, October 12, 1980. The full text of this article was printed in *Blessed Are the Pure of Heart*, the second in the original four-volume set of the TOB (Boston, MA: Pauline Books & Media, 1983).

absence of attention" to what the Pope was saying, which led to "misunderstandings, we hope in good faith." Unfortunately, some comments
were "so improvised and absurd as to be stupefying." Hence, the "suspicion arises," he concluded, "that not all the mistaken interpretations are
in good faith." Furthermore, Sorgi pointed out that to adulterate a
relationship simply means to distort it as compared with its original
meaning. "Now what is it," he asks, "if not adultery, to reduce the conjugal relationship to a mere satisfaction of sexual need?" Appealing to
modern sensibilities, Sorgi submits, "has it not been said and written
plainly in recent years that marriage often becomes a condition of slavery especially for the woman; that she is reduced to an erotic object or
even that in certain cases the conjugal relationship is only masked
prostitution?"

A Clarion Call to Uphold Woman's Dignity

John Paul's statement about adulterating sexual union within marriage is nothing but a clarion call for men to uphold the dignity of their
wives and vice versa. Both sexes are called to exist "for" the other sex
through the free and sincere gift of self. Yet lust—in this case of the
husband toward his wife—fundamentally changes the way in which
woman exists "for" the man. It reduces the deep riches of her attractiveness as a female person to the mere satisfaction of the husband's concupiscent urges and thereby robs her of her dignity as a subject made in
God's image. A man who uses woman's femininity to satisfy his own
"instinct" has assumed this attitude "deep down," inwardly deciding to
treat a woman in this way. This is precisely "adultery committed in the
heart." So a man can commit such adultery in the heart even with his
own wife, if he treats her as nothing but an object to satisfy his lusts
(see TOB 43:3).

Simply getting married does not suddenly justify a man and woman
using one another as a means of selfish gratification. For John Paul,
using is the antithesis of love. Sexual union is only justified (i.e., made
just, right, good, and holy) when—inspired by the love of God—man
and woman give themselves to each other in the divine image.
Marriage, while an absolute prerequisite, does not automatically guarantee that this will happen. Spouses must commit themselves all the
more to living according to the logic of "the truthful sign." They must

therefore guard against any thought or action that would make their union a *countersign* of God's love. Indulging concupiscent desire (like adultery) is just such a countersign.

■ How does this fit in with the traditional teaching that the "relief of concupiscence" is an end of marriage? This has often been interpreted to mean that marriage provides a legitimate outlet for indulging concupiscent desire. Such an interpretation all but gives men carte blanche to use their wives for their own selfish gratification. Because of this seriously misguided mindset, confessors and spiritual directors have often counseled wives that they are obligated to submit to their husbands' sexual needs upon request. But such "common wisdom" cloaks a terribly distorted anthropology. As Dr. John Crosby insists, "It is not too much to say that John Paul abhors any such interpretation" of the relief of concupiscence.[71] Such a misguided view fails entirely to take into account the new ethos to which Christ directs men and women in the Sermon on the Mount. A look at the Latin provides a window into understanding John Paul's perspective on the issue. *Remedium concupiscentiae* is actually better translated "*remedy* for concupiscence." While "relief" implies mere indulgence of concupiscent desire, "remedy" implies that the grace of marriage offers a healing of concupiscent desire. Through the healing power of the redemption of the body, men and women can progressively (re)experience sexual desire as God created it to be—the desire to love as he loves in the sincere gift of self. Only this understanding of *remedium concupiscentiae* is compatible with a personalist understanding of sexual ethics. As Cardinal Wojtyla wrote in a 1974 essay on marriage, "If it is true that marriage may also be a *remedium concupiscentiae* (see St. Paul: 'It is better to marry than to burn'—1 Cor 7:9), then this must be understood in the integral sense given it by the Christian Scriptures, which also teach of the 'redemption of the body' (Rom 8:23) and point to the sacrament of Matrimony as a way of realizing this redemption."[72]

---

71. See *The Legacy of John Paul II*, ed. Geoffrey Gneuhs (New York: Crossroads, 2000), p. 57.

72. "The Family as a Community of Persons," *Person and Community*, p. 327.

For those who have understood John Paul's thought up to this point, his teaching about the possibility of committing "adultery in the heart" within marriage makes complete sense. However, for those who are locked in a fallen view of sex, John Paul's statement seems to disqualify all sexual expression—hence, the media's barrage of criticism. Indeed, John Paul affirms that it is impossible to arrive at the second interpretation of Christ's words if we confine ourselves to the purely psychological interpretation of lust. Christ's words in the Sermon on the Mount call us to a theological understanding of lust as a reduction of God's plan "in the beginning."

The Real Possibility of Purity of Heart

A psychological understanding of lust sees the selfish sting of concupiscence as "normal." Yet, as John Paul insists in this crucial statement, Christ's words in the Sermon on the Mount demonstrate that "Christian ethos is characterized by *a transformation of the human person's consciousness and attitudes...such as to express and realize the value of the body and of sex* according to the Creator's original plan" (TOB 45:3). Psychology knows nothing of this "original plan" or the real hope of transforming the heart in this regard. Psychology knows only the reduction of lust. If *that* is wrong—if *that* is "adultery in the heart"—then men and women, husbands and wives, have no hope. They can only fear the severity of Christ's words and clamor against the Pope's interpretation of them.

In this sense, the Pope's critics understood John Paul correctly. Left solely to the forces of (fallen) nature, there is no hope for husbands and wives *not* to adulterate their own relationship, at least to some degree. But certain media reports completely missed that Christ's words (and John Paul's interpretation of them) are deeply imbued with the hope and *the real possibility* of redemption from the distortions of concupiscence. John Paul asks, "Should we *fear* the severity of...[Christ's] words or rather *have confidence* in their salvific content, in their power?" (TOB 43:7).

█████ The *Washington Post* article that reported on this address shows how much the secular media missed the "good news" of John Paul's call to sexual redemption. Judy Mann, in her article "A

Lesson on Lust for the Vatican," grants that the Pope's remarks on lust were "motivated only by the best of intentions." However, she then goes on to inform the Pope that "he may not be familiar with the role lust plays in the American family.... From the time Americans reach adolescence, lust is the life force." Mann seems to favor marriage and family life, but she seems blind to the real possibility of any alternative to lust as the foundation for marriage. She reports that in her day "one of the first things you learned at your mother's knee was that boys had only one thing on their minds—which was you-know-what—and that the road to the altar was paved with firm denials. I know for a fact," Mann says, "that in my generation lust led to hundreds of thousands of American marriages." Not only does lust lead to marriage, according to Mann, it can also aid marital fidelity. She concludes that "the Pope might want to bear in mind" that if "a man has lust in his heart for his wife, chances are he won't have adultery on his mind for somebody else."[73] These are the sad conclusions of a merely psychological interpretation of lust. Not only does it normalize lust, it asserts it as a good. Interestingly, however, Mann's tone hints that she may wish things were different. Unfortunately, she has resigned herself to the lesson (and attendant worldview) learned at her mother's knee: Lust is just the way it is. In light of this "lesson on lust for the Vatican," John Paul boldly calls Mann (and her mother) to "another vision of man's possibilities" (TOB 46:6).

John Paul II's interpretation of Christ's words are exacting, to say the least. If we are to live this new ethos, we must undergo a radical paradigm shift with regard to the way we think of and experience sexuality and sexual desire. We must allow "the innermost recesses of the human heart" to be thoroughly revealed. We must *"rediscover the lost fullness of...[our] humanity and want to regain it"* (TOB 43:7). In other words, we must perceive the true, liberating meaning of "purity of heart" and open ourselves to receive it as a gift of grace flowing from Christ's death and resurrection.

---

73. Judy Mann, "A Lesson on Lust for the Vatican," *Washington Post*, October 10, 1980, B1 and B2.

Of course, virtue does not come to fallen man without toil. If a person desires authentic liberation from lust, he must work in tandem with grace and firmly reject everything that stems from concupiscence. As Christ figuratively states, he must "pluck out his eye" and "cut off his hand" if these cause him to stumble. For "it is better that you lose one of your members than that your whole body go into hell" (Mt 5:29–30). Why are Christ's words so harsh and foreboding? One might observe in this context that lust and hell can both be defined with the same five words: *the absence of God's love.* This is why lust is so serious. If God's love constitutes man's origin, vocation, and destiny, then lust constitutes the antithesis of man's very existence.

The Guiding Thread of Existence

Christ takes such a firm stand against lust because lust is the most tenacious obstacle to an authentic communion between the sexes—and man and woman's call to form a communion of persons "is the deepest substratum of human ethics and culture" (TOB 45:3). Humanity stands or falls on this point. Impurity has consequences far beyond the bedroom. It leads to "the whole moral disorder that deforms both sexual life...and the functioning of *social, economic...*and even cultural *life*" (TOB 51, n. 61).[74]

John Paul observes that human life is by its nature "co-educational." The common life of men and women "makes up the pure and simple guiding thread of existence." Thus, the dignity and balance of human life "depend at every moment of history and in every place of geographical longitude and latitude on 'who' she shall be for him and he for her" (TOB 43:7). In short, a culture of lust degenerates into a culture that does not respect life—a culture of death. Only when men and women are freed from the grip of lust that strangles the spirit can they fulfill themselves in the freedom of the gift. And this freedom "is the condition of all life together in the truth" (TOB 43:6). Only in freedom can men and women realize "the sacramental unity" that the Creator himself

---

74. This statement certainly contradicts the idea that a person's "private" sexual behavior has no bearing on anyone outside the bedroom. A Jewish proverb recounts the story of a man on a boat drilling a hole beneath his seat. When the man sitting next to him protests, he replies, "Why should you care what I'm doing? It's under *my* seat."

willed (see Gen 2:24). Without this internal liberation from concupis-cence, a life together in the truth cannot exist. And the new dimension of ethos, John Paul says, "is always linked with the revelation of the depth that is called 'heart' and with the liberation of the heart from 'con-cupiscence' *so that man can shine more fully in this heart*" (TOB 43:6).

4. The "Heart"—Accused or Called?

In this section of the catechesis, John Paul shifts to a more practical analysis of Christ's words guided by the question: "Is the heart accused or called to the good?" (TOB 44:1). If humanity stands or falls on puri-ty of heart, how do we live so that we might stand? If we accept Christ's words, how are we to think? How are we to feel regarding sexuality, sexual attraction, and desire? Can anything in us reliably guide our thinking, feeling, and acting in this regard? If Christ's words do not merely accuse the human heart but also call us to good—what, exactly, is that good? "These questions are significant for human 'praxis,' and they indicate an organic link between 'praxis' itself and ethos. A living morality is always the ethos of human praxis" (TOB 44:2). In other words, as Christ himself indicated (see Mt 15:19), human actions (praxis) flow from the orientation of the human heart (ethos). A "living morality," then, takes us beyond mere duty. It flows from the super-abounding love in one's heart. With John Paul's shift to a more practi-cal analysis, he wants to show the way to attain that proper orientation of heart so that what flows from our hearts in practice will be a fulfillment of Christ's words.

The "how to's" of living according to Christ's words in the Sermon on the Mount have found multiform expressions throughout history. Currents of thought have drawn nearer to or moved further from the true ethos of Christ's words based on various historical factors. They have passed "from the pole of pessimism to the pole of optimism, from puritanical strictness to present-day permissiveness. It is necessary to realize this," according to John Paul, "so that the ethos of the Sermon on the Mount can always be sufficiently transparent when it confronts man's actions and behavior" (TOB 44:4).

With this statement, John Paul sets the stage for the proper appli-cation of Christ's words in human practice. At the dawn of the third

Christian millennium, having learned from the currents of history that have swung the pendulum from rigorism to license and back, it seems we can now penetrate Christ's words with more balance and accuracy. It seems we are now better prepared to establish the proper "ethos of human practice" in this vexing field of morality.

A. CONDEMNATION OF THE BODY?

Manichaeism

John Paul knows that if we are to think with the mind of the Church in understanding the proper sense of Christ's words, we must contend with the "Manichaean demon" that has plagued religious thought on the body to a greater or lesser degree throughout history. In its original form, Manichaeism saw the source of evil in matter, in the body, and therefore condemned everything physical in man. Since our bodiliness, as John Paul notes, manifests itself above all through a person's sex, Manichaeism particularly devalues all things sexual.[75]

John Paul knows that—like a wolf in sheep's clothing—such heretical thinking has seeped into many Christians' minds and hearts and must be uprooted. Some would even claim that the harshness of Christ's words in the Sermon on the Mount harmonize with a Manichaean devaluation of sex. Hence, the Holy Father firmly and repeatedly stresses that "the Manichaean way of understanding and evaluating man's body and sexuality is essentially foreign to the Gospel" (TOB 45:5). Therefore, anyone who wants to see in Christ's words a Manichaean perspective would be committing an essential error. "The adequate interpretation of Christ's words," as John Paul unambiguously affirms, "must be absolutely free from Manichaean elements in thought and in attitude" (TOB 45:3).

While the unaccustomed ear might equate the severity of Christ's words with the severity of Manichaeism, the essential difference lies in the assignment of evil. Manichaeism assigns evil to the body and sex itself. Christ assigns evil to man's heart, and not even to man's heart itself, but only to the distortion of lust. Lust devalues the body. Christ's statement in the Sermon on the Mount, then, springs "precisely from

---

75. John Paul offers a further explanation of the Manichaean ethos in the footnote of TOB 44.

an affirmation of the personal dignity of the body and of sex and only serves such dignity" (TOB 45:5). Thus, Christ's words in no way condemn the body and sex or deny their value. Instead they express a deep and mature affirmation of the body and sex. Christ calls his listeners to understand the body's supreme dignity both objectively and subjectively. John Paul poetically observes that Christ impresses this mature dimension of ethos on the pages of the Gospel in order to impress it subsequently in human life and human hearts. Only when the truth about good penetrates the heart—that is, only when ethic becomes ethos—can we speak of a "real" and a "human" morality.

Irreconcilable Difference in Mentality

John Paul summarizes the irreconcilable difference in mentality this way: "While for the Manichaean mentality, the body and sexuality constitute...an 'anti-value,' for Christianity, on the contrary, they always remain 'a value not sufficiently appreciated'" (TOB 45:3). Far from devaluing the body and sex, Christianity assigns to the body and sex a value beyond compare. Recall John Paul's thesis that the "body, in fact, and only the body, is capable of making visible what is invisible: the spiritual and the divine. It has been created to transfer into the visible reality of the world the mystery hidden from eternity in God, and thus to be a sign of it" (TOB 19:4). Now, in the context of countering Manichaeism, John Paul returns to his thesis and states that the "body in its masculinity and femininity has been called 'from the beginning' to become the manifestation of the spirit. It becomes such a manifestation also through the conjugal union of man and woman when they unite with each other so as to form 'one flesh.'" In this way the body "takes on the value of a sign, in a certain sense a sacramental sign" (TOB 45:2).

This is the value that the Manichaean mentality "insufficiently appreciates" (or fails to appreciate altogether): The body and sex are sacramental—through the veil of a sign they make the divine mystery visible. Christ calls men and women to rediscover this value and live according to the logic of "the truthful sign" both in thought and in action. Hence, the Pope insists that Christian praxis in this regard only concerns detaching oneself from the evil of lust. It *never* means transferring the evil of lust to its object. "Such a transfer would signify—perhaps not in a fully conscious way—a certain acceptance of the

Manichaean 'anti-value.' It would not constitute a real and deep victory over the evil of the act...; on the contrary, there would be concealed in it the great danger of justifying the act to the detriment of the object" (TOB 45:4).

In other words, in seeking to live according to Christ's words in the Sermon on the Mount, we must be sure that we are battling the true evil—lust. We must never project the evil in question onto the body and sexuality of the person toward whom our lusts are directed. Christ certainly demands detachment from the evil of lust, but John Paul insists that this never means that the object of that desire, that is, the woman who is "looked at lustfully," is an evil.[76] In fact, so long as man redirects the assignment of evil from his own lusts to the woman, he exempts himself from any need to overcome the evil in his heart. We can see, then, that the Manichaean condemnation of the body "might—and may always be—a loophole to avoid the requirements set in the Gospel" (TOB 44:6).

John Paul reproaches those who condemn the body and sexuality in the name of holiness, when, in fact, such "holiness" stems from a resistance of the demands of holiness. Mature holiness leads men and women to a thorough victory over the evil of lust through an ongoing transformation of the deep impulses of the heart. It demands an "ethos of seeing" with purity of vision. This is not only the ability to turn away from a potential object of lust. Even more so it is the ability, through the ongoing maturation of purity, to affirm positively with one's look that "object," which is always also a subject, a person.

███ This assignment of the Manichaean "anti-value" to the body can be seen in the tendency to describe sex or certain body parts as "dirty." No body part is "dirty." Nor is it ever accurate to call sex itself dirty. For God looked at all he had made and called it *very good*. What may be unclean or impure is the human heart and its view of certain body parts or its manner of engaging in sex. It would be misguided, for example, for a mother who catches her son viewing pornography to scold him for looking at "dirty pic-

76. John Paul notes that this important clarification seems to be lacking in some Wisdom texts. See, for example, Proverbs 5:1–6, 6:24–29, and Sirach 26:9–12.

tures." While it may be unconscious and unintentional on the mother's part, the assignment of evil is then on the body (since they are pictures of the body) instead of on the evil of lust behind the production and the viewing of pornography. As John Paul says, pornographic portrayals of the body raise objections "not because of their object, because in itself the human body always has its own inalienable dignity—but because of the quality or the way of its artistic reproduction" (TOB 63:5), which is intended to incite lust. This distinction is not just a matter of semantics but has to do with the proper assignment of evil. It has to do with conforming our language to authentic Christian teaching on the body. Consider also the common question asked when knocking on someone's bedroom door before entering: "Are you decent?" In light of the above, the only proper response to such a question—even if one is entirely naked—is an unequivocal "yes!" The body is *always* decent. Only the manner of another's "look" may lack decency. Thus, we cover the body out of reverence for its goodness, its decency—not to hide any supposed indecency.

Negation of the Body versus Victory over Lust

Sexuality is "deeply penetrated" by the mystery of the "redemption of the body" (see Rom 8:23). Only in this light can we properly understand Christ's words. If Christ accuses the heart of lust, he also calls man to experience a "real and deep victory" over the evil of lust in order that man may rediscover and live according to the true value of the spousal meaning of the body. On the other hand, John Paul says that the Manichaean attitude leads to "annihilation" and "negation" of the body and of sex, or at best to their "mere toleration" because of the necessity of procreation.

The idea that the Church thinks sex is bad, even if she grants the one reluctant exception of condoning it for procreation, is widespread. Many people, Catholics and non-Catholics alike, might actually believe that such heretical thinking is official Church teaching! Even some of the Church's otherwise esteemed thinkers have said things that lend credence to these ideas. In these addresses, John Paul II's ardent desire to set the record straight almost seems to leap off the page.

The Pope insists that in our efforts to overcome lust, we must contend with the "deep seated habits" springing from Manichaeism in our way of thinking and evaluating things (see TOB 46:1). A man struggling with lust, for example, can easily blame the woman after whom he is lusting rather than look deeply into his own heart. As John Paul observes, true victory over lust for such a man stems, rather, from his effort to "discover the authentic value" of the woman's body and sexuality and "to reaffirm them" so that the Manichaean "anti-value" does not take root in his consciousness and in his will (see TOB 45:5). This means much more than simply turning away in order to avoid looking with lust. Containing lustful impulse is the essential first step. But if a person's purity stops here, it is only a "negative" purity, so to speak. It is only a "turning away." As such, it carries the danger of slipping into the Manichaean error of assigning an "anti-value" to that from which a man is continually turning, that is, a woman, a person.

To gain a true victory over lust, John Paul says that purity must mature from the "negative" turning away to the more "positive" recognition and assertion of the real beauty, dignity, and value of the body and of sex.[77] This can only happen through the concerted effort, in this case, of the man, guided by grace, to see the true dignity of the woman's *personhood* revealed through her feminine body. Through the indwelling of the Holy Spirit, such dignity becomes not only a concept accepted by the mind but also a living reality "seen" by the eyes and "felt" by the heart. Indeed, the ethos of redemption enables man to be "moved to the good not only by his will alone, but also by his sensitive appetite."[78] This is the task that Christ gives us, and this is what the "redemption of the body" affords: the gradual reintegration of body and soul, of personality and sexuality, and the ability to *see* this and *experience* it—not perfectly in this life, but progressively and effectively. As we allow our diseased ways of thinking about the body to be crucified with Christ, we come to see the body as he sees it. Of course, most of us will experience setbacks on our journey, and we may sense that we are far from the ideal to which God calls us. Even so, as long as we keep

---

77. John Paul speaks of the "negative" and "positive" dimensions of purity more explicitly in TOB 54:3 and 129:5.

78. *CCC*, no. 1770.

our eyes fixed on Christ, he will bring to completion the work he has begun in us (see Phil 1:6).

■ From the moment of the very first sin, men have tended to blame women for their own disordered hearts (see Gen 3:11–12). Certainly women have a responsibility not to play on men's weaknesses. But whether women live responsibly in this regard or not, men have their own *prior* responsibility to battle lust and continually mature in purity to the point that they can see and assert *every* woman's true value and dignity.[79] If men do not take this responsibility seriously, they will almost inevitably project an air of blame toward women for their own lusts. And women, it seems, have antennas for picking up on this. This dynamic was exemplified in the comments of a young person who heard a talk of mine on woman's dignity. She attended a Catholic college where students, for the most part, genuinely desire to grow in holiness. She shared with me the emotional effects of having men for three years continually turn away or look at the sidewalk whenever she walked across campus. Those men may have needed to do this in order to avoid lusting. But was there not one man on that campus pure enough to look at her and in so doing affirm her dignity rather than lust after her? Every human being is crying out to be seen and loved—to be acknowledged positively as a person of value and worth. One can easily imagine that over time a woman in such circumstances might come to believe that there was something wrong with her—that *she* was responsible for causing men to stumble simply by being a woman. This woman said that what struck her most about the talk was that *she was good*; that she, herself, as a woman was not the problem. For she had a God-given dignity that shone in her femininity, whether the men on campus could see that or not. This is obviously a delicate situation, since it is better for a man not to look at a woman than to look at her with lust. But it is better yet to mature to the point where a man can look at a woman and, as master of himself, assert in positive affirmation the true dignity and value of the person.

---

79. See the concluding paragraphs of *Mulieris Dignitatem*, 10 and 14.

B. THE "HEART" UNDER SUSPICION?

"Masters of Suspicion"

We are approaching the crux of the matter for historical man: the crux of human practice. How is man to live? He is to live according to the purity of his origins. That is the norm; that is the standard; that is man's task. Through the ethos of redemption, he is called to regain what was lost. As Christ's words indicate in both his discussion with the Pharisees and in the Sermon on the Mount, man and woman are called progressively to reclaim the spousal meaning of the body as it was revealed "in the beginning."

This may sound a bit unrealistic. After all, in the state of original innocence—which, as the Church teaches, man has left irrevocably behind—man and woman did not need to contend with the threefold concupiscence. In the experience of historical man, however, the lust of the flesh always weighs him down and casts a shadow on all things sexual. Given that, it seems the best a man can hope for in this fallen world is to learn somehow to manage his unruly impulses and avoid the near occasions of sin. We have become so wounded and twisted that concupiscence, as common experience attests, will always have the upper hand in man's heart—at least in this life.

Will it? Those who believe that lust *inevitably* determines our experience of the body and sexuality can count themselves among those whom John Paul labels "the masters of suspicion." A master of suspicion is a person who does not know or does not fully believe in the transforming power of the Gospel. Concupiscence holds sway in his own heart, so he projects the same onto everyone else. In his mind the human body will always rouse concupiscence, especially if it is partially exposed, and all the more so if it is totally naked. It can do nothing else. So he holds the human heart in a state of continual and irreversible suspicion.

■ The story of the two bishops previously mentioned (see pp. 215–16) illustrates the interpretation of suspicion. The bishop who turned away readily assumed that his brother bishop was looking with lust. Having never experienced a real and deep victory over lust, he could not imagine any other way to look at the woman and he immediately accused his brother bishop of indulging lust. In this way, he held his brother's heart in a state of suspicion.

The Protestant scholar Paul Ricoeur coined the phrase "masters of suspicion" in describing the thinking of Freud, Marx, and Nietzsche. As John Paul points out, these thinkers have significantly influenced the way modern man understands himself and interprets morality. John Paul admits that we see a significant convergence in each of their systems of thought with a scriptural analysis of man, but we see also a fundamental and unmistakable divergence. Like Christ in the Sermon on the Mount, these men also "accuse" the human heart. The Holy Father even sees a particular correspondence in each of these thinkers' systems with one of the three forms of concupiscence described by St. John. John Paul suggests that Nietzschean thought corresponds in some sense with "the pride of life"; Marxist thought with "the concupiscence of the eyes"; and Freudian thought, of course, with "the concupiscence of the flesh."

But convergence ends here because these men make concupiscence "the absolute principle of anthropology and ethics" (TOB 46:2); they place concupiscence at the core of their interpretation of man. The Pope stresses that biblical anthropology does not allow us to stop here but opens us to the ethos of redemption. This is the fundamental divergence: the "masters of suspicion" see no hope of redemption from lust. This interpretation "is very different; *it is radically different* from the one we discover *in Christ's words* in the Sermon on the Mount." Christ's words "bring to light...another vision of man's possibilities" (TOB 46:6).

It is certainly true, as John Paul observes, that if man leaves himself at the mercy of the forces of fallen nature, "*he cannot avoid the influence of the concupiscence of the flesh*" (TOB 46:3). But it is equally true that man is not merely at the mercy of the forces of his fallen nature. The Pope insists that in Christ, fallen nature is always at the same time *redeemed* nature. With full confidence in the power of Jesus' death and resurrection to free us from sin, the Vicar of Christ stresses: "*Man cannot stop at casting the 'heart' into a state of* continual and irreversible *suspicion* due to the manifestations of the concupiscence of the flesh.... Redemption is a truth, a reality, in the name of which man must feel himself called, and 'called with effectiveness'" (TOB 46:4). Yes, *real power* gushes forth from Christ's crucified and risen body to *set us free from the domination of concupiscence*. As the Holy Father proclaims, we are "*called to rediscover,* or even better, to realize, the spousal meaning of the body...[through] that spiritual state and power that derive from mastery over the concupiscence of the flesh" (TOB 46:4).

Again it must be emphasized that the mature form of such mastery is not akin merely to corralling a wild horse (see p. 202). Certainly to the degree that concupiscence seeks to rear its ugly head, it must be "caged." But as one's mastery over lust matures, grace operatively transforms the horse so it no longer needs the corral. Of course, even a tame horse needs reins so that its master can guide and direct it. With mature self-mastery, as John Paul tells us, one enjoys "*the ability to orient* the respective *reactions* [of arousal and emotion] both as to their content and as to their character" (TOB 129:5). The freedom to do so is precisely "the freedom of the gift."

The Meaning of Life Is at Stake

Perfect freedom from concupiscence is reserved for the eschaton when we will be forever united with Christ in his resurrection. Until then we remain on the difficult and fragile pilgrimage of "becoming."[80] Yet "in a certain way...by virtue of the Holy Spirit, Christian life is already now on earth a participation in the death and Resurrection of Christ."[81] If we do not believe that men and women—even while still on the journey toward perfection—can die to lust and be raised to a new life of victory over it, then it seems that we do not fully believe in (or are not fully aware of) the *good news* of Christ's death and resurrection and how it can effectively operate in our lives.

Sin has wounded us deeply. Even so, as the Pope stresses, the original meaning of our humanity is "indestructible," and the "new man" risen with Christ is called with power to rediscover it. Hence, a continuity is established between "the beginning" and the perspective of redemption (see TOB 49:4). Christ does not invite man to return to the state of original innocence, since humanity has left it irrevocably

---

80. See *Veritatis Splendor,* 18.
81. *CCC,* no. 1002.

behind. Nevertheless, in Christ, we *can* live and love as God intended in the beginning. But a key difference exists between the original and historical state: Living the truth came naturally to original man, while historical man must engage in an arduous spiritual battle in order to see the body as God created it to be. But if we are willing to die with Christ, we too can come to share his victory over sin. We can *experience* and *know* this victory deep within our hearts—not easily, and not overnight, but progressively through suffering for the truth, we are purified inwardly, and the lies lose their power over us.

Doubt in this regard comes easily. Doubt, after all, takes us off the hook. If we consider Christ's appeal in the Sermon on the Mount hopelessly unrealistic, we do not have to challenge ourselves to grow or to change. It gives us a quick and easy detour around the cross (if such a thing exists). John Paul warns us not to detach Christ's appeal from the context of concrete existence (see TOB 46:6). The expectation that Christ places on us in the Sermon on the Mount (i.e., that we would *see rightly*) is entirely realistic in light of who he is, who we are, and what he came to do for us. If it seems hopelessly unrealistic, we need to ask ourselves what we really believe about who Christ said he is and what his death and resurrection mean in our lives. We must not fall into the trap of "holding the form of religion" while "denying the power of it" (2 Tim 3:5).

Much is at stake. In fact, even though Christ's appeal to overcome lust refers only to a certain sphere of human interaction, within this sphere it always means "the rediscovery of the meaning of the whole of existence, of the meaning of life" (TOB 46:6). If we close ourselves to the possibility of a real transformation of our hearts, we lock ourselves into an interpretation of man, a "hermeneutic," riddled with suspicion. And, as John Paul clearly states, "The meaning of life is the antithesis of the hermeneutics 'of suspicion'" (TOB 46:6).

Grace, Faith, and Man's Real Possibilities

Above we quoted John Paul saying that Christ's words in the Sermon on the Mount reveal "not only another ethos, but also another vision of man's possibilities" (TOB 46:6). Most people who contest Christ's teaching about lust in the Sermon on the Mount (and Christian teaching on sexuality in general) do so specifically because they do not believe it corresponds with the concrete possibilities of man. John Paul responds:

> But what are "the concrete possibilities of man"? And of *which* man are we speaking? Of man *dominated* by lust or of man *redeemed by Christ*? This is what is at stake: the *reality* of Christ's redemption. *Christ has redeemed us!* This means he has given us the possibility of realizing the *entire truth* of our being; he has set our freedom free from the *domination* of concupiscence. And if redeemed man still sins, this is not due to an imperfection of Christ's redemptive act, but to man's will not to avail himself of the grace which flows from that act. God's command is of course proportioned to man's capabilities, but to the capabilities of the man to whom the Holy Spirit has been given; of the man who, though he has fallen into sin, can always obtain pardon and enjoy the presence of the Holy Spirit.[82]

This bold papal proclamation brings us to the heart of the matter. John Paul, Christ's modern-day apostle, echoes the words of the Apostle Paul: "Do not empty the cross of its power!" (see 1 Cor 1:17). If we accept the Pope's challenge to ponder the *full power* of Christ's death and resurrection, we come to realize that this "other vision of man's possibilities" opens before us vistas of freedom and joy of which few men and women ever dream.

Returning to our image of the flat tires—despite the dysfunction of driving through life with the rubber shredding off the rims, many of us have become so accustomed to this that life with inflated tires might seem threatening. Such a vision demands that we reevaluate perhaps an entire lifetime of the diseased ways of thinking and relating we have grown accustomed to and may even have assimilated into a "deflated" notion of holiness. "Be not afraid!"

Grace Restored

As John Paul observes, only grace—life in the Holy Spirit—enables us to experience true liberation from lust and the joy that freedom brings. In the beginning, the grace given to man and woman constituted them in a state of original holiness and justice. This "beatifying gift" enabled them to see each other as God saw them, as evidenced by orig-

---

82. *Veritatis Splendor*, 103, emphasis in original.

inal nakedness (see p. 139). In the redemption, grace is given first for the remission of sins, yet it abounds in such a way that man can gradually reclaim God's original plan for human life. Christ's words in the Sermon on the Mount "testify that *the original power* (and thus also the grace) *of the mystery of creation becomes* for each one of...[us] *the power* (that is, the grace) *of the mystery of redemption*" (TOB 46:5). Recall that grace is "participation in the inner life of God himself, in his holiness." It is "that mysterious *gift made to man's innermost [being]—to the human heart—that allows* both the man and the woman *to exist* from the 'beginning' *in the reciprocal relationship of the disinterested gift of self*" (TOB 16:3).To be full of grace, then, means to be full of the Holy Spirit, of the very Love and Life of the Trinity, who *in*-spires the dust of our humanity with the capacity to love according to the image in which we are made.

The first Adam rejected this gift at the prompting of the deceiver. The New Adam restores this gift in fidelity to the Father. To experience this restoration, we need faith. For "*faith*, in its deepest essence, is *the openness* of the human heart to the gift: *to God's self-communication in the Holy Spirit.*"[83] We must open our hearts—yes, those same hearts accused and found guilty of lust—to Christ our Bridegroom. With utter trust and genuine humility we must submit our hearts to his judgment, to his justice. When we do, Christ returns to us a heart not condemned, but vivified. The more we surrender our hearts in this way, the more we experience the Holy Spirit impregnating our sexual desires "with everything that is noble and beautiful" with "the supreme value, which is love" (TOB 46:5).

The need for this transformation wrought by grace is essential. According to John Paul, it "concerns the very 'nature,' the very substrate of the humanity of the person, the deepest impulses of the 'heart'" (TOB 46:5). To be filled with God's grace is—in a less strict sense of the term—man's "natural" state, the way God created man to be "in the beginning." Without this transformation, without this grace, we cannot live according to the ethos of the Gospel. Without this transformation, the best we can do is "cope" with our lusts. Christ's words call us to so much more!

---

83. *Dominum et Vivificantem*, 51.

Christ's Call Wells Up from Within

Furthermore, as John Paul states, "Christ's words spoken in the Sermon on the Mount are not a call hurled into emptiness" (TOB 46:5). They find a home in man's heart precisely because man is not completely absorbed by the lust of the flesh. He *can* seek another form of mutual relations in the sphere of the perennial attraction of the sexes. In fact, even when experiencing lust, man feels within his own heart a deep need to preserve the dignity of the mutual relations of the sexes. The word of the Gospel calls him to this, so man experiences this call from "outside" himself. Yet at the same time the Holy Father insists that man also experiences this call from "inside" himself. This is what he means by saying Christ's words are not hurled into emptiness. When we let Christ's words act in us, they tap into that "echo" of our beginning deep within our hearts—that beginning that was "very good"; that beginning in which man and woman knew and lived the full truth of the body and, hence, were naked and felt no shame.

The more a person allows the echo of that good beginning to resound in his heart, the more he will realize, as John Paul says, that "the heritage of his heart" is deeper than the sinfulness inherited; *it is deeper than lust.* What cause for rejoicing! Lust is not the final word on man. Lust is not at man's core. The heritage of the human heart is deeper than all its distortions. And "Christ's words, set in the whole reality of creation and redemption, re-activate that deeper inheritance and give it real power in human life" (TOB 46:6).

To use an image, if the heart is a "deep well," the water—having been cut off from its source—often appears stagnant and murky. But beyond the mud and mire remains something of our "very good" creation—a spring with the capacity of yielding crystal clear waters. Christ reactivates that spring! Tapped into, these waters well up in us to purify us. Indeed, they well up in us to eternal life (see Jn 4:14). Despite our many sins and distortions, at our core, behold: we *are* very good!

C. EROS AND ETHOS

Is Eros Equated with Lust?

We have been discussing the "how to's" of growing in holiness according to the ethos of the Sermon on the Mount. Continuing with this theme, in his audience of November 5, 1980 (TOB 47), John Paul begins an analysis of the relationship between "eros" and "ethos"— between what is erotic and what is ethical. Do the words of Christ in the Sermon on the Mount condemn the erotic? Do they warn severely against eros? To answer these questions, we must clarify what we mean by "eros."

The Holy Father recounts that the Greek term "eros" passed from mythology into Plato's philosophy, then into romantic literature, and finally into its common usage today. He acknowledges that eros has a vast range of meanings according to its usage in different periods and cultures. Each of these shades of meaning points in its own way to the *"complex riches of the heart"* to which Christ appealed in the Sermon on the Mount (see TOB 47:4). Yet the sensual and sexual nature of eros forms the common thread woven in all these meanings.

John Paul defines "erotic phenomena" as "those actions and reciprocal forms of behavior by which man and woman approach each other and unite so as to be 'one flesh'" (TOB 47:4). The main point of the Pope's catechesis is to analyze these "erotic phenomena" and understand them in light of biblical revelation. John Paul wonders if the term "eros" leaves room for the ethos Christ announced. Does eros merely refer to the lust that Christ condemns? Or can eros also refer to that good and beautiful attraction of the sexes revealed "in the beginning" by the spousal meaning of the body?

Longing for the True, Good, and Beautiful

Ever determined to establish the fundamental goodness of sexual desire and sensuality, John Paul refuses to surrender the term eros to the distortion of lust. He creatively rehabilitates eros by appealing to Plato's philosophy. In Platonic usage, eros means the interior force that attracts man to the true, good, and beautiful. Within this sphere, the way opens toward what Christ expressed in the Sermon on the Mount. The Pope believes that people often see Christ's words about lust merely as a prohibition against eros without trying to discover "the truly deep and essential *values*" that this prohibition covers and ensures (see TOB 47:6). If we would open our hearts to the deeper meaning of Christ's words, we would find that Christ desires to liberate us to experience the true meaning of eros.

The Holy Father never tires of explaining that Christ not only accuses the heart of lust but also appeals to the heart to rediscover the goodness of God's original plan for sexuality. The ethos of redemption, then, "means *the possibility and the necessity of transforming* what has been weighed down by the concupiscence of the flesh" (TOB 47:5) so that we might experience eros as the desire for "what is true, good, and beautiful." John Paul firmly establishes that eros and ethos are not opposed to one another as many presume. Instead, through the transforming power of redemption, eros and ethos "*are called to meet in the human heart and to bear fruit in this meeting*" (TOB 47:5). When eros and ethos meet, they bear fruit in purity. Purity leads us in truth. Those with a mature purity of heart simply do not "look with lust." Even if concupiscence still tugs at them, the pure of heart can recognize it, resist it, and allow grace to "untwist" it. In this way man and woman come to participate to a significant degree in the original good of God's vision. Perfection in this regard comes only in the eschaton. Yet even now, purity enables us to see with God's vision, to view the body as a manifestation of divine beauty.[84] Men and women, husbands and wives who mature in this purity actually "taste" something of that experience of original nakedness. Yes, for the pure of heart, the erotic is true! It is good! It is beautiful!

The more we come to see this, the more the cloud of negativity and shame that tends to hover over all things sexual dissipates in our hearts. We no longer tend to condemn manifestations of sexuality with a sense of suspicion. Instead, we experience the very meaning of life and understand the fundamental place of sexuality in it. And we know it is *very good*.

The Problem of Erotic Spontaneity

If we are to progress on the road to holiness, if eros and ethos are to meet in our hearts and bear fruit, John Paul says that we must succeed in being an "interior man." We must allow our hearts to be transformed from "within." Caught up in our society's non-reflective, results-oriented mentality, we are often tempted to modify externals without addressing the deeper issues of the heart. Yet the only path to holiness

---

84. See *CCC*, no. 2519.

is to open one's deepest self to grace and accept the slow and often painful process of inner transformation. It is called taking up the cross daily and following Christ (see Lk 9:23). That alone produces "results."

To "succeed in being really an interior man...[means to be able] to obey right conscience, able to be the authentic master of...[our] own innermost impulses, like a watchman who watches over a hidden spring" (TOB 48:3). Only then are we free to draw from all those impulses what is truly pure. In this way we continually "rediscover the spousal meaning of the body and the true dignity of the gift in what is 'erotic.' This is the task of the human spirit," John Paul says, and "it is by its nature an ethical task. If one does not assume this task, the very attraction of the senses and the passion of the body can stop at mere concupiscence, deprived of all ethical value." If men and women stop here, they do "not experience that fullness of 'eros,' which implies the upward impulse of the human spirit toward what is true, good, and beautiful, so that what is 'erotic' also becomes true, good, and beautiful" (TOB 48:1). What joy! What hope! What truth, goodness, and beauty!

John Paul shows himself to be a true "interior man" with the penetrating insight he offers those who wish to watch over their "hidden spring" and draw pure waters from it. To paraphrase a lengthy passage, he says that we must learn with perseverance and consistency the meaning of our bodies and of our sexuality. We must learn this not only in the abstract (although this, too, is necessary), but above all in the interior reactions of our own "hearts." This is a "science," he says, that cannot be learned only from books because it concerns deep knowledge of our interior life. Deep in the heart we learn to distinguish between what, on the one hand, composes the great riches of sexuality and sexual attraction, and what, on the other hand, bears only the sign of concupiscence. And although these internal movements of the heart can sometimes be confused with each other, we have been *called by Christ to acquire a mature and complete evaluation allowing us to distinguish and judge the various movements of our hearts.* "One should add that this task *can* be carried out and that it is truly worthy of man" (TOB 48:4).

We have already noted the Pope's realism in this regard. Sometimes we can easily confuse love and lust. To be sure, on this side of perfection we will always recognize mixed motives in our hearts. This should not stifle us, however. In fact, the Holy Father affirms that the discernment we are speaking of has an essential relationship with spontaneity. It is often thought, as the Pope points out, that living according to Christ's words in the Sermon on the Mount puts a serious dent in the spontaneity of man and woman's relationship. Spontaneity is here understood as "doing what comes naturally" or acting immediately on what moves and attracts a person. Someone moved and attracted by lust views the moral path as a real impediment to eros. "Yet this opinion is mistaken and, at any rate, superficial. If we accept it and obstinately maintain it, we will never reach the full dimensions of eros" (TOB 48:2).

The full dimension of eros comes when men and women are free with the freedom of the gift; when they are free from the chains of lust that compel them to indulge concupiscence and degrade the true, good, and beautiful. A person experiences this full dimension of eros, therefore, when he is moved and attracted by that which is true, good, and beautiful—by the rich storehouse of values contained in sexuality as a God-given path to an authentic gift of self and communion of persons. Such a person chooses the truth *spontaneously*. The moral norm no longer acts merely as a constraint because his heart conforms significantly with the truth. Here we encounter the transforming power of Christ's words about lust. They do not only prohibit. As John Paul says, whoever accepts Christ's words about lust "should know that he or she is also *called to full and mature spontaneity* in relationships that are born from the perennial attraction of masculinity and femininity. Such spontaneity is itself the gradual fruit of the discernment of the impulses of one's own heart" (TOB 48:2).[85]

Mature Spontaneity and Noble Pleasure

Sexual excitement derived from concupiscence flares up in the immediate reactions of the heart with a *"subjective intensity"* that extends its dominion over man's emotions and involves his whole body (see TOB 47:3). Such a flaring up of lust demands immediate or "spontaneous" gratification. But this type of sexual excitement "is quite different from the deep emotion with which not only inner sensibility but also sexuality itself reacts to the integral expression of femininity and masculinity" (TOB 48:4). Through the gift of redemption, through the

---

85. See *CCC*, no. 1972.

meeting of eros and ethos, the character of sexual excitement is transformed and integrated with the dignity of the person and the supreme
value of love. The more we experience this transformation, the more
the desire to make a sincere gift of ourselves wells up from within us—
and with an intensity much more refined and grand than mere lust can
ever rouse.

> ■ The image of the burning bush can illustrate the difference
> between lust and a spiritually mature sexual desire. When lust
> flares up in us, it consumes us with such an intense heat that it
> devours any fuel we supply it. The heat not only chars the bush but
> also reduces it to ash. Christ wants to raise us up from our ashes!
> He wants to impregnate our sexual desire (eros) with the fire of his
> own passionate love (agape). When we experience the fire of
> redeemed sexual desire, we "burn" but are not consumed. Indeed,
> we rediscover our own humanity. We rediscover our primordial call
> to love and communion. We rediscover that we are made in the
> image of a God who revealed himself to Moses in a blazing bush
> that was not consumed.

Genuine erotic spontaneity actually leads, as John Paul says, to "a
noble pleasure" in the sexual sphere (see TOB 48:4). It taps into that
original beatifying experience because it forms man and woman in a
true communion of persons. This deep and mature spontaneity
remains unknown to those bound by concupiscence. Such a man refuses to pay the price of gaining self-control. And, paradoxically, the
authentic spontaneity to which Christ calls us all comes precisely at the
cost of self-mastery. Only by exercising such mastery can the human
heart rediscover "the spiritual beauty of the sign constituted by the
human body in its masculinity and femininity" (TOB 48:5). This is the
epiphany of the body referred to previously (pp. 134–35). When we see
and experience the body as a sign of God's eternal mystery of communion, this conviction comes to permeate our minds and hearts. The
value of the sign comes *spontaneously* to guide both our desires and our
choices. Hence, John Paul concludes that this mature spontaneity of
the human heart does not suffocate its noble desires and aspirations
but on the contrary, it liberates them and even facilitates them (see
TOB 48:5).

5. The Ethos of the Redemption of the Body

In the audience of December 3, 1980 (TOB 49), John Paul begins drawing his reflections on Matthew 5:27–28 to a close. He recaps the context in which Christ is speaking and summarizes some of the previous themes. He opens by stressing several times that this is a *new* ethos. It is new not only in regard to the Old Testament but also new in regard to every man of every period and culture. By stressing this "newness," it seems as though he is challenging us to recognize that even after two thousand years of Christian history, the new ethos still has not firmly established itself in many people's lives. People are still relying on their own resources in trying to live a Christian life. We have only two options in this case: repress our disordered desires in a misguided attempt to attain "holiness" (this leads to "angelism" and rigorism), or abandon the real demands of the Gospel for a watered-down version that allows us to indulge our disordered desires ("animalism" and laxity).

The new ethos fundamentally differs from both approaches. It demands a *radical* paradigm shift from typical perspectives and manners of living. Radical, of course, means "to the root." The new ethos is meant to do precisely this: return us to our roots, to the purity of our origins. As John Paul says, in the new ethos "the original ethos of creation was to be taken up anew" (TOB 49:4). This is why Christ refers to the beginning in discussing the problems surrounding man and woman's relationship. The new ethos, then, is "the ethos of redemption and especially the ethos of the redemption of the body" (TOB 49:2). Only the perspective of redemption justifies Christ's reference to "the beginning." Without this perspective, we have only our own resources. We have only concupiscence in its three forms. Even if a spark of God's original plan still remains in us, without the perspective of the redemption of the body, we have no hope of fanning that spark into flame.

The Whole Mission of Christ

By calling the man of concupiscence back to "the beginning" through the redemption of the body, Christ establishes a continuity between original man and historical man. Moreover, as we shall learn, the redemption of the body will be fully revealed only in the final resurrection, of which Christ speaks on another occasion. Hence, life in the body for historical man not only calls him to live in continuity with his origins. Life in the body here and now is also meant to lead him in continuity (while maintaining the important discontinuity) to his ultimate destiny: the consummation of all things; the resurrection of the body.

What John Paul is speaking about in terms of experiencing the restoration of God's plan for the body and sexuality is no footnote in the Christian life. Indeed, it pertains to the whole spectrum of God's plan for us. According to the Holy Father, this redemption of the body "is, in fact, the perspective of the whole Gospel, of the whole teaching, even more, of the whole mission of Christ" (TOB 49:3). Of course we will never open ourselves to the gift of redemption if we do not first have a profound realization of our *need* for redemption. John Paul reminds us that to aspire to virtue, purity of heart, and Christian perfection requires an awareness of our own sinfulness as a necessary starting point and an indispensable condition.

To grow in this perfection, we must "make an alliance" with the new ethos. We must give our entire selves to it. We must sell everything (see Mt 13:44), put our hands to the plow, and never look back (see Lk 9:62). When we do that, our "deepest and yet most real possibilities" manifest themselves and "the deepest layers of...[our] potentiality acquire a voice" (TOB 49:6). John Paul points out that those who surrender to lust, to suspicion, and/or to the Manichaean anti-value have no knowledge of those deepest layers of their own hearts. The ethos of redemption, on the other hand, "is based on a strict alliance with these layers" of the human heart (TOB 49:6). It is these layers of the heart that can recognize the value of the spousal meaning of the body. These layers can see in the body "the value of a transparent sign." This sign, in turn, reveals "the gift of communion, that is, the mysterious reality of...[God's] image and likeness" (TOB 49:5).

This is precisely the manner by which we experience "the whole mission of Christ" according to the call of the Sermon on the Mount. It means rediscovering and living according to the dignity and value of the human body as a sign of (and calling to) communion. And communion is man's origin, vocation, and destiny. *This* is the perspective of man's whole life, of Christ's whole teaching and mission. Those who, by God's grace, experience a mature purity are able to see and realize that this "whole perspective of the Gospel" is mysteriously contained in and revealed *through the human body* in its creation and redemption.

Growing in Holiness

Experiencing this mature kind of purity is not only theory for John Paul; it manifests an aspect of true holiness. And such holiness is truly attainable. But as already stated, a mature purity of heart does not come automatically. It is a gift of grace to be sure, but we must diligently cooperate with this grace. The Holy Father observes that when a person often yields to the lust of the flesh, turning from it is not only difficult, but also may give the impression of suspending sexual desire in a "void." This is especially true, he says, when a person makes up his mind to deny lust for the first time. "Yet, already the first time, and all the more so later when he has gained the ability, man gradually experiences his own dignity." He "attests to his own self-dominion and demonstrates that *he fulfills what is essentially personal in him*. In addition, he gradually experiences the freedom of the gift" (TOB 49:6).

Notice John Paul's emphasis on experience. Man is capable of *experiencing* his own dignity. He does so precisely when he exercises his freedom to choose the true, good, and beautiful. When someone acts against lust rather than allowing lust to act against him, he activates his self-determination and, hence, "*what is essentially personal in him.*" This is the battle for the dignity of our own personhood: will we *act* for the good; or will we forfeit our self-determination and let evil *act upon us*? Concupiscence is always ready to invade our hearts, dominate our senses, and assault our self-determination. We can acquiesce. Or we can *act* from our essence. This is the quintessential moment of truth. Much is at stake here, for in this moment man determines *the intentionality of his very existence*. Do man's passions determine what is good, or is there an objective reality of the good outside of man to which he must submit himself and toward which he must, with the help of grace, direct his passions?

If in this moment man conquers the enticing illusion of lust and acts in conformity with the truth of his humanity made in God's image, he regains his original dignity as a person. In fact, John Paul says that overcoming lust is a "reminiscence of original solitude" (TOB 49:7). The man who does so *experiences* his transcendence, his subjectivity, his freedom, and his call to live in a communion of persons. The more we overcome lust, the more we can be a real gift to another. And the more we *can* be a real gift to another, the more ardently we *desire* to be such a gift. We come to realize that the desire to love is *more powerful* than the desire to lust.

Redemption, Not Repression

The experience described above greatly differs from begrudgingly conforming one's behavior to an external norm. Of course, one only acquires this freedom in stages. If a person begins with the deception that views lust as a "good" to be pursued, the first essential stage of conversion is to recognize lust as an evil to avoid. The objective norm serves its essential purpose here. As St. Paul says, a man engrossed in sin does not know what sin is without the law (see Rom 7:7). Such a man will avoid lust only begrudgingly at first, out of obedience to the law. If he perseveres, however, lust itself becomes more and more distasteful to him. His subjective desires come more and more in tune with the true, the good, and the beautiful. In this way, the negative and prohibitive ethic of Christ's words in the Sermon on the Mount becomes a positive and liberating ethos.

This is how we appropriate the gift of our redemption. It is very different from repressing our lusts or merely seeking distraction from sexual temptations. John Paul's anthropological vision seeks to reclaim everything that is authentically human—everything that God created man to be "in the beginning." But this cannot happen if man ignores or represses his sexual desires.[86] Lust is the deceiver's plagiarization of the original power to love, the "twisting" of the fundamental drive within man to become a sincere gift to another. Man's sexual desires must be reclaimed according to this truth, "untwisted" and integrated within an adequate vision of the dignity and meaning of the human person. This means not running from our desires, but facing them and continually surrendering them to Christ—right at the moment lust flares up in us—so that grace might set our desires aright.

■   When a person struggling with lust seeks guidance, he will often hear from spiritual directors, confessors, and even otherwise sound chastity educators something like: "Just try to distract yourself from lustful thoughts. Try to ignore them. Do something con-

---

86. See *Love and Responsibility*, pp. 170–71.

structive. Take a walk. Take a bike ride. If need be, take a cold shower." While such advice may offer a helpful starting point—indeed, in the heat of a powerful temptation an immediate distraction is often essential—this approach offers only a temporary solution at best. Even when a person successfully distracts himself, that lust still lies "within" him. It will come back, and probably with more intensity. The "ethos of the redemption of the body" offers us a way of getting to the root of the problem. If we surrender our lustful desires to Christ, he can transform them by the power of the Holy Spirit. The *Catechism* proclaims that in the Sermon on the Mount "the Spirit of the Lord gives new form to our desires, those inner movements that animate our lives. Jesus teaches us this new life by his words; he teaches us to ask for it by prayer. The rightness of our life in him will depend on the rightness of our prayer."[87] As I wrote elsewhere, "When sexual feelings, desires, and temptations present themselves, as they inevitably do, instead of trying to ignore them or 'stuff' them by pushing them down and under, we need to bring them up and out. Not up and out in the sense of indulging them, but up and out and into the hands of Christ our Redeemer. You might simply say a prayer like this: *Lord Jesus, I give to you my sexual desires. Please undo in me what sin has done, so that I might know freedom in this area and experience sexual desire as you intend. Amen.*"[88]

Those men and women who continue diligently on this road of redemption—not repression—eventually see the threefold concupiscence for what it is: a cosmic tragedy that masks and even dismantles the very meaning of existence. To the degree that we internalize this, lust loosens its grip on us. Even if we continue to feel the pull of concupiscence, it loses its power to deceive us and lure us away. We know concupiscent desire is a cheap counterfeit for authentic eros. And we know that pursuing it can never satisfy. In this way we enter into the freedom for which Christ has set us free (see Gal 5:1). We experience purity as a vital power flowing from the Holy Spirit within us.

---

87. *CCC*, no. 2764.
88. *Good News About Sex and Marriage*, p. 82.

6. Purity as "Life According to the Spirit"

Blessed Are the Pure in Heart

John Paul devotes ten of his final addresses on historical man (TOB 50–59) to a scriptural analysis of purity of heart as an expression of "life according to the Holy Spirit." Such an analysis, he says, is "an indispensable completion of the words Christ spoke in the Sermon on the Mount on which we have focused the cycle of our present reflections" (TOB 50:1).

Most of the Pope's analysis of purity focuses on various passages from the Pauline Letters. However, in typical form, he begins with the words of Christ: "Blessed are the pure in heart, for they shall see God" (Mt 5:8). Here, as in Matthew 5:27–28, Christ appeals to the human heart, to the "inner man." His words remind us of that "beatifying beginning" in which man and woman, in beholding each other "naked without shame," saw the uniqueness and unrepeatability of the person from "within." Not only that, but in the visibility of their naked bodies they saw a sign that revealed the invisible mystery of God. Purity of heart specifically enabled them to *see* the body in this way, as a theology.

If we have been following the Pope's train of thought, we can say this: Blessed are the pure in heart, for they shall see God's mystery revealed in the human body. For, according to the Pope's thesis, the body, and it alone, is capable of making God's invisible mystery visible to us. And "in the beginning" nakedness manifested "the 'pure' value of man as male and female, the 'pure' value of the body and of [its] sex" (TOB 13:1).The Pope tells us that purity "is the glory of the human body before God. It is the glory of God in the human body, through which masculinity and femininity are manifested" (TOB 57:3). Of course, Christ's words do not limit purity merely to sexual morality. The Pope expresses that all moral good manifests purity, and all moral evil manifests impurity. Still, sexual purity is critical for all moral good to flourish, since the union of man and woman provides the deepest foundation of ethics and culture (see TOB 45:3).

"Purity is a requirement of love. It is the dimension of the inner truth of love in man's 'heart'" (TOB 49:7). Hence, purity concerns the innermost layers of man's being. It concerns his subjectivity and his realization in *solitude* of his call to *communion*—his call to love. Thus, as the Pope states, "Purity of heart is explained, in the end, by the relation to the *other subject, who is originally and perennially 'co-called'*" (TOB 49:7). Purity of heart enabled Adam to recognize Eve as the one who was called with him ("co-called") to live in a communion of persons. This same purity enabled them to experience nakedness without shame. Purity, then, is what man and woman lost due to sin, and it is what Christ came to restore in our hearts.

From Physical Purity to Moral Purity

John Paul points out that when we speak of purity as a moral virtue, we use the word in an analogous sense with physical cleanliness. Something pure contrasts with something unclean or polluted. The Old Testament tradition greatly valued physical cleanliness, as the abundance of ritual washings demonstrates. Many of these rituals concerned the cleansing of the body in relation to sexual impurity (see Lev 15). However, sexual impurity was understood almost exclusively in relation to physiology and its organic processes. John Paul suggests these may have corresponded to hygienic prescriptions according to the state of medical science at that time (see TOB 50:2). But such heightened attention to physical purity led to an erroneous way of understanding moral purity, which was often taken in the exclusively exterior and material sense.

Christ radically opposes this. His words indicate that none of the aspects of sexual uncleanness in the strictly physiological sense falls by itself into the definition of purity or impurity in the moral sense.[89] As John Paul stresses, referring to Christ's words from Matthew 15:11, nothing "makes a man unclean 'from the outside'; no 'material' dirtiness makes a man impure in the moral sense. No washing, not even ritual washing, is by itself suited to produce moral purity. Moral purity has its wellspring exclusively in man's interior: it comes from the heart" (TOB 50:3).

■ We can observe here the meaning of the rich symbolism of the wedding feast of Cana (see Jn 2:1–11). This is one of the few pertinent Scripture passages John Paul does not discuss in his

---

89. For example, a woman's menstrual flow does not make her "unclean" in any moral sense (see Lev 18:19).

TOB. Briefly we can recognize that, if wine is a symbol of grace, running out of wine speaks of the married couple's need for new life in Christ. If they are to love one another purely, they must drink deeply of the "new wine" that Christ gives and allow it to change them interiorly. The water Christ changed to wine was intended for the Jewish rites of purification. Christ's miracle symbolizes the fulfillment of Israel's ritual washings. Christ's "new wine" has the ability to purify our hearts. Furthermore, Christ, in referring to his "hour," points us to the marriage consummated on the cross.[90] There he will give himself up for his Bride to make her holy and without blemish (see Eph 5:25–27). The water and wine at Cana, therefore, prefigure the blood and water that flow from Christ's side on Calvary. Like the first Adam, Christ is put into a "deep sleep" on the cross. As figures of Baptism and Eucharist, the water and blood symbolize the life of God flowing from the side of the New Adam at the birth of the New Eve (remember that the "rib" symbolized the common life shared by the first Adam and Eve).[91] Like the first Adam, the New Adam calls the New Eve "woman" (compare Gen 2:23 and Jn 19:26). This evokes the re-creation or "resurrection" of man and woman's original relationship. And it is all prefigured at a *wedding feast* that takes place *on the third day*. All those who are "born again" through the waters of Baptism become the spiritual children of the New Adam and the New Eve—born not of a husband's seed but born of God (see Jn 1:13). And all those who drink the "new wine" of the Eucharist are purified and empowered from within to love others according to "the new ethos of redemption."[92]

Christ's shift of focus from external purity to "purity of heart" marks the turning point to the new ethos. Here we encounter the crux of the matter both for Christ and his Vicar. *This* is why John Paul II places so much emphasis on the subjectivity of man. This is why he finds so much benefit in the phenomenological method in coming to

---

90. See *CCC*, nos. 1335, 2618.

91. See *CCC*, nos. 766, 1067, 1225.

92. For an excellent discussion of the Cana account in light of spousal symbolism, see Ignace De La Potterie and Bertrand Buby, *Mary in the Mystery of the Covenant* (Alba House, 1992), pp. 157–208.

an adequate understanding of man. Purity certainly places objective demands on us. But to fulfill those demands, *we must be purified from within*. When we are, subjectivity becomes objective to the very depths. That suspicion toward the human heart previously mentioned tends also to oppose John Paul II's emphasis on "subjectivity." If the heart is always suspect and can never be transformed, a gulf will always remain between objective truth and subjective human desire. But to remain locked in this perspective is to empty the cross of its power. It is the antithesis of the meaning of life (see pp. 238–39).

"Flesh" and "Spirit" According to St. Paul

To recover the beatifying experience of purity, we must contend with the tension and conflict between the flesh and the Spirit that St. Paul outlined: "The desires of the flesh are against the Spirit and the desires of the Spirit are against the flesh" (Gal 5:17). As the Holy Father says, "The issue is not just the body (matter) and the spirit (the soul)." These "from the 'beginning' constituted man's very essence" (TOB 51:1). Their union and integration make man "very good" (Gen 1:31). As John Paul says elsewhere: "From the context it is clear that for the Apostle it is not a question of discriminating against and condemning the body, which with the spiritual soul constitutes man's nature and personal subjectivity."[93] What St. Paul is talking about in the opposition between the flesh and the Spirit is that disposition of forces formed in man with original sin.[94]

John Paul is careful to use a capital "S" for Spirit to indicate that the real opposition we experience "in the flesh" is with the Holy Spirit and what he desires for us (see TOB 50:5). In a footnote, the Pope also points out that "flesh" for St. Paul "is not to be identified with sex or with the physical body." In Pauline terminology, "flesh" seems almost to coincide with the threefold concupiscence of which St. John speaks. Thus, for Paul, the flesh indicates not only the "outer" man but also the man who is "interiorly" cut off from what is of the Father so that he lives according to what is of the world. To live according to the flesh, then, means to live according to our "un-inspired" or "ex-spired" desires.

---

93. *Dominum et Vivificantem*, 55 (see also *CCC*, no. 2516).
94. See *CCC*, nos. 2516–25.

It means to live according to the "dust" of our humanity, not filled with God's Spirit. John Paul says that the same idea is expressed in modern ethics and anthropology by terms like "humanistic autarchy" (man unto himself), "secularism," and "sensualism" (TOB 51:1).

The person who lives "according to the flesh" lives almost at the opposite pole as compared to how the Spirit would lead him (see TOB 51:2). The Spirit of God wants a different reality from the one that the flesh desires. The Holy Spirit, who is the "Person-Love" and the "Person-Gift" within the Trinity,[95] wants to fill our bodies with himself so that we might be a sincere gift in love to others. In other words, the Spirit wants to *in*-spire us to live according to the spousal meaning of our bodies. We could even say that by virtue of the Holy Spirit *in*-spiring our flesh, our bodies acquire a spousal meaning. In respect for our freedom, however, the Spirit never forces his own gift. We are free to reject the Spirit. If we do (and we are inclined to do so precisely because of concupiscence), we live according to our *un*-inspired "flesh." In this state we become bent on our own selfish gratification, even at the expense of others. This is the antithesis of the spousal meaning of the body; it is the antithesis of love, and the antithesis of life. As St. Paul expresses, "to set the mind on the flesh is death, but to set the mind on the Spirit is life and peace" (Rom 8:6).

Justification by Faith

The Holy Father observes that Paul's words regarding life "according to the flesh" and life "according to the Spirit" are at the same time a synthesis and a program (TOB 51:2). They synthesize very realistically the "fight" in man's heart between good and evil. But they do not simply leave man at the mercy of these interior forces. They provide a program for victory. "In this struggle between good and evil, man proves to be *stronger thanks to the power of the Holy Spirit*" (TOB 51:6).

St. Paul speaks of the interior battle between flesh and Spirit in the context of his discussion of justification by faith (see Rom 7, 8; Gal 5). Man cannot justify himself by observance of the law. If he seeks to do so, Christ is of no advantage to him, and he misses altogether the necessity and purpose of redemption. "You are severed from Christ, you

---

95. See *Dominum et Vivificantem*, 10.

who would be justified by the law; you have fallen away from grace"
(Gal 5:4). Condensing Paul's teaching, the *Catechism* says:

> The law entrusted to Israel never sufficed to justify those subject to it;
> it even became the instrument of "lust" (see Rom 7:7). The gap
> between wanting and doing points to the conflict between God's Law
> which is the "law of the mind," and another law "making me captive to
> the law of sin which dwells in my members" (Rom 7:23).
>
> "But now, the righteousness of God has been manifested apart
> from law, although the law and the prophets bear witness to it, the
> righteousness of God through faith in Jesus Christ for all who believe"
> (Rom 3:21–22). Henceforth, Christ's faithful "have crucified the flesh
> with its passions and desires"; they are led by the Spirit and follow the
> desires of the Spirit (Gal 5:24).[96]

Justice superabounds in man's heart by faith in Jesus Christ. This is
man's victory. This is how he *experiences* the power of the Holy Spirit—
by faith. We have previously quoted John Paul's definition of faith:
"*Faith*, in its deepest essence, is *the openness* of the human heart to the
gift: *to God's self-communication in the Holy Spirit.*"[97] Therefore, justification by faith "does not constitute simply a dimension of the divine
plan of man's salvation and of man's sanctification, but according to St.
Paul it is *a real power at work in man that reveals and affirms itself in his
actions*" (TOB 51:4). It is "*the power of Christ himself working in man's
innermost [being] through the Holy Spirit*" (TOB 51:3).

St. Paul speaks of this justification when he says: "He who raised
Christ Jesus from the dead will give life to your mortal bodies also
through his Spirit which dwells in you" (Rom 8:11). This "life" given to
our mortal bodies does not just refer to the eschaton. It is "*intended
already for 'historical man,'* for every human being of 'yesterday, today,
and tomorrow,' in the history of the world and also the history of salvation" (TOB 51:4). History, even if it remains the domain of struggle
and ambiguity, is also the domain in which salvation is given and
received. This means that historical man can truly be *vivified* by the
Holy Spirit; he can begin to live a resurrected life even now.[98]

In this way the Pauline theology of justification expresses faith in
"*the anthropological and ethical realism*" of redemption (see TOB 52:1).

---

96. *CCC*, nos. 2542, 2543.
97. *Dominum et Vivificantem*, 51.
98. See *CCC*, no. 1092.

In other words, Christ's redemption bears real fruit in changing man's heart (anthropological realism) and, consequently, changing his behavior (ethical realism). As the *Catechism* teaches, "Justification is not only the remission of sins, but also the sanctification and renewal of the interior man.... It frees from the enslavement to sin, and it heals."[99] In this way, justification, carried out by the Holy Spirit, enables justice to abound in man and in his behavior "in the measure God himself wills and expects" (TOB 52:1). This divine expectation is not only that man would meet the law's demands, but also that he would "fulfill" them through the superabounding justice poured into his heart through the Holy Spirit. This justification "is essential for the inner man and is intended precisely for that 'heart' to which Christ appealed when he spoke about 'purity' and 'impurity' in the moral sense" (TOB 51:4). Through the justification of the Holy Spirit, man "becomes himself" and enters his authentic ethos. Through the indwelling Spirit, objective reality enters human subjectivity, and what was once felt as an external law wells up as an intimate demand of the person. In this way, the Christian "incarnates" the Gospel; *logos*—that which is objective Truth —becomes *ethos*.

"Works of the Flesh" and "Fruit of the Spirit"

In his Letter to the Galatians, St. Paul says that "the works of the flesh are plain: fornication, impurity, licentiousness, idolatry, sorcery, enmity, strife, jealousy, anger, selfishness, dissension, party spirit, envy, drunkenness, carousing, and the like" (5:19–21). "But the fruit of the Spirit is love, joy, peace, patience, kindness, goodness, faithfulness, gentleness, self-control" (5:22–23). John Paul points out, as have many biblical scholars, that Paul distinguishes "works" of the flesh from the "fruit" of the Spirit. For Paul, "works" are the specific acts of man, whereas the term "fruit of the Spirit" emphasizes God's action in man. As John Paul says in a footnote, "This 'fruit' grows in...[man] as *the gift* of a life whose only Author is God; man can, at the most, provide for favorable circumstances that the fruit may grow and mature" (TOB 51:5, n. 62). In other words, everything that comes from "the flesh" is not of the Father but of the world. The goodness that springs from

---

99. *CCC*, nos. 1989–90.

man's heart, on the other hand, is of the Father and not of the world. It is the fruit of the indwelling Holy Spirit. Only from this perspective can we clarify fully the nature and structure of the ethos of redemption.

Reclaiming the purity of our origins does not mean pulling ourselves up by our boot straps. We "are speaking of a possibility opened up to man exclusively by grace."[100] The ethos of redemption is born in man when he forms an alliance with the Holy Spirit, allowing him to guide all his thoughts and behaviors. Behind each of the moral virtues that St. Paul outlines as a fruit of the Spirit lies a specific choice, an effort of the will, which is the fruit of the human spirit permeated by the Spirit of God. This cooperative action of the divine and human is always manifested in choosing that which is true, good, and beautiful. Again we see how this differs from merely following an external norm or law. "Healing the wounds of sin, the Holy Spirit renews us interiorly through a spiritual transformation. He enlightens and strengthens us to live as 'children of the light' through all that is 'good and right and true.'"[101] In other words, the Holy Spirit, operating deeply within man's heart, orients his desires rightly so that he comes to desire freely what the law demands of him. This is why St. Paul can say that "if you are led by the Spirit, you are not under the law" (Gal 5:18). You naturally live in love, joy, peace, patience, kindness, goodness, faithfulness, gentleness, and self-control. As St. Paul points out, no law forbids these things (see Gal 5:22–23).

In my lectures, to demonstrate what "freedom from the law" looks like, I will often ask a married man in the audience if he has any desire to murder his wife. A man with no desire to murder his wife does not need the commandment "Thou shalt not murder thy wife," because he has no desire to break it. He is free from this law. Similarly, men and women who have attained a mature level of sexual purity do not need a laundry list of sexual "thou shalt nots." The law is written on their hearts. In times of weakness and fragility, which seem inevitable, the law serves its purpose to guide them to the good. But, to the degree that people are free with the freedom for which Christ set them free, they needn't rely solely on

100. *Veritatis Splendor*, 24.
101. *CCC*, no. 1695.

the external norm to guide their behavior. They are guided from within and fulfill the law without experiencing it as a constraint. Christ did not die and rise from the dead to give us more laws to follow. His purpose was to purify our hearts so that we would no longer need the law. As the *Catechism* states, "The Law of the Gospel...does not add new external precepts, but proceeds to reform the heart, the root of human acts, where man chooses between the pure and the impure."[102]

The Freedom for which Christ Has Set Us Free

We have been reflecting on the opposition between the flesh and the spirit (or Spirit in reference to the Holy Spirit) in relation to reclaiming purity of heart. Of course, this antagonism between flesh and spirit is not "natural" to man. It results from the interior rupture caused by original sin (see TOB 13:1; 28:2). When we turned our backs on God, the breath of God's life died in us. We only had recourse to our *un*-inspired dust, what St. Paul calls "the flesh." The Apostle tells us that if we live according to the flesh, we will die. But if by the Spirit we put to death the deeds of the flesh, we will live (see Rom 8:13). According to the Pope, this putting to death the deeds of the body expresses precisely what Christ spoke about in the Sermon on the Mount, appealing to the human heart and exhorting it to mastery over lustful desires. This mastery, this putting to death the deeds of the flesh, "*is an indispensable condition of the 'life according to the Spirit'*" (TOB 52:4). In other words, we must die with Christ if we are to live with him in the power of the resurrection.

Life according to the flesh, as St. Paul describes it, effects the "death" of the Spirit in man. So, as John Paul explains, the term "death" means not only the death of the body but also the reality of mortal sin. Mortal sin is that which "kills" God's life, his Spirit, within us. Those who live according to the flesh (unless they repent and are filled once again with the Spirit) "shall not inherit the kingdom of God" (Gal 5:21). Elsewhere, as the Holy Father points out, St. Paul says that no fornicator or impure man has any inheritance in God's kingdom (see Eph 5:5). Only the pure man is capable of seeing God. That is the very definition

---

102. *CCC*, no. 1968.

of purity. Hence, impurity can be defined as the *inability* to see God. God desires to reveal his mystery in and through the mystery of our humanity as male and female, but the impure man cannot see it. Those who sin—sexually and otherwise—close their eyes to it. It is not that God will throw them into hell because of their sin. It is more accurate to say that the impure person is *ipso facto* incapable of the beatific vision.

How then does the impure person become pure? How does the blind person regain his sight? He does so by opening his flesh once again to the life of the Holy Spirit. As much as lust blinds man and woman to the truth of the body and deprives the heart of genuine desires and aspirations, so much does "life according to the Spirit" permit man and woman to regain the freedom of the gift and recover purity of heart (see TOB 101:5). Regaining purity, then, is not first a matter of "doing," but a matter of "letting it be done." Like the Immaculate One—that is, the woman totally pure of heart—we must offer our *fiat* to the Holy Spirit. Only then will Christ be "conceived" in our flesh.

John Paul concludes that justification comes "from the Spirit" (of God) and not "from the flesh." In other words, it comes from God's action in us as a fruit of the Spirit, not as a work of our own. Those who seek justification in following laws (in "doing" rather than "letting it be done") have been alienated from Christ. They have cut themselves off from the grace given by the Holy Spirit that empowers us to fulfill the law (see Gal 5:4–5). St. Paul therefore exhorts the Galatians to free themselves of the erroneous "carnal" concept of justification, and to follow the true one, the "spiritual" one. In "this sense he exhorts them to consider themselves free from the law, and even more so to be free with the freedom for which Christ 'has set us free'" (TOB 52:5).

Freedom and Purity

According to John Paul, we experience true purity of heart according to the measure that we experience the freedom for which Christ "has set us free." This is the crux of the new ethos: *freedom!* The Pope states that St. Paul touches the essential point right here, revealing the anthropological roots of the Gospel ethos. The "dimension of the new ethos of the Gospel is nothing other than an *appeal to human freedom*, an appeal for its fullest realization and in some way for the fullest 'use' of the powers of the human spirit" (TOB 53:1).[103] We have the potential to be *free* from sin. We have the potential to be *free* to desire and choose only what is good. We have the potential to be *free* with the freedom of the gift—not perfectly in this life, but progressively and substantially.[104] "For freedom Christ has set us free; stand fast therefore, and do not submit again to a yoke of slavery" (Gal 5:1).

For St. Paul, freedom is inextricably linked with love. "For you were called to freedom, brethren; only do not use your freedom as an opportunity for the flesh, but through love be servants of one another" (Gal 5:13). Notice, too, that St. Paul knows that the freedom necessary for love also provides the opportunity to indulge "the flesh." This is a key point. In our attempts to live the Gospel, we often seek to eradicate sin by eradicating our freedom to commit it. We must not remove the freedom we have to sin. For in the same stroke we eradicate the freedom necessary to love. To squelch freedom in order to avoid sin is not living the Gospel ethos of freedom at all. This approach knows not the freedom for which Christ has set us free. If we must chain ourselves in order not to commit sin, then we are just that—*in chains*. A person in this state remains bound in some way to his desire to sin and has yet to tap into the mature ethos of redemption. He has yet to experience in a sustained way life according to the Holy Spirit. For "where the Spirit of the Lord is, there is freedom" (2 Cor 3:17).

Here we put our finger on the pulse of the human mystery. Freedom is God's gift to man, a gift given as the capacity to love. But the flip side of the capacity to love is the capacity to sin. God respects our freedom. This means he respects our freedom to sin. He did not stay Adam and Eve's hands when they reached out to eat the fruit of the tree of the knowledge of good and evil. He told them what would happen, and then entrusted that to their freedom. Had God stayed their hands, he would have denied them the dignity he had bestowed on them. As the *Catechism* states, "God does not want to impose the good, but wants free beings." Thus, the *"right to the exercise of freedom, especially in moral and religious matters, is an inalienable requirement of the dignity of the human person."*[105] We inevitably sense the com-

---

103. See *CCC*, nos. 1730–48.
104. See *Veritatis Splendor*, 17.
105. *CCC*, nos. 1738, 2847.

promise of our dignity when we are forced to conform to the will of others. Even if the will of others is good, it can never be imposed. We must engage our freedom in choosing good if we are ever to experience that which *is* good *as* good.

■ This dynamic operates pointedly in the relationship of parents and children, especially when the children come of age. Parents have the delicate task of promoting the good without forcing it on their children. This means that, within appropriate limits, parents (like God the Father) must allow their children to choose wrongly, to sin. If parents "force" their children *not* to sin, they set up an unfortunate dynamic in which their children may feel compelled to rebel against what is good in order to assert their own dignity as self-determining persons. In such situations, the Church calls parents to "recognize the fragment of truth that may be present in some forms of [their children's] rebellion."[106]

A valuable lesson can be learned in this regard from John Paul II's struggle with Communism. Not all of the goals of Communism are evil. For John Paul, it seems the primary evil of Communism (and all totalitarian systems) lies in the way it annihilates human freedom to achieve its goals. Papal biographer George Weigel reports a conversation between John Paul II and General Pinochet (Chile's dictator) as follows: "Pinochet pressed the Pope: 'Why is the Church always talking about democracy? One method of government is as good as another.' John Paul politely but firmly disagreed. 'No,' he said, 'the people have a right to their liberties, even if they make mistakes in exercising them.'"[107] In other words, according to John Paul's read on the dignity of the person as a self-determining agent, a higher value is maintained when one exercises his freedom wrongly than when one is forced to do something objectively good.[108] In human affairs, the greatest good is the realization of the person, and this cannot come about without a steadfast respect for human freedom, which always implies (within due limits) respecting the freedom of others to choose wrongly. This

---

106. *The Truth and Meaning of Human Sexuality*, 51.
107. *Witness to Hope*, p. 533.
108. See *Karol Wojtyla: The Thought of the Man Who Became Pope John Paul II*, pp. 181–82.

deeply personalist affirmation of freedom, as expressed primarily in *Dignitatis Humanae*, is one of the main contributions of the Second Vatican Council.

Authentic Freedom

Society has much to say about sexual liberation. But society generally views it as the freedom to indulge one's lusts without restraint. It means never having to say no. This does not promote genuine freedom. This promotes bondage to libido. John Paul observes that the antithesis and, in a way, the negation of freedom occurs when freedom becomes a pretext for man to live according to the flesh (see TOB 53:3). Man chooses to indulge lust because he feels bound by lust. The man of concupiscence imagines he cannot *not* lust. Hence, in his view the moral law that condemns lust oppresses him. He must be "liberated" from it so he can live in his bondage to lust unhindered.[109] In essence, he wants to be free *from freedom* in order to embrace slavery without retribution.

Such a person is utterly deceived. To him, good is evil and evil good. Slavery is freedom and freedom slavery. Such a man will never find the happiness he seeks. As John Paul says, he *"ceases to be capable of this freedom* for which 'Christ has set us free'; he also ceases to be suitable *for the true gift* of self, which is the fruit and expression of such freedom. He further ceases to be capable of the gift organically linked with the spousal meaning of the human body"* (TOB 53:3). Therefore, so long as he lives in his bondage to lust, he can never fulfill the meaning of his being and existence.

Oh, the tragic deception of thinking Christ is against us! If the man of concupiscence would but open himself to the gift of redemption, through ongoing conversion, Christ would liberate his liberty from the oppression of lust. He would free him with a freedom so liberating that he would be free indeed. He would free him with the freedom of the gift—the freedom of receiving the gift of God (the Holy Spirit) and, in turn, the freedom of being a real gift to others. *This* is the meaning of life. *This* is the freedom for which we all long. This is the freedom for which Christ has set us free. To attain it, we must open our flesh to the indwelling of the Spirit.

---

109. See *Veritatis Splendor*, 18.

■ I will never forget my first experiences of this kind of freedom. Prior to returning to my faith as a young adult, I had dated a girl for four years. I could not *not* lust after her. Whenever I was with her, I was a man on a mission—not to love her as Christ loves, but to "get" what I wanted. Of course, I thought this was liberation because I had thrown off the oppressive "rules" of my Catholic upbringing and was indulging my lusts unhindered. I was utterly duped: even more so because, like everyone else, I called this love. I started dating my now-wife, Wendy, after about five years of deep purgation and healing from the indulgences of my past (discovering John Paul's TOB was instrumental in this healing). One day, early on in our relationship, Wendy and I were sitting on a mountainous ledge overlooking a river in Pennsylvania. Holding her in my arms, I had a flashback to my previous "mode of operation." And it dawned on me: I was free. *I was truly free!* My freedom had been set free from the domination of lust. I *did not desire* to "get" something from Wendy or to use her for my own gratification. I desired to be a gift to her, to bless and affirm her. Oh, what a feeling to be free with the freedom of the gift! I was flying. I was walking on water! I *knew* the power of redemption. I *knew* the power of the death and resurrection of Christ. I *knew* the power of the Holy Spirit. I felt his breath vivifying *my flesh* and impregnating my desires with everything noble and beautiful, with the supreme value of love.

Would that that exuberant experience had been constant ever since. Looking back, I remain grateful for that day, but it is clear that that was *only the beginning* of the journey toward the fullness of freedom, a journey I'll be on till the day I meet the Lord face to face. Years of trials and victories, of falling and rising have certainly confirmed what the *Catechism* observes: "Self-mastery is a *long and exacting work*. One can never consider it acquired once and for all. It presupposes renewed effort at all stages of life."[110]

Purity—Keeping the Body "in Holiness and Reverence"

St. Paul contrasts fornication, impurity, and licentiousness as works of the flesh with the self-control that is a fruit of the Spirit. According

---

110. *CCC*, no. 2342

to John Paul, this self-control is closely linked to purity of heart. The link becomes more explicit in Paul's First Letter to the Thessalonians: "For this is the will of God, your sanctification: that you abstain from unchastity; that each one of you know how to keep his own body in holiness and reverence, not in the passion of lust like the heathens who do not know God" (4:3–5). "God has not called us for uncleanness [i.e., impurity], but in holiness. Therefore, whoever disregards this, disregards not man, but God, who gives his Holy Spirit to you" (4:7–8).

According to John Paul, every word in this formulation has a particular meaning (see TOB 54:2). It is a "deeply *right, complete, and adequate*" (TOB 54:4) image of the virtue of purity, which emerges from the eloquent comparison of the function of "abstaining from unchastity" with that of "keeping one's body in holiness and reverence." The Pope further observes that these two functions—abstaining and keeping—are closely connected and dependent on each other. One cannot control his body "in holiness and reverence" if he cannot abstain from lust and that which leads to it. In turn, that recognition of the "holiness and reverence" due the body gives adequate meaning to abstention from lust.

John Paul shows his Thomistic foundations when he draws from the Angelic Doctor's teaching on virtues in order to compare it with St. Paul's image of purity. At the same time, it seems John Paul wants to deepen the understanding of purity found in Thomas. The Pope observes that, for Thomas, purity is a form of the virtue of temperance. Rooted in the will, it "consists above all in holding back the impulses of sense-desire, which has as its object what is bodily and sexual in man" (TOB 54:2). But, as John Paul observes, the same Pauline text turns our attention to another "more positive" function of the virtue of purity. The task of purity is not only a *turning away* from unchastity. This is a "negative," less mature purity. As St. Paul describes it, purity is also, and even more so, a *turning toward* the holiness of the body—a holiness that calls for our reverence, admiration, and respect.[111] Only when we

---

111. St. Thomas seems to speak to this same idea of the "positive" dimension of purity in his distinction between mere continence and authentic virtue. Continence involves the successful restraint of disordered desires, but this is not *virtue*. Virtue involves *ease and joy* in choosing the good because one's desires are rightly ordered toward that good. See *Summa, Prima Secundae*, q. 58, a. 3, ad. 2. See also pp. 565–66 of this work for a further discussion of this issue.

have such reverence for the body are we empowered from within to control the impulses of concupiscence that, if left unchecked, would degrade the spousal meaning of the body.

As John Paul expresses it, "*The reverence* born in man for everything bodily and sexual, both in himself and in every other human being, male and female, turns out to be the most essential power for keeping the body 'with holiness'" (TOB 54:4). When this reverence toward the body imbues us, we immediately sense when impulses of concupiscence rise up in us. And precisely that reverence toward the body and sexuality makes us ready and willing to submit our disordered desires to Christ, so that he might continually order them rightly. The Pope believes that this concept of reverence is perhaps the essential line of thought of the Pauline doctrine on purity (see TOB 54:6). So, in search of a more thorough understanding of what Paul means by reverence, the Holy Father turns his attention to Paul's description of the body in 1 Corinthians 12:18–25.

The Pauline Description of the Body

Although Paul's description of the human body in 1 Corinthians 12 is intended to outline an image of the Church as the body of Christ, it also has a fundamental meaning for the Pauline doctrine on purity. There St. Paul says:

> God arranged the organs in the body, each one of them, as he chose.... [T]he parts of the body which seem to be weaker are indispensable, and those parts of the body we think less honorable we invest with the greater honor, and our unpresentable parts are treated with greater modesty, which our more presentable parts do not require. But God has so adjusted the body, giving the greater honor to the inferior part, that there may be no discord in the body, but that the members may have the same care for one another. (vv. 18–25)

Paul's description here is obviously prescientific. His goal is not to present a biological study on the human organism. In fact, the Pope says that a mere biological description of the body can never be adequate since the human body is not just an organism. What is at stake when we deal with the human body is the truth about "*man who expresses himself by means of that body*, and in this sense," the Pope says, "'is' that body" (TOB 55:2). All descriptions of the body, therefore, must take this into account. Portraying the body is, in fact, "one of the perennial tasks and themes of all culture: of literature, sculpture, painting, as well as dancing, theater, and finally of the culture of daily life, private or social" (TOB 55:2). The Pope believes it is necessary to say how right it is to evaluate and portray the body in these various ways. However, all portrayals of the human body must have a proper spiritual attitude of reverence and respect, recognizing its holiness, which, as Christians know, springs from the mysteries of creation and redemption.

Restoring Harmony in the Body

John Paul observes that St. Paul's description of the body seems to correspond perfectly with the analysis of our creation, fall, and redemption that he has been outlining in the theology of the body (see TOB 55:5). God's arrangement of the body and all its parts is "very good." The experience of original nakedness was a participation in this original good of God's vision. Hence, prior to sin, man and woman experienced no discord in the body whatsoever, but a perfect harmony.

The Pope states that this harmony is precisely "purity of heart." Adam and Eve readily bestowed the "greater honor" on those parts of their bodies that revealed their call to communion. Nakedness, therefore, was entirely modest. Furthermore, this purity "allowed man and woman in the state of original innocence to experience in a simple way (in a way that made both of them originally happy) the unitive power of their bodies." This unitive power of their bodies was "the 'unsuspectable' substratum of their personal union or *communio personarum*" (TOB 55:6). In other words, the whole dynamic of attraction and arousal that led them to become "one flesh" was so integrated with their dignity as persons as to be taken for granted. There was no question of using one another. They had no need to hold one another in a state of "suspicion" when it came to the arousal of the body. For they lived their bodies "in holiness and reverence." Hence, they were naked and felt no shame.

St. Paul observes that we now consider some parts of our bodies "weaker," "less honorable," and "unpresentable." This corresponds to the shame Adam and Eve experienced after they ate from the forbidden tree. However, the Pope quickly affirms that in this same description of man's experience of shame, Paul indicates the path which leads to the gradual victory over that "discord in the body"—a victory that John Paul insists can and must take place in man's heart.

The key to rediscovering purity is to recognize that there is imprinted on our experience of shame "a certain 'echo' of the...original innocence of man: a photographic 'negative,' as it were, the 'positive' of which was precisely original innocence" (TOB 55:4). The negative provides a clue of the positive image. Similarly, that shame which leads us to consider our genitals "less honorable" and "unpresentable" is the negative. But shame's direct relation to our genitals provides a clue for understanding the true meaning and profound dignity of our creation as male and female. If we develop this negative or "flip it over," we realize that these parts of our bodies—far from being "less honorable"—deserve all "the greater honor." For these parts of our bodies distinguish the sexes and thus reveal our call to image God in life-giving communion.

The Need for a Pure Purity

We are learning that, for St. Paul, purity and modesty must be centered on the dignity of the body—on the dignity of the person who is always expressed through the body, through his masculinity and her femininity.[112] Thus, if one's "purity" is based on anything but a sincere appreciation for the value and dignity of the body, it is not authentic purity. Likewise, if one's modesty is based on a fear or devaluation of sexuality, it is not authentic modesty. What, then, is the path to a pure purity and an authentically modest modesty? As we have been stressing all along, it is openness to the gift of redemption. As John Paul says, the man of concupiscence must be "completely enveloped by the 'redemption of the body' achieved by Christ." He "must open himself to life according to the Spirit...in order to find again and realize the value of the body, freed by redemption from the bonds of concupiscence" (TOB 58:5).

> ■ As the future pope observed in *Love and Responsibility*, modesty is certainly connected with the way people dress, but the connection is not what most people tend to think. The following

---

112. See *CCC*, nos. 2517–27.

question can help us assess whether we have a proper understand-ing of purity and modesty in dress. If covering the sexual values of the body in public is a virtually universal manifestation of modesty, are we led to do so out of a sense that these parts of our body are "dishonorable"? Or do we cover our sexual values out of a profound sense of "the greater honor" they deserve because of the dignity God bestowed on them? Do we cover our sexual values because we attribute to them an "anti-value," or because we realize they mani-fest "a value not sufficiently appreciated"? (TOB 45:3). Under-standing this distinction is essential for an authentic modesty and for our purity to be just that—pure.

Tapping into some of the confusions regarding modesty, Wojtyla clearly states that accenting sexual values by dress is inevitable, and it can remain compatible with sexual modesty. Immodesty in dress, he says, is that which displaces the dignity of the person and aims deliberately to elicit lust in others. He also observes that partial and even total nakedness cannot simply be equated with immodesty. "Immodesty is present only when naked-ness plays a negative role with regard to the value of the person, when its aim is to arouse concupiscence, as a result of which the person is put in the position of an object of enjoyment." What happens then he calls "*depersonalization by sexualization*." But he adds that this is not inevitable.[113] Only a "master of suspicion" would conclude that the naked body always and *inevitably* leads a person to lust.

In summary, authentic modesty is a natural fruit of a proper—that is, a *pure*—understanding of the divine dignity God has bestowed on the body and sexuality. It cannot simply be equated with a certain manner of dress or lack thereof. As the *Catechism* states: "Teaching modesty to children and adolescents means awakening in them respect for the human person."[114] When a mother and father are concerned about the way their teenage daughter dresses, rather than focusing only on the clothes, they would do better to instill in her a sense of awe and wonder for the divine dignity of her body and the gift of her sexuality. A person

---

113. See *Love and Responsibility*, pp. 186–93.
114. *CCC*, no. 2524.

who consciously understands this *does not want to be cheapened by lust*. A woman who consciously understands this, for example, will (aided with a little education in male psychology) come to *know* interiorly when the attention she draws by her dress invites lust. She will naturally want to dress in a way that protects her dignity.

Purity as a Virtue and a Gift

As with all virtues, attaining purity certainly requires a personal effort. Ultimately, however, a man cannot make himself pure. Purity is also a gift to which a person must open himself. The Holy Father describes purity as "a new ability of the human being in whom the gift of the Holy Spirit bears fruit" (TOB 56:1). Thus, purity has not only a moral dimension as a virtue. Purity also has a charismatic dimension as a gift of the Holy Spirit.[115] These two dimensions of purity are present and closely connected in Paul's message. Among the seven gifts of the Holy Spirit (see Is 11:1–2), John Paul points out that the one most compatible with purity is piety.[116] Piety is the gift of reverence for God's designs. Piety, then, "seems to serve purity in a particular way by making the human subject sensitive to the dignity that belongs to the human body in virtue of the mystery of creation and of redemption" (TOB 57:2).

St. Paul is trying to awaken in us a sense of awe and respect for the great dignity God has bestowed on our bodies when he says:

> The body is not meant for immorality, but for the Lord, and the Lord for the body.... Do you not know that your bodies are members of Christ? Shall I therefore take the members of Christ and unite them to a prostitute? Never! ...Shun immorality. Every other sin which a man commits is outside the body; but the immoral man sins against his own body.... Do you not know that your body is a temple of the Holy Spirit within you, which you have from God? You are not your own; you were bought with a price (1 Cor 6:13–20).

These words "stigmatize" unchastity as the sin against the holiness of the body, the sin of impurity. They are severe words, even "drastic,"

---

115. See *CCC*, no. 1810.

116. Piety, the Pope says, "is a little known guiding thread of the theology of the body, but nevertheless deserves particularly deep study" (TOB 57:3). He gives this further attention in TOB 58:7; 89:1–3, 6; 95:1; 126:4; 131:2; 132:1, 6.

according to John Paul (see TOB 56:5). But St. Paul, full of the Holy Spirit and, hence, alive with the gift of piety, knows whereof he speaks. He knows that the "*redemption of the body* brings with it the establishment in Christ and for Christ of a new *measure of the holiness of the body*." By virtue of the Incarnation, "Christ inscribed in the human body—in the body of every man and of every woman—a new dignity, because he himself has taken up the human body together with the soul into union with the person of the Son-Word" (TOB 56:4). Through this union, this marriage with the Word, the human body now participates in the eternal exchange of bliss and love between the Father and the Son, which *is* the Holy Spirit.

John Paul says that the Holy Spirit dwells in man—in his soul and in his body—as fruit of the redemption carried out by Christ (see TOB 56:3). Through the gift of redemption, every man has received himself and his own body again from God as a new creation. So in redemption we receive a "new twofold gift"—the gift of the Holy Spirit *and* the gift of our own restored humanity. Sins of the flesh (or "carnal sins") not only entail a "*profaning of the body*"—of our own humanity—but also a "*profaning of the temple*" of the Holy Spirit. As St. Paul's tone indicates, *this is very serious*. Some might be tempted to see in the sternness of Paul's words a devaluation of the body and sexuality. Quite the contrary, his austere tone stems from his desire to protect and ensure the incomparable dignity that God has bestowed on the body and sexuality. By virtue of the Incarnation, the human body obtains "a new supernatural elevation in every human being, which every Christian must take into account in his behavior toward 'his own' body and obviously also toward another's body: man toward woman and woman toward man" (TOB 56:4).

"Do you not know that your body is a temple of the Holy Spirit within you, which you have from God? You are not your own; you were bought with a price" (1 Cor 6:19–20). It is precisely a living awareness of our redemption, a living awareness that we were "bought with a price," that enables us to "keep our bodies in holiness and reverence." St. Paul calls us to "shun immorality." We must certainly do so if we are to regain self-mastery. Yet St. Paul calls us to much more than shunning what is immoral. Tapping into that "holiness and reverence" of which he speaks "always bears fruit in the deeper experience of the love that has from the 'beginning' been inscribed in the whole human being and thus also in his body according to the image and likeness of God himself" (TOB 57:3). Thus, Paul's words "open fuller access to the experience of the spousal meaning of the body and of the freedom of the gift connected with it" (TOB 57:2).

Let us recall that freedom is the crux of the new ethos (see p. 262ff.). We only know true purity of heart to the extent that we are free from the domination of lust. But freedom in Christ is not so much freedom *from* as freedom *for*—freedom *for love*. Only in freedom is the profound aspect of purity and its organic link with love revealed. As we have already quoted John Paul saying, "Purity is a requirement of love. It is the dimension of the inner truth of love in man's 'heart'" (TOB 49:7). And love is impossible if we are not free with the freedom to be a sincere gift to others.

███   Since the freedom to which Christ calls us is so rarely proclaimed, we may think it impossible. Take a sincere engaged couple who honestly wants to save sexual intimacy for marriage. They will often think that in order to stay "chaste," they should never spend any extended time alone together. They fear, of course, that if they *were* alone, they could not refrain from sex. This may be the case, but this is not a mature experience of the freedom for which Christ has set us free. Attaining Christian freedom is obviously a process. A couple who choose not to be alone together in order to avoid sexual temptation should be commended. They should also be aware that they are called by Christ to a much deeper freedom.

Think about it: if the only thing that keeps a couple from having sex before marriage is the lack of opportunity, what does that say about the desire of their hearts?[117] Are they free to choose the good? Are they free to love? To use an image, if a man and woman need to chain themselves to two different trees in order to avoid sin, they are not free; they are in chains. As stated previously, if we chain our freedom to sin, with the same stroke we chain the freedom necessary to love. All the more dangerous in such an approach is the implicit attitude that marriage will somehow "justify" the couple's lack of freedom. The wedding night then becomes the moment when the couple are supposedly "allowed" to

---

117. See *CCC*, nos. 1768, 1770, 1775, 1968, 1972.

cut the chains loose, disregarding their previous need for con-
straints. Yet if this couple were not free to choose the good the day
before they got married, standing at the altar will not suddenly
make them free.

As John Paul has already made abundantly clear, marriage does
not justify lust, and we lust precisely in the measure that we lack
the freedom of the gift. For most people, to live as the free men
and women we are called to be demands a radical paradigm shift in
ways of thinking, living, and evaluating. Trusting our own freedom
to control concupiscence and to choose the good can be very
threatening. It is much easier to distrust ourselves and hold our
hearts in continual suspicion. But this is the antithesis of the
meaning of life. We are called to set our eyes on Christ, get out of
the boat, and walk on water. Many Christians, it seems, stay in the
boat for fear of sinking if they were to get out. This may seem like
a "safer" approach. We can't sink if we never leave the boat. But
neither can we walk on water. The truth of human life does not
reside in the boat! It can only be found on the water amidst the
wind and the waves—in the drama of putting faith to the test and
learning to walk with our eyes set on the Lord. Learning to love
always involves risk. There is nothing "safe" about it. But it is better to get out of the boat and accept the risk of sinking than to lock
up our freedom and throw away the key. As with Peter, Christ says,
"Come!" Yes, we might sink. If we do, we have a merciful Savior
ready to save us, as did Peter.

God's Glory Shining in the Body

After stating, "You are not your own; you were bought with a
price," St. Paul ends his passage in 1 Corinthians 6 with a significant
exhortation: "So glorify God in your bodies" (v. 20). John Paul states
that purity—in both its dimensions as a virtue and as a gift of the Holy
Spirit—"causes in the body such a fullness of dignity in interpersonal
relations that *God himself is thereby glorified.*" Hence, as mentioned earlier, purity "is the glory of the human body before God. It is the glory of
God in the human body" (TOB 57:3). Men and women who relate
with one another purely truly glorify God in their bodies. Far from
stifling their relationship, purity enables them to enter that authentic

communion they both long for—a communion that images the divine communion. They experience that "singular beauty" which permeates the whole of their lives together. This beauty makes it possible to express themselves in "the simplicity and depth, the cordiality and unrepeatable authenticity of personal trust" (TOB 57:3). In this way, purity enables men and women, husbands and wives, to rediscover something of that "beatifying beginning" in which the first man and woman were both naked and felt no shame.

To the degree that we are enveloped by the redemption of the body carried out by Christ, everything tainted by sin becomes pure. As purity swallows that sense of suspicion with which we so often consign our own hearts to irreversible lust, we see the entire universe with new eyes. We regain something of that original good of God's vision and realize that *everything* God has made is "very good." As John Paul II wrote elsewhere, to the degree that we enter into union with Christ, we "can find God in everything, we can commune with him in and through all things. Created things cease to be a danger for us as once they were, particularly while we were still at the purgative stage of our journey. Creation, and other people in particular, not only regain their true light, given to them by God the Creator, but also, so to speak, they lead us to God himself, in the way that he willed to reveal himself to us: as Father, Redeemer, and Spouse."[118]

Purity and Wisdom: To the Pure All Things Are Pure

St. Paul demonstrates that Christ's words about purity as the ability to "see God" not only have an eschatological meaning but also bear fruit already in time. As he writes in his Letter to Titus: "To the pure all things are pure, but to the corrupt and unbelieving nothing is pure; their very minds and consciences are corrupted. They profess to know God, but they deny him by their deeds" (Ti 1:15–16). The Pope points out that these words can refer to purity in the general sense of all moral good, but also to the more specific sense of sexual purity. Either way, in these two short sentences, St. Paul shows that our view of the whole universe shifts according to our purity of heart or lack thereof.

---

118. *Memory and Identity*, p. 30.

Impurity causes blindness. It prevents us from seeing God's glory in his creation—least of all, it seems, in manifestations of sexuality and the nakedness of the body. In turn, blindness can lock us into such suspicion toward the heart that purity seems impossible. When we see the freedom of those who are pure, we condemn it outright as an indulgence in sin. It could be nothing else. For, according to this mindset, sin can only be avoided when we chain freedom. To let freedom "loose" is *ipso facto* to fall into sin. This approach toward the body may seem consonant with Christian holiness. But it denies what John Paul calls "the supernatural realism of faith" (TOB 56:5) and *"the anthropology of rebirth in the Holy Spirit"* (TOB 57:5).

Such blindness shows a lack of wisdom that fails to recognize the rich sacramental, mystical vision of *the real*—of reality as God instituted it. As John Paul says, "Purity is, in fact, a condition for finding wisdom and for following her" (TOB 57:4). The Pope then quotes from the Book of Sirach: "I directed my soul to her [that is, to Wisdom], and through purification, I found her" (51:20). The pure see reality as it is— as *very good*. This instills in them a deep sense of awe and wonder toward the Creator. This instills in them that wholesome "fear of the Lord," which, as that famous line from Proverbs expresses, is the beginning of all wisdom (see Prov 1:7).

In this manner, John Paul points out that the Wisdom Books of the Old Testament prepare in some way for the Pauline doctrine on purity of heart. In fact, the twofold meaning of purity as a virtue and as a gift of the Holy Spirit already takes shape in the Wisdom texts. The virtue of purity is in the service of wisdom, and wisdom is a preparation for receiving the gift of the Holy Spirit. This divine gift strengthens a person's virtue and makes it possible for that person to enjoy, in wisdom, the fruits of a pure life (see TOB 57:4).

7. The Gospel of Purity of Heart—Yesterday and Today

In the audience of April 1, 1981 (TOB 58), John Paul recaps his reflections up to this point. Christ's words about God's plan for marriage "in the beginning," as well as his words about lust in the Sermon on the Mount, have "enabled us to outline the authentic *theology of the body*" (TOB 58:1). We have learned that our humanity has a theological basis. It is founded on the truth about God and, more specifically, the truth about God made man in Jesus Christ. An adequate anthropology, then, must ultimately be a theological anthropology. An adequate anthropology must be a "theology of the body." For only in the mystery of *the Word* (theology) *made flesh* (of the body) does the mystery of man take on light.[119]

As John Paul says, man's vocation "springs from the eternal mystery of the person as the image of God, incarnated in the visible and bodily fact *of the masculinity and femininity* of the human person" (TOB 58:2). *This* is the body's great dignity: it incarnates God's mystery, which is love. Man's vocation is to love as God loves, and it is revealed through the spousal meaning of his body. Through the inheritance of original sin, "historical man" has lost sight of the theology of his body. This is precisely why Christ—through the "expressive evangelical eloquence" of his words about man and woman's union in "the beginning" and his words about "looking lustfully"—recalls to the man of concupiscence the original experience of the body. The Pope affirms that Christ's words are entirely realistic. They do not try to make the human heart return to the state of innocence, but they indicate the way to a purity of heart that *is possible and accessible* to man even in the state of hereditary sinfulness (see TOB 58:5).

Summarizing his reflections on purity, John Paul says that purity constitutes the contrary of adultery committed in the heart. It is the deep recognition and affirmation of the goodness of the body and of sexuality according to the original good of God's vision. The purity Christ calls us to is not just abstention from unchastity (temperance). At the same time, Christian purity "opens the way toward an ever more perfect discovery of the [original] dignity of the human body" (TOB 58:6). If purity is first manifested as temperance, it eventually "matures in the heart of the human being who cultivates it and who *seeks to discover and affirm the spousal meaning of the body* in its integral truth. Precisely this truth must be known in an interior way; it must in some way be 'felt with the heart,' so that the reciprocal relations between man and woman—even mere looks—may regain that authentically spousal content of their meanings" (TOB 58:6). In mature purity, man experiences the "efficaciousness of the gift of the Holy Spirit," which enables

---

119. See *Gaudium et Spes*, 22.

him to reach the mystery and subjectivity of the person through his or her body. He thus "enjoys the fruits of victory over concupiscence." This victory restores to our experience of the body "all *its simplicity, its lucid clarity,* and also *its interior joy*" (TOB 58:7).

Such joy is *very different* from any momentary satisfaction that comes from indulging lust. John Paul compellingly expresses this reality in a passage that seems to summarize all his reflections on Christ's words about lust. He writes: "The satisfaction of the passions is, in fact, one thing, quite another is the joy a person finds in possessing himself more fully, since in this way he can also become more fully a true gift for another person. The words Christ spoke in the Sermon on the Mount direct the human heart precisely toward this joy. We must entrust ourselves, our thoughts, and our actions to Christ's words in order to find joy and give it to others" (TOB 58:7).

Theology and Pedagogy of the Body

In his audience of April 8, 1981 (TOB 59), John Paul closes his reflections on historical man. We have been reflecting on the human heart, in which, John Paul says, "*the innermost,* and in some way the most essential, *guiding thread of history* is inscribed. It is the history of good and evil...and, at the same time, it is the history of salvation whose word is the Gospel and whose power is the Holy Spirit, given to those who accept the Gospel with a sincere heart" (TOB 59:1).

John Paul has been constructing an adequate anthropology, which he calls the "theology of the body." His catechesis provides an education or a pedagogy in being human. Pedagogy aims at educating man, setting before him the requirements of his own humanity and pointing out the ways that lead to the fulfillment of his humanity. This is precisely the goal of the TOB. The words of Christ that John Paul has analyzed (concerning the man of innocence and the man of concupiscence) "contain a pedagogy of the body expressed in a concise and, at the same time, remarkably complete way" (TOB 59:2). By analyzing Christ's words "to the very root," we have learned that the Creator has assigned the body and the gift of sexuality to man *as a task*. It is the task of discovering the truth of our humanity and the dignity of the person. It is the task of embracing our redemption and growing in purity so that we can fulfill ourselves and bring joy to others through the sincere gift of ourselves—the sincere gift of our bodies that affords a true inter-personal communion. This is lived out particularly in marriage, but marriage is not the only way to live the sincere gift of self.

The task of the body and sexuality is, in fact, the task of discovering the truth and meaning of life and living it. It is the task of embracing "the perspective of the whole gospel, of the whole teaching, even more, of the whole mission of Christ" (TOB 49:3). As we have learned, if we follow through with this "task" of the body, if we follow all the traces of our hearts and all the stirrings of our sexuality to their source, we find ourselves at the edge of eternity catching a glimpse of the mystery of the trinitarian God. By way of this journey, men and women discover who they are. Ultimately, there is no other way but via God's revelation in the body. This is why John Paul asserts that "this *theology* of the body is the basis of the most appropriate method of the *pedagogy of the body*, that is, of man's education (or rather, self-education)" (TOB 59:3).

Here we encounter one of those key quotes that demonstrates the scope and purpose of the Pope's catechesis. It is not "just" a catechesis on sex and marriage. The truth about sex and marriage, in fact, provides the key for understanding what it means to be human. John Paul says that the pedagogy of the body, understood as "theology of the body," speaks not only of the sacramentality of married life but also of "the sacramentality of human life" itself (see TOB 59:7). However, we can-not understand and live the truth about life if concupiscence tyrannizes our hearts, and if our behavior contradicts the dignity of the person. A pedagogy of the body, therefore, must provide an anthropology that adequately explains the moral order regarding human sexuality and teaches men and women how to embrace it joyfully.

Spirituality of the Body

Perhaps the greatest threat facing man today is the ideology of dis-embodiment. As a person, man is spiritual. But the body must be under-stood "as a sign of the person, as a manifestation of the spirit" (TOB 59:3). The *human body*, in fact, in the full truth of its masculinity and femininity is given as a task to the *human spirit*. This is why John Paul speaks of a specific "*spirituality of the body*." Living a "spiritual" life *never implies disparagement for the body*. Instead, growing in spiritual maturity means becoming more and more integrated with the gift of one's own body in its masculinity or femininity. It means growing closer and closer to that original, rich, and far-reaching experience of holiness evidenced, as John Paul says, by the fact that the man and woman were both naked without shame. Holiness is certainly spiritual, but it is "felt" in the body (see TOB 19:5). Spiritual maturity, then, is intimately connected with rediscovering the spousal meaning proper to the body. The spiritually mature person comes to *see* the spousal meaning of the body, to *know* it, to *feel* it in his heart, and to *live* it. This is how men and women—and not only married men and women—*incarnate* the Gospel message. We are all called in this way to *put flesh on our spiritual lives*, so to speak.

This radical embodiment starkly contrasts with the modern view of things. An interior divorce between body and spirit is virtually taken for granted in our world today. In fact, the Pope points out that the whole development of modern science, despite its many contributions to human welfare, is based on the separation in man of body and spirit. This deprives the body of its personal meaning and dignity, and man, in turn, ceases to identify himself subjectively with his own body. In this milieu, the human body comes to be treated as an object of manipulation (see TOB 59:3).

In this context, John Paul makes a statement applicable to sex education. He says that purely biological knowledge of the sexual functions of the body can help people discover the true spousal meaning of the body only if an adequate spiritual maturity of the person accompanies this knowledge. Otherwise, as experience attests, it can have quite the opposite effect. We can gain two main points from this. First, the Holy Father does not condemn outright instruction in the sexual functions of the body. But it would be unwise to inundate those who are not spiritually mature with purely biological knowledge. Second, helping those who are not spiritually mature grow in such maturity requires that we help them discover the spousal meaning of the body. True education in sexuality is always an education in the theology of the body, which is the most suitable education in the meaning of being human.

The Church Applies Christ's Words Today

The Pope says that precisely in these divergent views of the body we touch upon the crux of the modern controversies surrounding the Church's teaching on marriage and sexual morality. The controversy grows most pointed in the teaching of the encyclical *Humanae Vitae*. The Church's teachings aim at applying Christ's words to the here and now. "From this point of view, one must consider the pronouncements of the contemporary Church in a clear-sighted way. Grasping and interpreting them adequately, and also applying them in practice (that is, pedagogy), requires that deepened theology of the body which we draw in its definitive form above all from the key words of Christ" (TOB 59:5).

With this statement, the Pope reveals the main goal of his project: to provide an adequate understanding of the Church's teaching on sexuality, particularly her teaching on contraception, which is the linchpin of all sexual morality.[120] Furthermore, he makes the explicit point that this adequate understanding derives *from the words of Christ*. It is rooted not only in natural law, on which the traditional emphasis has been placed in understanding sexual morality; it is also rooted in divine revelation. In this way, as John Paul says in a footnote from a previous audience, "the concept of the natural law acquires also a theological meaning" (TOB 25, n. 39).[121]

The above statement on the importance of the theology of the body not only reveals the essence of the Pope's project. It also outlines John Paul's great commission for the Church. The Church must plumb the depths of "that deepened theology of the body" if she is practically to apply Christ's words and help the world incarnate the Gospel in a new evangelization. At the heart of the new evangelization, at the heart of building a civilization of love and a culture of life, is marriage and the

---

120. While this might seem like an exaggeration to many modern minds, wise men and women throughout history have recognized the fact that once sexual pleasure is divorced from its intrinsic link with procreation, any sexual behavior can be justified. We previously noted Sigmund Freud's statement that the "abandonment of the reproductive function is the common feature of all sexual perversions" (*Introductory Lectures in Psychoanalysis*, p. 266). The inner logic is clear. If sexual relations need not be inherently related to procreation, why should sexual climax be limited to genital intercourse between a husband and wife? The logic that accepts intentionally sterilized intercourse, if it is to remain consistent with itself, must end by accepting any and every means to orgasm: from masturbation, to fornication and adultery, to sodomy, beastiality, etc.

121. As exemplified in his encyclical *Veritatis Splendor* (see especially no. 19), one of John Paul's seminal contributions to moral theology has been to reunite moral doctrine with faith in Christ. This reunion has been termed by some "a Christological approach to natural law."

family. And at the heart of marriage and the family is the truth about the body and sexuality. John Paul made the TOB the first catechetical project of his pontificate because it is the only adequate starting point for the renewal of the family, the Church, and the world. As he knew so well, such renewal cannot possibly happen if we do not go to the "deepest substratum of human ethics and culture" (TOB 45:3), if we do not embrace the truth of sexual morality, particularly the truth taught in the encyclical *Humanae Vitae.*

Plumbing the depths of the theology of the body means reconnecting with our own embodiment. It means living the very dynamism of the Incarnation by allowing the Word of the Gospel to penetrate our flesh and bones. It means realizing that *our bodies are sacramental,* that they reveal the mystery of our humanity and also point to the infinitely greater mystery of God's divinity. When this *incarnation of the Gospel* takes place in us, we see the Church's teaching on sexual morality not as an oppressive list of rules but as the foundation of a liberating ethos, a call to redemption, a call to rediscover in what is erotic the original meaning of the body. This, in turn, reveals the very meaning of life, and *this is the first step to take in renewing the world.*

Appendix:
The Ethos of the Body in Art and Media

In his encyclical *Humanae Vitae,* Pope Paul VI speaks of the need to create an atmosphere favorable to education in chastity.[122] As an appendix to his cycle on historical man, John Paul II devotes four addresses (TOB 60–63) to this need in relation to what he calls "the ethos of the image" (TOB 63:1). By this he means the manner in which we portray the human body in art and in the culture of the mass media. When dealing with such portrayals, he says that "we find ourselves continually within the orbit of the words Christ spoke in the Sermon on the Mount" (TOB 62:5).

Is it possible to portray the naked body artistically without offending the dignity of the person? This is a very delicate problem, the Pope

---

122. See *Humanae Vitae,* 22.

says, which intensifies according to various motives and circumstances. In the first three of these four audiences, as John Paul outlines the problem he seems so cautious at times that one might think he condemns nakedness in art altogether. Not so! In the restoration of the Sistine Chapel, he insisted on removing several of the loincloths that other clerics had had painted over Michelangelo's original nudes. In turn, when he dedicated the restored Sistine Chapel, he described it as *"the sanctuary of the theology of the human body."* Michelangelo, he said, had been guided by the evocative word of God in Genesis 2:25, which enabled him, "in his own way," to see the human body naked without shame. For "in the context of the light that comes from God, the human body also keeps its splendor and its dignity. If it is removed from this dimension, it becomes in some way an object, which depreciates very easily, since only before the eyes of God can the human body remain naked and unclothed, and keep its splendor and beauty intact."[123] The question then becomes: Is it possible to see the human body with the eyes of God? The perfect vision is reserved for the eschaton. But, quoting again from the *Catechism* in this regard: "Even now [purity of heart] enables us to see *according to* God...; it lets us perceive the human body—ours and our neighbor's—as a temple of the Holy Spirit, a manifestation of divine beauty."[124]

John Paul asserts that just because portraying the body in art raises "a very delicate problem...it does not at all follow that the human body in its nakedness cannot become the subject of works of art." It only means "that this issue is neither merely aesthetic, nor morally indifferent" (TOB 61:1). Therefore, John Paul does not intend to cast doubt on the right to this subject in art. He intends merely to demonstrate that its treatment is connected with a special responsibility (see TOB 63:4).

A Perennial Object of Culture

The Pope notes first that the human body is a perennial object of culture (see TOB 60:4). Sexuality and the whole sphere of love between

---

123. Homily preached by John Paul II at the Mass celebrating the restored Sistine Chapel, April 8, 1994 (published in *L'Osservatore Romano*, April 13, 1994).
124. *CCC*, no. 2519.

man and woman has been, is, and will continue to be a subject of art and literature. Indeed, the Bible itself contains that wonderful narrative of the Song of Songs that celebrates the intimate love of man and woman without shame. The body and sexuality's frequency in art and literature indicates their fundamental importance in each person's life and within culture at large. It speaks of that deep yearning we all have to understand "the spousal meaning of masculinity and femininity inscribed in the whole interior—and at the same time visible—structure of the human person" (TOB 63:3).

Herein lies the challenge for artists. If they are to portray *the visible structure of the person* (i.e., the human body), they must do so in a way that does not obscure but brings to light *the interior structure of the person*. In other words, art must integrate the body and soul of the person portrayed by bringing to light the body's spousal meaning. "The human body—the naked human body in all the truth of its masculinity and femininity—has *the meaning of a gift* of the person to the person" (TOB 61:1). Artists must work within this "*spousal system* of reference" if they are not to offend the dignity of the body, which is always the dignity of a person. The ethical norms that govern the body's nakedness are therefore inseparable from the personal truth of the gift.

John Paul affirms that this "norm of the gift" is even deeper than the norm of shame, understood as the need for privacy regarding the body (see TOB 61:2). Therefore, so long as the norm of the gift is properly and diligently respected, the body can be uncovered without violating its dignity. Occasions such as this are relatively rare and demand a "developed sensitivity." For overcoming the limits of shame, as the Pope observes, is accomplished "only with difficulty and inner resistance" (TOB 61:3). In this context, the Holy Father carefully distinguishes "overcoming" the limits of shame from "overstepping" the limits of shame. In the latter case, concupiscence is not conquered but shamelessly expressed. Nakedness then entails a violation of the personal dignity of the body.

The Ethos of the Image and the Ethos of Seeing

A danger exists of objectifying the body when it is portrayed in its nakedness. John Paul describes this as the danger of anonymity, which is a way of "veiling" or "hiding" the identity of the person reproduced (see TOB 60:5). Through photography in particular, the Pope observes that the body very often becomes an "anonymous" object, especially when images of a person's body are diffused on TV and movie screens around the world. Despite their similarities, John Paul notes an important difference between photographing the naked body and portraying the nude human form in the fine arts. In painting or sculpture, the body undergoes a specific elaboration on the part of the artist, whereas in photography an image of an actual, living person is reproduced (see TOB 60:4). Thus photography has even greater need of ensuring the visibility of the person. When this fails to happen, "the human body loses that deeply subjective meaning of the gift and becomes an object destined for the knowledge of many" (TOB 61:1). Hence, both the artist who portrays the body and those who view the artist's work must be aware of their obligation to uphold the dignity of the body as a sign of the gift of persons. From this perspective, John Paul speaks not only of the "ethos of the image" but also the "ethos of viewing" (TOB 63:1).

Creating an atmosphere favorable to chastity in the media and the arts, then, involves recognizing "a reciprocal *circuit* that takes place...between the ethos of the image and the ethos of seeing" (TOB 63:7). This can be explained by the mutual exchange found in actual interpersonal relationships. In genuine relationships, John Paul says that in its nakedness the human body becomes the source of "a particular interpersonal 'communication.'" It is "understood as a manifestation of the person and as the person's gift"—as a "sign of trust in, and of giving to, another person." Thus, we can conclude with the Holy Father that nakedness does not offend or elicit shame when man and woman are "aware of the gift" given and have "decided to respond to it in an equally personal way" (TOB 62:3).

> ■ This dynamic can be keenly observed within a loving marriage, but also in other rare situations. For example, I once heard the following story about a woman who modeled for art students. Having disrobed before the students, she immediately covered herself when she noticed that the shade had not been drawn on the window. When the teacher apologized and drew the shade, she again disrobed. This demonstrates that her nakedness before the students was not "shameless" but a form of "nakedness without shame." She trusted the students to respect her "gift" and to

respond to it in an equally personal way. However, shame immediately manifested itself (and rightly so) when she realized that her nakedness was being potentially exposed to an unknown (and, therefore, untrusted) audience.

A further problem arises, however. Even when an artist portrays the human body intending to illuminate its true spousal meaning, he cannot always know how the recipient of his work will respond. "In fact, that 'element of the gift' is, so to speak, suspended in the dimension of an unknown reception and of an unforeseen response" (TOB 62:3). In this way it is threatened in the sense that it may become an anonymous object of appropriation and abuse. "One cannot forget," John Paul reminds us, "that the fundamental inner 'situation' of 'historical' man is the state of the threefold concupiscence" (TOB 61:3). Through the ethos of redemption, concupiscence can be gradually overcome. Unfortunately, however, not everyone embraces the ethos of redemption. In our fallen world, that "shame, known already from the first chapters of the Bible, is a permanent element of culture and morality" (TOB 61:2). Furthermore, even if the negative sense of shame can be gradually overcome with fervent effort, we must not forget the positive function of shame that always maintains a steadfast respect for the dignity and mystery of others as persons.

True Art versus Pornography

Some works of art portray the naked body in a manner that does not arouse lust but "allows one to concentrate in some way on the whole truth of man, on the dignity and beauty—even 'suprasensual' beauty—of his masculinity and femininity." The Pope immediately adds that such works of art "*bear within themselves in a hidden way, as it were, an element of sublimation*" (TOB 63:5). A masterful artist can lead us through the naked body to the whole personal mystery of man and allow us to comprehend the spousal meaning of the body in purity of heart.[125] In contrast to these, other works of art—and perhaps even more often photographic images—epitomize man's degradation rather

---

125. For a fascinating and provocative study of nakedness in Renaissance art that strove to reveal a theology of the body, see Leo Steinberg's *The Sexuality of Christ in Renaissance Art and in Modern Oblivion* (Chicago, IL: University of Chicago Press, 1996).

than sublimation. Pornographic portrayals of the body raise objection, the Pope insists, not because they expose the human body per se. The human body in itself *always* retains its inalienable dignity. Rather, pornography raises objections because of *the way in which the human body is portrayed* (see TOB 63:5).

The difference between an authentic portrayal of the naked body in art and a pornographic[126] portrayal, then, lies in the artist's intention. Since the body itself always maintains an objective dignity, John Paul observes that the body can only be violated in the intentional order (see TOB 62:2). An artist's work manifests "his *inner world of values*" (TOB 63:4). The artist who not only understands the spousal meaning of the body in the abstract but also lives it himself interiorly can transfer this reality to his work. As experience confirms, the intentions of an artist are usually easy to ascertain. However, we must be careful not to project our own impurity onto artists whose intentions are pure. Those who subscribe to the "interpretation of suspicion" will tend to question the intentions of any artist who portrays the naked body. They will tend to label any portrayal of the naked body as obscene. Such was the case when various clerics, upon viewing Michelangelo's work in the Sistine Chapel, accused him of obscenity and subsequently covered his nudes with awkward drapes and loincloths. Doing so only demonstrated in some sense their own impurity; that is, their own *inability* to see the body as a theology, a revelation of the mystery of God.[127]

Michelangelo's nudes are not pornographic because he intended to reveal the spousal meaning of the body as a revelation of the trinitarian mystery. It is quite clear, however, that this is *not* the intention of pornographers, who portray the naked body with the explicit intention of rousing lust and profiting from concupiscence. By doing so, they explicitly violate "the intimate and constant *order of the gift and of reciprocal self-giving*" inscribed in the human being (TOB 62:1).

---

126. John Paul actually distinguishes between "pornography," which refers to literature and "pornovision," which refers to images. In common English usage, of course, the term pornography usually refers to both.

127. A documentary on the restoration of the Sistine Chapel reported this story. Apparently, Michelangelo liked to use the faces of actual people in painting his figures. It was already known that Michelangelo used the face of a cleric who condemned his nude paintings as the model for the demon in the lower right-hand corner of the Last Judgment. However, only when the loincloth on this demon was removed during the restoration did the modern world glimpse the full extent of Michelangelo's disdain for

██ The juxtaposition of the nudity on the billboards just outside the Vatican and the nudity portrayed in the art inside the Vatican vividly illustrates the difference between pornography and a respectful portrayal of the body in art (shall we call it "spousal-ography"?). On this point, those who subscribe to the "interpreta-tion of suspicion"—and think it holy or "Catholic" to do so —simply cannot justify their position after touring the Vatican. It would be impossible to count the number of depictions of the body that prudery would quickly label "obscene" in St. Peter's Basilica, the Sistine Chapel, and the Vatican museum.

The naked human body is not "obscene." What is "obscene" is that which specifically attempts to stir concupiscence. Professor Waldstein makes this important distinction:

> Some images [of the naked body] push us to concupiscence, others do not.... Going to the Sistine Chapel and looking at the naked women on the ceiling is for this reason a very different experience than watching a pornographic movie. It is not presumption, but the experience of many men, that one can look with purity at Michelangelo's nudes and take delight in their beauty. Michelangelo himself must have looked at his naked models in a pure way in order to be able to paint nudes in that pure way. It would most likely be presumption to think one can watch a pornographic movie with the same purity of heart. The "push" toward concupiscence in a porno-graphic movie is objectively contrary to the dignity of the person, regardless of how well one has mastered one's desires. That "push" is a sufficient reason to stop watching, even if one does not feel oneself sliding into a concupiscent way of looking. Of course, if one does feel a slide into concupiscence when looking at Michelangelo's nudes, it is a good idea to look away. That need to look away should also be a trumpet blast for recognizing that one is not living in accord with the redemption of the body, that one is in need of a seri-ous transformation.[128]

As the Pope says, pornographers will retort that their portrayal of the body is justified in the name of the realistic truth about man. Fur-thermore, they demand the right to "everything that is human" in

---

this cleric's prudery. What may have seemed like a vine coiled around this demon was actually revealed to be a serpent. Not only that—it was taking a generous chomp out of his genitals!

128. Michael Waldstein, private correspondence (December, 2006), printed with permission.

works of art. But, as John Paul insists, the problem with pornography is precisely that *it fails to portray everything that is human*. Precisely the lack of this truth about man—the *whole* truth about man—makes it necessary to condemn pornography (see TOB 62:2). The Holy Father confirms that this condemnation "*is not the effect of a puritanical mentality* or of a *narrow moralism*, nor is it the product of a way of thinking burdened by Manichaeism. What is at issue is rather an *extremely important* and fundamental *sphere of values* to which man cannot remain indifferent because of the dignity of humanity, because of the personal character and eloquence of the human body" (TOB 62:5). For John Paul, we could say that the problem with pornography is not that it reveals too much of the person, but that it reveals far too little. Indeed, it portrays the naked human body while obscuring *the person*.

What then are we to do in this world that incessantly bombards us with pornographic portrayals of the body? The Pope says that each person must decide whether he remains only a superficial "consumer" of the media's images, or commits himself to the effort of drawing near to the glorious truth of the human body in its masculinity and femininity (see TOB 63:7). The hunger we all experience to behold the human body in its nakedness is not the problem. This hunger manifests a God-given yearning for beauty, a God-given desire for the "great mystery" revealed by the body. The question is where will we go to feed that hunger—to the dumpster presented by our pornified culture, or to the banquet presented by this theology of the body?

Conclusion of Chapter 2

With these refreshingly balanced reflections on nakedness in art, John Paul closes his chapter on historical man. We have reflected on man's origins and on the historical drama of sin and redemption. Now, in order to complete the outline of an "adequate anthropology," we must look to the reality of embodiment and sexuality in the dimension of man's eternal destiny (see TOB 63:7).

On an interesting historical note, John Paul concluded this cycle of reflections on May 6, 1981. Exactly one week later, while driving through the crowd in St. Peter's Square at the beginning of his Wednesday audience, he was gunned down by the Turkish assassin Ali

Agca. Many years later John Paul II reflected: "Agca knew how to shoot, and he certainly shot to kill. Yet it was as if someone was guiding and deflecting that bullet." That "someone" was, according to the Pope, Our Lady of Fatima. "Could I forget that the event in St. Peter's Square took place on the day and at the hour when the first appearance of the Mother of Christ to the poor little peasants has been remembered [since 1917] at Fatima in Portugal? For in everything that happened to me on that very day, I felt that extraordinary motherly protection and care, which turned out to be stronger than the deadly bullet."[129]

Most people know the Pope was shot on the feast of Our Lady of Fatima. What many people don't know about that afternoon is that John Paul II had planned to announce the establishment of his Pontifical Institute for Studies on Marriage and Family—his main arm for promoting academic study of his theology of the body. It would be over a year later, on October 7, 1982, that John Paul officially established the institute. On that day—not coincidentally the Feast of Our Lady of the Rosary—in light of his extraordinary survival, John Paul II entrusted the institute to the care and protection of Our Lady of Fatima. As we continue our study of John Paul II's remarkable catechesis, we can be particularly grateful for the motherly intervention that saved his life on May 18, 1981, enabling him to continue delivering his TOB.

CHRIST APPEALS TO THE HUMAN HEART—IN REVIEW

1. Christ's words, which equate "looking lustfully" with committing adultery in the heart, announce the new ethos of redemption. Merely following an external ethic is not enough. It is necessary to penetrate inside the human heart (ethos) where man *experiences* the truth about good or fails to do so.

2. Fulfilling the law cannot be equated only with meeting the law's demands. It involves a super-abounding justice in man's heart that

---

129. *Memory and Identity*, p. 159.

readily goes beyond the demands of law out of genuine love for the truth. This is a "living morality" in which we realize the very meaning of being human.

3. The "heart" defines our humanity from "within." In a way it is equivalent to personal subjectivity. The heart is where we come to know and live the true spousal meaning of the body or fail to do so. For historical man, the heart is a battlefield between love and lust.

4. John Paul describes original sin as the "questioning of the gift." Man denies that "God is love" and therefore casts the Father from his heart. When the heart is *un*-inspired by God's love, it gives birth to concupiscence. The concupiscence of the flesh is a lack of God's love in sexual desire. Shame rises in the heart because man realizes that his body has ceased drawing from the power of the spirit.

5. Shame is cosmic (experienced in relation to all creation), immanent (experienced within oneself), and relative (experienced in relation to the "other"). Shame also has a twofold meaning. It manifests that man and woman have lost sight of the spousal meaning of the body, and it also indicates an inherent need to protect the spousal meaning of the body from the degradation of lust.

6. In the "second discovery of sex," what had once enabled man and woman's communion was suddenly felt to impede communion. It seems that the woman bears a particular burden in this new situation. Both man and woman are subject to lust, but the male tendency to dominate and control woman now places her in an apparent position of inequality.

7. The spousal meaning of the body continues to serve as the "measure of the heart" for historical man. The good news is that through the grace of redemption, Christ empowers man in the task of reclaiming the truth of the body and sexuality. Concupiscence has not completely suffocated the spousal meaning of the body, only habitually threatened it. Recognizing the distortions of our hearts should not lead us to distrust ourselves but should spur us on to reclaim self-mastery.

8. Maintaining the balance of the gift has been entrusted to both men and women, but it seems the man has a particular responsibil-

ity in this regard. If he is called in some sense to initiate the gift, he must ensure that the gift he initiates is genuine. He cannot seek to "possess" the woman's femininity, only to "receive" it. If men and women are to "belong" to each other, this can only come about through the sincere gift of self and never through lustful desire.

9. Old Testament legislation compromised with concupiscence, but the prophets point to the integrity of the covenant of marriage and to its sign. The bodily union of spouses is the regular sign of married love. Understanding this is essential for the entire theology of the body, from both an ethical and an anthropological point of view. For John Paul, sexual morality is understood through the logic of "the truthful sign."

10. The Wisdom literature of the Old Testament contains classic descriptions of carnal concupiscence and admonitions to avoid indulging it. However, it does not change ethos in any fundamental way. For such a change, we must wait for the gift of redemption in Christ.

11. A man "looks" in conformity with what he is. A "look" determines the intentionality of man's very existence. If a man looks with lust, he confirms his denial of the gift of God's love, the gift of the other person, and the gift of life itself. He reduces the value of the person to an object of self-gratification.

12. Marriage in no way "justifies" lust. Thus, a man can commit adultery in his heart with his own wife if he treats her as nothing but an object to satisfy his own instinct. A merely psychological definition of lust, however, cannot arrive at this conclusion, since it does not take man and woman's beginning in Genesis as the normative point of reference.

13. The common life of men and women constitutes the basic guiding thread of existence. Their call to communion is the deepest foundation of human ethics and culture. Hence, the freedom of the gift afforded by liberation from lust is the condition for all of life to be lived in the truth.

14. To understand Christ's words about lust properly, we must contend with the deep-seated habits of Manichaeism in our ways of thinking and evaluating. While the heresy of Manichaeism assigns to

the body and sex an "anti-value," Christianity recognizes in the
body and sex a value not sufficiently appreciated. The Manichaean
condemnation of the body often serves as a loophole to avoid the
demands of Christian purity.

15. If we are to gain a true victory over concupiscence, purity must
    mature from the "negative" turning away to the more "positive"
    assertion of the value and dignity of the body and sex. The "masters
    of suspicion" do not believe in the power of redemption to trans-
    form the heart in this way. But we must not stop at putting the
    heart in a state of irreversible suspicion. Redemption is a truth that
    calls man with efficacy to transformation of heart. The meaning of
    life, then, is the antithesis of the interpretation of suspicion.

16. Christ's call to overcome lust is not hurled into a void but taps into
    that "echo" of our beatifying beginning that remains within each of
    us. The heart is deeper than lust, and Christ's words reactivate that
    deeper heritage, giving it real power in our lives. The grace and gift
    of creation becomes renewed for each of us in the grace and gift of
    redemption.

17. The erotic and the ethical need not contradict each other. *Eros* and
    ethos are not inherently opposed. In fact, they are called to meet in
    the human heart and bear fruit. Eros is meant to be redeemed,
    transformed, and sanctified—not repressed or snuffed out.
    Through purification, the erotic becomes true, good, and beautiful.

18. Like a "guardian who watches over a hidden spring," we are called
    to discern the deep impulses of our hearts so we can draw forth
    what is fitting for the dignity of the gift and the communion of
    persons. Living this ethos of redemption, far from stifling eros,
    affords a mature spontaneity and a noble experience of pleasure.

19. Christ spoke his words about lust in the perspective of the
    redemption of the body, which is "the perspective of the whole
    Gospel, of the whole teaching, in fact of the whole mission of
    Christ." Christ's emphasis on purity of heart brings the Old
    Testament ethos to fulfillment in the New.

20. "Blessed are the pure of heart, for they shall see God." The pure
    can see the body as a making visible of God's mystery. Yet to attain
    this vision we must contend with the system of forces within us,

which St. Paul describes as a battle between the flesh and the Spirit. The "flesh" does not refer to the human body as such, but to the man of concupiscence—the man who has cut his heart off from the love and vision of God.

21. Justification by faith is not just a dimension of the divine plan of salvation, but is a real power at work in man to free him from the bonds of sin and, in this case, the concupiscence of the flesh. Justification by faith enables man to experience the power of "life according to the Spirit," which bears fruit in purity of heart and of action.

22. We experience purity of heart to the measure that we experience the "freedom for which Christ has set us free." The ethos of redemption is nothing but an appeal for the full flowering of human freedom. Freedom to sin is the flip side of freedom to love. If we seek to eradicate sin by eradicating our freedom to commit it, we also eradicate the freedom that is necessary to love.

23. Freedom is negated when it becomes a pretext for indulging "the flesh." Such a man is not free, but enslaved by his disordered passions. Freedom and purity come as we learn to refrain from unchastity and, more so, when we control our bodies "in holiness and reverence."

24. Authentic purity recognizes that those parts of the body we may think are "less honorable" actually deserve greater honor. Purity has a moral dimension as a virtue, but it also has a charismatic dimension as a gift of the Holy Spirit. It is connected with piety, which is respect for the work of God. Unchastity is a violation of piety because the body is a temple of the Holy Spirit.

25. St. Paul exhorts us to glorify God in our bodies. Purity is God's glory radiated in the human body. Christ's words about purity as the ability to "see God" have not only an eschatological meaning but also bear fruit here and now. "To the pure all things are pure, but to the corrupt and unbelieving nothing is pure." The latter deny the "supernatural realism of faith" and the "anthropology of rebirth in the Spirit."

26. The theology of the body is at the basis of the most suitable education of man in the meaning of his own humanity. It calls him to an

authentic Christian spirituality, which is *always* a spirituality of the human body. Furthermore, understanding and practically applying the pronouncements of the Church's magisterium regarding marriage and sexuality demand that deepened theology of the body that we derive from the words of Christ.

27. Portrayal of the naked body in art is connected with a special responsibility. It demands respect for the *"spousal system* of reference," which reveals the body as an intimate gift of the person. The body can be portrayed in its nakedness in a way that elicits awe and respect for the mystery of our humanity, but it can also be portrayed in a way that degrades our humanity. Pornography does not reveal too much of the person. It reveals far too little.

CHAPTER 3

Christ Appeals to the Resurrection

[Cycle 3—Eschatological Man
and Cycle 4—Continence for the Kingdom]

IN OUR QUEST FOR a "total vision of man" we have looked at our origin and our history; now we must look to our destiny. We must reflect upon the experience of embodiment for the man of the eschaton. In John Paul's original manuscript, this chapter also includes his reflections on celibacy for the kingdom. We will have more to say by way of introduction to that cycle in section 2 of this chapter.

As the *Catechism* affirms, "'On no point does the Christian faith meet with more opposition than on the resurrection of the body.' It is very commonly accepted that the life of the human person continues in a spiritual fashion after death. But how can we believe that this body, so clearly mortal, could rise to everlasting life?"[1] Christ's resurrection is the definitive word on the subject. Thus St. Paul attests that he who raised Christ from the dead will give eternal life to our mortal bodies as well (see Rom 8:11). Hence, man's destiny will be a *bodily* reality.

John Paul bases this cycle of reflections on Christ's discussion with the Sadducees. The Lord announces that men and women "neither marry nor are given in marriage" in the resurrection (see Mt 22:30; Mk 12:25; Lk 20:35). At the surface, Christ's assertion may seem to undermine all that the Pope has already said about the surpassing dignity of spousal union and the "eternal attraction" between the sexes. Certainly we know by now that John Paul's exegesis never remains at the surface. As we shall learn, Christ's words reveal a completely new

---

1. *CCC*, no. 996.

dimension of the human mystery, and thus point to the crowning glory of all the Pope has said.

"Eschatological Man" is the shortest cycle—only nine addresses delivered between November 11, 1981, and February 10, 1982 (TOB 64–72). But it is perhaps the most profound cycle and, thus, the most difficult at times to follow. Yet it is well worth every ounce of mental energy it requires. If we could but take in what this pontiff tells us about the joys to come, it would set us ablaze! John Paul weds his Carmelite mysticism to his phenomenological insights for an unsurpassed preview of the eschaton. To be sure, reflecting on the resurrection of the body stretches the Pope's use of the phenomenological method to the limit. How can we possibly talk about subjective experience in relation to the final resurrection when we have no experience of it whatsoever? We can do so in the same way we talk about original innocence—based on the principle of continuity. Christ, in his "revelation of the body," calls historical man to look in two directions. In Christ's conversation with the Pharisees, he calls us to look to the beginning. In his conversation with the Sadducees, Christ calls us to look to the future resurrection.

Even if a "discontinuity" separates the experience of original man, historical man, and eschatological man, as John Paul says, "*What the human body is in the realm of man's historical experience is not completely cut off from these two dimensions of his existence* revealed by Christ's word." Hence, these two "extensions of the sphere" of the experience of the body "are not completely beyond the reach of our...understanding." Based on the principle of continuity, "we can make a certain theological reconstruction of what might have been the experience of the body on the basis of man's revealed 'beginning' and also what it will be in the dimension of the other world" (TOB 68:5–6).

Applying this principle, we can say that if our origin and our history have something to do with the experience of trinitarian love in the human reflection of spousal union, then our destiny will also have something to do with that same experience. Of course, this "will be a completely new experience," as the Pope says. Yet,

> at the same time, it will not be alienated in any way from the experience man shared "from the beginning" nor from that which, in the historical dimension of his existence, constituted in him the source of the tension between the spirit and the body...with reference to the procreative

meaning of the body and of [its] sex. The man of the "future world" will find in this new experience of his own body *the fulfillment* of what he carried in himself perennially and historically. (TOB 69:5)

Returning to our image of the tires: If, in his discussion with the Pharisees and in the Sermon on the Mount, Christ calls historical man to reflect on "the beginning" when our tires were fully inflated, then in his discussion with the Sadducees, Christ calls us to reflect on the future, when tires will lose their *raison d'être* and will give way to flight.

1. Resurrection of the Body
as a Reality of the Future World

A. THE SYNOPTICS: "HE IS NOT THE GOD OF THE DEAD BUT OF THE LIVING"

The Third Part of the Triptych

Like the Pharisees who approached Jesus to question him about divorce, the Sadducees also tried to trap Jesus. The Sadducees did not believe in the resurrection. Appealing to the levirate law (see Deut 25:5–10), they brought a case to Jesus to prove their position. "'There were seven brothers; the first took a wife, and when he died left no children; and the second took her, and died, leaving no children; and the third likewise; and the seven left no children. Last of all the woman also died. In the resurrection, whose wife will she be? For the seven had her as wife'" (Mk 12:20–23). The Pope remarks that the Sadducees unquestionably treat the question of resurrection as a theory that can be disproved. Furthermore, as John Paul adds in a footnote, the Sadducees insinuate "that faith in the resurrection of the body leads to allowing polyandry, contrary to the law of God" (TOB 64:2, n. 68).

The Sadducees considered themselves highly educated experts in the Scriptures. But Jesus—an "uneducated," renegade prophet—responds:

> You are wrong, for you know neither the scriptures nor the power of God. For in the resurrection they neither marry nor are given in marriage, but are like angels in heaven. And as for the resurrection of the dead, have you not read what was said to you by God, "I am the God of

Abraham, and the God of Isaac, and the God of Jacob?" He is not God of the dead, but of the living. (Mt 22:29–33)[2]

John Paul says that Christ's response is "stupendous in its content." It forms the third element of "*the triptych*" of Christ's words that are essential for the theology of the body. His response, in fact, completes "the revelation of the body" and "is one of the key answers of the Gospel." It reveals "another dimension of the question, one that corresponds to the wisdom and power of God himself" (TOB 64:3).

Christ will eventually answer all doubts about the resurrection with the miracle of Easter. For now, however, he wants to demonstrate the truth about resurrection from the testimony of the Old Testament. Mark's account reports more details: "And as for the dead being raised, have you not read in the book of Moses, in the passage about the bush, how God said to him, 'I am the God of Abraham, and the God of Isaac, and the God of Jacob'? He is not God of the dead, but of the living; you are quite wrong" (Mk 12:26–27). John Paul mentions in a footnote that the immortality of their souls could seemingly explain why the Patriarchs are still "living." In other words, it need not prove the resurrection of the body. But Jesus was addressing himself to the Sadducees, who accepted "only the biblical psycho-physical unity of man, who is 'body and breath of life.' And so, according to them, the soul dies together with the body" (TOB 65:4, n. 73). For the Sadducees, Jesus' affirmation that the Patriarchs were "alive" could only have been understood in reference to the resurrection of the body.

Witness to the Power of the Living God

The synoptic accounts of the discussion "contain two essential elements: 1) the statement about the future resurrection of the body; 2) the statement about the state of the bodies of risen human beings" (TOB 65:2). The Holy Father examines each element. Regarding the simple truth of the resurrection, Jesus first shows the Sadducees "a mistake in their method: *they do not know the Scriptures.*" Then he shows them "an error of substance: they do not accept what is revealed by the Scriptures—*since they do not know the power of God*—they do not believe

---

2. See *CCC*, nos. 988–1008.

in the one who revealed himself to Moses in the burning bush" (TOB 65:3). Jesus demonstrates that mere literal knowledge of the Scriptures is not enough. In other words, just to be a Scripture scholar does not suffice. "Scripture is in fact and above all a means for knowing the power of the living God, who reveals himself in it, just as he revealed himself to Moses in the bush" (TOB 65:3). If we "know" the Scriptures inside and out but have not encountered the mystery of the living God within them, we have missed the whole point.

To reread the Scriptures correctly "means knowing and welcoming with faith the power of the Giver of life, who is not bound by the law of death, which rules over man's earthly history" (TOB 65:3). As John Paul says, "He who is—he who lives and is Life—constitutes the inexhaustible fountain of existence and of life, just as he revealed himself at the 'beginning' in Genesis" (TOB 65:5). Although we have turned our backs on Life by breaking the original covenant, and thus lost access to the "Tree of Life," John Paul affirms that throughout the Scriptures the living God continually extends his covenant of life to man and desires to renew it. "Christ is God's final word on this subject," the Pope says. The covenant that Christ establishes between God and mankind "opens an infinite prospect of Life." In Christ, "access to the Tree of Life—according to the original plan of the God of the covenant—is revealed to every man in its definitive fullness. This will be the meaning of Christ's death and resurrection; this will be the testimony of the paschal mystery" (TOB 65:6).

More than that, as we shall learn, the sacrament of marriage testifies to this, that sacrament which is consummated when husband and wife become "one flesh." If husband and wife are faithful to the truth of the sign of their covenant, they image and participate in that definitive covenant between Christ and the Church. Then their marriage, too, opens to "an infinite perspective of life." Tragically, spouses can, like the Sadducees, close themselves to this perspective of life. They can, like the Sadducees, "deprive" God of his life-giving power. Then, rather than becoming a truthful sign of the covenant of life, they (knowingly or unknowingly) become a countersign of it. And God, as in the case with the Sadducees, is seen as "the God of their hypotheses and interpretations" rather than "the true God of their Fathers" (TOB 65:7).

The New Meaning of the Body

John Paul defines marriage as "the union in which, as Genesis says, 'the man will...unite with his wife, and the two will be one flesh.'" He further states that if this union is "proper to man from the 'beginning,'" it does not "constitute man's eschatological future" (TOB 66:2). Indeed, Christ's words about the resurrection affirm that the "one flesh" union of marriage belongs exclusively to "this age" (Lk 20:34).

Many have thought Christ's words disparage sexuality and marital love. Some have seen his statement as proof positive that sexual love is inherently tainted and unfit for the holiness of heaven. Others have feared that it means an eternal sadness of separation from their spouses.[3] But, like the Sadducees, those who accept these interpretations "know neither the scriptures nor the power of God" (Mt 22:29).

The Fulfillment of Marriage

The resurrection will not eradicate marriage. Rather, marriage will be brought to its ultimate fulfillment in "the marriage of the Lamb" (Rev 19:7). From the beginning, the "great mystery" of spousal union was given to us to anticipate and prepare us for the "great mystery" of eternal union with Christ. This is why John Paul describes marriage as the *primordial sacrament*. But precisely as a sacrament—an earthly sign of a heavenly reality—marriage is not the final word on man. Man's ultimate end is heaven. Sacraments will not exist in heaven because they will have come to fruition.[4] When Jesus says men and women will not be given in marriage in the resurrection, it is as if he is saying, "You no longer need a sign to point you *to* heaven when you are *in* heaven." This is why the Pope says that in the resurrection, marriage and procreation "lose, so to speak, their *raison d'être*" (TOB 66:2). The reason they exist is to prepare us for heaven as the fruitful Bride of Christ.

In John Paul's vision of the resurrection, nothing essentially human is mitigated or eliminated. Everything we have learned about who the human person is as a subject (original solitude) and his perennial call to live in an incarnate communion of persons (original unity) reaches its ultimate realization. As the Pope says, the future age "means the

---

3. For a balancing view, see St. John Chrysostom's quote in *CCC*, no. 2365.
4. See *CCC*, no. 671.

definitive fulfillment of the human race." At the same time, however, this entails "the quantitative closure of that circle of beings created in the image and likeness of God" through conjugal union (TOB 66:2).

In other words, man's destiny is fulfilled only when the age in which men and women multiply through the union of their bodies comes to a close. This "closure" must never be perceived as a loss over which to lament. What a tragic misconception! This closure opens us to the fulfillment of every human desire that from the beginning was written in man's heart and stamped in his body as male and female. In fact, as John Paul points out, Christ reveals the new condition of the human body in the resurrection precisely by proposing a reference and a comparison with the condition in which man had participated since the beginning.

We Will Be "Like" Angels

The Pope carefully clarifies that when Christ says we will be "like angels in heaven" (Mt 22:30), he *does not* mean that we will be *dis*-incarnated or otherwise dehumanized. The context in which Christ is speaking, John Paul says, "indicates clearly that in the 'other world' man will keep his own psychosomatic nature. If it were otherwise, it would be meaningless to speak about the resurrection" (TOB 66:5). Unfortunately, Plato's belief that the body is the earthly prison of the soul has significantly influenced the thinking of many Christians. The Pope insists that "the truth about the resurrection clearly affirms that man's eschatological perfection and happiness cannot be understood as a state of the soul alone, separated (according to Plato, liberated) from the body." This idea is essentially alien to orthodox Christianity. Instead, man's ultimate beatitude "must be understood as *the definitively and perfectly 'integrated' state of man* brought about by such a [perfect] union of the soul with the body" (TOB 66:6).[5]

■ Philosopher Peter Kreeft writes: "A soul without a body is exactly the opposite of what Plato thought it is. It is not free but bound. It is in an extreme form of paralysis." The human soul *needs* the body to express itself—not only on earth but in heaven as

---

5. See *CCC*, no. 650.

well. "The body is the matter of the soul, and the soul is the form of the body. That is why the resurrection of the body is internal to the immortality of the soul, not a dispensable extra. When death separates the two," Kreeft continues, "we have a freak, a monster, an obscenity. That is why we are terrified of ghosts and corpses, though both are harmless: they are the obscenely separated aspects of what belongs together as one. That is why Jesus wept at Lazarus' grave: not merely for his bereavement but for this cosmic obscenity."[6]

John Paul mentions that faith in the resurrection of the body played a key role in the formation of theological anthropology. In fact, he says that theological anthropology could be considered simply as the *"anthropology of the resurrection"* (TOB 66:6). For only in light of the resurrection of the body do we fully understand who man is theologically and what he is destined for as a body-person. In fact, the Pope says that St. Thomas's reflections on the resurrection led him to draw closer to the conception of Aristotle. Unlike Plato, Aristotle taught that, together with the soul, the body constitutes the unity and integrity of the human being. Christian belief in the resurrection of the body confirms this.

But another question arises: Will we be raised as male and female? Some, granting the resurrection of the body, envision a sexless heaven based on St. Paul's teaching that in Christ "there is neither male nor female" (Gal 3:28). The Pope believes that our bodiliness belongs to our humanity more deeply than the fact that in our bodiliness we are either male or female (TOB 8:1). In other words, the experience of being a body-person (original solitude) is deeper than and "prior" to the experience of sexual differentiation and the call to communion (original unity). That being said, John Paul mentions three times in his audience of December 2, 1981 (TOB 66), and on other occasions throughout this cycle, that in the resurrection we reacquire our bodies *in their masculinity and femininity.* Sexual difference is the perennial sign and summons of the human race to communion. The resurrection fulfills not only the bodily experience of solitude, but also the bodily experience of

6. Peter Kreeft, *Everything You Ever Wanted to Know about Heaven* (San Francisco: Ignatius Press, 1990), p. 93.

communion—albeit in a completely new, virginal way. As John Paul expresses it, in the resurrection we rediscover not only "a new, perfect subjectivity of each person." At the same time we rediscover "a new, *perfect intersubjectivity of all*," that is, communion with other persons (see TOB 68:4).

Based on the Pope's modern philosophical language, we come to understand that sexual difference is not only retained but also is in some way essential to the communion of saints. Of course the resurrection means a completely new state of human life. Both the reality of sexual difference and the mystery of communion will be experienced in an entirely new way. As the *Catechism* says, "This mystery of blessed communion with God and all who are in Christ is beyond all understanding and description."[7] We must not, therefore, conceive of the eternal communion that awaits us as an expansion into infinity of the earthly reality of the male-female communion. Nonetheless, nothing genuinely human will be done away with or annihilated. All that is essentially human in the original experiences of solitude-unity-nakedness will be brought to ultimate fulfillment. Heaven, therefore, will be the experience of a great multitude of solitudes living in perfect unity without any fear of being seen and known by each and by all.

■ Does this mean we will be naked in heaven? Those who claim to have caught glimpses of the blessed report that it is hard to classify them as either clothed or naked.[8] The experience is simply "other" than we can imagine. If clothed, the blessed wear a "nuptial garment."[9] If naked, there is no fear because the original *raison d'être* of shame (in the negative sense) has ceased utterly. Interestingly, both the Gospel of Luke (24:12) and of John (20:5–7) mention that Christ's burial coverings were left behind in the tomb after his resurrection. The *Catechism* teaches that, together with the empty tomb, this signifies that "Christ's body had escaped the bonds of death and corruption."[10] Michelangelo sought to convey this truth by portraying his famous *Risen Christ*

---

7. *CCC*, no. 1027.
8. See Kreeft, *Everything You Ever Wanted to Know about Heaven*, p. 43.
9. See *CCC*, no. 1682.
10. *CCC*, no. 657.

naked without shame. It seems fitting that the New Adam would come forth from the ground just as the first Adam did. It also seems significant that Christ would come forth from the virgin tomb (see Jn 19:41) just as he came forth from the virgin womb. Yet in doing so, Christ's risen body was mysteriously "different," so much so that his own disciples did not immediately recognize him.

The Book of Revelation speaks of the saints in heaven wearing "white robes" (Rev 7:9). White is the color of light. When Christ was transfigured, his garments "became white as light" (Mt 17:2). Light reveals rather than conceals. In heaven, all is revealed by the light of Christ. "For nothing is hid that shall not be made manifest, nor anything secret that shall not be known and come to light" (Lk 8:17). Many Church Fathers speak both of Adam and Eve in paradise and of the blessed in heaven as being clothed in glory. "They shall have no need of woven raiment," says Ignatius of Antioch, "for they shall be clothed in eternal light."[11] St. John describes the "woman" who appeared in heaven as being "clothed with the sun" (Rev 12:1).

"Purity is the glory of the human body before God. It is the glory of God in the human body, through which masculinity and femininity are manifested" (TOB 57:3). White robes and nakedness are *both* symbols that the Church has used to convey Christian purity and new birth in Christ. St. Cyril of Jerusalem describes the symbolism of the once common practice of nude baptism as follows: "As soon as you entered [the baptismal font] you divested yourself of your garment; this gesture symbolized the divesting yourself of the old man in you with all his practices.... O marvelous thing, you were naked before everyone and yet you did not blush for shame. Truly you represented in this the image of the first man, Adam, who in paradise was naked but was not ashamed."[12] The resurrected state will recover whatever was essentially human in Adam's original experience of nakedness, but in an entirely new dimension, "beyond all understanding and description."[13]

---

11. *Epistle to the Philippians*, series 2, v. 13.
12. *Mystagogical Catecheses*, 2:2.
13. *CCC*, no. 1027.

Spiritualization of the Body

If the resurrection signifies man's perfect realization, this cannot consist in the opposition of spirit and body but only in a deep harmony between them. Of course, according to the "system of powers" within man (i.e., the spirit-body relationship), the spirit has primacy over the body. But original sin disrupted this system in man, and the body often rebels against the spirit. St. Paul expressed this well: "I see in my members another law at war with the law of my mind" (Rom 7:23). However, in the "other world," the primacy of the spirit will be realized and manifested in a "perfect spontaneity" without any opposition from the body.

John Paul carefully points out that this must not be understood as a definitive "victory" of the spirit over the body (see TOB 67:2). That would imply some remaining tension: an extrinsic domination of the spirit and a reluctant submission of the body. In the resurrection, however, no tension will exist. The body will return to perfect unity and harmony with the spirit. Thus, opposition between the spiritual and the physical in man will cease. John Paul says, "Here one could speak also about a perfect system of powers in the reciprocal relations between what is spiritual and what is bodily in man" (TOB 67:1).

Christ's comparison of men and women to angels points to a perfect "spiritualization" of the body. This means that the spirit will *"fully permeate the body and the powers of the spirit will permeate the energies of the body"* (TOB 67:1). Man and woman knew something of this in the beginning (see p. 139ff.). Indeed, the rupture of the harmony of body and spirit specifically caused the entrance of shame (see p. 182ff.). Furthermore, through the redemption of the body, historical man "can, as the fruit of persevering work," regain that harmony and "express a spiritually mature personality" (TOB 67:2). Even so, Christ's words about the resurrection refer to a dimension of spiritualization different from that of earthly life. John Paul adds that this is a spiritualization even different from that of the "beginning" itself.[14]

One of the main differences, John Paul says, is that the eschatological spiritualization of the body precludes any opposition between body

---

14. Here we gain insight into the soteriological principle (principle of salvation) that through Christ's redemption we gain even more than what we had in the state of original innocence. Heaven is not merely a return to Eden, but an entrance into a completely new fullness of our humanity.

and spirit. Original man, although fully integrated, had the possibility of disintegration (as original sin attests). Historical man can progressively regain integration, but he can still and often does fall prey to concupiscence. Eschatological man will experience a "perfect spiritualization," which makes it impossible that "another law" would be at war with the law of the mind (see Rom 7:23). Hence, this state "is essentially (and not only in degree) different from what we experience in earthly life" (TOB 67:2).

Divinization of the Body

Furthermore, the spirit that will totally permeate the body is not only man's own spirit. It is also the Holy Spirit. So the Pope speaks of a "divinizing spiritualization" (TOB 69:6). For "the sons of the resurrection" in Luke 20:36 are not only "equal to angels." They are also "sons of God." This is why "the degree of spiritualization proper to 'eschatological' man will have its source in the degree of his 'divinization'" (TOB 67:3). This means man's destiny is to participate in the very divinity of the Trinity through the *in*-spiration of his body by the Holy Spirit's power. All this is revealed in our bodiliness and sexuality. In the beginning, man's creation as male and female and his call to conjugal communion constituted a *primordial sacrament*, "understood as a *sign that efficaciously transmits in the visible world the invisible mystery hidden in God from eternity*. And this is the mystery of Truth and Love, the mystery of divine life, in which man really participates" (TOB 19:4).

Through their experience of original unity, man and woman participated in the *very humanity* of each other. This was an effective sign of their call to participate in the *very divinity* of God (see p. 148ff.). But the divinization to come will not be mediated by an earthly sign.[15] Hence, the future divinization is "incomparably superior to what can be reached in earthly life." Here "we are not dealing only with a different degree, but in some way with another kind of 'divinization'" (TOB 67:3).

This means that the consummate union of earth is consummated, so to speak, only in the consummate union of heaven. As the *Catechism* teaches, "*For man*, this consummation will be the final realization of the

---

15. See *CCC*, nos. 1023, 1136.

unity of the human race, which God willed from creation.... Those who are united with Christ will form the community of the redeemed, 'the holy city' of God, 'the Bride, the wife of the Lamb.'"[16] In the Lamb's gift of self to his Bride, John Paul says that "penetration and permeation of what is essentially human by what is essentially divine, will then reach its peak, so that the life of the human spirit will reach a fullness that was absolutely inaccessible to it before" (TOB 67:3). This is man's ultimate "participation in the divine nature." It is man's ultimate "participation in the inner life of God himself" (TOB 67:3). It is his ultimate participation in *grace*. This grace is "*God's self-communication in his very divinity*, not only to the soul but *to the whole of man's psychosomatic subjectivity*" (TOB 67:3)—his soul-body personhood. By virtue of this grace, man will "conceive" divine life within him and bear it continually in the Holy Spirit.

Of course the spousal analogy is woefully inadequate in conveying the mystery. Nonetheless, we see something of the mystery "stamped" in our very being as male and female and in our call to spousal union. How can we not, at this point, be reminded of Mary as the model of the Church and the archetype of humanity? She is the one who in this life was impregnated with divine life! She is the one who in this life allowed her entire person—body and soul—to be permeated by the Holy Spirit. Hence, she is our eschatological hope. In her, the redemption of the body is already brought to completion.

John Paul speaks of this divine communication to man's "psychosomatic subjectivity" (his soul-body personhood) and not only to a generic "human nature" in order to emphasize the personal and communal dimension of God's heavenly gift (see TOB 67:3). Heaven is a "union with God in his trinitarian mystery and of intimacy with him in the perfect communion of persons. This intimacy—with all its subjective intensity—will not absorb man's personal subjectivity, but, quite on the contrary, will make it emerge in an incomparably greater and fuller measure" (TOB 67:3). In other words, each person's uniqueness will not be lost or absorbed into the Trinity. Each person will shine in the full glory of his or her unrepeatability.

Once again, all of this was foreshadowed in some way through that original, beatifying union of man and woman who, full of grace, did not

---

16. *CCC*, no. 1045.

know shame in their nakedness. By surrendering themselves to each other, each person was not lost or absorbed in the other but, in fact, discovered his (her) true self through the sincere gift of self). In an infinitely greater dimension—in the definitive fulfillment of every human longing for union—we will discover our true selves in the resurrection when we respond to the gift of God with the sincere gift of ourselves to him.

The Beatific Vision: Seeing God "Face to Face"

From the beginning, human embodiment—connected as it is with erotic desire for union with an "other"—was meant to be a sign of and a preparation for that ultimate union with the ultimate Other. John Paul concludes that in "this 'spiritualization' and 'divinization' in which man will participate in the resurrection, we discover—in an eschatological dimension—the same characteristics that mark the 'spousal' meaning of the body." This time, however, all those characteristics (the complementarity of the sexes; the call to life-giving communion; the desire to see another and be seen by that other, etc.) are fulfilled "in the encounter with the mystery of the living God, which reveals itself through the face-to-face vision of him" (TOB 67:5). The *Catechism* speaks of this fulfillment when it says that the Church "longs to be united with Christ, her Bridegroom, in the glory of heaven," where she "will rejoice one day with [her] Beloved, in a happiness and rapture that can never end." [17]

John Paul asks whether it is possible to think of this eschatological experience of the spousal meaning of the body above all as the "*virginal*" meaning of being male and female—of the "virginal" experience of spousal communion (see TOB 67:4). To answer this question, the Holy Father says we must first penetrate more deeply into the "very essence" of the beatific vision. [18] In order to do that, we must "let ourselves be guided by that 'range of experience' of truth and love that surpasses the limits of man's cognitive and spiritual possibilities in temporality" (TOB 67:4).

With these words, John Paul shows himself to be a mystic. Only a mystic can let himself be guided by "a range of experience" beyond time

---

17. *CCC*, no. 1821.
18. See *CCC*, no. 1028.

while still living in time. In other words, beyond the principle of continuity, a phenomenological analysis of man's destiny can only be
attempted by someone who has mystically "experienced" something of
life beyond the veil. It seems John Paul had. In his letter marking the
beginning of the millennium, John Paul wrote: "The great mystical tradition of the Church of both East and West...shows how prayer can
progress, as a genuine dialogue of love...to the ineffable joy experienced
by the mystics as 'nuptial union.' How can we forget here, among the
many shining examples, the teachings of St. John of the Cross and St.
Teresa of Avila?"[19] "In this way," as the Pope wrote elsewhere, "we
somehow anticipate what is destined to be ours in eternity, beyond
death and the grave."[20]

In what follows, the Pope stretches words and ideas to their maximum capacity in his attempt to communicate to us something of his
own "eschatological anticipation." Here we will come to see the full
flowering of John Paul II's immersion in the spousal mysticism of John
of the Cross. Recall from our discussion in the Prologue the threefold
conviction that Wojtyla gained early in his life from the mystical
Doctor:

(1) Love involves the gift of self.
(2) The relationship of spouses is the paradigm of self-giving love
    in human experience.
(3) The relationship of Father, Son, and Holy Spirit is the source
    and model of all self-giving love.

In the beatific vision, the spousal paradigm of human self-giving
love will give way to the ultimate source of self-giving love in the
Trinity. Man will no longer need a sacrament (marriage, the "primordial
sacrament") to mediate the divine exchange of love and life. Through
bridal openness to the utterly gratuitous gift of the heavenly Bridegroom, man will participate immediately (without sacramental mediation) in the divine exchange itself. Man will thus enter the fullest
possible experience of union with God—something beyond all manner
of comprehension here on earth, but nonetheless, according to John of
the Cross, *"like the marriage union and surrender,* in which the goods of
both [God and man]...are possessed by both together. *They [will] say to*

---

19. *Novo Millennio Ineunte,* 33.
20. *Memory and Identity,* p. 30.

each other what the Son of God spoke to the Father.... 'All that is mine is yours and yours is mine' [Jn 17:10]."[21] In this way, the "mystical marriage" of which St. John so often spoke will be forever consummated.

The Eschatological Experience

As stated previously, from the beginning man was created to be a "partner of the Absolute" (see p. 99ff.). He was called to enter into a covenant with God—a relationship of eternal communion analogous to the union of spouses (see p. 126ff.). Man broke this original covenant with God by eating from the forbidden tree. Yet God's gift of himself to man is irreversible (see p. 139ff.). Christ's coming is the ultimate testimony of God's irreversible gift. If historical man is willing to pass by way of the cross, not only can he recover that original communion with God, but he also opens himself to the living hope of the eschatological fulfillment of this communion.

In this eschatological fulfillment, we will know "in a living and experiential way, the *'self-communication'* of God to everything created." In particular, we will know and experience the self-communication of God to us. This *"is God's most personal self-giving: in his very divinity"* because we are "that being who has from the beginning borne his image and likeness" within ourselves (TOB 67:5). We are that being who bears the inner dimension of the gift (see p. 149). In this eschatological experience, the inner dimension of the gift in man—expressed and made visible "in the beginning" through the nakedness of the body—will meet its divine prototype "face to face." All our energies will be concentrated on receiving the gift of the living God and reciprocating that love by giving ourselves back to him. This "eschatological communion (*communio*) of man with God," the Pope says, "will be nourished by the vision 'face to face'...of the most perfect communion —because it is purely divine—which is, namely, the *trinitarian communion of the divine Persons* in the unity of the same divinity" (TOB 68:1).

In other words, our union with the living God springs from the beatific vision of his innermost mystery—his trinitarian exchange of

---

21. John of the Cross, *The Living Flame of Love*, commentary on st. B3, pars. 78–80 (cited also in the introduction of TOB, pp. 27–28).

love. Beholding the total, perfect, and incessant reciprocal giving of the Trinity will inspire us to enter the mystery by giving ourselves incessantly to God in response to his eternal gift to us. His gift is nothing other than to share in his own bliss, his own communion. Recall that key teaching of the *Catechism*: "By sending his only Son and the Spirit of Love in the fullness of time, God has revealed his innermost secret: God himself is an eternal exchange of love, Father, Son, and Holy Spirit, and he has destined us to share in that exchange."[22] In this way we come to understand that the object of the beatific vision, *what we will see face to face*, "will be that mystery hidden from eternity in the Father, a mystery that has in time been revealed in Christ to be fulfilled unceasingly by the work of the Holy Spirit" (TOB 67:5).

The Body: A Witness to Love

In a word, that mystery we shall behold "face to face" is love (see 1 Jn 4:8). Love is gift; and gift is grace; and grace received is communion *with the divine*. Recalling John Paul's thesis, this mystery of love and gift (and grace and communion) hidden in God from all eternity and definitively revealed in Christ was made visible from the beginning by the sign of the body in its masculinity and femininity. Man and woman embody the reality of gift. Hence, the body has a spousal meaning. As previously quoted, John Paul says, "This is *the body: a witness* to creation as a fundamental gift, and therefore a witness *to Love as the source from which this same giving springs*. Masculinity-femininity—namely, sex—is the original sign of [God's] creative donation." At the same time, "man, male-female, becomes aware of [this sign] as a gift lived so to speak in an original way" (TOB 14:4).

This "original way" of living the gift of God's love (grace) was revealed in the experiences of original solitude, unity, and nakedness. The "historical way" of living the gift seeks to recover the grace of creation through the redemption of the body. Finally, the "eschatological way" of living the gift not only fully recovers the original purity but also takes us infinitely beyond to an entirely new dimension—to an *immediate bodily participation* in the trinitarian mystery of love and gift. This trinitarian mystery will become "the content of eschatological experi-

---

22. *CCC*, no. 221.

ence and the 'form' of human existence as a whole in the dimension of the 'other world'" (TOB 67:5). Therefore, the Pope says that eternal life in the resurrection must be understood as the full and perfect experience of grace.

Our first parents experienced the original dimension of this grace in the beginning. We participate in it now through faith and the sacraments. However, this grace will only reveal itself "in all its penetrating depth" to those who partake in the "other world." There, the grace already given in creation and restored in redemption will "be experienced in its beatifying reality" (TOB 67:5).

The Perfection of Subjectivity

This ultimate participation in grace—in the very life and love of God through the beatifying vision of him face to face—is what enables all that is physical in man to participate perfectly in all that is spiritual in him. At the same time this experience will consist in the perfect realization of what is personal in man. According to the "great mystery," we are created to be the Bride of Christ. In giving ourselves totally to Christ, we do not lose ourselves. We discover ourselves (see Mk 8:35). In submitting ourselves as a Bride to our eternal Bridegroom, we are not dominated; we are not abased. We are loved (see Eph 5:25). We are served (see Mt 20:28). We are filled to the full with life (see Jn 10:10). If we don't believe that surrendering totally to God provides the key to our freedom and the fulfillment of our personal subjectivity, we are still duped by the father of lies. We are still "doubting the gift" (see p. 178ff.). If we only knew the gift of God and who it is that offers it to us (see Jn 4:10)!

Not only will participants in the other world rediscover their authentic subjectivity, but the Pope repeatedly affirms that they will also acquire it to a far more perfect extent than in earthly life. By living in "perfect communion with the living God," they will enjoy a perfectly mature subjectivity. This confirms what John Paul calls "the law of the integral order of the person" (TOB 68:2). According to this law, as a personal subject, man is created for his own sake (solitude), but he is not called to live for his own sake. He can only perfect his subjectivity through the sincere gift of self, that is, through a perfect experience of inter-subjectivity (unity). In turn, the perfection of communion is conditioned by the spiritual maturity of the subjects who enter that communion. We can see this clearly in the case of marriage. A marriage is only as healthy as those who enter it. However, at the same time, and according to the same law of the integral order of the person, the perfection of communion determines the perfection of the participants in that communion. In marriage, as the spouses' communion grows in perfection, so do the spouses.

Man and woman knew the earthly model (the primordial sacrament) of this perfect communion in the beginning. To the extent that we allow the ethos of redemption to permeate us, we can rediscover and live according to this original earthly model. But in the resurrection, the earthly model will give way to the divine prototype, and human subjectivity will be perfected through an immediate experience of inter-subjectivity with the divine Subject who, himself, lives an eternal mystery of divine inter-Subjectivity. *This* is why men and women are no longer given in marriage in the resurrection. Their call to communion will be fulfilled in an eternal communion with *the* Eternal Communion!

The Marriage of Divinity and Humanity

A New Threshold for Understanding Man

In his exchange with the Pharisees, Christ speaks of the state of marriage "in the beginning." In his exchange with the Sadducees, he speaks of the state of marriage in the future. These two "words" of Christ are linked together as bookends in John Paul's "total vision of man." They correspond to the bookends of the Bible itself—the marriage of Adam and Eve in Genesis and the "marriage" of the New Adam and the New Eve in Revelation.

John Paul says that Christ's words about the resurrection enable us to understand the meaning of that original "one flesh" unity in a whole new dimension. Recall that in John Paul's first cycle of reflections, he indicated that Genesis 2:24 ("the two shall become one flesh") "was to have a broad and far-reaching perspective in God's revelation" (TOB 9:5). In this cycle the Pope says that Christ's words about the resurrection and the state of male and female in the resurrection "have a decisive meaning, not only for what concerns the words of Genesis ...but also in what concerns the whole Bible" (TOB 69:8).

Christ's words on the resurrection "allow us in some way to reread in a new way—that is, in all its depth—the whole revealed meaning of the body, the meaning of being man, that is, an 'incarnated' person, of being, as a body, male or female" (TOB 69:8). In the beginning, the meaning of our creation as male and female was revealed as "gift." Man and woman were created first to receive the gift of God's gratuitous love, to return it to him, and then to recapitulate that love by being gift to each other. "Therefore," as Genesis 2:24 proclaims, "a man leaves his father and his mother and cleaves to his wife, and they become one flesh." This was the consummate expression of the gift in the beginning, which established that incarnate communion of persons (see p. 110).

The words of Genesis 2:24 direct us "especially toward 'this world,'" the Pope says, but "not completely" (TOB 69:8). These words "are constitutive of the sacrament of Marriage" (TOB 19:5). Hence, like all sacraments, the "one flesh" unity of marriage points in some way to the "other world." There, the gift will be consummated in an eternal, eschatological dimension of "incarnate communion" inclusive of all who respond to the wedding invitation of the Lamb. If, as John Paul says, the words of Genesis (and from the context it seems the Pope is speaking specifically of Genesis 2:24) "were the threshold, as it were, of the whole theology of the body," Christ's words about the resurrection "are like a new threshold of this integral truth about man, which we find again in the revealed Word of God. It is indispensable for us to dwell on this threshold," the Pope says, "if we wish our theology of the body—and also our Christian 'spirituality of the body'—to be able to use it as a complete image" (TOB 69:8). It is Christ himself, through the "triptych" of his words about the body, that provides us with the "complete image" of man.

Divine-Human Communion

John Paul explains the absence of marriage in the resurrection not only with the end of history, but also—and above all—with what he calls the "eschatological *authenticity*" of man's response to God's self-giving (see TOB 68:2). In the consummation of the gift in the resurrection, the divine Subject (God) will give himself to the human subject (man) in a beatifying experience "absolutely superior to every experience proper to earthly life. The reciprocal gift of oneself to God...will be the response to God's gift of himself to man" (TOB 68:2–3). By virtue of the eternal Word made flesh, this too will be an *incarnate* gift, an incarnate communion.

Keeping in mind the ever greater dissimilarity in the analogy while also focusing on the intrinsic similarity, we are talking about the ultimate consummation of the marriage of divinity and humanity. We are talking about the eternal, beatifying experience of a perfect divine-human inter-subjectivity, a perfect divine-human *communio personarum*. We are talking about the eschatological fulfillment of the prophecy of Genesis 2:24. As St. Paul says, the union in one flesh is a "great mystery," and it refers to the union of Christ and the Church (see Eph 5:31–32). Christ left his Father in heaven; he left the home of his mother on earth—to give up his body for his Bride so that we, the Bride of Christ, might become "one flesh" with him. What was foreshadowed from the beginning in the incarnate communion of man and woman (marriage) and definitively revealed in the incarnate communion of Christ and the Church (Eucharist) will be lived eternally in the resurrection.

This is the ultimate meaning of "being a body," of being male and female in the divine image. Sexual difference and our longing for union reveal that we are created for eternal communion with *the* eternal Communion: Father, Son, and Holy Spirit. Participation in this eternal Communion will be a completely new experience, but it will not be alienated in any way from the earthly experience of communion. The earthly communion, then, will not be erased or deleted—it will be definitively fulfilled and completed in the marriage of the Lamb.

Again, we can see Satan's reason for attacking man and woman's communion in the beginning and throughout history. It is the primordial sign in creation of God's plan to take on flesh and be one with us. This is precisely what the enemy wants to thwart. But all he can do in his attempts to counter God's plan is plagiarize the sacraments. All he can do is twist what God created to be true, good, and beautiful. This means that all the sexual confusion in our world—and in our own hearts—is simply the human desire for heaven gone berserk. Untwist it and we rediscover the image of God in every human being; we rediscover the deep human longing—that God put there—for union with him. G. K. Chesterton expressed the same idea when he wrote: "Every man who knocks on the door of a brothel is looking for God."[23]

Knowledge of God

John Paul speaks of the beatific vision as a "concentration of knowledge ('vision') and love on God himself." This concentration of knowledge "cannot be anything but full participation in God's inner life, that is, in trinitarian Reality itself" (TOB 68:4). We can recall at this point our previous discussion of biblical "knowledge." Through their knowledge of each other in Genesis, man and woman came to know "a third." In some sense they came to participate in a created version, so to speak, of the Uncreated relations of the Trinity.

The entire cosmos, in fact, bears the mark of its Creator; the mark of trinitarian relations.[24] John Paul says the knowledge of God in heaven will be at the same time the discovery, in God, of "the whole 'world' of relations" that are part of God's perennial order in the cosmos (TOB 68:4). In other words, the eschatological experience will not only be man's full participation in the *Uncreated* world of relations (the Trinity), but it will also be a full participation in the *created* world of relations. This includes a full participation in man's original harmony with creation[25] *and* in the original created communion of persons.

All this means that created relations will not be annulled or overridden by participation in the Uncreated relation. As John Paul says, "The concentration of knowledge and love on God himself in the trinitarian communion of Persons can find a beatifying response in [man] ...only *through realizing...communion commensurate with created persons.*

---

23. David Dooley, ed., *The Collected Works of G. K. Chesterton*, vol. 1 (San Francisco: Ignatius Press, 1986).

24. See *CCC*, no. 237. See also *Dominum et Vivificantem*, 50, for a concise statement of the cosmic dimensions of trinitarian relations as manifested by the Incarnation.

25. See *CCC*, nos. 1047–48. As St. Paul says, "We know that the whole creation has been groaning in travail [awaiting] the redemption of our bodies" (Rom 8:22–23). Despite the exaggerations of some environmentalist and "animal rights" groups, there is nonetheless a fundamental rightness in man's concern and love for creation (see *CCC*, nos. 2415–18). When we untwist the distortions, we rediscover a fundamental longing for harmony with creation that was part of God's original plan. John Paul previously described the "cosmic shame" that manifests the breaking of this harmony with creation (see p. 184ff.).

And for this reason," he says, "we profess faith in the 'communion of saints'" (TOB 68:4).[26]

Communion of Saints: Fulfillment of the Spousal Meaning of the Body

Christ's words do not fall in a void, whether he speaks of the beginning or of the future resurrection. If we experience an "echo" of our beginning deep within our hearts, we also experience a kind of "premonition" of our destiny. In fact, the earthly experience of the body "provides the substratum and the basis" (TOB 69:2) of the heavenly experience of the body. Although "*it is difficult to construct a fully adequate image* of the 'future world,'...at the same time, there is no doubt that with the help of Christ's words at least a certain approximation to this image is possible and reachable" (TOB 69:7).

The spousal meaning of the body gives John Paul the key for constructing an image of the "future world." The call to be gift (to love as God loves) is inscribed in the interior and exterior structure of the human person from "the beginning." This primordial truth finds its eschatological realization in the reciprocal gift of God and man to each other in an eternal divine-human communion of persons. However, as mentioned above, man's participation in the Uncreated Communion of the Trinity is also a perfect realization of the created communion of persons. Not only will we be "one" with God; we will be "one" with everyone who responds to the wedding invitation of the Lamb.

A Union of Communion

To paraphrase John Paul, the communion of saints consists of many created communions united with each other by contemplating the vision of that Uncreated Communion (the Trinity). In turn, man's beatific vision of the Trinity constitutes a real communion with this Uncreated Communion. This "union of communion," as the Pope describes it (see TOB 68:4), is an eternal and mysterious unity of created communions with the Uncreated Communion. In this ultimate reality we will see all and be seen by all. We will know all and be known by all. And God will be "all in all" (Eph 1:23).

---

26. See *CCC*, nos. 1474–77.

If you find yourself lost in the communion of these communions, drawing from the logic of the spousal meaning of the body, we can say this: In the eschatological experience, we who are many as male and female will form one body (see 1 Cor 10:17). In a manner beyond our present comprehension,[27] all that is masculine in humanity will be in union with all that is feminine in humanity. In turn, this "one body" will form the one Bride of Christ who, through eternal union with her Bridegroom, will live in eternal communion with the Trinity. As the Pope says, and we have already quoted, we must think of this reality in terms of "the rediscovery of a new, perfect subjectivity of each person and at the same time of the *rediscovery* of a new, *perfect intersubjectivity of all.*" This reality, the Pope continues, "means the true and definitive fulfillment of human subjectivity and, on this basis, the definitive fulfillment of the 'spousal' meaning of the body" (TOB 68:4). In other words, the original mystery and experience of solitude—of being "alone" as *a person* before God and with God—will be blissfully fulfilled. And, on this basis, so too will the call to communion inscribed in the body from the beginning be fulfilled.

The Pope continues: "The total concentration of created, redeemed, and glorified subjectivity on God himself, will not take man away from this fulfillment, but—on the contrary—will introduce him into it and consolidate him in it." In other words, our complete focus on God will not diminish our own fulfillment as individual persons and as persons in communion, but will enable it. Our vision of the trinitarian Reality of three distinct Persons living in perfect Communion will enable us to mirror that Uncreated Communion in the created communion of the saints. As the Pope concludes, "in this way the eschatological reality will become the source of the perfect realization of the 'trinitarian order' in the created world of persons" (TOB 68:4).

When the Pope speaks of "the trinitarian order," he is speaking of unity-in-plurality, oneness-in-multitude, a communion-of-solitudes. In the beginning, biblical "knowledge" signified a communion so intimate and unifying that man and woman became "one single subject, as it were, of that act and that experience, although they remain two really distinct subjects in this unity" (TOB 20:4). In a similar way, the great multitude of subjects that form the communion of saints in commun-

---

27. See *CCC*, nos. 1000, 1027.

ion with the Trinity will be the one single subject, as it were, of that act and experience of eternal self-giving, while remaining, in this unity, a great multitude of different subjects (both human and divine). Human participation in the "trinitarian order" means a participation in the perfect unity and distinction found within the Trinity itself.[28] "That 'spousal' meaning of being a body will, therefore, be realized," according to John Paul, "as a *meaning that is perfectly personal and communitarian at the same time*" (TOB 69:4).

A Virginal Communion

John Paul says that in man's beatifying gift of himself to God, "as the response worthy of a personal subject to God's gift of himself, the...virginal state of the body will manifest itself completely as the eschatological fulfillment of the 'spousal' meaning of the body" (TOB 68:3). Recall the deeper meaning of man's "virginal value" understood as the original integrity of body and soul—as the state of man in "solitude" before God, belonging *first and last* to God and God alone. Respecting the primacy of communion with God, the original incarnate communion of man and woman did not rob them of their "virginal value," but affirmed it, because it also affirmed the full truth of man in "solitude" before God.

Therefore, if man's destiny is to be understood as the definitive fulfillment of his origin, the incarnate communion of saints in union with the Trinity must be understood as a *virginal* communion. For, as we have already quoted the words of John Paul, man's ultimate beatitude "must be understood as *the definitively and perfectly 'integrated' state of man* brought about by such a [perfect] union of the soul with the body" (TOB 66:6). According to the Pope, virginity is "the specific sign and authentic expression of personal subjectivity as a whole" (TOB 68:3). It is the specific sign of man's psychosomatic integration as the fruit of a perfect communion with God and God alone. "In this way, then, the eschatological situation in which they 'will take neither wife nor husband' has its solid foundation in the future state of the personal subject" (TOB 68:3); that future state of perfect *virginal* integration.

Again, eschatological virginity does not mean absence of union but, rather, perfection of union. The "'spousal' meaning of the body in the res-

---

28. See *CCC*, nos. 254–55, 689.

urrection to the future life will perfectly correspond both to the fact that man as male-female is a person, created 'in the image and likeness of God' [recall original solitude], and to the fact that this image is realized in the communion of persons [recall original unity]" (TOB 69:4). And the Pope affirms that this will be a "union that is proper to the world of [human] persons in their psychosomatic constitution" (TOB 68:4).

The Perfect Freedom of the Gift

"This will be a completely new experience," the Pope says. Yet

at the same time, it will not be alienated in any way from the experience man shared "from the beginning" nor from that which, in the historical dimension of his existence, constituted in him the source of the tension between the spirit and the body...with reference to the procreative meaning of the body and of [its] sex. The man of the "future world" will find in this new experience of his own body *the fulfillment* of what he carried in himself perennially and historically. (TOB 69:5)

In the beginning the body was a sign of the person and his call to communion. Throughout history, the original meaning of that sign has been obscured. John Paul observes that the heritage of concupiscence has weighed us down with endless limitations, struggles, and sufferings. In the resurrection, however, that original sign will not only be restored; it will also be fulfilled. The body, as it was created to do from the beginning, will reveal the eternal mystery hidden in God and enable us to participate in it.

"That perennial meaning of the human body...will then be revealed again and will be revealed at once in such *simplicity and splendor* that everyone who shares in the 'other world' will find in his glorified body the fountain of the freedom of the gift" (TOB 69:6). Can we imagine *such splendor* revealed through the glorified human body? The longing we all have to *see* and *be seen*—to behold the "gratuitous beauty" of the body in purity and freedom from all taint of sin—will be superabundantly fulfilled. And that beauty of the human body will be but a reflection of the glory of the trinitarian life itself.

▄▄ What is pornography if not the diabolic mockery of the theology of the body? Recall that all the enemy can do is twist and distort what God created to be true, good, and beautiful. The body is not inherently porno-graphic! Rather, the body is inherently *theo-graphic*! The union of the sexes is a "great mystery" that is meant to point us to Christ and the Church, and, in turn, to the inner life of the Trinity (see Eph 5:31–32). What we long for is the beatific vision—to *see* the eternal exchange of love of the three divine Persons that the body "and only the body" can reveal to us (see TOB 19:4). What we turn to instead with pornography are so many pixels portraying creatures in a mock exchange of love. The hunger, the desire to *see*, is not the problem. The problem with pornography is that we are trying to feed that hunger by eating out of a dumpster. We are trying to feed that hunger with a grossly distorted vision of the body. In the process, as St. Paul says, we come to worship the creature rather than the Creator. So God gives us up in the lusts of our hearts to the dishonoring of our bodies (see Rom 1:22–25).

But herein lies the gift, "the pearl" of John Paul II's teaching, based as it is on the "good news" of the Gospel itself. As we submit the pornographic vision of the body to the "redemption of the body," that is, as we allow grace to untwist all the distortions, we discover sacramental reality! Untwist the *porno-vision* and we regain a true *theo-vision*: we see the body and the union of man and woman as a "great mystery," a "great sacrament" that points to Christ and the Church. This is obviously not a once and done transformation, but demands a steadfast commitment each day to "take up one's cross and follow." As we continue on "the way" of following Christ, we gain a truly catholic, mystical, sacramental vision of *the real*. We can say, "I once was blind, but now I see." And our vision deepens and expands—not, of course, without various trials and sometimes even setbacks—as we await that glorious day when we will behold the Mystery face to face.

The splendor of our glorified bodies, the Pope says, will allow us to rediscover "the fountain of the freedom of the gift." What was that fountain in the beginning? It was *grace*: the indwelling of God's breath in the dust of our humanity, the spiritualization of the body, the perfect integrity of body and soul. Therefore, the *"glorification of the body*, as the eschatological fruit of its divinizing spiritualization, will reveal the...perfect 'freedom of the sons of God' (see Rom 8:21)" (TOB 69:6).

"This freedom lies exactly at the basis of the spousal meaning of the body" (TOB 15:1) and "is indispensable *in order for man to be able to*...'find himself fully' though a 'sincere gift of self'" (TOB 15:2). The eschatological reality is precisely every man and every woman finding himself or herself through the sincere gift of self. It is precisely every man and every woman living in perfect virginal communion via the ultimate fulfillment of the spousal meaning of his or her body. In this way, the perfect freedom of the gift (the Holy Spirit) will nourish "all the communions that will constitute the great community of the communion of saints" (TOB 69:6).

A Development of the Truth about Man

Man and woman's call to marriage and procreation is fundamental in the mystery of creation. It touches the very "bone marrow" of anthropological reality (see p. 109ff.). When Christ explains that in the resurrection we neither marry nor are given in marriage, it is clear that "we are dealing with a development of the *truth about the same man.*" Even so, "man will always be the same, just as he came from the hand of his Creator and Father" (TOB 69:3). Christ does not state that eschatological man will no longer be male and female as he was "from the beginning." He merely indicates that the meaning of being male or female in the eschaton must be sought outside marriage and procreation. However, John Paul affirms that "there is no reason to seek it outside of that which (independently from the blessing of procreation) derives from the very mystery of creation and thereafter also forms the deepest structure of man's history on earth, given that this history was deeply co-penetrated by the mystery of redemption" (TOB 69:3).

Communion Is Fundamental

What is it that derives from the very mystery of creation, forms the deepest structure of man's history on earth, and will, therefore, also form the basis of the meaning of the body in the resurrection? Man is created as male and female to form a "unity of the two." The Pope says that in his solitude, man is revealed to himself as a person in order to reveal, at the same time, the communion of persons. In both states (solitude and communion) the human being is constituted as an image and likeness of God (see TOB 69:4).

In the purity of original nakedness, man discovered his fundamental call to communion in the spousal meaning of the body. Throughout history the primary way man has entered into this communion is through the call to marriage and procreation. However, as those crucial words of Christ make clear, this will not be the case in the resurrection. Summarizing his previous reflections, John Paul says that this "indicates that there is a condition of life without marriage, in which man, male and female, finds at one and the same time the fullness of personal giving and of the intersubjective communion of persons, thanks to the glorification of his whole psychosomatic being in the eternal union with God" (TOB 73:1). He also summarizes his vision of the eschaton when he says that "the divinizing depth" of the beatific vision will enable men and women to live the spousal meaning of their bodies in a simultaneous experience of "perpetual 'virginity'" *and* "perpetual 'intersubjectivity.'" The Holy Spirit dwelling *in our flesh* will be "the inexhaustible source" of this perfect, eternal, virgin-union (see TOB 71:5).

For historical man, this means that earthly marriage is not his be-all and end-all. It is given only to prepare for and anticipate the "marriage" to come. John Paul expresses the same idea in this striking statement: "Marriage and procreation do not definitively determine the original and fundamental meaning of being a body nor of being, as a body, male and female. Marriage and procreation only give concrete reality to that meaning in the dimensions of history" (TOB 69:4). In other words, earthly marriage is actually preparation for the heavenly marriage, the marriage of the Lamb. If historical man has lost his bearings due to sin and has been adrift on a meaningless sea, the Pope's above quoted statement guides him back to shore. Even more, disembarking from his wayward vessel, the truth contained in this statement is the terra firma on which man stands in order to be rightly oriented in *his-story* between the echoes of his origin and the premonitions of his destiny.

▬ It is entirely human to yearn for marital love. Yet we must be careful never to "hang our hats on a hook that cannot bear the weight." Anyone who looks to marriage as his ultimate fulfillment is setting himself up for serious disillusionment. Realizing that earthly marriage is only a sign of the heavenly marriage to come, and that the union to come is a gift extended to everyone without exception, takes a tremendous burden off people's expectations for ultimate happiness through marriage in this life. Only within this perspective does marriage even take on its authentic purpose and meaning. Only within this perspective will a person who enters marriage be able to avoid suffocating his spouse with his expectations and hopes for ultimate fulfillment. Then and only then can marriage bring the true measure of happiness and joy it is intended to bring. As a married man, I am the first to extol the joys of married life. But these are only a foretaste, only a foreshadowing of the eternal joys to come.

Icon or Idol?

As soon as man steps off this terra firma, he forgets that marriage is only a temporal icon of an eternal reality. The image is only that—an image, an icon. Icons are meant to point us to something far greater than themselves. When we lose sight of this, we worship the icon itself. Then the "one flesh" union becomes an idol.

To use another image, that deep spiritual-physical craving that man experiences for union in "one flesh" is like the energy of a rocket that, when rightly directed, launches us into the stars and even to the edge of eternity itself. When spousal union is understood and lived in this way, even the beatifying joys of the marital embrace are experienced as a kind of earthly foreshadowing of the eternal joys of heaven.[29] But what would happen if we inverted the rocket's engines, aiming them away from the stars and back upon ourselves? The rocket could only backfire in a blast of self-destruction. And we would be left trying desperately to make sense out of the charred remains of our lives and our deepest aspirations.

In many ways, this icon-idol distinction summarizes the cultural crisis that the sexual revolution ignited. The greater the gift (human sexuality), the greater the temptation to idolize it. However, when we exchange the truth for a lie—that is, when we exchange the icon for an idol—love becomes lust and we experience all the tragic consequences

---

29. See *CCC*, no. 1642.

sin brings.[30] As we shall learn, viewing the "one flesh" union of marriage in light of the celibate vocation is the sure remedy for the world's false, idolatrous cult of the body and sex.

B. PAULINE INTERPRETATION OF THE RESURRECTION IN 1 CORINTHIANS 15:42–49

John Paul concludes his reflections on eschatological man by devoting three addresses to what he calls "the 'anthropology of the resurrection' according to St. Paul" (TOB 72:1). St. Paul expresses his faith in the resurrection throughout his letters, but primarily in chapter 15 of 1 Corinthians. Christ's response to the Sadducees was "pre-paschal." He appealed only to the truth of the Old Testament to demonstrate the resurrection—to the truth that the living God "is not the God of the dead, but of the living" (Mk 12:22). Paul, however, in his "post-paschal" argumentation, refers above all to the reality of Christ's own resurrection. In fact, Paul defends this truth as the foundation of the Christian faith in its integrity: "If Christ has not been raised, then our preaching is in vain and your faith is in vain.... But, in fact, Christ has been raised from the dead" (1 Cor 15:14, 20).

God's Reply to Death

John Paul describes Christ's resurrection as "the answer given by the God of life to the historical inevitability of death." It "is *the final* and the fullest word *of the self-revelation* of the living God as '*God* not of the dead, but *of the living*' (Mk 12:27)" (TOB 70:3). St. Paul presents Christ's resurrection as the beginning of our own eschatological fulfillment, our own victory over death. Paul, in fact, following the other apostles, experienced the state of Jesus' glorified body in his encounter with the risen Christ on the road to Damascus (see Acts 9). When Paul proclaims resurrection, he knows of what he speaks. If we

---

30. Who cannot think in this context of the often self-inflicted proliferation of sexually transmitted diseases (some fatal, such as AIDS), the abortion holocaust, and the social plague of divorce that has resulted from the idolatry of lust promoted incessantly by the culture of death? And these are only some of the measurable consequences. Although we see the symptoms all around us, the havoc wrought on the souls of hundreds of millions of people cannot be quantified.

are to live according to the full truth of our bodies—to live according to the image in which we are made—we too must have our own "encounter with the risen Christ." Indeed, the road to human happiness begins and ends in this meeting.

Admitting that it is difficult to sum up here and comment adequately on Paul's "stupendous and far-ranging argument" (TOB 70:2), the Pope focuses primarily on the following passage:

> What is sown is perishable, what is raised is imperishable. It is sown in dishonor, it is raised in glory. It is sown in weakness, it is raised in power. It is sown a physical body, it is raised a spiritual body. If there is a physical body, there is also a spiritual body. Thus it is written, "The first man, Adam, became a living being"; the last Adam became a life-giving spirit. But it is not the spiritual which is first but the physical, and then the spiritual. (1 Cor 15:42–46)

This teaching is essentially consistent with Christ's words on the resurrection. However, whereas Christ called us to reflect on the resurrected state of the male-female communion, Paul's teaching seems to remain in the sphere of the individual person and his inner structure. Paul focuses on that interior "system of powers"; that tension between the flesh and the spirit well known to him (see Rom 7:17–25). However, through the "divinizing spiritualization" of the body, he demonstrates that this "system of powers" will undergo a radical change in the resurrection (see TOB 71:5–6).

Taking account of various misinterpretations, John Paul carefully points out that Paul's seemingly pejorative description of the body cannot be interpreted in the spirit of dualistic anthropology (see TOB 71:6). This would imply an inherent dishonor to man's bodily constitution contrary to the original good of God's vision. When Paul writes that the body is "weak," "perishable," and "in dishonor," he speaks from the experience of historical man whose body is weighed down by concupiscence. These descriptions, as John Paul says, indicate what revelation describes as the consequence of sin—what Paul himself in Romans 8:21 calls "bondage to decay" (see TOB 70:7).

However, according to St. Paul, this "bondage to decay" also conceals within itself the hope of resurrection, just as a woman's labor pains portend the hope of new life (see Rom 8:22). Paul can make this connection between "decay" and "hope" because he understands that the

Holy Spirit has been poured out upon us for the redemption of our bodies (see Rom 8:23). As John Paul says, "Redemption is the way to the resurrection. The resurrection constitutes the definitive accomplishment of the redemption of the body" (TOB 70:8).[31]

The First Adam Bears Potential for the New Adam

It is quite significant that Paul unites man's eschatological perspective with reference to the "first Adam" as well as a deep awareness of man's historical situation. As the Pope points out, by doing so, St. Paul synthesizes all that Christ had announced in his three "key words" about "the beginning," about lust in the "heart," and about the "resurrection of the body." Paul's synthesis "plunges its roots deeply into the whole of the revealed mystery of creation and redemption." Man's creation "is an act of enlivening matter by the spirit." It involves the "animation of the body" by God's breath (TOB 70:7). In this way, as St. Paul says, "Adam became a living being" (1 Cor 15:45). Man's redemption-resurrection is to be understood in a similar way. If man ex-pired (breathed the Spirit out) when he sinned so that we return to dust (see Gen 3:19), our redemption-resurrection must be the (re)quickening or re-inspiration of our dust with the Spirit. Hence, we see again that St. Paul does not negate the body but speaks of its ultimate dignity as the temple of the Holy Spirit (see 1 Cor 6:19).

▬ Notice that in the New Adam's resurrection he, like the first Adam, comes forth from the ground at the moment of the Spirit's *in*-spiration. Describing the earth as a "mother" has a definite element of truth. Significantly, both John and Luke mention that Christ was put in a tomb not previously used (see Jn 19:41 and Lk 23:53). As stated earlier, Christ was born of a virgin womb and "born again" of a virgin tomb. Similarly, on the last day, at the moment of the Spirit's *in*-spiration, the earth will in some sense "give birth" virginally to all those who have returned to dust in joyful hope of the coming of their Savior, Jesus Christ.[32]

31. See *CCC*, no. 1026.
32. See *CCC*, no. 1683.

The re-quickening of the body by the Spirit, however, does not only restore man's original state before sin. According to the Pope, that would "not correspond to the inner logic of the whole economy of salvation, to the deepest meaning of the mystery of redemption." The re-inspiration of the flesh in the redemption-resurrection "can only be an *introduction to a new fullness*. It will be a fullness that presupposes man's whole history, formed by the drama of the tree of the knowledge of good and evil" (TOB 72:3).

In contrasting the first Adam with the last Adam (Christ), Paul tries to show that historical man has been placed in a sort of tension between two poles. John Paul says that between these two poles— between the first and the second Adam—takes place the process that St. Paul expresses as follows: "As we have borne the image of the man of earth, so we will bear the image of the man of heaven" (1 Cor 15:49). Yet the Pope stresses that the "man of heaven" is not so much the antithesis and negation of the "man of earth." He is above all his fulfillment and confirmation. Already in our creation, our humanity "carries within itself," the Holy Father says, "*a particular potentiality* (which is capacity and readiness) *for receiving* all *that the 'second Adam' became*, the heavenly Man, namely, Christ: what he became in his resurrection" (TOB 71:3).

Viewing this through the lens of the spousal analogy, we can say that just as a bride is made in her very being as a woman to receive her bridegroom, so too is man (male and female) made to receive Christ. John Paul observes that among all the bodies in the cosmos, the human body bears in itself the "potentiality for resurrection"—that is, it bears the aspiration and capacity to become definitively "imperishable, glorious, full of power, spiritual." This is possible because right from the beginning man is made in the image of God as male and female, body and soul. In this way, John Paul says that man "*can gather and reproduce in this 'earthly' image and likeness of God also the 'heavenly' image of* the last Adam, *Christ* " (TOB 71:4).

Since "everyone bears in himself the image of Adam," it can be said that "everyone is also called to bear in himself the image of Christ, the image of the Risen One." While this mystery will only be consummated in the other world, "it is already in some way a reality of this world, given that it was revealed in...[this world] through the resurrection of Christ" (TOB 71:4).

The Spiritual Body

Christ's resurrection is a reality "implanted" in our humanity. Even though our bodies are sown "in weakness" and are "perishable," we carry in ourselves at the same time, the Pope says, "the desire for glory" (TOB 71:3). God put it there "in the beginning"—not to frustrate us by dashing our hopes, but to lead us to fulfillment in him. All hopes, therefore, must be placed in our resurrection. Then the body that we experience as perishable will be raised imperishable. The body that we experience as weighed down in dishonor and weakness will be raised in glory and power. For what is sown a physical body is raised a spiritual body.

"Body" in this sense refers to the whole person in his psychosomatic subjectivity. Thus, Paul is not contrasting a material reality with a nonmaterial reality. The "physical body" is the whole person inasmuch as he resists and opposes the Holy Spirit. It is the man who lives "according to the flesh" (see p. 256ff.). The "spiritual body" is the whole person inasmuch as he remains under the influence of the vivifying Spirit of Christ. As the Pope states in a footnote, in contrast to any dualistic notion of the person, in St. Paul there "is insistence on the fact that body and soul are capable of being...spiritual" (TOB 71:6, n. 81). While spirituality has a just supremacy over sensuality, we must not think that the sensual life fundamentally opposes the spiritual life.[33] If we experience sensuality as "a force that often undermines man," this is due only to sin. Man's senses are "often urged or pushed, as it were, toward evil" only because of concupiscence (TOB 72:4).

At the same time he denies the lustful cravings of disordered sensuality, the man of concupiscence must open sensuality to the total penetration and permeation of the Spirit. Then he experiences "the fundamental function of the senses that serves to liberate spirituality" (TOB 72:4). This is what Paul means by the "spiritual body." It is, as the Holy Father expresses, "precisely *the perfect sensitivity of the senses, their perfect harmonization with the activity of the* human *spirit* in truth and in freedom" (TOB 72:4). Thus, as the *Catechism* says, "The virtuous

---

33. As Wojtyla said in *Love and Responsibility*, "An exuberant and readily roused sensuality is the stuff from which a rich—if difficult—personal life may be made. It may help the individual to respond more readily and completely to the decisive elements in personal love" (p. 109).

person tends toward the good with all his sensory and spiritual powers."[34] For those who have entered an alliance with the Holy Spirit, this
spiritual-sensual unity is a reality already developing in them toward
final completion.

> ■   With the dualistic worldview we have inherited from Des-
> cartes, it is very difficult for modern men and women to under-
> stand the Pauline concept of a "spiritual body." As Peter Kreeft
> observes: "'Spiritual' to premodern cultures did not mean 'immate-
> rial.' Pre-Cartesian cultures did not divide reality into two mutual-
> ly exclusive categories of purely immaterial spirit and purely
> nonspiritual matter. Rather, they saw all matter as in-formed, in-
> breathed by spirit." Kreeft elaborates: "Descartes initiates 'ange-
> lism' when he says, 'My whole essence is in thought alone.' Matter
> and spirit now become 'two clear and distinct ideas.'... This is our
> common sense; we have inherited these categories, like nonremov-
> able contact lenses, from Descartes, and it is impossible for us to
> understand pre-Cartesian thinkers while we wear them. Thus we
> are constantly reading our modern categories anachronistically into
> the authors of the Bible."[35] Proof of Kreeft's assertion is that St.
> Paul's "spiritual body" seems like a pure contradiction in terms to
> most moderns.

2. Continence for the Kingdom of Heaven

[Cycle 4]

In John Paul's original manuscript, his treatment of "continence for
the kingdom" appears, as it does here, as the second section of Part I,
Chapter 3. Pedagogically speaking, we can recognize that this section
marks a shift from the development of an "adequate anthropology" to
its application in the field of vocation—from the question, *What does it
mean to be human?* to the question, *How do I live my life in accord with
the truth of my humanity?*

---

34. *CCC*, no. 1803.
35. Kreeft, *Everything You Ever Wanted to Know about Heaven*, pp. 86–87.

The human mystery is one of love and gift. The Creator gives man his very being as a gratuitous gift of love. He is created in the image of God as male and female and endowed with freedom (self-determination) in order to recapitulate the mystery of love and gift. "Therefore a man leaves his father and his mother and cleaves to his wife, and they become one flesh" (Gen 2:24). Yet in the same discussion in which Christ reestablishes God's original plan for marriage, he also invites some to sacrifice marriage "for the sake of the kingdom of heaven" (Mt 19:12). Thus, as John Paul says in *Familiaris Consortio,* "Christian revelation recognizes two specific ways of realizing the vocation of the human person, in its entirety, to love: marriage and virginity or celibacy. Either one is in its own proper form an actuation of the most profound truth about man, of his being 'created in the image of God.'"[36]

This cycle on celibacy for the kingdom consists of fourteen addresses delivered between March 10, 1982, and July 21, 1982 (TOB 73–85). For good reason John Paul reflects on the celibate vocation prior to his cycle on the marital vocation. As we shall learn, only by understanding the meaning of Christian celibacy can we understand the sacramentality of marriage. For celibacy is a more immediate participation (even if only by way of anticipation) in what marriage signifies sacramentally—the eternal "virginal union" of Christ and the Church.

Using our former image, Christians called to the marital vocation are in some way meant to reclaim the "inflated tires" of the beginning as a sacramental sign of man's ultimate end. In a sense, Christians called to the celibate vocation move in the other direction. They look to the future, anticipating in the here-and-now the life of flight "beyond tires." In this way they shed light on God's ultimate plan right from the beginning. Recall the Pope's provocative statement that marriage does "not definitively determine the original and fundamental meaning of being a body nor of being, as a body, male and female. Marriage and procreation only give concrete reality to that meaning in the dimensions of history" (TOB 69:4). In a way, men and women who are celibates "for the sake of the kingdom of heaven" step outside the dimensions of history—while living within its dimensions—and proclaim to the world that "the kingdom of God is here."

---

36. *Familiaris Consortio,* 11.

A. THE WORDS OF CHRIST IN MATTHEW 19:11–12

Christ's Words Mark a Turning Point

The "call to an exclusive gift of self to God in virginity and celibacy plunges its roots deeply into the evangelical soil of the theology of the body" (TOB 73:1). Based on our reflections on the resurrection, we can see clearly that this vocation "is a charismatic orientation toward that eschatological state in which human beings 'take neither wife nor husband'" (TOB 73:4).[37] However, as John Paul demonstrates, it is very significant that Christ does not refer to celibacy in his discussion with the Sadducees about the resurrection. Instead, he refers to it in his conversation with the Pharisees about God's plan for marriage "in the beginning" (see TOB 73:5).

When Christ firmly established the indissolubility of marriage, his disciples said: "If such is the case of a man with his wife, it is not expedient to marry" (Mt 19:10). Christ does not respond to their line of reasoning. Instead, he takes the discussion to a new level by introducing an even more radical way of living according to God's plan for creating us male and female. He replies:

> Not all men can receive the precept, but only those to whom it is given. For there are eunuchs[38] who have been so from birth, and there are eunuchs who have been made eunuchs by men, and there are eunuchs who have made themselves eunuchs for the sake of the kingdom of heaven. He who is able to receive this, let him receive it. (Mt 19:11–12)

As concise as these words are, John Paul states that they "are wonderfully rich and precise, rich with a set of implications both doctrinal and pastoral in nature" (TOB 78:1). At the same time, it is hard to overestimate how incomprehensible these words would have been to the Israelites. In the tradition of the Old Testament, marriage was a religiously privileged state, privileged by revelation itself. Marriage had acquired a deeply religious significance because of God's covenant with Abraham and the promise of countless offspring. The Pope observes

---

37. See *CCC*, nos. 1618–19.

38. A eunuch is a person who, either by birth defect or acquired malady, is physically incapable of engaging in sexual intercourse. Definitive and perpetual impotence is to this day a canonical impediment to marriage (see canon 1084). See Christopher West, *Good News About Sex and Marriage*, pp. 54–57, for an explanation.

that only persons with physical impotence could constitute an exception. Such people (eunuchs) were seen as outcasts, accursed by God because they could not participate in fulfilling the promise given to Abraham. In such a climate it would have been inconceivable for someone actually to *choose* to "make himself a eunuch." And for the kingdom of heaven? Outlandish!

Christ certainly acknowledges this difficulty in the way he introduces the idea to his listeners. As John Paul puts it, it is as if Christ wished to say: "I know that what I am going to tell you now will raise great difficulties in your consciousness, in your way of understanding the meaning of the body; I shall speak to you, in fact, about continence, and this will undoubtedly be associated in you with a state of physical deficiency, inborn or acquired by human cause. I want to tell you, by contrast, that continence can also be voluntary and chosen by man 'for the kingdom of heaven'" (TOB 74:4).

John Paul says that from the theological perspective—that is, from the perspective of the revelation of the body's meaning—Christ's words mark a decisive *turning point* for historical man and his call to marriage. However, they "do not express *a commandment* that is binding for all, but *a counsel* that regards only some persons" (TOB 73:4). Therefore, the Holy Father says that continence is a kind of exception to the general rule of this life, which is to marry (see TOB 73:5).

Voluntary, Supernatural, Virginal Communion

The Pope stresses that celibacy is a "personal choice" empowered by a "particular grace." Hence, this vocation must be understood as *voluntary* and *supernatural*. Without these two specific characteristics, it does not fall within the scope of Christ's words. On the one hand, this means continence for the kingdom can never be imposed on anyone. It is a gift given by God that must be received and freely chosen.[39] On the other hand, even if freely chosen, if continence is not "for the kingdom," it does not correspond to Christian celibacy. Thus, Christ's phrase "for the kingdom" expresses not only the *objective* orientation of this vocation, it also indicates the need for a *subjective* motivation "corresponding in an adequate and full way to...[this] objective finality"

---

39. See *CCC*, no. 1599.

(TOB 76:3). For example, if a person were to choose celibacy out of fear of marital intimacy or disdain for sexuality, this would not be celibacy *for the kingdom*.

At the same time, while Christ stresses the supernatural dimension of this vocation, he wishes to root the vocation to such continence "deeply in the reality of earthly life" (TOB 74:1). In a way, the celibate person steps *beyond* the dimensions of history into that state of the body where men and women are no longer given in marriage. But all the while he remains grounded *within* the dimensions of history and, in this way, becomes a prophetic witness *in his body* to the future resurrection. In other words, the celibate man or woman witnesses to the definitive accomplishment of the "redemption of the body" while still awaiting its ultimate consummation.

Christian celibacy, therefore, exists in the heart of that tension of "already, but not yet." For, as the Holy Father points out, this vocation is "not a question of continence *in* the kingdom of heaven, but of continence '*for* the kingdom of heaven'" (TOB 73:5). It is an anticipation and "eschatological sign" of the life to come. Thus, an essential difference exists between celibacy for the kingdom as an earthly vocation and that glorified state of the body in which all men and women will "neither marry nor be given in marriage." Because in this world marriage remains part of man's normal and noble inclination, the celibate "choice is connected *with renunciation* and also with a determined *spiritual effort*" (TOB 74:5). However, if celibacy anticipates the future world, the virginal state of the future world does not indicate an absence of real interpersonal communion. Virginity and communion are not opposed to one another. Rather, in the eschatological reality—as the fulfillment of the beginning—they are fulfilled in each other. Thus, the celibate vocation—while renouncing the genital expression of incarnate communion—does not renounce the human vocation to live in a communion of persons.

Continence for the kingdom is *a charismatic sign* that "points out the eschatological 'virginity' of the risen man, in which," the Pope says, "the absolute and eternal spousal meaning of the glorified body will be revealed in union with God himself, by seeing him 'face to face.'" At the same time the body will be "glorified moreover through the union of a perfect intersubjectivity that will unite all the 'sharers in the other world,' men and women, in the mystery of the communion of saints"

(TOB 75:1). In this way "that continence 'for the kingdom of heaven'—inasmuch as it is an indubitable sign of the 'other world'—bears within itself above all the inner dynamism of the mystery of the redemption of the body" (TOB 76:3). Through that dynamism we will all recover our "original virginal value" in an eschatological dimension through the perfect integration of body and soul in union with the Word made flesh. All the saints will live in the eternal "virginal" communion of one body. *This* is what the celibate vocation anticipates.

Continence for the Kingdom and Spiritual Fruitfulness

Earthly continence for the kingdom "is a sign that the body, whose end is not death, tends toward glorification; already by this very fact," John Paul says, Christian celibacy is "a testimony among men that anticipates the future resurrection" (TOB 75:1). In this state, men and women no longer marry—not because the deep truth of marriage is deleted, but because the sacrament is fulfilled in the eternal reality of Christ's union with the Church. In this sense, those who are celibate for the kingdom are "skipping" the sacrament in anticipation of the real thing. They wish to participate in a more direct way—here and now—in the "marriage of the Lamb."

> ■ The term "celibacy" speaks more about what this vocation is not rather than what it is. It seems that some of the confusion and negativity surrounding this vocation could be avoided if it were defined more in terms of what it embraces—the heavenly marriage—instead of what it gives up.

John Paul says that the person "who consciously chooses such continence chooses in some sense a particular *participation in the mystery of the redemption (of the body)*; he wishes to complete it in a particular way in his own flesh (see Col 1:24)." In doing so, the celibate person finds a distinctive "imprint of a likeness with Christ," who himself was continent for the kingdom (TOB 76:3). The Pope observes that the departure from the Old Testament tradition, in which marriage and procreation were a religiously privileged state, had to be based on the example of Christ himself. From the moment of his virginal conception, Christ's whole earthly life, in fact, was a witness to a new kind of fruitfulness. This mystery, however, remained hidden from those to whom Christ first spoke about continence for the kingdom. The Pope points out that only "Mary and Joseph, who lived the mystery of his birth, became the first witnesses of a fruitfulness different from that of the flesh, that is, the fruitfulness of the Spirit: 'What is begotten in her comes from the Holy Spirit' (Mt 1:20)" (TOB 75:2). The miracle surrounding Christ's virgin birth would only gradually be revealed to the eyes of the Church on the basis of Matthew and Luke's Gospels.

Joseph and Mary's Virginal Marriage

John Paul remarks that although Christ "is born from her like every man...still Mary's motherhood was virginal; and to this virginal motherhood corresponded the virginal mystery of Joseph" (TOB 75:2). Joseph's and Mary's virginity is certainly in keeping with that continence for the kingdom that Christ will one day announce to his disciples. However, at the same time, they were a legitimate husband and wife.[40] As John Paul says, "*The marriage of Mary with Joseph...conceals within itself*, at the same time, *the mystery* of the perfect communion of persons, of Man and Woman in the conjugal covenant and at the same time the mystery of this *singular 'continence for the kingdom of heaven'*: a continence that served the most perfect '*fruitfulness of the Holy Spirit*' in the history of salvation. Indeed," the Pope continues, "it was in some way the absolute fullness of that spiritual fruitfulness, because precisely in...Mary and Joseph's covenant in marriage and continence, the gift of the Incarnation of the Eternal Word was realized" (TOB 75:3).

> ■   John Paul II may be developing here the Church's understanding of St. Joseph's role in the Incarnation. For John Paul, St. Joseph is not a kind of "tack-on" provided to lend some legitimacy in the public eye to Mary's motherhood. Mary and Joseph were already married (see Mt 1:18; Lk 1:27). Joseph's virginal "yes" to God (and virginal love for Mary) played an important role in the mystery of the Incarnation, albeit of a different nature than Mary's

---

40. For those interested in the finer points of canon law, the Church teaches that a couple must be capable of consummating their marriage at the time they enter marriage (see canon 1084), but they are not absolutely obligated to consummate their marriage.

"yes." Mary responded to the Annunciation with her *fiat*. John Paul writes in *Redemptoris Custos* that "*at the moment of Joseph's own 'annunciation'* he said nothing; instead he simply '*did* as the angel of the Lord commanded him' (Mt 1:24)."[41] This typically masculine "doing" could be considered the spousal counterpart to Mary's feminine "let it be done." And this virginal complementarity of Joseph and Mary expressed the absolute fullness of spiritual fruitfulness. Although we typically refer to Joseph as Jesus' "foster father," John Paul insists that Joseph's fatherhood is not less real because of his virginity. In a way, it is even more real. The Pope writes: "*In this family, Joseph is the father: his fatherhood* is not one that derives from begetting offspring; but neither is it an 'apparent' or merely 'substitute' fatherhood. Rather, it is one that *fully shares in authentic human fatherhood.*"[42] Human fatherhood becomes all the more authentic to the degree that it becomes a transparent sign of God's Fatherhood. Joseph's fatherhood is the most transparent sign of God's Fatherhood and is, therefore, all the more real.

In a profound paradox that simultaneously embraces the heavenly marriage (i.e., continence for the kingdom) *and* the earthly marriage, Joseph and Mary's virginal communion of persons literally effected the marriage of heaven and earth. This is the grace of the hypostatic union—the marriage of the human and divine natures in the Person of Christ. This grace is connected precisely with the absolute fullness of the spiritual fruitfulness that comes from embracing continence for the kingdom. John Paul concludes that every man and woman who authentically embraces continence for the kingdom in some way participates in this superabounding spiritual fruitfulness.

Marriage and Celibacy Both Flow from the Ethos of Redemption

The marriage of Joseph and Mary sheds a bright light on both Christian vocations. The Pope observes that it helps us understand the profound sanctity of marriage *and* a certain personal "disinterestedness"

41. *Redemptoris Custos*, 17.
42. Ibid., 21.

in marriage on the part of those who prefer to remain continent for the kingdom. John Paul will go to great lengths reflecting on the sanctity of marriage in his next cycle. For now let us linger on this question, posed by the common perspective of our day: "Why would a Christian be 'disinterested' in marriage? After all, for the Christian, this is the only legitimate opportunity for sex, right? Who in his right mind would actually prefer a life without sex?"

This widespread perspective ultimately stems from a failure to understand the redemption Christ won for us. So much confusion about the Church's teaching—not just on sex but on the whole economy of salvation—results from the tunnel vision that comes from normalizing concupiscence. For those whose hearts are bound by lust, the idea of choosing a life of total continence is absurd. But for those who are being liberated from lust by the ethos of redemption, the idea of sacrificing the genital expression of their sexuality "for the sake of the kingdom of heaven" not only becomes a real possibility—it also becomes quite attractive, even desirable.

When authentically lived, the Christian call to lifelong continence witnesses dramatically to the freedom for which Christ has set us free. Of course, a truly chaste marriage witnesses to the same freedom. Contrary to the tunnel vision perspective mentioned above, marriage *does not* provide a "legitimate outlet" for indulging one's lusts. Thus, whoever has a genuine Christian understanding of marriage at the same time gains a real Christian understanding of lifelong celibacy. Such an understanding comes from the ethos of redemption. As John Paul says, behind the call to continence in Matthew 19 and the call to overcome lust in Matthew 5, "*one finds the same anthropology and the same ethos*" (TOB 77:4). In other words, both vocations (marriage and celibacy) flow from the same vision of the human person and the same call to experience the redemption of our bodies, which includes the redemption of our sexual desires.

John Paul says that the invitation to celibacy for the kingdom even "enlarges" the perspectives of the ethos of historical man in light of the future anthropology of the resurrection. This does not mean that the anthropology of the resurrection replaces the anthropology of historical man. Men and women who choose celibacy for the kingdom, just like those who choose marriage, must contend with concupiscence. But historical man is also redeemed man. "Redemption is a truth, a reality, in the name of which man must feel himself called, and 'called with effectiveness'" (TOB 46:4). Only the man or woman living this "effective redemption" is properly prepared to embrace a life of continence for the kingdom. Lest we fall into the trap of thinking marriage legitimizes concupiscence, we must insist that living the effectiveness of redemption is also required of those who embrace marriage. The Holy Father expresses this when he says that the person who chooses continence for the kingdom must submit "*the sinfulness of his own humanity to the powers that flow from the mystery of the redemption of the body*...just as every other person does...whose way remains marriage. What is different," the Pope observes, "is only the kind of responsibility for the chosen good, just as the kind of good chosen is different" (TOB 77:4).

The difference between marriage and continence for the kingdom must *never* be understood as the difference between having a legitimate outlet for concupiscence on the one hand and having to repress concupiscence on the other. Christ calls *everyone* to overcome the domination of concupiscence through the redemption of the body. Only upon experiencing a true level of freedom in this regard do the Christian vocations (celibacy *and* marriage) make sense. For *both* flow from the same experience of the redemption of the body and of sexual desire. Both flow from the same spousal meaning of the body and the call to become a gift in and through masculinity and femininity. Without experiencing the freedom of the gift for which Christ has set us free, celibacy is seen as hopelessly repressive and marriage as legitimately indulgent. How far from the Gospel ethos these perspectives are!

Correct Understanding of the "Superiority" of Celibacy

History has seen some serious distortions of the Church's teaching that celibacy is a calling "superior" to marriage. Tragically, many Catholics have thought that this means marriage is only a second-class vocation for those who "can't handle" celibacy. The sentiment often goes like this: "If celibacy is so good, marriage must be so bad. If refraining from sex makes one pure and holy, having sex must make one dirty and unholy." Yet nothing could be further from the mind of the Church in promoting the value of celibacy. Such a belief smacks of the Manichaean heresy.

In response to such distortions, John Paul stresses that the "*superi-ority' of continence to marriage never means, in the authentic tradition of the Church, a disparagement of marriage* or a belittling of its essential value. It does not even imply sliding, even merely implicitly, toward...a Manichean understanding of the body and of sex" (TOB 77:6). He continues by saying that Christ's words about celibacy point to a "supe-riority" of this vocation only by virtue of its motive "for the kingdom of heaven." We may admit only this superiority. In Christ's words "we do not find any basis whatsoever for the disparagement of marriage" (TOB 77:6).

In Christ's words about continence "there is not a hint of any 'infe-riority' of marriage related to the 'body' or to the essence of marriage consisting in the fact that man and woman unite with each other in...'one flesh'" (TOB 78:1). This is God's *good* and *holy* design. Hence, the "superiority" of continence *does not* rest on the mere fact of absti-nence from sexual union. The Pope insists that on "this point Christ's words are decidedly clear." Christ proposes continence not "with pre-judices against *conjugal 'union of the body,'* but *only for the 'kingdom of heaven'*" (TOB 78:1).

How, then, are we to understand the exceptional value of celibacy in relation to the marriage vocation? John Paul points out that "if *marriage* possesses its full fittingness and value for the kingdom of heaven, a *fun-damental*, universal, and ordinary *value*," then it makes sense that "con-tinence on its part possesses *a particular and 'exceptional' value* for this kingdom" (TOB 76:2). From the context of Christ's words, John Paul says that "it is sufficiently clear that the point is not to diminish the value of marriage to the advantage of continence" (TOB 77:2). Marriage certainly has a *great* value as an earthly sacrament of the eter-nal communion of heaven. But celibacy is not a sacrament of heaven on earth. Because it directly anticipates the eschatological reality, it *is* (if only in this anticipatory sense) "heaven on earth." It is a sign that *the kingdom of God is here*. Celibacy could be understood as "better" than marriage, then, in the same way that heaven is better than earth. In this way Christian celibacy "is particularly valid and important 'for the kingdom of heaven.' It must be so," John Paul says, "given that Christ himself chose it" (TOB 76:2).

But celibacy for the kingdom is only "better" in an objective sense and because of its objective orientation. Subjectively speaking, what is better for a given person is the vocation to which God calls him or her. Those who choose celibacy as their Christian vocation must do so, the Pope says, not because of "a supposedly negative value of marriage...but in view of the particular value which is connected with this choice" (TOB 73:3). Those men and women to whom this calling is given must discover and welcome this value as their own personal vocation. Marriage with its own value remains the normal calling in this life. It is in this sense that the value of celibacy is *exceptional*—it is the exception to the rule.

Solitude, Communion, and the Spousal Meaning of the Body

As our study of the Genesis texts revealed, men and women are "made" for marriage according to the normal and noble inclinations of their nature. The Pope describes continence as a conscious "breaking away" from these noble inclinations in anticipation of their eschatological fulfillment. Because of the great good that marriage entails as a divine institution, choosing to renounce marriage demands real self-sacrifice. As John Paul expresses: "This break also becomes the beginning of further renunciations and voluntary self-sacrifices that are indispensable if the first and fundamental choice is to be consistent in the breadth of one's entire earthly life" (TOB 77:3).

The Pope remarks that Christ, in calling some men and women to renounce marriage, has no desire to "hide *the travail*" that continence and its enduring consequences can bring. In some sense, those who choose continence are choosing to remain in the "ache" of man's original solitude—the "ache" to which the Lord himself refers when he said, "It is not good that the man should be alone" (Gen 2:18). The conscious choice to refrain from marriage "for the sake of the kingdom of heaven" becomes a powerful testimony to the fact that God and *God alone* can ultimately fulfill that "ache" of solitude. Marriage is a sacrament of our ultimate fulfillment, but it is not our ultimate fulfillment. Men and women who vow to a life of celibacy devote their yearning for communion directly toward God. As John Paul says, "continence must demonstrate that man, in his deepest constitution, is...'alone' before God and with God." Nevertheless, John Paul stresses that what "is an invitation to *solitude for God* respects at the same time both the 'dual nature of humanity' (that is, its masculinity and femininity) and also that *dimension of the communion* of existence that is *proper to the person*" (TOB 77:1). Recall that the eschatological reality is not only man's perfect communion with God. It is also the perfect communion of all men and women with each other. Thus, John Paul says that Christ enables the continent person, in anticipation of the perfect communion of saints, "to discover in this solitude...a new and even *fuller form of intersubjective communion with others*" (TOB 77:2).

Christ, therefore, while calling some to renounce marriage, does not thereby call the continent person to renounce his nature as a sexual being. As John Paul says, the continent person, like everyone else, remains "a 'dual' being (that is, directed as a man toward woman, and as a woman toward man)" (TOB 77:2). We recognize this in the "trinitarian meaning" of our creation as male and female in God's image. Whoever properly comprehends Christ's call to continence "preserves the integral truth of his humanity without losing along the way any of the essential elements of the vocation of the person created in 'the image and likeness of God'" (TOB 77:1). This trinitarian image is *always* fulfilled in man through the spousal meaning of the body, which calls man to the sincere gift of self and establishes a true communion of persons.

Far from renouncing this most fundamental meaning of sexuality, the celibate person is able "to realize himself 'differently,' and in some sense 'more' than in marriage, by becoming a 'sincere gift for others'" (TOB 77:2). Differently in that the celibate person does not become a gift via the one flesh union; and "more" in that the celibate person can participate to a higher degree in the "intersubjectivity of all." Hence, John Paul says that the decision to remain celibate for the kingdom must be "made *on the basis of the full consciousness* of the *spousal meaning* [of the body], which masculinity and femininity contain in themselves. If this choice were made by artificially 'prescinding' from this real richness of every human subject, it would not correspond appropriately and adequately to the content of Christ's words" (TOB 80:7). In fact, the Holy Father insists that only in relation to "the deep and mature *consciousness of the spousal meaning of the body*...does *the call to voluntary continence* 'for the kingdom of heaven' *find a full guarantee and motivation.*" Then he adds: "Only and exclusively in such a perspective does Christ say, 'Let anyone understand this who can' (Mt 19:12)" (TOB 80:6).

Marriage and Celibacy Explain
and Complete Each Other

Papal biographer George Weigel has described John Paul as a clergyman with a "lay soul."[43] He also observes that perhaps no more priestly priest has sat in the chair of Peter than Pope John Paul II. Yet Weigel's point is that in some sense this Pope had the heart of a layman. For John Paul, the focal point of the Church's life is not found inside the Vatican. Instead, the focal point of Christian life resides where lay men and women live out their call to holiness: in the home, the family, the streets, the fields, the factory, the office.

Having internalized his own call to holiness as a layman, Wojtyla was one of the main forces behind the Second Vatican Council's emphasis on the universal call to holiness. Prior to this renewed emphasis, many Catholics thought that only priests and nuns were called to sanctity. Since those who bound themselves by the evangelical counsels (poverty, chastity, and obedience) embraced what is traditionally called "the state of perfection," lay people often felt consigned to "the state of imperfection." John Paul's "lay soul" shows itself in his efforts to transcend this false dichotomy. He insists that marriage and celibacy do not "divide the human (and Christian) community into two camps...[as if there were] those who are 'perfect' because of continence, and those who are 'imperfect' or less perfect because of the reality of conjugal life" (TOB 78:2). Perfection in the Christian life is not measured by whether or not one is celibate. "*The perfection of Christian life is measured*, rather, *by the measure of love*" (TOB 78:3).

This means that "perfection is possible and accessible to every human being, whether in a 'religious institute' or in the 'world.'" In fact, a person who does not live in "the state of perfection" can nonetheless "reach a higher degree of perfection...than a person who lives in the 'state of perfection' with a lesser degree of love" (TOB 78:3). Far from being opposed to one another, John Paul demonstrates at great length the profound complementarity between these vocations, which is essential to the life and health of the Church. Marriage and continence, the Pope says, are meant to "explain or complete each other" (TOB

---

43. George Weigel, "The Soul of John Paul II," lecture delivered at Oxford, March 6, 2001.

78:2). Marriage reveals the spousal character of the celibate vocation just as the celibate vocation reveals the sacramentality of marriage. He even says that in "the life of an authentically Christian community, the attitudes and the values proper to the one and the other state...*in some sense interpenetrate*" (TOB 78:4).

Marriage Reveals the Spousal Character of Celibacy

John Paul says that the conjugal fidelity of spouses and the irrevocable gift they make to each other provide the foundation of celibacy for the kingdom. Marriage, in fact, reveals the very nature of the love expressed by the person who is continent for the kingdom. Thus "the nature of the one as well as the other love is 'spousal,' that is, expressed through the complete gift of self" (TOB 78:4).

Christ is the ultimate example of spousal love lived in a celibate way. While remaining celibate, Christ revealed himself as Spouse of the Church, "to whom he has given himself to the end in the mystery of his Passover and of the Eucharist" (TOB 79:9). In this way, Christ gave the ultimate revelation of the spousal meaning of the body. Through the light that marriage sheds on this vocation, we come to realize, as John Paul says, that celibacy for the kingdom has "*acquired the meaning of an act of spousal love.*" Continence for the kingdom is "a spousal gift of self with the end of answering in a particular way the Redeemer's spousal love" (TOB 80:1). Furthermore, since spousal love is ordered by its nature toward fatherhood and motherhood, the Pope says that continence for the kingdom must lead in its normal development to fatherhood and motherhood in a spiritual sense (see TOB 78:5). Thus the familial terms husband, bride, father, mother, brother, and sister are applicable to marriage and family life *and* to the celibate vocation.

This means that the choice of marriage *and* the choice of celibacy for the kingdom require and presuppose "the consciousness and inner acceptance of the spousal meaning of the body, which is connected with the masculinity and femininity of the human person" (TOB 80:7). For *both* vocations flow from the true meaning of human sexuality and the deepest meaning of sexual desire. To the degree that sexual desire is freed from the distortion of concupiscence, it becomes the desire to make a sincere gift of one's body (one's very self) to another. As the Holy Father expresses it: "On the basis of the same disposition of the personal subject and on the basis of the same spousal meaning of being, as a body, male and female, there can be formed the love that commits man to marriage for the whole duration of his life (see Mt 19:3–9), but there can be formed also the love that commits man for his whole life to continence 'for the kingdom of heaven' (see Mt 19:11–12)" (TOB, 80:6). According to John Paul, this is the significance of Christ's words in Matthew 19 where he speaks of marriage according to God's original plan *and* celibacy for the kingdom.

The point is that no one can escape the spousal meaning of his or her body. Every man, by virtue of the spousal meaning of his body, is called in some way to be both a husband and a father. And every woman, by virtue of the spousal meaning of her body, is called in some way to be both a wife and a mother. This is lived on earth either through marriage or, in a different way, through the celibate vocation.[44] But, according to Christ's words, John Paul says that anyone who chooses marriage must do so just as it was instituted by the Creator "from the beginning." Similarly, anyone who pursues continence for the kingdom of heaven must seek in it the proper values of this vocation (see TOB 79:6).

■ What about the place of the single person in living out the spousal meaning of the body? Many more people are in this situation today than was typical in the past. This "new" reality calls for a pastoral response from the Church that has yet to be adequately developed. In brief, I would say that there is a difference between one who is single by choice in order to devote himself to worthy causes[45] and a person who is single not by choice but by circumstance.[46] The former has made a definitive vocational choice in some ways parallel to the celibate vocation. The latter is still waiting to make a definitive vocational choice. This does not mean such a person's life need remain "on hold." He or she can live a very fruitful life serving others while maintaining the hope of finding a spouse or continuing to discern a call to consecrated celibacy. In every way that single men and women give and receive the "sincere

---

44. See *CCC*, no. 923.
45. See *CCC*, no. 2231.
46. See *CCC*, no. 1658.

gift of self"—through prayer, work, leisure, service of friends, families, neighbors, the poor, etc.—they are living the truth of the spousal meaning of their bodies, which is nothing other than the call to give and receive love. In any case, the ultimate fulfillment of the spousal meaning of the body for everyone is to be found, not in any earthly vocation, but in the heavenly marriage of Christ and the Church.

Celibacy Reveals the Sacramentality of Marriage

Christian celibacy is not a sacrament. Why? Sacraments mediate heavenly realities on earth. But in the future world the sacraments lose their *raison d'être* because we will participate in the divine mystery *immediately* (without sacramental mediation).[47] Celibacy is not a sacrament because it is a more direct participation (if only by way of anticipation) in the life to come. It anticipates the life *beyond* sacraments. It is precisely "with regard to this dimension and orientation," John Paul says, that "continence 'for the kingdom of heaven' has a particular importance and particular eloquence for those who live a conjugal life" (TOB 78:2). Because celibacy is *not* a sacrament, it demonstrates why marriage *is* a sacrament. It demonstrates that marriage's ultimate purpose is to point men and women toward their eschatological destiny—toward the consummation of the marriage of the Lamb, which immeasurably exceeds anything possible in earthly life. John Paul reminds us that "the one and only key for understanding the sacramentality of marriage is the spousal love of Christ for the Church" (TOB 81:4). This is the primordial value and meaning of man and woman's call to become "one flesh" (see Eph 5:31–32).

Hence, the Holy Father says that renouncing conjugal union at the same time affirms the deepest meaning of conjugal union because it "*highlights* that meaning in all its inner truth and in all its personal beauty" (TOB 81:3). The Pope admits that this may seem paradoxical. Yet many truths of the Gospel are paradoxical—and these are often the most profound truths. The personal beauty and inner truth of conjugal union lies in its establishment of a true communion of persons so intimate and profound as to image something of the inner life of the

---

47. See *CCC*, no. 1023.

Trinity and the marriage of Christ and the Church. *This* is what celibacy—as a more direct participation in the heavenly marriage—affirms about the union of husband and wife.

Celibacy's affirmation of marriage arises when we discover the dimension of "gift" proper to each vocation. In this way, the Pope says, the celibate gift of self indirectly serves to highlight what is most lasting and most profoundly personal in the marriage vocation (see TOB 81:6). It highlights the fact that conjugal union—in its totality and in its consummate expression—is the temporal manifestation of the eternal reality of "gift." Furthermore, the spiritual fruitfulness of celibacy even reveals something about the physical fruitfulness of marriage. John Paul says that physical procreation fully responds to its meaning only if it is completed by fatherhood and motherhood in the spirit. This spiritual counterpart to physical procreation is expressed in all that the parents do to educate the children born from their conjugal union (see TOB 78:5).

For all these reasons, as John Paul says, continence "is in some sense indispensable for the clearer recognition of the same spousal meaning of the body in the whole ethos of human life and above all in the ethos of conjugal and family life" (TOB 81:3). Without the eschatological reminder of the celibate vocation, the call to become "one flesh" easily turns in on itself and loses its orientation toward the eternal union yet to be consummated. In this way, celibacy provides an essential remedy for the world's false, idolatrous cult of the body.

Celibacy Anticipates Man's Definitive Fulfillment

Before he begins reflecting on St. Paul's teaching on the celibate vocation, John Paul offers some concluding remarks on Christ's words about eunuchs for the kingdom. In his audience of April 21, 1982 (TOB 79), the Pope reviews and summarizes previous themes. He reiterates that Christ wants to impress on his disciples that because continence entails renouncing a great good, it demands great sacrifice. But in this instance John Paul nuances his statement by emphasizing that celibacy is a renunciation only when "*seen in the categories of the temporal order*" (TOB 79:8). We must remember that celibacy makes no sense apart from those key words of Christ: "*for the sake of the kingdom of heaven.*"

Christ established the kingdom of heaven in time and also foretold its eschatological fulfillment. All are called to participate in and prepare for the coming of the kingdom (the Pope points to the parable of the wedding banquet in Matthew 22 as an illustration of this). Yet John Paul concludes that those who are continent for the kingdom are called "to participate uniquely in the establishment of the kingdom of God on earth, through which the definitive stage of the 'kingdom of heaven' is begun and prepared" (TOB 79:2).

Taking up one's cross every day and following Christ can reach the point of renouncing marriage and raising a family of one's own. If Christ calls some to sacrifice so great a good—a good that God established from the beginning as a sign of his own covenant love—this sacrifice must involve an even greater realization of *the same great good* that marriage and family life serves. It must involve a supernatural potential for realizing the kingdom of God both in its earthly dimension and in its ultimate consummation. Masculinity and femininity reveal that the human person is created "for" another—to be a gift "for" the other. Christ's words about celibacy "show accordingly that this *'for,'* which has been present 'from the beginning' at the basis of marriage, *can also stand at the basis of continence 'for' the kingdom of heaven!*" (TOB 80:6).

Being "for" another always implies a spousal relationship of sorts. Thus, "to clarify what the kingdom of heaven is for those who choose voluntary continence for its sake, *the revelation of the spousal relationship between Christ and the Church* has particular significance" (TOB 79:7). A decisive text for John Paul in this regard is Ephesians 5. The Pope says that the "great mystery" of spousal union outlined there by St. Paul (see vv. 21–32) is equally valid both for the theology of Christian marriage and for the theology of Christian celibacy. The kingdom of heaven is the consummation of Christ's union with the Church. As John Paul reminds us, this is "the definitive fulfillment of the aspirations of all human beings, to whom Christ addresses his message: it is the fullness of the good that the human heart desires beyond the limits of all that can be its portion in earthly life; it is the greatest fullness of God endowing man with the gift of grace" (TOB 79:7).

When viewed as a choice for this, celibacy is not a renunciation at all (and it *must* be viewed in this light if is to concur with Christ's words). It is embracing in the here and now—if only by anticipation—the ultimate reality of communion, that maximum fullness of God's bounty toward man. As previously mentioned, we live in the tension of "already, but not yet" in relation to the coming of the kingdom. One could say that Christian celibacy emphasizes the "already," whereas Christian marriage emphasizes the "not yet." In order for a person to discern properly if he is called to celibacy (and, equally so, to discern the call to marriage), he must have a mature understanding of this "tension" emphasized by the complementarity of celibacy and marriage in the life of the pilgrim Church.

In view of the "already," celibacy is not a renunciation. In view of the "not yet," however, celibacy demands not only renunciation and sacrifice but also a weighty responsibility. Even so, the Pope says, "through all this, through the seriousness and depth of the decision, through the severity and responsibility it brings with it, what shines and gleams is love: *love as the readiness to make the exclusive gift of self for the 'kingdom of God'*" (TOB 79:8). "It is a characteristic feature of the human heart to accept even difficult demands," the Pope observes, "in the name of love, for an ideal, and above all *in the name of love for a person.*" Then he adds that "love is, in fact, oriented by its very nature toward the person" (TOB 79:9). And for those who choose celibacy for the kingdom, that person is Christ himself.

Liberation from Concupiscence

The Holy Father recognizes that a proper examination of the way in which the celibate vocation is *formed, or rather "transformed"* in a person would require an extensive study beyond the scope of his analysis (see TOB 81:5). Suffice it to say that it is impossible to receive the "gift" of this vocation if one accepts the modern view that man has a sexual instinct akin to animals. Applying this naturalistic concept to man is woefully inadequate. It greatly limits the full truth of human subjectivity revealed and expressed through the spousal meaning of the body. The spousal meaning of the body, deduced from the first chapters of Genesis (especially Gen 2:23–25), is "the only appropriate and adequate concept" in which to discover man's personhood and subjectivity in the sphere of sexuality. As revealed in the experience of original solitude, man, even when he is understood from the viewpoint of species, cannot be qualified merely as an *animal,* but as a *rational animal* (see TOB 80:4).

Man is a subject because he is free to determine his own actions. He is not bound by instinct like an animal. If he feels that he is, then he does not experience the truth of his own humanity, but the domination of concupiscence that greatly diminishes the truth of his humanity. Only to the degree that a person has experienced liberation from concupiscence—and is, thus, in possession of his own sexual subjectivity—can he properly receive the vocation of celibacy as a gift. This is why John Paul says that the celibate vocation is a matter not only of formation but also of *transformation*.

Anyone who has doubts or reservations about God's plan for sexuality and marriage will have similar doubts and reservations about the vocation of celibacy. For only to the degree that a person adequately understands the beauty and sacredness of God's plan for sex and marriage can he properly understand what it means to renounce them for the kingdom. John Paul concisely expresses this when he says: "In order for man to be fully *aware of what he is choosing* (continence for the kingdom), he must also be fully aware of *what he is renouncing*." He adds parenthetically that "the consciousness at stake here is exactly the consciousness of the value in the 'ideal' sense; nevertheless," he concludes, "this consciousness is completely 'realistic'" (TOB 81:2).

The Holy Father stresses that Christ explicitly requires this full and mature understanding when he says, "He who is able to receive this, let him receive it" (Mt 19:12). Only with this *full* understanding do Christ's words convey what John Paul calls their "convincing stamp and strength" (TOB 79:8). Only with this *full* understanding do we comprehend why John Paul says that the call to continence "has a capital importance not only for the Christian ethos and spirituality, but also for anthropology and for the whole theology of the body" (TOB 81:7).

B. Paul's Understanding of the Relation Between Virginity and Marriage (1 Cor 7)

Christ's Statement and the Teaching of the Apostles

John Paul devotes four of his final five audiences of this cycle (TOB 82–85) to a reflection on St. Paul's teaching on celibacy as outlined in chapter seven of his First Letter to the Corinthians. Paul answers some concrete questions that troubled the first generation of Christians in

Corinth regarding the relationship of celibacy and marriage. The Pope reflects that he might have been responding to the concerns of a young man who wanted to marry, or a newlywed who wanted to give direction to his married life. A father or guardian may have asked Paul for counsel regarding whether or not his daughter should marry. As the Pope reminds us, Paul was writing in a time when marriage decisions belonged more to parents than to young people (see TOB 82:5). He also notes that a particular asceticism then existed in Corinth that may have been influenced by dualistic currents of thought that devalued the body. This asceticism may have led some to question whether marriage itself was a sin. If such ideas were circulating in the Corinthian community, this certainly would have led to troubled consciences for the married and for those who wished to marry.

Understanding this context helps us better appreciate not only the content of Paul's response but also his manner and style. He demonstrates a keen understanding of the human condition and counsels his audience with the greatest realism. Furthermore, Paul presents the truth proclaimed by Christ in all its authenticity. At the same time, the Pope says, "he gives it his own tone, in some sense his own 'personal' interpretation" (TOB 82:1). Paul offers opinions and accents distinctively his own while carefully distinguishing them from the Lord's commands. Although moralists often turn to Paul's teaching in 1 Corinthians 7 seeking resolutions to difficult questions, the Pope reminds us that ultimate resolutions must be sought in the life and teaching of Christ himself (see TOB 82:2). This is significant since, as we shall see, Paul seems to make concessions that we do not find in the life and teaching of Christ. Paul's Letter to the Corinthians certainly demands full respect as the Word of God. Nonetheless, the life and words of Christ in the Gospels hold preeminence,[48] and Paul's teaching must be interpreted in light of Christ's teaching.

Paul's Argumentation

It may appear as though Paul paints a rather negative picture of marriage in this passage from 1 Corinthians. Based on some of the Apostle's statements, John Paul himself asks at one point if Paul might

---

48. See *CCC*, nos. 125–27.

not express a personal aversion to marriage (see TOB 83:3). "I wish that all were [celibate] as I myself am" (v. 7). "Do not seek marriage" (v. 27). "[L]et those who have wives live as though they had none" (v. 29). The married man's "interests are divided" (v. 34). Admittedly, it may seem difficult to reconcile John Paul II's personalist vision with statements like these. It may even appear as though St. Paul were leaning toward a Manichaean view of marriage. But John Paul asserts that in a thoughtful reading of the whole text "we do not find any premise for what was later to be called 'Manichaeism'" (TOB 85:5).

Paul obviously wants to spare his flock the "troubles in the flesh" that marriage brings with it (see v. 28). But the Holy Father maintains that Paul's desire is not based on any supposed negative value of marriage. It is a "realistic observation," the Pope says, in which "one should see a justified warning for those who think—as at times young people do—that conjugal union and life should bring them only happiness and joy. The experience of life shows that spouses are not seldom left disappointed in what they expected most" (TOB 83:3). The Holy Father rightly observes that conjugal love—that love precisely by virtue of which the two become "one flesh"—is a difficult love. It places serious demands on the couple. If this is what St. Paul intends to say, John Paul argues that "he certainly remains on the grounds of evangelical truth, and there is no reason to detect any symptoms of...Manichaeism" (TOB 83:3).

The Pope finds a personalist key to interpreting Paul's teaching in verse seven. There the Apostle states in relation to the choice of vocation that "each has his own special gift from God, one of one kind and one of another." The Holy Father places great weight on this statement. He believes that it leads us to see differently St. Paul's teaching as a whole. With this assertion as our interpretive key, we realize that, according to St. Paul, both celibacy *and* marriage stem from a special grace given by God.[49] While Paul clearly encourages abstention from marriage to the Corinthians, this most definitely does *not* stem from a view that marriage is somehow evil. Paul explicitly wants to counter the idea circulating in Corinth that marriage is a sin (see vv. 28, 36). To this end he states clearly, as the Pope repeatedly reminds us, that in both vocations "the 'gift' is at work that each one receives from God" (TOB

---

49. See *CCC*, no. 1620.

85:4). This gift is the grace that makes the body a "temple of the Holy Spirit," as St. Paul stated in the previous chapter of his letter (see 1 Cor 6:19). This gift continues in both vocations (celibacy and marriage) if the person remains faithful to his gift and, according to his state, does not "dishonor" this temple of the Holy Spirit, which is his body.

Does Paul View Marriage as an Outlet for Concupiscence?

Various distortions were prevalent in the Corinthian community that dishonored the temple of the Holy Spirit. St. Paul writes "fully aware of the weakness and sinfulness to which...[they were] subject, precisely by reason of the concupiscence of the flesh" (TOB 85:4). It even seems he is willing to concede to some weakness for the sake of avoiding a greater dishonor to the body. For instance, he says that couples should "come together again, lest Satan tempt you through lack of self control." And then he adds: "I say this by way of concession" (v. 6). And also: "But if they cannot exercise self-control, they should marry. For it is better to marry than to be aflame with passion" (v. 9).

John Paul asks if Paul, based on these words, might not view marriage as an ethical outlet for concupiscence. To this legitimate question, the Pope, in my opinion, fails to give an altogether satisfying answer. Do we not find here the basis of that traditional understanding that one of the ends of marriage was "relief of concupiscence" in the sense of *indulging* lustful desire? Again it may seem difficult to reconcile John Paul's teaching with St. Paul's. The Holy Father has insisted throughout his entire catechesis that there is "real power" in Jesus Christ's death and resurrection to *set men and women free* from the domination of concupiscence. Based on the ethos of redemption that Christ preached in the Sermon on the Mount, John Paul has held out this freedom as the norm and the task for all Christians and stressed that marriage does *not* justify indulging concupiscence.

This, it seems, is why John Paul reminds us that we must look to the teaching of Christ himself for ultimate resolutions to these difficult questions. He also rightly cautions against making judgments about what the Apostle was thinking or teaching about marriage solely based on his statements in 1 Corinthians 7 (see TOB 82:6). For example, we can recognize that indulging concupiscence at the expense of one's wife would blatantly contradict Paul's call for husbands to love their wives "as Christ loved the Church" in Ephesians 5. Recall John Paul's pre-papal statement quoted previously: "If it is true that marriage may also be a *remedium concupiscentiae* (see St. Paul: 'It is better to marry than to burn' —1 Cor 7:9) then this must be understood in the integral sense given it by the Christian Scriptures, which also teach of the 'redemption of the body' (Rom 8:23) and point to the sacrament of matrimony as a way of realizing this redemption."[50]

Despite the qualifications the Pope offers, the reader of his exegesis is left desiring more explanation for the apparent incongruity between the Sermon on the Mount (and John Paul's interpretation of it) and Paul's teaching that it "is better to marry than to burn." The Pope does say that Paul certainly characterizes marriage "from the 'human' side" based on the particular struggles with concupiscence found among the Corinthians. But John Paul believes, based on the Apostle's statement about the "gift" in verse seven, that "at the same time he brings out, and with no less strength of conviction,...the action of grace in every human being—in the one who lives in marriage no less than in the one who voluntarily chooses continence" (TOB 84:9). This statement seems to indicate that John Paul believes there is no incongruity in what he has been teaching and in what Paul says to the Corinthians. In the final analysis, there may not be. Unfortunately (although the Pope does revisit this issue at the end of Part II, Chapter 1), John Paul does not take us to that stage of the discussion.

> ■ It does not seem to me that Paul holds out the power of grace to set the Corinthians *free* from the domination of concupiscence with equal strength of conviction. It seems more plausible to me that Paul offers some concessions to human weakness (specifically, lack of self-control caused by the domination of concupiscence) without a bold proclamation of the full power of redemption because, as he said earlier in his letter, they were not ready for it. He could only feed them with milk, not with solid food, because they were still "babes in Christ"; they were still "of the flesh" (see 1 Cor 3:1–3).

---

50. "The Family as a Community of Persons," *Person and Community*, p. 327.

Why Celibacy Is "Better" According to St. Paul

As previously noted, Paul is responding to various questions and erroneous ideas found among Christians in Corinth. Paul counters the idea that marriage is itself sinful by stating explicitly that he who marries "does well." But he encourages celibacy because he believes that "he who refrains from marriage will do better" (v. 38). To clarify any confusion on this point, John Paul stresses that Paul is not speaking of the difference between good and evil, but only between good and better. But why does he say that refraining from marriage is "better"? While he affirms the reasons we already discussed (see p. 352ff.), he adds some personal insights.

First, Paul clearly states that celibacy is better than marriage only given the appropriate circumstances (see TOB 82:6). In keeping with the words of Christ, celibacy must be a voluntary response to a special grace (see v. 7), and it must be chosen because "the form of this world is passing away" (v. 31). In other words, it must be chosen for the sake of the kingdom (which does not pass away).

The Holy Father spends much time reflecting on the following words as the basis of Paul's teaching that celibacy is "better" than marriage. "The unmarried man is anxious about the affairs of the Lord, how to please the Lord; but the married man is anxious about worldly affairs, how to please his wife, and his interests are divided" (vv. 32–34). John Paul says this passage indicates the spousal nature of the celibate vocation. We try to please the people we love, especially a spouse (see TOB 84:1). A form of spousal love, then, is at the foundation of the celibate's desire to "please the Lord." Of course, as the Pope notes, every Christian who lives his faith is anxious to please the Lord. But the celibate person, free from the obligations of marriage and family life, can devote himself to the affairs of the Lord in an exclusive or "undivided" way. Furthermore, John Paul observes that people can "be anxious" only about what occupies their hearts. The "affairs of the Lord" occupy the hearts of those who are celibate for the kingdom. They have chosen the "better part," the "one thing necessary" (see Lk 10:41; see TOB 83:7).

What are the "affairs of the Lord"? John Paul says they signify in the first place the building up of Christ's body, the Church. But they also signify "solicitude...[for] the whole world!" (TOB 83:8). For, as St. Paul says, "the earth is the Lord's and everything in it" (1 Cor 10:26).

According to John Paul, this love that Paul has for the Lord, his Church, and his whole world—and his ability to devote himself totally to their service—motivates him to write that "I wish that all were as I myself am" (v. 7).

The Holy Father says that a celibate person with such love and devotion to Christ is marked by an *inner integration*—a unification that allows him to dedicate himself completely to the service of God's kingdom in all its dimensions. Do we not see here, perhaps, an echo of that "original virginal value of man" who was characterized by a perfect inner integration? In any case, it is not celibacy per se that enables such "virginal" integration. John Paul notes that an unmarried person can also experience an inner "division." When an unmarried person lacks a clear goal for which to sacrifice marriage, he or she often faces a certain emptiness (see TOB 84:5). At the same time, as John Paul has already affirmed, a married couple devoted to Christ can rediscover in some sense that original "virginal" integrity.

Both Vocations Are a Call to Holiness

Paul mainly desires to help the Corinthians live in "undivided devotion to the Lord" (v. 35). Marriage in itself is no obstacle to Christian devotion. But, as experience attests, married men and women can easily get distracted by the "affairs of the world." As John Paul says, "The Apostle seems to know all this well and takes pains to make clear that he does not want to 'cast a snare' [v. 35] on the one whom he counsels not to marry" (TOB 84:3). His overall point is to call the Corinthians to holiness in body and spirit (see v. 34).

"In order to grasp the whole depth of Paul's thought," John Paul says, "one must observe that 'holiness,' according to the biblical conception, is a state rather than an action; it has first of all an ontological character and then also a moral one" (TOB 84:5). In other words, holiness is not first a matter of "doing." It is first a matter of "being." Holiness is first a gift that we must *receive*, not a commodity that we must *produce*. The moral goodness of our actions then flows forth as a fruit of and response to the gift we have received.

▰ Recall John Paul's statement that "holiness is measured according to the 'great mystery' in which the Bride responds with the gift of love to the gift of the Bridegroom."[51] Holiness is a gift of love given by the Bridegroom to which we give our consent, our *"fiat."* This is why the *Catechism* teaches that "Mary goes before us all in the holiness that is the Church's mystery as 'the bride without spot or wrinkle.'"[52]

Furthermore, as St. Paul states and John Paul emphasizes, both celibacy *and* marriage are a special *gift* from God. When received as such, both are vocations to holiness. However, as the Apostle to the Gentiles stresses, in a sense the married person finds it more difficult to understand and live this. As Christ affirmed in his discussion with the Sadducees, marriage is part of what Paul calls "the form of this world [which] is passing away" (v. 31). And if man is to be holy, he cannot become too attached to the goods of a perishable world. "Desire for true happiness frees man from his immoderate attachment to the goods of this world"—including marriage—"so that he can find his fulfillment in the vision and beatitude of God."[53] Thus, for marriage to lead to holiness, the Christian must live it in light of his definitive vocation. In other words, he must not let it tie him down to "earthly affairs." He must live it as a sacrament of the life to come. This is what St. Paul means when he says "let those who have wives live as though they had none" (v. 29). Obviously, a celibate for the kingdom is not locked in the world's transience in the same way a married person is. "Exactly for this reason," John Paul asserts, "the Apostle declares that the one who chooses continence 'does better'" (TOB 85:2).

The Grace Operative in Married Life

John Paul closes his reflections on Paul's First Letter to the Corinthians with some comments on the operation of grace in the conjugal union. The Pope observes that Paul writes about it with the same realism that marks the advice he gives throughout the seventh chapter of this letter. "The husband should give to his wife her conjugal rights, and likewise the wife to her husband. For the wife does not rule over

---

51. *Mulieris Dignitatem*, 27.
52. *CCC*, no. 773.
53. *CCC*, no. 2548.

her own body, but the husband does; likewise the husband does not rule over his own body, but the wife does" (vv. 3–4).

John Paul notes that this language of "rights" and "ruling over the body" has passed from Paul's vocabulary into the whole theology of marriage. Unfortunately, these phrases have not always been understood in a way that upheld the dignity of the spouses and the personal nature of the one flesh union. The contractual "rights" and "duties" of spouses have been emphasized at times to the neglect of the love proper to a personal covenant. Hence, ever on guard against anything that obscures the dignity of the person, John Paul insists that these Pauline phrases "cannot be explained by abstracting from the proper dimension of the marriage covenant" (TOB 85:6). In his catechesis up to this point, the Holy Father has tried to clarify precisely this deeply personal nature of conjugal relations. And he will clarify it even more fully in Part II of his catechesis.

John Paul also has an intriguing and original way of applying the following passage from St. Paul's letter: "Do not refuse one another except perhaps by agreement for a season, that you may devote yourselves to prayer; but then come back together again" (v. 5). According to the Holy Father, "St. Paul clearly says that both conjugal relations and the voluntary periodic abstinence of the spouses must be a fruit of the 'gift of God,' which is their 'own.'" By knowingly cooperating with this gift, the couple "can keep up and strengthen their reciprocal personal bond together with the dignity that being 'temple[s] of the Holy Spirit who is in [them]' (see 1 Cor 6:19) confers on their bodies" (TOB 85:7). With these statements, the Holy Father is clearly laying the foundation for his future reflections on the value of periodic abstinence to an authentic marital spirituality (pp. 562–84).

Furthermore, he interprets Paul's call to periodic abstinence as an indication of "the need to consider all that in some way corresponds to the subjectivity, so highly differentiated, of man and woman" (TOB 85:8). All the subjective richness of man and woman is expressed differently, John Paul indicates, according to their different levels of sensitivity. If these differences are to produce harmony rather than discord, they must remain under the influence of that particular gift (grace) given to married people. Based on the subject matter of the Pauline passage, the Pope's statements seem a clear reference to the different rise in sexual arousal in man and woman of which he (as Karol Wojtyla) wrote in detail in *Love and Responsibility*. Because the man typically experiences a more rapid rise in sexual arousal than the woman, the virtue of continence is necessary if the man is to respond tenderly and lovingly toward his wife.[54] Such tenderness is aided by the practice of periodic abstinence and prayer, of which St. Paul spoke. Here again we see John Paul applying familiar Scripture passages in excitingly innovative ways.

Conclusion of Part I

The Redemption of the Body and the Hope of Every Day

John Paul concludes Part I of his catechesis in his audience of July 21, 1982 (TOB 86), with a summary of his reflections up until this point. "Everything we have tried to do in the course of our meditations in order to understand the words of Christ," the Pope says, "has its definitive foundation in the mystery of the redemption of the body" (TOB 86:8). Historical man can begin to reclaim God's original plan for his humanity only in this context. It is the only basis for man's hope to attain ultimate fulfillment in his eschatological destiny.

The Holy Father reminds us that St. Paul speaks of the redemption of the body in both an *anthropological* and a *cosmic dimension*. It is anthropological because "it is the redemption of man." It is cosmic because, at the same time, the Pope says, "it irradiates in some way on all creation, which has from the beginning been tied to man in a particular way and subordinated to him (see Gen 1:28–30)" (TOB 86:2). According to John Paul, "The whole visible creation, the whole cosmos, carries the effects of man's sin" (TOB 86:1). As St. Paul writes, "creation was subjected to futility." But it was subjected "in hope: because the creation itself will be set free from its bondage to decay and obtain the glorious liberty of the children of God" (Rom 8:20–21). The hope of man and the hope of the entire universe, then, rests on the redemption of the body.

---

54. See *Love and Responsibility*, p. 275.

Christ Fulfills the Proto-Evangelium

Recalling the *proto-evangelium* (i.e., the first announcement of the Gospel) in Genesis, John Paul says that the hope of the body's redemption was planted in man's heart immediately after the first sin. The Lord said to the serpent, "I will put enmity between you and the woman, and between your seed and her seed; he shall bruise your head, and you shall bruise his heel" (Gen 3:15). The Church sees in these words a foreshadowing of the New Adam and the New Eve, of Jesus and Mary.[55] Satan will continue to attack the woman and her call to bear life (e.g., see Rev 12). The devil will wound the woman's offspring (Jesus). Yet in the very process of what seems like a victory for Satan, Christ will deal a fatal blow to his head and restore man and woman (and all creation) to the purity of their origins.

Through John Paul's TOB we come to realize that this cosmic battle between good and evil, while fought on a spiritual plane (see Eph 6:12), is always a battle for the truth of the body. It is an attack on the spousal meaning of the body. This is why "the redemption of man" is the redemption of his body. In fact, what the *proto-evangelium* announces is the restoration of the spousal meaning of the body. For Christ defeats the devil and fully reveals man to himself precisely through the spousal gift of his body on the cross and the "rebirth" of his body in the resurrection.

The triptych of Christ's words upon which John Paul has been reflecting (i.e., Christ's words about the beginning, about the man of concupiscence, and about the resurrection) flow *"from the very divine depth of the mystery of redemption."* And this redemption finds its specific "historical" subject precisely in Christ himself because the redemption of the body has already been accomplished in him (see TOB 86:3). Christ fulfills the hope of the *proto-evangelium* "not only with the words of his teaching, but above all with the testimony of his death and resurrection" (TOB 86:3).

The Hope of Every Day

St. Paul indicates that the redemption of the body is something we "wait for...with patience" (Rom 8:25). We are saved in hope. But who

---

55. See *CCC*, no. 411; for the Marian interpretation, see *Lumen Gentium*, 55, and *Redemptoris Mater*, 7, 11, 24.

hopes for what he has already attained (see v. 24)? In this sense Paul speaks of the ultimate fulfillment of the redemption of the body—the eschatological victory over death, to which Christ gave testimony above all by his resurrection. Those who limit themselves to this sense of Paul's words might resign themselves merely to coping with concupiscence until Christ returns. We will certainly always feel the pull of concupiscence in this life, but John Paul insists that the redemption of the body can and *must* bear fruit in the here and now of historical man's life. Recall from our reflection on historical man that "*the 'redemption of the body' is already an aspect of human life on earth.* This redemption is not just an eschatological reality but a historical one as well. It shapes the history of the salvation of concrete living people...in keeping with the intent of the Creator announced to the first parents before the fall."[56]

Thus, in the Sermon on the Mount, Christ calls historical man to overcome concupiscence not only by observing external norms of behavior, but "even in the exclusively inner movements of the human heart." This call "is not a question of the eschatological hope of the resurrection, but of the hope of victory over sin." With humble faith and buoyant optimism, John Paul calls this "the hope of everyday" (TOB 86:6). The "hope of everyday," the Pope observes, "shows its power in human works and even in the very movements of the human heart, clearing a path in some sense for the great eschatological hope tied to the redemption of the body" (TOB 86:7).

Whether man chooses marriage or celibacy for the kingdom, he must daily give a living witness of fidelity to his choice. For both vocations, such fidelity is only possible when man draws "from the mystery of the redemption of the body the inspiration and strength to overcome the evil that is dormant in him in the form of the threefold concupiscence." This victory comes from "*the hope of everyday,* which in the measure of normal tasks and difficulties of human life helps to overcome 'evil with good' (Rom 12:21)" (TOB 86:7). Thus John Paul affirms that the redemption of the body "expresses itself not only in the resurrection as victory over death. It is present also in the words of Christ addressed to 'historical' man" (TOB 86:6).

---

56. "The Family as a Community of Persons," *Person and Community,* p. 326.

The Theology of the Body Is Fundamental

John Paul states that there is a "bond that exists between the dignity of the human being (of the man or the woman) and the spousal meaning of his body." The more we live and experience daily a victory over concupiscence, the more we "discover and strengthen...[that] bond" (TOB 86:8). As this bond establishes itself firmly in man's conscience, he discovers the true dignity of every human being by readily recognizing the spousal meaning of that person's body. In fact, we could even say that to the extent that concupiscence dominates us, we are blind to the dignity of the person precisely because we are blind to the spousal meaning of his or her body. Or, perhaps more aptly, to the extent that we are bound by concupiscence, the dignity of the person remains only an idea, a concept we may well accept, but which we do not *feel* and *experience* in the movements of the heart.

The triptych of Christ's words affords us that "hope of every day" which enables us progressively to rediscover and, more, to experience in our hearts the spousal meaning of the body. Through the mature freedom of the gift, we can fulfill our body's spousal meaning either through marriage or celibacy for the kingdom. Both vocations "provide a full answer to one of man's underlying questions: namely, the question about the meaning of 'being a body,' that is, the meaning of masculinity and femininity" (TOB 85:9). "In these different ways," John Paul says, enlisting his anthem from Vatican II, "Christ 'fully reveals man to man himself and makes his supreme vocation clear'" (TOB 86:8). What is man's supreme vocation? It is to be taken up into the eternal ecstasy of the trinitarian mystery through union with the eternal Word, which St. Paul compares to the union of spouses (see Eph 5:31–32). And this vocation, the Holy Father reminds us, "is inscribed in man according to his whole psycho-physical *compositum* [makeup] precisely through the mystery of the redemption of the body" (TOB 86:8).

Apart from the redemption of the body, all interpretations of man—or what John Paul calls "anthropological hermeneutics"— inevitably fall short of the full truth of man's greatness, of his supreme vocation. Thus, John Paul boldly proclaims that the "theology of the body proves to be something truly fundamental and constitutive *for anthropological hermeneutics* as a whole" (TOB 85:10). In other words, unless we understand the truths of the theology of the body, we do not—and cannot—understand fundamentally and adequately who man is and who he is meant to be. Nor can we understand how he is meant to live. For the theology of the body is "equally fundamental for ethics." And, if we are to penetrate man's subjectivity, it is fundamental in constructing "*the theology of the human ethos*" (TOB 85:10).

CHRIST APPEALS TO THE RESURRECTION—IN REVIEW

1. When the Sadducees questioned Jesus about the resurrection with a marriage case that they thought would lead to the admission of polyandry, Christ responded by saying that in the resurrection, men and women "neither marry nor are given in marriage." This stupendous response is the third element in the "triptych" of Christ's words that constitute and, in this case, complete "the revelation of the body."

2. God is the God of the living, not of the dead. He is the God of life! Christ's resurrection is the ultimate word on the subject. Marriage and its consummate expression also testify to God as the God of life. But in the resurrection, marriage and conjugal union lose their *raison d'être*. They exist "from the beginning" to point us to the marriage of the Lamb. When this marriage is consummated, the primordial sacrament will give way to the divine reality.

3. When, in referring to the resurrection, Christ says we will be "like angels in heaven," this does not mean we will be disincarnated. Since man was constituted "from the beginning" as male and female in a unity of body and soul, his eschatological perfection cannot be understood as a state of the soul alone. His body will be raised and glorified in an infinitely perfected masculinity and femininity.

4. In our resurrected integration, the mutual opposition between body and soul that resulted from original sin will cease utterly. The forces of the spirit will fully permeate the energies of the body.

This eschatological "spiritualization of the body" will differ essentially (and not only in degree) from what we experience in earthly life. It is different even from what man and woman experienced "in the beginning."

5. The spirit totally permeating the body is not only man's spirit but also the Holy Spirit. Hence, the eschatological "spiritualization" is also a "divinization." In the marriage of the Lamb, penetration and permeation of what is essentially human by what is essentially divine will then reach its peak. God will communicate himself in his very divinity not only to man's soul but also to his whole embodied personhood. This will be man's ultimate participation in grace, in the divine nature.

6. In the "divinizing spiritualization" of the resurrection, we rediscover—in an eschatological dimension—the same spousal meaning of the body in the beatific vision, which is a meeting with the mystery of the living God face to face. This is God's most personal self-giving of his very divinity. All of our energies will be concentrated on receiving this divine gift and reciprocating it through the gift of ourselves to God.

7. Christ's words about the resurrection enable us to reread with new depth the meaning of that perspective text of Genesis 2:24 (the two become "one flesh"). These words refer especially to "this world," but they also point in some way to the "other world"—to the eschatological dimension of communion. The ultimate meaning of our creation as male and female is found in our call to incarnate communion with the Trinity in and through the incarnate Christ.

8. If in the eschaton we are to participate in the uncreated relations of the Trinity, this participation must be adapted in some way to the communion of created persons. For this reason we profess belief in the communion of saints. Not only will we be "one" with the divine Persons. We will also be "one" with every human person who responds to the wedding invitation of the Lamb.

9. We must think of the resurrection as the rediscovery of a new, perfect subjectivity of everyone (fulfillment of original solitude) and at the same time of a new, perfect intersubjectivity of all (fulfillment of original unity). This reality means the definitive fulfillment of

human subjectivity, and, on this basis, the definitive fulfillment of the spousal meaning of the body.

10. The eschatological state will become the perfect realization of the trinitarian order in the created world of persons. This implies a participation in the perfect unity and distinction found within the Trinity itself. Thus the spousal meaning of the body will be experienced in a way that is "perfectly personal and communitarian at the same time."

11. In the resurrection, the body will be experienced in its perfect "virginal" state due to the perfect integration of body and soul. As the fulfillment of the beginning, in the eschaton there will be no contradiction between virginity and communion. The resurrected spousal meaning of the body will correspond perfectly both to man and woman's creation in the image of God as individuals and to the fact that this image is realized through the incarnate *communio personarum*.

12. The eschatological communion of persons will be a completely new experience, yet it will not be alienated in any way from the original and historical dimension of the procreative meaning of the body and sex. The perennial meaning of the human body will be revealed in an eschatological splendor when men and women rediscover in their glorified bodies the perfect freedom of the gift. In turn, this freedom will nourish each of the communions that will make up the great community of the communion of saints.

13. Christ's response to the Sadducees presents a profound development of the truth about man. It teaches us that marriage did not definitively determine the original meaning of being created male and female. Marriage and procreation merely give concrete expression to that meaning within history. In other words, earthly marriage is not man's end, but only preparation for the heavenly marriage yet to come.

14. In St. Paul's teaching on the resurrection in 1 Corinthians 15, he unites the "last Adam" with the "first Adam" in the context of a deep awareness of the effects of sin. By doing so, the Apostle synthesizes all that Christ said in his three "key words" about man's origin, history, and destiny.

15. Historical man lives in a sort of tension between the poles of the first and the last Adam. Since every man bears the image of the first Adam, every man is called to bear the image of Christ. Already in creation our humanity bears the potential to receive Christ, just as a bride bears in herself the potential to receive her bridegroom.

16. According to St. Paul, the body that historical man experiences as perishable will be raised imperishable. What we experience as weighed down in dishonor and weakness will be raised in glory and power. For what is sown a physical body is raised a spiritual body. Paul is not contrasting a material reality with a nonmaterial reality. He is speaking of the spiritualizing divinization of the whole man, body and soul. In the resurrection, the dust to which we have returned will be re-quickened by a new fullness of the breath of God, which is the Holy Spirit.

17. Christ's words about those who make themselves eunuchs "for the sake of the kingdom" form the basis of the Pope's reflection on the celibate vocation. This voluntary and supernatural calling serves as a charismatic sign of the future resurrection when men and women "neither marry nor are given in marriage" but participate eternally in the marriage of the Lamb. Based on the covenant with Abraham, preferring to be a eunuch was virtually unthinkable for a Jew.

18. The departure from the Old Covenant was effected especially in the celibate example of Christ. The celibate lives of Joseph and Mary also speak to this new dimension. In a profound paradox, they simultaneously embrace the marriage of earth and the marriage of heaven. By doing so, they participate in the most fruitful marriage of the cosmos—the union of the human and divine natures in the Person of Christ. All those who live an authentic celibate vocation participate in some way in this new superabounding spiritual fruitfulness.

19. Behind both marriage and the celibate vocation we find the same anthropology and the same ethos. In other words, both vocations flow from the same vision of the human person and the same call to experience the redemption of our bodies, which includes the

redemption of our sexual desires. Without understanding the ethos of redemption, lifelong continence is viewed as hopelessly repressive and marriage as a "legitimate outlet" for lust.

20. An authentic understanding of the "superiority" of continence never means disparaging marriage. It is not based on any prejudice toward the "one flesh" union, which, as the essential element of marriage, is part of God's good and holy design. The celibate vocation is "superior" only in its more direct orientation toward man's superior heavenly destiny.

21. Christ does not wish to hide the real sacrifice involved in choosing lifelong continence. Historical man is "made" for marriage. However, continence in no way rejects man's dual nature as a sexual being. It participates in the ultimate purpose and meaning of masculinity and femininity. The celibate person fulfills the spousal meaning of his body differently and even "more" than the married person by being a sincere gift to others.

22. Marriage and celibacy do not divide the Church into two camps of those who are "perfect" and "imperfect." Perfection is measured by love, not by whether or not one is celibate. Celibacy and marriage, in fact, explain, complete, and in some sense interpenetrate each other.

23. Marriage reveals that continence, too, is an expression of spousal love, which leads to a spiritual fatherhood and motherhood. Continence, by anticipating the heavenly union of Christ and the Church, reveals that marriage is a sacramental participation in the same mystery. Each vocation, in its own way, expresses the reality of "gift" inscribed in the body.

24. Masculinity and femininity reveal that the human person is created to be a gift "for" another. Christ's words reveal that men and women can express this in choosing celibacy "for" the kingdom. This is only a renunciation when viewed in temporal categories. The kingdom for which some choose celibacy expresses the fullness of God's grace given to man and is the ultimate fulfillment of all that man desires.

25. The celibate vocation is not only a matter of formation but also of *transformation*. Only to the degree that a person is liberated from

lust and is in possession of his own sexual subjectivity can he be a gift to others—whether in the celibate vocation or in marriage. Only one who understands and embraces the beauty and sacredness of God's plan for sex and marriage can renounce them in the mature sense that Christ requires.

26. In 1 Corinthians 7, St. Paul presents the truth about celibacy proclaimed by Christ, yet at the same time he employs a style totally his own. It can seem as though Paul has a rather negative view of marriage, but in a thoughtful reading of the text we see no introduction to Manichaeism. In fact, Paul insists that both marriage and the celibate vocation are a special "gift" (grace) from God.

27. Many have thought that Paul's statement "it is better to marry than to burn" justifies indulging concupiscence within marriage. It may seem difficult to reconcile John Paul II's teaching with St. Paul's. Yet Paul's words cannot be interpreted apart from Christ's words about lust nor apart from Paul's teaching as a whole, which includes "the redemption of the body" and the call of husbands to love their wives "as Christ loved the Church."

28. The Apostle writes that he who marries "does well," but he who refrains "does better," since he can devote himself in an undivided way to "the affairs of the Lord." Marriage itself is a vocation to holiness and therefore concerns the "affairs of the Lord." But experience attests that the responsibilities of marriage and family life can distract men and women from their ultimate vocation and tie them down to "earthly affairs." It is in this sense that Paul exhorts married people to live as though they were not married.

29. When Paul speaks of granting "conjugal rights" and spouses "ruling over the body" of the other, these expressions cannot be explained apart from the context of the love proper to the marriage covenant. Grace is poured out on the couple in their conjugal life to harmonize their different levels of sensitivity. The periodic abstinence that Paul recommends can aid this.

30. Christ fulfills the "proto-evangelium" of Genesis not only in his teaching but especially with his death and resurrection. In this way Christ "re-creates" man and woman and redeems the spousal meaning of the body. This redemption is not only a hope for the

eschaton but is also a "hope of every day." It already begins here and now and clears a path for future glory.

31. A deep bond exists between the dignity of the person and the spousal meaning of his or her body. To the extent that concupiscence binds us, the dignity of the person is not "felt." Thus, the theology of the body and the redemption to which it calls us is fundamental for all interpretations of man and for constructing an adequate and authentic human ethos.

Part II

THE SACRAMENT

CHAPTER 1

The Dimension of Covenant and of Grace

[Cycle 5—The Sacramentality of Marriage]

THE THEOLOGY OF THE BODY has emerged along the lines Christ provides in the triptych or three-part "revelation of the body." Having reflected on this "total vision of man" and then applied it to the vocation of celibacy for the kingdom, we are now prepared to penetrate the "great mystery" of *the sacrament*.

As stated in the Prologue, this refers, of course, to marriage as a sacrament, but the Pope's title for Part II of his catechesis—"The Sacrament"—refers also to the manner in which the mystery hidden in God from eternity "has *become visible* and thereby *entered into the sphere of the Sign*" (TOB 95b:6). In the beginning the divine mystery became visible through the primordial sacrament of marriage. In the "fullness of time" this same mystery became visible through the sacrament of Christ's union with the Church (see TOB 97:4). As we will come to understand more deeply in this chapter, the "great mystery" of *the sacrament* is to be found precisely in the fact that these two signs, these two "great sacraments," have become *one*. These two "great signs"—the union of husband-wife and the union of Christ-Church—express *one mystery* and thus form one "great sacrament": *the* Sacrament (see TOB 95b:7).

For John Paul, reflecting on the sacrament of marriage does not mean reflecting merely on one sacrament out of the seven. For him, marriage serves in some way as *a prototype of all the sacraments*, as a model for understanding the whole mystery of salvation (see TOB 98:2). For the goal of all of the sacraments is to unite the Bride (the Church) with the Bridegroom (Christ) and to "impregnate" (in-fill, in-spire) her with divine life. Marriage, then, "is the visible and efficacious *sign* of the covenant with God in Christ, that is, of *grace*" (TOB 103:6).

Here we see that there are "*two dimensions* essential to this *sacrament* (as to every other sacrament), namely, the [divine] dimension of covenant and grace and the [human] dimension of the sign" (TOB 133:2). In this chapter—consisting of seventeen addresses delivered between July 28, 1982, and December 15, 1982 (TOB 87–102 [includes 95b])—the Pope explores the divine dimension. What is the *covenant* with God, the *grace* that marriage communicates to spouses? John Paul will provide a searching study of this question. Then, in the next chapter, he will explore *how* this divine gift is communicated through the *sacramental sign*.

In the cyclical structure of the catechesis, these two chapters combine to make Cycle 5. This first chapter of Cycle 5 provides a fresh analysis of what John Paul calls another "key" and "classical" text of Scripture: Ephesians 5:21–33. The mystery of God's spousal love for humanity was only "half open" in the Old Testament. In Ephesians 5:21–33, "it is fully unveiled (without ceasing to be a mystery, of course)" (TOB 95:7). Building on all the Pope has mined from Christ's three key statements about man and woman, the text of Ephesians 5 brings our understanding of the body and spousal union to a "mystical" level. The Pope wants to understand how the sacramentality of marriage emerges from this text. He also wants to understand the sense in which Ephesians 5 speaks about the human body as an image of the Church (as "Christ's body") and in its concrete masculinity and femininity. "We must ask ourselves these questions, expecting not so much immediate and direct answers, but possibly deeply thought-through and 'long-term' answers that our earlier analyses have prepared us for" (TOB 87:3). As we will discover, in the process of providing these "thought-through" answers, John Paul presents some of the most profound and provocative theological assertions of the entire catechesis. So rich are his insights here that it will take theologians centuries to unfold them.

1. Ephesians 5:21–33

A. INTRODUCTION AND CONNECTION

The Text of Ephesians 5:21–23

One would be hard-pressed to find a passage in the Scriptures that has been more maligned and dismissed by today's "politically correct" society than Ephesians 5. In light of such polemics—which have even seeped into the Church—John Paul is at pains to resurrect the true meaning of St. Paul's[1] words and to show their fundamental importance. Here is the full passage:

> Be subject to one another out of reverence for Christ. Wives, be subject to your husbands, as to the Lord. For the husband is the head of the wife as Christ is the head of the church, his body, and is himself its Savior. As the church is subject to Christ, so let wives also be subject in everything to their husbands. Husbands, love your wives, as Christ loved the church and gave himself up for her, that he might sanctify her, having cleansed her by the washing of water with the word, that he might present the church to himself in splendor, without spot or wrinkle or any such thing, that she might be holy and without blemish. Even so husbands should love their wives as their own bodies. He who loves his wife loves himself. For no man ever hates his own flesh, but nourishes and cherishes it, as Christ does the church, because we are members of his body. "For this reason a man shall leave his father and mother and be joined to his wife, and the two shall become one flesh." This is a great mystery, and I mean in reference to Christ and the church; however, let each one of you love his wife as himself, and let the wife see that she respects her husband.

The Crowning of the Themes of Scripture

When this controversial passage from Ephesians is correctly understood in the full biblical context, we realize that it contains "central themes and essential truths" that cannot be dismissed. John Paul even

---

1. The Holy Father acknowledges in a footnote that some exegetes question the Pauline authorship of Ephesians. John Paul provides a provisional solution to the dispute "by an intermediate *supposition* that we accept here as *a working hypothesis*: namely, that St. Paul entrusted some concepts to his secretary, who then developed and finished them" (TOB, n. 87). For this reason, he alternately references "the author of the letter to the Ephesians," the "Apostle," and "St. Paul."

says in his poetic fashion that we should consider this passage "as the 'crowning' of the themes and truths that ebb and flow like long waves through the Word of God revealed in Sacred Scripture" (TOB 87:4). He reiterates this and even goes a step further in his *Letter to Families* by describing this passage from Ephesians as "the compendium or *summa*, in some sense, *of the teaching about God and man* which was brought to fulfillment by Christ."[2] John Paul wants to penetrate this "summa" to help us "understand if possible 'to the very depths' what wealth of truth revealed by God is contained within the scope of that stupendous page" (TOB 87:6). To do so we must presuppose the triptych of Christ's words about the human body in the beginning, in history, and in the resurrection.

As John Paul points out, the words of Ephesians 5 "are centered on the body" (TOB 87:3). They speak of the body in both the *metaphorical sense* of the body of Christ, which is the Church, and the *concrete sense* of the human body in its sexual complementarity and its "perennial destiny for union in marriage" (TOB 87:3). The convergence of these two meanings of the body gives us the key to understand the "great mystery" St. Paul speaks of in verses 31–32. There the Apostle links the primordial meaning of the "one flesh" union of spouses with the union of Christ and the Church. What is the relationship between these two holy communions? John Paul will provide a profound and studied answer.

Precisely at this point—in the relationship of that perennial union in "one flesh" with the union of Christ and the Church—we find ourselves on the threshold of the meaning and mystery of the universe. We find ourselves on the threshold of discovering the glory and greatness that God has bestowed on us by creating us as male and female and calling us to incarnate communion. This is why, using again his anthem from *Gaudium et Spes*, John Paul says that this passage from Ephesians "reveals—in a particular way—*man to man himself* and makes *his supreme vocation* clear" (TOB 87:6).

The Incarnate Person: Body and Sacrament

By linking this passage from Ephesians with the key anthropological statement of Vatican II, we glimpse from yet another angle the

---

2. *Letter to Families*, 19.

exceptional importance John Paul places on St. Paul's words here. However, a person can only see this link with *Gaudium et Spes* 22 "inasmuch as he participates in the experience of the incarnate person" (TOB 87:6). This phrase "the experience of the incarnate person" in some way penetrates and describes the Pope's entire catechesis. This is what the TOB—and this passage from Ephesians—are all about. They seek to ground man in the *experience* of his own *incarnate personhood*. The modern view of man, however, has effectively severed man from his body. In the often vehement dispute over Ephesians 5, we glimpse the great clash of two competing humanisms and, in particular, their respective views of the human body and the meaning of sexuality.

In the modern view, the body has been relegated to the realm of subhuman nature. It may serve as a biological reference point, but it has nothing to say about the human person and the order of human relationships. Much less does the body say anything about *theology*—about the nature of the divine mystery and God's love for humanity. In this view, the person stands over and against his body. The body does not call him to anything. It makes no demands on him. Modern man owns his body like a thing, and, as such, he believes he can do anything he wants with it. The body and sexuality are then used as tools and as a means to selfish pleasure, even profit. The "word" (or anti-word) inscribed in the body for modern man is "self-gratification."

St. Paul, on the other hand, is deeply rooted in a sacramental, theological view of the body. He knows the body "speaks" a mystical language. It speaks not only about the truth of the human person as male and female. It also speaks about the "great mystery" hidden in God from all eternity. For St. Paul, the truth about who man is as male and female can only be understood in light of this "great mystery." Recalling God's plan in Genesis for man and woman to join in "one flesh," he builds on the analogy of the spousal love of God for Israel and shows the fulfillment of this Old Testament image in Christ's love for the Church. In doing so, he calls man and woman to embrace the sublime vocation inscribed in their bodies from "the beginning"—to love as God loves. The Word inscribed in the body in Ephesians 5, therefore, is "self-donation."

Even at first glance we see how Ephesians 5 confirms John Paul's thesis statement: "The body, in fact, and only the body, is capable of making visible what is invisible: the spiritual and the divine. It has been created to transfer into the visible reality of the world the mystery hidden from eternity in God, and thus to be a sign of it" (TOB 19:4). In Ephesians 5, the Apostle is speaking precisely of that "great mystery" hidden from eternity in God that, according to John Paul, the body "and only the body" is capable of making visible to us. It is the mystery of divine love and life—of trinitarian communion—in which man and woman are called to participate through the intimacy of "spousal union" with Christ. This is the very essence of what this passage from Ephesians reveals about the sacramentality of marriage and its consummate expression of conjugal intercourse. The Pope seeks gradually to unfold precisely this point.

The Pope reiterates his thesis at the beginning of Cycle 5 when he affirms:

> In some way, therefore—even if in the most general way—the body enters into the definition of sacrament, which is "a visible sign of an invisible reality," namely, of the spiritual, transcendent, and divine reality. In this sign—and through this sign—God gives himself to man in his transcendent truth and in his love. The sacrament is a sign of grace, and it is *an efficacious sign.*

In other words, the Pope says that the sacrament "does not merely *indicate* and express grace in a visible way, in the manner of a sign, but *produces* grace." The sacrament "contributes efficaciously to cause that grace to become part of man and to *realize and fulfill the work of salvation* in him, the work determined ahead of time by God from eternity and fully revealed in Christ" (TOB 87:5).

This is a grand statement of incarnational theology. It grounds God's plan of salvation *in the body* by grounding the action of God's grace in the body. It beautifully echoes Tertullian's famous saying: "the flesh is the hinge of salvation."[3] Man is an incarnate person. This is the only way he can encounter God and be himself. This means that, contrary to popular opinion, in his quest for transcendence man need not shed his skin. In an act of utter *kenosis* (self-emptying), Transcendence himself took on man's skin, thus *divinizing the body.* In the Bridegroom, Jesus Christ, "the whole fullness of deity dwells bodily" (Col 2:9). The Incarnation, then, as John Paul said at the conclusion of his first cycle, is "the definitive source of the sacramentality of marriage" (TOB 23:4). The Incarnation, in fact, is the definitive and ultimate

---

3. See *CCC*, no. 1015.

"spousal" union. It is the union of divinity and humanity in the Person of the Word. It is the indissoluble sign of the Father's covenant love for humanity, of the super-abounding grace bestowed upon the incarnate—that is, the human[4]—person.

This is precisely the affirmation of the body and of spousal union found in St. Paul's proclamation of the "great mystery" in Ephesians 5. The modern view of man and of human sexuality cannot tolerate and, in fact, radically opposes this great *incarnational* mystery. Such a grand vision places far too many demands on man and challenges his utilitarian view of the body at its roots. Thus, those who embrace the vision of the body and of marriage proclaimed in Ephesians 5 can expect persecution. It is no coincidence, as John Paul indicates, that St. Paul's proclamation of the "great mystery" is followed by "a stupendous encouragement to spiritual battle (see Eph 6:10–20)" (TOB 88:5). It is also important to realize that St. Paul began his letter by presenting the eternal plan of humanity's salvation in Christ (see Eph 1). This is the battle we are fighting—the battle of salvation. It is a *spiritual* battle but it is waged against the truth of the *body*. And, as we learn from the Letter to the Ephesians, the sacramentality of marriage stands at the center of the clash. If we are to win this battle, the first thing we must do is "gird our loins with the truth" (Eph 6:14).

B. DETAILED ANALYSIS

The Context of Ephesians

In his audience of August 4, 1982 (TOB 88), John Paul outlines the overall structure of the Letter to the Ephesians before analyzing chapter 5. This helps us position St. Paul's detailed instructions to husbands and wives in the broader context of the moral obligations of the family, the larger Christian community, and society as a whole. It also helps us understand the spiritual climate that the Apostle believes should animate the lives of Christians. Sinful humanity is called to new life in Jesus Christ. Only by living this "new life"—that is, only through the encounter with the risen Christ—are men and women empowered to live as St. Paul exhorts them to live.

---

4. There is only one "incarnate person" who is not a *human* person: Jesus Christ, who is an incarnate *divine* Person.

For this reason the Apostle bends his knee "before the Father" and asks him to grant that the readers of his letter would "be strengthened with might through his Spirit in the inner man, and that Christ may dwell in your hearts through faith; that you, being rooted and grounded in love, may have power to comprehend with all the saints what is the breadth and length and height and depth, and to know the love of Christ which surpasses knowledge, that you may be filled with the fullness of God" (3:14–19). If the Apostle holds husbands and wives to a high standard, he assures his readers that the "fullness of God" and the love of Christ within us affords a "power" that can do far more in us than anything we could ask or imagine (see Eph 3:20).

Modern Sensitivities and St. Paul's Interpretive Key

John Paul II inaugurated his pontificate echoing Christ's declaration: "Be not afraid!" We can certainly apply this to St. Paul's words in Ephesians 5. We need not be afraid of what this passage reveals about man and woman's relationship. John Paul certainly is not. He presses into it without hesitation. In the process he shows that far from promoting an imbalance or inequality between spouses, this passage provides the only means of ensuring the proper ordering of love between them—reverence for the mystery of Christ revealed through their bodies.

In speaking of the wife's subjection (or "submission") to her husband, the Holy Father affirms that the "author of Ephesians is not afraid to accept the concepts that were characteristic of the mentality and customs of that time.... Certainly, our contemporary sensitivity is different," the Pope observes, "and the social position of women in comparison with men is different" (TOB 89:5–6). But if we simply dismiss St. Paul's words because of modern sensitivities, we miss his evangelical genius altogether. Like any great evangelist, he seeks to inject the language and customs of his day with the Christian mystery.

Since the first chapter of his letter, the Apostle has been outlining the divine plan of man's salvation—that mystery hidden in the Father which has been made known through Christ's union with the Church. He has also been seeking to outline the vocation of those who are baptized into this mystery. According to John Paul, these are the *two main guiding lines* of the entire letter, and St. Paul's "classical" teaching on marriage appears at the meeting of these guiding lines (see TOB 88:3). The mystery of Christ's union with the Church and the vocation of Christians to "walk in love, as Christ loved us" (5:1–2) provide the interpretive key to Paul's teaching. This is *crucial* to a proper understanding of the passage.

The Apostle insists that those who accept their vocation in Christ "must no longer live as the Gentiles do, in the futility of their minds; they are darkened in their understanding, alienated from the life of God...due to their hardness of heart" (4:17–18). Then he exhorts his readers: "Put off your old nature which belongs to your former manner of life and is corrupt through deceitful lusts, and be renewed in the spirit of your minds, and put on the new nature, created after the likeness of God in true righteousness and holiness" (4:22–24). Do we not see here reference to that same "hardness of heart" and that same "lust" Christ referred to in his words about God's original plan for marriage and in the Sermon on the Mount? Do we not also see the call to a radical transformation of the conscience and attitudes of men and women according to the image and likeness of God in which they were made?

In light of the ethos of redemption, St. Paul's exhortation to husbands and wives takes on a whole new meaning. Indeed, it turns the typical interpretation (i.e., that St. Paul is justifying male domination) on its head. Knowing that male domination flows from sin (see Gen 3:16), the Apostle is actually calling husbands and wives to live according to God's original plan in which there was a perfect balance, complementarity, and equality between the sexes. Based on the Holy Father's exegesis, we might conclude that Paul is saying something like this to his readers: "You are accustomed to speaking of 'submission' within marriage. This means one thing to the Gentiles who are darkened in their understanding and corrupted by lust. But here is how this looks in light of the mystery of Christ. Here is what this means for the vocation of Christians."

Mutual Submission "Out of Reverence for Christ"

The first thing St. Paul calls spouses to do is to "submit to one another out of reverence for Christ" (5:21). John Paul emphasizes this passage in order to highlight the often overlooked fact that submission within marriage, according to St. Paul, is *mutual*. It is not, as often thought, a unilateral submission of the wife to the husband. At this point the questions multiply. What does it mean to "submit" to one another? And why out of reverence for Christ? Furthermore, does it not seem like Paul then stresses the wife's submission to her husband more than the husband to his wife? As we shall see, these questions can only be properly answered if we believe in "the gift." They can only be properly answered if we understand that the truth of masculinity and femininity lies in the sacramental ability of the body to convey the covenant relationship of God and man. "The gift" is the love the the Heavenly Bridegroom gives to humanity as Bride. But men and women must *believe* in the gift if they are to *receive* it and *recapitulate* it in their love for one another.

Remove this element of "gift" and, in relation to divinity, humanity can only assert itself in the face of a supposed tyranny. In turn, this same dynamic will be played out in the relationship of the sexes. "Submission" then means a self-abnegating surrender to domination, particularly in the relationship of the wife to the husband. Void of "the gift," the feminist revolt against Ephesians 5 is quite understandable. But we are not void of the gift! *The gift has been given in superabundance* through the "great mystery" of which Ephesians 5 speaks. But we must "believe in the good news" (Mk 1:15). We must reclaim the original meaning of the body—of masculinity and femininity—and the original way of living the body as a gift.

Recall one of John Paul's key statements from his reflections on Genesis: "This is *the body: a witness* to creation as a fundamental gift, and therefore a witness *to Love as the source from which this same giving springs.* Masculinity-femininity—namely, sex—is the original sign of...[God's] creative donation." At the same time, "man, male-female, becomes aware of [this sign] as a gift lived so to speak in an original way" (TOB 14:4).

The original way of living "the gift" was manifested in the perfect balance of love between the sexes as exhibited by the peace of original nakedness. As we all know from experience, however, original sin shattered this "original way." Concupiscence does not live the reality of gift. Instead, it appropriates and dominates the other. This is felt in a particularly pointed way by woman in relation to man. But through the power of the Holy Spirit, the author of Ephesians calls spouses to put off their old nature corrupted by lust and put on the new nature made in God's image (see 4:22–24). In other words, through the mystery of redemption, St. Paul calls spouses back to that "original way" of living the gift. And, as we have been learning throughout our study, there is *real power* flowing from the mystery of the redemption to empower spouses to reclaim God's original plan in their lives.[5]

From this perspective we come to understand with John Paul that to "submit" to one's spouse means to be "completely given" (TOB 90:2). In turn, mutual submission means "a reciprocal gift" of self (TOB 89:4). In other words, to submit to one another means to live the sincere gift of self "in everything" (v. 24) according to the spousal meaning of the body, of masculinity and femininity. This is the radical paradigm shift St. Paul calls for by informing the customs of his day (which concupiscence certainly influenced) with the mystery of Christ. In this way, John Paul says that Christian marriage, according to Ephesians, "excludes this element of the contract, which weighed on this institution and at times does not cease to weigh on it" (TOB 89:3). Husbands and wives are called to mutual subjection *out of reverence for Christ*. This means that their mutual relations should flow from their common relationship with Christ. They should flow from a profound and lived experience of the redemption of the body and, in this way, reclaim something of that original harmony of the beginning.

This reverence for Christ, John Paul points out, is analogous to "fear of the Lord" or piety. Such "fear" is not a defensive attitude before God as if he posed a threat. It is a gift of the Holy Spirit that inspires a profound respect for the holy, the sacred, and the expression of this gift is love (see TOB 89:1–3). The mystery of Christ is, in fact, inscribed in the very bodies of husband and wife and in their "one flesh" union. This is what makes marriage a sacred mystery. When "awe" for this mystery penetrates the spouses' hearts, it engenders in them that holy "reverence for Christ" and leads them to be "subject to one another." This confers a deep and mature character on the conjugal union (see TOB 89:2–4).

With Christ as both the source and the model of their subjection (of their giving), the Holy Father observes that the psychology and moral nature of the spouses is so transformed as to give rise to "a new and precious 'fusion'" of their relations and conduct (TOB 89:4).

---

5. See *CCC*, no. 1615.

Husband and wife become "fused" in this sense not only with one another but also with the Holy Spirit who inspires them to live the "sincere gift of self." Filled with the Spirit (see v. 18), husbands are inspired to love their wives "as Christ loved the church" (v. 25); and wives are inspired to be subject [or given] to their husbands "as the Church is subject to Christ" (v. 24).

The Spousal Analogy

Christian spouses must model their relationship after the relationship of Christ and the Church. According to the great "spousal analogy," the wife is an icon of the Church as Bride and the husband is an icon of Christ as Bridegroom. Hence we read: "Wives, be subject to your husbands *as* to the Lord. For the husband is the head of the wife *as* Christ is the head of the church" (vv. 22–23). John Paul stresses, "When he expresses himself in this way, the author does not intend to say that the husband is 'master' of the wife and that the interpersonal covenant proper to marriage is a contract of domination by the husband over the wife" (TOB 89:3). Recall that Christ says any proper leadership among his followers must *not* be modeled after the Gentiles who lord it over their subjects and make their authority felt. Instead, the "lord" must serve others in love and in self-sacrifice (see Lk 22:25–26).

St. Paul could not be clearer on this point when he says: "Husbands, love your wives *as* Christ loved the church." How did Christ love the Church? He "gave himself up for her" (v. 25). Christ said that he came not to *be* served but *to serve*, and to lay down his life for his Bride (see Mt 20:28). Thus, John Paul insists that the love to which St. Paul calls husbands clearly "excludes every kind of submission by which the wife might become a servant or slave of the husband, an object of one-sided submission. Love makes the *husband simultaneously subject* to the wife, and *subject* in this *to the Lord himself*, as the wife is to the husband" (TOB 89:4).

But one might still ask why St. Paul, having called spouses to a mutual subjection, subsequently specifies the wife's subjection to her husband, whereas he calls the husband to "love his wife." The Holy Father might respond that in this manner the Apostle maintains the complementarity of the sexes that is indispensable in living "the gift." Husband and wife are certainly called to a mutual subjection, but, according to the nature of sexual difference, each lives this subjection in different, complementary ways.

■ The feminist debate arises precisely here, in the admission that any fundamental and meaningful *difference* between the sexes exists. But, again, it arises only in a paradigm void of "the gift." In the face of man's historical domination of woman, many feminists think that the only way to claim their equality with men is to level sexual difference. They prefer words like "mutuality" to "complementarity" when discussing the interrelationship of the sexes. Of course, there is a proper place for "mutuality," such as in the expression "mutual self-donation." But the original call of mutual self-donation is only possible in and through the beauty, mystery, and complementarity of sexual *difference*. The point is that equality between the sexes does not and must not mean "sameness." As John Paul expresses, the equal dignity of man and woman results from their "specific diversity and personal originality.... Consequently, even the rightful opposition of women to what is expressed in the biblical words, 'He shall rule over you' (Gen 3:16) must not under any condition lead to the 'masculinization' of women." He continues, "In the name of liberation from male 'domination,' women must not...*deform and lose what constitutes their essential richness.*"[6] Tragically, by leveling sexual difference we also eradicate the spousal mystery proclaimed by our humanity. In other words, we blind ourselves to the theology of the human body in its maleness and femaleness.

Giving and Receiving the Gift

As John Paul states in his reflections on original man, the reality of gift "indicates the one who gives and the one who receives the gift, as well as the relation established between them" (TOB 13:4). The Pope is referring specifically to the covenant of creation established between God and man. But it also applies to the spousal relationship of man and woman that images and participates in God's covenant love with humanity. As John Paul expresses, in imaging the spousal mystery of

---

6. *Mulieris Dignitatem*, 10.

Christ's love for the Church, "*the husband* is above all *the one who loves* and the wife, by contrast, is *the one who is loved*" (TOB 92:6). In other words, it corresponds to the spousal meaning of the husband's body to "initiate the gift," whereas it corresponds to the spousal meaning of the wife's body to "receive the gift." This complementary, sacramental reality is written in our very anatomy—and, thus, because the body is the "sacrament" of the person, it is written in our very personality as male and female.

> ■ This giving and receiving of the gift is *not* to be equated with "activity" and "passivity." Nor is it correct to limit "giving" to the masculine and "receiving" to the feminine. Recall John Paul says that the "giving and accepting [of] the gift interpenetrate in such a way that the very act of giving becomes acceptance, and acceptance transforms itself into giving" (TOB 17:4). We could qualify the complementarity of the sexes in their giving and receiving, as Dr. William E. May expresses it, by stating that the man "gives in a receiving way," whereas the woman "receives in a giving way."[7]

Through our analysis it comes to light, as the Holy Father proposes, that "the wife's 'submission' to the husband, understood in the context of the whole of Ephesians 5:22–23, means above all 'the experiencing of love.' This is all the more so, because this 'submission' refers to the image of the submission of the Church to Christ, which certainly consists in experiencing his love" (TOB 92:6).

By drawing this analogy between spousal love and Christ's love for the Church, we realize that, despite modern sensitivities and cultural differences, the fundamental moral principle of the Letter to the Ephesians remains the same for all times and cultures. When properly understood and lived, the Pope observes that it always produces that deep and firm supporting structure of the true communion of persons in marriage (see TOB 89:6). It enables men and women to live the sincere gift of self stamped in the spousal meaning of their bodies. In this way, husband and wife, in their own complementary ways, image God and thus fulfill the very meaning of their being and existence.

---

7. See *Marriage: The Rock on which the Family Is Built* (San Francisco: Ignatius Press, 1995), p. 50.

Two Directions of the Spousal Analogy

As we are seeing, the sacramentality of marriage emerges in the Letter to the Ephesians via the spousal analogy of Christ's love for the Church. The Pope tells us that St. Paul inserts his teaching on marriage into *the very reality of the mystery* hidden from eternity in God and revealed to mankind in Jesus Christ. In this way we are "witnesses...of a particular encounter of this mystery with the very essence of the vocation to marriage" (TOB 89:7). This means that the sacramentality of marriage is not merely some holy thing tacked onto marriage as a natural institution. Marriage's participation in the divine mystery is of its very essence. Of course, in the strict sense of the term, marriage is only a sacrament when both spouses are already baptized in Christ. Yet even in the marriages of non-Christians there remains a "figure" in some sense of the primordial sacrament, a certain—even if not sacramentally efficacious—sign of Christ's union with the Church (see TOB 97:1).

John Paul observes that marriage clarifies and illuminates the mystery of Christ and the Church, at least to a certain degree. Yet at the same time, the mystery of Christ and the Church "*reveals the essential truth about marriage*" (TOB 90:2). Thus John Paul tells us that the spousal analogy operates in two directions. In analyzing the text of Ephesians 5, we must look at both.

When we reread St. Paul's analogy "inversely"—that is, beginning with Christ's relationship with the Church and then moving to husband and wife—we realize that "marriage, in its deepest essence, *emerges from the mystery* of God's eternal love for man and humanity: from the salvific mystery that Christ's spousal love fulfills in time for the Church" (TOB 90:4). As John Paul asserts, this means "that marriage corresponds to the vocation of Christians only when it mirrors the love that Christ, the Bridegroom, gives to the Church, his Bride, and which the Church...seeks to give back to Christ in return. This is the redeeming, saving love, the love with which man has been loved by God from eternity in Christ" (TOB 90:2).

This is quite a lofty calling. Who by his own strength can live this divine love? Only the grace of salvation makes it possible. And the sacrament of marriage affords precisely this. As John Paul says, marriage "is a revelation and realization in time of the mystery of salvation, of the election of love 'hidden' from eternity in God" (TOB 90:1). So once again we learn that "at the basis of the understanding of marriage in its very essence stands Christ's spousal relationship with the Church" (TOB 90:4). From the beginning, marriage found its *raison d'être* as a visible sign of the divine eternal mystery, as an image and foreshadowing of Christ's union with the Church. In this way, John Paul says that the Letter to the Ephesians leads us to *the very foundations of the sacramentality* of marriage.

Accordingly, we must conclude that in the spousal analogy St. Paul does not find merely a coincidental or extrinsic resemblance that affords a convenient way of making his point. This is not the wistful thinking of a dreamy evangelist. Instead, "one must admit," according to the Holy Father, "that the very essence of marriage contains *a particle of the...[divine] mystery*. Otherwise, this whole analogy would hang in a void." It "would be deprived of a real basis, as if it had no ground under its feet" (TOB 90:3). The cross of Christ is planted in the ground under the feet of this spousal analogy. Here we witness the totality of Christ's spousal love for the Church. "That gift of self to the Father through obedience to the point of death (see Phil 2:8) is at the same time, according to Ephesians, an act of 'giving himself for the Church.' In this expression, *redeeming love* transforms itself," the Pope says, "*into spousal love*: by giving himself for the Church, with the same redeeming act, Christ united himself once and for all with her as the Bridegroom to the Bride, as the husband with the wife" (TOB 90:6).

In this way we can see that "the mystery of the redemption of the body conceals within itself in some sense the mystery 'of the marriage of the Lamb' (see Rev 19:7)." Through the Bridegroom's sincere gift of self "the whole salvific gift of redemption penetrates the Church as the body...[of Christ], and continually forms the deepest essential substance of her life" (TOB 90:6). This is the mystery stamped in our bodies, in the gift of sexual difference and our call to become "one flesh." Hence, we can understand why in *Familiaris Consortio* John Paul describes spouses as "the permanent reminder to the Church of what happened on the cross." "Their belonging to each other," he says, "is the real representation, by means of the sacramental sign, of the very relationship of Christ with the Church."[8]

---

8. *Familiaris Consortio*, 13.

Head and Body Analogy

All of this is confirmed and deepened by the head and body analogy St. Paul also uses.[9] The Pope suggests that this analogy seems even more central to the Apostle in his proclamation of the truth about Christ's relationship with the Church. However, John Paul says we must equally affirm that St. Paul has not placed the head-body analogy next to or outside of the spousal analogy. In fact, the Apostle speaks as if in marriage the husband is also the "head of the wife" and the wife "the body of the husband" (see TOB 91:2). Thus, these two images are deeply interrelated, so much so that the one "passes over" into the other (see TOB 90:6). We see the link between these two analogies in the "one flesh" union the Apostle speaks of, quoting from Genesis. Speaking of the spousal relationship in terms of the head-body relationship, it is as if St. Paul is saying that spouses, in becoming "one body," are united so intimately as to form "one organic union"—one "organism" (see TOB 91:2, 3).

And since the body is the expression of human subjectivity, John Paul goes so far as to say that, by becoming "one body," spouses also become in some manner "*a single subject.*" The Apostle indicates this when he says, "He who loves his wife loves himself" (v. 28). The Holy Father quickly clarifies, however, that *this does not blur the spouses' individuality.* An essential and dominant "bi-subjectivity" always remains at the basis of "uni-subjectivity." Otherwise, spouses would be lost or swallowed up in the other, rather than finding their true selves through the sincere gift of themselves.[10]

We can see this distinction clearly in the relationship of Christ with the Church. John Paul states that there "is no doubt" that Christ is a subject different from the Church. Nonetheless, he is united with her in a particular relationship as in one organic union of head and body (see TOB 91:3), or, as the *Catechism* expresses, as "one mystical person."[11] Even so, the unity of Christ and the Church, like the unity of husband

---

9. See *CCC*, nos. 787–96.

10. These reflections are closely related with the themes of solitude being "prior" to unity (see pp. 92ff., 304), of double solitude as the foundation for unity (see p. 107), of unity-in-plurality (see p. 320), and of the rediscovery of a perfect subjectivity and intersubjectivity (see pp. 314–15, 317).

11. See *CCC*, nos. 795, 1119, 1474.

and wife, does not remove their distinction.[12] Precisely in the tension of unity-in-plurality, the trinitarian mystery is manifested in a real way, and man's own mystery is revealed to himself.

The Holy Father further specifies that the spouses' "uni-subjectivity" does not have a "real character" but only "intentional." It is a *unity through love* established not in an ontological sense but in a moral sense (see TOB 92:5). Still, in this moral sense, conjugal love is so unifying that it allows spouses "to interpenetrate each other, belonging spiritually to one another, to the point that the...'I' becomes in some way the 'you,' and the 'you' the 'I'" (TOB 92:7). In other words, spousal love makes the "I" (that is, the subjectivity) of the other person his own. The "wife's 'I,'" the Pope suggests, "becomes through love the husband's 'I'" (TOB 92:6). Hence, at the close of his passage, St. Paul reiterates that each husband is to "love his wife as himself" (v. 33).

As John Paul stresses, all of this is rooted in and expressed through the body. "The body is the expression of this 'I' and the foundation of its identity. The union of husband and wife in love expresses itself also through the body" (TOB 92:6). So, in loving their wives "as Christ loved the Church" (v. 25), husbands are to "love their wives as their own bodies" (v. 28). For this is how Christ loves the Church, which is his body. John Paul says that the body of the "other" becomes "one's own" in the sense that one cares for the welfare of the other's body as he cares for his own. "For no man ever hates his own flesh, but nourishes and cherishes it, as Christ does the church, for we are members of his body" (vv. 29–30). All of these references to the body (see vv. 23, 28, 29, 30, 31) find their logic in "the motif" of one flesh that Paul presents as a "great mystery." This *bodily love* that unites the spouses expresses the most general and at the same time the most essential content of the entire passage of Ephesians 5. This incarnate love signifies divine love. In this way, John Paul demonstrates that "bodily love"—far from being base or innately corrupt as often suspected—is meant to express "the language of '*agape*'" (TOB 92:7).[13]

---

12. *CCC*, no. 796.

13. See Pope Benedict XVI's encyclical *God Is Love*. See also *The Way of Love: Reflections on Pope Benedict's Encyclical* Deus Caritas Est (Ignatius Press, 2006), and Christopher West, *The Love That Satisfies: Reflections on Eros and Agape* (Ascension Press, 2007).

In *Love and Responsibility*, Karol Wojtyla offers a practical application for how a husband is to care for his wife's body as he does his own within the intimacy of marital relations. In the final chapter, entitled "Sexology and Ethics," the future pope tells us that if a man is truly to love his wife, "it is necessary to insist that intercourse must not serve merely as a means of allowing [his] climax." Love, he says, "demands that the reactions of the other person, the sexual 'partner,' be fully taken into account." He continues: "Sexologists state that the curve of arousal in woman is different from that in man—it rises more slowly and falls more slowly.... The man must take this difference between male and female reactions into account...so that climax may be reached [by] both...and as far as possible occur in both simultaneously." The husband must do this, Wojtyla insists, "not for hedonistic, but for altruistic reasons." In this case, if "we take into account the shorter and more violent curve of arousal in the man, [such] tenderness on his part in the context of marital intercourse acquires the significance of an act of virtue." Wojtyla is speaking here not so much of the "technique" of marital relations, but of an atmosphere of tenderness, communication, and affection that creates the proper "culture" of marital relations. This culture of love reflects Christ's tender, incarnate love for the Church.[14]

Sacredness of the Body

At the end of the Pope's reflections on the head-body analogy, he tells us that St. Paul's teaching in Ephesians 5 provides us with a profound sense of the *sacredness* of the human body in general, and especially in marriage (see TOB 92:8). We can already see from our analysis that St. Paul had a keen grasp of the human body's capacity to signify sacred mysteries—to convey theology. The head-body and groom-bride analogies he employs can carry the tremendous load he places on them because the human body, in the mystery of sexual difference and the call to union, "has been created to transfer into the visible reality of the world the mystery hidden from eternity in God, and thus to be a sign of it" (TOB, 19:4). From this perspective, St. Paul does not place

---

14. *Love and Responsibility*, pp. 272, 274, 275.

an excessive load on the body at all. God created the body to carry this "load." God created the body as a theology—as a visible sign of his own divine mystery.

This sign in no way exhausts the mystery; it is not a complete or adequate image. As stated previously, we must be careful never to reduce the spiritual and divine mystery to its physical and human sign. This would involve a heretical blurring between Creator and creature. Nonetheless, with that understood, the body is an *efficacious* sign and in a real way communicates the divine mystery it symbolizes.

Baptism Expresses Christ's Spousal Love for the Church

In examining the spousal character of Christ's love for the Church in Ephesians 5, we notice that the scope and goal of Christ's love is the Church's sanctification: "Christ loved the church and gave himself up for her, that he might sanctify her, having cleansed her by the washing of water with the word, that he might present the church to himself in splendor, without spot or wrinkle or any such thing, that she might be holy and without blemish" (vv. 25–27).

The Church understands this "washing of water" as a reference to Baptism. John Paul describes Baptism as "the first and essential fruit of Christ's gift of self for the Church" (TOB 91:6). In this way Baptism takes on a spousal character. It is "*the expression of spousal love*," the Pope says, "in the sense that it prepares the Bride (the Church) for the Bridegroom...[and] makes the Church the Bride of Christ" (TOB 91:7). Baptism, of course, is applied to individual persons. But within the spousal analogy, St. Paul speaks of this "washing" in reference to the Church as a whole. As John Paul affirms, "The spousal love of Christ refers to her, to the Church, every time that a single person receives in her the fundamental purification by Baptism. The one who receives Baptism becomes at the same time—by virtue of the redemptive love of Christ—a participant in his spousal love for the Church" (TOB 91:7).

To accent the spousal character of Baptism, the Pope points to an intriguing insight of various biblical scholars. They observe that the washing with water recalls the ritual of the nuptial bath, which at one time commonly preceded a wedding. This was an important religious rite, John Paul notes, even among the Greeks.[15]

---

15. See *CCC*, no. 1617.

Baptism, however, is only the beginning of our spousal relationship with Christ. St. Paul also points to Baptism's eschatological fulfillment when he speaks of the Church "in splendor without spot or wrinkle or any such thing" (v. 27). Christ will "present the Church to himself" in radiance. The Pope says that this "seems to indicate that moment of the wedding when the bride is led to the bridegroom already clothed in the wedding dress and adorned for the wedding." John Paul continues: "The quoted text highlights that the same Bridegroom, Christ, takes care to adorn the Bride, the Church, in order that she might be beautiful with the beauty of grace, beautiful in virtue of the gift of salvation in its fullness, already granted from the moment of the sacrament of Baptism" (TOB 91:8).

Physical Beauty as an Image of Holiness

It is significant, according to the Holy Father, that St. Paul presents the image of the Church in splendor *"as a bride all beautiful in her body"*—as a bride without spot, wrinkle, blemish, or "any such thing." This is certainly a metaphor, but the Pope pauses to demonstrate its eloquence in showing how deeply important the body is in the analogy of spousal love. According to John Paul, "spot" seems to signify ugliness and "wrinkle" growing old and senile (see TOB 92:2). Both terms, according to the metaphor, indicate not a defect of the body, but a defect of the spirit, a moral defect. The Pope also adds that, according to St. Paul, the "old man" signifies the man dominated by sin (see Rom 6:6). Therefore, Christ's redemptive and spousal love ensures "that the Church not only becomes sinless, but remains 'eternally young'" (TOB 92:2).

Recall that the body is the outward expression of the person. With this deeply integrated understanding of body and soul, St. Paul presents physical beauty as a sign of spiritual beauty. Spiritual beauty is goodness and purity—in a word, it is holiness. And what is holiness? Holiness "is measured according to the 'great mystery' in which the Bride responds with the gift of love to the gift of the Bridegroom."[16] Having received the Bridegroom's (Christ's) love, the Bride (each member of the Church as well as the Church understood as a corporate person) can

---

16. *Mulieris Dignitatem*, 27 (see also *CCC*, no. 773).

respond also with that same love. And this holiness is manifested *in the body*. Holiness, John Paul affirms, "permits man to express himself deeply with his own body, precisely through the 'sincere gift' of self." It is "in his body as man or woman [that] man senses himself as a subject of holiness" (TOB 19:5). For St. Paul, then, the physical beauty of the body without spot, wrinkle, or blemish is an image of the holiness to which we are all called as the Bride of Christ.

> ■ In our day and age, the desire for youthfulness and beauty has spawned its own religion. This false "cult of the body"[17] is saturated with a million and one "sacraments" that promise the "grace" of remaining forever young and attractive. Thousands of beauty aids promise skin without spot or wrinkle or "any such thing." Thousands of creams, soaps, scrubs, and medications pledge to free us from our blemishes. Thousands of other products—from power shakes to thigh-busters—guarantee to reshape our metabolisms and our figures in order to restore our shapeliness and youthful vigor. Untwist this distorted cult of bodily youth and beauty, and what do we have? Our desire for holiness; our desire for sanctification, for purity and innocence; our desire for heaven, where we will share in the radiant beauty and eternal youth of Christ's Bride.

By using the image of physical beauty to convey holiness, St. Paul shows a masterful understanding of the sacramentality of the body. For him, the human body indicates "attributes and qualities of the moral, spiritual, and supernatural order" (TOB 92:3). By virtue of this "sacramentality," St. Paul can explain the mystery of sanctification, the mystery of Christ's redemptive love, and the mystery of humanity's union with the divine all "through the likeness of the body and of the love by which the spouses...become 'one flesh'" (TOB 92:3).

Yet again we must clarify that this is not a wishful projection of the Apostle's ideals on the body and sexual union. The body and sexual union are *meant* to convey this. God inscribed this in our humanity by creating us as male and female and calling us to become "one flesh." It all proclaims the mystery of Christ—not adequately and perfectly, but

---

17. See *CCC*, no. 2289.

wonderfully, beautifully, and efficaciously. In this way we "see how deeply the author of Ephesians looks into sacramental reality when he proclaims the great analogy: both the union of Christ with the Church and the spousal union of man and woman in marriage are in this way illuminated by a particular supernatural light" (TOB 91:8).

The Husband Must Desire His Wife's Beauty

Using St. Paul's image of the Bride's beautiful body as a metaphor for holiness, and following the logic of the spousal analogy in which husbands and wives are to mirror the love of Christ and the Church, we discover a remarkable truth that helps us understand the attractiveness of the human body. Of course our attraction toward the body has been confused by concupiscence. If we are to understand beauty and attractiveness in its proper perspective, we must listen to that "echo" of God's original plan still deep within us; we must recognize the distortions of sin; and we must trust in the power of redemption to restore holiness in our lived experience of the body. With that in mind, let us open our hearts to absorb what the Holy Father has to say.

If Christ, in his self-giving love for his Bride, desires her beauty—that beauty of inner holiness which is also manifested in the body—then husbands, in loving their wives "as Christ loved the Church," must also desire their beauty. "Love binds the bridegroom (husband)," according to John Paul, "to be concerned for the good of the bride (wife); it commits him to desire her beauty and at the same time to sense this beauty and care for it" (TOB 92:4). Of what beauty is the Pope speaking? Calling us again, not to be merely more "spiritual" but more *incarnational*, John Paul adds: "What is at stake here is also visible beauty, physical beauty" (TOB 92:4). Precisely at this point we must recall the tension and conflict that exist between the manner of appreciating the beauty of the body for original man, and the manner of appreciating the beauty of the body for the man of concupiscence. Right in the crux of that tension the man of concupiscence is called to faith in the power of redemption.

We could say that for original man, the appreciation of the other's beauty was disinterested. In appreciating the beauty of Eve's body, Adam was not seeking his own gratification in any selfish or grasping way. He certainly took delight in her. But, without the least tinge of lust, he would have appreciated her beauty as a person created for "her own sake." He would have seen woman's beauty as a marvel and image of God's beauty. Nakedness without shame enables us to discern this. Likewise, the entrance of shame enables us to recognize a profound change in man and woman's understanding of and appreciation for the beauty of the other's body. A spark still flickers within us of that original, holy appreciation of the beauty of the body, but we must contend now with self-seeking. We have lost the self-mastery that afforded "the peace of the interior gaze" (see pp. 126ff., 189).

Woman feels the resulting pain of this distortion in a particularly keen way. It seems the beauty of woman is more often objectified and exploited in society. And men with their disordered attractions can seem more to blame at times for society's false standard of "beauty" than women. In turn, this illusory standard contributes to a deep-seated sense of inadequacy and even self-loathing in many women because they fail to meet it. And those women who come closer to society's impossible standard of beauty must continuously stake the claim of their own dignity in the face of men's lustful attractions in order to avoid constant degradation. In both situations, men fail to recognize, desire, appreciate, and care for the true beauty of woman.

> ■ Two personal stories might illustrate how grace can enable men to appreciate woman's true beauty. The first regards a woman who seemed to capture society's standard of beauty, and the other regards a woman who was far from it. Several years ago, during a Mass at the National Shrine of the Immaculate Conception, I noticed a very beautiful woman sitting a few pews ahead of me. At one point she casually flipped her red hair over her shoulder. Whoa! This gesture tapped into some deep well in my soul. It captured all that was so beautifully "feminine" about her. "Lord, what was *that*?" I prayed. Rather than repress the stirrings of my heart, I surrendered them to Christ so he could purify them and show me their true meaning. As I prayed, it dawned on me that the beauty of woman—if we have the purity to see it—lies in her being a living, incarnate symbol of heaven, of the New Jerusalem, of God's dwelling place. Through Mary, woman's womb has become the dwelling place of the Lord! And yes, when all is purified, man's desire to enter woman's gates seems to point in some way to his

desire to dwell in the house of the Lord. This is what purity of heart affords and how grace reorients us when we let it. The deepest truth of my attraction to this woman confirmed my desire for heaven. Some might suspect that my attraction to this woman during Mass would be a source of distraction—or worse, an occasion of sin. Yet as I allowed the distortions to be crucified, this woman helped me enter into true worship. She helped me understand what the Mass is all about. I realized that right then and there, in that basilica dedicated to Mary, I was already in "woman's womb," and I was about to witness the Word being made flesh. In this realization the words of John Paul II ring out: Christ instituted the Eucharist to express in some way "the relationship between man and woman, between what is 'feminine' and what is 'masculine.'"[18]

The next story is closely related. Several months later I was vacationing at the beach. Seeing many shapely, bikini-clad women, I found myself engaged in a lively battle to reclaim this heavenly vision of woman's body.[19] Then I noticed a very overweight woman, and my initial thought was, "Oh, what a relief. No struggle there." But then I realized that my reaction to her was simply another dimension of a distorted view of the person. *My heart sank.* The dignity of the person is so great that he—or, in this case, she—is never meant to be used as a means of selfish gratification. Again, in the case of this heavy woman, "No problem there." But wait! Is a person meant to be disregarded and discarded, pushed aside as if inconsequential? I did have a problem there: a big problem. *Oh the tragedy of being blinded by our culture and our own sin to the true dignity and beauty of every human being!* As I had been praying to see the true personal beauty in all of the "shapely" women at the beach, so too did I begin to pray to see the true personal beauty in all the "unshapely" women at the beach. Coming to do so is another dimension of our struggle to see others as Christ sees them. By God's grace I experienced a new level of integration

---

18. *Mulieris Dignitatem,* 26.

19. By telling this story, I do not mean to give license to those who might be so bound by lust that going to a beach would be an "occasion of sin." For the man bound by lust, the admonition "Turn away your eyes from a shapely woman" (Sir 9:5) retains all its wisdom (see p. 211ff.).

that day, a new level of purity of heart. Regaining the purity of our origins is a lifelong journey. It won't be completed until we reach the eschaton. But, as the *Catechism* says, "Even now...[purity of heart] enables us to see *according to* God...; it lets us perceive the human body—ours and our neighbor's—as a temple of the Holy Spirit, a manifestation of divine beauty."[20]

True Love Recognizes Woman's True Beauty

How, then, is that appreciation of beauty to which John Paul calls husbands to be lived out? Only to the degree that a man experiences freedom from the domination of concupiscence in Christ can he look beyond the illusory measures of beauty to woman's true beauty—a beauty in which *every* woman shares. It is the beauty of the human story, the beauty of the mystery of humanity. For, as John Paul says elsewhere, woman is "the archetype of the whole human race: she *represents the humanity* which belongs to all human beings, both men and women."[21] Woman's body, then, in a unique way—and even more particularly according to the personal characteristics of each woman—bears testimony to the original good of creation, the tragedy of the fall, and the hope of full redemption.

■ We see this preeminently in *the* woman—Mary, the Mother of God. Without a doubt, *this woman* is the most beautiful creature God has ever created. Her body radiates the glory of God, the splendor of holiness like no other body (next to Christ's own body, which, of course, originates from his mother's body). For, like no other human person, she lives in her body the mystery of the human drama of creation and redemption. As the *Catechism* expresses, "Mary goes before us all in the holiness that is the Church's mystery as the 'bride without spot or wrinkle.'"[22] In this sense we speak of Mary as "our hope." For she lives already in her body what we hope for—the fullness of redemption. In this light we can also understand the interconnectedness of Mary's

---

20. *CCC*, no. 2519.
21. *Mulieris Dignitatem*, 4.
22. *CCC*, no. 773.

Immaculate Conception and bodily Assumption into heaven. One who has received the fullness of redemption (Immaculate Conception) does not experience decay but lives the final resurrection "already" (Assumption).[23]

The husband who believes wholeheartedly in the human story (in other words, the husband who believes wholeheartedly in the Gospel) embraces his wife's humanity *as she is*. He sees even in her blemishes and disfigurations an "echo" of the beginning and the hope of eternal glory. Such a husband, the Pope says, "examines his bride attentively, as though in a creative loving restlessness, to find all that is good and beautiful in her." Good and beauty is what "he desires for her" (TOB 92:4). He desires that all that is good and beautiful in her would blossom and radiate through her body. This is what he *sees* in her. This *is* his wife's beauty—the radiation of her goodness. In this way he reclaims something of the original good of God's vision (see Gen 1:31).

The Holy Father even says that the husband's love in some sense "creates" the goodness that he sees in the one he loves. In this way the husband imitates the love of *the* Creator whose love "*gives rise to the good and is well pleased with the good*" (TOB 13:3). The husband's ability to see that good, the Pope continues, "is like a test of that same love and its measure" (TOB 92:4). In other words, the husband who does not recognize this good, this beauty in his wife, cannot be said to love his wife. In any case, he does not love his wife "as Christ loved the Church." All men, of course, will be found wanting in this regard. But when we are weak, then we are strong (see 2 Cor 12:10).

■   Is beauty definable? Is it not in the eye of the beholder? Certainly every man and woman—whether they meet the idealized standard of beauty or not—reflects something of the beauty of God. Granting this, why do we find some bodies more "attractive" than others? Research indicates that even infants will stare at an "attractive" face longer than an "unattractive" one.[24] What mystery

---

23. See *CCC*, no. 2853.

24. See Cathy Newman, "The Enigma of Beauty," *National Geographic* (January 2000): pp. 95–121.

of our humanity is revealed by the spectrum of physical appearances we find in the human family?

Obviously standards of beauty are deeply influenced by cultural conditioning. Even so, I would imagine every culture could relate, each in its own way, to a general scale of "normally attractive," "unattractive," and "very attractive." Extending the Pauline metaphor of physical beauty as an image of holiness, I would hazard the idea that within this scale or spectrum we see something of original man, historical man, and eschatological man. Furthermore, recognizing that Christ fully reveals man to himself, I would suggest that in this spectrum we can see something of a parallel in Christ's own life. Christ was *figured* to our "normally attractive" humanity in the Incarnation, *disfigured* by our sin in his passion, and *transfigured* by God's glory in his resurrection.

It seems in some way we all bear this spectrum in our bodies, some visibly emphasizing one element of the spectrum more than other elements. Yet recall the continuity in the human drama. In Christ, the "figure" of original man, the "disfigure" of historical man, and the "transfigure" of eschatological man are all one man, one mystery, which is the final Adam—and this one mystery is radiantly beautiful! We fail to see authentic human beauty when we fail to recognize how the body of historical man, with all its blemishes and disfigurations, contains the echo of the beginning and the hope of eternal glory. Without this "total vision of man"— with the final Adam's death and resurrection at the center of it all—real human beings are not beautiful. We much prefer fantastic images and air-brushed ideals. Without Christ at the center of the human drama, not only do we prefer fantasy, we actually become repulsed by the real. Many people who have indulged their fantasy in the illusionary world of pornography have found it terribly difficult to love the real flesh and blood they married.

Those who cannot love a person with blemishes grasp at glory. They fail to reckon with the "mystery of iniquity" and grope in some sense for eschatological man without the cross of history. Perfect human beauty will come, but not as the world desires. The radiance of the "spotless Bride" is given as a gift, but we must be willing to be *configured* to the whole Adam (Christ) in his figure, disfigure, and *then* his transfigure.

Spousal Love and the Eucharist

Covered with the blemishes, spots, and wrinkles of sin—Christ loved his Bride all the more. He saw her goodness, her beauty still, and longed to tell her of it by the testimony of his death on the cross. "God shows his love for us in that while we were yet sinners Christ died for us" (Rom 5:8). Thus, the husband who commits himself to "nourishing" and "cherishing" the beauty of his wife's body must give himself to her in the most disinterested way "as Christ does the Church" (v. 29). This is the measure of love, as St. Paul tells us and as the Pope reiterates.

According to many Scripture scholars, this "nourishment" the Apostle refers to is "a reference *to the Eucharist* with which *Christ, in his spousal love, 'feeds' the Church*" (TOB 92:8). In this way we glimpse how this nourishment (the Eucharist) indicates, even though in a muted tone, "the specific character of conjugal love, especially," the Pope observes, "of the love by which the spouses become 'one flesh'" (TOB 92:8).[25]

We will later return to the eucharistic character of marital love and conjugal union. It will profoundly influence the rest of John Paul's reflections on the body, specifically his reflections on *Humanae Vitae.* For now, the Pope merely states that the expressions of nourishment and caring for the body help us understand in a general way the dignity of the body and the moral imperative to care for its good. They also give us a profound sense of the sacredness of man and woman's relationship and their call to become "one flesh."

This Is a Great Mystery-Sacrament

In his audience of September 8, 1982 (TOB 93), the Holy Father launches into a specific analysis of the riches of sacramental theology. In one of the most interesting footnotes of the entire catechesis, John Paul helps us understand the multilayered texture of the word "sacrament" by tracing its history and usage.[26] This term "has traveled a long way in the course of the centuries" (TOB 93:5, n. 88). The journey begins with the Greek word "*mysterion*" (mystery), which in the Book of Judith referred

---

25. See *CCC*, no. 1621.
26. See *CCC*, no. 774.

to the king's secret military plans (see Jdt 2:2). In the Book of Wisdom (2:22) and in the prophecy of Daniel (2:27), however, "mystery" came to signify God's creative plans for man and the purpose that he assigns to the world. St. Paul's usage marks a turning point. For him "mystery" is not merely God's eternal plan, but the accomplishment on earth of that plan in Jesus Christ (see Eph 3:4; Col 2:2, 4:3).

It was not until the third century that the most ancient Latin versions of the Scriptures translated *mysterion* with the word "*sacramentum.*" Interestingly, this term originally referred to the military oath taken by the Roman legionaries. Tertullian pointed out that since these soldiers were initiated into a new form of life, made a commitment without reserve, and pledged faithful service even unto death, the term "sacrament" was fitting for those sacred rites of Christian initiation: Baptism, Confirmation, and Eucharist. St. Augustine emphasized that sacraments are sacred signs which contain and confer in some way what they symbolize. St. Thomas then further specified that not all sacred signs are sacraments, but only those signs that actually sanctify our humanity. From this point forward, the word "sacrament" was restricted to mean one of the seven sources of grace instituted by Christ.[27]

Recovering the Broader Meaning of "Sacrament"

Only in the last century have theologians sought to recover that broader and more ancient understanding of sacrament as the revelation and accomplishment of the mystery hidden in God from time immemorial. Although closely related, "mystery" and "sacrament" are not synonymous (see TOB 93:5). We can understand the relationship of "mystery-sacrament" in the tension of that "hidden-revealed" marvel that is God and his plan for humanity. Within this tension, "mystery" signifies primarily what is hidden, whereas "sacrament" signifies primarily what is revealed.[28] The *good news* of the Gospel is found precisely here, what has been *hidden* from time immemorial in God has been definitively *revealed* to us in Jesus Christ (see Rom 16:25–26).

---

27. See *CCC*, no. 1117.
28. See *CCC*, nos. 774, 1075. See also Gerard Beigel, *Faith and Social Justice in the Teaching of Pope John Paul II* (New York: Peter Lang, 1997), p. 35.

Yet, even so, in the age of the sacraments (that is, on this side of the final resurrection) this "hidden-revealed" tension will always remain. For the divine mystery so far exceeds the human capacity of comprehension that, as the Pope reminds us, "even after its proclamation (or revelation) it does not cease to be called 'mystery'" (TOB 93:5). "For now we see in a mirror dimly, but then face to face. Now I know in part; then I shall understand fully, even as I have been fully understood" (1 Cor 13:12).

John Paul speaks of the sacrament—or "sacramentality"—of the body in this broader sense. He points out that the Fathers of the Second Vatican Council also revived this meaning of the word when they described the Church in *Lumen Gentium* as "the universal sacrament of salvation." Earlier in the same document they proclaimed that the "Church is in Christ in the nature of a sacrament—a sign and instrument, that is, of communion with God and of unity among all men."[29] The Pope observes that the phrase "in the nature of a sacrament" was used to recover that broader sense of the term without confusing this with the seven sacraments (see TOB 94:6). Speaking in this way, the Council Fathers indicate that the Church, in her existence as Bride and Body of Christ, proclaims and accomplishes the mystery of salvation. This is the mystery hidden in God from eternity: that all members of the human race would live in fruitful communion with the Trinity and with one another through communion with Christ. This is the "great mystery" of spousal communion of which St. Paul speaks in Ephesians. This mystery, John Paul tells us, "is *'great' indeed*: as God's salvific plan for humanity, that mystery is in some sense the central theme of the whole of revelation, its central reality. It is what God as Creator and Father wishes above all to transmit to mankind in his Word" (TOB 93:2).

Keystone of the Spousal Analogy

As St. Paul indicates, marriage has participated in this "great mystery" as a sign and proclamation from the beginning. Hence, while the sacramentality of the Church is related to each of the seven sacraments,

---

29. *Lumen Gentium*, 1, 48; see also *CCC*, nos. 747, 774–76, 780, 1045, 1108, 1140.

we must recognize "that *the sacramentality of the Church remains in a particular relationship with marriage,* the most ancient sacrament" (TOB 93:7). This "particular relationship" comes to full light in verses 31–32 of St. Paul's marvelous passage. Directly following his words about the eucharistic gift through which Christ "nourishes" the Church with his own body, St. Paul references the original biblical call to spousal self-donation. "For this reason a man shall leave his father and mother and be joined to his wife and the two shall become one flesh" (v. 31). Then, in a stroke of inspired mystical illumination, St. Paul immediately links this to the eucharistic mystery of which he just spoke. The two becoming one flesh "is a great mystery, and I mean in reference to Christ and the church" (v. 32).

John Paul says that here St. Paul writes not only of the great mystery hidden in God, but also, and above all, of the mystery that Christ accomplishes through his act of redemptive-spousal love. In this act of love, Christ gives his body up for the Church and is thereby united with her "in a spousal way...as husband and wife are reciprocally united in marriage instituted by the Creator" (TOB 93:6). Thus, the Pope observes that the Apostle's reference to Genesis 2:24 is necessary not so much to recall the "one flesh" unity of spouses, but to present the mystery of Christ's union with the Church (see TOB 93:1).

This linking of the union of marriage with the union of Christ and the Church is, according to John Paul, "the most important point of the whole text, *in some sense its keystone*" (TOB 93:1). Only by comprehending this linking can we understand how Ephesians 5 "reveals man to man himself and makes his supreme calling clear." In this linking we witness God's salvific initiative toward man in the different phases of its revelation. St. Paul is speaking of the revelation of the "great mystery" in its *most ancient* phase according to Genesis 2:24 ("they become one flesh") and in the phase of "the fullness of time" (Gal 4:4) when Christ is united to the Church (see TOB 93:3). This "keystone" of Ephesians 5 *"unites, in God's salvific plan, marriage* as *the most ancient revelation* (and 'manifestation') of that plan in the created world *with the definitive revelation* and 'manifestation,' namely, the revelation that 'Christ loved the Church and gave himself for her' (Eph 5:25)" (TOB 93:1).

In this way "St. Paul highlights the continuity between the most ancient covenant...and the definitive covenant." God established the most ancient covenant "by constituting marriage already in the work of creation," according to Genesis 2:24. And he established the definitive covenant in Christ, who, "having loved the Church and given himself for her, unites with her in a spousal way, that is, corresponding to the image of spouses. This *continuity of God's salvific initiative*," the Pope concludes, "constitutes the essential basis of the great analogy contained in Ephesians" (TOB 93:3).

John Paul asks if St. Paul might be speaking of marriage as a sacrament in the sense that we understand sacraments today (i.e., the seven sacraments). He concurs, however, with the widespread opinion of biblical scholars and theologians that Paul is not. Nonetheless, John Paul says, it seems "that in this biblical text he speaks *about the bases of the sacramentality* of the whole of Christian life and in particular about the bases of the sacramentality of marriage." Even if he speaks of marriage as a sacrament in an indirect way, still he does so "in the most fundamental way possible" (TOB 93:4).

The Sacrament Proclaims and Accomplishes the Mystery

Recall that early in his catechesis John Paul said the words of Genesis 2:24—"they become one flesh"—would have "a broad and far-reaching perspective in God's revelation" (TOB 9:5). This broad and far-reaching perspective finds fulfillment in Ephesians 5:31–32. In view of the entire Bible, John Paul says that the words of Genesis 2:24 can be considered "the fundamental text on marriage" (TOB 93:1). Since these words are "constitutive of the sacrament of Marriage" (TOB 19:5), becoming "one flesh" never expresses merely the joining of two bodies. According to the Holy Father, this is a "'sacramental' expression, which corresponds to the communion of persons" (TOB 31:2).

Summarizing our above reflections, "sacrament" (in the broader and more ancient sense of the term) refers to the revelation of the divine mystery. The Pope adds that it also presupposes man's acceptance of the mystery by means of faith. At the same time, however, John Paul says that "sacrament" is something more than this. Sacramental reality is such that the mystery proclaimed is also effectively *accomplished* in those who believe. Man *really participates* in the mystery of divine life signified by the sacrament. "The sacrament consists in '*manifesting*' that *mystery in a sign* that serves not only to proclaim the mystery but also *to accomplish it* in man. The sacrament is a visible and efficacious sign of grace. It is a means for accomplishing in man the mystery hidden from eternity in God, about which Ephesians speaks" (TOB 93:5).

2. Sacrament and Mystery

Christ Reveals the Mystery Hidden for Ages in God

In his audience of September 15, 1982 (TOB 94), the Holy Father reflects once again on the first chapter of the Letter to the Ephesians. There St. Paul outlines the revelation of "the mystery...set forth in Christ" (1:9). The Pope tells us that in the rest of the letter, St. Paul exhorts those who have received this revelation and accepted it in faith to model their lives according to the truth they have received. This truth is not a concept but a person. This Truth is Jesus Christ.

The greater part of Paul's letter provides moral instruction (or *parenesis*). But John Paul stresses that the Apostle's moral instructions are intimately intertwined with the "great mystery" revealed in Christ. They are given to those in whom the grace of redemption is efficaciously at work by virtue of the sacraments, especially Baptism (see TOB 94:4). The point is that the moral life can never be divorced from life in Christ. Christian morality is not a sterile ethical code but a living ethos vivified by the resurrected life of Jesus Christ.

This indispensable truth has a particular bearing on the moral life of husbands and wives, since their union is a sign and actuation of the mystery of salvation. In that climactic moment of Ephesians 5:31–32, we learn that "the mystery hidden for ages in God" (3:9) was foreshadowed "from the beginning" in the union of Adam and Eve. But it is the New Adam who definitively reveals the mystery by leaving his Father in heaven and leaving the home of his mother on earth to "cleave to his wife" (the Church) and become "one flesh" with her. Christ is the meaning of embodiment. Christ is the meaning of morality. Christ is the meaning of marriage. Throughout this audience (and throughout the entire catechesis on the body), the Holy Father underscores *the centrality of Christ*.

Christ stands at the *heart and center* of the "great mystery" proclaimed by St. Paul. "In him—precisely in him—humanity has been eternally blessed 'with every spiritual blessing.'" When "this eternal mystery is realized in time, this is brought about also...in Christ and through Christ. Through Christ the mystery of divine Love is revealed. Through him and for him it is accomplished" (TOB 94:5). We have been chosen in Christ to "be holy and blameless before him"; to be part of God's family; to be adopted as "his sons through Jesus Christ." This is possible despite humanity's fall because we now "have redemption through his blood, the forgiveness of our trespasses, according to the riches of his grace which he lavished upon us." This is "the mystery of [God's] will"; this is his "plan for the fullness of time": to "unite all things in [Christ]" (Eph 1:3–5, 7–10).

The Mode of Gift and the Veils of Faith

This eternal mystery is accomplished in time in the mode of "gift"—the gift God gives to man in Jesus Christ. St. Paul likens this divine gift to the gift of spouses who through mutual self-donation become "one flesh."[30] In Ephesians 5, the "supernatural *gift of the fruits of the redemption* accomplished by Christ gains the features of a spousal gift of self by Christ himself to the Church according to the likeness of the spousal relationship between husband and wife. Thus, not only the fruits of redemption are a gift, but above all Christ himself is a gift: he gives himself to the Church as to his Bride" (TOB 94:5).

John Paul says that when we accept the gift offered to us through faith in Christ, we really become sharers in the eternal mystery, even though it works in us under the veils of faith. The "veils of faith" can also be described as the veils of sacramental signs. For, as John Paul said in his previous audience, participation in the eternal plan of God "is accomplished in a mysterious way, under the veil of a sign; nevertheless, that sign always 'makes visible' the supernatural mystery that is at work in man under its veil" (TOB 93:5).

Various saints have observed that God veils his mystery in sacramental signs out of mercy, for if we saw his glory as he is we would die. No one can see God's glory and live (see Ex 33:20). But herein lies our privileged calling. God's gift to us is his own self-disclosure, his own self-communication. We shall see his face and live! Indeed, we are

---

30. See *CCC*, no. 772.

called with "unveiled face," St. Paul tells us, to behold the glory of the Lord. This vision transforms us into God's likeness "from one degree of glory to another" (2 Cor 3:18).

Through this ongoing transformation we reclaim and experience the sacramentality of our bodies. Even if it does so in a veiled way, the human body is meant to proclaim God's eternal mystery. The more we are transformed "from glory to glory" according to the likeness of God, the more we can see the divine mystery stamped in our bodies—in every*body*. Furthermore, we come to understand, just as spouses come to experience, that the communion of male and female in "one flesh" participates in God's glory as well. All that St. Paul illuminates in this regard builds on the analogy of spousal love from the Old Testament.

The Spousal Analogy: From the Old Testament to the New

The Holy Father reminds us of many passages from the Old Testament that employ the spousal analogy in order to help us better understand the context in which St. Paul speaks. Isaiah, Hosea, and Ezekiel speak of God's love for Israel in spousal terms. Furthermore, the vivid celebration of eros in the Song of Songs has long been understood as an image of God's love for his people (see TOB 94:7).

St. Paul preserves the Old Testament analogy of spousal love while transforming it and deepening it according to the "great mystery" now revealed through Christ's union with the Church. This "*christological and ecclesiological dimension*," John Paul says, "was present only in embryonic form" in the Old Testament. It was "something merely foreshadowed." But what was "barely outlined," only "half-open," is now "fully unveiled" in the Letter to the Ephesians. Fully unveiled, but of course, the Pope reminds us, "without ceasing to be a mystery" (TOB 95:7).

Your Maker Is Your Husband

To show the continuity and development of the spousal analogy from the Old to the New Testament, John Paul II devotes an entire audience (TOB 95) to analyzing the following text from Isaiah in light of that classic passage from Ephesians 5.

[Y]ou will forget the shame of your youth, and the reproach of your widowhood you will remember no more. For your Maker is your husband, the LORD of hosts is his name; and the Holy One of Israel is your Redeemer, the God of the whole earth he is called. For the LORD has called you like a wife forsaken and grieved in spirit, like a wife of youth when she is cast off, says your God. For a brief moment I forsook you, but with great compassion I will gather you,...with everlasting love I will have compassion on you, says the LORD, your Redeemer.... For the mountains may depart and the hills be removed, but my steadfast love shall not depart from you, and my covenant of peace shall not be removed, says the LORD, who has compassion on you. (Is 54:4–8, 10)

The Pope states that this text "has a theological content of extraordinary richness" (TOB 95:4). "These words overflow with the authentic ardor of love," he says. And this "is perhaps the strongest 'declaration of love' by God, joined with a solemn oath of faithfulness forever." Furthermore, these words indicate "the true *character of the gift* that God's love is for Israel." It is "a gift coming entirely from God's initiative...indicating *the dimension of grace*, which is contained in this love from the beginning" (TOB 95:3).

▬ Recall that God's initiative as Bridegroom and humanity's response as Bride are essential in understanding how the bodies of male and female reveal the spousal mystery. The spousal meaning of the man's body calls him to image God's initiation of the gift, whereas the spousal meaning of the woman's body calls her to image humanity's receptivity and response to the gift. This is why the Pope describes woman as the "archetype of the whole human race."[31] Of course this does not mean that it is "wrong" for wives to initiate the gift of self. It is also crucial that husbands learn how to receive and respond. Even so, since the body is the revelation of the person, initiation and receptivity speak not only of male and female anatomy but also of male and female personality. It is not mere social convention, for example, that men most often propose marriage to women. It speaks of the masculine call to image God in the initiation of the gift. Whatever resistance we might have to this truth ultimately stems, it seems, from a failure to believe in and live the reality of gift. As soon as the element of the "sincere gift" is removed, the initiation

31. *Mulieris Dignitatem*, 4.

of God and, in turn, the initiation of the male, is seen (understandably so) as a threat. In turn, woman retreats (understandably so)
from her natural receptivity.

John Paul comments that the "shame of your youth" and the
"reproach of your widowhood" mentioned by Isaiah indicates the mentality of the time when it was disreputable for a marriageable woman to
remain unmarried (see TOB 95:3). While the Holy Father does not
mention this, we might also recognize an echo of that shame of Eden
which man and woman experienced having broken their covenant with
God. Only through the love of our Redeemer and the restoration of the
covenant can a man and woman regain something of that original
vision of the body that enables them to "forget" their shame. Indeed,
authentic love "swallows shame," as Wojtyla expresses it.[32]

From Isaiah to Ephesians: New Aspects of Revelation

Comparing the text of Isaiah with that of Ephesians, we certainly
recognize a continuity, but we also recognize "new revealed aspects"—
the trinitarian, christological, and eschatological moments (see TOB
95:6). Isaiah obviously could not consciously speak to these new
aspects. God as a Trinity of Persons; Christ as the Incarnate Son,
Bridegroom, and Redeemer; and the ultimate consummation of the
spousal mystery in which Christ's Bride will be "holy and blameless
before him" (Eph 1:4) are realities only revealed in their fullness in the
historical event of Christ. From this perspective, St. Paul can distinguish the work of the Father, the Son, and the Holy Spirit throughout
his letter in a way that Isaiah could not.

In fact, John Paul points out that in Ephesians St. Paul presents the
mystery hidden for ages in God first in the dimension of fatherly love
rather than conjugal love (see TOB 95:5). The Father "destined us in
love to be his sons through Jesus Christ, according to the purpose of his
will" (Eph 1:5). Of course the prophets also spoke of the fatherhood of
God (see Hos 11:1–2; Is 64:8; Mal 1:6). But what Isaiah did not and
could not know in speaking of God as Redeemer was that the "figure of
the Redeemer is...proper to him who is the first 'beloved Son' of the

---

32. *Love and Responsibility*, p. 181.

Father (Eph 1:6)" (TOB 95:6). According to John Paul, God as "husband" in some way parallels God as "Redeemer." Christ the Redeemer is the heavenly Bridegroom. Without knowing the full implications, Isaiah himself spoke to this reality. In fact, Isaiah uses the analogy of spousal love only when the Creator and the "Holy One of Israel" is manifested as Redeemer.

Thus the Holy Father observes that St. Paul no longer repeats: "your Maker is your Husband." Instead, St. Paul reveals Christ the Son as Redeemer and Bridegroom. Christ's salvific love "consists in his gift of self for the Church." In this way St. Paul reveals redemptive love as *"a spousal love by which he [Christ] marries the Church* and makes her his own Body" (TOB 95:7). Thus John Paul says that Christ's gift of self for the Church is equivalent to carrying out the work of redemption. In this way the "Creator Lord of hosts" spoken of by Isaiah becomes the "Holy One of Israel" as her Redeemer. But John Paul adds that in this case, we are speaking of "the new Israel," the Church (see TOB 95:6). Here we see the continuity and the deepening of the spousal analogy from the Old Covenant to the New Covenant.

The Reality of the Gift, the Meaning of Grace

Through the different phases of the spousal analogy—from the embryo of the Old Covenant, to the full revelation of the New—we come to see both the full extent and limitations of this analogy. John Paul believes that "the analogy of conjugal or spousal love helps us to penetrate into the very essence of the mystery"—but, of course, only "up to a certain point" and only "by way of analogy." The Pope continues: "It is obvious that the analogy of earthly...spousal love cannot offer an adequate and complete understanding of that absolutely transcendent Reality, the divine mystery.... *The mystery* remains *transcendent with respect to this analogy* as with respect to any other analogy with which we try to express it in human language" (TOB 95b:1).[33] That being said, the Pope believes that the "analogy of spousal love contains a characteristic of the mystery that is not directly emphasized by...any other analogy used in the Bible" (TOB 95b:3). He also mentions that this even includes the analogy of fatherly love.

---

33. See *CCC*, nos. 42, 239, 370.

What specific characteristic does John Paul mean? "The analogy of spousal love," he says, "allows us in some way to understand the mystery...as the love proper to a total and irrevocable gift of self by God to man in Christ" (TOB 95b:2). John Paul points out that this is a question of "man" both in the personal and in the communal sense. Isaiah expresses the community dimension as "Israel" and St. Paul expresses it as "Church." In both cases these terms indicate a *"reduction of the community to the person"*—Israel and the Church are considered as "Bride-person" in relation to the "Bridegroom-person" (Yahweh and Christ). Thus every "concrete 'I' must find itself in that biblical 'we'" (TOB 95b:2). That biblical "we" is the one Bride who has received God's irrevocable gift of self.

John Paul says that this gift of God to man is certainly "radical" and therefore "total." He adds, however, that we cannot speak of this "total" giving of God to man in its transcendental fullness. As a creature, man cannot receive divinity as such. Such a "total" and uncreated gift "is shared only by God himself in the 'trinitarian communion of Persons'" (TOB 95b:4). Nevertheless, through God's gift of self—which by virtue of the Incarnation is a bodily gift and, analogously, a spousal gift—we do *participate in the divine nature* (see 2 Pet 1:4). As the Eucharistic Prayer indicates, we "come to share in the divinity of Christ who humbled himself to share in our humanity." According to this measure, God's self-gift *is* "total" in that he gives all that he *can* give of himself to us considering our limited faculties as creatures.

The Single "Great Sign" Communicates the Radical Character of Grace

In this way the spousal analogy, like no other analogy in the Bible, indicates the radical character of grace (see TOB 95b:4). Recall that in this chapter the Pope is unfolding marriage in the divine dimension of "covenant and grace." Here John Paul says that the analogy of marriage—as a human reality that *incarnates* spousal love—helps us *understand the mystery of grace* both as an eternal reality in God and as a historical fruit of mankind's redemption in Christ. But recall that the analogy works in two directions. Marriage not only illuminates the divine mystery (of grace), but the divine mystery also defines the proper way in which to understand marriage. For we see in marriage, according to all we have been learning through John Paul's catechesis, the *image and likeness of the divine Mystery* (see TOB 95b:5).

"By presenting the relationship of Christ with the Church according to the image of the spousal union of husband and wife, the author of...[Ephesians] speaks...about the realization of the eternal divine mystery" within time. But he also speaks "about the way in which that *mystery* has expressed itself in the visible order, about the way it has *become visible* and thereby *entered into the sphere of the Sign*" (TOB 95b:6). By "sign" John Paul simply means the visibility of the Invisible (see TOB 95b:7). According to St. Paul, two intimately related "signs" make the divine Reality visible. The union of husband and wife is the most ancient sign of the mystery. And the union of Christ and the Church is the definitive sign of this mystery revealed in "the fullness of time." John Paul credits St. Paul with "a particular merit" for bringing "these two signs together, making of them *the single great sign*, that is, *a great sacrament*" (TOB 95b:7).

Here we find the surest foundation for speaking of the eucharistic —or "liturgical," as John Paul will later say (see TOB 117b)—nature of marital love and of the "spousal" nature of the Eucharist. The love of husband and wife (consummated when the two become "one flesh") and the love of Christ and the Church (consummated sacramentally in Eucharistic Communion) are so intimately related as to form, according to St. Paul and as John Paul II expresses, a *"single great sign."* This sign not only reveals to man the mystery hidden for ages in God that all would be one in Christ (see Eph 3:9, 1:10). It also accomplishes this oneness in man.

Conjugal Union in Light of the Incarnation

Since this linking of the union of husband-wife and Christ-Church is the most important point and "keystone" of the entire text, we should try to penetrate even further the interrelationship of these two "signs" that form the "one great sacrament." The Pope has already described the conjugal union of spouses as the original and "most ancient" revelation of the mystery. Given this, his following statement might seem odd. The Holy Father asserts that the divine Mystery "became visible first of all *in the historical event itself of Christ*" (TOB 95b:7). The words "first of all" are puzzling within the confines of historical chronology.

However, by recalling the first sentence of John Paul II's first encyclical, we solve the puzzle: "The Redeemer of man, Jesus Christ, is *the center of the universe and of history.*"[34]

History is measured by Christ. In a sense, history does not begin "in the beginning" and move forward in time. The human drama, we could say, "begins" with the Incarnation at *its center* and moves outward in both directions. The point here is that, as Pope Leo XIII said in his encyclical on marriage, the "one flesh" union of man and woman "has been even from the beginning a foreshadowing of the Incarnation of the Word of God."[35] Conjugal union, therefore, can only be fully understood in light of Christ's union with the Church. For it is the "relationship of Christ to the Church," John Paul emphasizes, which "constitutes the fulfillment and concretization of the visibility of the same mystery" (TOB 95b:7). Looking backward in time from the vantage point of Christ's incarnate union with the Church, John Paul says our attention turns "toward what we presented previously—in the context of the very mystery of creation—as the 'visibility of the Invisible,' toward the very 'origin' of man's theological history" (TOB 95b:7).

Here John Paul wants us to recall his thesis: "The body, in fact, and only the body, is capable of making visible what is invisible: the spiritual and the divine. It has been created to transfer into the visible reality of the world the mystery hidden from eternity in God, and thus to be a sign of it" (TOB 19:4). This sacramental understanding of the body is constituted by means of man's visible masculinity and femininity. Therefore, the body also communicates the mystery "through the conjugal union of man and woman when they unite with each other so as to form 'one flesh.'" In this way, through the unity of masculinity and femininity, John Paul tells us that the body "takes on the value of a sign, in a certain sense a sacramental sign" (TOB 45:2).

The Foundation of the Sacramental Order

Now a key text of the Holy Father's comes to light—a text that in some way captures the full weight of glory that the Pope believes God has ascribed to marriage and to the consummate union of spouses.

---

34. *Redemptor Hominis*, 1, emphasis added.
35. *Arcanum*.

"One can say," John Paul asserts, "that the visible sign of marriage 'in the beginning,' inasmuch as it is linked to the visible sign of Christ and the Church on the summit of God's saving economy, *transposes* the eternal plan of love *into the 'historical' dimension* and makes it *the foundation of the whole sacramental order*" (TOB, 95b:7). This is one of those stunning statements that the Pope plants in his catechesis without commentary. It is destined to become one of those texts that theologians chew on for centuries, only gradually unpacking its implications.

If the union of Christ and the Church is "on the summit of God's saving economy," we might say that at the trailhead marking the path to this summit, we have marriage and its consummate expression of conjugal intercourse. Inasmuch as this "trailhead" points to the summit, the visible sign of marriage is the foundation upon which God reveals and actuates his hidden designs—revealing his plan for man and for the universe that all things in heaven and on earth might be "one" in fruitful union with Jesus Christ (see Eph 1:10). This is the deepest essence and meaning of human embodiment, of erotic desire, and of spousal love. They are meant to point us to Christ and to God's hidden designs for the universe. Thus, inasmuch as the spousal union points us (analogically) to Christ's union with the Church, the visible sign of marriage constitutes *"the foundation of the whole sacramental order"*—that order by which God *incarnates* his own mystery, making it visible in the order of "signs" in order to communicate it to incarnate men and women.

Perhaps now we can sense with what awe and reverence St. Paul referred to the "one flesh" union as "a great mystery." Perhaps now we can better understand what St. Paul means when he calls spouses to submit to one another *out of reverence* for Christ. Words fail when we come in contact with such a mystery. It seems the only proper response is silence offered as praise and tears offered in reparation for the desecration of this sacramental mystery so prevalent in our world and often in our own hearts.

Marriage as the Primordial Sacrament

In his audience of October 6, 1982 (TOB 96), John Paul begins to reexamine marriage's "beginning" in light of what we have learned in Ephesians about the "great mystery." The Pope says that the Letter to the Ephesians authorizes us to do this because the Apostle himself refers to the "beginning." He refers specifically to the words of Genesis 2:24, which instituted marriage as a sacramental reality right from the beginning. The Holy Father wants to return to these words regarding the "one flesh" union in order to understand better how they illuminate marriage as the primordial sacrament.

"Ephesians opens before us the supernatural world of the eternal mystery, of the eternal plans of God the Father in regard to man. These plans," the Pope reminds us, "precede the 'creation of the world' and thus also the creation of man. At the same time, these divine plans begin to be realized already in the whole reality of creation" (TOB 96:3). This sheds new light on the nature and origin of the grace of original innocence. "Ephesians leads us to approach this situation— man's state before original sin—from the point of view of the mystery hidden from eternity in God" (TOB 96:2). According to this mystery, God chose us in Christ *not only after we sinned* and in order to redeem us from sin. God chose us in Christ "before the foundation of the world" (Eph 1:4). This means that "before sin...man carried in his soul the fruit of eternal election in Christ" (TOB 96:4).

It seems that John Paul cannot stress this point enough. Comparing the testimony of the "beginning" with the testimony of Ephesians, he says that "we must deduce that *the reality of the creation of man* was already *permeated* by the perennial election of man in Christ.... From the 'beginning,' man, male and female, shared in this supernatural gift." And again he says that this supernatural endowment in Christ "took place before original sin" (TOB 96:4, 5). Rereading the account of creation in light of the New Testament, we realize that man's destiny in Christ is already implied in his creation in the image of God. For it is Christ who "is the image of the invisible God." Thus, it is in Christ that we image God right from the beginning (see Col 1:15–16).[36]

With these statements, the Holy Father appears to be adding his input to a centuries-old theological debate: Would Christ have come had man not sinned? In any case, John Paul II's opinion on the matter seems clear. For him, Jesus Christ—the *incarnate* Christ—"is *the center of the universe and of history.*"[37] For him, it seems even to entertain

---

36. See *CCC*, nos. 280, 1701.
37. *Redemptor Hominis*, 1, emphasis added.

the idea of a universe without an incarnate Christ is to miss the central point of the "great mystery" of God's love for humanity.[38]

Christ is "the first-born of all creation" (Col 1:15). Everything— especially man in his original unity as male and female—was created for him, through him, and in expectation of him. When we reread man's beginning in view of the "great mystery" of Ephesians, we can see that Christ's *incarnate* communion with the Church is already antici- pated and in some sense "contained" and communicated in the *primor- dial sacrament*—in the original incarnate communion of man and woman in marriage. And this original unity in "one flesh" was consti- tuted by God *before* sin. Man and woman's original unity, therefore, was a beatifying participation in grace (see p. 140). This grace made original man "holy and blameless" before God. Here John Paul reminds us that their primordial (or original) holiness and purity were also expressed in their being naked without shame (see TOB 96:4). The Holy Father then asserts that this original bounty was granted to man in view of Christ, who from eternity was "beloved" as Son, "although—according to the dimensions of time and history—it preceded the Incarnation" (TOB 96:5).

If this is the case, the Incarnation is not an afterthought—a second plan intended to rectify the first, supposedly thwarted when man sinned. Of course sin put man on a major detour, one might say, in real- izing God's plan. But sin is not an insurmountable roadblock. Sin is not more powerful than God's eternal plan to unite us with Christ. God's plan for man and for the universe continues in spite of sin.

The grace of original innocence, John Paul tells us, "was brought about precisely *out of regard for...[Christ]*, while chronologically antici- pating his coming in the body" (TOB 96:5). And, recalling our reflections on Genesis, that grace was given "irrevocably, despite the subsequent sin and death" (TOB 16:2). It is true that man lost this grace as a result of sin. The entrance of shame attests to this. But he did not lose it forever. Christ's resurrection bears witness that the grace of the mystery of creation becomes, for anyone open to receiving it, the grace of the mystery of redemption (see TOB 46:5). "Redemption was to become the source of man's supernatural endowment after sin and, in a certain sense, despite sin" (TOB 96:5). In this way God's eternal plan

---

38. See *CCC*, nos. 280, 381, 653.

for man—remaining the same yesterday, today, and forever—is definitively accomplished in his beloved Son.

John Paul wants to stress the *continuity* between God's plan in the mystery of creation and his plan in the mystery of redemption. But at the same time we can deduce a "new" dimension to God's self-gift—the revelation of his mercy.[39] After sin, in order to fulfill "the mystery hidden for ages in God" (Eph 3:9), Christ would first have to reconcile man to the Father. This means that his Incarnation and his bodily gift of self would now entail his suffering and death. "In him we have redemption through his blood, the forgiveness of our trespasses" (Eph 1:7). This forgiveness is essential to Christ's mission. Still, it is not the only purpose of his mission. Forgiveness of our sins is only part of "the riches of his grace which he lavished on us" (Eph 1:7–8). One might call it the necessary prerequisite for the fulfillment of God's eternal plan for us "to be his sons through Jesus Christ" (1:5). From the perspective of the spousal analogy, if spouses have been at enmity with each other, they must first reconcile before they reunite in "one flesh." Christ's self-gift on the cross is the reconciliation of estranged spouses that opens the way for their eternal consummate communion.

Let us recap the themes expressed above. The eternal plan of God the Father is to unite us in an incarnate communion with Christ. These plans precede the creation of the world and therefore also our creation as male and female. Furthermore, man's sin did not and could not thwart God's plan. The Father continues to carry out the mystery of his will to unite all things in Christ despite sin. John Paul asks: "*In what way can one verify the reality of the sacrament,* of the primordial sacrament, in this context?" (TOB 96:6) We will now seek to answer this question.

The Body Pervaded by Grace

The Holy Father says that the following phrases sum up his entire analysis of the creation accounts in Genesis. He quotes himself: "Man appears in the visible world as the highest expression of the divine gift, because he bears within himself the inner dimension of the gift. And with it he carries into the world his particular likeness to God.... A

---

39. See *Dives in Misericordia*, 7.

reflection of this likeness is also the primordial awareness of the spousal meaning of the body pervaded by the mystery of original innocence" (TOB 96:1; 19:3).

God *is* "Gift" just as "God *is* Love" (1 Jn 4:8). Man is the highest expression of the divine gift in the visible world because he is created as a person who is called *from within* to love. This is "the inner dimension of the gift." But in the perfect integration of body and soul, this "inner dimension" is also manifested outwardly in the body—in the spousal meaning of the body. To say that their awareness of the spousal meaning of the body was "pervaded by the mystery of original innocence" is to say that their experience of the body was "pervaded by grace." This is that grace of election in Christ which was already granted in the mystery of creation. The effect of that grace is, as John Paul says (quoting again from his earlier catechesis on Genesis), that "in his body as man or woman, man senses himself as a subject of holiness [TOB 19:5]. 'He senses himself' and he is from 'the beginning'" (TOB 96:6).

And what is holiness? "The holiness of God is the inaccessible center of his eternal mystery."[40] Human holiness is our participation in this mystery enabled by God's utterly gratuitous gift of himself to us. Therefore, human holiness is measured according to the response of the Bride (man) to the gift (grace) of the Bridegroom (Christ). In turn, holiness "permits man to express himself deeply with his own body...precisely through the 'sincere gift' of self" (TOB 19:5). In this way we see how the *invisible* divine reality of gift-grace-holiness (in a word, love) was originally made *visible* through the human body and in the incarnate self-gift of man and woman to each other. Therefore the Holy Father adds that the holiness that the Creator conferred originally on man pertains to what he calls the "sacrament of creation."

The Sacrament of Creation

When John Paul speaks of the "sacrament of creation," he indicates that all of the created universe in some way makes the invisible mystery of its Creator visible. As the psalmist proclaims: "The heavens are telling the glory of God" (Ps 19:1). The sacrament of creation reaches its highest expression in the crown of creation: man, male and female.

---

40. *CCC*, no. 2809.

Man, in turn, reaches his fulfillment through the sincere gift of self, which was realized in an original way through that rich personal union of man and woman in "one flesh." It is the *incarnate communion* of man and woman that in some way sums up or *consummates* the "sacrament of creation" (see p. 152).

The Holy Father expresses this when he says: "*The words of Genesis 2:24*, 'the man will...unite with his wife, and the two will be one flesh,'...*constitute marriage as an integral part* and in some sense the central part of the '*sacrament of creation.*'... In this sense," the Pope concludes, marriage "is the primordial sacrament" (TOB 96:6). Quoting himself again, John Paul reminds us that the primordial sacrament is to be "understood as a sign that efficaciously transmits in the visible world the invisible mystery hidden in God from eternity. And this is the mystery of Truth and Love, the mystery of divine life, in which man really participates" (TOB 96:1; 19:4). Thus, John Paul tells us that the "*institution of marriage*, according to the words of Genesis 2:24, expresses not only the beginning of the fundamental human community." At the same time "*it expresses the Creator's salvific initiative*, which corresponds to man's eternal election [in Christ] spoken about in Ephesians" (TOB 96:7).

Here we reach the summit of the "great mystery" of our creation as male and female and our call to become "one flesh." Here we touch the deepest essence of the body and of spousal union *as theology*. It is this: When we allow the grace of redemption to "untwist" what is disordered in our sexuality, we realize that our entire incarnate personalities as male and female—lived in the current of our erotic desire for union—proclaim, express, and summon us to receive as utter "gift" our eternal election in Jesus Christ. This election invites us to *participate* in the glory of the divine self-giving for all eternity. This divine life of triune self-giving is "the mystery hidden from eternity in God." And this is what the body—through its visible masculinity and femininity—proclaims and in what it summons us to participate. Once again, the Pope recalls his thesis:

> The sacrament, as a visible sign, is constituted with man, inasmuch as he is a "body," through his "visible" masculinity and femininity. The body, in fact, and only the body, is capable of making visible what is invisible: the spiritual and the divine. It has been created to transfer into the visible reality of the world the mystery hidden from eternity in God, and thus to be a sign of it. (TOB 96:6; 19:4)

The primordial sacrament as instituted in Genesis 2:24 contains a supernatural efficacy because already in creation man was "chosen in Christ."[41] In this way the Pope says we must recognize that the original "sacrament of creation" draws its efficacy from Christ (see TOB 96:7). John Paul indicates that St. Paul speaks of this grace in Ephesians 1:6—the "grace which [the Father] freely bestowed on us in the Beloved." Marriage—this primordial sacrament of sexual love—is intended, therefore, not only to advance the work of creation through procreation. God also intends that it serve "to spread the same sacrament of creation to further generations of human beings, that is, to spread the supernatural fruits of man's eternal election by the Father in the eternal Son" (TOB 96:7).

▄▄ Based on this, is it any wonder why Satan attacks right here? Recall that sin "and death have entered into man's history *in some way through the very heart of that unity that had from the 'beginning' been formed by man and woman,* created and called to become 'one flesh' (Gen 2:24)" (TOB 20:1). Satan's goal is to keep man from his eternal election in Christ. He does so by plagiarizing the primordial sacrament. Satan wants to twist man and woman's union into an "anti-sacrament"—an effective denial of the gift of God's life and love. He plagiarizes the Word inscribed in the body ("self-donation") and makes it his own anti-word ("self-gratification"). At this point we are getting closer to understanding why Karol Wojtyla, just a few months before his election as Pope John Paul II, described the teaching of *Humanae Vitae* as a "struggle for the value and meaning of humanity itself."[42]

Marriage: Platform for the Realization of God's Eternal Plans

We have been chosen in Christ "before the foundation of the world to be holy and blameless before him" (Eph 1:4). This is the mystery of God's will that St. Paul announced in the first chapter of Ephesians: to unite us (and all things) with Christ according to the riches of his grace

41. See *CCC*, no. 257.
42. Cited in *Crossing the Threshold of Hope*, p. 113.

(see vv. 4, 8–9). According to John Paul, this is all realized by the "great mystery" proclaimed in Ephesians 5 (see TOB 97:3).

We have learned that marriage—instituted by the union of male and female in "one flesh"—was already "in the beginning" an image of and a participation in this eternal election in Christ. This lofty theological concept may seem hopelessly removed from the "real life" experience of ordinary men and women. From the experience of men and women dominated by concupiscence, yes. But for husbands and wives who are being freed from the domination of concupiscence through ongoing conversion to Christ, this "lofty theology" gradually becomes what they *live* and *experience* as a foretaste of the marriage of the Lamb.

In what way? How actually is marriage and its consummate expression supposed to image and participate in our eternal election in Christ? To answer this question we must attune ourselves to that "echo" of our origins deep within us. We must recall the original experiences we reconstructed in our analysis of Genesis—solitude, unity, and nakedness—and believe in the power of the grace "which God lavishes on us in his Beloved" to restore what was lost.

Being Chosen and Being Able to Choose

The Holy Father recalls that in all of creation, the election to the dignity of adopted sonship was proper only to the "first Adam"—to the man created in the image and likeness of God as male and female (see 96:5). This "Adam" realized he was alone in the visible world as a *person*. The deepest meaning of this solitude is that Adam was "set into a *unique, exclusive, and unrepeatable relationship with God himself*." He alone among all the body-creatures was a "partner of the Absolute" (TOB 6:2).

The experience of original solitude, then, was an experience of "being chosen" and of "being able to choose." God *chose* Adam in love. He chose him *in Christ*. For, as John Paul's favorite passage from Vatican II tells us, "Adam, the first man, was a figure of him who was to come, namely Christ the Lord."[43] Furthermore, in "being chosen," Adam was also given the ability *to choose* to love God in return *and* to

---

43. *Gaudium et Spes*, 22.

choose to love another human person in order to recapitulate the love God had given to him. In this way original solitude leads to the experience of original unity. For it is not good for the man to be alone.

But the experience of original nakedness in particular enables us to see how man and woman's original unity was an image of and participation in man's eternal election in Christ. Nakedness without shame revealed that they were "free with the very freedom of the gift." Adam had no compulsion to satisfy an "urge" at the sight of woman's nakedness. Her body inspired nothing in Adam but the desire to make a "sincere gift" of himself to her: to *choose* her in freedom as his bride, as God had chosen him in Christ "before the foundation of the world." Furthermore, knowing that she was a person made for "her own sake," he knew he could not "take" her or "grasp" her. He had to trust that she—in her freedom—would desire to open herself to the gift he initiated and respond freely with the gift of herself to him, which she did. Free from any compulsion and selfish sting, their union was a mutual choice—a choice made *for* the good of the other and *because of* the good of the other (and also, of course, for the good experienced by oneself in loving and being loved). It was a participation in that original good of God's vision that affirms his choosing of us.

In this way their conjugal union was a "beatifying experience," imaging and participating in their having been "elected" or chosen by eternal Love. John Paul describes this participation as the "supernatural efficaciousness" of the primordial sacrament. In other words, the experience of original unity truly communicated God's life and love to man and woman. This "supernatural efficaciousness is identical with the very act of the creation of man in the state of original innocence" (TOB 96:7).

Sin and the Loss of Supernatural Efficacy

This reality, however, as experience attests, became obscured by the heritage of original sin. As John Paul expresses, "the heritage of grace was driven out of the human heart when man broke the first covenant with the Creator." In this way "marriage, as the primordial sacrament, was deprived of the supernatural efficaciousness it drew at the moment of its institution from the sacrament of creation in its totality. Nevertheless," the Pope continues, "also in this state, that is, in the state of man's hereditary sinfulness, *marriage never ceased being the figure of the sacrament, about which we read in Ephesians* 5:22–33." Despite sin, John Paul deduces that "marriage has remained the platform for the realization of God's eternal plans" (TOB 97:1).

Even if crippled in its ability to do so, man and woman's longing for marital union has spoken in some way of the "great mystery" to all the generations of history. The universal cultural heritage of romantic poetry, literature, music, and art often points to a basic intuition that the love of the sexes is meant to be a merging of the human and the divine.[44]

While marriage entails many trials under the inheritance of sin, a "spark" of that beatifying beginning remains. In fact, this spark prepares men and women for the gift of redemption. The heart longs for "something more" than this life can offer. To tap into that desire for "something more" is to tap into that "echo" deep within our hearts of God's original plan for us. Despite formidable foes that seek to snuff it out, that yearning cannot and will not be repressed.[45] It is a yearning to live in the grace of our eternal election in Christ. It is a yearning to live in the eternal embrace of the marriage of the Lamb. Nothing else can satisfy. Nothing else can fulfill. And all else is destined to pass away.

■ It is precisely this yearning that Satan targets and toys with in order to manipulate us in his direction. The myriad pleasures of this world that he parades before us as "the prince of the power of the air" (Eph 2:2) purport to satisfy our longings but leave us empty. Still, we must always keep in mind that all Satan can do to attract us is plagiarize the joys God created for us in this world to foreshadow the joys of heaven. All the authentic pleasures of this world are in some way sacramental, whereas all the counterfeit pleasures of this world are in some way sacrilegious. This is where the battle is fought: between sacraments and their counterfeits, between icons and idols, between signs and anti-signs. One foreshadows an eternity of fulfillment and communion, the other an eternity of emptiness and alienation.

---

44. See *Gaudium et Spes*, 49.

45. See Lorenzo Albacete, *God at the Ritz: Attraction to Infinity* (New York: Crossroads, 2002).

Sacrament of Creation Fulfilled
in Sacrament of Redemption

The "echo" of God's original plan that resounds in the human heart despite sin is irrepressible. We might call this an echo of the sacrament of creation. And this echo prepares men and women to receive the sacrament of redemption. John Paul speaks to this when he suggests that "the sacrament of creation had come near to human beings and prepared them for the sacrament of redemption, introducing them into the dimension of the work of salvation" (TOB 97:1). What does the Pope mean by the "sacrament of redemption"? To answer this, let us first recall what he means by the sacrament of creation.

The sacrament of creation is that which in the totality of creation makes visible the mystery hidden in God from all eternity. This is the mystery of divine life and love—of *communion*—in which original man really participated through the grace of the sacrament of creation.[46] Marriage as instituted by the words of Genesis 2:24 is the central and consummate point of the sacrament of creation. In this sense it is the primordial sacrament, which was at work in man and woman with supernatural efficaciousness. Marriage, however, lost its efficacy as the central point of the sacrament of creation with the dawn of sin. When man and woman broke their covenant with the Creator, the "life" with which they had been *in*-spired, *ex*-spired in their hearts. Shame in their nakedness attests to this loss of grace and holiness. Even so, as John Paul suggests, "marriage has remained the platform for the realization of God's eternal plans" (TOB 97:1). "In fact, the original 'unity in the body' of man and woman does not cease to shape man's history on earth, although it lost the lucid clarity of the sacrament, of the sign of salvation, which it possessed 'at the beginning'" (TOB 100:1).

When St. Paul links this "unity in the body" of the first Adam and Eve with the incarnate communion of the New Adam and Eve (Christ and the Church), he speaks of it as a "great mystery." According to the Holy Father, this linking of Genesis 2:24 with Christ and the Church "seems to point out not only the identity of the Mystery hidden in God from eternity, but also the continuity of its realization." This continuity exists "between the primordial sacrament connected with man's super-

---

46. See *CCC*, no. 375.

natural gracing [that is, endowment with grace] in creation itself, and the new gracing—which was brought about when 'Christ loved the Church and gave himself for her, in order to make her holy' (Eph 5:25–26)." It is this "new gracing," the Pope emphasizes, "*that can be defined in its entirety as the sacrament of redemption*" (TOB 97:2).

According to St. Paul, Christ gives himself *for* the Church and *to* the Church in the image of the spousal union of husband and wife in marriage. In this way John Paul says that the sacrament of redemption "clothes itself, so to speak, in the figure and form of the primordial sacrament." The marriage of the first man and woman was a sign of the supernatural gracing of man in the sacrament of creation. To this there "corresponds the marriage, or rather the analogy of the marriage, of Christ with the Church, as the fundamental 'great' sign of man's supernatural gracing in the sacrament of redemption" (TOB 97:2). This "new gracing" definitively renews the covenant of the grace of election, which was broken in the beginning by sin. The Pope also says that this "new gracing" of the sacrament of redemption is "a new realization" of that Mystery hidden in God from eternity. It is new in relation to the sacrament of creation because this new grace is in a certain sense a "new creation" (see TOB 97:3). As St. Paul proclaims: "Therefore, if anyone is in Christ, he is a new creation; the old has passed away, behold, the new has come" (2 Cor 5:17).

While John Paul stresses the continuity between the original gracing and the new gracing, he also notes an important difference. The original gracing given in the *sacrament of creation* constituted man in the state of original innocence. The new gracing given in the *sacrament of redemption* is given first for the remission of sins. But, as discussed previously, forgiveness of sins is only part of "the riches of his grace which he lavished on us" (Eph 1:7–8). In this context the Holy Father quotes from Romans 5:20: "Where sin increased, grace abounded all the more" (see TOB 97:3).

Signs of Creation and Redemption

But in what manner is the grace of the sacraments of *creation* and *redemption* actuated and realized? John Paul observes that "when we speak about the realization of the eternal mystery, we are speaking also about the fact that it becomes visible with the visibility of the sign"

(TOB 97:5). There is a sign that actuates and realizes the sacrament of creation by making the mystery of creation visible. And there is a sign that actuates and realizes the sacrament of redemption by making the mystery of redemption visible. What are these signs? John Paul himself tells us that the "Mystery hidden from all eternity in God...in the sacrament of creation became *a visible reality through the union* of the first man and the first woman in the perspective of marriage." This same mystery "becomes in the sacrament of redemption *a visible reality in the indissoluble union of Christ with the Church,* which the author of Ephesians presents as the spousal union" (TOB 97:4).

As John Paul said earlier: "It is a particular merit of the author of Ephesians that he brought these two signs together, making of them *the single great sign,* that is, *a great sacrament*" (TOB 95b:7). When we speak of these signs—of the union of spouses and of the analogous union of Christ and the Church, which Paul united as a *"single great sign"*—according to John Paul, "we are also speaking about the sacramentality of the whole heritage of the sacrament of redemption in reference to the entire work of creation and redemption" (TOB 97:5). This is the power of sacramental signs. They actualize that which they symbolize. In the beginning, marital unity was created to symbolize the eternal mystery of life-giving Communion in the Trinity.

> Just as the "first Adam"—man, male and female—who was created in the state of original innocence and called in this state to conjugal union (in this sense we speak about the sacrament of creation) was a sign of the eternal Mystery, so also the "second Adam," Christ, who is united with the Church through the sacrament of redemption by an indissoluble bond analogous to the indissoluble covenant of spouses, is the definitive sign of the same eternal Mystery. (TOB 97:5)

From this perspective John Paul tells us that the Church itself is the "great sacrament," the new sign of the covenant and of grace. Just as marriage emerged from the sacrament of creation as a primordial sign of the covenant and of grace, now the new sign of the covenant and of grace "draws its roots from the depths of the sacrament of redemption." Thus, the "primordial sacrament is realized in a new way in the 'sacrament' of Christ and the Church" (TOB 99:2).

John Paul is talking about the profound interrelationship of the marriage of the first Adam and Eve and the marriage of the New Adam and Eve (Christ and the Church). We could even say these two marriages are *married* to each other. In this way they form *"the single great sign"* that reveals the One "great Mystery." Of course sacramental signs do not fully explain the mystery. As an object of faith, the mystery remains veiled even in the expression of its sign. Yet grace is communicated with power under the veil of the sign (see TOB 97:5).

Christ's Spousal Love Is Unitive and Life-Giving

In the densely packed audience of October 13, 1982 (TOB 97), John Paul stresses that the spousal gift of Christ to the Church, as the analogy indicates, has both a unitive and a "life-giving dimension." We see the unitive dimension in the reciprocity of the gift between Christ and the Church. Christ initiates the sacrament of redemption by giving up his body for the Church with the desire of "uniting with her in an indissoluble love, just as spouses, husband and wife, unite in marriage." But the gift given must also be received. Through her response to the gift, the Church "on her part completes this sacrament, just as the wife, in virtue of spousal love, completes her husband" (TOB 97:4). This "completion" of the husband by his wife was already pointed out, the Pope says, when the first man found in woman "a helper fit for him."

Recall that the wife's mystery *"manifests and reveals itself in its full depth through motherhood"* (TOB 21:2). Hence, along with the "unitive dimension" of Christ's spousal love for the Church, we also recognize the "life-giving dimension." In this context John Paul says we can "add that the Church too, united with Christ as the wife with her husband, draws from the sacrament of redemption her whole spiritual fruitfulness and motherhood" (TOB 97:4). St. Peter testifies to this in some way when he writes that we have been "reborn not from a corruptible, but from an incorruptible seed, through the living and enduring word of God" (1 Pet 1:23).

At this point we are close to understanding the importance of the encyclical *Humanae Vitae.* The "one flesh" union of spouses is meant to be a sign of the "great mystery" of Christ's union with the Church. And, as John Paul has already said, we can speak of moral good and evil in the sexual relationship based on whether the couple gives to their union "the character of a truthful sign" (TOB 37:6). Anyone can recognize that an attack on the unitive dimension of sexuality—for instance, physical abuse inflicted on one's spouse—would contradict utterly the sign of Christ's love for the Church. Why then is it so difficult to recognize that an attack on the life-giving dimension also utterly contradicts this sign of Christ's love for the Church? This is the context in which the Holy Father will reflect on the issue of contraception in the final chapter of his catechesis.

Marriage: Prototype of All the Sacraments

Nature and Grace

John Paul II's analysis of Ephesians demonstrates the profound interrelationship of creation and redemption in the human drama. In this same context it also demonstrates the profound interrelationship of nature and grace. Some conceive of man as capable of a purely "natural fulfillment" apart from grace. Grace is then "added on" to man's nature, it seems, as if it were a two-story structure. But based on John Paul II's analysis of Genesis and Ephesians, we know that God gave grace to man in his creation *as man*. In the human being's creation, "*the heritage of original grace*...was given by God as soon as he infused the rational soul" (TOB 97:1). To be full of grace, then, is man's natural state—if by "natural" we mean God's one and original plan for man.

Just as a bride is created in her very being to receive her husband, so too is man created in his very being to receive grace; to receive divine life as the Bride of Christ. This insight is found already in the work of St. Thomas Aquinas, who taught that man is naturally capable of grace because he is made in God's image.[47] In this sense we cannot speak of a purely "natural" state of man detached or divorced from grace. The only natural state is that willed by God in the beginning. When man fell from grace, he did not become a "natural" man. He stooped lower than his nature. This is why Christ, in revealing the mystery of the Father and his love—that is, in revealing the mystery of grace—fully reveals man to himself.

---

47. See *Summa Theologica*, I–IIae, q. 113, a. 10. Fathers Hogan and LeVoir also point this out in their discussion of nature and grace in their book *Covenant of Love: Pope John Paul II on Sexuality, Marriage, and Family in the Modern World* (San Francisco: Ignatius Press, 1992), p. 35. For a discussion of Wojtyla's intervention at the Council on the issue of nature and grace, see Rocco Buttiglione, *Karol Wojtyla: The Thought of the Man Who Became Pope John Paul II*, pp. 195–99.

This grace, of course, is not man's due, any more than being created in the first place is his due. We need not dissociate nature and grace, as some might imagine, in order to maintain this important truth. Man's creation—and his creation with a graced nature—is not owed him. It is a sheer gift.[48]

Grace of the Primordial Sacrament Restored

We see this "marriage" of nature and grace in Ephesians 5:31–32, where St. Paul weds the consummate sign of the sacrament of creation with the consummate sign of the sacrament of redemption. Quoting from Genesis, he says: "For this reason a man shall leave his father and mother and be joined to his wife, and the two shall become one flesh." Then he adds: "This is a great mystery, and I mean in reference to Christ and the church."

According to the Holy Father, a careful analysis of this key text shows that the Apostle's linking of the original union of spouses with the union of Christ and the Church "is not only a comparison in the sense of a metaphor." This passage speaks "of a real *renewal* (or 're-creation,' that is, a new creation) of *what constituted the salvific content* (in a certain sense the 'salvific substance') of the primordial sacrament" (TOB 98:8). In other words, the grace of the primordial sacrament that was lost through sin is now restored, re-created, or *resurrected* in the sacrament of redemption.

Marriage regains its efficaciousness—its power to actualize that which it signifies. This time, however, it draws this efficaciousness not from the sacrament of creation, but from the sacrament of redemption. With this efficaciousness, John Paul points out that marriage is not merely a model and figure of Christ's union with the Church. It "constitutes an *essential part* of the new heritage" (TOB 98:1). "In his dia-

---

48. This brief sketch barely begins to introduce a very complex debate that lies at the heart of the theological problem of our time. At the core of the contemporary controversy regarding the relationship between nature and grace is the teaching of the French Jesuit theologian Henri de Lubac. For a summary of the debate as it centers on his thought, see David Schindler's introduction to de Lubac's book, *The Mystery of the Supernatural* (New York: Crossroad Herder, 1998), pp. xi–xxxi. For a more comprehensive discussion, see Hans Urs von Balthasar's *The Theology of Karl Barth* (San Francisco: Ignatius Press/*Communio* Books, 1992), especially Part III, pp. 251–358.

logue with the Pharisees (see Mt 19), Christ not only confirms the existence of marriage instituted from the 'beginning' by the Creator, but he declares *also that it is an integral part of the new sacramental economy*" (TOB 98:3). The new sacramental economy is the new order of "salvific signs" that derives its origin and efficaciousness from the sacrament of redemption.

Marriage Provides the Basic Structure of Salvation

In referring to these new "salvific signs," John Paul moves from the broader sense of "sacrament" to the more specific sense in which sacrament refers to those signs instituted by Christ and administered by the Church (see p. 403ff.). The Pope emphasizes that this new sacramental economy differs from the original economy in that it is directed not to the man of original innocence, but to the man burdened with the heritage of sin (see TOB 97:3). While in the original bestowal of grace marriage was "the one and only sacrament" (TOB 98:3), in the new economy there are seven sacraments instituted to give grace to the man of concupiscence. It is almost as if the original sacrament was "fractured" by sin into seven sacraments—like light, which, when fractured, reveals the seven colors of the rainbow. And just as each color of the rainbow carries forth an aspect of the light from which it derived, so too do each of the seven sacraments bear something of the spousal mystery of the primordial sacrament.

Based on the integral relationship of creation and redemption, we can conclude that the primordial sacrament already foreshadowed and "contained" in some way the grace that was to become the gift of redemption. This grace is now given to the man of concupiscence through the spousal union of Christ and the Church poured forth in each of the seven sacraments. It is given first for the remission of sins, but also in superabundance for the sake of eternal communion with the Trinity through Christ.

Recall that God's original plan for man continues despite sin. Sin did not thwart it. Accordingly, marriage—which was the central point of the sacrament of creation in its totality—also provides the figure "according to which the underlying, weight-bearing structure of the new economy of salvation and the sacramental order is built, which springs from the spousal gracing that the Church receives from Christ"

(TOB 98:2). In other words, Christ assumes into the whole economy of redemption the same spousal imprint that permeated creation. As the *Catechism* teaches, "The entire Christian life bears the mark of the spousal love of Christ and the Church."[49]

Therefore John Paul observes that marriage, as a primordial sacrament, is "assumed and inserted into the integral structure of the new sacramental economy...from its very basis." In this way we see how marriage arises from redemption, as the Holy Father emphasizes, "*in the form...of a prototype*.... If we reflect deeply on this dimension, we have to conclude that all the sacraments of the New Covenant find their prototype in some way in marriage as the primordial sacrament" (TOB 98:2).

This idea is closely related with what the Holy Father said earlier when he described the visible sign of marriage as "*the foundation of the whole sacramental order*" (TOB 95b:7). Marriage serves as a kind of foundation, model, and prototype of all of the sacraments because all of the sacraments draw their essential significance and their sacramental power from the *spousal love* of Christ the Redeemer. John Paul points out that Ephesians 5 shows the spousal character of Baptism (v. 26) and the Eucharist (v. 29) in a particularly impressive, if somewhat illusive, manner. Moreover, we can recognize that each of the seven sacraments is imbued with a spousal meaning. Each of the sacraments, in its own way, unites us *in the flesh* with Christ our Bridegroom. When we as Bride are open to the gift, the sacraments infuse—or, in keeping with the analogy, we could say "impregnate"—us with divine life.

> ■ A person can go through the motions of receiving the sacraments while denying the life-giving grace they afford; an example of this would be a person who receives the Eucharist in a state of defiance toward God. This would be a serious sacrilege. A question then arises. If the consummate expression of the sacrament of marriage is meant to symbolize the gift of Christ and the receptivity of the Bride to divine life, what does contraception do to this picture?

The "great mystery" of Christ's union with the Church was foreshadowed from the beginning in our creation as male and female and in

---

49. *CCC*, no. 1617.

our call to become one flesh. As if this has not been emphasized enough, we shall say it again: Sexuality—when given its full biblical, theological-sacramental, and anthropological meaning—is all about Christ. And Christ "is the center of the universe and of history."[50]

3. Sacrament and "Redemption of the Body"

A. THE GOSPEL

Those who glimpse the vision of marriage as presented in John Paul II's TOB cannot help but marvel at the beauty of it. But is this sublime vision of marriage possible to live? In the final section of this chapter, John Paul is at pains, yet again, to point men and women to the real power flowing from the redemption of the body. Left to their own resources, the best men and women can do is admire this theological vision from a distance. But *men and women are not left to their own resources!* As the *Catechism* teaches, "By coming to restore the original order of creation disturbed by sin, [Christ] himself gives the strength and grace to...'receive' the original meaning of marriage and live it."[51]

In his audiences of October 27 and November 24, 1982 (TOB 99–100), John Paul revisits those key words from the Gospel about God's original plan for marriage and about lust as "adultery committed in the heart." We can now understand the power and importance of these key words of Christ with even more precision in light of the "great mystery" of Ephesians 5. John Paul reminds us that these words have a profound theological, anthropological, and ethical significance. "Christ speaks from the depth of that divine mystery. At the same time, *he penetrates into the very depth of the human mystery*" (TOB 100:7). In this way the God-Man witnesses to a theological anthropology. Christ "fully reveals man to himself" by unveiling the God-like dignity bestowed on men and women in the mystery of creation and redemption. It is a dignity that calls men and women to greatness. In other words, it makes demands on them—ethical demands. But the gift of redemption also provides us with the grace necessary to meet those demands.

---

50. *Redemptor Hominis*, 1.
51. *CCC*, no. 1615.

The Anthropology of Redemption

When Christ refers to God's original plan for man and woman's joining in "one flesh," as well as when he condemns the lust in man's heart, his words penetrate "into what man and woman are (or rather into who the man and the woman are) in their own original dignity as image and likeness of God." John Paul immediately stresses that historical man inherits this same dignity despite sin. In fact, the dignity of original man is "continuously 'assigned' to man as a task through the reality of redemption" (TOB 100:5).

Christ's key words flow *"from the divine depth of the 'redemption of the body'* (Rom 8:23)" (TOB 99:4). Christ thereby opens marriage (and male-female relations in general) "to the salvific action of God, *to the powers flowing 'from the redemption of the body,'* which help to overcome the consequences of sin and to build the unity of man and woman according to the Creator's eternal plan" (TOB 100:2). As we have already seen, redemption, in fact, signifies a *"new creation."* It assumes all that is created to express it anew according to "the fullness of justice, equity, and holiness planned for it by God" (TOB 99:7)—especially in man who is created as male and female in the divine image. Thus, the "salvific action deriving from the mystery of redemption takes into itself God's original sanctifying action in the very mystery of creation" (TOB 100:2). Christ's words bear within them the leaven of this hope. The Pope reminds us that this is not only a hope reserved for our state in the final resurrection. This is also a hope that can be progressively realized in "the dimension of daily life" (TOB 99:5)—what John Paul called earlier "the hope of every day" (see TOB 86:6–7).

John Paul insists that it is truly possible for historical man to "find again the dignity and holiness of conjugal union 'in the body' on the basis of the mystery of redemption" (TOB 100:6). What hope! Man and woman need not be continually wounded by the blades of concupiscence that stab at the heart of their dignity and their communion. Married life need not be only an ongoing coping with or mere channeling of wounded and wounding desires. Marriage invites us to participate *consciously* and *conscientiously* (see TOB 100:4) in the redemption of the body. Spouses who are committed to doing so (Christian spouses are supposed to commit to this) can progressively rediscover, reclaim, and live according to their original dignity. They can—by daily embracing their trials and taking up the redeeming cross of Christ—experience a real measure of the harmony, peace, and happiness of original unity.

The Ethos of Redemption

Christ's words about marriage not only show us who we are in the mystery of creation and redemption. They have at the same time a "very expressive ethical eloquence." In other words, Christ's words provide the foundation both for an "*adequate anthropology*" and for an "*adequate ethos.*" John Paul has already described this as "*the ethos of redemption*" (see TOB 100:3).

Christ not only confirms marriage as a primordial sacrament. In referring to "the beginning," he also draws moral conclusions: "Whoever divorces his wife and marries another commits adultery against her" (Mk 10:11). The Pope points out that St. Paul also places his teaching on marriage in the context of moral exhortations, which outline the ethos that should characterize the life of Christians. John Paul then defines what a Christian is: "Christians...[are] those who are aware of their election, which is realized in Christ and the Church" (TOB 98:5). Precisely such awareness empowers us by grace to understand and live the "ethos of redemption." Those who are not aware of the power of this grace will inevitably see the demands of Christian morality as an imposition. They will see an external ethic that burdens rather than an internal ethos that liberates.

> ■ Tragically, it seems that few people who fill the pews of our churches are "aware of their election, which is realized in Christ and the Church" (TOB 98:5). Rarely, though, is this lack of awareness the people's fault. An evangelical and catechetical crisis in the West seems to have left a great many Catholics with little knowledge of the "great mystery." More specifically, my experience in sharing the TOB with Christians around the world indicates that most people who fill the pews do not realize that this election—the mystery of the Gospel itself—is stamped mysteriously in their own bodies as male and female. Hence, as John Paul II repeatedly insists, a crucial need exists for a "new evangelization"—new because it is largely directed to the baptized. The Epilogue will address how John Paul II's TOB provides a foundation, both in substance and methodology, for the new evangelization.

While the Christian ethos can be explained philosophically (and John Paul adds through a *personalist* philosophy)—nonetheless, Christian ethos is essentially theological, since it is an ethos of redemption. More specifically, according to John Paul, it is an ethos of *the redemption of the body* (see TOB 100:3). Ultimately, the Christian ethos is only fully tenable to those who are living their election in Christ—to those who are living the grace of the redemption of their bodies. Redemption is "the basis for understanding the particular dignity of the human body, which is rooted in the personal dignity of man and woman" (TOB 100:3). This dignity forms the basis of all morality.

All of the Church's teachings on sexual morality, then, are a call for men and women to embrace and uphold their own greatness. As the Holy Father says, in defining the ethos of sexual morality in the Sermon on the Mount, Christ "assigns the dignity of every woman as a task to every man; at the same time (although this conclusion follows only indirectly from the text) he assigns also the dignity of every man to every woman. Finally," the Pope concludes, "he assigns to each—both to the man and to the woman—his or her own dignity." John Paul defines this dignity as the "*sacrum*"—the "sacredness"—of the person. And he adds that this sacredness of men and women is "*specifically with respect to* the person's femininity or masculinity, *with respect to the 'body'* " (TOB 100:6). The body reveals man's greatness—man's dignity.

Living according to our own dignity is a continuous and often arduous struggle. In this context Christ appeals to the heart—"that 'intimate place,' in which good and evil, sin and justice, concupiscence and holiness fight each other in man" (TOB 100:7). However, if Christ wants all men and women to realize that they are subject to concupiscence, he also wants them to realize that he makes the grace of redemption available to them with *real power* to transform their hearts.

John Paul observes that "*redemption is given* to man *as the grace* of the New Covenant with God in Christ—and at the same time it is *assigned to him as ethos*" (TOB 100:4). This is a demanding ethos, to be sure. Christ assigns it to man's heart and, as John Paul adds, "to his conscience, to his looks, and to his behavior" (TOB 100:7). If the man of concupiscence feels powerless in himself to meet these demands, he must not forget his election in Christ.

Here John Paul reminds us that the new ethos is "the form of morality that corresponds to the action of God in the mystery of redemption" (TOB 100:4). What was God's action in the mystery of redemption? It was grace poured out in superabundance to conquer sin (see Rom 5:20). It was the death of sin "so that as Christ was raised from the dead to the glory of the Father, we too might walk in newness of life" (Rom 6:4). If we once yielded our bodies to impurity, now the Spirit enlivens our mortal bodies and empowers them for righteousness (see Rom 6:19; 8:11). When the power of the Holy Spirit vivifies us in this way, we come to *know* the sacredness of the body and of conjugal relations. Living from this awareness—even if we still recognize the tug of concupiscence—we simply do not desire to profane the sacred. We would prefer to be crucified.

As St. Peter learned, if we keep our eyes on Christ we can walk on water. Even if our faith wanes and we begin to sink, Christ always reaches out to save us if we but turn to him again (see Mt 14:25–31). But we must first *believe* in the power of Christ and step out of the boat. As we observed previously, the drama of redemption—in this case the drama of conquering concupiscence in our hearts, our looks, and our behavior—lies not in the "safety" of the boat, but amidst the wind and the waves. That is where Christ is, and he beckons us, "Come!"

Marriage Reveals God's Will to Save Us from Sin

Sacraments are given for man and woman's salvation. The Church firmly believes that Christ instituted each of the seven sacraments for this purpose.[52] Traditionally theologians have pointed to Christ's presence at the wedding feast of Cana as the biblical evidence of Christ's institution of marriage as a sacrament.[53] John Paul II also points to Christ's discussion with the Pharisees as such evidence. Based on these words, the Pope concludes that marriage is not only a sacrament from the very "beginning," but it is also a sacrament arising from the mystery of the "redemption of the body" (see TOB 100:7). At the beginning of the same audience, John Paul says that "Christ's words to the Pharisees (see Mt 19) appeal to marriage as a sacrament, or to the primordial revelation of God's salvific will" for man (TOB 100:1).

---

52. See *CCC*, nos. 774, 1123, 1680.
53. See *CCC*, no. 1613.

This definition of the sacrament of marriage deserves comment. What is God's salvific will for man? Christ summarizes it when he says: "This is my commandment, that you love one another as I have loved you" (Jn 15:12). This is the meaning of our creation as male and female and our call to become "one flesh." It is a call to love as God loves "from the beginning." John Paul then links this call revealed already in Genesis 2:24 with the teaching of *Gaudium et Spes*, number 24:

> the Lord Jesus, when praying to the Father "that they may all be one...even as we are one" (Jn 17:21–22), opened up new horizons closed to human reason by implying that there is a certain parallel between the union existing among the divine persons and the union of the sons of God in truth and love. It follows, then, that if man is the only creature on earth that God has wanted for its own sake, man can fully discover his true self only in a sincere giving of himself.

"In virtue of God's salvific will and action, man and woman, uniting with each other in such a way as to become 'one flesh' (Gen 2:24), were at the same time destined to be united 'in truth and love' as sons of God," according to the above teaching of *Gaudium et Spes*. John Paul continues by saying that Christ directs his words about marriage as the primordial sacrament to "such unity and such a communion of persons, according to likeness with the union of divine Persons" (TOB 100:1), as the above teaching of the Council also indicates. In his *Letter to Families*, John Paul states that every man and woman "fully realizes himself or herself through the sincere gift of self. For spouses the moment of conjugal union constitutes a very particular expression of this. It is then that a man and a woman, in the 'truth' of their masculinity and femininity, become a mutual gift to each other." [54]

John Paul illuminated for us early on that this teaching of the Council on communion among human persons through the sincere gift of self is incarnated in the spousal meaning of the body (see p. 131ff.). The human model for all the "sons of God" who are united "in truth and love" is the union of husband and wife in "one body." For we are all "one body" in Christ (see 1 Cor 12:12–13). Here we see very clearly the threefold conviction that John Paul II gained from John of the Cross: (1) Love involves the gift of self; (2) Spousal donation is the

---

54. *Letter to Families*, 12.

model of self-giving love in human experience; (3) The self-giving of the three Persons of the Trinity is the source and model of all self-giving love.

Marriage Is a Call to "Life in the Spirit"

Overcoming Concupiscence

When husband and wife are united "in truth and love," marriage becomes "an efficacious expression of the saving power of God" (TOB 101:1). This "saving power" enables man and woman to overcome concupiscence and gain mastery over the tendency toward an egoistic gratification. "A fruit of this mastery is the unity and indissolubility of marriage and, in addition, the deepened sense of the woman's dignity in the man's heart (as also the man's dignity in the woman's heart)." This deepened appreciation for the dignity of the opposite sex becomes evident both "in conjugal life together and in every other sphere of reciprocal relations" (TOB 101:1).

John Paul already said that "the freedom of the gift" afforded by the "liberation of the heart from 'concupiscence'...is the condition of all life together in the truth" (TOB 43:6). If we want to build a culture that respects life and acknowledges human dignity, we must begin by overcoming concupiscence in our own hearts. There is no other starting point. There is no other solution. It all begins right here. But how can we do it? Concupiscence is ever ready to rear its ugly head and blind us to our great dignity. True enough. But when we open our flesh to the "life of the Holy Spirit," we find a power at work in us infinitely greater than the force of concupiscence. Listen to these words of hope: "Just as 'concupiscence' darkens the horizon of interior vision and deprives hearts of the lucid clarity of desires and aspirations, so 'life according to the Spirit'...allows man and woman to find the true freedom of the gift together with the awareness of the spousal meaning of the body" (TOB 101:5). John Paul specifies that this "life according to the Spirit"—while available to everyone—is also the specific grace poured out in the sacrament of marriage.

As a sacrament of the Church, the Pope says that marriage is also "a word of the Spirit" that exhorts man and woman to model their whole

life together by drawing power from the mystery of the redemption of
the body. In this way, man and woman "are called to chastity as to the
state of life 'according to the Spirit'" (TOB 101:4). Marriage, then, is a
sacrament of redemption given to the man of concupiscence as a grace
and at the same time as an ethos. In this case John Paul says that the
redemption of the body signifies "the everyday hope, the hope of temporality" that overcomes the domination of concupiscence (see TOB
101:4).

Better to Marry Than to Be Aflame with Passion

In this context, the Holy Father wishes to stress again that the
chaste love of husband and wife excludes the idea that marriage provides a "legitimate outlet" for indulging concupiscence. To this end he
turns again to St. Paul's words in 1 Corinthians 7 in order to clarify the
common but—in John Paul's mind—erroneous interpretation of the
Apostle's teaching.

There St. Paul recommends marriage "because of the temptation to
immorality" (v. 2). He would prefer that his readers remain single as he
is. "But if they cannot exercise self-control, they should marry. For it is
better to marry than to be aflame with passion" (v. 9). On first reading,
this passage seems to justify the indulgence of concupiscence in marriage. We previously asked if an incongruity exists between the teaching
of St. Paul and the teaching of John Paul II on this point. It was my
opinion that John Paul's explanation of the apparent incongruity was
not altogether satisfying. This time, however, the Pope's explanation is
more compelling.

The Holy Father again stresses the Apostle's teaching that
Christian marriage, like Christian celibacy, is a special gift of grace (see
v. 7). For John Paul, grace always signifies the new ethos. Hence,
he concludes that St. Paul "simply expresses the thought in his words,
suggestive and paradoxical as they are, that marriage is assigned to
the spouses as an ethos" (TOB 101:3). To demonstrate this, the
Pope points out that in Paul's words, "it is better to marry than to be
aflame [with passion]," the word "*aflame*" signifies *the disorder of the passions* deriving from concupiscence. But "to marry" signifies *the ethical
order*, which Paul consciously introduced in this context. So, according
to this reasoning, St. Paul is saying that the ethos of marriage (which

transforms the desires of the heart into sincere self-giving) is better than being ruled by concupiscence (see TOB 101:3).

John Paul reminds us that marriage is meant to be "the place of the encounter of eros and ethos and of their reciprocal interpenetration in the 'heart' of man and woman, and likewise in all their reciprocal relations" (TOB 101:3). Purity of desire is the fruit born when eros and ethos meet in the human heart. Such purity excludes the indulgence of concupiscence. Such purity never leads a person to appropriate the other for one's own selfish gratification—only to love the other as God loves, in the sincere gift of self.

Marital Intercourse as "Life in the Holy Spirit"

In the beginning, the body and erotic desire was the trustworthy foundation of man and woman's communion. Due to the distortions of concupiscence, however, men and women often question the trustworthiness of the body and of erotic desire. Concupiscence, one might say, has introduced a multi-pronged thorn into the relationship of the sexes. This jagged barb has pricked and pierced many men and women so often that they have become numb to their aspirations for authentic love and communion in marriage. In such case, "double solitude"—rather than leading toward a "unity of the two" in which the sexes really *participate* in each other's humanity—stagnates, leading them to withdraw into what could be called a protective "double alienation" (see pp. 39, 188).

Nonetheless, men and women who mutually overcome the concupiscence of the flesh through "life in the Spirit" can rediscover marriage as "the sacramental covenant of masculinity and femininity." Through this ongoing transformation, the same "flesh" that is held suspect due to concupiscence "becomes the specific 'substratum' of a lasting and indissoluble communion of persons...in a manner worthy of persons" (TOB 101:4). This means that Christ gives us hope of healing. To continue with the above image, can we not recognize in Christ's own thorn-pierced flesh his willingness to take upon himself those very wounds that keep the sexes from true unity and communion? The Bridegroom's gift of self on the cross proclaims at the same time both the depth of our woundedness *and* the possibility of reestablishing a true life-giving marital communion.

We must recall that living "according to the Spirit" does *not* mean eschewing the body. It means the integration of body and spirit. It means opening our flesh to the Holy Spirit's *in*-spiration. For spouses, this also means opening the "one flesh" they become in marital intercourse to the indwelling of the Spirit. John Paul does not hesitate to say that "life 'according to the Spirit' expresses itself also in the reciprocal 'union' or 'knowledge' (see Gen 4:1) by which the spouses...become 'one flesh'" (TOB 101:6). And this life "according to the Spirit," the Pope says, is "the grace of the sacrament of Marriage" (TOB 101:5). Husband and wife are meant to experience this grace when, through the sincere gift of self, they become "one flesh."

Sexual union, then, is meant to be not only the union of husband and wife but also of God and man. In this way, sexual pleasure itself (understood integrally) is meant to be a participation in God's own mystery—in the joy of loving as God loves. Recall that Christ gave us the commandment to love as he loves so that his joy might be in us and that our joy might be complete (see Jn 15:11). Of course this pleasure greatly differs from the "egoistic gratification" toward which concupiscence tends. Authentic sexual pleasure always corresponds to the dignity of the spouses themselves. The husband and wife who are fully aware of their dignity as expressed in the spousal meaning of their bodies strive to uphold it in all of their expressions of intimacy and affection.

Furthermore, when marital intercourse is "in the Holy Spirit," it is never closed in on itself. Spouses, in opening their flesh to the Holy Spirit, are also conscious that this Spirit is "the Lord and Giver of Life." If their sexual union is to be "according to the Spirit," spouses must trustingly "submit their femininity and masculinity to the blessing of procreation" (TOB 101:6). As John Paul explicitly affirms, the spouses' dignity cannot be divorced from their potential to become parents. The pulse and intensity of authentic pleasure in marital intercourse is naturally integrated with "*the deep awareness of the holiness of the life*...to which both give rise, thereby participating in the powers of the mystery of creation" (TOB 101:6). Would not any intentional divorce from these "powers of the mystery of creation," in fact, be a specific closing off of one's flesh to the Lord and Giver of Life—a closing off to "life according to the Spirit"?

Procreation: An Integral Part of Creation and Redemption

Since the mark of spousal love permeates both the mystery of creation and the mystery of redemption (see p. 432), so too does its fruitfulness. As the Scriptures demonstrate, procreation is an integral part of both the mystery of creation (see Gen 1:28) and the mystery of redemption (see Lk 1:35; 1 Tim 2:15). Recall John Paul's statement that every conception of a child reproduces the mystery of creation (see TOB 10:4). Now he also states that every child conceived is a testimony to the hope of redemption (see TOB 101:6). He relates this once again to St. Paul's words about the hope of the redemption of the body (see Rom 8).

In light of this hope, John Paul says that each "new human life, the new human being conceived and born from the conjugal union of his father and mother, opens himself to the 'first fruits of the Spirit' (Rom 8:23) 'to enter into the freedom of the glory of the children of God' (Rom 8:21)" (TOB 101:6). In other words, every time a child is conceived, the very mystery of that child's conception proclaims the work of the Spirit. It proclaims the mystery of trinitarian love and the mystery of our being chosen in Christ to be children of God in communion with him for all eternity.

Because of sin, however, this hope that the child represents is not realized without suffering. Since the dawn of man's shame, an element of the cross has also been written into the mystery of spousal union and procreation. Authentic love between the sexes is determined right here: Will men and women embrace the cross or run from it? Love leads to redemptive suffering. Lust leads to resisting suffering. Sexual sin, in fact, always involves a specific attempt to divorce love from the cross of Christ. In all truth, there is no love apart from this cross.

When spouses "take up their cross and follow" Christ, the suffering of spousal love and procreation is redemptive. Indeed, it plunges men and women—husbands, wives, and their offspring—headfirst into the mystery of Christ's death and resurrection. Spouses who live in the "good news" of redemption are not crippled by fear of the sufferings they must endure. They may well taste fear, but it does not lead them to sterilize their union. When spouses become "one body" in accord with the divine plan, fear does not keep them from opening their "one body" to the Lord and Giver of Life. In fact, when they do open their union in this way, they effect in some way what their sacrament signifies. They recapitulate the entire mystery of creation and redemption (see p. 427ff.).[55] For the marital embrace "bears in itself the sign of the divine mystery of creation and redemption" (TOB 131:5).

Marriage and the Eschatological Hope of Redemption

The more we are aware of the "great mystery" marital union signifies and in which it participates, the more marriage "constitutes the basis of hope for the person, for the man and the woman, for the parents and the children, for the human generations" (TOB 101:7). John Paul speaks of this hope when, quoting again from Romans 8, he declares: "And if 'the whole creation groans and suffers until now in labor pains' (Rom 8:22), a particular hope accompanies the mother's labor pains." This is "the hope of the 'revelation of the sons of God' (v. 22)" (TOB 101:6). Every newborn babe who comes into the world bears within himself a spark of this hope, says John Paul. Recognizing this spark, however, can be difficult in a world engulfed by darkness. John Paul affirms with St. Paul that the hope of redemption is "in the world." It penetrates the whole of creation. However, this hope is not "of the world." It is of the Father (see TOB 101:7). Herein lies the struggle. In order to live in the hope of redemption, we must trust in the Father's love. But man has called the Father's love into question since "the beginning."

Recall that original sin is the mystery of man turning his back on the Father. "*Original sin attempts, then, to abolish fatherhood*, destroying its rays which permeate the created world, placing in doubt the truth about God who is Love."[56] Through original sin, man casts God out of his heart, detaching himself from what is "of the Father" so that all that remains in him is what is "of the world." In this way, we witness the birth of human lust (see p. 177ff.). As the Apostle John tells us, lust "is not of the Father but is of the world" (1 Jn 2:16). However, the

---

55. If we do not hesitate to describe spouses as co-creators with God, could we not also describe them in this sense as "co-redeemers" with God? (I owe this provocative idea to Steve Habisohn, founder and president of the GIFT Foundation.)

56. John Paul II, *Crossing the Threshold of Hope*, p. 228.

Pope tells us that marriage, including the sexual love proper to spouses, is not "of the world" but "of the Father." Deep in the human heart a battle rages for dominance between the two—between that which is *of the Father* and that which is *of the world*. A battle rages between love and lust, between hope and despondency, between life and all that opposes life.

Genesis tells us with certainty that fertility is a blessing from the Father (see Gen 1:28). However, because of the suffering it entails, men and women often question the value of bringing another life into the world. Without a living faith in Christ's resurrection, the suffering connected with procreation can even lead people to the point of counting the original blessing of fertility itself as a curse (see p. 160). Such people will often seek to avoid procreation not by avoiding sexual intercourse, but by defrauding this sacred act of its procreative potential. Closing their union in this way to the Lord and Giver of Life, they close themselves to that which is "of the Father," and there remains what is "of the world." There remains sexual desire *un*-inspired by God; *eros* cut off from *agape*. This cannot *not* be lust.

In this way we see that the blessing of fertility forces us to choose between that which is "of the Father" and that which is "of the world." This choice has eternal consequences. The Holy Father quotes again from the Apostle John: "On the one hand, 'the world passes away with its concupiscence,' and on the other [hand], 'the one who does the will of God will remain in eternity' (1 Jn 2:17)" (TOB 101:7). John Paul then states that the grace of "marriage as a sacrament immutably serves the purpose that man, male and female, by mastering concupiscence, does the will of the Father. And the one who 'does the will of God will remain in eternity' (1 Jn 2:17). In this sense, marriage as a sacrament also bears within itself the germ of man's eschatological future" (TOB 101:10–11). In other words, the chaste love of spouses, as proof of the indwelling of the Holy Spirit, becomes a foreshadowing and even a "guarantee" in some sense of eternal life (see Eph 1:13–14). As the *Catechism* says, "Chastity is a promise of immortality."[57]

In this context John Paul briefly revisits Christ's words about the future resurrection. Recall that Christ's exclusion of marriage in the

---

57. *CCC*, no. 2347.

resurrection does not mean that the deep truth of marriage will be done away with. It means it will be fulfilled in the marriage of the Lamb. Earthly marriage serves as the indispensable precursor to heavenly marriage. Of course, in order for marriage to prepare people for heaven, the earthly model must accurately image the divine prototype. John Paul describes marriage as "a sacrament of the human 'beginning'" (TOB 101:11). As man's origin, marital intercourse enables man to have a future not merely in the historical dimensions but also in the eschatological. Thus John Paul observes that every man brings into the world his vocation to share in the future resurrection because his origin lies in the marriage (more specifically, the marital embrace) of his parents. In this way marriage fulfills an "irreplaceable service" with regard to man's ultimate destiny (see TOB 101:11).

Hope of eternal life: this is the living hope in which spouses participate when they become "one flesh" and open their bodies to life according to the Spirit. They choose what is of the Father. In the face of all that assails their hope, they choose life—not only in its earthly, temporal dimension, but also in its heavenly, eternal dimension.

B. EPHESIANS

The Spousal and Redemptive Meaning of Love

In his audience of December 15, 1982 (TOB 102), John Paul summarizes and concludes his analysis of that classic text from Ephesians 5. In doing so, he takes us for yet another lap in his ever deepening spiral of reflections. The Pope tells us that the "great mystery" St. Paul speaks of is above all the mystery of Christ's union with the Church. But, according to the continuity of God's saving plan, the Apostle links this "great mystery" to the primordial sacrament in which the two become "one flesh." Here John Paul says we find ourselves in "the sphere of the great analogy" that *presupposes* and *rediscovers* the sacramentality of marriage. Marriage is presupposed as "the sacrament of the human 'beginning,' linked with the whole mystery of creation." But it is rediscovered "as the fruit of the spousal love of Christ and the Church, linked with the mystery of redemption" (TOB 102:1).

Presupposing the original meaning of marriage, St. Paul calls spouses to "*learn this sacrament anew*" in light of the spousal unity of

Christ and the Church. This means modeling their lives and their unity not only on the original unity of man and woman, but also and more so on the unity of Christ and the Church. As John Paul states: "That original and stable image of marriage as a sacrament *is renewed* when Christian spouses—aware of the authentic depth of the 'redemption of the body'—unite 'in the fear of [or out of reverence for] Christ' (Eph 5:21)" (TOB 102:3). This is not just an abstract theological concept. It is meant to be *lived* and *experienced* by couples. Uniting "out of reverence for Christ" means uniting with a deep respect and awe for the "great mystery" stamped in and revealed through the spousal meaning of the male and female body.

But notice the Pope says this is possible only when spouses are "aware of the authentic depth of the 'redemption of the body.'" In other words, spouses must be aware of the gift of the Holy Spirit poured out in Christ's death and resurrection. They must allow the life and love of Christ to vivify their entire body-soul personalities. To the extent that men and women are not vivified in this way, the distortions of concupiscence will continue to obscure the "great mystery" inscribed in their bodies. But to the degree that spouses allow their lusts to be "crucified with Christ" (see Gal 5:24), the grace poured out in and through the sacraments (including, if not especially, the sacrament of Marriage) can free spouses (and men and women in general) from the blinding effects of concupiscence. The more we cooperate with this grace, the more the scales fall off our eyes. As this happens, we come more to see, experience, and "feel" the true dignity of the body and its spousal meaning as a revelation of the mystery of Christ. Precisely in this way we gain that "reverence for Christ" of which St. Paul speaks. In fact, John Paul boldly observes that this "reverence for Christ" is nothing but a spiritually mature form of the mutual attraction of the sexes (see TOB 117b:4).

This is what authentic marital love affords. Spousal love is itself redemptive. "The Pauline image of marriage...brings together the redemptive dimension of love with its spousal dimension. In some sense it unites these two dimensions...[into] one. Christ...has married the Church as his bride because 'he gave himself for her' (Eph 5:25). Through marriage as a sacrament...*both of these dimensions of love, the spousal and the redemptive...*penetrate...into the life of the spouses" (TOB 102:4). In this way, the spousal meaning of the body—and an authentic reverence for it—is confirmed and, in some sense, John Paul says, "created anew." At the same time husband and wife—via their spousal-redemptive love—"share in the creative love of God himself. They share in it both by the fact that, created in the image of God, they have been called in virtue of this image to a particular union (*communio personarum*, the communion of persons), and because this union has itself been blessed from the beginning with the blessing of fruitfulness (see Gen 1:28)" (TOB 102:2).

Understanding Human Existence

John Paul says that the linking of the spousal meaning of the body with its "redemptive meaning" is obviously important with regard to marriage and the Christian vocation of spouses. But then he adds that it "is equally essential and *valid for the hermeneutics of man* in general: for the fundamental problem of understanding him and for the self-understanding of his being in the world" (TOB 102:5). This is another one of those striking statements that almost stops the reader in his tracks. According to John Paul II, the meaning of human existence is contained right here: in Ephesians 5 where St. Paul links the spousal meaning of the body from Genesis 2:24 (the two become "one flesh") with the redemptive meaning of the body revealed by Christ's union with the Church. John Paul believes that the "great mystery" of Christ's union with the Church "obliges us" to link *the spousal meaning of the body with its redemptive meaning*. In this link, John Paul reiterates that all men and women "find the answer to the question about the meaning of 'being a body'"—which is the meaning of being a human being (TOB 102:5).

Our creation as male and female—our sexuality—is inextricably intertwined with the questions we all have about the meaning of life. Sexuality, as John Paul says, is "deeply inscribed in the essential structure of the human person" (TOB 102:6). And it is a call "from the beginning" for men and women to participate in the divine nature by loving as God loves—in a fruitful communion of persons (*communio personarum*). This is the deepest meaning of human existence: We are created *by* eternal Love and Communion to participate *in* eternal Love and Communion. This is the spousal meaning of the body. Yet, because of sin, we cannot fulfill the meaning of our existence unless we are redeemed. Christ's incarnate union with the Church affords this redemption, and this is the redemptive meaning of the body. Thus in the spousal-redemptive meaning of the body lies the very meaning of human existence.

Love, in a word, is man's origin, vocation, and destiny. While Love in its divine mystery is purely spiritual, in its revelation and human realization it is always *incarnational*. This mystery of love and communion was revealed in the original spousal meaning of the body. But the body's original meaning is "completed," John Paul tells us, in the redemptive meaning of Christ's incarnate union with the Church (see TOB 102:8). Christ initiates his spousal-redemptive love as a gift. We are created to receive it, but never forced to do so. If we engage our freedom and open ourselves to the gift (keeping in mind that the desire and freedom to do so are themselves divine gifts), like a bride we conceive that gift within us. Life then becomes thanksgiving (*eucharistia*) for the gift received, and we experience an incessant desire to extend the divine-human communion of persons to the ends of the earth.

Spousal Love Embraces the Universe

The "great mystery" of spousal and redemptive love is clearly recapitulated (although differently) in the vocations to marriage and celibacy. However, John Paul stresses that the spousal and redemptive meanings of the body pertain to everyone in every human situation. They are not only lived in marriage and celibacy for the kingdom, he says. They are lived on the many "different roads of life and in different situations:...for example, in the many kinds of *human suffering*, indeed, in man's very *birth and death*" (TOB 102:8). Spousal love marks all of human life, and marriage provides the paradigm for all of human life. No one is excluded from this "great mystery." It embraces "every human being and, in some sense, everything created" (TOB 102:7). John Paul goes so far as to say that through "the New Covenant of Christ with the Church, marriage is inscribed anew in the 'sacrament of man,' which embraces the universe" (TOB 102:8).

Everyone without exception is called to the "great sacrament" of Christ's union with the Church. Marriage is organically inscribed in this new sacrament of redemption just as it was inscribed in the sacrament of creation. This means that the sacrament of marriage remains "a living and life-giving part" of the process of salvation "until the measure of definitive fulfillment is reached in the kingdom of the Father" (TOB 102:8).

In all of this John Paul wants to underscore yet again the profound unity—the marriage of sorts—between creation and redemption. When we take this unity and continuity seriously, the implications multiply: We recognize a profound and original unity between nature and grace, between God and man, between man and woman, and between man and all creation. We also recognize that *all* of these unities—all of these marriages—find their foundation and draw their efficacy from the ultimate unity manifested in flesh, the ultimate marriage: that of *the divine and human natures in the incarnate person of Christ*. He is "the center of the universe and of history."[58] Christ "fully reveals man to himself and makes his supreme calling clear."[59] Only when we take the profound link between creation and redemption seriously does the meaning of our humanity and our lofty vocation as men and women come into focus.

As John Paul states: "Man, who is 'from the beginning' male and female, must seek the meaning of his existence and the meaning of his humanity by reaching all the way to the mystery of creation through the reality of redemption. There he finds also the essential answer to the question about the meaning of the human body, about the meaning of the masculinity and femininity of the human person" (TOB 102:8). It is Christ. We were created from the beginning as male and female and called to communion to prepare us for *communion with Christ*.

THE DIMENSION OF COVENANT AND OF GRACE—IN REVIEW

1. In Part II, Chapter 1 of his catechesis on the body, John Paul unfolds the mystery of "the sacrament" (of marriage) in the divine dimension of covenant and grace by resurrecting the meaning of

---

58. *Redemptor Hominis*, 1.
59. *Gaudium et Spes*, 22.

Ephesians 5. He wants to demonstrate this "classical" text's fundamental importance not only for understanding the sacramentality of marriage, but for understanding the entire Christian mystery and the very meaning of human existence.

2. The Apostle's outline of the spousal mystery in Ephesians 5 reveals man to himself in a particular way and makes him aware of his lofty vocation. But man can only see the importance of Ephesians 5 for his own existence to the extent that he participates in the experience of the incarnate person. Modern rationalism, with its radical split between body and soul, is perpetually at odds with the "great mystery" of Ephesians 5.

3. In a general way the body enters the very definition of "sacrament" as a visible sign of the invisible. The body, then, through its sacramentality, is an efficacious sign of grace; it is "the hinge of salvation." Thus, man need not shed his skin in his quest for transcendence. He need not eschew his body and sexuality. This is the affirmation of Ephesians 5—bodiliness and spousal union are a "great mystery" that refer to Christ and the Church.

4. In calling wives to "submit" to their husbands, St. Paul appeals to the custom of the day in order to inject this mentality with the mystery of Christ's love for the Church and the vocation of Christians to "walk in love, as Christ loved us." In this light, the Apostle calls spouses to "submit to one another out of reverence for Christ." Subjection within marriage, then, is not one-sided, but mutual, and it must be modeled on the love of Christ.

5. When viewed through the paradigm of the "gift," we come to understand that to be "subject" to one's spouse means to live the sincere gift of self. In turn, mutual subjection means reciprocal self-donation. According to the spousal analogy, the husband must image Christ in his self-giving, and the wife is called to image the Church in her receptivity to the gift and in her giving of herself back to her husband.

6. Since the husband is to love his wife "as Christ loved the Church," this clearly excludes male domination. Domination results from original sin. When properly understood, the wife's "submission" to her husband signifies above all the experiencing of love. This seems

even more obvious because the wife's "submission" is related to the submission of the Church to Christ, which certainly consists of experiencing his love.

7. The spousal analogy operates in two directions. To a certain degree marriage illuminates the mystery of Christ and the Church. At the same time Christ's relationship with the Church unveils the essential truth about marriage. The very essence of marriage captures a particle of the Christian mystery. If it were otherwise, the analogy would hang in a void.

8. The spousal analogy is intimately related with the head-body analogy. In becoming "one body," the spouses almost form "one organism," like a head and a body. In this way they almost become "one subject" while maintaining an essential "bi-subjectivity." This is a unity-in-plurality through the mystery of love in which the "I" of the other in some sense becomes one's own. In this way "carnal love" images the Trinity and expresses the language of agape.

9. Ephesians 5 shows that the purpose of Christ's self-gift is our sanctification. Christ cleanses us "by the washing of water with the word." This is a reference to the "spousal bath" of Baptism, which applies and extends the spousal and redemptive love of Christ to all who are bathed so that we might become a glorious bride, "without spot or wrinkle or any such thing."

10. By using physical beauty as a metaphor for holiness, St. Paul demonstrates a masterful understanding of the sacramentality of the body. For him, the human body indicates attributes of the moral, spiritual, and supernatural order. St. Paul explains the mystery of sanctification, the mystery of Christ's redemptive love, and the mystery of humanity's union with the divine all through the resemblance of the body and of the spousal union in "one flesh."

11. Love obliges the husband to desire his wife's beauty, to appreciate it, and to care for it. A husband who loves his wife "as Christ loved the Church" wants all that is good in her to blossom and radiate through her body. He sees even in her blemishes and disfigurations an "echo" of the beginning and the hope of eternal glory. Christ saw his Bride covered with the blemishes and disfigurations of sin and loved her all the more.

12. The "nourishment" Christ offers his Bride is his own body in the Eucharist. Thus, in Ephesians 5 we glimpse the manner in which the Eucharist indicates the specific character of spousal love, especially of that gift of self in "one flesh."

13. Since the time of Aquinas, the term "sacrament" has referred almost exclusively to the seven signs of grace instituted by Christ. Only in the last century have theologians sought to recover the broader and more ancient understanding of "sacrament" as the revelation and accomplishment of the mystery hidden in God from eternity. The words "sacrament" and "mystery" are related but not synonymous. Mystery connotes that which is hidden, and sacrament that which is revealed.

14. The "great mystery" revealed by the sacrament is God's plan of salvation for humanity. In some sense this is the central theme of divine revelation. St. Paul indicates that the "one flesh" union of spouses has participated in this "great mystery" from the beginning. His linking of Genesis 2:24 with Christ's union with the Church is *the keystone* of Ephesians 5. It establishes the continuity between the most ancient covenant and the definitive covenant.

15. Christ is at the heart of the "great mystery" proclaimed in Ephesians. In him we have been blessed "with every spiritual blessing" and chosen "before the creation of the world." The eternal mystery is accomplished in Christ and through Christ. Christ reveals the mystery of divine love. Christ is the meaning of embodiment and marriage. Christ is the meaning of the moral instruction given by Paul. Christ is the center of *everything*.

16. The "great mystery" is accomplished in the mode of gift, of the spousal donation of Christ himself to his Bride. We participate in the eternal mystery of Love and Communion when we open ourselves to the gift and accept it through faith. The divine Mystery is at work in us under the veil of faith and the veil of a sign that makes the Invisible visible.

17. The spousal love of God for humanity was only "half open" in the Old Testament. In Ephesians 5, it is fully revealed. Paul presents new revealed moments unknown prior to Christ. We now learn with clarity what Isaiah already intuited: that there is a certain

parallel between God as "spouse" and God as redeemer. Christ's spousal gift of self to his Bride is equivalent to carrying out the work of redemption.

18. The spousal analogy is certainly not adequate or complete, yet it contains a characteristic of the mystery not emphasized by any other analogy in the Bible—the aspect of God's "total" gift of self to man. In Christ, God gives all that he can give of himself to man considering man's limited faculties as a creature. In this way, the spousal analogy provides a vivid image of the radical character of grace.

19. The sacrament manifests the divine mystery in a sign that serves not only to proclaim the mystery, but accomplish it in man. The image of conjugal union in Genesis 2:24 speaks of the most ancient way in which the divine mystery was made visible, while the union of Christ and the Church speaks of the definitive sign of this mystery given in the fullness of time. To his special merit, St. Paul makes of these two signs *one great sign*—the single "great sacrament."

20. Conjugal union foreshadowed the Incarnation right from the beginning. Thus, the visible sign of marriage—inasmuch as it is analogically linked to the visible sign of Christ and the Church, the summit of God's revelation—transfers God's eternal plan of love into history and becomes the "foundation of the whole sacramental order."

21. Man was chosen in Christ "before the foundations of the world." Thus, the grace of original innocence was accomplished in reference to Christ, while anticipating chronologically his coming in the body. Christ's coming, therefore, is not merely the result of sin. God's eternal plan for man in Christ remains the same yesterday, today, and forever. The redemption became the source of grace for man after sin and, in a certain sense, despite sin.

22. Genesis 2:24 constitutes marriage as the primordial sacrament inasmuch as it is the central point of the "sacrament of creation." All creation makes God's mystery visible in some way. Yet the "sacrament of creation" reaches its highest expression in man, male and female, who fully realizes himself through the sincere gift of

self. The inner dimension of the gift in man is revealed through the grace-filled awareness of the spousal meaning of the body.

23. The primordial sacrament contains a supernatural efficacy because already in creation man was "chosen in Christ." Hence the original "sacrament of creation" draws its efficacy from Christ. Marriage is intended, therefore, not only to advance the work of creation through procreation. God also intends that it serve to extend his eternal plan of love and election in Christ to further generations.

24. The heritage of sin dimmed the beatifying experience of original unity. As the primordial sacrament, marriage was deprived of its supernatural efficaciousness. Yet even in the state of man's hereditary sinfulness, marriage always remained the figure of that sacrament—the platform for realizing God's eternal plans. The original unity in the body still molds human history, even though it lost the clarity of the sign of salvation.

25. The "sacrament of redemption" refers to the totality of the new gracing of man in Christ. St. Paul links it with Genesis 2:24, showing that it takes on the same form as the primordial sacrament. The sacraments of creation and redemption are realized in the visibility of their signs—*through the union* of the first Adam and Eve in creation, and *through the union* of the New Adam and Eve (Christ and the Church) in redemption. These signs, which St. Paul made one "great sign," refer to the entire work of creation and redemption.

26. Christ's spousal relationship with the Church, as the analogy would indicate, has both a unitive and a life-giving dimension. The unitive dimension is completed when the Church receives and responds to the gift of her Bridegroom, just as Eve completed her husband as a "helper fit for him." In turn, the Church manifests the life-giving dimension in her fruitfulness and spiritual motherhood.

27. The Apostle's linking of the original union of spouses with the union of Christ and the Church is not merely a metaphor, but speaks of a real renewal of that which constituted the salvific content of the primordial sacrament. In other words, the grace of the primordial sacrament, which was lost through sin, is now *resurrected* in the sacrament of redemption.

28. In some way Christ assumes into the whole economy of redemption the same spousal imprint that permeated creation. As a primordial sacrament, marriage is assumed and inserted from its very basis into the integral structure of the new sacramental economy. Thus, marriage arises from redemption *in the form of a prototype.* In some way all of the sacraments find their prototype in marriage as the primordial sacrament.

29. Marriage constitutes an exhortation to participate *consciously* and *conscientiously* in the redemption of the body. Spouses who are committed to doing so can progressively rediscover, reclaim, and live according to their original dignity. They can—by daily taking up the redeeming cross of Christ—experience a real measure of the harmony, peace, and happiness of original unity.

30. Christian ethos can be explained philosophically but, ultimately, it is only fully tenable to those who are living the grace of a redeemed life in Christ. Christ assigns the ethos of redemption to man's heart, his conscience, his looks, and his behavior. The sacred and personal dignity of the body forms the basis of all morality, sexual or otherwise. To the degree that we are vivified by the Holy Spirit, we are consciously aware of this sacred dignity and do not desire to profane it.

31. There is a deep link between the call to become "one flesh" in Genesis 2:24 and the teaching of *Gaudium et Spes*, 24, that man can only find himself "through the sincere gift of self." The egoistic gratification of concupiscence is incompatible with such self-giving. Yet as much as concupiscence distorts the heart and its desires, so much does "life according to the Holy Spirit" permit men and women to find again the true freedom of the gift in their bodily union.

32. St. Paul's words—"it is better to marry than to be aflame with passion"—do not justify indulging concupiscence. "To be aflame" signifies the disorder of the passions, whereas "to marry" signifies the ethical order and the ethos of redemption. Marriage is meant to be the meeting place of eros with ethos—a meeting that bears fruit in purity of heart.

33. The mutual union in "one flesh" and its accompanying pleasure is meant to be an expression of "life according to the Spirit"—of the specific grace of the sacrament of marriage. Authentic pleasure, however, is not egoistic, nor is it ever closed in on itself. If marital intercourse is to be "according to the Spirit," spouses must open their union to that Spirit who is the Lord and Giver of Life.

34. Every child conceived of the marital union not only reproduces the mystery of creation, but also proclaims the hope of redemption. Openness to life in conjugal intercourse, therefore, has not only a temporal dimension but also an eternal dimension. The blessing of fertility forces men and women to choose between what is "of the Father" and what is "of the world." "The world passes away and the lust thereof; but he who does the will of God abides forever" (1 Jn 1:17).

35. In light of Ephesians 5, spouses are called to model their lives not only on the original unity of man and woman, but even more so on the unity of Christ and the Church. In this way the original meaning of marriage is *presupposed* and *rediscovered*, but only if spouses consciously experience the redemption of the body. Authentic spousal love is itself redemptive. St. Paul unites these two dimensions of love into one.

36. The linking of the spousal meaning of the body with its redemptive meaning is obviously important with regard to marriage, but it is equally essential if man is to comprehend the very meaning of his existence in the world. Man is called *in his body* to love as God loves. This is the spousal meaning of the body. Yet, because of sin, he cannot fulfill the meaning of his existence unless he is redeemed. Christ's union with the Church affords this redemption, and this shows the redemptive meaning of the body.

37. By reaching out to the mystery of creation through the reality of redemption, we discover the meaning of human existence, the meaning of sexuality, and the meaning of marriage. Spousal love marks all of human life. In Christ's union with the Church, marriage is again inscribed in that "sacrament of man" which embraces the universe.

The Dimension of Sign

[Cycle 5—The Sacramentality of Marriage, cont'd.]

IN PART II, CHAPTER 1, we explored "the sacrament" in the dimension of *covenant and grace* (this is the divine dimension). Now, in Part II, Chapter 2, we will explore the meaning of "the sacrament" in the dimension of *the sign* (this is the human dimension).

John Paul has already said much about the nature of marriage as a sacramental sign. Still, in these sixteen addresses delivered between January 5, 1983, and July 4, 1984[1] (TOB, 103–117b), the Pope penetrates more deeply into the very "structure" of the sign in order to define it in a more adequate and exhaustive way. He does so first by developing the concept of the "language of the body" and the need to speak this language truthfully. Then he looks to the lovers in the Song of Songs and to the marriage of Tobias and Sarah as biblical examples of couples who, each in their own way, speak the language of the body truthfully. As John Paul II says, both couples "find their place in what constitutes the sacramental sign of marriage. Both share in the formation of this sign" (TOB 116:5). Finally, the Holy Father returns to the "great mystery" of Ephesians 5 in order to find "definitive" confirmation of the sacramental sign.

The Holy Father's teaching regarding what constitutes the sacramental sign of marriage offers a welcome resolution to a centuries-old

---

1. John Paul II's catechesis on the body was interrupted in February of 1983 by the celebration of the Holy Year of Redemption. He resumed on May 23, 1984.

theological discussion. What *visible* reality of marriage (human dimension) symbolizes and effects the *invisible* mystery (divine dimension) of grace? Theological debates about what constituted marriage as a sacramental sign came to the fore around the tenth and eleventh centuries, when marriage was placed more fully under the jurisdiction of the Church.[2] Most theologians and canonists followed the lead of Hugh of St. Victor, who posited the sign of marriage in the words of consent (the wedding vows) and their mutual exchange in the rite of marriage. Other currents of thought posited the sign in the bodily act of consummation. The latter view was resisted for various reasons. For example, how could such a view account for the virginal marriage of Joseph and Mary? Furthermore, emphasis on consummation was probably resisted, at least in some cases, because of the "interpretation of suspicion" and the inability of those who adhere to this interpretation to imagine the sexual act as a participation in grace.

John Paul's faith in the *real power* of the redemption of the body removes the taint of suspicion from the marital act. For him, there is no question that the sexual union of spouses is meant to be a participation in grace. He has already affirmed that God intends the "one flesh" union as a vehicle of the Holy Spirit in married life—of the specific grace of the sacrament of marriage (see TOB 101:5–6).

Does this mean he simply sides with those theologians who posited the sign of marriage in the act of consummation? For John Paul conjugal intercourse certainly plays a fundamental role in understanding the sacramental sign of marriage. He has already said as much in various ways throughout his catechesis (see pp. 148ff., 198, 209, 231, 429). But John Paul does not resolve the debate by picking sides. He creatively demonstrates that, in effect, both "sides" are correct. The

---

2. These debates were closely related with the question about what established the indissoluble bond of marriage. Roman law recognized the mutual consent as the "contractual moment" of marriage. However, the various cultures of northern Europe being evangelized in the tenth and eleventh centuries recognized marriage either at the moment of betrothal (when the father handed the bride over to the husband) or at the moment of *consummation*. In light of these debates, Pope Alexander III decreed that marriage is *ratified* at the moment of consent. However, marriage is not constituted in its full reality until the moment of consummation. In some cases, therefore, prior to sexual union a marriage can be dissolved by papal dispensation. See canons 1061, 1142. For an overview of the history outlined here, see Peter J. Elliot, *What God Has Joined* (Homebush, Australia: St. Paul/Alba House, 1990), pp. 73–117.

key to this innovation lies in understanding the rich and mysterious "language of the body."

1. "Language of the Body" and the Reality of the Sign

Words "Made Flesh"

The purpose of all language is to give expression to meaning, to truth. All that John Paul has said about *the truth of the body* and its *spousal meaning* is expressed—or, is *meant* to be expressed—through the body's "language." According to John Paul, the body "speaks" a language without words (see TOB 109:1). It speaks the deepest truth of man's personal existence as male and female and of his call to love as God loves in a life-giving communion of persons. And man "is *in some sense unable to express* this singular language of his personal existence and vocation *without the body*" (TOB 104:7). From the beginning, man was constituted in such a way as to express spiritual realities in and through his flesh. This means that "the deepest words of the spirit—words of love, gift, and faithfulness—call for an appropriate 'language of the body.' And without this language, they cannot be fully expressed. We know from the gospel that this point applies both to marriage and to continence 'for the kingdom of heaven'" (TOB 104:7). To divorce the language of the spirit from the language of the body, as John Paul says elsewhere, breaks "the personal unity of soul and body [and] strikes at God's creation itself at the level of the deepest interaction of nature and person."[3]

What bearing does this have on determining the structure of the sacramental sign of marriage? John Paul says that the exchange of wedding vows gives an intentional expression on the level of the intellect and will, of consciousness and heart to the spiritual reality of love, of giving, and of fidelity (see TOB 103:5). However—if, according to the Pope's thesis, the body *and only the body* is capable of making spiritual realities visible—the spoken language of the vows is not "complete" without an adequate and corresponding language of the body. The spiritual expression of intellect and will *must* have a corresponding bodily

---

3. *Familiaris Consortio*, 32.

expression. What is that corresponding bodily expression? Conjugal intercourse.

The marital embrace, one might say, is where the words of the wedding vows *become flesh*. The "language" inscribed in sexual intercourse and expressed by those who perform the sexual act is and should always be the language of wedding vows. John Paul states: "In fact, the words themselves, 'I take you as my wife/as my husband'...can only be fulfilled by...conjugal intercourse." With conjugal intercourse "we pass *to the reality* that corresponds to these words.[4] Both the one and the other element," he says, "are important *with regard to the structure of the sacramental sign*." And by means of this sign, the Pope reminds us, "the saving reality of grace and the covenant is expressed and realized" (TOB 103:2, 3).

> ■ St. Bonaventure offered a profound reflection on the interrelationship of the exchange of vows and consummation in marriage. He taught that in the moment of consent when spouses commit their will to marriage, they are with Christ in his agony in the garden. There Christ committed his will to "giving himself up" for his Bride. In the moment of consummation, spouses are with Christ on the cross, living out in their bodies what they committed to at the altar, just as Christ is living out what he committed to in the garden.[5]

John Paul concludes that the "sacramental sign is constituted in the intentional order inasmuch as it is simultaneously constituted in the real order" (TOB 103:3). He continues by saying that the words spoken by the bride and groom "would not of themselves constitute the sacramental sign" of marriage unless these words corresponded to the awareness (or consciousness) of the body, linked to their masculinity and femininity. Here John Paul says we must recall the whole series of our previous analyses of Genesis. Most specifically, the Holy Father recalls that the Creator himself instituted conjugal intercourse from the very beginning according to those familiar words of Genesis 2:24: "For this

---

4. See *CCC*, no. 1627.
5. See St. Bonaventure, "On the Integrity of Matrimony," *Breviloquium*, Part VI, chap. 13.

reason...the two become one flesh." Hence, the Pope affirms that the structure of the sacramental sign remains in essence the same as "in the beginning." It is communicated in "*'the language of the body*,' inasmuch as the man and the woman, who are to become one flesh by marriage, express in this sign the reciprocal gift of masculinity and femininity as the foundation of the conjugal union of the persons" (TOB 103:4). Through their mutual exchange of vows, in fact, "the man and the woman express their readiness to become 'one flesh' according to the eternal truth established in the mystery of creation" (TOB 103:3). Recall John Paul's statement that marriage only corresponds to the vocation of Christians if they choose it just as the Creator instituted it "from the beginning."

This means the exchange of vows is a sacramental sign by reason of its content—by its expressed readiness to actuate the vows in "one flesh." However, John Paul tells us that in and of itself the exchange of consent is "only a sign of the coming to be of marriage. And the coming to be of marriage is distinct from its consummation, so much so that without this consummation, marriage is not yet constituted in its full reality" (TOB 103:2). While marriage is contracted at the moment of consent—and a ratified marriage exists at this moment—it is not *fully* constituted as a marriage until the moment of consummation.

The Interplay of Form and Matter

According to the scholastic tradition, sacraments are constituted by the creative interplay of the words spoken (the "form") and the physical reality (the "matter") (see TOB 98:7). The vows make up the "form" of the sacrament of marriage and the bodies of husband and wife make up the "matter." Accordingly, as John Paul says: "*Both of them, as man and woman*, being ministers of the sacrament at the moment of contracting marriage, at the same time *constitute the full and real visible sign* of the sacrament itself" (TOB 103:4).

The words spoken correspond to the "human subjectivity of the engaged man and woman" in their masculinity and femininity and in their call to become "one flesh." In the marital embrace the "form" and the "matter" (their vows and their bodies) in some sense become one and the same sacramental mystery—one and the same sacramental sign. "In this way," John Paul says, "the perennial and ever new 'language of the body' *is not only the 'substratum,' but in some sense also the constitutive content of the communion of the persons*" (TOB 103:5). Of course, the communion of persons in marriage does not refer only to the specific moment of joining in "one flesh." Conjugal intercourse is meant to be a sign that encompasses and sums up (*con*-summates) the whole reality of married life. "As spouses, the man and woman bear this sign throughout the whole of their lives, and they remain this sign until death." At the beginning of their lives together, the "liturgy of the sacrament of Marriage gives a form to that sign: directly, during the sacramental rite...; indirectly, throughout the whole of life" (TOB 103:7).

So, does the liturgical exchange of vows make up the sign? Do the man and woman themselves make up the sign? Does conjugal intercourse make up the sign? Does the whole of married life make up the sign? Yes, yes, yes, and yes. The entire reality of the gift of man and woman to each other "until death" is the unrepeatable sign of marriage. And, as John Paul says, this is a "*sign with...manifold contents*" (TOB 105:6). It is first established by the liturgical rite in the exchange of consent, and it is then embodied and brought to fulfillment in marital intercourse. In turn we come to realize that this "is not merely an immediate and fleeting sign, but a sign that looks toward the future and produces a lasting effect, namely, the conjugal bond, one and indissoluble" (TOB 105:6). In its manifold contents, the sacramental sign of marriage "is the visible and efficacious *sign* of the covenant with God in Christ, that is, of *grace, which is to become...[the spouses'] portion in this sign as 'their own gift'* (according to the expression of 1 Cor 7:7)" (TOB 103:6).

In summary: the sacramental sign of marriage is expressed through the language of the irrevocable self-giving of man and woman to each other. It is a gift given "in good times and bad, in sickness and in health...all the days of my life." This language of the spirit—of the heart, will, and intellect—has a corresponding "language of the body." This body-language is expressed throughout married life, but especially in the act of marital intercourse. As the Holy Father says in his *Letter to Families*: "All married life is a gift; but this becomes most evident when the spouses, in giving themselves to each other in love, bring about that encounter which makes them 'one flesh.'"[6] This confirms the Pope's statement that "the 'language of the body' also enters essentially into

---

6. *Letter to Families*, 12.

the structure of marriage as a sacramental sign" (TOB 104:1). Just as the body is the visible sign of a person's soul, the "one body" that spouses become serves in some way as the visible sign of their marriage's "soul." In turn, if the whole of married life is a sign, we might say that conjugal intercourse is a *sign* of that sign. The Pope seems to express this idea when he states that "the sign of spousal union...has become...a sign of marriage as a sacrament" (TOB 108:5).

The "Prophetism of the Body"

Although John Paul gives a fresh voice to this idea of the body possessing a language, he points out that it has a long biblical tradition. This tradition begins in Genesis (especially 2:23–25), passes through the prophets, and finds its definitive culmination in Paul's Letter to the Ephesians (see Eph 5:21–33). John Paul believes that the prophetic books of the Old Testament have a particular importance for understanding marriage in the dimension of sign. In the text of the prophets the body speaks the language of God's covenant love for his people. Based on this tradition, John Paul says we can even "speak *about a specific 'prophetism of the body,'* both because we find this analogy above all in the prophets and also in regard to its very contents. Here the 'prophetism of the body' signifies precisely the 'language of the body'" (TOB 104:1).

The analogy the prophets use seems to have two levels. "*On the first level*, the fundamental level, the prophets *portray the covenant as a marriage* established between God and Israel (which in turn allows us to understand marriage itself as a covenant between husband and wife; see Prov 2:17; Mal 2:14)" (TOB 104:2). The other books of the Old Testament present Yahweh's absolute "lordship" in terms of his dominion as Lord of the covenant and Father of Israel. But the prophets add a new and "stupendous" dimension, "namely, the...spousal dimension. In this manner, the absolute of lordship turns out to be the absolute of love" (TOB 104:3). Thus, in the prophets, a breach of the covenant involves not only a breaking of the law of the supreme Legislator, but infidelity and betrayal of God's love. This is "a blow that directly pierces his heart as Father, Bridegroom, and Lord" (TOB 104:3).

This more fundamental level of the analogy reveals a second level, which is precisely the language of the body. If God's covenant love is presented as a spousal love, the language of the body is meant to express faithfully that same covenant love of God. It is in this way that the language of the body is understood as prophetic. As John Paul points out: "A 'prophet' is one who expresses with human words the truth that comes from God, one who speaks this truth in the place of God, in his name and in some sense with his authority" (TOB 105:2). This is precisely what God created the human body to do. From the beginning God created the body to proclaim his own truth, his own mystery of life and love—of communion.

Man: The Author of His Own Language

However, John Paul points out several times that the body per se is not the author of this prophetic language. "*Its author is man*" (see TOB 104:7; 105:2,6). The language of the body, to be sure, has an objective dimension—a meaning given by God which is pre-inscribed in the body, so to speak. However, man must take up this language as its subject. He must make it his own. In this way man becomes the "author" of the language of his own body. If he is to speak the truth with his body, every man must ensure that the *subjective* language he authors corresponds with its *objective* meaning.

Here we glimpse the very foundations of morality for man. Throughout his catechesis, John Paul—in accord with modern sensitivities—fully recognizes man as a personal subject. In this context he affirms again that "man—male and female–is a conscious subject capable of self-determination. Only on this basis can he be the author of the 'language of the body'" (TOB 107:5). However, man's liberation as a subject comes not by a self-assertive divorce from objective reality. It comes by wedding himself to it—not because it is imposed upon him, but because he trusts in it and desires it freely. He subjects himself to it as a subject. If man's "authorship" of the language of his own body speaks of his freedom to choose between good and evil, it does not thereby give him authorship over what *is* good and evil. This is a "tree" from which man cannot eat, lest he die (see Gen 2:17). The moment man divorces himself from the objective good and seeks to author his own reality is precisely the moment of abuse of his own subjectivity. It is the moment of broken trust in his Creator and of infidelity to the covenant.

Recall that the prophets use the language of the body both in praising God's fidelity to his covenant and in condemning Israel's infidelity
as "adultery." In this way the prophets outline ethical categories, setting
moral good and evil in mutual opposition (see TOB 104:8). This has
immediate implications for the union of man and woman. In their relationship, "it is the body itself that 'speaks'; it speaks with its masculinity
or femininity, it speaks with the mysterious language of the personal
gift, it speaks...both in the language of faithfulness, that is, of love, and
in the language of conjugal unfaithfulness that is, of 'adultery'" (TOB
104:4).

What does all this mean? If man, as a self-determining subject, is
the author of his own body's language, he can choose to speak the
truth. But he can also choose to speak lies. In other words, if the body is
prophetic, the Pope points out that we must also keep in mind the biblical distinction between true and false prophets (see TOB 106:4). The
categories of truth and falsity are essential to every language (see TOB
104:8). Everyone can recognize that it is possible to speak a lie with the
body. The Scriptures give a plain example in Judas's kiss. Here an
expression of love became instead an act of betrayal.

"Language of the Body" Reread in the Truth

When spouses exchange the words of consent, they explicitly
confirm the essential "truth" of the language of the body and implicitly
exclude any "falsity." In other words, they commit to being true
prophets according to the original biblical meaning of joining in "one
flesh." The body speaks the truth "through conjugal love, faithfulness,
and integrity." It speaks lies "through all that negates conjugal love,
faithfulness, and integrity" (TOB 105:1). John Paul says that in this
way the essential truth of the sign will remain organically linked to the
morality of the spouses' marital conduct (see TOB 105:6). Recall that
we can speak of moral good and evil in the marital/sexual relationship
based on whether the couple gives to their union "the character of a
truthful sign" (TOB 37:6).

In this context, John Paul specifically reminds us that the language
of consent in marriage—to which the language of the body in sexual
intercourse corresponds—must include an affirmative answer to the
following question: "Are you willing to accept children lovingly from

God?" This question that the priest or deacon poses to the couple is an essential part of the liturgical rite. If the language of consent says "yes" to this question but the language of the body says "no," would we not encounter a specific negation of conjugal love, faithfulness, and integrity?

As the author of his own body's language, man must learn to reread the spousal meaning of the body as integrally inscribed in each person's masculinity or femininity. "A correct rereading 'in the truth' is an indispensable condition for proclaiming this truth or instituting the visible sign of marriage as a sacrament" (TOB 105:2). Indeed, John Paul says that "the essential element for marriage as a sacrament is the 'language of the body' reread in the truth. It is precisely through this that the sacramental sign is constituted" (TOB 104:9).

Through "the whole of the 'language of the body'...the spouses decide to speak to each other as ministers of the sacrament" (TOB 105:6). They not only proclaim the truth coming from God, John Paul even says that they proclaim this truth *in God's name* (see TOB 105:2). In constituting the marital sign in the moment of consent and fulfilling it in the moment of consummation, the spouses "*perform an act of prophetic character.* They confirm in this way their share in the prophetic mission of the Church" received from Christ (TOB 105:2).

By speaking the language of the body in truth, spouses "*also reach in some sense the very sources* from which this sign each time draws its prophetic eloquence and sacramental strength. One must not allow oneself to forget," the Pope insists, "that before being spoken by the lips of the spouses, the ministers of the sacrament as a sacrament of the Church, 'the language of the body' was spoken by the word of the living God, from the beginning in Genesis through the prophets of the Old Covenant all the way to the author of Ephesians" (TOB 105:4). Hence, John Paul reaffirms that this enduring language of the body bears within itself the whole richness and depth of the divine-human mystery: first of creation, then of redemption (see TOB 105:4).

"Language of the Body" and Victory over Concupiscence

The entire question of the sacramental sign of marriage has "a highly anthropological character," the Holy Father tells us. "We build it on the basis of theological anthropology and in particular on...the 'theology of the body'" (TOB 106:5). In turn, the understanding of the sacramental sign as John Paul presents it confirms his theological anthropology, his specific interpretation of man.

The body is understood as a "theology" specifically because God created it from the beginning to be a sign of his own divine mystery. He created it as such in its sexuality—its masculinity and femininity—and the call to form "one body." We know, however, that original sin obscured the truth of the body as a sign of the divine mystery. The man of concupiscence is almost blind to the value of the body as a sacramental sign. How then is he to "reread" the language of the body in truth? Precisely at this point we stand at the thresholds of two competing and irreconcilable anthropologies. We either open to the possibility of rebirth in the Holy Spirit, or we condemn man with an irreversible suspicion.

Rereading the language of the body "in the truth" is given as a task to the man of concupiscence. But is such a man up to the task? Is the man of lust not bound to falsify the language of the body? At this point John Paul once again, in proclaiming the power of the Gospel, is at pains to ensure us that the redemption of the body is *effective* in saving man from his sins, in enabling him to be victorious in his fight with concupiscence. He recalls his reflections on "the masters of suspicion," who believe man is determined by lust and has no alternative but to lust (see p. 236ff.). John Paul insists again that the redemption of the body is not only a divine mystery, but also—in Christ and through Christ—*a human reality that reaches us*, that reaches every human being (see TOB 107:2). Christ does not merely accuse the heart of lust in the Sermon on the Mount. Above all, Christ *calls* the man of concupiscence to overcome the lust in his heart through the ethos of redemption (see p. 199). Christ calls man with tenderness and compassion, with mercy and forgiveness.

We see this foreshadowed already in the prophets. John Paul points out that Hosea in particular "highlights the whole splendor of the covenant, of the wedding in which Yahweh shows himself as a sensitive Bridegroom or husband ready to forgive and at the same time demanding and severe" (TOB 104:5). Christ's words about lust are indeed severe. However, should "we *fear* the severity of these words, or rather *have confidence* in their salvific content, in their power?" (TOB 43:7). They have power to save us because the man who speaks them is the

Lamb of God who takes away the sin of the world. This means that the man of concupiscence need not be determined by lust. If such were the case, man would "be condemned...to essential falsifications." He would be "condemned to suspecting himself and others in regard to the truth of the language of the body. Because of the concupiscence of the flesh, he could only be 'accused,' but he could not be truly 'called'" (TOB 107:6). However, John Paul assures us that "the 'hermeneutics of the sacrament'"—that is, the interpretation of man in light of the grace poured out through the sacrament—"allows us to draw the conclusion that man is always *essentially 'called' and not merely 'accused'*" (TOB 107:6).

"The analysis of Christ's words in the Sermon on the Mount leads us to understand...that the human 'heart' is not so much 'accused and condemned' by Christ because of concupiscence...but first of all 'called.' Here we find a decisive divergence between the anthropology...of the Gospel and...the so-called masters of suspicion." Although "man naturally remains the man of concupiscence...he is at the same time *the man of the 'call.'* He is 'called' through the mystery of the redemption of the body" (TOB 107:1–2). The Pope insists, therefore, that concupiscence *"does not destroy the capacity to reread the 'language of the body' in the truth."* In fact, the light of the Gospel and of the New Covenant revealed in Christ's body enables us to reread the true language of the body "in an ever more mature and full way" (TOB107:3). Thus, John Paul affirms that despite the heritage of original sin, men and women are able—from the evangelical and Christian perspective of the problem—to constitute the sacramental sign in faithfulness and integrity. And they are able to do so "as *an enduring sign*: 'To be faithful to you always, in joy and in sorrow, in sickness and in health, and to love you and honor you all the days of my life'" (TOB 107:4).

Spouses establish this enduring sign at the moment of their consent in the exchange of vows. However, that initial sign will be continually fulfilled and completed by the "prophetism of the body." The spouses' bodies will continue to speak *"for"* and *"on behalf of"* each of them—*in the name of and with the authority of* each of the spouses. In this way, in and through the language of their bodies, husband and wife will carry out "the conjugal dialogue" proper to their vocation (see TOB 106:2). They will continually and mutually speak of their commitment to their marital covenant (or their lack thereof).

John Paul says that spouses are called to form their life and their living together as a communion of persons on the basis of that language of the body. And, as he exclaims, "it is necessary that it is reread in the truth!" (TOB 106:2). In this sphere John Paul says that the spouses are both the cause and the authors of conjugal actions, which have "clear-cut meanings." These "conjugal actions" refer, of course, to the acts of conjugal intercourse. But they also refer to "the whole of the 'language of the body' with which the spouses decide to speak to each other as ministers of the sacrament" (TOB 105:6). The Pope observes that all the meanings of the language of the body are initiated and "programmed" in the content of conjugal consent. Day by day, the spouses draw from that program the same sign, identifying themselves with it throughout their lives (see TOB 106:3). In all that they do—and especially in the consummate expression of their union—the spouses remain faithful to their original consent, or they fail to do so. They deepen their love and faithfulness, or they weaken and cheapen it.

In this way we see that there "*is an organic link between rereading* the integral meaning of the 'language of the body' in the truth and the consequent *use* of that language in conjugal life" (TOB 106:3). Spouses "are explicitly called to bear witness—by correctly using the 'language of the body'—to spousal and procreative love, *a testimony worthy of 'true prophets.'* In this consists the true significance and the greatness of conjugal consent in the sacrament of the Church" (TOB 106:4). The "greatness" of conjugal consent is precisely its prophetic witness to the "mystery hidden from eternity in God"—the mystery of trinitarian life and love that flows through the spousal union of Christ with the Church, reaching the concrete lives of men and women within history.

It is this divine life and love alone that enables spouses to offer a "testimony worthy of true prophets." Such a testimony is impossible if men and women are left to their own resources. Without the powers coming from the Holy Spirit, spouses cannot overcome the domination of concupiscence, which condemns them to essential errors in reading and speaking the language of the body. But here is the *good news* of the Gospel as proclaimed so powerfully by John Paul II: "While concupiscence...brings about many 'errors' in rereading the 'language of the body'...nevertheless, in the sphere of the ethos of redemption there is always the possibility of passing from 'error' to the 'truth' as well as the possibility of...conversion, from sin to chastity as an expression of a life according to the Spirit (see Gal 5:16)" (TOB 107:3).

Concretely, what does this conversion from sin to chastity entail? "How might love be experienced so that it can fully realize its human and divine promise? Here we can find a first, important indication in the Song of Songs, an Old Testament book well known to the mystics."[7]

2. The Song of Songs

The whole sphere of erotic love, as John Paul says, "has been, is, and will be the subject of literary narrative. Such a narrative found its place also in the Bible...in the text of the Song of Songs.... Indeed," he continues, "one must note that in the whole history of literature or art, in the history of human culture, this *subject seems to be particularly frequent* and is *particularly important*" (TOB 63:3). The Pope, far from being skittish about the celebration of erotic love in the Song of Songs, believes that this biblical poetry speaks of eros in a "way worthy of the greatest works of human genius" (TOB 111:6). The fact that Sacred Scripture also celebrates eros should not surprise us. To the degree that we are free of a Manichaean ethos, we can recognize that such themes "contain a primordial and essential sign of holiness" (TOB 109:2). For holiness is what "permits man to express himself deeply with his own body...precisely through the 'sincere gift' of self." It is "in his body as man or woman [that] man senses himself as a subject of holiness" (TOB 19:5).

Thus, it is with good reason that the Song of Songs is the favorite biblical book of so many of the mystics. The erotic poetry of the Song provides a language—certainly inadequate, but in the experience of many saints, the *least* inadequate—for expressing the burning passion of God's love and the experience of "nuptial union" to which all are called with God. John Paul II, himself a mystic, mines exquisite treasures from the text of the Song.[8] According to Michael Waldstein, this

---

7. Pope Benedict XVI, *God Is Love*, 6.

8. Many of these treasures were only unveiled to the English-speaking world in 2006, when Michael Waldstein translated addresses on the Song of Songs that were part of the Pope's original manuscript but that were never delivered at the Wednesday audiences. See TOB 108–12.

section is "clearly one of the most important" in the whole of the Pope's catechesis.[9] If we are to benefit from his insights here, in a particular way, we must remember to "do theology on our knees." It is in prayer that the riches of this erotic love poetry resound *as a song within one's own heart.*

John Paul observes that the Song of Songs provides "a rich and eloquent text of the truth about human love." Commentaries on this "deeply original book" take on many possible forms. The Pope's analysis, however, "*is not a commentary* in the proper sense of this term. It is only a little fragment of reflections on the sacrament of Marriage." His goal, once again, is to see how the visible sign of marriage is constituted through a truthful reading of the language of the body. "For such reflections, the Song of Songs has an altogether singular significance" (TOB 113:6). Through the witness of the lovers' duet, we come to understand that the body not only "speaks"—the body *sings.* And it not only sings, but it sings the greatest of all songs—*the Song of Songs.*

Interpreting the Song of Songs

In light of various misunderstandings and controversies surrounding this book, how are we to understand the Song of Songs? We might begin with a passage from St. Paul: "All scripture is inspired by God and profitable for teaching, for reproof, for correction, and for training in righteousness" (2 Tim 3:16). Unfortunately, some churchmen throughout history have seemed to think these words of the Apostle do not apply to the erotic poetry of Solomon's Song. As John Paul observes, to many this book has seemed "profane." Its reading has often been discouraged and even forbidden (see TOB 108:2). Such a perspective seems to stem from the "interpretation of suspicion" (see TOB 46). The Song's unabashed celebration of erotic love should rather be seen as the precise biblical antidote to such suspicion. The Song of Songs teaches us to love human love with the original good of God's vision. With just such a love, the greatest mystics have drawn lasting inspiration from this sacred, erotic poetry, and the Church has inserted its verses into her liturgy (see TOB 108:2). One must understand that

---

9. See Introduction, TOB, p. 119.

this mystical and liturgical tradition—rather than the parallel history of suspicion—reflects *the authentic mind of the Church* regarding the Song of Songs. For as the Church prays, so does she believe.

John Paul observes that the marital love of the Song is connected in some way with the whole biblical tradition of the great spousal analogy. It certainly serves to illuminate the prophets' description of God's spousal love for Israel. In turn, the Song of Songs also sheds light on Christ's union with the Church, as St. Paul describes in Ephesians 5. However, the Pope immediately adds that the *"theme of spousal love* in this singular biblical 'poem' lies *outside that great analogy.* The love of bridegroom and bride in the Song of Songs is a theme by itself, and in this lies the singularity and originality of that book" (TOB 108:1).

John Paul expands on this idea in four extensive footnotes. Quoting from various scholars, the Holy Father is critical of those who rush to disembody the Song, seeing it only as an allegory of God's "spiritual" love. It is "the conviction of a growing number of exegetes," the Pope maintains, that the Song of Songs (quoting biblical scholar J. Winandy) is "to be taken simply as what it manifestly is: a song of human love" (TOB 108, n. 95). For "human love, created and blessed by God, can be the theme of an inspired biblical book" (TOB 108, n. 97). John Paul seems to agree with the view of Alonso-Schockel that those who have "forgotten the lovers" or "petrified them into pretense" have not interpreted the Song correctly. "'He who does not believe in the human love of the spouses, he who must ask forgiveness for the body, does not have the right to rise higher....With the affirmation of human love, by contrast, it is possible to discover the revelation of God in it'" (TOB 108, n. 96).

This confirms an essential element of incarnational/sacramental reality. Grace—the mystery of God's life and covenant love—is communicated *through* the "stuff" of our humanity, not despite it. Presenting the position of A. M. Dubarle, John Paul says that "a faithful and happy human love reveals to human beings the attributes of divine love." This means, as D. Lys notes, "that the content of the Song of Songs is at the same time sexual and sacred." When we ignore the sacred, we see the Song merely as a secular erotic poem. But when we ignore the sexual, we fall into *allegorism*. "It is only by putting these two aspects together that one can read the book in the right way" (TOB 108, n. 97).

Mutual Fascination with the Body

As we have seen throughout our study of John Paul II's work, integrating the sexual and the sacred is essential—not only to a proper interpretation of the Song of Songs, but also to a proper interpretation of what is authentically human. Integrating the sexual and the sacred is one of the precise goals of a *theology* of the *body*. Hence, the Song of Songs evokes all the themes already discussed in the Pope's catechesis. John Paul says that the entire Song testifies to that "beginning" Christ referred to in his decisive conversation with the Pharisees. It demonstrates all the richness of the language of the body whose first expression is already found in Genesis 2:23–25 (see TOB 108:3).

Recall John Paul's description of Adam's fascination with woman as the biblical prototype of the Song of Songs. Now he says that what "was barely expressed in the second chapter of Genesis (vv. 23–25) in just a few simple and essential words is developed here in a full dialogue" (TOB 108:5). And yet, when "one reads the Song of Songs, it even seems that its verses—with all their poetic wealth—are a weaker expression of...the statement—so simple and apparently poor—of Genesis. Therefore, one should interpret this poverty [of Genesis] by this wealth [of the Song]—but also vice versa, this wealth [of the Song] by this poverty [of Genesis] and in its light" (TOB 111:4).

In the Song, the lovers express the same sentiments of Genesis in a complementary duet in which the bridegroom's words are interwoven with the bride's. A wonder, admiration, and fascination similar to Adam's runs "in a peaceful and even wave from the beginning to the end of the poem" (TOB 108:5). And just like Genesis, the "point of departure as well as the point of arrival for this fascination—reciprocal wonder and admiration—are in fact the bride's femininity and the bridegroom's masculinity, in the direct experience of their visibility." The body reveals the person and the body summons them to love. Thus, their words of love are "concentrated on the 'body'" (TOB 108:6).

Fascination with the human body in its masculinity and femininity—often considered innately prurient—is here, in the Bible's Song of Songs, a means "for training in righteousness" (2 Tim 3:16), that is, for training in *love*. Concupiscence has certainly distorted our vision and our sentiments. Yet, when we tap into that deep well of human desire and fascination that remains beyond the distortions of concupiscence,[10] we discover that our attraction to the body is God-given. And it is *very good* (see Gen 1:31).

Of course attraction to the body in an integral sense must always be and always is *attraction to a person*. It is a vision of another person not only with the eyes but with the heart. A look determines the heart within the one who looks, and it determines whether or not he sees the heart of the person at whom he looks. To the degree that one's heart is pure, so is his look. And to the degree that a person looks with purity of heart, he sees not just *a* body, but *some*body. In the inspired duet of this Song, the lovers not only "look" at each other. They *see* each other. Their attraction toward the other's body is an *attraction toward the other person*. And seeing *the other person*, they do not use the person as an object of egoistic gratification. Rather, as John Paul says, this attraction that lingers directly and immediately on the body *generates love* in the inner impulse of the heart (see TOB 108:6).

While attraction toward the body is *meant* to generate love, tragically, for the man of concupiscence, the human body often generates lust. Of course, through the gift of redemption, we can overcome the domination of concupiscence, but not without a lively spiritual battle. John Paul observes that it is as if the spouses of the Song live and express themselves in an ideal world in which the struggle in the heart between good and evil did not exist (see TOB 115:2). "The words, movements, and gestures of the spouses, their whole behavior, correspond to the inner movement of their hearts" (TOB 108:4). And the movement of their hearts is a pure flame of love. Is it not precisely the inner strength and truth of love that enables man to win in his struggle with concupiscence? (see TOB 115:2). The more that love purifies the heart, the less concupiscence can deceive us.

Experience of the Beautiful

"In addition, *love unleashes a special experience of the beautiful*, which focuses on what is visible, although at the same time it involves the

---

10. Recall John Paul's statement that the heritage of our hearts "is deeper than the sinfulness inherited." And the good news is that Christ came to "re-activate that deepest inheritance and give it real power in human life" (TOB 46:6).

entire person" (TOB 108:6). An integrated understanding of beauty always involves the whole person. The lover exults: "Behold, you are beautiful, my love, behold, you are beautiful! Your eyes are doves behind your veil. Your hair is like a flock of goats moving down the slopes of Gilead" (Song 4:1). The Pope acknowledges that such metaphors of beauty may surprise us today since we are not familiar with the life of shepherds and goat herders. Nonetheless, "that which they express as well as the very force with which they are expressed have kept their value" (TOB 109:1). Although they sound archaic, the metaphors of the Song show us how the language of the body seeks support and confirmation in the whole visible world (see TOB 108:8).

As John Paul tells us, the bridegroom rereads this "language" at one and the same time with his heart and with his eyes (see TOB 108:8). In other words, the bridegroom is integrated internally and externally. If a "look" determines the very intentionality of existence (see p. 219), the lover has determined to live in the truth of the *gift*. He respects woman as a gift. His look concentrates "on the whole female 'I' of the bride." He sees her as a *person*—a subject—created for her own sake. And her personhood "speaks to him through every feminine trait, giving rise to that state of mind that can be defined as fascination, enchantment" (TOB 108:8).

In this way the language of the body finds a "rich echo" in the bridegroom's words. He speaks in poetic transport and metaphors, which attest to the experience of beauty, to "a love filled with pleasure" (TOB 108:8). Yet in the end the lover's metaphors fall short. Leaving them behind, the bridegroom says, "You are all beautiful, my beloved, and there is no blemish in you" (4:7). And further on, with the plea, "Open to me," he calls her "my perfect one" (5:2). John Paul tells us that the bridegroom's desire—which is "born of love" on the basis of the language of the body—is "a search for integral beauty, for purity free from every stain; it is a search for perfection that contains...*the synthesis of human beauty, beauty of soul and body*" (TOB 112:3). Recall John Paul's statement that love *obliges* the husband to desire his wife's beauty, to cherish it and care for it, desiring all that is good for her. The husband's ability to see his wife's beauty is, as we learned earlier, a test and measure of his love.

John Paul continues: "And if the words of the bridegroom just quoted ["Open to me...my perfect one"] seem to contain the distant echo of the 'beginning'—that first search-aspiration of the male man for a being still unknown—they resound much nearer in Ephesians where Christ, as Bridegroom of the Church, desires to see his Bride without 'spot,' desires to see her 'holy and immaculate' (Eph 5:27)" (TOB 112:3). In other words, the bridegroom of the Song, like Christ, points us in two directions. He points us back to the beginning, to God's original plan for married love, and to the eschatological future when the marriage of the Lamb will be consummated. Then the Bride will be made *perfect forever*. She will shine radiantly—without blemish, wrinkle, or any such thing (see Eph 5:27). Then, in the marriage of the Lamb, we will discover the true, integral beauty of everyone who forms the great communion of saints. It will be a beauty "free from every stain," a *"beauty of soul and body,"* as John Paul says. And this dazzling beauty of every human being will be but a dim reflection, a little glimmer of the beauty of the Eternal One whom we will behold "face to face."

"Eyes of the Body" and "Eyes of the Heart"

This vision of integral beauty is seen both with the "eyes of the body" and the "eyes of the heart." Both the bridegroom and the bride in the Song see with this integral vision, although each with a different emphasis. As John Paul observes, the man seems to see his beloved's attractiveness more with the "eyes of the body" while the woman's affection is aroused more by the "eyes of the heart." In other words, the visible expression of femininity seems to prevail in the bridegroom's song, whereas for the bride, their physical closeness causes "the *growth* of the intimate *'language of the heart'*" (TOB 111:2). Both dispositions, however, find balance in the other. And both dispositions, properly integrated, lead to wonder and amazement at the mystery of the other as a body-person and to wonder and amazement at the *love* through which the mystery of the other is revealed (see TOB 109:1).

Through this integral vision of beauty, both the bridegroom and the bride enjoy "a particular *experience of values that irradiates over everything* that stands in relation to the beloved person" (TOB 109:2). This, in turn, helps us understand who the man *is* for the woman and who she *is* for him. John Paul tells us that this is of essential importance for the theology of the body and for the theology of the sacramental sign of marriage—"to know...*who the feminine 'you' is for the male 'I'* and vice versa" (TOB 109:3).[11] The poetic duet of the lovers in the Song of Songs expresses with particular eloquence who man and woman "are" for each other. John Paul focuses on two themes or plots from the Song that exemplify this. The first could be called the "fraternal" theme (see TOB 110:5), and the second the theme of "inviolability" (see TOB 110:8).

"My Sister, My Bride"

Several times throughout the Song, the lover refers to his bride first as his sister. "You have ravished my heart, my sister, my bride, you have ravished my heart with one glance of your eyes.... How sweet is your love, my sister, my bride!" (4:9–10) According to John Paul, these expressions say much more than if he had called her by her proper name. They illustrate how love reveals the other person. "The fact that in this approach the feminine 'I' is revealed for the bridegroom as 'sister'—and that *she is bride* precisely *as sister*—has a particular eloquence" (TOB 109:4). The lover's words are "impregnated with a particular content" (TOB 110:1). They reveal that he sees her not as a thing to be appropriated, but as a *person* to be loved. To be a person "means both 'being a subject,' but also 'being in relation'" (TOB 109:4). The term "sister" denotes this. It speaks of the two different ways in which masculinity and femininity "incarnate" the same humanity, and it speaks of their being in reciprocal relationship.

Obviously, the term "sister" also allows the man to be understood as brother. "O that you were like a brother to me, that nursed at my mother's breast!" (8:1). John Paul observes that recognizing each other as brother and sister presents a certain *challenge* for the man (see TOB 109:4). It challenges him to assess his motives. Is he motivated by love or by lust, by the sincere gift of self or merely by a desire to gratify himself? The bridegroom of the Song accepts this challenge and gives a spontaneous answer to it (see TOB 109:4): "Do not stir up nor awaken love until it please [before she wants it!]" (8:4). And further on he says,

---

11. This is also vitally important for life in general. Recall the Pope's statement that the dignity and balance of human life depend at every moment of history and at every point on the globe on who woman will be for man and who man will be for woman (see TOB 43:7).

"We have a little sister, and she has no breasts. What shall we do for our sister, on the day when she is spoken for?" (8:8). These verses are sufficient proof, according to John Paul, that the bridegroom accepts the challenge of being a "brother" to her and of recognizing her as "sister."

As the Pope poignantly expresses, the "bridegroom's words tend to reproduce...the history of the femininity of the beloved person; they see her still in the time of girlhood ('We have a little sister, and she still has no breasts')." In this way, the bridegroom's words "embrace her entire 'I,' soul and body, *with a disinterested tenderness*" (TOB 110:2). This same tenderness carries through when the term "sister" gives way to the term "bride." The transition from "sister" to "bride" maintains—and it must maintain—the same recognition of her personhood, of her dignity as "sister." This is the special eloquence of calling her "sister" *before* calling her "bride." It reveals that the lover's *modus operandi* in desiring her as bride is love, not lust. And love forms "a reciprocal relation ...through marriage similar to the one that unites brother and sister." In fact, "through marriage man and woman become brother and sister in a special way" (TOB 114:3). They become brother and sister in a way that is actually rooted in authentic spousal love.

"This is the reason," as the Pope states, "for *the convergence (and not divergence) of both expressions and both references.* The term 'sister' used in the Song belongs certainly to the 'language of the body'...reread in the truth of reciprocal spousal love" (TOB 109:6). Calling her "sister-bride" demonstrates that the language of the body is not determined by "libido" alone. Left to itself, "libido" would not recognize the woman as "sister." And for lack of such recognition, it could not recognize her properly as "bride." She would be for him only an object of appropriation. But the lovers of the Song bear witness precisely to the fact that authentic *eros* is not aimed at appropriation and selfish satisfaction. Rather, true eros expresses itself "in the reciprocal ecstasy, as it were, of the good and the beautiful in love.... The terms 'my sister, my bride' seem to arise precisely from this deep level and only on the basis of that level can they be interpreted adequately" (TOB 110:3).

███ I have observed differing reactions between men and women when I have presented the "sister-bride" concept in the classroom and at seminars. For whatever reason, most women, it seems, tend to respond readily, as if such an idea confirms their deepest hopes for a relationship. Men, on the other hand, often seem taken aback. To consider a potential "sex partner" as a "sister" cuts right at the heart of what most men seem to desire in a relationship. A man revolts at the idea of indulging lust with his "sister." This is precisely the point! He should also revolt at the idea of indulging lust with his bride. Women certainly have their own distortions to contend with, but coming to recognize woman first as "sister" compels men in a particular way to face the distortions of lust and to seek grace in "untwisting" those distortions. I also offer the following observation. The whole concept of "dating" in popular culture today—with its expectations of immediate romantic involvement and often immediate sexual activity—serves to skip the "fraternal plot" of man and woman's relationship altogether. Men and women who have never come to love one another fraternally are without a proper foundation for spousal love. They are in grave danger of mistaking lust for love. Building a marriage on such a foundation is equivalent to building a house on sand.

Common Belonging Brings Peace

The "fraternal plot" speaks of their common humanity and a shared sense of belonging. It is as if "they descended from the same family circle, as though from infancy they had been united by memories of the common hearth. In this way, they reciprocally feel as close as brother and sister who owe their existence to the same mother" (TOB 110:1). We can recall what John Paul said in his reflections on Genesis: "Before they become husband and wife..., man and the woman *come forth from the mystery of creation* first of all *as brother and sister in the same humanity*" (TOB 18:5). The first man and woman had a "sense of belonging to the Creator as their common Father." This experience of common belonging—of being "brother-sister" in the same humanity—provided "the first foundation of the communion of persons" (TOB 110:3). In other words, the original experience of unity (spousal unity as the "primordial sacrament") rested upon the original experience of sharing the same humanity as brother and sister—together as son and daughter of the same Father.

John Paul observes that these themes from Genesis are "wonderfully developed in the Song of Songs" (TOB 110:3). Both Genesis

2:23–25 and the Song of Songs demonstrate that rereading the "language of the body" in the truth demands that men and women recognize each other *first* as brother and sister in the same humanity. Failure to build the spousal relationship on this foundation detaches men and women from the richness of the "primordial sacrament." Here John Paul specifically reminds us that the goal of his reflections on the Song of Songs is to understand marital love as a "sign" communicating divine grace (see TOB 110:3). This sign is constituted and divine grace communicated by rereading the "language of the body" according to the truth of the primordial sacrament—according to the truth of God's intention for man and woman "in the beginning." The lovers in the Song successfully reread the original "language" that God inscribed in their bodies and speak it—or, rather, *sing* it—to each other truthfully, in splendid harmony.

In turn, the Holy Father says that the sincerity of their love allows them to live their mutual closeness in security and to manifest it without fearing the unfair judgment of others. They are not ashamed of their love because they are confident in its purity. As the beloved says, "If I met you outside, I would kiss you, and none would despise me" (8:4). From this experience a deep inner tranquility arises, reminiscent of the "peace of the interior gaze" in the experience of original nakedness. "So I was in his eyes as one who finds peace" (8:10). While this is a peace found deep in the human heart, nonetheless John Paul says it is also a "peace of the body." Above all, John Paul describes it as *the peace of the encounter* of man and woman as the image of God *by means of a reciprocal and disinterested gift of self* (see TOB 110:2). This is the richness and the challenge of the words "my sister, my bride."

"A Garden Closed, a Fountain Sealed"

John Paul uncovers the second plot of the Song of Songs—what we have called the plot of "inviolability"—in the following passage of the poem: "A garden locked is my sister, my bride, a garden closed, a fountain sealed" (4:12). John Paul sees in the poetic beauty of these metaphors "not only a beauty of language, but a beauty of the truth expressed by this language." These metaphors both confirm and surpass what was expressed by the name "sister," revealing another vision of the feminine mystery (see TOB 110:6).

John Paul says that from the "beginning," femininity determines
the mystery of "union" about which Genesis speaks (the "one flesh" of
Genesis 2:24 and the "knowledge" of Genesis 4:1). The Holy Father
seems here to indicate not only the fact that without woman union is
impossible (the same could be said of the man), but that the feminine
body "says more" or "reveals more" about the mystery of union. It is the
woman who expresses "the whole theological depth" of the mystery of
union and procreation (see TOB 21:6). John Paul says that in the Song
of Songs, we find ourselves in the "vestibule" of that union (see TOB
110:8)—just on the verge of entering into its mystery. The metaphors
"garden closed" and "fountain sealed" remain in a very strict relation
with the union of the sexes and, thus, help us understand its mystery,
especially the mystery of "the woman" (see TOB 110:7).

We can see the great value of these expressions, the Pope says, in
their ability to convey the profoundly personal dimension and meaning
of the union of the lovers. "The language of metaphors—poetic language—seems to be especially appropriate and precise in this sphere"
(TOB 110:8). Both of these metaphors—"garden closed" and "fountain
sealed"—express the whole *personal dignity of the female sex*. They speak
with profound reverence of the mystery of the feminine body and—
since the body expresses the person—of the feminine personality. These
metaphors speak of

> what seems most profoundly hidden in the entire structure of her
> feminine "I," which also constitutes the strictly personal mystery of
> femininity.... One can say that both metaphors, "garden closed" and
> "fountain sealed," express the whole *personal dignity*...of that femininity
> which belongs to the personal structure of self-possession and can con-
> sequently decide not only the metaphysical depth, but also the essential
> truth and authenticity, of the personal gift. (TOB 110:7)

To speak of the woman's "personal structure of self-possession" means
she holds the key to her own "closed garden." She is her own person
with her own will to choose, and as such she is inviolable. She is in total
possession of herself and stands before her lover as such.

As John Paul II poignantly expresses it, "The bride *presents herself to
the eyes of the man as the master of her own mystery*" (TOB 110:7).
Recognizing this, the lover knows he cannot "take" her or "grasp" her. If
they are to live in a common union (*communio personarum*), it must be
based on the freedom of the gift (see p. 134). For the language of the

body reread in the truth keeps pace with *the discovery of the inner invio-*
lability of the person (see TOB 110:8). When we fail to reread the language of the body truthfully—that is, when we lust—we inevitably
violate the mystery of the person. We take what is not given. We
become master over another person. And persons—precisely because
they are persons—are meant to be their own masters. Their dignity
demands it. "What becomes apparent in this inner necessity, in this
dynamic of love, is *the impossibility*, as it were, *of one person being appro-*
priated and mastered by the other. The person is someone who stands
above all...[measures] of appropriation and domination, of possession
and satisfaction" (TOB 113:3). If the man were to barge into this
"closed garden" (in thought or deed), or if he were to manipulate her
into surrendering the key, he would not be loving her, he would be violating her—raping her.

Declaring her a "closed garden" and a "sealed fountain" attests to the
sincerity of his own gift of self. He is knocking at the door, not breaking in. He presents himself to her as a gift, placing himself in her hands
and entrusting himself to her freedom. He initiates the gift, making his
desire clear: "Open to me, my sister, my love, my dove, my perfect one;
for my head is wet with dew" (5:2). And she hears him: "Listen, my
beloved is knocking" (5:2). But, respecting her fully as "master of her
own mystery,"[12] he puts "his hand to the latch" (5:4) only with her
freely given "yes"—a yes given without any hint of being coerced or
manipulated. Indeed, the bride knows that the bridegroom's "longing"
is *for her*—for her whole feminine person, not merely a reductive desire
for her body—so she goes confidently to meet him with the gift of herself. In total freedom, she surrenders to him; she opens her garden to
him, making it *his*: "Awake, O north wind; and come, O south wind!
Blow upon my garden, let its fragrance be wafted abroad. Let my
beloved come to his garden, and eat its choicest fruits" (4:16).

Thus, in the course of their dialogue of love, *"the 'garden closed' opens*
up in some way before the eyes of the bridegroom's soul and body" (TOB
111:4). And with profound reverence and awe ("Submit to one another
out of reverence...") he beholds her mystery unveiled—that mystery of
which she remains the master. Her openness is offered with the full

---

12. Interestingly, when one abbreviates this expression, we see that the man must
respect the woman as "m.o.m."

freedom of her own choice, in the full freedom of the gift. She and she alone is able to unveil her mystery, and the bridegroom of the Song is fully aware of this. He will *never* extort her gift. As she opens to him, he approaches her with tenderness, ever desiring to assure her that her trust of him is not in vain. He comes to her delighting in her gift, remaining ever in awe of her freely opened garden: "I come to my garden, my sister, my bride, I gather my myrrh with my spice, I eat my honeycomb with my honey, I drink my wine with my milk" (5:1).

Oh the delight of satisfying this holy desire! And that is what it is— *holy.* As John Paul says, "The presence of these elements in this book that enters into the canon of Sacred Scripture shows that they...contain a primordial and essential sign of holiness" (TOB 109:2). The boldly erotic verses of the Song—verses dripping with fragrant sensuality, yet remaining reverently veiled—reveal the mystery of "authentic love" (TOB 110:9). And authentic love is holiness. If we are to enter through this *gateway to holiness* opened to us by the Song of Songs, all suspicion must be abandoned at the threshold; all depreciations of sexuality—be they of the angelistic or animalistic kind—must be crucified; and all fear of our own desires surrendered to the purifying fire of the Mystery. The suffering we must bear, the crucifixion we must endure to "passover" into this mystery is well worth it. For through this gateway lies "the ineffable joy experienced by the mystics as 'nuptial union.'" [13]

▬   Speaking of the call of every Christian to enter mystically into this "garden closed," St. Louis de Montfort remarks, "But how difficult it is for us sinners to have the freedom, the ability and the light to enter such an exalted and holy place." [14] "Some," he says "—the great majority—will stop short at the threshold and go no further. Others—not many—will take but one step into its interior. Who will take a second step? Who will take a third? Finally who will remain in it permanently? Only the one to whom the Spirit of Jesus reveals the secret." [15] Lest we accuse de Montfort of a kind of gnosticism ("secret knowledge"), we must recognize that the

---

13. John Paul II, *Novo Millennio Inuente*, 33.
14. *True Devotion to the Blessed Virgin* (Bay Shore, NY: Montfort Publications, 1993), p. 263.
15. Ibid., p. 119.

"secret" of which he speaks is whispered throughout the Scriptures to all those with "ears to hear." It is whispered especially, perhaps, in the Song of Songs. Elsewhere de Montfort writes:

> Fortunate and happy, incredibly happy, is the soul to which the Holy Spirit reveals the Secret.... To that soul the Paraclete opens the "Garden Enclosed." He permits it to drink deep draughts of the living waters of grace from the "Fountain Sealed"! That soul will find God alone in his most glorious garden. It will find God infinitely holy and exalted yet adapting Himself to the weakness of the soul.[16]

Oh what glorious divine condescension! God comes right down to our level in the "garden" of Mary's womb. This, according to de Montfort, is where we meet God and he meets us.

This kind of "entering" the divine mystery, according to John Paul II, "is the lived experience of Christ's promise: 'He who loves me will be loved by my Father, and I will love him and manifest myself to him' (Jn 14:21)." Offering the context for what I already quoted above, the Pope continues: "[This entering of the Mystery] is a journey totally sustained by grace, which nonetheless demands an intense spiritual commitment and is no stranger to painful purifications (the 'dark night'). But it leads, in various possible ways, to the ineffable joy experienced by the mystics as 'nuptial union.' How can we forget here, among the many shining examples, the teachings of St. John of the Cross and St. Teresa of Avila?"[17]

The Bride Remains "Inviolate": Reciprocal Belonging

Authentic love, as proclaimed by the Song of Songs, means initiation into the mystery of the person without ever violating that mystery (see TOB 111:1). The bride-sister of the Song remains "inviolate in the deepest experience of the man-bridegroom, herself master of the intimate mystery of her own femininity" (TOB 111:6). Remaining "inviolate" in this way, we can observe that when the lovers in the Song "unite with each other (in the conjugal act)," they are "reliving in some way

---

16. *The Secret of Mary* (Bay Shore, NY: Montfort Publications, 1998), p. 17.
17. *Novo Millennio Inuente*, 33.

man's original virginal value, which emerges from the mystery of his solitude before God" (TOB 10:2). Concupiscence—not love—violates the person. Concupiscence—not love—robs men and women of their "original virginal value." If a person's "love" violates the one loved, if it attacks the person's "virginal value," then *it is not love* and should not be called love. It is love's counterfeit—lust.

If lust seeks to grasp and possess the other, true love "expresses the authentic depth of the reciprocal belonging of the spouses" (TOB 110:8). John Paul observes that the spouses in the Song are aware of "belonging" to each other, of being "destined" for each other: "My beloved is mine and I am his" (2:16). But recall the "personal analogy of belonging" of which the Holy Father spoke previously (see p. 205ff.). In the language of authentic love, when spouses speak of "belonging" to each other it "indicates the reciprocity of giving, it expresses the equilibrium of the gift...in which the reciprocal *communio personarum* is established" (TOB 33:4). As John Paul states: "When the bride says, 'My beloved is mine,' she means at the same time, 'It is he to whom I entrust myself,' and therefore she says, 'and I am his' (Song 2:16)" (TOB 110:9). The words "my" and "mine," according to the Holy Father, affirm the whole *depth of the entrustment* in a way that corresponds to the inner truth of the person. This reciprocal "belonging" and act of "entrusting" seems to be generated above all from masculine desire, as the Pope observes. But the bride has a corresponding desire and, recognizing his purity, a trusting acceptance of his desire (see TOB 113:1).

■ In man and woman's being "destined" for each other we can even see a sign of our being destined in Christ (see Eph 1:4). Similarly, if a Christian speaks of "belonging" to Christ, this is not an "ownership" on Christ's part. God may indeed have a "right of ownership" over his creatures. But here is the mystery of the "divine respect" he shows toward humanity—he does not assert such a right of ownership. He, too, respects us—his Bride—as "masters of our own mystery." Wojtyla makes this point unambiguously in the following provocative statement:

> Nobody can use a person as a means toward an end, no human being, nor yet God the Creator. On the part of God, indeed, it is totally out of the question, since, by giving man an intelligent and

> free nature, he has thereby ordained that each man alone will decide
> for himself the ends of his activity, and not be a blind tool of some-
> one else's ends. Therefore, if God intends to direct man toward cer-
> tain goals, he allows him to begin with to know those goals, so that
> he may make them his own and strive toward them independently.
> In this amongst other things resides the most profound logic of rev-
> elation: God allows man to learn his supernatural ends, but the deci-
> sion to strive toward an end, the choice of course, is left to man's free
> will. God does not redeem man against his will.[18]

Sensuality and Spirituality

The authentic love of which the Song speaks is nothing other than
a rereading of the language of the body in the truth. John Paul lists several verses of the lovers' duet that reveal this authentic love in an ever
growing marital intimacy between them. Here is a sample: "As an apple
tree among the trees of the wood, so is my beloved among young men.
With great delight I sat in his shadow and his fruit was sweet to my
taste" (2:3).[19] The "masculine eros" (TOB 111:4) expresses itself as follows: "Your rounded thighs are like jewels, the work of a master hand.
Your navel is a rounded bowl that never lacks mixed wine.... Oh, may
your breasts be like clusters of the vine, and the scent of your breath like
apples, and your kisses like the best wine that goes down smoothly,
gliding over lips and teeth" (7:1–2, 8–9).

The bridegroom's words "contain not only a poetic description of
the beloved, of her feminine beauty,...but these words *speak about gift
and self-gift.* In them we always hear the echo of the very first words of
Genesis (2:23) by which the sign of the primordial sacrament was constituted" (TOB 111:4). In this way the lovers discover each other as a
gift and, as John Paul observes, they even "taste" each other as a gift.
"*The 'language of the body' speaks to the senses....* The love that unites them
is of a spiritual and sensual nature together" (TOB 111:5). In other

---

18. *Love and Responsibility*, p. 27.

19. One cannot help but recognize an inverse parallel here with the sin of Eve in
Genesis. Both Eve and the bride in the Song desire a fruit and find delight in it. It seems
the difference, however, is that of *grasping* versus *receiving*. Eve, having accepted the *paradigm of denial*, cast doubt on the gift of the Heavenly Bridegroom (Yahweh) and
grasped at what was not given. The Bride in the Song lives in the *paradigm of gift* and
opens herself to receive the "fruit" of her bridegroom, which he freely bestows upon her.

words, their spiritual love is integrated with and even rooted in their bodies—in their sexuality and sensuality. The pining of their hearts for authentic love is expressed in the pining of their bodily senses, apparently without the disturbance and "disconnect" of concupiscence.

■ The erotic poetry of the Song of Songs is full of sensual references to foods and fragrances, to smelling, tasting, eating, and drinking each other's goodness (see, for example, 1:12–14; 2:3–6; 4:10–5:1). This indicates a profound interconnection between spousal love, smelling, tasting, eating, and drinking. Are not these senses (and, in fact, all of the senses) fully engaged in erotic love? What does the passionate kiss of lovers say if not in some sense "I want to taste you; I want to take you into myself and consume you; 'eat' you; 'drink' you"? Furthermore, does not the very fragrance of the body stir men and women to love? Perhaps we look on the senses with suspicion because they often rouse concupiscence. But to the degree that men and women live from that vivification of the Holy Spirit, all things sensual stir them to love. Yes, our senses—all of our senses—were created by God to inspire love! This is the nature of incarnational/sacramental reality. Analogously, the interconnections between spousal love, smelling, tasting, eating, and drinking are fully revealed in the Eucharistic liturgy. Here, more than in any earthly encounter, Christ invites us to "taste and see" his own goodness (see Ps 34:8). The fragrance of incense, oils, and candles all add to the sensual experience of the union of Bridegroom and Bride. And how is the marriage of Christ and the Church sacramentally consummated? The deepest desire of the Heavenly Bridegroom is that we, his Bride, might *eat his flesh* and *drink his blood*. Stunning!

Love Is "Strong as Death"

In this way "the rereading of the spousal meaning of the body in the truth is achieved, because the man and the woman together must constitute the sign of the reciprocal gift of self, which *impresses the seal on their whole life*" (TOB 111:5). Consummation of the marriage is the specific moment in which the marriage bond is rendered absolutely indissoluble by anything but death. To reread the language of the body truthfully, men and women must recognize that sexual intercourse proclaims: "I am totally yours unto death. I belong to you and you to me until death do us part." The bride confirms that she knows this truth when she says, "Set me as a seal upon your heart...for love is strong as death.... Its flashes are flashes of fire, a most vehement flame. Many waters cannot quench love, neither can floods drown it. If a man offered for love all the wealth of his house, it would be utterly scorned" (8:6–7).

John Paul says that these words bring us to "the peak" of the Song's declaration of love. They seem to present the final chords of the Song, the "final chords in the 'language of the body.'" When we read that "love is strong as death," we discover "the closure and crowning of everything in the Song of Songs that begins with the metaphor of the 'garden closed' and 'fountain sealed'" (TOB 111:6). Recall that with these words, the lover presented himself to his beloved not as one superficially attracted to her feminine "otherness." Rather, he presented himself as one who is captivated and fascinated by her entire mystery as a woman, as one ready to uphold the whole personal dignity of her sex, as one desirous of honoring her as a feminine person, as a sister and a bride—until and even unto death.

Now we see that a woman can only open her "closed garden" to her lover and remain inviolate if she is assured that he is ready and willing to commit his *entire life* to her, if she is assured that he has set her *as a seal upon his heart*, if she is assured that his love will be *strong as death*. The beloved of the Song is confident in the sincerity of her lover's gift. And so, in "the moment in which the bride of the Song of Songs...asks, '*set me as a seal upon your heart*,' the whole delicate structure of spousal love *closes*, so to speak, in its own inner interpersonal circle" (TOB 111:6). In other words, the bride responds with the gift of herself and in *opening* her garden to her bridegroom, an "inner interpersonal circle of love" *closes* around the spouses. We might even say that this circle encloses them *within her garden*, as it were.

This closure seems to speak of the exclusivity and fidelity essential to spousal love. As John Paul says, "It is in this closure [this exclusive, lifelong commitment] that the visible sign of the perennial sacrament matures, born of the 'language of the body,' reread, so to speak, to the end in the truth of the spousal love between man and woman" (TOB 111:6). It is precisely in this commitment to reread the language of the body faithfully "to the end" that we see the power of the sacrament of marriage *really and truly* to communicate the mystery of Christ's love for the Church. For Christ committed himself to his Bride "to the end" (Jn 13:1) and with his final breath uttered "it is consummated" (Jn 19:30).

Eros and Agape

John Paul concludes his reflections on the Song of Songs by examining the relationship of *eros* (human, erotic love) and *agape* (divine, sacrificial love).[20] The Pope observes "that this biblical poem reproduces the human face of eros, its subjective dynamism as well as its limits and its end, with authenticity free from defects" (TOB 112:1). As we shall see, eros can overcome its limits only by opening itself to the fire of agape (Love's "flashes are flashes of fire, a most vehement flame," 8:6). And if eros has a "human face," agape has a divine one. These different "faces" of love meet in Christ, for he is "the human face of God and the divine face of man."[21] Based on this illuminating truth, we might also describe Christ as the *eros of God* and the *agape of man*. In the love of Christ the Bridegroom, these different faces of love become one "great mystery."[22]

Recall from our earlier reflections that John Paul refuses to surrender the word "eros" to the corruption of lust. Lust is an inversion of eros. Eros in its proper orientation refers to the heart's aspiration toward what is true, good, and beautiful (see p. 243ff.). But for eros to be experienced in this way, it must open itself to *agape*. We witness this opening of eros to agape in the verses of the Song of Songs. The erotic attraction of the lovers expresses itself "in the frequent refrains that speak of the search full of longing and of the spouses' reciprocal rediscovery. This brings them joy and calm, and at the same time seems to lead them to a new search, a continual search" (TOB 112:1). John Paul observes that in their search for each other and even in their reaching

---

20. For further discussion on this relationship, see Pope Benedict XVI's encyclical *God Is Love*. See also *The Way of Love: Reflections on Pope Benedict's Encyclical* Deus Caritas Est (Ignatius Press, 2006); and Christopher West, *The Love That Satisfies: Reflections on Eros and Agape* (Ascension Press, 2007).

21. John Paul II, *Ecclesia in America*, p. 67.

22. As Pope Benedict XVI said, "God loves, and his love may certainly be called *eros*, yet it is also totally *agape*" (*God Is Love*, 9).

each other, "*they ceaselessly continue to tend toward something*" (TOB 112:1). Their duet clearly shows their readiness to respond to the call of *eros*. But it also intimates that they desire something more. That "something more" is *agape*.

This "*process of tension and search*," as John Paul puts it (TOB 112:2), is clearly expressed in the following verses of the Song: "Upon my bed by night I sought him whom my soul loves; I sought him, but found him not; I called him, but he gave no answer. I will rise now and go about the city...; I will seek him whom my soul loves" (3:1–2). Here we see that "human eros reveals the face of *love* ever *in search* and, as it were, *never satisfied*" (TOB 112:4). This kind of restlessness runs throughout the verses of the Song: "I opened to my beloved, but my beloved had turned and gone. My soul failed me...I found him not; I called him but he gave no answer.... I am sick with love" (5:6, 8). John Paul asks whether such restlessness is part of the nature of eros. Then he adds that if it is, "such restlessness would indicate...*the need for [eros] to surpass itself*" (TOB 113:2), to go beyond its own limitations. Authentic love extends to the furthest limits of the language of the body in order to overcome those limits (see TOB 113:3).

Limitations in the Language of the Body

What are the limitations of eros? John Paul speaks of three: (1) *eros is limited by the body's weakness*, (2) *by the prospect of death*, and (3) *by jealousy*. Let us look at each of these limitations *and* at how spouses can overcome them.

(1) *Eros is limited by the body's weakness*. When the bride in the Song exclaims, "I am sick with love," John Paul says it is as if she wanted to bear witness to her own fragility, to her own weakness. Earlier in this chapter, John Paul told us that man cannot fully express love without the body (see TOB 104:7). Now he states that due to the body's weakness, love—and here it seems he means the divine dimension of Love— ultimately "shows itself *as greater than what the 'body' is able to express*" (TOB 112:5). For in the final analysis, the infinitude of Love is *too much* for the finitude of the body. A body that were to take it in would "break"—more aptly, "explode." Infinite Love inevitably *wounds* the body. And as we see in Christ, it is a mortal wound.

■ What *is* Jesus' passion and death? Certainly, it is all manner of human and diabolic hatred hurled at the body of Christ. In this sense the Lord's passion and death comes from "without." But is the Lord's passion and death not also the visible "explosion" of divine love *within* a human body? Might we look upon Christ's wounds—his sweating drops of blood, his lacerations from the scourging, his flesh pierced by thorns, nails, and a sword—not only as *wounds of hatred* inflicted from "without," but also as *wounds of love* expressed from within? For within, "contained" in his beating heart, was something the human body *simply cannot contain*—the *infinite love* of the Trinity. Is it not *that love* that bursts through the pores of his brow in drops of blood, rends his flesh in multiple lacerations, punctures his hands and feet, and finally bursts the membranes of his heart in a gushing surge of blood and water? Is this not precisely the infinite love of the Trinity "exploding" in a human body?

And what of Mary? Her finite body also "contained" infinite Love. He whom all the universe cannot contain came in her body to dwell. And because of it, a sword pierced her heart also (see Lk 2:35). Like Jesus and Mary, all who wish to experience and express divine love in their bodies must "passover" into this divine mystery through suffering, making up in their own flesh what is "lacking" in the sufferings of Christ (see Col 1:24). For all those who accept this way as their own ("Take up your cross and follow..."), a sword will pierce their hearts also. How can we not be reminded in this context of Bernini's famous statue "The Ecstasy of St. Teresa"? Memorialized in stone, we see the angel of love poised to thrust his wounding arrow into Teresa's readied heart. Her face—masterfully sculpted by Bernini—tells the story of a saint who is tasting, as John Paul describes it, "the paradoxical blending of bliss and pain" as *"something akin to Jesus' experience on the cross."*[23]

How can spouses overcome the weakness of the body? Precisely by embracing the mortal wound of love, the body "passes over" to another

---

23. *Novo Millennio Inuente*, 27.

dimension of love, and the mortal becomes clothed with immortality (see 1 Cor 15:54). In this way the body's weakness itself becomes a kind of "language of the body" (see TOB 112:5). In other words, the very weakness of the body—its very *inability* to express the fullness of Love—when humbly accepted, becomes itself in some way the body's *ability* to express that Love. "For when I am weak, then I am strong" (2 Cor 12:10).

(2) *Eros is limited by the prospect of death.* "Love is strong as death" (Song 8:6). According to John Paul, these words express the power and force of erotic love to draw man and woman into a loving union—and it is precisely *from the depth of this union* that the words "Love is strong as death" come forth (see TOB 112:5). But these words also point to the fact, at least indirectly, that the love expressed in the "language of the body" finds its conclusive end in death (see TOB 112:5). Marriage itself is a commitment that ends with death. Can eros surpass death? Can the "language of the body" overcome the "strength" of the grave?

Recall what the Pope said early on in his catechesis: "In man, consciousness of the meaning of the body...come[s] into contact with the consciousness of death.... And yet, in man's history...life struggles always anew with the inexorable prospect of death, and always overcomes it" (TOB 22:7). Now, at this stage of his reflections, John Paul observes that if the body conceals within itself the prospect of death, love does not want to submit to it. "In fact—as we read in the Song of Songs—love is 'a flame of the Lord' that 'the great waters cannot quench... / neither can the rivers drown it' (Song 8:6–7)." John Paul considers these words, among all the words of world literature, to be "particularly fitting and beautiful" (TOB 113:1). When eros opens itself to the "flame of the Lord"—that is, to agape—rivers cannot drown it; death cannot conquer it. When eros is inflamed with agape, "death is swallowed up in victory" (1 Cor 15:54) and "love never ends" (1 Cor 13:8). We will see this truth all the more clearly when we reflect on the marriage of Tobias and Sarah in section 3 of this chapter.

(3) *Eros is limited by jealousy.* In the same verse in which we discover that "love is strong as death," we also discover that love involves a "jealousy as cruel as the grave" (8:6). Jealousy, from one perspective, confirms *"the exclusivity and indivisibility of love."* That said, it "is nevertheless difficult to deny that jealousy manifests...a spiritual kind of limitation" (TOB 113:1). It manifests a lack of trust, a lack of freedom,

and a possessiveness not in keeping with the dignity of the person. It is true in a way that the spouses "belong" to each other ("My beloved is mine and I am his," Song 2:16). However, when this degenerates into a jealous "possession" of the other, authentic love "demands from both that they take a further step on the staircase of such belonging, always seeking a new and more mature form of it" (TOB 113:2). Authentic love recognizes "*the impossibility, as it were, of one person being appropriated and possessed by the other*" (TOB 113:3). The problem, however, as John Paul acknowledges, is that erotic desire by itself "is not able to pass beyond the threshold of jealousy" (TOB 113:1).

But erotic desire need not be left to itself. Eros can overcome jealousy by opening itself to agape. In light of the death and resurrection of Christ, St. Paul proclaimed that "Love is patient and kind; love is *not jealous*" (1 Cor 13:4). Where "human eros closes its own horizon," Paul's words opens us to "another horizon of love that speaks another language." This love "seems to emerge from another dimension of the person," and invites us "to another communion" (TOB 113:5). "*This love has been called 'agape,'* and agape brings eros to fulfillment while purifying it" (TOB, p. 591).[24]

Sign and Reality

By looking at the limitations of eros and the power of agape to enable men and women to overcome those limitations, we learn ever more deeply what it means to read the "language of the body" in truth. If it is true that the erotic language of the body has limitations, it is *not true* that spouses are bound by those limitations. Erotic desire must open itself to that eternal flame of agape if men and women are to constitute the sign of married love in truth. Indeed, if the human reality of "the sign" is meant to express the divine reality of "covenant and grace," then eros *must* express agape. In this way, as John Paul says, spouses will be able "*to reach* what constitutes *the very nucleus of the gift of person to person*" (TOB 113:3).

Still, the sacramental mystery of spousal union in the Song of Songs—as beautiful and wonderful as it is—remains only a sign of the

---

24. This quote is taken from the unnumbered address of June 6, 1984, which, in Waldstein's translation, was left unnumbered. Hence, the provision of a page number.

divine mystery itself. Even spouses must be open to "breaking away," the Pope says, from the earthly means of expressing eros-agape in order to reach that *nucleus of the gift of person to person* (see TOB 113:3). The ultimate reality of the gift of person to person can be none other than the relationship found within the Trinity itself. That communion alone can satisfy the desire that is ever seeking and (in this life) never satisfied. In short, what we are realizing is that if eros is to become an earthly sign of that divine communion, then the *language of the body* must be taken up into the *language of the liturgy*. It is precisely here—in the liturgy—that the divine and human meet, that heaven and earth "kiss."

3. When the "Language of the Body" Becomes the Language of the Liturgy (Reflections on Tobit)

In the final five addresses of Part II, Chapter 2 (TOB 114–117b), John Paul develops the idea that the language of the body—if it is to be reread in truth, thus constituting the sign of marriage as a sacrament—must become an expression of the Church's liturgy. In other words, the life and love of spouses—if it is to overcome all that threatens it—must become part of the Church's prayer to the Father by which we enter into the "great mystery" of Christ's love for the Church. Conjugal life must become, and is meant in fact to be, *liturgical*. As John Paul confirms, "the dimension of the liturgy that belongs to the sign of marriage as a sacrament...plays a defining role for this sign" (TOB 115:4).

"The dimension of the liturgy *takes up into itself* the 'language of the body' reread in the truth of human hearts—as we know this language from the Song of Songs. At the same time, however, it seeks to set this 'language' into the context of the integral truth of man, reread in the word of the living God. This is what the prayer of the new spouses in Tobit expresses" (TOB 115:4), which we will examine below. After looking at the marriage of Tobias and Sarah in the book of Tobit, and especially at their spousal prayer, the Pope then revisits the "classical" text of Ephesians 5 to confirm this mystical linking of conjugal and liturgical life.

In some sense these reflections bring us to the climax of John Paul's dramatic proposal about the "greatness"—the God-likeness—of spousal love as a sacramental sign. Here we cross the threshold and enter into the most profound integration of the sexual and the sacred. But before we turn directly to the Pope's reflections, we should seek a better understanding of "liturgy" so we can understand the sense in which conjugal life is "liturgical."

Conjugal Life and Liturgical Life

Turning to the *Catechism*, we learn that in Christian tradition, liturgy "means the participation of the People of God in 'the work of God.'"[25] The work of God refers above all to the "great mystery" of our redemption in Jesus Christ accomplished through his death and resurrection. To say that conjugal life is liturgical is to say that it participates in this "great mystery." As such, the union of man and woman in conjugal love is meant to sanctify the world as a living sign of redemption—a constant reminder of what happened in the death and resurrection of Christ. "It is this mystery of Christ that the Church proclaims and celebrates in her liturgy so that the faithful may live from it and bear witness to it in the world."[26] Spouses do precisely this when they live in fidelity to the language God inscribed in their bodies as male and female.

The *Catechism* also says that liturgy is the Church's "celebration of divine worship." In fact, it is "a participation in Christ's own prayer addressed to the Father in the Holy Spirit."[27] So, too, is conjugal life. When lived according to the "great mystery" of God's designs, even the marital embrace itself becomes a profound prayer. It becomes eucharistic as an act of thanksgiving offered to God for the joyous gift of sharing in his own life and love. According to the analogy, we might even view the marital bed as an altar upon which spouses offer their bodies in living sacrifice, holy and acceptable to God. This is their spiritual act of worship (see Rom 12:1).

Liturgy also refers "to the proclamation of the Gospel and to active charity" carried out by the Church "in the image of her Lord."[28] So does conjugal life. Conjugal life is a profound and continuous proclamation of the "Gospel of the body" lived in the image of Christ's love for the

---

25. *CCC*, no. 1069.
26. *CCC*, no. 1068.
27. *CCC*, nos. 1070, 1073.
28. *CCC*, no. 1070.

Church. Quoting from the Second Vatican Council, the *Catechism* concludes: "The liturgy then is rightly seen as an exercise of the priestly office of Jesus Christ. It involves the presentation of man's sanctification under the guise of signs perceptible by the senses and its accomplishment in ways appropriate to each of these signs."[29] In conjugal life, the sanctification of spouses is presented and appropriately accomplished through the sign of their faithful union, lived out day-to-day and consummated in becoming one flesh. In this way spouses are initiated into the mystery of Christ through an ongoing marital-liturgical catechesis that proceeds "from the visible to the invisible, from the sign to the thing signified, from the 'sacraments' to the 'mysteries.'"[30]

The idea that conjugal life is liturgical is not surprising when we consider that the whole liturgical life of the Church revolves around the sacraments.[31] Marriage is not only one of the sacraments, but is in some sense the prototype or model of all the sacraments (see p. 431ff.). Hence, not only is conjugal life liturgical. When we read the spousal analogy in the other direction, we realize that the Church's liturgical life is in some way conjugal. As the heading of this section indicates (see p. 498), John Paul wants to unfold how the "language of the body" is founded on the language of the liturgy. However, he will also demonstrate that the language of the liturgy is *modeled after the "language of the body"* (see TOB 117:6). As the *Catechism* expresses, "The entire Christian life bears the mark of the spousal love of Christ and the Church."[32] According to this analogy, the Church's liturgical life is where she enters into the "great mystery" of spousal union with Christ. It is where the Bride receives the spousal love of her Bridegroom in an eternally fruitful embrace (*fiat*) and offers endless praise and thanksgiving for so great a gift (*magnificat*).

The Marriage of Tobias and Sarah

John Paul looks at the marriage of Tobias and Sarah in the book of Tobit yet again to understand how the sacramental sign of marriage is constituted through the "language of the body" reread in the truth.

---

29. *CCC*, no. 1070.
30. *CCC*, no. 1075.
31. See *CCC*, no. 1113.
32. *CCC*, no. 1617.

"When one compares Tobit with the Song of Songs or the prophets, it is right to raise the question as to whether or not the text we are examining speaks about this 'language.' While the Song offers us the whole richness of the 'language of the body,' reread with the eyes and hearts of the couple,...the Book of Tobit falls short from this point of view, because it is extremely spare and sober" (TOB 115:1). Yet, as we shall see, precisely in its spareness and sobriety we find a rich, concentrated confirmation of the main themes of the theology of the body.

We read in the book of Tobit that, before marrying Tobias, Sarah had already married seven others. But through the work of a demon (the evil spirit Asmodeus), each man died in the bridal chamber on the wedding night before consummating the marriage (see Tobit 6:13–14). With this in mind, let us place ourselves in Tobias's shoes. The angel Raphael tells Tobias that he is to marry Sarah. John Paul II—man of keen insight that he is—observes that Tobias *had reason to be afraid*! (see TOB 114:5). In fact, Sarah's father was so convinced of Tobias's immanent death that on the wedding day he was already digging Tobias's grave (see Tobit 8:9).

In the face of Tobias's understandable reluctantce to take Sarah as his wife (see Tobit 6:14), the angel Raphael encouraged him: "Now listen to me, brother, for she will become your wife; and do not worry about the demon, for this very night she will be given to you in marriage.... Do not be afraid, for she was destined for you from eternity. You will save her, and she will go with you, and...you will have children by her." Then we read: "When Tobias heard these things, he fell in love with her and yearned deeply for her" (Tobit 6:15, 17).

Love as a Test of Life-or-Death

Here we see all the components of good and evil gearing up for a great spiritual battle: angels and demons; life and death; God's eternal salvific will and man's fearful and rebellious designs; love and all that is opposed to love. How can the spouses overcome the demon, conquer death, cast out fear, and enter into God's saving plan so that life and love triumph? *Only by entering into the "great mystery" of the liturgy.* And in what context does this great clash, this decisive battle, occur? As John Paul says, "Everything, in fact, happens during the couple's wedding night" (TOB 114:8). Just as the "great mystery" centers on a man and woman joining in "one flesh," so does the "great battle." Precisely in this "union of the two," John Paul tells us, "the choices and acts...[of the spouses] take on the whole weight of human existence" (TOB 115:3).

These are heavy words, but they should not surprise us. We have seen that the weight of human existence rests on man and woman's union from the outset of our study. The first pages of Genesis reveal that sexuality and procreation are intimately linked with the great contest of good and evil, life and death. "And so," as John Paul starkly expresses, when spouses "unite as husband and wife, they must find themselves in the situation in which *the powers of good and evil fight against each other*" (TOB 115:2). Husbands and wives live this great *spiritual* contest in their *bodies*. We see this vividly in the case of Tobias and Sarah. From the first moment of their marriage, their love had *to face the test of life-or-death*. "The words about love 'strong as death,' spoken by the spouses of the Song of Songs...here take on the character of a real test" (TOB 114:6).

In the Song of Songs, we see the spouses rereading the true "language of the body" through an ongoing loving dialogue of heartfelt sentiment, affection, and erotic longing. We see also how eros overcomes its own limits by opening to agape. In Tobit, by contrast, "the distressing situation of the 'limit' together with the test of life-or-death brings *the loving dialogue of the spouses in some way to silence*" (TOB 115:3). In the Song of Songs, the spouses experience a mutual fascination, joy, and pleasure in reading the language of their bodies. In Tobit, Tobias and Sarah soberly recognize that "the touchstone of a test of life-or-death [is] also part of the 'language of the body'" (TOB 115:3). They realize that "in the sacramental sign of conjugal unity...the body expresses itself also through *the mystery of life and death*. It expresses itself through this mystery more eloquently perhaps than ever" (TOB 115:3).[33]

Doesn't the body's inevitable corruption ("to dust you shall return," Gen 3:19) demonstrate that "death" is, in some way, the last word to be spoken by the body's "language"? Most couples have little to remind them of this distressing fact on the day of their wedding—indeed, it is

---

33. The French seem to recognize this connection in their common reference for orgasm—*la petite mort*, which means "the little death."

usually the furthest thing from a bride and groom's mind. Tobias and Sarah, however, had to stare this distressing word "death" in the face right from the outset of their marriage. "What depth does their love acquire in this way...?" asks the Pope (TOB 115:3). And we might also ask, what depth does their love *require* if they are to stare death in the face and overcome it?

The Prayer of Tobias and Sarah

Tobias knows that if he is to conquer death through love, he must be mindful of Raphael's instructions. The angel had given him various pieces of advice on how to free himself from the demon's grip. Above all, however, Raphael recommended prayer (see TOB 114:7): "When you enter the bridal chamber," the angel had said, "when you approach her, rise up, both of you, and cry out to the merciful God, and he will save you and have mercy on you" (Tobit 6:16–17).

"With this promise," John Paul says, "it was easier for both to face the test of life-or-death awaiting them on the wedding night" (TOB 114:8). In Tobit we find neither a dialogue nor a duet between the spouses, as with the lovers in the Song of Songs. Instead, as John Paul observes, Tobias and Sarah "decide above all *to speak in unison*—and this unison is nothing other than prayer. In that unison...man and woman are united not only through the communion of hearts, but also through the union of both in facing the great test" (TOB 115:4). Nothing solidifies spousal union more than the shared experiences of deep, intimate prayer coupled with a common goal of facing *and overcoming*—with the help of God's grace—great trials. Tobias and Sarah witness to the fact that there is no trial in married life—*not even the prospect of death!*—that cannot be overcome by prayer. Tobias and Sarah's prayer "becomes the one and only word in virtue of which the new spouses meet the test" (TOB 115:5). As we read in Tobit:

> When the door was shut and the two were alone, Tobias got up from the bed and said, "Sister, get up, and let us pray that the Lord may have mercy upon us." And Tobias began to pray, "Blessed are you, O God of our fathers, and blessed be your holy and glorious name forever. Let the heavens and the whole creation bless you. You made Adam and gave him Eve his wife as a helper and support. From them the race of mankind has sprung. You said, 'It is not good that the man should be

alone; let us make a helper for him like himself.' And now, O Lord, I am not taking this sister of mine because of lust, but with sincerity. Grant that I may find mercy and grow old together with her." And she said with him, "Amen." (Tobit 8:4–8)

Tobias's prayer "sets the 'language of the body' on the terrain of the essential terms of the theology of the body" (TOB 116:4). Notice that, just as Christ will eventually direct the Pharisees to do, Tobias and Sarah set their hearts on God's original plan for marriage. Notice Tobias calls her "sister" like the bridegroom in the Song of Songs. Notice that he contrasts lust with the "sincere gift of self." Notice that he intends to spend his whole life with her ("What therefore God has joined together let no man put asunder," Mt 19:6). And notice that Tobias knows they cannot live this sublime calling by relying on their own strength. They need God's mercy deeply; they need God's grace to *empower* them to overcome the *diabolic plan* of lust and death and live the *divine plan* of love and life.

"One can say that in this prayer...*the dimension of the liturgy* proper to the sacrament is outlined against the horizon of the 'language of the body'" (TOB 114:8). Their prayer itself is an entering into the liturgy—an entering into the worship of God and the sanctification of man. And it is all a preparation for their joining in "one flesh." Much is riding on the disposition of Tobias and Sarah's hearts in this dramatic moment. The prospect of choosing between *love* and *lust* presents them with a test of good and evil, life and death, and not only in some abstract way. Their actions in this moment will determine whether they experience "a good or bad lot—in the dimension of life as a whole" (TOB 115:5).

■ So few married people (and men and women in general) seem to understand the far-reaching consequences of their sexual choices and, even more, the disposition of heart with which they approach sexual union. These serve as a barometer, of sorts, that can measure and predict "a good or bad lot" in the whole of their life together. Indeed, one would be hard-pressed to find any marital difficulty that cannot be traced, directly or indirectly, to a failure to read the language of the body truthfully. Wojtyla touched upon this in *Love and Responsibility* when he observed that "the realiza-

tion of [a lasting union of persons] in each particular sexual act"—
we could also say a rereading of the language of the body in
truth—"presents...the internal problem of every marriage."[34] But
for all our failures in this regard, hope is not lost. We, like Tobias
and Sarah, can always cry out for mercy.

Love Is Victorious Because It Prays

Tobias and Sarah "realize that the evil that threatens them on the
part of the demon can strike as suffering, as death, destruction of the
life of one of them. But *in order to repel the evil* threatening to kill the
body," and this is one of John Paul's key points, "one must *prevent the
evil spirit from having access to the soul,* one must free oneself within oneself from his influence" (TOB 115:5).

His influence goes right back to "the beginning," when the first
man and woman exchanged the truth of God for a lie and the original
"man of the covenant" became the "man of concupiscence." In this
moment, eros was cut off from its proper ethos, and, ever since, men
and women have struggled to express the true "spousal meaning" of
their bodies. But let us never forget the good news! If "concupiscence...brings about many 'errors' in rereading the 'language of the
body'...nevertheless, in the sphere of the ethos of redemption there is
always the possibility of passing from 'error' to the 'truth'...the possibility of...conversion from sin to chastity as an expression of a life according to the Spirit (see Gal 5:16)" (TOB 107:3).

Eros cut off from ethos is death dealing, as Sarah and her seven
previous husbands discovered quite dramatically. But Tobias's love for
Sarah is not a diseased form of eros. Tobias's "love is confirmed and
validated by ethos, that is, by the will and the choice of [authentic] values" (TOB 115:1). Recall that eros and ethos "*are called to meet in the
human heart and to bear fruit in this meeting*" (TOB 47:5). Tobias's
prayer, as a liturgical reality, reveals the meeting of eros and ethos in his
heart and it indeed bears *abundant fruit.* It enables the newlywed
spouses to be confident in love's victory. It enables them to "go without
hesitating toward this...test of life-or-death." And in this test "*life has
the victory,* because, during the test of the first wedding night, *love*

---

34. *Love and Responsibility*, p. 225.

supported by prayer is revealed as stronger than death." Love "is victorious because it prays" (TOB, pp. 597, 601).[35] From within the bridal chamber, Tobias and Sarah transform the "language of the body" into a single voice of prayer—"And Sarah said with him, 'Amen'" (Tobit 8:8). This voice, this act of praying in unison, "allows both of them to pass beyond the 'limit situation,' beyond the threat of evil and death, inasmuch as they open themselves totally, in the unity of the two, to the living God" (TOB 115:6).

That Good May Conquer

Recall that all of this is preparing us to understand what is at stake in the Church's teaching on contraception. Spouses can only overcome the diabolic threat of evil and death if they open their union totally to the presence of the living God, who has revealed himself at one and the same time as "Love" and as "Father," as "Communion" and as "Lord and Giver of Life." This is the "Word" written by God into the theological language of the body. But as we see from the first pages of Genesis and confirmed here in Tobit, there is a meddling force at work, an "anti-Word" who wants to write "death" into this language.

If Tobias had "reason to be afraid" in taking Sarah as his wife, St. John tells us: "There is no fear in love, but perfect love casts out fear" (1 Jn 4:18). In a clarion call for all men and women to embrace that perfect love—almost repeating his signature phrase "be not afraid"— John Paul declares: "The truth and strength of love are manifested in the ability of [love] to place itself between the forces of good and of evil that fight within man and around him, because love is confident in the victory of good and is ready to do everything in order that good may conquer" (TOB 115:2). No sacrifice is too great for true lovers—no suffering too much to bear—when it is needed to ensure the victory of good over evil, love over lust, life over death. This is precisely the testimony of the cross, of Christ's spousal love for the Church. This is precisely the perfect love in which every husband and wife are called to participate. And, as we shall see in the next chapter, this is precisely what the teaching of *Humanae Vitae* calls spouses to embrace.

---

35. These quotes are taken from the unnumbered address of June 27, 1984. See also TOB 114:6, which offers a slightly different rendering.

The Spouses' "Conjugal Creed"

One of the high points of the Church's liturgy is the profession of her Creed. The Creed encompasses in just a few words the whole knowledge contained in both the Old and New Testaments.[36] To say it with faith is to enter into communion with the Trinity and with the whole Church.[37] In other words, to say the Creed with faith is to enter into the "great mystery" of Christ's spousal union with the Church.

When Tobias and Sarah express the language of the liturgy with the language of their bodies, their prayer becomes a profession of their "conjugal creed" (see TOB 116:2). As we have seen, this conjugal creed encompasses in just a few words the whole truth of the theology of the body contained in both the Old and New Testaments. This creed originates from the depth of *love* in the new spouses' hearts and expresses itself in the *life*-giving language of their bodies. As such, this "creed" serves as a precise antidote to the demon's plot to write *lust* into their hearts and *death* into their bodies. A look at each of its components reveals the precise way for spouses of all times and places to *prevent the evil spirit from having access to their hearts*, so as *to repel the evil* threatening to kill the body (see TOB 115:5).

In Genesis, the serpent wanted the first spouses to question God's benevolence, so he aimed his attack straight at God's character: "Did God *really* say..." (Gen 3:1). As a precise antidote to this attack on God's name, Tobias and Sarah begin their prayer with praise and thanksgiving: "Blessed are you, O God of our fathers, and blessed be your holy and glorious name forever. Let the heavens and the whole creation bless you" (Tobit 8:5). In this way, John Paul says that Tobias and Sarah speak in some sense for all of creation—both visible and invisible. It is on this vast and "*cosmic*" background that both recall with gratitude the creation of man as male and female (see TOB 116:1): "You made Adam and gave him Eve his wife as a helper and support. From them the race of mankind has sprung. You said, 'It is not good that the man should be alone; let us make a helper for him like himself'" (Tobit 8:6).

The Pope infers that the truth expressed here—the truth of God's plan for man and woman "in the beginning"—is at the center of Tobias

36. See *CCC*, no. 186.
37. See *CCC*, no. 197.

and Sarah's "religious consciousness." Indeed, it constitutes "*the very bone marrow of their conjugal 'creed'*" (TOB 116:2). By turning to these words of Genesis—and, as John Paul points out, their prayer references *both* creation accounts (see TOB 116:1)—the couple fully expresses the desire within their hearts. They long "to become a new link in the chain that goes back up to man's very beginnings." Precisely in this moment, before joining in conjugal union, "they commit themselves together to rereading the '*language of the body*' proper to their state in its divine source" (TOB 116:2). In this way, their conjugal creed becomes the specific antidote to the lust that the evil spirit wants to write into their hearts. If men and women of history are crippled by lust, Tobias and Sarah realize that "from the beginning it was not so" (Mt 19:8).

Tobias and Sarah "see with the eyes of faith the holiness of this vocation" (TOB 116:4). However, they are not granted an "automatic" sanctity. As fallen human beings, the new spouses sense their "need for a full purification," as the Pope puts it. Tobias expresses the purity of his intention: "And now, O Lord, I am not taking this sister of mine because of lust, but with sincerity." But he also knows that he is not able to carry out this intention without divine assistance: "Grant that I may find mercy.... And Sarah said with him, 'Amen'" (Tobit 8:7–8). Here we witness "*the moment of purification*" to which spouses must submit themselves if they wish, in becoming "one flesh," to express truthfully the sacramental sign of their covenant. Sexual intercourse "must serve to build the reciprocal communion of persons, by reproducing the spousal meaning of the body in its inner truth" (TOB 116:3).

Tobias's words, "not because of lust," should be understood in the integral context of all that we have learned about the "man of concupiscence" and the *ethos of redemption*. Recall that "Christian ethos is characterized by *a transformation of the human person's consciousness and attitudes...such as to express and realize the value of the body and of sex* according to the Creator's original plan" (TOB 45:3). This, John Paul says, is the way in which the "language of the body" becomes the language of the liturgy. It must be "anchored in the deepest way possible, namely, by being set into the mystery of the 'beginning'" (TOB 116:2). Hence, the prayer of Tobias and Sarah—their "*conjugal creed*"— "becomes in some way the deepest *model of the liturgy*" and a precise antidote to the diabolical scheming of the evil one. For liturgical prayer "is *a word of power*...drawn from the sources of the covenant and of grace." This grace is precisely "the power that frees [us] from evil and purifies. In this word of the liturgy, the sacramental sign of marriage is fulfilled, built in the unity of man and woman on the basis of the 'language of the body' reread in the integral truth of the human being" (TOB 115:6).

It is precisely the *power* of the liturgy that enables spouses to overcome the pull of lust in order to become "true prophets." For, *as ministers of the sacrament* (ministering a sacrament is clearly a liturgical act!), spouses express and bring into being "the mystery" that has its source in God himself (see TOB 116:4). This mystery is that God is an *eternal exchange of life-giving love*. And the good news of the Gospel is that the eternal Father, by extending an eternal covenant to man, has destined us to share in that exchange.[38] The "conjugal covenant is in fact the image...of the covenant that draws its origin from eternal Love." It is "the primordial sacrament of the covenant of God with man, with the human race" (TOB 116:4).

Tobias's love for Sarah, then, is a type of Christ's love for the Church. Christ stared death in the face on the "marriage bed" of the cross, thus consummating his love for the Church and conquering death by rising to new life. Tobias also stared death in the face on his marriage bed, and inspired with sacrificial (Christ-like) love, he also conquered death. After seven men had succumbed, Tobias *consummates the marriage and lives!* When God's design for marriage is your "conjugal creed," death has no chance. Life refuses to surrender. Because of the eros-agape love that united them in "one flesh," Tobias and Sarah witness to God as *the God of life*. Their union joyously proclaims: "Where, O death, is your victory? Where, O death, is your sting?" (1 Cor 15:55).

Ephesians 5: The Language of the Liturgy Becomes the "Language of the Body"

In Part II, Chapter 1, John Paul spent a considerable amount of time examining Ephesians 5 in order to understand "the sacrament" in the divine dimension of covenant and grace. In the final two addresses of Part II, Chapter 2 (TOB 117–117b), the Pope returns to the "classi-

---

38. See *CCC*, no. 221.

cal" text of Ephesians 5 to glean more insight into the nature of "the sacrament" in the human dimension of *the sign*.

John Paul observes that if the sacramental sign of marriage is based on the "language of the body" reread in the truth of love, then Ephesians 5 offers us the "*definitive*" expression of this sign reread in the truth of love. We read that the "one flesh" union is a "great mystery" that is meant to express and proclaim the love of Christ and the Church. While the Song of Songs contains "the language of the body' in all the richness of its subjective meaning," Ephesians 5 "contains *the 'objective' confirmation of this language* in its entirety, a solid and complete confirmation" (TOB 117:2).

The author of Ephesians offers "*above all a commentary* on those older, original *biblical words*, in which the nature of the sacramental sign of marriage finds its expression: 'The two will be one flesh' (Gen 2:24)." It is clear from our previous analyses of this text that this sign of unity in "one flesh" must be understood, as John Paul says, "*in a fully personalistic way*" (TOB 117:3). In other words, one cannot determine the goodness of the sexual act based only on objective and external criterion. Conforming one's behavior to an objective sexual *ethic* is not enough. One's *ethos*—his inner world of values—must correspond to the true dignity of the person and the true meaning of love. For example, the mere fact that a man and a woman are married to each other does not guarantee the goodness of their sexual acts. Their sexual acts must express *subjectively* as well as *objectively* the truth of their marital commitment.

In both the Song of Songs and the marriage of Tobias and Sarah we see spouses rereading the language of the body in the truth. Both couples witness to the deepest meaning of the sacramental sign of marriage. They understand the truth of this sign not only in an *objective* sense. They also desire it *subjectively*. They long for it in their hearts. When this profound integration between objective reality and subjective experience occurs, John Paul says that spouses experience the language of the body for what it is. They experience it as *the language of the liturgy* (see TOB 116:5).

The sacramental sign of marriage is built on the foundation of the language of the liturgy and of the whole liturgical ritual (see TOB 117:5). Indeed, the normal context in which to enter the sacrament of marriage is the sacrament of the Eucharist—the Mass. Here we see vividly in the liturgical ritual the link that Ephesians 5 draws between the union of spouses and the union of Christ and the Church. Here we see vividly that the liturgy itself brings "these two signs together, making of them *the single great sign*, that is, *a great sacrament*" (TOB 95b:7). The manifold richness of the Church's liturgy "reveals above all how in this sign the dimension of the covenant and of grace is realized" (TOB 117:5). It is realized through *the union of spouses*—Christ and the Church and, in turn, man and woman, husband and wife.

We are seeing here that the liturgical mystery of marriage finds its "definitive biblical model" in Ephesians 5 (see TOB 117:5). In the prism of this model, John Paul says we can see with particular clarity how the "language of the body" is founded on the language of the liturgy. However, working in the other direction, we can also see "the way in which *the language and ritual* of the liturgy *form (ought to form!) the 'language of the body'*" (TOB 117:6). The spousal analogy operates in two directions (see TOB 90:4). Through that "keystone" passage in Ephesians 5—where the author links the union of spouses with the union of Christ and the Church (vv. 31–32)—we recognize Marriage as the *sacrament of Christ and the Church*...and we recognize the Eucharist as the *sacrament of the Bridegroom and the Bride*.[39]

John Paul asks if the Christian "style" of spousal relations set forth in Ephesians 5 does not show how the language and ritual of the Church's liturgy are modeled after the language of the body and marital love (see TOB 117:6).[40] The Christian "style" is for spouses to "submit to one another *out of reverence for Christ*." Husbands are to love their wives "as Christ loved the Church"—they must love them "as their own bodies," serving and caring for their wives as Christ does the Church. And wives are to receive the love of their husbands and respond to it as the Church receives and responds to the love of Christ. According to John Paul, this rich personalistic affirmation of spousal union reveals *the "absolute" sense* of the *language of the body*, its most perfect expression.

---

39. See *Mulieris Dignitatem,* 26.

40. A clear example of this would be the blessing of the baptismal font at the Easter Vigil. When the Easter candle is plunged into the font "in the name of the Father, and of the Son, and the Holy Spirit," it serves as a symbol of the Heavenly Bridegroom impregnating the womb of the Church from which many children will be born again— not of a husband's seed, but born of God (see Jn 1:13). As for the Eucharist, the baldacchino in the West and the icon screen in the East indicate that the priest has entered the bridal chamber to "give up his body" for his bride, the Church.

Men and women can reach it only by penetrating the "great mystery" presented in Ephesians 5 (see TOB 117:6).

The Sacramental Sign—Mystery and Ethos

The text of Ephesians 5, John Paul says, "brings us to a dimension of the 'language of the body' that could be called 'mystical.' It speaks in fact about marriage as a 'great mystery'" (TOB 117b:1). It is true that St. Paul says this "great mystery" refers to Christ's union with the Church. Nevertheless, St. Paul *does not hesitate to extend that mystical analogy* to the sacramental sign of marriage. He extends it "to the *'language of the body,'* reread in the truth of spousal love and of the conjugal union of the two" (TOB 117b:1). It is the liturgy that *"elevates the conjugal covenant* of man and woman, which is based on the 'language of the body' reread in the truth, *to the dimensions of the 'mystery,'* and at the same time enables that covenant to be realized in these dimensions through the 'language of the body.' It is precisely about this that the sign of the sacrament of Marriage speaks" (TOB 117b:2).

If we ponder this "great mystery," John Paul observes that the text of Ephesians 5 radically frees our thinking both from elements of Manichaeism and from a non-personalistic view of the body. At the same time it "brings the 'language of the body,' which is contained in the sacramental sign of marriage, closer to the dimension of *real holiness*" (TOB 117b:2). When spouses unite in conjugal intercourse, this great sign of married love expresses not only "an interpersonal event full of intense personal content." It also expresses "a sacred and sacramental reality rooted in the dimension of the covenant and of grace, in the dimension of creation and redemption. In this way," John Paul continues, "the liturgical language assigns love, faithfulness, and conjugal integrity to both man and woman through the 'language of the body.' It assigns them the unity and indissolubility of marriage in the 'language of the body.' *It assigns them as a task the whole 'sacrum' [sacredness] of the person and of the communion of persons,* and in the same way their masculinity and femininity, *precisely in this language*" (TOB 117b:2). The language of the body—expressed in the whole of married life and consummated in becoming "one flesh"—is sacred. It is holy. *It is mystical and liturgical!*

When we let these truths sink in, we cannot persist in our suspicion toward the body. We cannot persist in the heretical belief that the body and sexuality are somehow inherently tainted (Manichaeism). We cannot persist in the dualistic error that views the body as an inherent obstacle to the spiritual life. Instead we realize that our male and female bodies are the vehicle of the Holy Spirit, in all of life but particularly in married life. Our bodies are created to be infused with holiness, with grace. Even if we have lost this grace due to sin, we can receive it once again through the sacraments. As John Paul evangelically proclaims: "The sacraments infuse holiness into the terrain of man's humanity: they penetrate the soul and body, the femininity and masculinity of the personal subject, with the power of holiness" (TOB 117b:2).

This is not an abstract theological concept. John Paul insists that we can *experience* this in the depths of our subjectivity. He adds that all of this is expressed in the body and brought about through the language of the liturgy. When spouses understand marriage as an integral part of the liturgical life of the Church, they are empowered to live their sacrament as the vocation to holiness that it is. They experience and express the true language of their bodies not only in the moments of joining in "one flesh," but in "an uninterrupted continuity of liturgical language" (TOB 117b:3)—in the whole series of acts and tasks that make up their daily lives as spouses.

When spouses strive with God's grace to speak the liturgical language of the body honestly in the consummate sign of their union, the whole ensemble of their conjugal dialogue becomes an extension of that fidelity. Living the true language of the body becomes a way of life, *a liturgical way of life*, a life of prayer. Married life, one might say, becomes a "song"—the *Song of Songs*. Every sacrifice, every diaper change, every meal cooked, every commute to work, every trial and suffering born in love, every task and responsibility carried out day-to-day is understood and lived as a continuation of the faithful gift, that unconditional "yes" spoken by the body in the marital union of bodies. The good times and bad, the sickness and health, the better and worse all become an offering to God as an ongoing participation in the Church's liturgy. It all serves to sanctify the family and the world.[41] In

---

41. See *CCC*, nos. 1368, 2031.

this way, John Paul affirms that "liturgical language becomes the 'language of the body.'" And all of life's acts and tasks serve to "form the '*spirituality*' of marriage, its 'ethos'" (TOB 117b:3).

Spiritually Mature Sexual Attraction

A profound sense of the holiness of the body and of conjugal union—of the person and the communion of persons—must form the essential "ethos" and "spirituality" of married life. St. Paul calls spouses precisely to this when he exhorts them to be "subject to one another out of reverence for Christ" (Eph 5:21). In fact, John Paul says that this Pauline image of reverence for Christ "is nothing other than *a spiritually mature form* of that reciprocal *fascination* [or attraction]...of the man for femininity and of the woman for masculinity" (TOB 117b:4). Mature sexual attraction inspires deep awe and wonder at the mystery of God revealed through the gratuitous beauty of the masculine and feminine body. The Pope remarks that this is the same sexual fascination and attraction that the book of Genesis revealed for the first time (see 2:23–25) and that "seems to run like a wide torrent" through the verses of the Song of Songs. It also finds a concentrated expression in the marriage of Tobias and Sarah. The spiritual maturity of this fascination and attraction, John Paul tells us, is nothing but *the fruit born of the gift of reverence* and awe for the mystery of the sacred which, as the Pope also reminds us, is one of the seven gifts of the Holy Spirit (see TOB 117b:4).

Living a chaste life *does not* mean annihilating erotic desire. It means opening erotic desire to the divine fire and inspiration of *agape*, so that the love, affection, and consummate embrace of spouses can be a true image of Christ's love, affection, and consummate union with the Church. Chastity does not impoverish the love of the sexes. On the contrary, the divine fire of *agape* makes these experiences "spiritually more intense and thus *enriches* them" (TOB 128:3). This *mature, intense* experience of sexual fascination-attraction-desire *is actually a gift of the Holy Spirit*, according to John Paul II. By "stirring their desire for 'reverence' in conjugal relations, Ephesians...[calls couples to] chastity as a virtue and as a gift" (TOB 117b:5). We must certainly cultivate chastity as a human virtue, doing all within our ability to resist the concupiscence of the flesh. But in the end, that spiritually mature attraction of the sexes of which Ephesians speaks is a gift of God. And it is a gift God *longs* to give to us—the gift of his Spirit dwelling in our flesh.[42]

To the degree that we turn from concupiscence and live "according to the Spirit," the desires of our hearts conform to the truth, dignity, and sacredness of the body and the call to communion. As the Holy Father says: "Both the man and the woman, provided they turn away from concupiscence, find the proper dimension of the freedom of the gift, united with femininity and masculinity in the true spousal meaning of the body." In this way they experience the mysterious language of the body "in a depth, simplicity and beauty hitherto altogether unknown" (TOB 117b:5). Such a statement is not merely a projection of a celibate pontiff but also the observation of a pastor who worked intimately and extensively with countless married couples over the course of many years.

John Paul concludes that *this seems to be the integral meaning of the sacramental sign* of marriage. "In this way, through the 'language of the body,' man and woman encounter the great '*mysterium*' in order to transfer the light of this mystery...into the 'language of the body.'" The Pope affirms that through the ethos of redemption married couples are able to transfer the "light of truth and of beauty expressed in liturgical language" to their practice "of love, of faithfulness, and of conjugal integrity" (TOB 117b:6). Through the gift of redemption, man and woman are called, just as they were "in the beginning," to be the visible sign of God's creative love. Ephesians 5 fully discloses the "great mystery" of this sign, but it plunges its roots "into the mystery of the creation of man, male and female, in the image of God" (TOB 117b:3).

If redeemed man—joining as male and female so intimately as to be "one flesh"—is called to image God as the visible sign of his creative love, what happens to this "sign" if the spouses rob it of its procreative potential? If the lovers of the Song of Songs proclaim the joy of living the true sign of marital love while Tobias and Sarah face a test of life-or-death to reclaim the truth of that sign, what light does this shed on the teaching of *Humanae Vitae*? John Paul will provide us with that answer in the final chapter of his extended catechesis.

---

42. See *CCC*, nos. 1810, 1811, 2345.

THE DIMENSION OF SIGN—IN REVIEW

1. In Part II, Chapter 2, John Paul unfolds the mystery of "the sacrament" (of marriage) in the human dimension of the sign. The wedding vows give an intentional expression to this sign. Yet, these words of the spirit demand a corresponding "language of the body." The wedding vows can be fulfilled only by means of conjugal intercourse, which constitutes marriage in its full reality. Both the vows and the marital embrace, then, are important for the sacramental sign of marriage.

2. The sacramental sign of marriage is one of manifold contents. It is first established by the liturgical rite in the exchange of consent and is then consummated in marital intercourse. In turn, the sacramental sign endures in the man and woman themselves and their indissoluble bond throughout their lives.

3. Since the language of the body proclaims the mystery of God's life and love, we can speak of a specific "prophetism of the body." Man, as a subject, becomes the author of this language. He can choose to speak the truth with his body, but he can also choose to speak lies. If the body is "prophetic," we must carefully distinguish true from false prophets.

4. Spouses must learn to reread and "speak" the language of their bodies truthfully. Indeed, the essential element of the sacramental sign of marriage is the language of the body spoken in truth. During the liturgical rite of marriage, the priest or deacon asks the couple if they promise to receive children lovingly from God. If the language of consent says "yes" but the language of the body says "no," this falsifies the sacramental sign.

5. All the meanings of the language of the body are initiated and synthesized in the content of conjugal consent. Day by day, spouses draw from that synthesis the same sign, identifying themselves with it throughout their lives. In all that they do—and especially in

the consummate expression of their union—the spouses remain faithful to their original consent, or they fail to do so. They deepen their love and fidelity, or they cheapen it.

6. Rereading the language of the body in truth is given as a task to the man of concupiscence. Even if concupiscence causes many "errors" in rereading the language of the body and gives rise to sin, man is not determined by concupiscence. Through the ethos of redemption, the possibility always remains of passing from "error" to the "truth"—the possibility of conversion from sin to chastity through life according to the Holy Spirit.

7. The erotic poetry of the Song of Songs provides a rich affirmation of the language of the body reread in the truth. John Paul criticizes those exegetes who quickly disembody the Song of Songs, seeing nothing more than a "spiritual" allegory. Precisely in the Song's profound affirmation of erotic love—not despite it—we are able to discern God's revelation. In the lovers' mutual fascination with the body we see the divine mystery made visible in "the sign" of married love.

8. What was expressed in Genesis in just a few short words ("At last, this one is bone of my bones, flesh of my flesh...") is developed in the Song in a full dialogue. The same kind of wonder and fascination that Adam and Eve originally took in each other runs throughout the Song in a peaceful and even wave. Fascination with the human body in its masculinity and femininity is presented in the Song as a means for training in righteousness, for training in authentic love.

9. The bridegroom's fascination with the visible femininity of his beloved reveals an aspiration born of love on the basis of the language of the body. It is a search for integral beauty, the beauty of body and soul free of all stain. It is a love and appreciation not just for *a* body but for *some*body, for her entire feminine person. Both the bridegroom and the bride see each other with the eyes of the body *and* the eyes of the heart.

10. In calling his beloved first his "sister" before his "bride," the bridegroom speaks of their common humanity, reproducing in some

way the whole history of the femininity of the person he loves. "Sister" demonstrates the disinterested tenderness of his desire toward her, demonstrating the sincerity of his self-gift. Unless lovers first recognize each other as brother and sister, they are unable to love one another properly as husband and wife.

11. Because their love goes right back to the truth of the primordial sacrament in Genesis, the lovers in the Song of Songs experience a sense of "common belonging." They are children of the same Father in heaven, sharing the same humanity. This brings an experience of peace reminiscent of the "peace of the interior gaze" that Adam and Eve experienced in the beginning.

12. The expressions "garden closed" and "fountain sealed" bring us into the vestibule of the union of the sexes, helping us understand its mystery, especially the hidden mystery of "the woman." These metaphors express the whole personal dignity of the female sex, revealing her as "master of her own mystery." The lover knows that he cannot grasp or possess her. He must trust in the freedom of the gift.

13. The bride opens her "garden closed" before the eyes and heart of the bridegroom with the freedom of a trusting surrender. He delights in entering this garden and, because of the purity of his intention, she remains "inviolate." Authentic spousal love—which is simultaneously spiritual and sensual—enables an initiation into the mystery of the person without ever violating the mystery of the person.

14. The words "Love is strong as death" bring us to the peak of the Song's declaration of love, presenting the final chords in the language of the body. They show how far it is necessary to go—*unto death!*—if spousal love is to be true to itself. The bride can only open her "closed garden" and remain inviolate if the bridegroom pledges himself to the very end, all the days of his life.

15. The restlessness of their desire for a love that is "ever in search" but "never satisfied" speaks of their desire for integration of eros with "something more"—with agape. Left to itself, eros is limited by *bodily weakness*, the *prospect of death*, and by *jealousy*. Agape, however, reveals a love made *strong in weakness*, a love that *overcomes*

death, and a love that is *not jealous*. Spouses, then, can only reach the very nucleus of self-giving love by allowing agape to penetrate and purify eros.

16. Spousal love—if it is to overcome all that threatens it—must become part of the Church's prayer to the Father by which we enter into the "great mystery" of Christ's love for the Church. In other words, spousal love must become *liturgical*. Spousal love and all of conjugal life become liturgical (an effective act of prayer, worship, sanctification) to the degree that, through the ethos of redemption, men and women reclaim God's original plan for their humanity.

17. If the spouses in the Song of Songs experience joy and pleasure in the language of their bodies, the spouses of Tobit recognize that the language of the body also expresses a test of life-or-death. We see very pointedly in the marriage of Tobias and Sarah that in becoming one flesh, spouses find themselves at the center of the great contest between good and evil, life and death, love and all that is opposed to love.

18. Tobias's prayer shows that he desires not to lust for Sarah but to be a sincere gift to Sarah according to God's original plan. Hence, in calling upon God's grace and mercy, Tobias and Sarah face the test of life-or-death—and their love, supported by their prayer, is revealed as "stronger than death." In this way, their "one flesh" union bears witness to God as the God of life.

19. With the prayer of Tobias and Sarah, the language of their bodies becomes liturgical. Their prayer is a profession of their "conjugal creed" and, as such, provides the specific antidote to the diabolical scheming of the demon. For liturgical prayer is a *word of power* drawn from the mystery of God's covenant and grace. This power restores in spouses the original ethos of marital love and union.

20. Ephesians 5 offers us the definitive expression of the sign of marriage reread in the full truth of eros-agape love. Here we read that the one flesh union is a "great mystery" that is meant to express Christ's love for the Church. This is a solid and complete confirmation of all that we have learned about the true meaning of the body's "language" presented in a *fully personalistic* way.

21. Because the analogy in Ephesians 5 works in two directions, conjugal life is not only liturgical; liturgical life is also modeled after the love of spouses. We not only recognize marriage as the sacrament of Christ and the Church, but we recognize the sacrament of Christ and the Church (the Eucharist) as the union of the bridegroom and the bride.

22. Ephesians 5 brings us to the "mystical" and "liturgical" dimensions of the language of the body. Above all, liturgical life involves the celebration of the sacraments. Marriage is not only one of the sacraments but also a kind of prototype for all of them. The sacraments penetrate both soul and body, the entire male and female personality, with the power of holiness.

23. The ethos and spirituality of married life is formed by that "reverence for Christ" to which St. Paul exhorts spouses. This reverence is nothing but a mature form of sexual fascination-attraction. It is a gift of the Holy Spirit (piety) that frees men and women to experience the language of the body in a depth, simplicity, and beauty altogether unknown to men and women dominated by concupiscence. It enables spouses to be a true *sacramental sign* of God's eternal, creative love.

He Gave Them the Law of Life as Their Inheritance

[Cycle 6—Love and Fruitfulness: Reflections on *Humanae Vitae*]

"THE REFLECTIONS ABOUT human love in the divine plan carried out so far would remain in some way incomplete," the Pope observes, "if we did not try to see their concrete application in the area of conjugal and familial morality" (TOB 118:1). The concrete application of which he speaks is the regulation of births. Thus, in fifteen concluding addresses delivered between July 11, 1984, and November 21, 1984 (TOB 118–32), John Paul II applies everything he has thus far taught to the teaching of Pope Paul VI's landmark encyclical *Humanae Vitae*. Taking this further step "will bring us to the conclusion of our, by now, long journey" (TOB 118:1).

It has been a long journey indeed. Every step has led us to this point. Recall that John Paul sees his entire catechesis on the body as "*an extensive commentary* on the doctrine contained precisely in *Humanae Vitae*" (TOB 133:2). Questions come from this encyclical, which, according to John Paul, "run in some way through the whole of our reflections." Therefore, it "follows that this final part is not artificially added to the whole, but is organically and homogeneously united with it" (TOB 133:4). Introducing his reflections on *Humanae Vitae*, the Holy Father states: "It seems to me, in fact, that what I want to set forth in the coming weeks is, as it were, the crowning of what I have explained" (TOB, p. 549).

The fierce denunciation of the encyclical's teaching had inspired John Paul II to develop his TOB in the first place. He made this the first major teaching project of his pontificate because it is absolutely impossible to build a civilization of love and a culture of life if we do not understand and embrace the teaching of *Humanae Vitae*. And it is impossible to understand the full importance of *Humanae Vitae* without a "total vision of man." As Paul VI himself recognized: "The problem of birth [regulation], like every other problem regarding human life, must be considered beyond partial perspectives." It must be seen "in light of a total vision of man and of his vocation, not only his natural and earthly, but also his supernatural and eternal vocation."[1] As we mentioned in the Prologue, this was John Paul's cue. This "total vision of man" is precisely what the TOB provides for us. This thoroughly biblical–theological–sacramental–personalistic vision of man and of conjugal union not only provides a new and winning context for understanding the Church's constant teaching on the immorality of contracepted intercourse. It also places it on the surest foundation possible: that of divine revelation itself (see TOB 119:4; 133:3).

Much is at stake in the teaching of *Humanae Vitae*. Recall Waldstein's observation that all "the fundamental questions of our age—questions about the meaning of the body, about the meaning of love, about nature, technology, and progress—come together in the issue of *Humanae Vitae* as in a tight knot." This is why "John Paul II does not view the teaching of *Humanae Vitae* as a particular moral prohibition, but as a precious inheritance from the Creator that is closely connected with fostering life as a whole."[2] The phrase "a precious inheritance" reminds us of the title the Pope gave this chapter: "He Gave Them the Law of Life as Their *Inheritance*." While so many people consider Church teaching on sex as a scolding reminder of sin, John Paul's reflections on *Humanae Vitae*—still within the framework of his catechesis on "The Sacrament" and all the redemptive power connected with it—remind us that the inheritance of our hearts "is deeper than the sinfulness inherited." God's law of life reactivates "that deepest inheritance" and gives it "real power in human life" (TOB 46:6).

Only to the degree that we are vivified with this "power" do we see what a precious inheritance *Humanae Vitae* is. Hence, John Paul's goal

---

1. *Humanae Vitae*, 7.
2. Waldstein, Introduction, TOB, pp. 107, 109.

in this cycle of his catechesis is not only to provide a compelling apologetic for the Church's moral norm—which he does in section one, called "The Ethical Problem." Even more he wants to demonstrate *the power* flowing from Christ that makes living the moral norm not only a possibility but also a *joy*. He does this in section two, called "Outline of Conjugal Spirituality."

Wojtyla wrote in his book *Sources of Renewal* that the "key problem of life as actually lived by Christians is that of the link between faith and morals." We discover "Christian morality understood in all its fullness"—that is, "not only in the field of...norms, but still more in the field of...*ethos*"—only by participating "in the priestly and kingly mission of the Redeemer." Christian morality, therefore, "combines the element of *sacrifice*, proper to a priesthood, with the kingly element of *victory*, of man's dominion over himself and the world of nature. These two elements," Wojtyla concludes, "constitute the very root of [Christian] morality."[3] For these two elements—sacrifice and victory—take us to the heart of the Christian mystery of love: *death* and *resurrection*. Only those willing to embrace the *sacrifice* required by authentic conjugal love will ever taste the *victory* over concupiscence that comes through the redemption of the body. Only through such sacrifice and victory can man and woman's union shine as a transparent sign of God's love in the world. This is precisely what the teaching of *Humanae Vitae* seeks to protect and ensure—the value of conjugal love as a transparent sign of divine love.

Conjugal love takes its origin from the God who has revealed himself to us at one and the same time as "Love" and as "Father."[4] Thus, as Wojtyla once observed, Paul VI's encyclical *"responds basically to a single question*: what must conjugal love be like in order to discover God's eternal plan of love in it? Under what conditions does conjugal love reflect its prime exemplar, God as Love and God as Father?" According to Wojtyla, this is "the very summit of the issue." And this "is the level upon which we must consider the entire encyclical and the teaching on conjugal love contained therein."[5]

---

3. *Sources of Renewal*, p. 99, emphasis added.
4. See *Humanae Vitae*, 8.
5. "The Teaching of the encyclical *Humanae Vitae* on Love," *Person and Community*, pp. 303, 304.

1. The Ethical Problem

The Moral Norm and the Truth of the "Language of the Body"

The Pope's appeal to human subjectivity throughout his catechesis makes it clear that he believes it virtually impossible to explain the Church's teaching on sexual morality to the modern world without incorporating the way modern men and women think. *Humanae Vitae*, in fact, is one of the first documents of the Church's magisterium to draw from modern philosophy's "subjective turn" in its approach to married life and conjugal morality. John Paul relates that the Fathers of the Second Vatican Council had already discussed the necessity for a deepened analysis of human subjectivity in this regard (see TOB 129:3). In turn, the Council clearly integrated personalistic language into its teaching on marriage.[6] Even prior to that, there were a few seeds of such personalism in Pope Pius XI's *Casti Connubii* of 1930.[7] Still, *Humanae Vitae* is the first magisterial document that attempts to frame a major moral pronouncement in largely personalistic terms.

███ Here it is easy to recognize the influence of a certain Polish prelate in the paragraphs of Paul VI's encyclical. In fact, historians and other Vatican observers often credit Karol Wojtyla as the main architect behind *Humanae Vitae*. Papal biographer George Weigel, however—while recognizing Wojtyla's influence—argues that the encyclical did not adopt in full the rich personalistic context that Wojtyla proposed to his predecessor. Weigel even suggests that the encyclical might have been better received and the aftermath not so ugly had Paul VI more fully heeded Wojtyla's advice.[8] Perhaps, but it seems *Humanae Vitae* was rejected primarily because of its conclusion, not because of its inadequate argumentation.

Humanae Vitae reaffirms the constant teaching of the universal Church that in each and every marriage act "there must be no impair-

---

6. See *Gaudium et Spes*, 47–52.
7. See par. 24 of *Casti Connubii*, for example.
8. See *Witness to Hope*, pp. 209–10.

ment of its natural capacity to procreate human life."[9] There is nothing new here. The novelty of Paul VI's encyclical, however, is that it bases this teaching "on the inseparable connection, established by God which man on his own initiative may not break, between the unitive meaning and the procreative meaning which are both inherent to the marriage act."[10] Without analyzing the whole encyclical, John Paul focuses primarily on this passage.

This new basis of defense for the Church's teaching marks a clear turn to the subject. To focus on the "meaning" of the act rather than its "end" is to evaluate the sexual act from the interior perspective of the persons performing it. As Wojtyla wrote in a pre-papal essay, "One can detect in this part of the encyclical *a very significant passage from what some might call a 'theology of nature' to a 'theology of person.'*"[11] The purpose is not to separate "nature" from "person," but to link them in a deep and organic way.[12] In an integral "theology of person," an appeal to the "meaning" of the conjugal act does not imply that persons are free to assign their own meaning to the act. Paul VI avoids the pit of "subjectivism" by linking this subjective turn with objective reality. These two meanings of sexual intercourse, he says, are rooted in the "innermost structure" of the act and "the actual nature of man and of woman."[13] Through this "innermost structure" and because of the "actual nature" of the persons engaging in the act, anyone can observe that sexual intercourse both "deeply unites husband and wife" and at the same time "makes them able to generate new lives." Logic recognizes both meanings as essential to the integrity of the act as nature (God) designed it. Thus, it follows by logical necessity—unless we have a split view of nature and person, body and soul (as most of the "modern world" does, and herein lies the precise problem)—that both meanings of the act are essential to the integrity of the subjects themselves who are performing the act (see TOB 118:6).

---

9. *Humanae Vitae,* 11. This passage is typically and less accurately translated: "...each and every marriage act must remain open to the transmission of life."

10. Ibid., 12.

11. "The Teaching of the Encyclical *Humanae Vitae* on Love," *Person and Community,* p. 308.

12. For a discussion of the importance of linking "nature" and "person," see Michael Waldstein's Introduction, TOB, pp. 60, 94–99.

13. *Humanae Vitae,* 12.

Here John Paul insists that morality is not based merely on evaluating an "act" in the abstract. It is based on the truth of the acting person(s) and their dignity.[14] Only persons, in fact, are capable of morality. In evaluating sexual morality, nothing else is at stake here than reading the "language of the body" truthfully (see TOB 118:6). He also stresses, therefore, that the inseparability of the unitive and procreative meanings of intercourse is "strictly linked with our earlier reflections about *marriage in the dimension of the (sacramental) sign*" (TOB 118:3). The sacramental sign is based on the faithful and ongoing *incarnation* of the vows freely professed at the altar—vows of fidelity, permanence, and openness to children. "In fact, as man and woman live in marriage 'until death,' in some sense they continuously re-propose the sign they themselves gave—through the liturgy of the sacrament—on the day of their wedding" (TOB 118:4).

Signs and Countersigns

If all of married life constitutes the sacramental sign, there is also a consummate moment in which spouses renew and express this sign in a very particular way—the moment of the marital embrace. The "sign of spousal union...has become a sacramental sign" (TOB 108:5). Here couples are called to speak and renew the vows they made at the altar *with their bodies*. As John Paul stresses: "Precisely *in this moment, so rich in meaning*, it is also particularly important that the 'language of the body' be reread in the truth. This reading," he continues, "becomes an indispensable condition for *acting in the truth* or for behaving *in conformity with the value and the moral norm*" (TOB 118:4). Notice the words "value" and "moral norm." John Paul observes that in Paul VI's encyclical, the Church not only wants to recall an objective moral norm, but also demonstrate its subjective value and foundation (see TOB 118:5). In his TOB, John Paul frames the objective truth and the subjective value of the norm in terms of the sacramental sign, that is, in terms of the objective language of the body and its subjective "rereading in truth."

Recall that statement we have repeated several times: "One can speak of moral good and evil" in the sexual relationship based on whether the couple gives to their union "the character of a truthful

---

14. It is significant to note that the very first line in the section of the *Catechism* that deals with morality is "Christian, recognize your dignity" (*CCC*, no. 1691).

sign" (TOB 37:6). John Paul reasonably maintains that "the 'language of the body' should *express*, at a determinate level, *the truth of the sacrament*. By participating in the eternal plan of Love, '*Sacramentum absconditum in Deo*' [the mystery hidden in God], the 'language of the body' becomes in fact a 'prophetism of the body'" (TOB 123:2). In other words, the language of the body—throughout all of married life, but especially in the conjugal act—is meant not only to proclaim the mystery of God's life and love, but to enable spouses to participate in it. From this perspective, as Professor Mary Rousseau has expressed, morally upright sexual behavior is simply another way of saying "sacramentally efficacious" sexual behavior.[15] Waldstein observes that the "key terms of John Paul II's whole argument" are brought into play right here—in "the spousal meaning of the body linked with the gift of self, and the efficacious sacramental transmission of trinitarian life by the body in its spousal meaning."[16]

For sacramental signs to be *efficacious*, however, they must accurately signify the spiritual reality they are intended to communicate. The "one flesh" union of husband and wife—inasmuch as it is a sign of Christ's union with the Church (see Eph 5:31–32)—is meant to signify "the entire work of creation and redemption" (TOB 97:5). It is meant to signify the trinitarian mystery hidden in God from all eternity (see TOB 19:4–5). This is the mystery of eternal life-giving Love and Communion in which man is called to participate through the "great mystery" of Christ's union with the Church—a union that gives life and gives it to the full (see Jn 10:10). But what does a contracepted act of intercourse—that is, an act of intercourse that the spouses themselves defraud of its procreative potential—do to this sacramental picture? We can certainly argue against contraception purely from natural law (i.e., human reason). But John Paul's catechesis on the body demonstrates the ultimate *theological* reason for the immorality of contraception: it is fundamentally sacrilegious. It profanes the "great mystery"—the "great sacrament"—by falsifying the sign.[17] As the Pope

---

15. See Mary Rousseau, "Eucharist and Gender," *Catholic Dossier* (September/ October, 1996): pp. 19–23. This article is an insightful and provocative treatment of sacramental efficacy as applied to sexual morality and especially the reservation of priestly ordination to men.

16. Waldstein, Introduction, TOB, p. 121.

17. See *CCC*, no. 2120.

says, by virtue of their sacrament, spouses have a divine mission "fundamental for all humanity" to "witness to Love and to Life." But if marital love is falsified, "communion is broken, the mission destroyed."[18]

In his insightful book *Sex and Sacredness* (*A Catholic Homage to Venus*), Christopher Derrick frames his entire discussion of sexual morality in terms of the profane and the sacred. In doing so, he takes the insights of John Paul's TOB to their logical conclusions. To "profane," he observes, "refers to whatever we find in front of the temple (*pro fanum*), and therefore outside it, to whatever lacks the religious kind of importance. The 'sacred' will then be whatever *does* have the religious kind of importance." As the Church sees it, sex is supremely sacred. "If the word 'sacrament' means anything at all in this connection," Derrick writes, "it means that the symbolic is here the actual—that God is actively present in the marital bedroom and deeply involved in what happens there.... He's right in there where the action is; and we, on our side, are correspondingly involved with him." In response to the notion that the Church harps disproportionately on sexual sin, Derrick responds that we may well be tempted to commit any number of sins. "But unless we go in for Satanism and the Black Mass, there is only one kind of sin which allures us powerfully and constantly and which (if committed) will involve the profanation of a sacrament." This applies particularly, Derrick believes, to contraception. "In order to avoid the Cross, we shall be separating love from creativity." Contracepted intercourse

> will still have a theological meaning. But this will now be Manichaean instead of Christian: we shall be enacting [not faith in Christ, but] the faith of those who denied the possibility of any direct relationship between God's love and the existence of this troubled world. The Venus whom we then serve will be daemonic in the rather specialized sense of being heretical or worse.[19]

Sexual union is not only a *biological* process; it is also a *theological* process. When we override the divine Word written in our bodies with

---

18. Homily on the Feast of the Holy Family, December 30, 1988.
19. *Sex and Sacredness*, pp. 23, 97, 99, 100.

contraception, we speak *against* (we *contra*-dict) the "great mystery" of God's life and love that our bodies were created and redeemed to proclaim. Insert contraception into this sacramental sign of married love, and (knowingly or unknowingly) a couple engages in a *countersign* of the "great mystery" of creation and redemption. Their union becomes an objective *denial* of God's creative and redemptive love. In this way, the objective language of the body turns the spouses (knowingly or unknowingly) into "false prophets." In contracepted intercourse, the language of the body is akin to blasphemy. It speaks not the *symbolic* Word, but the *diabolic* anti-Word.

Such are the logical, moral, practical, and pastoral conclusions of an authentic theology *of the body*. If we are to embrace our own greatness—our own God-like dignity—as revealed in the Scriptures, we must also embrace the demands incumbent upon our dignity. For those who come to understand the "great mystery" of joining in one flesh, contraception is simply *unthinkable*. As John Paul will say in the course of his reflections: such couples have a "salvific fear" of ever "violating or degrading what bears in itself the sign of the divine mystery of creation and redemption" (TOB 131:5). Every human being proclaims this mystery through his (or her) own body. If we are to be ourselves, we must learn to read this divine body-language "in truth." As the Pope says, "What is at stake here is the *truth*, first *in the ontological dimension* ('innermost structure') and then—as a consequence—in the *subjective and psychological dimension* ('meaning')" (TOB 118:6). Here the Pope stresses the primacy of objective reality but also indicates its link with subjective experience. Through this linking, *Humanae Vitae* attempts to demonstrate how its moral norm is not imposed from "outside," but wells up from "within" man. In other words, it is in accord with the deepest truth about man and, hence, his deepest desires.[20]

Recall that moral norms are not hurled into emptiness. When we learn to read the objective truth of the body, it then enters the person's consciousness (his subjective dimension) and finds a home there. We

---

20. Many would argue that *Humanae Vitae* did not persuasively demonstrate this. It is no injustice to Paul VI to recognize that his personalistic argument, although groundbreaking, needed refinement. But John Paul II's TOB compensates in abundance for whatever might have been lacking in Paul VI's argument. It imbues precisely that rich and developed personalism that makes the teaching of *Humanae Vitae* ring true.

are created for truth, and the honest person knows it when he finds it. Demonstrating his trust in people's good-will, Paul VI writes: "We believe that our contemporaries are particularly capable of seeing that this teaching [on the immorality of contraception] is in harmony with human reason."[21] John Paul adds that we should also be capable of seeing its profound conformity with all that Tradition has given us, which stems from biblical sources (see TOB 119:4).

The Rightness of the Norm and Its Practicability

John Paul acknowledges that the moral norm taught by *Humanae Vitae* is not found literally in Sacred Scripture.[22] Nonetheless, we find the basis for this teaching in the Scriptures, "particularly," the Pope says, "in biblical anthropology." Hence, while some would claim the Bible has little or nothing to say on the matter of contraception, the Holy Father believes that it is "entirely reasonable" to look precisely to a biblical "theology of the body" for the foundation of the truth taught by *Humanae Vitae* (see TOB 119:4). Precisely within this full biblical context we realize that the norm upheld by the encyclical belongs not only to the natural moral law, but also, John Paul stresses, "to the *moral order revealed by God*" (TOB 119:4). It is an integral part of the *ethos of redemption*. "Based on this 'ethos,' the norm of the natural law finds not only a new expression, but also a *full* anthropological and ethical *foundation* in the word of the Gospel as well as in the purifying and strengthening action of the Holy Spirit" (TOB 119:5).

In other words, the immorality of contraception is not the teaching of men but the teaching of God, a teaching based on God's revelation. Therefore, as the magisterium has stated, "This teaching is to be held as definitive and irreformable."[23] It cannot be changed, nor is it open for theological debate. Furthermore, insofar as it is a norm of natural law, it concerns all men and women everywhere—not only members of the Church. Yet the Church, in particular, is called to witness to this

---

21. *Humanae Vitae*, 12.

22. Many argue that a prohibition against contraception is to be found directly in the Scripture, especially in the incident of Onan "spilling his seed on the ground" (see Gen 38:8–10). For a Protestant argument against contraception based solely on Scripture, see Charles D. Provan, *The Bible and Birth Control* (Monongahela, PA: Zimmer Printing, 1989).

23. *Vademecum for Confessors Concerning Some Aspects of the Morality of Conjugal Life*, 4.

norm before men. In this context, John Paul appeals to every believer and in particular every theologian to "reread and understand ever more deeply the moral teaching of the encyclical in this integral context" (TOB 119:5). Then he adds that his own catechesis on the body is precisely an attempt at this rereading.

Development of the Council's Teaching

Many claim that the teaching of *Humanae Vitae* was a step backward from the forward-looking teaching of Vatican II. On the contrary, the Council issued strong statements affirming the constant teaching of the Church on the immorality of contraception. In this context the Council also referenced some of the most authoritative statements of the modern magisterium in this regard, Pius XI's *Casti Connubii* being first on the list.[24] As John Paul states: "Not only is...[*Humanae Vitae*] aligned with the conciliar teaching, but it also constitutes *the development and completion* of the issues raised there, particularly in regard to the question of the 'harmony between human love and reverence for life'" (TOB 120:1).

> ■ Note 14 of *Gaudium et Spes* number 51 reveals part of the reason why so many people were expecting the Church's teaching to change. The Council Fathers stated that they reserved judgment on certain "questions which need further and more careful investigation." These "have been handed over...to a commission for the study of population, family, and births, in order that, after it fulfills its function, the Supreme Pontiff may pass judgment." The point in question was the birth control pill. Faulty natural law arguments that posited the immorality of contraception primarily in the physical obstruction of semen (i.e., barrier methods and withdrawal) found no grounds against the pill. This new historical situation raised new considerations. It also pointed to the need for a renewal in moral theology—away from a physicalistic interpretation of natural law to a personalistic one (a personalism that integrated person and nature, spirit and matter, soul and body). Just such a renewal was already underway in Poland with the guidance of

---

24. See *Gaudium et Spes*, 51, n. 14.

Karol Wojtyla. The personalistic understanding of the moral law that he helped develop at the University of Lublin left no doubt about the immorality of the pill. But the Council's tacit admission of uncertainty on this point gave people the idea that the Church was considering a change in her teaching. Indeed, as the familiar story goes, the papal commission rendered a split decision to Paul VI: the majority advocating not only acceptance of the pill, but a complete change in teaching on contraception. In turn, this "Majority Report" was leaked to the press, fueling false hopes that an unprecedented Catholic about-face was imminent. So a maelstrom of opposition was poised and ready when Paul VI, inspired, no doubt, by the Holy Spirit, saw the wisdom of the "Minority Report" and issued *Humanae Vitae*.

Perhaps the most common argument for contraception is that it enables couples to foster their love for one another when conception is undesirable. With this argument in mind, John Paul recalls the Council's statement that "a true contradiction cannot exist between the divine laws pertaining to the transmission of life and those pertaining to the fostering of authentic conjugal love."[25] In fact, since the unitive and procreative meanings of the sexual act are truly *inseparable*, if the couple violates one, they also damage the other.

Every time a husband and wife join in "one flesh," their union is meant to be a sign of the mystery hidden from eternity in God—the mystery of God's eternal life and love and his plan for us to participate in that life and love through Christ. But when men and women are detached from the original vision of God's plan, they will have difficulty recognizing that their sexual union is a "sign" of anything beyond their own desire for a gratifying experience of shared pleasure. They will want to call this "love," but in reality what is often called love, "if subjected to searching critical examination turns out to be, contrary to all appearances, only a form of 'utilization' of the person"[26] stemming from concupiscence. When man and woman are cut off from their own dignity and lofty calling, concupiscent "love" seems quite normal to them. Sadly, it may be all they know and all they have ever known.

---

25. *Gaudium et Spes*, 51.
26. *Love and Responsibility*, p. 167.

Such a couple may desire a few children along the way. But prior to that, or once they have the desired number, they will almost inevitably view contraception (or even surgical sterilization) as the most expedient way to continue "loving" one another without fear of an "unwanted pregnancy."[27] If they are Catholic, they will probably brush off the Church's teaching as "out of touch," impractical, and not "pastoral."

True Pastoral Concern

John Paul II responds to such accusations by defining the true nature of pastoral concern. "Pastoral concern," he insists, "means seeking the *true* good of man, promoting the values impressed by God in the human person." In this context, there is indeed a "rule of understanding." But this does not consist in watering down the true dignity of man. Instead, the rule of understanding "aims at the ever clearer discovery of God's plan for human love, in the certainty that the *one and only true* good of the human person consists in putting this divine plan into practice" (TOB 120:6).

John Paul remarks that whoever believes that *Humanae Vitae* does not sufficiently take into account the difficulties present in concrete life does not understand the pastoral concern at the origin of the document (see TOB 120:6). Throughout his encyclical, Paul VI is solicitous of the real problems and questions of modern men and women in all their import and states explicitly that he has no desire to pass over these concerns in silence. He acknowledges that some might find the encyclical's teaching "very difficult" and "even impossible to observe." He states plainly, in fact, that men and women cannot live this teaching "unless God came to their help with that grace by which the good will of men is sustained and strengthened."[28] If God makes serious demands on us, at the same time he pours out all the grace needed for men and women not only to meet those demands but also to fulfill them super-abundantly. Thus, *Humanae Vitae* is not only concerned with reaffirming a

---

27. Dr. William E. May is keen to point out that the slogan of contraception and abortion proponents is "No unwanted child ought ever to be born." However, the truth proclaimed by the Church in the name of Christ is that "No person ought to be unwanted" (see *The John Paul II Institute 1993–1995 Academic Catalogue*, p. 41). This sums up well the disparity between secular and Christian humanisms.

28. See *Humanae Vitae*, 3, 20, 25.

moral norm. Beyond this "normative dimension," the encyclical has an explicitly "pastoral dimension" that aims to uphold and demonstrate the real possibility of living according to the demands of the Gospel (see TOB 122:4).

If one is to have a correct view of *Humanae Vitae*, John Paul observes that one must interpret both the "normative dimension" (the moral principle it affirms) and the "pastoral dimension" (the possibility of fulfilling the moral norm) in light of the theology of the body that emerges from Sacred Scripture (see TOB 122:4). Having built his TOB on the solid foundation of Christ's own words, the Pope concludes: "The theology of the body is not merely a theory, but rather a specific, evangelical, Christian pedagogy of the body" (TOB 122:5). It is an education—and the most appropriate method of education—in the meaning of being human (see TOB 59:3).

John Paul says that the importance of the theology of the body derives from its source—the Bible, especially the Gospels and the words of Christ himself. The Gospel is a message of salvation "revealing *what man's true good is* for the sake of shaping...his life on earth in the perspective of the hope of the future world." This is what the encyclical *Humanae Vitae* proclaims. It points to "man's true good as a person, inasmuch as he is male and female" (TOB 122:5). It proclaims what married love must look like if it is to enable spouses not only to receive the gift of a human life, but to receive the gift of divine life— *eternal life*. By doing so it shows how the problem of birth regulation can be addressed in a way that corresponds to man's true dignity and lofty vocation, how sexual relations can be lived in a way that truly prepares a couple for eternal life.

Paul VI's choice was either to trust in the power and word of the Gospel or not. What is the truly loving, the truly "pastoral" thing to do? As Paul VI stated in his encyclical: "To diminish in no way the saving teaching of Christ constitutes an eminent form of charity for souls."[29] *Humanae Vitae*, in fact, is nothing other than a call for men and women to embrace their own "greatness"—to embrace the full truth of what it means to be created in the image and likeness of God and redeemed in Jesus Christ. Is this not pastoral? Is this impractical? Is this only an

---

29. *Humanae Vitae*, 29.

ideal that needs to be adjusted in light of man's so called "concrete possibilities"? We have already recorded John Paul's response to this question:

> But what are "the concrete possibilities of man"? And of *which* man are we speaking? Of man *dominated* by lust or of man *redeemed by Christ*? This is what is at stake: the *reality* of Christ's redemption. *Christ has redeemed us!* This means he has given us the possibility of realizing the *entire truth* of our being; he has set our freedom free from the *domination* of concupiscence. And if redeemed man still sins, this is not due to an imperfection of Christ's redemptive act, but to man's will not to avail himself of the grace which flows from that act. God's command is of course proportioned to man's capabilities; but to the capabilities of the man to whom the Holy Spirit has been given; of the man who, though he has fallen into sin, can always obtain pardon and enjoy the presence of the Holy Spirit.[30]

Humanae Vitae, then, is a call to faith in the *real power* of redemption. It is a call to a radical paradigm shift in which we listen attentively to that "echo" of God's original plan deep within us and refuse to normalize concupiscence. Yes, *Humanae Vitae*, so often viewed as oppressive, calls us to liberation! It calls us to live in the true freedom of love. It calls us to respond to the unreserved gift God gives to us with the unreserved gift of ourselves to him.

Responsible Parenthood

Anyone familiar with the authentic teaching of the Church realizes that her opposition to contraception does not mean that couples must leave the number of children they have entirely to "chance." Both the teaching of Vatican II and *Humanae Vitae*, in calling couples to a responsible love, call them also to a responsible parenthood.

As John Paul II expresses, responsible parenthood requires that the "couple observe in this area 'their own duties toward God, toward themselves, toward the family, and toward society, in a correct hierarchy of values' (HV 10). Thus, one cannot speak here of 'proceeding at will.' On the contrary, the couple must conform their activity to the creative intention of God' (HV 10)" (TOB 121:6). This, of course, implies a

---

30. *Veritatis Splendor*, 103.

mature ability on the part of husband and wife to discern God's intention for the size of their family. The counsel of a priest or spiritual director can certainly assist them in this regard. However, the Church wisely teaches that it "is the married couple *themselves* who must in the last analysis arrive at these judgments before God."[31] No one else can make this judgment for them. And John Paul states that this point is "of particular importance in determining...*the moral character of 'responsible fatherhood and motherhood'*" (TOB 121:2).

The Council limits the guidance it gives couples to the following: Husband and wife should consider "their own good and the good of the children already born or yet to come." They should "read the signs of the times and of their own situation on the material and spiritual level." Finally, they should consider "the good of the family, of society, and of the Church."[32] One couple might prudently reflect on these considerations and choose to have a large family. Another couple might prudently reflect on these considerations and choose to limit their family size. So long as both couples are acting in a way that respects the meaning of sexual union—in a way that never falsifies the language of the body— the Church teaches that they are *both* exercising responsible parenthood.[33]

It is a myth that the Catholic Church teaches that couples must have as many children as is physically possible. The Church readily recognizes, particularly in our day and age, that in the course of married life couples might have just reason to avoid a pregnancy. As John Paul points out, *Humanae Vitae* admits that even those who use contraception can be motivated by "*acceptable reasons*" for avoiding pregnancy. However, the Holy Father also emphasizes that the end never justifies the means. Contraception remains a grievous violation of the sacramental sign of married love regardless of the motives for using it. In this context John Paul refers to the following teaching of the Council:

> When it is a question of harmonizing married love with the responsible transmission of life, it is not enough to take only the good intention and the evaluation of motives into account; objective criteria must be used, criteria drawn from the nature of the human person and human

---

31. *Gaudium et Spes*, 50, emphasis added.
32. Ibid.
33. See *Humanae Vitae*, 10.

action, criteria which respect the total meaning of mutual self-giving and human procreation in the context of true love; all this is possible only if the virtue of married chastity is seriously practiced.[34]

"The relative principle of conjugal morality is thus faithfulness to the divine plan manifested in the 'innermost structure of the conjugal act' and in the 'inseparable connection between the two meanings of the conjugal act'" (TOB 121:6). How, then, might a couple who have a just reason for avoiding pregnancy do so without violating the "innermost structure of the conjugal act" and without divorcing the unitive and procreative meanings of the act? In order to answer that question, we must clarify still further the essential evil of the contraceptive act.

The Truth of the Language of the Body and the Evil of Contraception

As we have learned throughout our study of John Paul II's TOB, the *raison d'être* of joining in "one flesh" is for the spouses to form a true "communion of persons" in the image of divine love and communion. "The communion of the Holy Trinity," the *Catechism* observes, "is the source and criterion of truth in every relationship."[35] Recognizing this, we can readily see that when a couple engages in contracepted intercourse—that is, when they engage in sexual intercourse but willfully defraud it of its procreative potential—they negate the divine image in their union. As John Paul says, they may engage in a union of bodies, but they fail to achieve a true *communion of persons* (see TOB 123:7). In fact, contraception introduces a divorce at the very heart of the spouses' body-soul integrity. By doing so, it "strikes at God's creation itself at the level of the deepest interaction of nature and person."[36] If contracepted intercourse claims to express love for the other person, it can only be a *dis*-embodied person. It is not a love of the person for his or her "own sake." It is not a love for the person as God created him or her to be in the full truth and integrity of masculinity and femininity. Instead, by using contraception, spouses implicitly (or even explicitly) reject the way God made them as persons. In essence, they say, "I 'love' you, *but*

---

34. *Gaudium et Spes*, no. 51.
35. *CCC*, no. 2845.
36. *Familiaris Consortio*, 32.

not your fertility." In this way they reject the God-ordained unity of body and soul. Consequently, by attacking the procreative meaning of the sexual act, contracepted intercourse "also *ceases to be an act of love*" (TOB 123:6).

Truth and love go hand in hand. "As ministers of a sacrament that is constituted through consent and perfected by conjugal union, man and woman are called *to express* the mysterious *'language' of their bodies in all the truth that properly belongs to it.*" At this point the Holy Father presents one of his most vivid images of sexual love. "Through gestures and reactions, through the whole reciprocally conditioned dynamism of tension and enjoyment—whose direct source is the body in its masculinity and femininity, the body in its action and interaction—through all this, *man, the person,* 'speaks'" (TOB 123:4).

What does the body-person say? Based on the Pope's teaching on the prophetism of the body, we can conclude that if the husband loves his wife "as Christ loved the Church," he says: "This is my body which is given for you" (Lk 22:19). If the wife responds in love to her husband as the Church responds to Christ, she says (as the model of the Church says): "Let it be done to me according to your word" (Lk 1:38). By speaking this prophetic language honestly, spouses faithfully and continually minister their sacrament to each other in the true image of the union of Christ and the Church. By joining in "one flesh" in this way "man and woman reciprocally express *themselves* in the fullest and most profound way made possible for them by the [bodily] dimension itself of their masculinity and femininity." They "express themselves in the measure of the whole truth of their persons" (TOB 123:4). Then the whole "dynamism of tension and enjoyment" that they experience is a participation in the joy Christ promised when we love as he loves (see Jn 15:11). Indeed, the whole dynamism of tension and enjoyment is a vehicle of the Holy Spirit, a participation in divine life, an experience of the very grace of the sacrament of marriage.

But insert contraception into this picture and it changes *everything.* Void of the sincere gift of self, the whole "dynamism of tension and enjoyment" becomes an end in itself rather than a fruit of love. In the final analysis, contracepted intercourse amounts to little more than an act of mutual (or at least one-sided) use and self-seeking. In this regard, contracepted intercourse is closer to an act of (mutual) masturbation than to an act of spousal love and self-donation.

Rendering the sexual union sterile effectively scrambles the sacramental language of the body. Continuing with the above image, by refusing to give his own potency, the husband declares: "This is my body *not* given for you." And by denying the fruitfulness of her own womb, the wife declares: "Let it *not* be done to me according to your word." Right at the great mystery's "*moment of truth*," the truth is exchanged for a lie. Far from imaging the union of Christ and the Church, contracepted intercourse becomes a "countersign" of the great mystery. Likewise, far from imaging the inner life of the Trinity, contracepted intercourse becomes a "countersign" of this mystery—we might even say an "*anti*-sacrament."

Is this not the deceiver's goal from the beginning? The father of lies wants us to speak his own language! He wants the Word of the Gospel inscribed in our bodies (self-donation) to become his anti-word (self-gratification). He wants us to *lie* with our bodies. According to the Holy Father: "Such a violation of the inner order of the conjugal communion, a communion that plunges its roots into the very order of the person, *constitutes the essential evil of the contraceptive act*" (TOB 123:7). He adds that the reflections about the "sign" of marriage as a sacrament are "especially important for this interpretation" (TOB 123:8).

■ In an address entitled "The Church: a Bride Adorned for Her Husband," John Paul contrasted the biblical, feminine figure of Christ's Bride with "the hostile and furious presence of another female figure, 'Babylon,' the 'great harlot' (see Rev 17:1, 5)." John Paul points out a major difference between the two: the Bride of Christ (the Church) "is endowed with an inner fruitfulness by which she constantly brings forth children of God.... These are the children who form that 'assembly of the first-born who are enrolled in heaven.'" Thus, in union with the Holy Spirit (the Lord and Giver of Life), the Bride cries, "Come, Lord Jesus!" (Rev 22:20) In contrast, John Paul says we recognize the "great whore" of Babylon as the one who embodies "death and inner barrenness." With an understanding of the symbolic language of the body gained from John Paul's catechesis on the body, we might ask which figure from Revelation does contracepted intercourse signify—the life-giving Bride of Christ, or the adulterous one who *chooses* barrenness?

If this imagery speaks more to the contracepting bride, what are we to say about the contracepting bridegroom? In this light, we might remember the Pope's "key" for interpreting reality: "*Original sin attempts...to abolish fatherhood.*"[37] Does not contraception, in a given act of intercourse, attempt to do the same? "Called to give life, spouses share in the creative power and fatherhood of God." Indeed, the "divine fatherhood is the source of human fatherhood."[38] The question then arises: Can an act of sexual intercourse that the couple willfully *renders sterile* possibly image and communicate to the world the eternal mystery of God who has revealed himself to us at one and the same time as "Love" and as "Father"?

The desire to avoid a pregnancy (when there is sufficient reason to do so) is not what vitiates contracepted intercourse. What vitiates the act is the specific choice to *render sterile* a potentially fertile union. This changes entirely (*contra*-dicts) the symbolic meaning of the act with drastic consequences to the whole "economy" of the sacramental sign. When spouses have sufficient reason to avoid a pregnancy, it is entirely possible to do so without ever rendering a potentially fertile act sterile, without ever mocking and adulterating the sacramental meaning of the act. We will explore this ethically legitimate means below.

The Ethical Regulation of Births

Suppose a couple understands the true language of their bodies and is committed to express that language faithfully—as all couples should be. But suppose this couple also has serious reason not to conceive another child. What could they do that would not violate the God-given "language" of their union? (Hint: I'm sure you're doing it right now...) They could *abstain.*

Every time a couple engages in the marital embrace, they must speak the language of their bodies in truth. In other words, they must renew honestly (with their bodies) the commitments they freely made at the altar—commitments of fidelity, permanence, and openness to

---

37. *Crossing the Threshold of Hope,* p. 228.
38. *CCC,* nos. 2214, 2367.

children. But couples are not always obligated to engage in the marital embrace. Indeed, on multiple occasions in married life, even if a heightened desire to unite arises, love demands abstinence. Perhaps one's spouse is ill. Perhaps it is after childbirth. Or, perhaps the couple has a serious reason to avoid a pregnancy. In these and in many other cases, love demands abstinence, and if one *cannot* abstain in these situations, that person's love is called into question.

In itself, refraining from marital union to avoid a pregnancy in no way violates the truth of intercourse as a "sign." In order actively and directly to violate the sign of intercourse, a couple must first engage in it. Only then could they defraud it of its meaning. Furthermore, what if a couple who were abstaining from intercourse to avoid a pregnancy were to discover—based on the very way God designed human fertility—that an act of intercourse on a given day would be naturally infertile. Would they be doing anything that objectively violated the sign of conjugal union by engaging in intercourse then? Would they be contracepting? In other words, would they be doing anything to impede the procreative potential of that act of intercourse?

Herein lies the specific moral difference between contraception and the natural means of regulating fertility. It is true, as *Humanae Vitae* recognizes, that "in each case married couples, for acceptable reasons, are both perfectly clear in their intention to avoid children." Paul VI even states that "they mean to make sure none will be born."[39] However, in the one case, infertile intercourse is an *act of God*. In the other case, the couple take the powers of life *into their own hands* with the intent of thwarting God's creative design.

Anyone who thinks the moral difference here is a matter of splitting hairs must answer the following question. What is the moral difference between euthanasia and natural death? The result is the same—the person dies. But one is an "act of God," and in the other, human beings take the powers of life into their own hands. As John Paul says elsewhere: "Contraception is to be judged so profoundly unlawful as never to be, for any reason, justified. To think or to say the contrary is equal to maintaining that in human life, situations may arise in which it is lawful not to recognize God as God."[40]

---

39. *Humanae Vitae*, 16.
40. *L'Osservatore Romano*, October 10, 1983, p. 7.

Married couples who recognize God as God realize, as Paul VI
points out, that they are not the masters of the source of life, but rather
the ministers of the design established by the Creator.[41] As Creator,
God calls married couples to be *procreative* (see Gen 1:28). Spouses
may at times have a just reason to be *non*-procreative. But it would
violate the very essence of married love to be *anti*-procreative. Abstaining from intercourse and engaging in naturally infertile intercourse are both *non*-procreative behaviors. In this way, as *Humanae
Vitae* states, couples can "control birth without offending moral principles."[42] However, to render an act of intercourse sterile is to engage
in *anti*-procreative behavior. One harmonizes with the nature of the
human person and of marital love, while the other grievously contradicts both.

> ■   We speak of "natural" family planning (NFP) specifically
> because of this; it harmonizes with the *nature* of the human person
> and of marital intercourse. NFP is morally acceptable not because
> it is not "artificial," but because it is not contraceptive. Couples
> who use NFP *never* impede the procreative potential of any of
> their acts of intercourse. In this way, the value of the "sign" of inter-
> course remains objectively intact. Likewise, artificial birth control
> is not immoral *because* it is artificial, but because it is *contra-
> ceptive*—because it objectively violates the sign. In my opinion, the
> term "artificial" should be dropped from the discussion altogether
> as it only confuses the issue. Most confusing of all is the phrase
> "artificial contraception," as it implies that NFP is somehow "natu-
> ral contraception." NFP is not contraception at all! This, in fact, is
> the key distinction.

Two Irreconcilable Views of the Person

Some object that the Church's teaching reduces morality to the
laws of biology. Faulty and impersonal interpretations of natural law
may merit such an accusation. However, when the accusation of "biolo-
gism" is leveled outright against the Church's teaching on the proper

---

41. See *Humanae Vitae*, 13.
42. Ibid., 16.

regulation of births, it conceals within itself a pernicious vision of the human being that effectively divorces body and soul.

As John Paul wrote in *Familiaris Consortio*: "The difference, both anthropological and moral, between contraception and recourse to the rhythm of the cycle...is much wider and deeper than is usually thought, one which involves in the final analysis two irreconcilable concepts of the human person and of human sexuality."[43] In the one view, the body—including its fertility—is seen as integral to the person and, hence, as integral to self-giving love. In the other view, the body is seen as part of the realm of subhuman "nature" over which the person has dominion. From the latter perspective, man sees no moral problem in applying the same techniques of dominion to his body and fertility that he exerts over the forces of nature. In fact, doing so is necessary, they say, in order to "humanize" the processes of reproduction.[44] But such language betrays a radical divorce between the physical and the personal in man.

We have previously quoted the Holy Father saying that the "whole development of contemporary science...is based on the disjunction between what is bodily and what is spiritual in man" (TOB 59:3). In his *Letter to Families* John Paul writes: "The separation of spirit and body in man has led to a growing tendency to consider the human body not in accordance with...its specific likeness to God, but rather on the basis of its similarity to all the other bodies present in the world of nature, bodies which man uses as raw material in his efforts to produce goods for consumption." (We engineer tomatoes and cattle to suit our preferences. Why not engineer our own bodies?) John Paul concludes: "When the human body...comes to be used as *raw material* in the same way that the bodies of animals are used...we will inevitably arrive at a dreadful ethical defeat."[45]

---

43. *Familiaris Consortio*, 32.

44. The "Majority Report" of what came to be dubbed the "Papal Birth Control Commission" used precisely such language. In seeking to justify contraception it spoke of "the duty to humanize...what is given in nature." For "it is natural to man to use his skill in order to put under human control what is given by physical nature." The processes of fertility do not need to be "humanized." They are *already* fully human! See Michael Waldstein's Introduction (TOB, pp. 36–44, 99–105) for an excellent discussion on how the roots of this dualistic view can be traced to Francis Bacon and René Descartes.

45. *Letter to Families*, 19.

Humanae Vitae stands as a constant reminder that "biological laws...involve human personality."[46] When we tinker with the human body, we tinker not just with laws of biology, but with *human persons* in their body-soul integrity. Marital love and responsible parenthood require that spouses come to embrace the harmony of biology and personality. Dominion over the "forces of nature," when applied to the important question of regulating births, must never mean obliterating some integral aspect of human nature and personality. The only proper "dominion" to speak of in this case is that of *self-mastery* of one's drives and desires. Unfortunately, as John Paul observes, modern man shows a tendency to transfer the methods proper to the dominion of drives and desires to the domination of his physical constitution. Man looks to dominate his biology through medicine and technology in an attempt to dodge the ascetic effort required by spiritual and moral responsibility.

In fact, according to John Paul, the essence of the Church's teaching on contraception lies right here—in maintaining *the adequate relationship* between dominion of the forces of nature and mastery of self (see TOB 123:1). Without self-mastery, men and women put their intelligence at the service of manipulation rather than love. In turn, when intelligence is no longer informed by love, it exults in what it *can* do rather than in what it *should* do. Man comes to relate to himself and to all of creation not with loving care and respect but with a selfish will to dominate and control. Man's proper dominion over creation, therefore, always begins with a proper understanding and experience of self-mastery in the male-female relationship. Man's freedom—or lack thereof—to choose the good in his sexual life will always reveal the manner in which he exercises dominion over creation. Our study of Genesis already revealed the profound interrelationship between the male-female communion and human dominion over the earth.

Self-Mastery and the Freedom of the Gift

Paul VI acknowledges that man "has made stupendous progress in the domination and rational organization of the forces of nature to the point that he is endeavoring to extend this control over every aspect of

---

46. *Humanae Vitae*, 10.

his own life—over his body, over his mind and emotions, over his social life, and even over the laws that regulate the transmission of life."[47] Yet John Paul asserts that dominating the natural processes of fertility through contraception "threatens the human person for whom the method of 'self-mastery' is and remains specific" (TOB 123:1). Self-mastery corresponds to the fundamental constitution of the person as a subject. In this sense exercising self-mastery is a "natural" method of birth regulation because it is "natural" to man to be in control of his own drives and desires. Resorting to contraception, on the contrary, "*breaks* the constitutive dimension of the person, deprives man of the subjectivity proper to him, and turns him into *an object of manipulation*" (TOB 123:1).

In other words, the only type of "birth control" in keeping with human dignity is *self-control*. Why do we spay or neuter our pets? Precisely because they cannot say no to the urge to mate. We can. If we say otherwise, we deny our original solitude before God. We deny that which distinguishes us from the animals. We deny our dignity as subjects. We deny the essence of our humanity. As the Pope observes: "Man *is person precisely because he possesses himself and has dominion over himself.* Indeed, inasmuch as he is master over himself he can 'give himself' to another. And it is this dimension—the dimension of the freedom of the gift—that becomes essential and decisive for the 'language of the body' in which man and woman express themselves reciprocally in conjugal union" (TOB 123:5).[48]

Without self-mastery, no true gift of self takes place, but only something akin to the copulation of animals. In other words, if one cannot say "no" to sexual intercourse, his "yes" is emptied of its meaning. He is no different from the animals, and he cannot express love. All he can do is indulge concupiscence. The man who fails to master himself—to master his own drives and desires—will inevitably seek to master others in order to satisfy those drives and desires. Manipulation replaces love.

From this perspective, a little-recognized fact comes to light. In the final analysis, contraception was not invented to prevent pregnancy. We already had a perfectly safe, infallibly reliable way of doing that—

---

47. Ibid., 2.
48. See *CCC*, no. 2339.

abstinence. Certainly other motives came into play, but ultimately, if necessity is the mother of invention, the "necessity" that mothered contraception was the desire to indulge sexual instinct without restraint—without abstinence. This can only stem from concupiscence.

In these ways we see how John Paul's defense of *Humanae Vitae* plunges its roots deep into the soil of the garden of Eden—into the truth of man's original solitude, unity, and nakedness, which empowered him to image God as a subject in the freedom of self-giving love. This is the "full truth" about man, the truth he must reclaim if he is ever to be himself. And contraception attacks this truth at its roots.

> ■   Magisterial statements on what constitutes responsible parenthood provide the appropriate balance sometimes lacking in various circles of those who accept the Church's teaching against contraception. In general, there seem to be two poles in a "mentality conflict" among such people. One pole seems to minimize the necessity of having just reasons to avoid pregnancy, while the other seems to think that couples are obligated to procreate unless avoiding pregnancy is a matter of life and death. The primary danger of the former mentality is that of selfishness in avoiding children.[49] Couples with the latter mentality, however, may end up practicing another less obvious form of selfishness. Large families are often the result of prudent consideration and selfless giving. Other times, however, large families may be a result of the couple's lack of freedom to abstain from intercourse. Self-mastery is an absolute prerequisite of authentic conjugal love. This is why the practice of periodic continence is such an aid to marital love. The freedom to say "no" demonstrates the authenticity of the couple's "yes." Thus, even if a couple has prudently concluded that they have no serious reason to avoid pregnancy, occasional periods of abstinence should be practiced (obviously these need not be during the fertile period) in order to foster authentic freedom in self-giving. The point is that parenthood can only be considered "responsible" when either the choice to avoid intercourse during the fertile time, or the choice to engage in it, is free of any selfish sting.

---

49. See *CCC*, no. 2368.

The Integral Vision of Natural Fertility Regulation

If we are to understand how natural fertility regulation differs substantially from contraception, we must have an "integral vision of man" and of his vocation. We must understand who man is as a person made in God's image as male and female. We must understand who man is as a subject created "for his own sake," who can only find himself through "the sincere gift of himself." Safeguarding these anthropological truths is the *raison d'être* of the encyclical *Humanae Vitae*. For contraception directly attacks the truth that man is created in God's image and likeness. It directly attacks man's subjectivity and his call to sincere selfgiving. Yes, the very identity of man is at stake in the debate about contraception. Contraception is a *betrayal of our humanity*.

The Holy Father insists that the whole question of the encyclical *Humanae Vitae goes back to the very subjectivity* of the human person (see TOB 129:3). Anyone would certainly misinterpret the encyclical who would see in "responsible parenthood" merely a reduction to a "biological rhythm of fertility." John Paul insists that the "author of the encyclical energetically disapproves of and contradicts every form of reductive ...interpretation and with insistence proposes the integral understanding" (TOB 126:3).

When we view the issue of birth regulation with this "integral understanding"—that is, with an understanding of the human person's incarnate subjectivity—we realize that this "problem belongs not so much to biology, but to psychology: from biology and psychology, it then passes into the sphere of conjugal and family spirituality" (TOB 129:3). It passes into the sphere of religion and theology—a theology that seeks God's revelation *in the body*. John Paul observes that without this perspective, the method of natural birth regulation is frequently separated from its proper ethical dimensions and is, therefore, put into effect in a merely functional, even utilitarian, way. In this situation "one no longer sees the difference between it and the other 'methods'...and one ends up speaking about it as if it were just another form of contraception" (TOB 125:4).

Such is the case when the "naturalness" of natural birth regulation is viewed only at the level of biology. But the integral vision recognizes, as John Paul insists, that "this is 'naturalness' on the level of the person. One cannot, therefore, think of it as a mechanical application of biological laws. By itself, knowledge of the 'rhythms of fertility'—though indispensable—does not yet create that interior freedom of the gift that is...[needed] in order to allow the *gift* of self to the other" (TOB 130:4). The call to regain this interior freedom is at the heart of *Humanae Vitae's* integral vision of natural birth regulation.

Personalistic Interpretation of Natural Law

Being free with the interior freedom of the gift is man's natural state. It was man's state "in the beginning." The call to regain this freedom—inherent in the encyclical *Humanae Vitae*—is also inherent in John Paul's personalistic understanding of the natural law.[50]

The natural law is often confused with the "laws of nature." The laws of nature pertain to those laws that govern irrational beings, whereas natural law pertains to man's rational participation in the divine law.[51] Thus, in speaking of the teaching of *Humanae Vitae* as a norm of the natural law, "we understand here the 'order of nature' in the field of procreation inasmuch as it is understood by right reason" (TOB 124:6). Linking the objective truth of natural law with the modern "turn to the subject," John Paul stresses that the natural law refers to man "not only in the 'natural' aspect of his existence, but also in the integral truth of his personal subjectivity" (TOB 123:3). The order of the natural law "is the expression of the Creator's plan for the human person." Hence, the Holy Father states that the virtue expressed in natural fertility regulation "is determined *not so much* by faithfulness to an impersonal '*natural law,' but to the personal Creator*, the source and Lord of the order that is shown in this law" (TOB 124:6).

Although John Paul himself does not explicitly point this out, we see here a link between the natural law and the sacramentality of the body. The body reveals the mystery and plan of God for man. This plan, inscribed in our bodies, is only impersonal if our bodies are impersonal. But the body is the "sacrament" of the person. Furthermore, in Christ, the human body is the sacrament of the divine Person of the Word. Thus, from the perspective of the theology of the body, the natural law is anything but impersonal. It is the law of the gift. It is the law

---

50. See *CCC*, nos. 1954–60.
51. See *CCC*, no. 1955.

of the freedom of the gift of persons. In other words, it is the law of life-giving love written in our persons by a personal God who destines us for the communion of persons—human *and* divine. John Paul repeats that from this perspective, the reduction to a mere biological regularity, separated from the Creator's plan, deforms the authentic thought of the encyclical *Humanae Vitae* (see TOB 124:6). So, in the case of conforming to the natural law in regulating fertility, the Pope emphasizes that it is not a question of "biologizing ethics" (that is, of "reducing ethics to biology"), as some have mistakenly held. The "question is, *What is the true good of human persons and what corresponds to the true dignity of the person?*" (TOB 125:2).

Having a Procreative Attitude

The integral intention of natural fertility regulation also presupposes of spouses a positive attitude toward family and procreation. That is to say, "it demands 'that they acquire and possess solid convictions concerning the true values of life and of the family' (HV 21)" (TOB 124:3). In a contraceptive culture, children are often looked upon as a burden to be resisted rather than a blessing to be embraced. In such a milieu, couples often enter marriage with an attitude toward children that assumes they will not have them *unless* or *until* they "want" them. Without thinking much of it, couples who take this approach will simply look for the most expedient way to carry out their plan of avoiding "unwanted" children.

Suppose such a couple chose to use the natural method of avoiding pregnancy. This would not correspond to *Humanae Vitae's* integral vision of responsible parenthood. Although they would not objectively violate the value of the sign of conjugal intercourse, they would violate that sign subjectively. They would violate that sign "in their hearts." The Holy Father clarifies: "*As regards the immediate motivation, Humanae Vitae* requires that 'in order to space births there must be serious reasons that stem either from the physical or psychological condition of the couple or from external circumstances...' (HV 16)" (TOB 124:5). John Paul II concludes: "The use of 'infertile periods' in conjugal shared life can become a source of abuses if the couple thereby attempt to evade procreation without just reasons, lowering it below the morally just level of births in their family" (TOB 125:3).

"*Humanae Vitae* presents 'responsible parenthood' as an expression of a high ethical value. *In no way* does it *aim one-sidedly* at limiting, even less at excluding, children; it means also the willingness to welcome a greater number of children" (TOB 125:3). The integral vision of natural fertility regulation, then, does not involve merely a "mode of behavior" in a certain field. It involves an attitude based on the integral moral maturity of the spouses. John Paul says that this morally mature attitude can be described in biblical terms as "living by the Spirit" (see TOB 124:6). He then adds that confusion arises about the difference between contraception and periodic abstinence precisely when this moral maturity is lacking. Herein lies the importance of the theology of the body understood as a pedagogy of the body. Instruction in the truth of the body and its language of divine-human (agape-eros) love fosters just such moral maturity in men and women.

■■■ Building on the natural death-euthanasia distinction referenced earlier can help us understand the necessary moral attitude that must accompany the integral intention of natural family planning. Our natural attitude toward others should be one that desires their life and good health. Circumstances, however, could lead us to have a righteous desire for God to call someone on to the next life. Suppose an elderly relative was suffering greatly with age and disease. You could have a noble desire for his passing. It is one thing in such a situation to suffer with your loved one while waiting patiently for his natural death. In such a situation there would be nothing blameworthy even to be grateful for his death when it occurred. This would be akin to having a righteous desire to avoid a pregnancy, waiting until the naturally infertile time to consummate your marriage, and even rejoicing that God has granted a time of infertility. But, returning to the elderly relative, it would be quite another thing to take the powers of life into your own hands and kill him because you cannot bear his sufferings. This would be akin to rendering yourself sterile because you cannot bear the suffering of abstinence. Taking this analogy a step further, it is also possible that your desire for your relative's death might be unrighteous. You may feel some sort of hatred toward him that would lead you to wish him dead. You may not kill him yourself; indeed, he may die of a natural cause. Nonetheless, your rejoicing in his death would be blameworthy. This is akin to a couple who uses natural family planning with an unrighteous desire to avoid a pregnancy. Their rejoicing in the infertile time would also be blameworthy because it is motivated by a selfish, anti-child mentality.

"The concept of a morally right regulation of fertility is nothing other than rereading the 'language of the body' in the truth." And, as John Paul continues: "One should keep in mind that the 'body speaks' not only with the whole outer expression of masculinity and femininity, but also with the inner structures of the organism." Perhaps the most decisive "inner structure" of the human body-person is his and her fertility and the preparedness of the woman's womb to bear new life. "All this should find its fitting place in the language with which the spouses dialogue as persons called to communion in the 'the union of the body'" (TOB 125:1).

In this way the Pope observes that the theology of the body, understood as the pedagogy of the body, leads to the *"theology of the family."* In other words, when we understand the meaning of the body as a theology, we understand that its potential procreativity—its potential to establish or increase the family—is an integral part of the body's capacity to image and participate in the creative love of God. Hence, the theology of the family flows directly from the theology of the body (see TOB 124:3).

2. Outline of Conjugal Spirituality

The Power that Flows from Sacramental "Consecration"

Once again, having presented a "hard teaching," John Paul follows it up with a proclamation of the *power* of redemption to enable men and women not only to follow the law but also to *fulfill* the law joyfully. Throughout the catechesis we have seen this pattern. John Paul always presents the Christian *ethic* in light of the power of Christian *ethos*. He always presents the *law* in light of the power of *grace*. And here he presents the *normative dimension* of *Humanae Vitae* in light of the *pastoral dimension* of a "conjugal spirituality."

According to John Paul, the feasibility of the norm confirmed by *Humanae Vitae* constitutes "one of the most essential (and right now also one of the most urgent) questions in the area of conjugal spirituality" (TOB 129:2). If we are to understand its feasibility, we must bear in mind the whole teaching about purity understood as the life of the Spirit (see Gal 5:25) (see TOB 124:4; 51–57). Conjugal spirituality is nothing other than a spousal commitment to remain open to the powers of the Holy Spirit. It consists in opening one's flesh—and the "one flesh" spouses become—to the *in*-spiration of the Spirit who empowers spouses not only to understand the true meaning of their bodies and of marital love, but to live according to their great dignity and lofty vocation. Since John Paul has been developing precisely these themes throughout his catechesis, he concludes that education in the theology of the body ("theology-pedagogy") "constitutes already by itself the essential core of conjugal spirituality" (TOB 126:2).

Christian Realism

Many people, in light of human weaknesses, look at Church teaching as hopelessly unrealistic. Paul VI, as a faithful witness to Christ, wants to reassure his readers that God's power is made perfect in weakness (see 2 Cor 12:9). He proclaims that through the sacrament of Marriage spouses "are strengthened and...consecrated to the faithful fulfillment of their duties; to realizing to the full their vocation." In this way spouses bear witness "to Christ before the world."[52] This "strength" and "consecration," as John Paul emphasizes, is none other than "*the love planted in the heart* ('poured out into our hearts') *by the Holy Spirit*" (TOB 126:5). And the sketch of conjugal spirituality found in *Humanae Vitae* intends to place in relief precisely those "powers" that make the authentic Christian witness of married life a living possibility.

Humanae Vitae is certainly aware of man's weaknesses, but it does not base its conclusions on them. To do so would empty the cross of its power. To do so would drain Christianity of its lifeblood. *Humanae Vitae* bases its conclusions on the *reality* of the power of God that has been poured into our hearts through Christ's death and resurrection. This is authentic *Christian* realism. As John Paul observes, *Humanae Vitae's* view of married life is marked at every step by such realism (see

---

52. *Humanae Vitae*, 25.

TOB 127:4). *Humanae Vitae* preaches Christ crucified—a stumbling block to Jews and foolishness to Gentiles. But to those whom God has called, *Humanae Vitae* proclaims the wisdom and power of God (see 1 Cor 1:23–24). It calls Christ's followers to take up their crosses and travel on the narrow path of salvation (see Mt 7:14).

Can men and women live the teaching of *Humanae Vitae* relying on their own resources? A realistic assessment of human weaknesses says "no." But to whom is this teaching given? To men and women who remain slaves to their weaknesses, or to men and women who have been *set free by Jesus Christ* to love as he loves? As Christ says in the verses following his discourse on the "one flesh" union: "With men this is impossible, but with God all things are possible" (Mt 19:26). As both Paul VI and John Paul II remind us, the Church does not only lay down the demands of God's law and then leave men and women to their own resources in attempting to carry it out. The Church also "'announces the tidings of salvation, and by means of the sacraments flings wide open the channels of grace, which makes man a new creature.'" In his new creation man is "'capable of corresponding with love and true freedom to the design of his Creator and Savior, and of finding the yoke of Christ to be sweet' (HV 25)" (TOB 126:1).

Here our previous reflections on the *ethos of redemption* are most pertinent. Ultimately the teaching of *Humanae Vitae* is a question of faith. Do we believe in the gift of God? Do we believe that Christ died and rose again to free us from our sins and empower us to live according to God's original plan? Do we believe that the Holy Spirit—the very power and love of God—has been poured into our hearts? These could not be more crucial questions with which to confront men and women, husbands and wives, of today. To fault the Church for her teaching in *Humanae Vitae* is to fault the Church for calling men and women to holiness—to faith in the Gospel of Jesus Christ.

Let us recall John Paul II's definition of faith: *"faith,* in its deepest essence, is *the openness* of the human heart to the gift: *to God's self-communication in the Holy Spirit."* [53] Without such faith, it is impossible to live an authentic conjugal spirituality. And without such a spirituality, it's impossible to live the teaching of *Humanae Vitae*. But with such

---

53. *Dominum et Vivificantem,* 51.

faith, men and women can move mountains (see Mt 17:20); men and women can walk on water (see Mt 14:29); men and women can live God's plan for marital love as it was established "in the beginning" (see Mt 19:8).

Infallible Means of Conjugal Spirituality

The encyclical also marks the road spouses must travel in living this spirituality. Paul VI admits that spouses must pass through the "narrow gate" and travel along the "hard way." But this, for all Christians, is the way that leads to eternal life.[54] John Paul adds that even if the gate is narrow, awareness of the future life opens up "*a wide horizon of the powers*" that can and must guide spouses along their way. *Humanae Vitae* "goes on to point out how the spouses must implore [God] for such 'power' and for every other 'divine help' in prayer; how they must draw grace and love from the ever-living fountain of the Eucharist; how 'with humble perseverance' they must overcome their own faults and sins in the sacrament of Penance." Prayer and the sacraments—especially the Eucharist and Penance—these are the "*infallible and indispensable*" means, John Paul stresses, "to form the Christian spirituality of conjugal and familial life. With their help, that essential and *spiritually creative 'power' of love* reaches human hearts and, at the same time, human bodies in their subjective masculinity and femininity" (TOB 126:5).

This, in a nutshell, is the threefold "program" for *living* the theology of the body, whatever one's state in life: (1) *prayer*, (2) *Eucharist*, and (3) *Penance*. It is the same "program" for living the Christian life itself— for living according to the theology of our bodies is nothing other than living the Christian life to the full. Let us reflect briefly on each of these *infallible* and *indispensable* means for living the truth of our masculinity and femininity.

(1) *Prayer*. Christians are called to live from within the "great mystery" of the spousal love of Christ for the Church. This "vital and personal relationship with the living and true God...is prayer."[55] Prayer is where we "let our masks fall and turn our hearts back to the Lord who

---

54. See *Humanae Vitae*, 25.
55. *CCC*, no. 2558.

loves us, so as to hand ourselves over to him as an offering to be purified and transformed."[56] As we already quoted John Paul saying,

> The great mystical tradition of the Church...shows how prayer can progress, as a genuine dialogue of love, to the point of rendering the person wholly possessed by the divine Beloved, vibrating at the Spirit's touch, resting filially within the Father's heart. This is...a journey totally sustained by grace, which nonetheless demands an intense spiritual commitment and is no stranger to painful purifications (the "dark night"). But it leads, in various possible ways, to the ineffable joy experienced by the mystics as "nuptial union."[57]

This "ineffable joy" is the promise given to all those who persevere in prayer. In turn, only to the degree that we are living in "nuptial union" with God are we capable of living in authentic "nuptial union" with others.

(2) *Eucharist.* To receive the Eucharist and live it with faith is to receive and live all that we have learned in the theology of the body. In this sacred and holy consummation of love between Bridegroom and Bride, the Church and her individual members are infused, in-filled, "impregnated" with divine life. He who consumes this bread "eats fire and Spirit," as St. Ephrem said.[58] Here we receive *all* that Christ gave us in the "great mystery" of our redemption. As John Paul wrote in his encyclical on the Eucharist, "In the Eucharist we have Jesus, we have his redemptive sacrifice, we have his resurrection, we have the gift of the Holy Spirit, we have adoration, obedience and love of the Father. Were we to disregard the Eucharist, how could we overcome our own deficiency?"[59]

(3) *Penance.* Regular confession of all sins and imperfections in the sacrament of Penance is critical if we are to become holy, without blemish, wrinkle, or any such thing (see Eph 5:26–27). "Indeed, the regular confession of [even] our venial sins helps us form our conscience, fight against evil tendencies, let ourselves be healed by Christ and progress in the life of the Spirit."[60] Through this sacrament of mercy we are not only reconciled to God through the forgiveness of our sins. We also

---

56. *CCC*, no. 2711.
57. *Novo Millennio Inuente*, 33.
58. See John Paul II, *Ecclesia de Eucharistia*, 17.
59. Ibid., 60.
60. *CCC*, no. 1458.

receive "an increase of spiritual strength for the Christian battle."[61] Anyone who wishes to live the theology of the body must avail himself regularly of this spiritual strength.

Holiness: Logic of the Sincere Gift of Self

If man "cannot find himself except through the sincere gift of self,"[62] then man cannot find himself without the power of grace that flows through the sacraments. "The sacraments...penetrate the soul and body, the femininity and masculinity of the personal subject, with the power of holiness" (TOB 117b:2). And holiness is what "permits man to express himself deeply with his own body...precisely through the 'sincere gift' of self" (TOB 19:5).

As John Paul wrote in his *Letter to Families*, "When a man and a woman in marriage mutually give and receive each other in the unity of 'one flesh,' the logic of the sincere gift of self becomes a part of their life. Without this, marriage would be empty."[63] In other words, when the consummate expression of the sign of married love is lived faithfully, it bears fruit in the whole life of the married couple. Conversely, when the whole of married life is lived faithfully, it bears fruit in the faithful expression of its consummate sign. The opposite is also true. If sexual union is lived as a countersign of authentic love, it undermines the whole reality of married life. And if the whole of married life is marked by a lack of commitment to the demands of love, sexual union will be marked by the same. In fact, it will be inherently dishonest.

Once again we see a parallel with the Eucharist. If we receive Christ's body worthily, our communion bears fruit in our whole life. Conversely, if we live a faithful Christian life, it affords a worthy reception of Christ's Body in the Eucharist. However, if we receive Christ's Body unworthily, it affects our whole Christian life. In fact, we profane our union with Christ and eat and drink judgment upon ourselves (see 1 Cor 13:27–29). And if our life is marked by a blatant lack of commitment to Christ, receiving his Body in the Eucharist is dishonest. All of our failures in this regard, however, can be forgiven and all can be

---

61. *CCC*, no. 1496.
62. *Gaudium et Spes*, 24.
63. *Letter to Families*, 11.

reconciled to God, once again, through the gift of the sacraments—in this case, the sacrament of Penance.

In the final analysis, men and women have two choices—holiness or the betrayal of their humanity. Spouses, too, must choose between holiness in their conjugal union or the betrayal of their marriage. God does not force us to participate in the marriage covenant according to his designs. He sets forth his designs in creation and confirms them in Christ and in the teachings of his Church. He offers us the grace to respond to his invitation *and* the grace to fulfill his law. But he does not force our wills. He places us in the freedom of our own counsel. As John Paul says, God calls every husband and wife "to be a witness and interpreter of the eternal plan of Love" (TOB 123:3). These expressions indicate a profound and even stunning act of entrustment on God's part. God places the primordial revelation of his own mystery in human hands, and then he "lets go." In turn, every couple interprets this mystery—faithfully or unfaithfully—"by becoming the minister of the sacrament, which has 'from the beginning' been constituted in the sign of the 'union of the flesh'" (TOB 123:3).

Why such self-abandoned trust on God's part? He knows we will be unfaithful to his plan. Yes, but he also knows that a spark of our "beatifying beginning" remains despite the distortions of concupiscence, and he is always looking for ways to fan that spark into flame. The "sincere gift of self" is the only way to "revive" our authentic humanity. He is willing to take that risk of *entrusting himself to us* even if we take advantage of that trust: even if we shun him—*even if we crucify him*—in his very act of entrustment. Some might ask: "Why does God even give us the possibility of spoiling his plan?" Here again we contemplate the mystery of human freedom. If we did not have the ability to forsake God's plan—to twist, distort, and malign it—we would not have the ability to enter into it. For love to be love, it must be free. In other words, as discussed previously, without the possibility of sin there is no possibility of love.

And yet, even when we have sinned, God continually holds out to us the possibility of conversion. Even if spouses have sinned grievously and repeatedly, God's love and mercy, poured into the spouses' whole spiritual-sexual being through the *infallible* and *indispensable* means of prayer and the sacraments, "allows the spouses to build up their whole life together *according to* the 'truth of the sign.'" In this way "marriage is built up in its sacramental dignity, as the central point of...[*Humanae Vitae*] shows (HV 12)" (TOB 126:5).

The Role of Conjugal Love in the Life of Spouses

In his audience of October 10, 1984 (TOB 127), John Paul again, even if very quietly, seems to offer a solution to an ongoing theological debate. This time it regards the role of conjugal love in the life of spouses. Some background information on the issue is needed if we are to realize the importance of the Holy Father's contribution.

According to John Paul, conjugal love—inspired by the Holy Spirit (by the Person-Love[64])—is the key element of the spirituality of spouses and parents (see TOB 127:5). This may seem like an obvious observation. However, it actually represents a new emphasis in both Catholic theology and magisterial teaching influenced by the personalistic turn of the twentieth century. Traditional theological and magisterial treatments of marriage are marked by what, today, seems like a glaring underemphasis of the role of conjugal love in the life of spouses. The interpretation of suspicion may have played its role in some theologian's treatment of marriage, but this deficiency can also be explained, at least in part, by the conventional way of "doing theology." Love as lived and experienced in marriage is primarily an *interior reality*. Objective analyses of marriage, important as they are, cannot penetrate the subjective dimensions of love. Hence, traditional formulations—in keeping with their objective methodologies—focused on the specific and ordered *ends* of marriage: procreation being the primary end; mutual help and the remedy for concupiscence being secondary ends.

The Poles of the Debate

The modern shift in consciousness is much more attune to the need of incorporating the interior dimensions of love into a theology of marriage. Karol Wojtyla/John Paul II was not only one of the main proponents of this need, but he was also one of the main architects behind the construction of a theology of marriage that successfully develops this need. As we have already quoted him saying, without this interior

---

64. See *Dominum et Vivificantem*, 10.

perspective we "consider quite abstract concepts rather than the human person as a living subject" (TOB 4, n. 8). From the start of his catechesis on the body, John Paul has "attempted to show in a systematic way how the dimension of man's personal subjectivity is an indispensable element present in theological hermeneutics" (TOB 60:1). John Paul finds this penetration into consciousness and experience in the biblical texts themselves and this requires "that one considers and reflects them in theology" (TOB 60:1). This is especially true in a theology of marriage and sexuality.

Even prior to the work of Karol Wojtyla, the twentieth century witnessed some promising theological developments in this regard.[65] But the sorely needed process of wedding conventional formulas of marriage with modern sensitivities has had its share of growing pains. Some, in their desire to read an affirmation of spousal love into the traditional schema of ends, have equated "mutual help" with conjugal love. Such a reading is not only erroneous, but results in an unnecessary "power struggle" of sorts between procreation as the "primary end" and conjugal love as the assumed "secondary end." Displeased with such a conclusion, some theologians have scrapped the traditional hierarchy of ends altogether in favor of placing all primacy on love. Such a move, however, can lead—and has led in many cases—to an interpretation of conjugal love divorced from the objective goods and purposes of marriage. Marriage then becomes relativized according to personal preferences.

In anticipation of (or in reaction to) this error, currents of thought on the other end of the spectrum have been reluctant to accept any incorporation of conjugal love into the Church's traditional schema on marriage. Such thinking is suspicious of emphasizing subjectivity because of the dangers of relativizing the objective meaning of marriage. Ultimately, errors on both poles of the debate stem from a failure to link the objective and subjective dimensions of marriage. Herein lies the value and importance of Karol Wojtyla/John Paul II's philosophical

---

65. For example, Dietrich von Hildebrand's book *Marriage* (originally published in German in 1929 as *Die Ehe*) broke new ground with its bold emphasis on conjugal love as the primary *meaning* of marriage, distinguished from procreation as its primary *purpose*. This short, innovative volume is now published in English under the title *Marriage: The Mystery of Faithful Love* (Manchester, NH: Sophia Institute Press, 1991).

project. Once this problem is viewed through his creative linking of
metaphysics and phenomenology (objectivity and subjectivity)—which,
with all its modern sensitivities also has strong biblical and Carmelite
roots—a relatively simple and much needed solution emerges.

Authentic Love Rejoices with the Truth

Notice how the Pope, in the following definition of love, links subjectivity with objective truth. He states that "*love is a 'power'*—from the
subjective point of view—that is...*given to the human person to participate* in the love with which God himself loves in the mystery of creation and redemption" (TOB 127:1). In other words, love has an
anchor. It has an objective reference point. That reference point is
Ultimate Truth itself: for *God is Love* (1 Jn 4:8).

The Pope continues by quoting St. Paul: Authentic love "is the love
that 'rejoices in the truth' (1 Cor 13:6)." It is that love "in which spiritual joy...about every authentic value is expressed: a joy similar to the joy
of the Creator himself who saw in the beginning that everything 'was
very good' (Gen 1:31)" (TOB 127:1). Prior to sin, subjectivity was
completely objective. The relativizing of love only occurs with man and
woman's distancing from God. But a love cut off from God is not really
love at all, only the counterfeit of concupiscence. Such a counterfeit is
not "of the Father" but "of the world." Authentic love, however, is
always "of the Father" (see 1 Jn 2:16). Thus, it is "actively oriented
toward the fullness of the good, and for this reason toward every true
good" (TOB 127:2).

Is this authentic love possible? Or are men and women simply
"stuck" in the reality of a counterfeit love because of sin? If we are stuck
in an impure love, marriage can only be understood within two main
schemas: the *subjectivism* of a "love" cut off from the objective good, or
the *objectivism* of a sterile and loveless conformity to abstract principles.
But John Paul repeatedly insists that we are not stuck in our impurities.
The new ethos that flows from the redemption of the body is a reality
in the name of which man must feel called, and *called with power!* This
means "the subjective profile of love" can gradually become "objective to
the very depths" (see TOB 19:1).

In other words, emphasizing authentic conjugal love does not mean
abandoning the ends of marriage. It means fulfilling them! Nor does

maintaining these ends mean de-emphasizing conjugal love. It means—and must mean—calling couples to the fullness of conjugal love. For only love can give "*adequate content and value* to conjugal acts *according to the truth*" (TOB 127:3).

Conjugal Love Fulfills the Ends of Marriage

So, in assessing the proper role of conjugal love in the life of spouses, we come to realize that love it is not an *end* of marriage at all. Instead, conjugal love is the inner form—the "soul"—of marriage. It coordinates the actions of the spouses in the sphere of the purposes of marriage. In other words, the ends of marriage are also the ends of conjugal love. The Council Fathers make this clear when they state: "Marriage *and conjugal love* are by their nature ordered toward the begetting and educating of children."[66]

While John Paul acknowledges that neither *Gaudium et Spes* nor *Humanae Vitae* use the language of the hierarchy of ends, he nonetheless maintains that they "speak about that to which the traditional expressions refer." By linking the objective ends of marriage with the subjectivity of the spouses, these documents clarify "the same moral order," but they do so "in reference to love" (TOB 127:3). In this way they avoid the danger of an objectivized morality and a subjectivized love. Hence, the traditional teaching on the ends of marriage is not done away with, as some might think. As John Paul affirms: "In this renewed orientation, the traditional teaching on the ends of marriage (and on their hierarchy) is confirmed and at the same time deepened from the point of view of the interior life of the spouses, of conjugal and family spirituality" (TOB 127:3).

We see here a parallel with Christ's own words: "I have come not to abolish [the law and the prophets] but to fulfill them" (Mt 5:17). How is the law fulfilled? Precisely through love understood as life in the Holy Spirit. As St. Paul says, "Love is the fulfillment of the law" because "it does no wrong" (Rom 13:10). This is exactly what an

---

66. *Gaudium et Spes*, 50, emphasis added. See Ramon Garcia de Haro's *Marriage and the Family in the Documents of the Magisterium* (San Francisco: Ignatius Press, 1993), pp. 200, 234, 244, etc., for a discussion of the role of conjugal love and the error of considering it an *end* of marriage. See also Rocco Buttiglione's *Karol Wojtyla: The Thought of the Man Who Became Pope John Paul II*, pp. 98–99.

authentic conjugal spirituality is—the fulfillment of the objective demands (or ends) of marriage through the subjective vivification of love understood as life in the Spirit. *This* is the role of conjugal love in the life of spouses.

Analysis of the Virtue of Continence

We have established that love is not rightly considered an end of marriage. Instead, as John Paul expresses it, love is poured out into the hearts (see Rom 5:5) of the spouses as "the fundamental spiritual power of their conjugal covenant" (TOB 127:4). In turn, conjugal love orients spouses toward the fulfillment of the ends of marriage by protecting both the value of the true communion of the spouses and the value of truly responsible parenthood. Therefore, as the Holy Father concludes: "The power of love—of authentic love in the theological and ethical sense—expresses itself in this: that love *rightly unites 'the two meanings of the conjugal act'*" (TOB 127:4). This crucial statement takes us to the heart of the debate over *Humanae Vitae*. The real debate over this encyclical is a debate about the meaning of human love. Hence, it is a debate about the very meaning *of human life*—as the title of the encyclical itself indicates.

As John Paul notes, the idea that the teaching of *Humanae Vitae* deprives spouses of the opportunity to express their love is the most frequent objection to the encyclical (see TOB 127:4). But what kind of "love" are we speaking of here? Authentic love, the Pope maintains, excludes "not only in theory, but above all in practice, the 'contradiction' that could come about in this area" (TOB 127:4). In other words, those who are vivified by the life and love of the Holy Spirit realize internally that there is no contradiction "between the divine laws pertaining to the transmission of life and those pertaining to the fostering of authentic conjugal love."[67] In fact, they realize that the teaching of *Humanae Vitae* provides them with the proper measure to ensure that what they express when they become "one flesh" is truly love and not merely a cheapened counterfeit.

If we are going to speak of a "contradiction" in this matter, the contradiction is contraception. It blatantly speaks *against* (contra-dicts)

---

67. *Gaudium et Spes*, 51.

the very meaning of the marital embrace as a participation in the life-giving mystery of God's love. With regard to the Church's teaching, as John Paul says, there is no "contradiction" involved, only a "difficulty." This difficulty

> derives from the fact that *the power of love is planted in man threatened by concupiscence*: in human subjects, love comes up against the threefold concupiscence (see 1 Jn 2:16), particularly against the concupiscence of the flesh, which deforms the truth of the "language of the body." And for this reason also love is not able to realize itself...except through mastery over concupiscence. (TOB 127:4)

In effect John Paul is saying that those who seek to justify contraception in order to express their "love" for one another have actually (and perhaps unwittingly) confused love with concupiscence. Love does not seek to justify what is wrong but "rejoices in the truth" (1 Cor 13:6)—whatever the cost. Concupiscence, on the other hand, is not concerned with maintaining the truth of sexual union as a *sacramental sign* of God's life-giving love. It is concerned with seeking its own satisfaction and is "afraid" of the cost of authentic love. As we observed previously, contraception was not invented to prevent pregnancy. Ultimately, it was invented to skirt the sacrifice required by continence (see p. 553ff.). Contraception can certainly seem like an attractive alternative to the difficulties inherent in attaining self-mastery. However, to the degree that one is not master of himself, it is impossible to be a true gift to another. To this degree it is impossible to express love in sexual union.

Precisely at this moment—in the moment of recognizing the "difficulty" involved in true love—man and woman must make a decision. They must activate their self-determination and decide what power will hold sway in their relationship: love or concupiscence; truth or counterfeits? Much is at stake in such a decision. As the story of Tobias and Sarah illustrates so well, it is a test of life-or-death (see p. 501ff.). Precisely in this decision, as stated previously, the choices and the actions of man and woman "take on the whole weight of human existence" (TOB 115:3). Precisely in this decision men and women "find themselves in the situation in which *the powers of good and evil fight against each other*." But those who love are not afraid. For the "truth and the strength of love are manifested in the ability of [love] to place itself between the forces of good and of evil that fight within man and around him, because love is confident in the victory of good and is ready to do everything in order that good may conquer" (TOB 115:2).

Authentic conjugal love leads one to prefer to suffer—even to die—for the truth ("Husbands, love your wives *as Christ loved the Church*"). If the powers of concupiscence try to detach the language of the body from the truth, *the power of love* instead always renews and strengthens the language of the body in that truth, so that the mystery of the redemption of the body can bear fruit in the spouses' sexual union (see TOB 127:1). And the fruit that the redemption of the body bears is precisely an ongoing liberation from concupiscence through an ongoing strengthening of the virtue of continence. According to John Paul, the virtue of continence is so critical here that without a proper understanding of it we can never arrive at "the core of the moral truth nor the core of the anthropological truth of the problem" presented by *Humanae Vitae* (TOB 125:5).

Continence Is a Permanent Moral Attitude

John Paul says that if the key element of the spirituality of spouses is *love*, this love is by its nature linked with the chastity that is manifested as self-mastery. Such self-mastery is also known as continence (see TOB 127:5). As stated above, only one who is master of himself can make a gift of himself. In other words, only one who is continent can love.

In speaking of the natural regulation of births we speak of practicing "periodic continence." However, John Paul indicates that such continence should not be viewed merely as a temporary "technique." Properly understood, "*continence* itself is a definite and permanent moral attitude; *it is a virtue*, and thus the whole mode of behavior guided by it becomes virtuous" (TOB 124:4). In other words, not only does exercising one's freedom to abstain from intercourse when there is sufficient reason to avoid a pregnancy constitute an act of virtue. Exercising continence in this way also fosters the freedom necessary to ensure that when spouses do become "one flesh" they act out of authentic love and do not merely indulge concupiscence. In this way we begin to see, as John Paul points out, that the role of continence lies not only in protecting the procreative meaning of intercourse, but also the unitive meaning. How so?

Continence, John Paul reminds us, is part of the more general virtue of temperance (see TOB 128:1). Unfortunately, it seems both words tend to have a negative connotation, as if they were only a "saying no" to something. Continence certainly involves "saying no" to lust. As John Paul says, "The conviction that *the virtue of continence* 'opposes' the concupiscence of the flesh is correct, but it is not entirely complete" (TOB 128:2). The Pope observes that continence does not act in isolation, but always in connection with the other virtues such as prudence, justice, fortitude, *and above all with love*. As the Holy Father insists, "Continence is not only—nor even mainly—*the ability to 'abstain'*...this sort of function can be defined as 'negative.' But there exists also another function of self-mastery (which we can call 'positive'): and it is *the ability to orient* the respective *reactions* [of arousal and emotion] both as to their content and as to their character" (TOB 129:5).The virtuous person does not tyrannize his passions. The virtuous person works with grace to order his passions so that he "tends toward the good with all his sensory and spiritual powers."[68]

■■■ In speaking of continence itself *as a virtue*, we should note that John Paul uses the word differently than St. Thomas. Thomas, basing his teaching on Aristotle, used the word "continence" in reference to a very imperfect state of moral development. From this viewpoint, the "continent" person is able to restrain himself from sin, but only by force of will—that is, only by acting *against* the disorder of his passions. True virtue, by contrast, implies effortless joy in choosing the good because even one's passions are ordered *toward* that good. As the *Catechism* teaches, "*Human virtues*...order our passions.... They make possible ease, self-mastery, and joy in leading a morally good life."[69]

In his *Summa*, St. Thomas writes:

Continence...falls short of being virtue: since intellectual virtue, which makes reason to hold itself well in respect of moral matters, presupposes a right desire of the end...and this is lacking in the continent and persevering man.... Hence if the sensitive faculty, which is moved by the rational faculty, is not perfect; however perfect the

68. *CCC*, no. 1803.
69. *CCC*, no. 1804.

rational faculty may be, the resulting action will be imperfect: and consequently the principle of that action will not be a virtue. And for this reason, continence, desisting from pleasures, and perseverance in the midst of pains, are not virtues, but something less than virtue, as the Philosopher [Aristotle] maintains (Ethic, vii, 1,9).[70]

The example of the two bishops and the scantily clad prostitute used earlier (see p. 215) demonstrates the difference between "continence" and "virtue" in the language of Thomas. The bishop who looked away was *continent*, but the bishop who saw rightly was *virtuous*. Although their terminology is different, John Paul develops the same Thomistic distinction between "continence" and "virtue" in distinguishing one who merely follows the *ethic* from one who is vivified with *the ethos of redemption*, in one who practices a "negative" form of purity and a "positive."

Continence, understood in the mature sense as a *virtue*, in connection with the other virtues, enables men and women gradually to experience sexual desire as God intended it to be—as the desire to make a free and sincere gift of self according to the true meaning of love and the spousal meaning of the body. This is why the virtue of continence is so crucial in the relationship of the sexes. Without it, men and women are pulled to and fro by the tides of concupiscence. And for lack of knowledge of anything else, more often than not they will make the tragic mistake of calling that love. As stated previously, if a marriage were to be built upon such a foundation, it would be akin to building a house on sand.

Continence Upholds the Incomparable Value of the Body

As discussed in the second cycle of reflections, concupiscence tends to flare up in man like an unquenchable fire. It "invades his senses, arouses his body, draws the feelings along with itself, and in some way takes possession of the 'heart'" (TOB 39:2). It also causes the "outer man" to reduce the "inner man" to silence. In other words, because passion aims at satisfaction, "it blunts reflective activity and disregards the

---

70. *Summa, Prima Secundae*, q. 58, a. 3, ad 2.

voice of conscience" (TOB 39:2). Those who continually indulge con-cupiscence remain blind to the gospel of the body. If men and women wish ultimately to experience the transformation of the very "content and character" of sexual desire according to the truth of love—if they want to see and experience the body as an efficacious sign of the very mystery of God—they must progressively acquire mastery over concu-piscent impulses and desires.

John Paul observes that "conjugal chastity (and chastity in general) manifests itself at first as the ability to resist the concupiscence of the flesh." Then, the more such mastery is acquired, the more chastity "gradually reveals itself as a *singular ability* to perceive, love, and realize those meanings of the 'language of the body' that remain completely unknown to concupiscence itself" (TOB 128:3). "Self-mastery is a *long and exacting work*. One can never consider it acquired once and for all. It presupposes renewed effort at all stages of life."[71] If men and women are to acquire self-mastery, they must commit themselves to a progres-sive education in self-control of their will, their sentiments, and their emotions. And this must develop, according to John Paul, by beginning with the simplest gestures in which it is relatively easy to put the inner decision into practice (see TOB 128:1). Notice the Pope's wise pastoral counsel. In effect, he is saying, if you want to experience the mature virtue of continence, you must be patient with yourself and start small. It is similar to lifting weights. A beginner should not expect to bench-press 350 pounds. However, if he begins with a realistic appraisal of his own abilities and commits himself to a progressive program of training, he will increase his strength day by day. And what was once impossible will eventually become reality.

Of course, in this whole process of strengthening virtue, unlike a weightlifter our progress does not depend merely on our natural capac-ities. Recall that continence is not only a human virtue, but even more a divine gift—a gift of the Spirit dwelling in our flesh. At every step of the way the supernatural gift of grace aids us, if we avail ourselves of it. As the following plea of St. Augustine illustrates, continence is not only something to work for, but something to pray for: "I thought conti-nence arose from one's own powers, which I did not recognize in

---

71. *CCC*, no. 2342.

myself. I was foolish enough not to know...that no one can be continent unless you grant it. For you would surely have granted it if my inner groaning had reached your ears and I with firm faith had cast my cares on you."[72]

The Holy Father says that willingness to commit to ongoing growth in virtue also presupposes the clear perception of the values expressed in God's law (see TOB 128:1). These are the values of the personal and sacramental meaning of the body and sex. The person who wishes to practice true virtue must set his will like flint on these values. He must put his hand to the plow and never look back (see Lk 9:62). He must prefer to die a martyr's death than to lust. Indeed, if some are willing *to kill* to indulge their lusts (this is what abortion, for example, amounts to), Christians, on the other hand, must be willing *to die* rather than give in to lust. If one does not prefer death to lust, he is not yet fully ready to overcome lust. As John Paul states, it is precisely such "firm convictions that give rise to the corresponding virtue, provided they are accompanied by the *corresponding disposition* of the will. This is precisely the virtue of continence (self-mastery)" (TOB 128:1).

Thus, the continent person exercises "control" precisely in order to uphold the incomparable *value* of sexuality—to protect it from the degradation of lust. This is an essential point. We cannot speak of continence as a virtue if one's "control" in sexual matters is based on a fear or *devaluation* of sexuality. That would imply acceptance of the Manichaean anti-value (see p. 234). Prudery and repressiveness may masquerade as virtue, but in reality they point to its lack.[73] In fact, at their root we often find the "interpretation of suspicion," which is the antithesis of the meaning of life. Such an interpretation leads either to the repression of all things sexual or to the regular indulgence of concupiscence. People in either case remain under the dominion of concupiscence, which makes man "in some way blind and insensitive to the deeper values that spring from love" (TOB 128:2).

We expressed this previously when we stated that a person who gives place to lust, to suspicion, and/or to the Manichaean anti-value has no knowledge of the innermost layers of his own heart where that

---

72. Cited in *CCC*, no. 2520.
73. See *Love and Responsibility*, p. 188.

"echo" of the beatifying beginning resounds. True chastity, however, flows from the "ethos of redemption," and this ethos is based on a close alliance with those deepest layers of the heart. It is those layers of the heart that can recognize the value of the spousal meaning of the body. Those layers can see in the body the value of a "transparent sign." This sign, in turn, reveals the gift of communion, that is, the mysterious reality of God's image and likeness (see TOB 49:5). Only when self-control is motivated by these values can we speak of continence *as a virtue* and as a participation in "life according to the Spirit."

Continence Purifies and Deepens Spousal Union

We can recognize authentic continence versus a repressive continence based on the fruits each bears in man and woman's relationship. For example, does the exercise of self-control open a couple to those more profound and more mature values inherent in the spousal meaning of the body? Does their exercise of self-control lead them to experience the authentic freedom of the gift? Or, does their exercise of "control" lead to an impoverishment of affection and an increase in tension and conflict?

If self-control leads to the latter, the solution is not to abandon self-control. This would only justify the unrestrained indulgence of concupiscence, leading to far worse conflict. The solution is to open to the conversion of heart that leads to authentic virtue. The asceticism necessary to practice continence as a virtue does not impoverish the relationship of the sexes. Quite the contrary! As the Holy Father expresses, it progressively enriches "the spousal dialogue of the couple by purifying, deepening, and at the same time simplifying it." Thus, expressions of affection are not dampened. The virtue of continence actually "makes them spiritually more intense" (TOB 128:3).

Authentic continence does not repress sexual attraction. As the virtue matures, it enables men and women to live from that place of redeemed sexual attraction. These pure, deep, simple, and spiritually intense experiences of which John Paul speaks flow directly from that mature sexual attraction that St. Paul writes about when he calls spouses to submit to one another "out of reverence for Christ" (Eph 5:21). According to John Paul, this "reciprocal submission" signifies the shared concern for the truth of the language of the body. And submitting "out of reverence for Christ" indicates the Holy Spirit's gift of "fear of the Lord," which accompanies the virtue of continence (see TOB 128:1). We have already described this reverent "fear" or "awe" as the gift of piety. Authentic conjugal love matures in a couple in measure with this piety, this "reverence for Christ." John Paul relates that such reverence seems to open that "interior room" in both man and woman that makes them ever more sensitive to the most profound and mature values of the spousal meaning of the body and the true freedom of the gift (see TOB 128:3).

When a husband and wife *see* each other's bodies as a sign of God's own mystery, when they *know* that their incarnate union is a sign of the "great mystery" of Christ's union with the Church—in other words, when the theology of the body is not just a concept but an *experience*— sexual attraction takes on the pure, simple, deep, and intense character of which John Paul speaks. It is precisely through "this inner maturation," John Paul says, that *"the conjugal act itself* acquires the importance and dignity proper to it in its potentially procreative meaning" (TOB 128:5).

Furthermore, not only does the marital embrace take on its full and glorious meaning. Conjugal chastity also reveals to the awareness and experience of the couple all the other possible "manifestations of affection" that can express the couple's deep life of communion. Although marital intercourse remains the consummate expression of spousal love, other expressions of affection are also revealed in their pure, simple, deep, and most intense character "in proportion to the subjective richness of femininity and masculinity" (TOB 128:5). Countless wives, for example, upon experiencing the maturation of continence in their marriage, can attest to the joy of being kissed, embraced, or tenderly touched by their husbands without the suspicion that he is selfishly out to "get" something. A virtuous husband is not out to "get" something. His manifestations of affection are truly that. He has no ulterior motive.

Harmony, peace, sincere affection, and spiritually intense communion—these are the fruits of the virtue of continence.[74] "In this way, the

---

74. See *Humanae Vitae*, 21. There Paul VI outlines the "beneficent influence" of continence on marriage and family life. Those who practice continence as a virtue know precisely whereof he speaks.

essential character of conjugal chastity also becomes clear in its organic link with the 'power' of love, which is poured out in the hearts of the spouses together with the 'consecration' of the sacrament of Marriage" (TOB 128:3). When spouses live from that "power of love" granted by God—when they live the "consecration" of their sacrament—marriage works! Using our former image, to the degree that we allow our tires to be inflated, we experience the car the way it is meant to be experienced. And it works! This is not to say, of course, that tires can't lose their air. All cars (marriages) require regular maintenance to keep their tires properly inflated. And it is always possible that some obstacle in the road or even an undetected nail can cause a flat. But a committed life of prayer, Eucharist, and Penance will *infallibly* allow couples, whatever their difficulties and trials, to live this vision in their lives.

Continence: Arousal and Emotion

If John Paul extols the harmony of married life that flows from conjugal chastity (understood also as the virtue of continence), some couples might look at their own experience and retort that continence is more often a cause of conflict—first within oneself and, in turn, within their common life as a married couple. But is such an experience of continence an experience of the *virtue* in its integral sense? Has such a couple crossed the threshold from continence as a "constraint" to continence as the interior freedom of the gift?

John Paul observes: "It is often thought that continence causes inner tensions from which men and women should free themselves." But he immediately emphasizes: "In the light of the analyses offered...[above], continence, integrally understood, is, on the contrary, the one and only *way to free oneself from such tensions*" (TOB 129:1). "Tensions" here would commonly be understood as pent-up sexual energy that seeks release. In this context John Paul speaks of sexual "arousal" as distinguished from "emotion." Arousal, he says, is first of all a bodily and sexual phenomenon. It seeks release in the sexual act. Emotion, on the other hand, is stirred more by the whole reality of the person in his masculinity or femininity. It is not immediately aimed at the sexual act but more toward other "manifestations of affection" (see TOB 129:4, 6).

■   It is easy to recognize that, according to these definitions, most men tend more toward "arousal" while most women tend more toward "emotion." Both arousal and emotion have their concupiscent expressions, which treat the opposite sex as a means toward selfish gratification. But both arousal and emotion also have their original and redemptive expressions, which open men and women to the possibility of an authentic communion of persons. In *Love and Responsibility,* Wojtyla describes such arousal and emotion as the "raw material" of love. But it is a mistake to consider the raw material as the "finished form." In our fallen state, mere arousal and emotion often stem from a utilitarian outlook contrary to the very nature of love as self-donation.[75]

If continence is understood only as a means of "containing" sexual arousal (and emotion) then, yes, such continence will lead to inner tensions from which men and women will seek to "free" themselves. Freedom, in this sense, of course, would come—it is supposed—by releasing one's tensions without restraint. In this paradigm, people view continence as the enemy of freedom. But does indulging one's desires without restraint lead to freedom or to slavery? If one cannot say no, is he free or is he in chains? And is such uncontrollable desire love or is it lust? The mere stirring of arousal and emotion is no guarantee of love. In fact, "if they are not held together by the correct gravitational pull," arousal and emotion "may add up not to love, but to its direct opposite."[76]

Recall the Pope's statement that the "antithesis and in some way the negation of...freedom takes place when it becomes 'a pretext for living according to the flesh'" (TOB 53:3). In essence, those who want to be "free" from continence want to be free *from freedom* so they can embrace their bondage to concupiscence unhindered. Continence as an authentic virtue calls us to a radical paradigm shift. It calls us to *the freedom for which Christ has set us free* (see Gal 5). This is the freedom of the ethos of redemption. It is the freedom *from* the domination of concupiscence that frees us *for* the sincere gift of self. As John Paul repeatedly insists, the virtue of continence is "not only the ability to 'contain' bodily and

---

75. See *Love and Responsibility,* p. 139.
76. Ibid., p. 146.

sensual reactions, but even more the ability to control and guide the whole sensual and emotive sphere of the human person." Therefore, continence is "the *ability both to direct the line of arousal* toward its correct development, *and also* to direct the line of *emotion* by orienting it toward the deepening and inner intensification of its 'pure' and, in a certain sense, 'disinterested' character" (TOB 130:1).

Disinterested desire is interested in love, not its own selfish satisfaction. Only to the degree that we experience this mature level of continence are we truly *free* from those inner "tensions." And only to the degree that we are free from those inner tensions can we become a real gift to another person. Precisely through such freedom we discover and experience that "mature spontaneity" and "noble pleasure" spoken of previously (see TOB 48:4–5).

Balance Between Arousal and Emotion

The Holy Father clarifies that in distinguishing between arousal and emotion, he does not mean to imply that they are opposed to one another. The distinction only demonstrates the subjective richness of human persons in their sexual body-soul constitution. Furthermore, the virtue of continence affords a balance between arousal and emotion, enabling them to be lived as different components in the same experience (see TOB 129:5). Arousal informed by virtue is stirred not *merely* by the body, but by the body as the expression of the person. In turn, the virtuous conjugal act is not merely sensual but involves "a particular intensification of emotion." Virtuous intercourse, as an authentic communion of persons, is both physically and emotionally intense. And John Paul emphasizes that "*it ought not to be otherwise*" (TOB 130:2).

We can observe that an *in*continent act of intercourse can also be a physically and emotionally intense experience. But such an experience is not anchored in the incarnate truth of persons and their call to communion. Such an act may hint at love, but it is not integrated with *the truth of love* and communion revealed by the spousal meaning of the body. An incontinent act of intercourse, therefore, cannot *not* be an indulgence of concupiscence. As John Paul reminds us: "The spousal meaning of the body has been deformed almost at its very roots by concupiscence." The mature virtue of continence, on the other hand, "gradually reveals the 'pure' aspect of the spousal meaning of the body. In this way, continence develops *the personal communion* of man and woman, a communion that *cannot be formed* and developed in the full truth of its possibilities *on the ground of concupiscence alone.*" And the Pope adds: "This is precisely what *Humanae Vitae* affirms" (TOB 130:5).

Thus, the Vicar of Christ firmly maintains that the Church is "fully convinced" of the correctness of the teaching of *Humanae Vitae* (see TOB 129:2). It "teaches responsible fatherhood and motherhood 'as the verification of a mature conjugal love,' and thus it contains not only the response to the concrete question raised in the area of the ethics of conjugal life, but, as has been said already, it also indicates a sketch of conjugal spirituality" (TOB 130:3).

The Gift of Reverence

In his audience of November 14, 1984 (TOB 131), the Holy Father takes us for a final lap in his deepening spiral of reflections by reviewing the key concepts of an authentic conjugal spirituality. By doing so it seems as if he is preparing us for what might be considered the summit of his commentary on *Humanae Vitae*, which he delivers in the following audience of November 21, 1984 (TOB 132).

John Paul recalls that the fundamental element of the spirituality of married life as taught by *Humanae Vitae* is the love poured out into the hearts of the couple as a gift of the Holy Spirit (see Rom 5:5). Through their own sacrament, the couple receive this divine gift along with a special "consecration." An integral element of this love is "conjugal chastity, which, manifesting itself as continence, realizes the inner order of conjugal life together" (TOB 131:1). What is the inner order of conjugal life? It is precisely that purity of heart to which Christ calls couples in the Sermon on the Mount. As a fruit of "life in the Spirit," this purity enables the inner reality of the heart to conform to the objective truth of the spousal meaning of the body. In turn, this "inner order" enables man and woman to establish an authentic *communion of persons* in all of married life through the mutual gift of self. This is why chastity stands "at the center of conjugal spirituality" (see TOB 131:2). For it is precisely the virtue of chastity that orders sexual arousal and emotion toward the truth of an authentic communion of persons.

"Chastity means living in the order of the heart," John Paul says. This order allows the development of the spouses' manifestations of affection according to their proper meaning. "In this way, *conjugal chastity* is also confirmed *as 'life by the Spirit'* (see Gal 5:25)" (TOB 131:1). In other words, Christian chastity, as we have affirmed previously, should be understood "not only as a moral virtue (formed by love), but equally as a virtue connected with the gifts of the Holy Spirit—*above all with the gift of reverence for what comes from God*" (TOB 131:2). John Paul defines this "reverence" as the gift of *piety* and reminds us that the author of Ephesians has this gift in mind when he exhorts married couples to "submit to one another out of reverence for Christ" (Eph 5:21). Through this reverence for the mystery of Christ, the one flesh union "finds its humanly mature form thanks to life 'according to the Spirit'" (TOB 131:6). In fact, as the Holy Father emphasizes, "These 'two,' who—according to the most ancient expression of the Bible—'will be one flesh' (Gen 2:24), cannot realize such a union on the level of persons (*communio personarum*) *except through the powers that come...from the Holy Spirit*, who purifies, enlivens, strengthens, and perfects the powers of the human spirit" (TOB 131:3). In other words, spouses who, in their own spirit, desire to speak the truth of love in their sexual union, cannot do so except by a divine gift, except by the powers that come from the Holy Spirit.

In this assertion we see vividly how sexual intercourse is not only meant to be the union of spouses, but also *the union of the spouses with God*. In fact, according to John Paul, sexual union is only what it is meant to be as an authentic communion of persons when it is performed in union with God as an expression of his own trinitarian life— the life of the Holy Spirit. There is no two-tiered distinction between nature and grace here. It is of sexual union's very "nature" to be full of grace—to be a sacramental expression of the mystery and inner life of the Trinity.

Conjugal Spirituality from "the Beginning"

"It follows from this that the essential lines of conjugal spirituality are 'from the beginning' inscribed in the biblical truth about marriage. This spirituality is also 'from the beginning' *open to the gifts of the Holy Spirit*" (TOB 131:3). Recall that we described the original gracing of creation as a special state of "spiritualization" in man (see p. 139). This enabled the first man and woman's *created* communion to participate in some way in God's *Uncreated* Communion. Loving one another as God loves—that is, loving according to the "breath" of the Spirit which *in*-spired their flesh (see Gen 2:7)—they experienced a beatifying immunity from shame (see Gen 2:25).

Through this experience of original nakedness, we discerned that man and woman understood and lived the body as an efficacious sign of the very mystery of creation. In turn, the entrance of shame marked the loss of this original gracing and, thus, the loss of this understanding of the body as a sign. However, the good news of the Gospel is that through the death and resurrection of Christ, the "new gracing" of redemption restores God's original plan for the body and for the "one flesh" communion of marriage. Through this new gracing the body (and the personal union of bodies) recovers its efficacy as a sign (see pp. 428–30).

Thus, when a husband and wife open themselves to the gift of piety—the gift of reverence and awe for what is sacred—the Holy Spirit instills in them a particular sensitivity to everything that is a created reflection of God's wisdom and love. In turn, as the Pope says, they regain "a singular *sensibility for all* that in their vocation and shared life carries *the sign of the mystery of creation and redemption*" (TOB 131:4). When spouses sense the "great mystery" proclaimed and revealed in their union, it instills in them a profound reverence for the two inseparable meanings of the conjugal act. This reverence develops as spouses sense the *personal dignity* of what is intrinsic to *masculinity* and *femininity*. Inscribed in their bodies and "released" in their union is the *power* to generate a new human life. This is not only a biological reality but also a deeply *personal* and *theological* reality. It is a "*sign of the mystery of creation and redemption*," as John Paul says. Thus, the spouses' sense of reverence toward each other and their union develops "inseparably in reference to the *personal dignity of the new life* that can spring from...[their] conjugal *union*" (TOB 131:4).

Through the *in*-spiration of the Holy Spirit, this profound reverence for the inseparability of the unitive and procreative meanings of intercourse wells up *from within* the couple. It is not imposed on them from "outside." They come to *see* the body and sexual union with something of the original good of God's vision and, as John Paul says, they are "full of veneration for *the essential values of conjugal union*" (TOB 131:5).

When a couple interiorizes the glorious plan of God for sexual union, they experience a "salvific fear" of ever "violating or degrading what bears in itself the sign of the divine mystery of creation and redemption" (TOB 131:5).[77] But, of course, they do not *live* in fear. Instead, loving as Christ loves, they taste something of the eternal joy that Christ himself promised (see Jn 15:11). To the degree that they embrace the sacrifices involved in remaining faithful to the language of the body, they re-create something of that beatifying experience of the beginning. Indeed, through the sincere gift of their body-persons to each other, they fulfill *the very meaning of their being and existence* (see p. 131).

In this way the sacramentality of marriage and the gospel of the body become not only religious concepts but also lived experiences. In this way spouses come to experience the marital embrace as a mystical and liturgical reality, as a window that opens onto the "great mystery" of Christ's love for the Church and even allows them to catch a glimpse of the inner life of the Trinity. At this point the apparent contradiction in this area "disappears" and the difficulty arising from concupiscence fades. Is it possible to get to this point? Yes—not without a willingness to die with Christ and not based on one's own resources, but thanks to the power of the Holy Spirit's gift.

The Exceptional Meaning of the Conjugal Act

The audience of November 21, 1984 (TOB 132), brings us to the pinnacle of John Paul's analysis of the conjugal spirituality implicit in the teaching of *Humanae Vitae*. In these final reflections, one cannot help but be struck by the clarity of insight with which this celibate pontiff penetrates the inner life of spouses. He is able to enter their longings and aspirations and, in turn, point husbands and wives to the path that leads to their authentic fulfillment. In the process he demonstrates that—despite any surface interpretation to the contrary—contracepted intercourse is antithetical to the true love and affirmation for which men and women long.

As John Paul stated in his catechesis on Genesis, the spousal meaning of the body reveals both the call to become a gift, and the capacity

---

77. See *CCC*, no. 1432.

and deep availability for the "affirmation of the person." This affirmation means living "the fact that the other—the woman for the man and
the man for the woman—is through the body someone willed by the
Creator for his own sake." This someone is "unique and unrepeatable,
someone chosen by eternal Love" (TOB 15:4). When we first read
these words we asked: Is there any man or woman alive who does not
ache in the depths of his or her being for such affirmation? Is this not
what men and women are looking for in their mutual relationship—in
all of their "manifestations of affection"? Are they not looking to be
affirmed for *who they are* as God created them to be in their own
uniqueness and unrepeatability? At the deepest level of the human
heart, no one wants to be treated as an object for someone else's
gratification. Men and women want to be loved sincerely, disinterested-
ly, for their own sake.

   As John Paul says, such love "can be realized only through a deep
understanding of the personal dignity of both the feminine and the masculine 'I' in reciprocal shared life. This spiritual understanding is the
fundamental fruit of the gift of the Spirit that impels the person to reverence for the work of God. It is from this understanding," the Pope
continues, "that all the 'affective manifestations' that form the fabric of
the stability of conjugal union draw true spousal meaning" (TOB
132:4). This true spousal meaning is the giving and receiving of the
gift, which affords the love and affirmation for which men and women
long in marriage. And it is precisely an uncompromising reverence for
the work of God (piety) that ensures this love and affirmation. As John
Paul says, such reverence "creates and enlarges, so to speak, the interior
space of the mutual freedom of the gift, in which the spousal meaning
of masculinity and femininity is fully manifested" (TOB 132:3).

   The interior constriction of concupiscence presents the main obstacle to this freedom. Concupiscence does not bless the other "I" as a person created for his or her own sake. Instead, it is directed toward the
other person as an object of enjoyment or pleasure (see TOB 132:3). If
the aim is merely to satisfy desire, one can do this in any number of
ways (and with any number of persons). The person who is the object
of concupiscence gradually realizes the sentiment of the other: "You
don't need *me*. You don't desire *me* as the person I am. You desire only a
means of gratification." Hence, far from feeling loved and affirmed as a

unique and unrepeatable person, those objectified by concupiscence feel used and debased as an insignificant and repeatable commodity.

As John Paul indicates, herein lies the "enormous *significance*" of the attitude of *reverence for the work of God*, which the Spirit stirs up in the spouses (see TOB 132:4). As men and women come to reclaim something of that original good of God's vision, they stand in "awe" of the mystery of God revealed in the other. In other words, when men and women come to see the body as a theology, they gain "the capacity for profound pleasure in, admiration for, [and] disinterested attention to the 'visible' and at the same time the 'invisible' beauty of femininity and masculinity." They gain "a profound appreciation for the disinterested gift of the 'other'" (TOB 132:4).

It is precisely this "awe" and reverence that frees men and women from the interior constriction of concupiscence. It frees them from all that reduces the other "I" to a mere object of enjoyment and strengthens in them the freedom of the gift. When men and women live from this place of reverence and interior freedom, all their manifestations of affection "protect in each of them that 'deep-rooted peace'...which is in some way the inner resonance of chastity" (TOB 132:5).

The Inner Harmony of Marriage

Chastity is not a "negative" virtue; it "is above all positive and creative."[78] It resonates in the hearts of men and women as a deep peace reminiscent of that original "peace of the interior gaze" (see p. 126ff.). One is at total peace when he knows he is loved. He can be himself without fear of rejection. He can be *naked without shame*. Such peace creates the fullness of the intimacy of persons.

This is what authentic chastity affords. It affords "the *inner harmony of marriage*" because "the spouses live together in the inner truth of the 'language of the body'" (TOB 132:6). Far from eschewing the body, conjugal chastity involves "a deep and all-encompassing *attention to the person* in his or her masculinity or femininity." Such attention brings with it the deep affirmation of the person, "thus creating the interior climate suitable for personal communion" (TOB 132:5). When spouses

---

78. *Love and Responsibility*, p. 171.

open themselves to "life in the Spirit," chastity becomes profoundly liberating. Spouses taste the freedom for which Christ set them free. And *all* of their manifestations of affection take on their true meaning in building their communion.

Even so, while all expressions of marital affection are certainly significant, according to John Paul, spouses who live "in the Spirit" come to realize "in the whole of conjugal shared life" the particular importance of *"the act* in which, at least potentially, the spousal meaning of the body is linked with the procreative meaning." The Holy Father expounds:

> In the spiritual life of the spouses...the gifts of the Holy Spirit are at work and, in particular...the gift of reverence for that which is God's work. This gift, united with love and chastity...guides one to understand, among the possible "manifestations of affection," the singular and even exceptional meaning of...[the conjugal] act: its dignity and the consequent grave responsibility connected with it. (TOB 132:1–2)

In fact, John Paul concludes that recognizing and protecting the dignity of the sexual act is the specific goal of conjugal spirituality. As he states: "The virtue of conjugal chastity, and even more so the gift of reverence for that which comes from God, shapes the spirituality of the spouses *for the sake of protecting the particular dignity of this act*, of this 'manifestation of affection,' in which the truth of the 'language of the body' can be expressed only by safeguarding the procreative potential" (TOB 132:2).

Antithesis of Authentic Conjugal Spirituality

Now we approach John Paul's ultimate conclusion about the importance of the encyclical *Humanae Vitae* for an authentic conjugal spirituality. Keep in mind that without such a spirituality, we do not know *who man is* as male and female and *who he is meant to be*. Without an adequate understanding of marriage, we cannot have an adequate anthropology. For "the two, man and woman, were created for marriage" (TOB 18:5).

As we stated above, "life in the Spirit" leads to understanding "the singular and even exceptional meaning" of the conjugal act. "Therefore," the Pope concludes, "the antithesis of conjugal spirituality is constituted in some sense by the subjective lack of such understanding, connected with anti-conceptive practices and mentality" (TOB 132:2). All that

John Paul has told us in the course of his extensive catechesis has led us to this conclusion: Contracepted intercourse and the mentality behind it demonstrate in some way the "antithesis of conjugal spirituality."

From the beginning God created man as male and female and called them to "be fruitful and multiply" in order to reveal (make visible) his own invisible mystery of life-giving love and communion. But this primordial sacrament not only imaged the mystery—it was also supernaturally efficacious. In other words, through their own life-affirming communion, man and woman actually *participated* in the eternal communion of God right "from the beginning." This is the Word that the language of the body speaks. The anti-Word, however— that enemy of God and the enemy of our humanity—wants to keep man from participating in God's life-giving communion. Thus, Satan attacks *"in some way through the very heart of that unity that had from the 'beginning' been formed by man and woman,* created and called to become 'one flesh' (Gen 2:24)" (TOB 20:1). As John Paul says in his encyclical on the Holy Spirit, Satan "seeks to *'falsify'...creative love."* [79] *"This is truly the key for interpreting reality.... Original sin attempts, then, to abolish fatherhood."* [80] Is this not the precise effect of contracepted intercourse?

Spousal union is meant to bear witness to "creative love." As John Paul II wrote in *Mulieris Dignitatem*, every time a new life is conceived, man and woman share in the "eternal mystery of generation, which is in God himself, the one and Triune God." In fact, he says, "All 'generating' in the created world is to be likened to this absolute and uncreated model" that "belongs to the inner life of God." [81]

"The communion of the Holy Trinity is the source and criterion of truth in every relationship." [82] An authentic conjugal spirituality calls spouses to open their bodies to *this truth*, to the *in*-spiration of the Holy Spirit so that they might image and participate in the communion of the Holy Trinity. Insert contraception into this picture and we witness a specific and determined "closing off" of the spouse's flesh to the presence of the Holy Spirit—a closing off to "the Lord and Giver of Life." This is precisely why contraceptive practice and mentality manifests the antithesis of an authentic conjugal spirituality.

---

79. *Dominum et Vivificantem*, 37.
80. *Crossing the Threshold of Hope*, p. 228.
81. *Mulieris Dignitatem*, 8 and 18.
82. *CCC*, no. 2845.

■ A woman at one of my lectures once asked a question that exemplified this "closing off." Recognizing the role of the Holy Spirit in the marital embrace and the conception of a child, she asked: "*What if I want to have sex with my husband, but we don't want the Holy Spirit there?*" This is exactly what the language of contracepted intercourse says. Conjugal life, and the marital embrace in particular, is meant to be liturgical. As the *Catechism* says, "In every liturgical action the Holy Spirit is sent in order to bring us into communion with Christ and so to form his Body. The Holy Spirit is...the Spirit of communion.... Communion with the Holy Trinity and fraternal communion [in this case, spousal communion] are inseparably the fruit of the Spirit in the liturgy."[83]

By using contraception, spouses are performing an "anti-epiclesis" of sorts. The *epiclesis* refers to the invocation of the Holy Spirit that is at the heart of each sacramental and liturgical celebration, especially the Eucharist:[84] "Let your Spirit come upon these gifts to make them holy, so that they may become for us the body and blood of our Lord, Jesus Christ." It would be an utter sacrilege for a priest to go through the motions of celebrating the Eucharist—"*the sacrament of the Bridegroom and of the Bride*," as John Paul described it[85]—and say, "Let your Spirit *not* come upon these gifts...." In some sense, this is what spouses are doing when they render their union sterile. They are profaning and thus negating communion with each other and with the Trinity. They are draining their union of the "'powers that come forth' from the Body of Christ, which is ever-living and life-giving."[86] But would spouses continue to make such a choice if they *knew* that this is what their actions implied? It seems apparent that in most cases spouses simply "know not what they do."

Someone might argue that couples who practice natural family planning are also closing themselves to the Holy Spirit. This *may* be the case, but not necessarily. Let us return to the priest and his celebration of the Eucharist. A priest may have legitimate reason

---

83. *CCC*, no. 1108.
84. *CCC*, nos. 1105, 1106, 1624.
85. *Mulieris Dignitatem*, 26.
86. *CCC*, no. 1116.

to abstain from saying Mass on a given day. He does nothing wrong in this case. This is worlds apart from going through the motions of a Mass but profaning it through an "anti-epiclesis." However, a priest may also have an illegitimate reason for abstaining from Mass—perhaps out of contempt for the demands of being a priest, perhaps out of anger at God or his congregation. Such motives would indicate some sort of closure to the Holy Spirit. Similarly, if spouses have a contempt toward children, abstaining so as to avoid having children might indicate a closure of some sort to the Spirit. Here is a test for determining whether or not a couple is open to the Holy Spirit in their acts of intercourse. Can they honestly pray every time they join in one flesh: "Come, Holy Spirit, if it is *your* will, let there be life"? Spouses who use natural family planning responsibly would have no problem praying this prayer every time they unite. They may, in fact, have a legitimate hope that it *not* be God's will to bring forth a child. They may also be assured that it is a biological impossibility. But they are content to leave that entirely in the Holy Spirit's hands.

Ethical, Personal, and Religious Content of Sexual Union

"In addition to everything else," John Paul says that the contraceptive practice and mentality causes "enormous harm from the point of view of the inner culture of the human person" (TOB 132:2). Whether they know this or not, by using contraception spouses are cutting themselves off from the very source of married love. Since conjugal intercourse is meant to be a sign of and inspiration to their whole married life, spouses who sterilize their union inevitably weaken and cheapen their entire relationship. Every time they engage in contracepted intercourse, rather than consummating and strengthening their marriage bond, they are being unfaithful to the promises they made at the altar. How healthy would a marriage be if husband and wife were continually unfaithful to their wedding vows?

Spouses know all too well that sexual relations can become merely a "habit" drained of their appropriate *meaning*. As the Pope observes, reverence for the work of God contributes to ensuring that the conjugal act is not deprived of its proper personal and ethical "contents" (see TOB 132:3). Furthermore, the gift of the Spirit fills the sexual life of spouses with its proper "religious contents." Sexual union itself, when spouses live it in union with the Holy Spirit, becomes an act of "veneration for the majesty of the Creator...and for the spousal love of the Redeemer." This veneration instills in the couple an unwavering conviction that God is "the only and the ultimate depository of the source of life" (TOB 132:3). Spouses realize that to take this power into their own hands would be to make themselves "like God" (see Gen 3:5). In a way it would be to commit the original sin all over again—*grasping* at the divine likeness rather than *receiving* it.

Conclusion

Humanae Vitae and the Authentic Progress of Civilization

John Paul delivered the final address of his TOB on November 28, 1984 (TOB 133). He concluded his catechesis with a brief sketch of the extensive project he had just completed, outlining his goals and purposes and the structure and method of his analysis.

He says the entire catechesis can be summed up under the title: "Human Love in the Divine Plan," or more precisely, "The Redemption of the Body and the Sacramentality of Marriage" (TOB 133:1). He describes the phrase "theology of the body" as a "working term" that places the theme of the redemption of the body and the sacramentality of marriage on a wider basis. However, he says that we "must immediately observe, in fact, that the term 'theology of the body' goes far beyond the content of the reflections presented here." Multiple problems (the Pope lists suffering and death as primary examples) not addressed specifically by this catechesis belong to a theology of the body.[87] And John Paul adds: "One must say this clearly" (TOB 133:1).

The Pope's priority, of course, was to propose the biblical vision of embodiment in terms of erotic desire and man's call to communion. As he says, the words of Genesis 2:24 (the two become one flesh) were "originally and thematically at the basis of our argument." These words

---

87. John Paul states that his apostolic exhortation *Familiaris Consortio* outlines the direction for the progressive completion and development of the theology of the body. We could also add that the entire library of John Paul II's teaching constitutes a building on the foundation of his "adequate anthropology" found in his first major catechetical project.

confirm, among other ways, "the moment in which the light of revelation touches the reality of the human body" (TOB 133:1).

John Paul observes once again that he made his reflections in order to face the questions raised by the encyclical *Humanae Vitae*. The largely negative reaction that the encyclical aroused confirms both the importance and the difficulty of these questions. As the Pope's entire catechesis demonstrates, these questions do not concern only biology or medicine. To frame the discussion merely in such terms is to stop at the surface of the issue. These questions remain "in organic relation both with the sacramentality of marriage and the whole biblical problematic of the theology of the body, which is centered on the 'key words' of Christ" (TOB 133:2). Hence, the Pope's final cycle of reflections on *Humanae Vitae* "is not artificially added to the whole" of his catechesis "but is organically and homogeneously united with it." In fact, the part "located at the end, is at the same time found at the beginning" (TOB 133:4). John Paul adds that this last statement is important from the point of view of "structure and method," thus indicating how his deepening spiral of reflections returns to its origin by reaching its destiny.

John Paul is convinced that adequate answers to the questions raised by *Humanae Vitae* must be sought in "the sphere of anthropology and theology that we have called 'theology of the body'" (TOB 133:2). In other words, the Pope maintains that adequate answers to man's perennial questions—and also to the difficult questions of our modern world—concerning marriage and procreation must focus on the "biblical and personalistic aspects" of these issues.

Biblical and Personalistic Aspects

John Paul focuses on the *biblical aspects* in order to place the Church's doctrine on the foundation of divine revelation. In light of some trends that tend to develop theology apart from the Scriptures, the Holy Father stresses that progress in theology takes place through a continual restudying of the deposit of revelation (see TOB 133:3).[88]

---

88. John Paul II has certainly made this point most emphatically by his own example. Virtually all his encyclicals, apostolic letters, and other magisterial statements begin with a reflection on the word of God.

Countering the fears of others who are leery of his engagement with and incorporation of modern thought, John Paul states that the Church is always open to people's questions and also uses the instruments most in keeping with modern science and today's culture (see TOB 133:3). In other words, if the Church is going to evangelize the modern world, she must enter into the mind of the modern world and appeal to that mind in presenting the unchanging truths of the Gospel. She must readily accept and thoughtfully respond to the questions men and women pose regarding Church teaching. (We might observe that 129 Wednesday audience addresses spanning five years is a thoughtful response indeed.[89])

Justifying his turn to the subject, the Holy Father states: "It seems that in this area the intense development of philosophical anthropology (in particular the anthropology that stands at the basis of ethics) *meets very closely with the questions* raised by the encyclical *Humanae Vitae*" (TOB 133:3). John Paul even says that examining the Church's teaching with a *personalistic* approach is essential for man's authentic development, since modern civilization tends to measure progress on the basis of "things" rather than on the basis of the person. "The analysis of the personalistic aspects of the Church's teaching...highlights a resolute appeal to measure man's progress with the measure of the 'person,' that is, of that which is a good of man as man, which corresponds to his essential dignity." Thus, "*the fundamental problem* the encyclical [*Humanae Vitae*] presents is the viewpoint of the *authentic development of the human person*; such development should be measured, as a matter of principle, by the measure of ethics and not only of 'technology'" (TOB 133:3).

Technology, Ethics, and Progress

Modern technology has provided incalculable benefits for humanity. But technology is only a good insofar as it is at the service of the true good of the human person. In other words, technology is answerable to ethics. Regarding the issue at hand, the Catholic response to contraceptive technology is that it is *not* in keeping with the true good of the

---

89. Recall that six of the original 135 addresses derived from the Pope's manuscript were not delivered.

human person. This is precisely what the Pope's TOB has sought to demonstrate "from the beginning."

As John Paul II states: "In *Humanae Vitae*, Paul VI expressed what many authoritative moralists and scientists, including non-Catholics, affirmed elsewhere, namely, precisely that in this field, which is so deeply and essentially human and personal, one must before all else look toward the human being as a person, toward the subject who decides about himself or herself, and not toward the 'means' that turn him into an 'object' (of manipulations) and 'depersonalize' him." John Paul concludes that the teaching of *Humanae Vitae* is a question nothing short of the "authentically 'humanistic' meaning of the development and progress of human civilization" (TOB 129:2).

Precisely on this point we see the dramatic clash of two irreconcilable visions of the human person, of human sexuality, and of human progress. Some emphatically claim that contraception provides a key (if not *the* key) to solving many of the problems that hinder the progress of human civilization. In turn, such people accuse the Church of fostering such travesties as poverty, starvation, the abuse of women, abortion, and the spread of AIDS because of her insistence on the immorality of contraception.

What, however, is the root cause of poverty, starvation, the abuse of women, abortion, and sexually transmitted diseases? Do they not stem precisely from rejection of the "great mystery" of God's plan for human life inscribed in our bodies? Is not the proclamation of this plan and the universal invitation to participate in it precisely the road to authentic human flourishing? Of course this does not mean merely delivering a message. We must be willing to join in solidarity with those who suffer from poverty or those who are dying of AIDS. We must love them where they are and as they are precisely because of their great dignity as men and women made in the divine image. These are the issues at stake—the truth of love, the dignity of the human person, the very meaning of being created male and female in the divine image.

If what the Church proposes about the great dignity and meaning of our humanity is correct, contraception can *never* be the solution to our problems but only the source of a terrible setback for humanity. Whether the problem at hand is a pregnant woman living in a Brazilian favela and struggling to feed the children she already has, or the pandemic of AIDS in Africa—the Church believes that a return to the "great mystery" of God's plan for man and woman is the *only real and lasting solution* to the problems we face.

Humanization and Evangelization

As we previously quoted John Paul saying, the relationship of the sexes "makes up the pure and simple guiding thread of existence." Thus, the dignity and balance of human life "depend at every moment of history and in every place of geographic longitude and latitude on 'who' she shall be for him and he for her" (TOB 43:7). Enslavement to concupiscence is the basic and fundamental force disrupting the relationship of the sexes and, in turn, the dignity and balance of human life. Give people contraceptives and we keep them in their chains. Give them the "great mystery" of God's plan for life and love as proclaimed in John Paul's TOB and we bring good news to the poor, we set captives free, we give sight to the blind (see Lk 4:18). We set men and women on the path to fulfilling the very meaning of their being and existence.

An authentically "humanistic" meaning of the development and progress of civilization consists precisely in this. When we take John Paul II's anthem to heart—that "Jesus Christ fully reveals man to himself"—we realize why, for this Polish pontiff, humanization and evangelization are simply two sides of the same coin.[90] This is what the new evangelization *is* and must be—the universal proclamation of and invitation to participate in the "great mystery" of God's plan for human life. This great mystery is inscribed in our bodies "from the beginning." It is inscribed in masculinity and femininity and the call of the "two" to become "one flesh." And it is definitively revealed in the Word made flesh, in Christ's incarnate communion with his Bride, the Church.

We learn all this in John Paul II's TOB—the *good news* of the Gospel is written in human flesh, in everyone's flesh, in every*body*. Our concluding reflections will seek to demonstrate how this theology of the body plays an indispensable role in the new evangelization. In some sense, the new evangelization is and must be a proclamation of the gospel of the body.

---

90. See Phillip Egan, "Priesthood in the Teaching of John Paul II," in *The Wisdom of John Paul II* (London: CTS Publications, 2001), p. 37.

He Gave Them the Law of Life
as Their Inheritance—In Review

1. John Paul's final cycle of reflections applies all that we have learned in the preceding chapters to the fiercely resisted teaching of Pope Paul VI's encyclical *Humanae Vitae*. Questions come from this encyclical that permeate the Pope's entire catechesis. Thus, this final cycle is homogeneously united with the preceding reflections.

2. *Humanae Vitae* bases its teaching on "the inseparable connection" between "the unitive and procreative meanings" of sexual intercourse. This formulation appeals to modern philosophy's "subjective turn." Couples, however, are not free to assign their own meaning to the conjugal act. Its twofold meaning is already objectively pre-inscribed in the fundamental structure of the act and the actual nature of man and of woman.

3. The immorality of contraception is revealed (theologically) in the integral truth of marriage as a sacramental sign. It is especially important in the consummate sign of married love that the language of the body be reread in truth. Contraception negates this truth and falsifies the divine Word inscribed in the body. It turns the spouses into "false prophets." Rather than proclaiming the "great mystery" of God's life-giving love, they blaspheme with their bodies.

4. The moral norm of *Humanae Vitae* belongs not only to natural law but also to the moral order revealed by God. It is based on a biblical theology of the body, which is not merely a theory but rather a specific, evangelical, Christian pedagogy of the body. Pastoral concern means the search for man's true good and the proclamation of God's plan for human love. In turn, God calls every couple to be a witness and interpreter of his plan.

5. The teaching of *Humanae Vitae* presents an integral aspect of the message of salvation for the purpose of modeling earthly life on the hope of life eternal. *Humanae Vitae*, then, is a call to faith in the real power of redemption. It is a call to a radical paradigm shift in

which we listen attentively to that "echo" of God's original plan deep within us and refuse to normalize concupiscence.

6. In the responsible exercise of parenthood, couples prudently and generously decide to have a large family, or—for serious reasons and with total respect for the language of the body—they choose to space births or limit family size. It is the married couple themselves and no one else who must discern before God the proper size of their family. This is of particular importance in determining the moral character of responsible parenthood.

7. Since the two meanings of intercourse are inseparable, by attacking the procreative meaning, contracepted intercourse also ceases to be a communion of persons and an act of love. Through the whole dynamism of tension and enjoyment, the bodies of husband and wife are meant to speak the mystery of God in all its truth. But contraception, by violating the interior order of conjugal union, turns the language of the body into a lie. This constitutes the essential evil of the act.

8. A couple who resorts to contraception may have an acceptable reason to avoid a pregnancy, but the end never justifies the means. Abstaining from that which causes pregnancy is the only means of avoiding pregnancy that does not objectively violate the language of the body. Through abstinence, couples show themselves capable of authentic freedom in self-giving.

9. Responsible parenthood requires that spouses embrace the harmony of biology and personality. When we suppress fertility, we tamper with the body-soul integrity of the human person. The essence of the Church's teaching on contraception lies in maintaining an adequate relationship between dominion of the forces of nature and mastery of self. Self-mastery corresponds to man's dignity as a subject with self-determination. Suppressing fertility deprives man of his subjectivity, making him an object of manipulation.

10. In the integral vision of natural family planning presented by *Humanae Vitae*, there can be no thought of a mechanical application of biological laws. Responsible parenthood requires a mature freedom in self-giving and a positive family and procreative attitude. It requires that the language of the body—including its inter-

nal structures—be reread in truth. Thus, in no way is responsible parenthood exclusively directed to limiting, much less excluding children.

11. Natural law refers to the Creator's plan for man insofar as it is understood by right reason. Fidelity to the natural law is not a reduction of ethics to "impersonal" laws of biology but is rightly understood as fidelity to a personal Creator who inscribed his will for us in our own body-persons. It is therefore a question of what corresponds to the true dignity of persons.

12. *Humanae Vitae* outlines an authentic conjugal spirituality, and the theology of the body constitutes the essential nucleus of such spirituality. Spouses must pass through the "narrow gate" and travel the "hard way," yet they are strengthened and "consecrated" by the power of the Holy Spirit to bear authentic witness to Christ in their married life. Prayer and the sacraments—especially the Eucharist and Penance—are the "infallible and indispensable" means for forming an authentic conjugal spirituality.

13. The Church's renewed formulation, with its emphasis on the subjective dimension of love, reaffirms the traditional teaching on the objective purposes of marriage (and their hierarchy) and at the same time deepens this teaching from the viewpoint of the interior life of the spouses. Thus, conjugal love is not an "end" of marriage but the inner form of married life. Conjugal love directs spouses to the fulfillment of the ends of marriage.

14. Authentic love correctly unites the two meanings of the conjugal act. There is no contradiction involved here, only a "difficulty," since love must do battle in the heart with concupiscence. If the powers of concupiscence try to detach the language of the body from the truth, the power of love strengthens the language of the body ever anew in that truth. In this way spouses bear witness to the mystery of the redemption of the body.

15. Continence (self-mastery) certainly involves "saying no" to lust. But continence is not only—and not even principally—the ability to say no. This is the negative role of continence, but it also has a positive role. Mature self-mastery enables one to direct the very "content and character" of physical and emotional reactions toward

sincere self-giving. If chastity is first manifested as the capacity to resist concupiscence, it gradually reveals itself as the capacity to perceive, love, and live the true, sacramental meaning of the body and of sex.

16. To acquire self-mastery a person must be committed to a progressive education in self-control of the will, feelings, and emotions—beginning with the most simple acts in which it is fairly easy to practice control. The continent person exercises "control" precisely in order to uphold the incomparable *value* of sexuality—to protect it from the degradation of lust. We cannot speak of continence as a virtue if our "control" in sexual matters is based on a fear or *devaluation* of sexuality. That would imply acceptance of the Manichaean anti-value.

17. The asceticism necessary to marital chastity does not impoverish the relationship of the sexes. It progressively enriches their dialogue, purifying it, deepening it, and simplifying it. Expressions of affection are not dampened but become spiritually more intense. If marital intercourse remains the consummate expression of spousal communion, through conjugal chastity other expressions of affection are also revealed in their purest, simplest, deepest, and most intense character. Harmony reigns in married life as the fruit of a mature continence.

18. It is often thought that continence causes inner tensions from which man must free himself. Yet, when understood integrally, continence is the only way to free man from such tensions. Continence is not only the capacity to "contain" sensual reactions, but even more the capacity to control and guide the whole sphere of man's sensuality and emotions. Mature continence directs arousal and emotion toward the sincere gift of self.

19. Man and woman's personal communion cannot be formed in the full truth of its possibilities only on the level of concupiscence. In fact, the spousal meaning of the body has been distorted by concupiscence almost at its very roots. The teaching of *Humanae Vitae* affirms the possibility of overcoming these distortions with God's grace and living conjugal love in its pure, integral truth. This is also love's most physically and emotionally intense form.

20. Chastity lies at the center of conjugal spirituality as a manifestation of "life in the Holy Spirit." In fact, spouses cannot experience conjugal intercourse on the proper level of persons (*communio personarum*) "except through the powers coming from the Holy Spirit who purifies, enlivens, strengthens, and perfects the powers of the human spirit." Through the Holy Spirit, man and woman are filled with veneration for the values of the conjugal union.

21. The gift of piety—of reverence and awe for what is sacred—instills in the couple a profound reverence for the twofold meaning of the conjugal act. When men and women interiorize God's glorious plan for sexual union, they have a "salvific fear" of ever violating or degrading what bears in itself the sign of the divine mystery of creation and redemption. Thus, when spouses live by the Holy Spirit, contracepted intercourse becomes *unthinkable*.

22. Men and women who are the object of concupiscence gradually realize that they are not loved for their "own sake," but only insofar as they satisfy the other's selfish needs. Herein lies the enormous significance of reverence for the work of God, which the Spirit stirs up in those who are open to it. When men and women live from this place of reverence, all their manifestations of affection protect and affirm in each of them a "deep-rooted peace." This peace is the "interior resonance" of chastity.

23. The gift of piety, together with love and chastity, leads the couple to understand *the singular and exceptional meaning* of the conjugal act. Recognizing and protecting the dignity of this act is the specific goal of conjugal spirituality. Thus "the antithesis of conjugal spirituality" is constituted, in some sense, by a couple's lack of understanding of the exceptional significance of intercourse demonstrated by contraceptive practice and mentality.

24. Reverence for what is sacred contributes to seeing that the conjugal act does not become an empty "habit"—and that there is expressed in it a sufficient fullness of ethical, personal, and religious content. Through the gift of the Spirit, the sexual union of spouses becomes an act of veneration for the majesty of the Creator and for the spousal love of the Redeemer.

25. Birth regulation is not only a biological problem, but is organically related to the whole question of the theology of the body. Thus, answers to man's pressing questions must focus on the biblical and personalistic aspects of the issue. The biblical emphasis demonstrates that the Church's teaching against contraception is rooted in divine revelation. The personalistic emphasis demonstrates that authentic human progress must be measured not merely on the basis of technology but on the basis of the essential dignity of the human person.

26. Enslavement to concupiscence is the basic and fundamental force disrupting the dignity and balance of human life. Contraception only fosters this concupiscence. But the "great mystery" of God's plan for the sexes proclaimed by John Paul's TOB sets men and women on the path to fulfilling the very meaning of their being and existence. *Humanae Vitae*, therefore, is a question nothing short of the authentically "humanistic" meaning of the development and progress of civilization.

The Gospel of the Body
and the New Evangelization

―――――――⟡―――――――

HAVING UNDERTAKEN THE MAMMOTH task of studying John Paul II's TOB from start to finish, we will now conclude by looking briefly at its importance for the Church at this historical moment. Describing this moment in his apostolic letter at the close of the Great Jubilee, John Paul wrote: "A new millennium is opening before the Church like a vast ocean upon which we shall venture, relying on the help of Christ."[1] Though rough waters abound, John Paul beckons us to set sail without fear and to "put out into the deep" for a catch: "*Duc in altum*" (Lk 5:4).[2] Two millennia ago, led by Peter's faith in Christ—"at your word I will let down the nets" (Lk 5:5)—the first disciples cast their nets and caught a multitude of fish.

Peter's 263rd successor has reflected with great faith on Christ's words in his TOB. He has sought—and found—in the Master's words the deepest answers to the most pressing questions of modern men and women concerning the meaning of our creation as male and female and the call of the two to communion in "one flesh." These are always questions about the meaning of life itself, the meaning of love, the meaning of existence. These are questions that take us to "the deepest substratum of ethics and culture." Our answers to these questions determine

---

1. *Novo Millennio Inuente*, 58.
2. Ibid., 1.

culture—whether men and women flourish in a culture of life or lan-
guish in a culture of death. If there is to be a great catch of fish in a
"new evangelization," we sons and daughters of the Church must first
recover the sense of having an urgently important message for the salvation of the world. The gospel of the body proclaimed by John Paul II
is that message. *How urgently it is needed!* We must follow Peter's example of faith and "put out into the deep" for a catch—*"Duc in altum!"*

As we reflected at the start of this book, the twentieth century,
which began with the hope of unlimited progress, ended as the bloodiest century known to history. Modern man had placed his hopes for a
messiah in his own genius—in science, technology, medicine.
Whenever man loses sight of the "great mystery" and sets his sights on
this world, he always meets disappointment, even despair. "The world
is not capable of making man happy. It is not capable of saving him
from evil, in all of its types and forms—illness, epidemics, cataclysms,
catastrophes, and the like. This world, with its riches and its wants,
needs to be saved, to be redeemed."[3]

We now stand in great need of a "passover" from death to life. Even
after two thousand years of Christianity, Christians themselves are still
coming to terms with the fact that salvation comes only by way of the
cross. We are much like the disciples on the road to Emmaus—baffled
by the tragic events of our own day, wondering what it all means and
why it has all gone so sour. Yet, through his TOB, the Vicar of Christ
has walked with us, opening up the Scriptures for us. Those who have
heard his words can certainly say, "Were not our hearts burning within
us as he unfolded the 'great mystery' of God's designs?" (see Lk 24:32)
And just as the disciples on the road came to recognize Christ "in the
breaking of the bread"—in his body given for them in the Eucharist—
so, too, have we come, through our study of John Paul's catechesis, to
see Christ revealed in his body, that is, in our bodies, because we,
though many, are "one body" with him.

Inasmuch as John Paul's TOB takes us to the deepest roots of the
modern crisis and outlines so clearly the path to the "redemption of
the body"; inasmuch as John Paul's TOB appeals to the modern turn to
the subject, incarnating the Gospel in the everyday experiences of men
and women, it seems indispensable in the Church's efforts to reconnect

---

3. *Crossing the Threshold of Hope*, p. 56.

the modern world with the "great mystery" of God's spousal love for humanity, Christ's spousal love for the Church. It seems an indispensable foundation for the "new evangelization" and for the building of a culture of life.

1. The Antidote to the Culture of Death

Ramifications for All of Theology

We are living in an age that Christians of the future will likely describe as the near triumph of "the anti-life heresy." They will recount that this heresy threatened to destroy civilization at its roots with its resulting culture of death. However, as has always been the case in the history of theological development, the Christians of the future will recognize that this attack against God's original plan for human life—commonly referred to in the future as his "marital plan"—will have been vanquished by a precise theological elaboration of the place of the spousal meaning of the body and the marital covenant at the very heart and center of the economy of salvation.[4]

This is the gift of John Paul II's TOB to the Church and the world. It is the antidote to the culture of death and the theological foundation of the culture of life. Indeed, if the future of humanity passes by way of marriage and the family,[5] we could say that the future of marriage and the family passes by way of John Paul II's TOB. Put simply, there will be no renewal of the Church and of the world without a renewal of marriage and the family. And there will be no renewal of marriage and the family without a return to the full truth of God's plan for the body and sexuality. Yet that will not happen without a fresh theological proposal that compellingly demonstrates to the modern world how the Christian sexual ethic—far from the cramped, prudish list of prohibitions it is assumed to be—is a liberating, redeeming ethos that, even if it involves the element of the cross, corresponds perfectly to the most noble aspirations of the human heart. This is precisely what John Paul II's TOB is. But, as we have seen in our extensive study, it is also so much more.

---

4. These ideas expressed with gratitude to Sean Innerst.
5. *Familiaris Consortio*, 86.

As George Weigel writes, "John Paul's *Theology of the Body* has ramifications for all of theology. It challenges us to think of sexuality as a way to grasp the essence of the human—and through that, to discern something about the divine." Weigel continues, "Angelo Scola, [Patriarch of Venice and former] rector of the Pontifical Lateran University in Rome, goes so far as to suggest that virtually every thesis in theology—God, Christ, the Trinity, grace, the Church, the sacraments—could be seen in a new light if theologians explored in depth the rich personalism implied in John Paul II's theology of the body."[6]

This is a striking proposal. Indeed, it is no exaggeration to say that the Pope's TOB will leave the Church reeling in self-discovery for centuries to come. Much like the thinking of Augustine or Aquinas, John Paul II's insights—in the whole corpus of his thought but particularly in this catechesis on the body, his masterwork—inaugurate a new era in the history of Christian thinking and set a new standard for theological inquiry. Yet theologians have hardly begun to unpack the great riches of the Pope's teaching. As George Weigel observes: "John Paul's portrait of sexual love as an icon of the interior life of God has barely begun to shape the Church's theology, preaching, and religious education. When it does, it will compel a dramatic development of thinking about virtually every major theme in the Creed."[7]

Understanding the human body as a theology must not be relegated to the level of an obscure interest of a few specialized theologians. It needs to be the interest of every man and woman who desires to understand the meaning of human existence. Indeed, ultimate reality itself is revealed through the human body—through the Word made *flesh*. If we stay the course, curiosity about the meaning of the body and of sexuality—so often considered innately prurient—actually leads us into the heart of the mystery hidden in God from eternity. Indeed, that biblical "one flesh" union "bears in itself the sign of the divine mystery of creation and redemption" (TOB 131:5). Hence, as we have learned, understanding Christ's revelation regarding the human body and its redemption "concerns the whole Bible" (TOB 69:8). It plunges us head first into "the perspective of the whole gospel, of the whole teaching, even more, of the whole mission of Christ" (TOB 49:3).

---

6. *Witness to Hope*, p. 343.
7. Ibid., p. 853.

Mainstream Mysticism

Some might ask: "If this theology of the body is *so* important, where has it been for two thousand years?" This is a legitimate question. However, while recognizing that John Paul is presenting a clear development of thinking, we must also recognize that the fundamental message of the TOB is nothing new. It is the same Gospel that has been proclaimed since the descent of the Holy Spirit upon Mary and the apostles in the upper room. It is the same Gospel that has transformed the saints throughout history. John Paul II has penetrated that Gospel—which is the same yesterday, today, and forever—with new clarity, new insight, new depth. He has rooted the revelation of that Gospel—as it always has been, even if it has not always been so well understood—in the biblical truth of the human body, of the incarnate person made, as male and female, in the image and likeness of God. But the essence of this message is nothing new.

Mystics throughout history have plumbed the depths of the "great mystery" of the divine-human "nuptial union." But their ecstatic visions and the insights they afforded were not exactly mainstream. With the deep Carmelite roots of the TOB, we might say that Pope John Paul II is bringing John of the Cross's "nuptial mysticism" to the whole Church, proposing it in some sense as the "normal" Christian view of the world. In fact, John Paul II once observed that the union John of the Cross described with God was intended for everyone as "the final and grandiose goal of all evangelization."[8]

Why has it taken two thousand years for such a liberating mysticism to be presented by a pope as food for the whole Church? We must recognize that the Church matures through time in some ways similar to the maturing of a human person. The analogy is certainly imperfect, but we would not expect a child to understand himself the same way an adult does. We might even say that with John Paul II's TOB, the Church, as a corporate person, has reached puberty—a new "awakening" of sorts regarding the meaning of the body and the communion of the sexes. We might also observe that puberty is not full maturity, but only the beginning of the process that brings one into adulthood. Thus,

---

8. John Paul II, homily at Buenos Aires (March 10, 1987), cited in Introduction, TOB, p. 33.

if this comparison is at all accurate, the Church still has a good deal of maturing ahead of her, and a good deal of "growing pains."

Finally, if the Pope's insights are the fruit of two thousand years of "communal reflection" on the word of God,[9] they have also been forged by the unprecedented triumphs and tragedies of this particular historical "moment." In the Easter Vigil liturgy we exult in the "happy fault of Adam which won for us so great a Redeemer." We might also exult in the "happy fault" of the sexual revolution of the twentieth century, which won for us so great a theology of the body. For where sin abounds, grace abounds even more (see Rom 5:20).

Incarnating the Gospel Message

In his encyclical *Redemptoris Missio*, John Paul wrote: "I sense that the moment has come to commit all of the Church's energies to a new evangelization and to the mission *ad gentes*. No believer in Christ, no institution of the Church can avoid this supreme duty: to proclaim Christ to all peoples."[10] He also wrote: "If we look at today's world, we are struck by many negative factors that can lead to pessimism. But this feeling is unjustified: we have faith in God our Father and Lord and in his mercy.... God is preparing a great springtime for Christianity, and we can already see its first signs."[11]

John Paul first used the expression "the new evangelization" in a pastoral visit to Latin America in 1983. Ever since, he "unstintingly recalled the pressing need for a *new evangelization.*"[12] This urgency stemmed not only from the fact that the number of those not yet reached by the Gospel is still immense,[13] but also because "entire groups of the baptized have lost a living sense of the faith, or even no longer consider themselves members of the Church, and live a life far removed from Christ and his Gospel."[14]

Therefore, one thing "new" about this evangelization is the fact that it entails not only the mission *ad gentes*, or "to the nations" who

---

9. See *Fides et Ratio*, 101.
10. *Redemptoris Missio*, 3.
11. Ibid., 86.
12. *Fides et Ratio*, 103.
13. See *Redemptoris Missio*, 86.
14. Ibid., no. 33; see also Pope Paul VI, *Evangelii Nuntiandi*, no. 52; Pope John Paul II, *Catechesi Tradendae*, 19, 42.

have not heard the Gospel, but also a mission toward men and women who are already baptized. The widespread phenomenon of the "baptized non-believer" has come to light as the social structures favoring Christianity have fallen in the West. Previous generations of men and women may have conformed in varying degrees to the Christian ethic, but as the social pressures to do so waned, the essential Christian ethos was found lacking. Men and women in large numbers were "culturally Christian," but had not experienced a conversion of heart to Jesus Christ and his teachings. The recovery of an authentic Christian "ethos," in fact, was one of the main goals of Vatican II. As the Council understood well, this can only happen through an authentic, compelling, evangelical proclamation of salvation through Jesus Christ.

Bringing Heavenly Mysteries Down to Earth

As John Paul clarified in his apostolic letter at the close of the Great Jubilee, the new evangelization is not "a matter of inventing a 'new program.' The program already exists: it is the plan found in the Gospel and in the living Tradition, it is the same as ever."[15] What is essential in order to meet the unprecedented needs of our day is a proclamation of the Gospel that is "new in ardor, methods, and expression."[16]

According to John Paul, "*the new evangelization* [involves] a vital effort to come to a deeper understanding of the mysteries of faith and to find meaningful language with which to convince our contemporaries that they are called to newness of life through God's love." It is the task of sharing with modern men and women "the 'unsearchable riches of Christ' and of making known 'the plan of the mystery hidden for ages in God who created all things' (Eph 3:8–9)."[17] This is *precisely* what John Paul II's TOB provides: a deeper understanding of the mysteries of faith and a meaningful way to share them with men and women of today.

---

15. *Nove Millennio Inuente*, 29.
16. Address to the Assembly of CELAM, March 9, 1983.
17. *Springtime of Evangelization: The Complete Texts of the Holy Father's 1998 Ad Limina Addresses to the Bishops of the United States* (San Diego: Basilica Press, 1999), pp. 53, 55.

Once the Pope's scholarship is actually comprehended (or presented in a way that people can understand), the Pope's TOB has a remarkable ability to bring the heavenly mysteries down to earth. These are
not theological abstractions. They "ring true" in the human heart
because the Pope's teaching is the fruit of a constant confrontation of
doctrine with experience. As the Holy Father observes, "God comes to
us in the things we know best and can verify most easily, the things of
our everyday life, apart from which we cannot understand ourselves."[18]
What do we know better, what can we verify more easily, what is more
"everyday" than the experience of embodiment? This is where God
meets us—*in the flesh*. And this is where the Church must meet the
world in the new evangelization.

The *Catechism* teaches that the Church "in her whole being and in
all her members...is sent to announce, bear witness, make present, and
spread the mystery of the communion of the Holy Trinity."[19] This
sums up well the essential goal of evangelization. This eternal mystery
of communion becomes a practical, incarnate reality through the lens of
the TOB. It becomes *close* to us, we realize that it is *part* of us. The
divine mystery of love and communion is stamped not only in our
deepest spiritual reality but also in our physical reality—in our whole
personal experience of being "a body," and of being, as a body, male or
female. This—our creation as male and female—is "the fundamental
fact" of human existence (see TOB 18:4).

The Human Question and the Divine Answer

John Paul defines the basic task of evangelization as "the Church's
effort to proclaim to [all men and women] that God loves them, that
he has given himself for them in Christ Jesus, and that he invites them
to an unending life of happiness."[20] This basic message is in itself
"good news." But it needs to be *incarnated* if men and women are to
find their link with it. Of course, this message was and *is* incarnated in
Jesus Christ. However, someone might still respond, "What does some
man who lived two thousand years ago have to do with me?"

---

18. *Fides et Ratio*, 12.
19. *CCC*, no. 738.
20. *Springtime of Evangelization*, p. 55.

As a professor of mine once said, we can proclaim that "Jesus is the *answer*" until we are blue in the face. But unless people are first in touch with the *question*, we remain on the level of theological abstraction. Herein lies the gift of grounding the Gospel in the body. It is the antidote to theological abstraction. It roots us in what is truly human and by so doing prepares us to receive what is truly divine. In other words, it puts us squarely in touch with the *human question*, thus opening our hearts to the *divine answer*.

Nothing puts us in touch with the enigma of human existence like the reality of our own embodiment. In some sense, embodiment *is* the human question. What does it mean to be a man? What does it mean to be a woman? There is no more important question for men and women to ask. As we observed early on, these are inherently sexual questions. Of course, the very ability to question and to wonder points to our deeper, metaphysical (beyond the physical, beyond the body) dimension. But the human anomaly is that the metaphysical dimension of man is manifested in his physical dimension. The body reveals the person. The body reveals man's solitude, and it is this solitude that *is* the human question.

As we have learned throughout our study, the human being's solitude is his own experience of being a person. This is the basic universal human experience. But what does it mean? This is the basic universal human question! Where do we find the answer? The same place we found the question—in our experience of embodiment. If solitude is the question, *communion* is the answer.

However, if the question (solitude) arises from within oneself as a person, the answer (communion) is discovered only by looking outside oneself toward the "other" person and in relation to that "other" person. By contemplating the "other" in the mystery of sexual difference, we realize that the body has a *spousal* meaning. We realize that "man can only find himself through the sincere gift of himself."[21] This is the very meaning of "being a man" and "being a woman"—we are called to be a gift for one another, a gift that leads to a true communion of persons.

This is not abstract. Even if sin has distanced us from the beauty and purity of the original experience, everyone knows the "ache" of solitude and the longing for communion. Everyone knows the "magnetic

---

21. *Gaudium et Spes*, 24.

pull" of erotic desire. This basic human longing for communion, in fact, is the most concrete link in every human heart with "that man who lived two thousand years ago." How so? Experience also attests that even in the most harmonious human communion, that "ache" of solitude is not entirely satisfied. The heart and body yearn for "something more." Indeed, the male-female communion (as the paradigm of all human communions) is only a preliminary answer to the enigma of our existence. It is only a glimmer, only a foreshadowing, only a sacrament of something far greater. And only the divine prototype, to which the biblical "one flesh" points, can ultimately satisfy the human longing for love and communion.

"For this reason...the two become one flesh." For what reason? To reveal, proclaim, and anticipate the union of Christ and the Church (see Eph 5:31–32). The eternal, ecstatic, "nuptial" communion with Christ and the entire communion of saints—so far superior to anything proper to earthly life that we cannot begin to fathom it—this alone can satisfy the human "ache" of solitude. This is the North Pole to which that magnetic pull of erotic desire is oriented. And *this* is why "Jesus is the answer." If the spirit of the Gospel is not *incarnated* as such, it will forever remain detached from what is essentially human. It will forever remain outside the scope of essentially human experiences (see pp. 92ff., 171ff.). Yet, Christ took on flesh to wed himself indissolubly to that which is essentially human. Hence, if the Gospel is not incarnated with what is essentially human, it is essentially not the Gospel of Jesus Christ.

Notice how, in the following passage from *Evangelium Vitae*, John Paul II not only summarizes the call of the new evangelization, but roots it in the call to communion through the sincere gift of self, which, as he also affirms, is rooted in the truth of the body and sexuality.

> We need to bring the *Gospel of life* to the heart of every man and woman and to make it penetrate every part of society. This involves above all proclaiming *the core* of this Gospel. It is the proclamation of a living God who is close to us, who calls us to profound communion with himself and awakens in us the certain hope of eternal life. It is the affirmation of the inseparable connection between the person, his life and his bodiliness. It is the presentation of human life as a life of relationship, a gift of God, the fruit and sign of his love. It is the proclamation that Jesus has a unique relationship with every person, which enables us to

see in every human face the face of Christ. It is the call for a "sincere gift of self" as the fullest way to realize our personal freedom....

[As a consequence] the meaning of life is found in giving and receiving love, and in this light human sexuality and procreation reach their true and full significance.[22]

In light of all we have learned in the study of the TOB, this passage takes on its full, incarnate meaning. The "God who is close to us" is so, in the most concrete sense, in and through the *Incarnation*, in and through human flesh. The call to an eternal life of "communion with himself" is stamped in our creation as male and female right from the beginning—in our interior spiritual reality and our exterior physical reality. Thus, there is an "inseparable connection between the person, his life and his bodiliness." The spousal meaning of the body reveals human life "as a life of relationship." In the original human communion, we see the "gift of God" revealed through the primordial sacrament that is "the fruit and sign of his love." In the life of the first Adam, we already see a foreshadowing of the New Adam's "unique relationship with every person." And because the human body speaks of the great mystery of Christ, we "see in every human face the face of Christ." In light of all this, "personal freedom" can only be realized in the freedom of the gift—the sincere gift of self in imitation of Christ. This is the meaning of the Gospel—"giving and receiving love"—and it is all stamped in the meaning of the body, of human sexuality and the call to fruitful communion.

John Paul asserts: "To make the Church *the home and school of communion:* that is the great challenge facing us in the millennium which is now beginning, if we wish to be faithful to God's plan and respond to the world's deepest yearnings."[23] The new evangelization, therefore, is not first an appeal to abstract, objective principles. It is an appeal to the deepest yearnings of the human heart for communion and a living witness to the truth that only Christ can fulfill this yearning. Furthermore, in the new evangelization, Christians must help men and women realize that their longing for Christ is written in the "great mystery" of the human body and its spousal meaning.

---

22. *Evangelium Vitae*, 80–81.
23. *Novo Millennio Inuente*, 43.

But Christians can only pass this good news on to others if they are first infused with it and vivified by it themselves. As Pope Paul VI said in his great apostolic exhortation on evangelization, "The Church is an evangelizer, but she begins by being evangelized herself."[24] There is no doubt that, in delivering his TOB, John Paul II's intended audience was, first and foremost, the Church herself. Very few Christians seem to understand that the "great mystery" hidden from eternity in God is stamped in their own bodies and in their erotic yearning for communion. Large numbers of Catholics have been caught up in the false humanism of the day and are hostile toward much of the Church's teaching. Hence, unless the tide is turned within the Church—unless the Church is first evangelized—she cannot evangelize others.

2. The Church's Response to Modern Rationalism

The Spousal Analogy and the "Analogy of Faith"

John Paul II's TOB provides great hope for the urgently needed renewal within the Church. When we view the Gospel message through the interpretive key of man and woman's call to incarnate communion, not only does the Gospel message take on flesh, but even the most controversial teachings of the Church (virtually all of which are related to the meaning of gender and sexuality) begin to make sense. Spousal theology demonstrates how all of the various puzzle pieces of the Christian mystery fit beautifully together. The truth of Catholicism "clicks" when viewed through the lens of the TOB. In other words, through the spousal analogy we become attentive to the "analogy of faith"—that is, to the coherence of the truths of faith among themselves and within the whole plan of revelation centered on Christ.[25] The TOB allows the Church's wisdom to shine in all its brilliance.

This is why the TOB will lead to a dramatic development of thinking about the Creed. This is why the *Catechism* speaks of the important connection between sexual rectitude, believing in the articles of the Creed, and *understanding* the mysteries we profess in the Creed. In other words, the *Catechism* points to the intimate connection between

---

24. *Evangelii Nuntiandi*, 15.
25. See *CCC*, nos. 90, 114, 158.

purity of heart, love of the truth, and orthodoxy of faith.[26] Conversely, Christianity unravels at the seams—its inner logic collapses and virtually everything it teaches becomes contested—as soon as we divorce ourselves from the "great mystery" of spousal communion revealed through the body.

Modern rationalism, with its absolutizing of the conscious mind, effects just such a divorce. The body becomes divorced from the spirit and cannot be viewed as a theology. As John Paul wrote in his 1994 *Letter to Families*:

> St. Paul's magnificent synthesis concerning the "great mystery" appears as the compendium or *summa*, in some sense, *of the teaching about God and man* which was brought to fulfillment by Christ. Unfortunately, Western thought, with the development of *modern rationalism*, has been gradually moving away from this teaching. The philosopher who formulated the principle "*Cogito, ergo sum*"—"I think, therefore I am"— also gave the modern concept of man its distinctive dualistic character. It is typical of rationalism to make a radical contrast in man between spirit and body, between body and spirit. The body can never be reduced to mere matter: it is a *spiritualized body*, just as man's spirit is so closely united to the body that he can be described as *an embodied spirit*. The richest source for knowledge of the body is the Word made flesh. *Christ reveals man to himself*. In a certain sense, this statement of the Second Vatican Council is the reply, so long awaited, which the Church has given to modern rationalism.[27]

We proposed *Gaudium et Spes* 22 as the Church's response to modern rationalism in the Prologue, and said we would return to it after our study of the Pope's catechesis. In what way is *Gaudium et Spes* 22— "Christ fully reveals man to himself"—a response to modern rationalism? And how does the Pope's TOB, as an extended commentary on *Gaudium et Spes* 22, shed light on this?

Man as "Absolute" or "Partner of the Absolute"

If modern rationalism makes of man an absolute, then man determines his own self by himself. He is answerable to nothing greater than himself and his own subjectivistic "reality." He is not ordered to anything or anyone else. He is not called to communion. He is a self-

26. See *CCC*, no. 2518.
27. *Letter to Families*, 19.

defined island. Fulfillment is attained by self-assertion and selfish gain. Other human beings become a utilitarian means to that gain or, if they are found to be an obstacle, they are crushed, discarded, even exterminated.

In such a worldview, freedom means doing whatever one wants without any outside constraint. The Supreme Court of the United States, reaffirming the right of men and women to exterminate their own unborn children, concisely expressed this individualistic, rationalistic ideology when it asserted: "At the heart of liberty is the right to define one's own concept of existence, of meaning, of the universe, and of the mystery of human life."[28] It almost sounds like a religious statement. But it is the religion of the deceiver. The Supreme Court might simply have repeated his perennial lie: At the heart of liberty is the right to "make oneself like God" (see Gen 3:5).

Insert *Gaudium et Spes* 22 into the equation and it unmasks the sham of modern rationalism. "The religion of the God who became man," said Paul VI in his closing speech at the Council, encounters "the religion (for such it is) of man who makes himself God."[29] Man does not define himself. Christ fully reveals man to himself. Man is not the absolute. The mystery of the Father and his love is the absolute. And how is this revealed? Through the gift and mystery of Christ's body— through the Word made flesh! Our humanity is not divine, but in Christ's humanity, we see our humanity wed indissolubly to divinity. In Christ we see that profound link between theology and anthropology that we spoke of in the Prologue and unfolded throughout our study (see p. 21ff.).

Asserting his own dignity as a free creature does not place man in a contest of wills with the Absolute. Such would be the case only if God were a tyrant, jealous of his own rule and leery of the freedom he bestowed upon his creature. This is the original anti-Word promulgated by the deceiver. The foundation of the universe is that *God is Love.* Man is not the absolute, but he is called to open his heart to the greatest gift that the Absolute could possibly bestow upon a creature: Man is invited to be *"partner of the Absolute."* This, in fact, sums up the key

---

28. *Planned Parenthood v. Casey*, 1992.

29. Cited in *Closing Speeches: Vatican Council II* (Boston: Pauline Books & Media), p. 10.

distinction between secular and Christian humanism. Either human freedom determines man as the absolute, or freedom is given to man so as to enter into "partnership" with the Absolute. If the former, man is not ordered in any fundamental way toward anything but himself, and freedom is fulfilled in his own egoistic, "masturbatory" gratification. If the latter, man is ordered toward *communion with the Absolute*, and freedom is fulfilled in the sincere gift of self to the "Other."

Furthermore, as we learn from John Paul's TOB, man determines himself in one direction or the other based on his understanding of his own body and sexuality. The body is either *narcissistic* or *nuptial*. It either throws man back on himself, or points him to relationship with an "other." As Stanislaw Grygiel, a professor at the John Paul II Institute in Rome, once stated, "If we don't live the sexual differences correctly that distinguish man and woman and call them to unite, we will not be capable of understanding the difference that distinguishes man and God and constitutes a primordial call to union. Thus, we may fall into the despair of a life separated from others and from the Other, that is, God."[30]

▇▇ We can also recognize how man and woman's approach to regulating births pivots them either in the direction of a secular or Christian humanism. When a couple chooses to contracept, they take the powers of life into their own hands. They determine for themselves that this act of intercourse will be sterile. By doing so, they make themselves the "Absolute." However, when a couple chooses to cooperate with the way God designed human fertility, exercising the freedom to abstain from intercourse when serious reasons call for the avoidance of pregnancy, they show respect for God as the Absolute. They enter into "partnership" with the Absolute. Furthermore, if they choose to engage in intercourse during the infertile period, they *receive* infertility as a gift rather than *grasp* at it.

When we understand the body's spousal meaning, we understand how *Gaudium et Spes* 22 leads us to *Gaudium et Spes* 24: If man is the only creature that God willed for "its own sake," man can only find

---

30. Quoted in "The Church Must Guide the Sexual Revolution," Zenit International News Agency, August 31, 1999.

himself through "the sincere gift of himself." This is how Christ fully reveals man to himself—by showing him that God is Gift and empowering him to live a life of sincere self-giving. In other words, Christ reveals man to himself by making the sincere gift of his body on the cross ("this is my body, given for you") and filling our bodies with new life in the Holy Spirit. In turn, this "life in the Holy Spirit" restores in us the freedom of the gift.

Living in this freedom, we realize that other human beings are not means to my own selfish end. They are created for *their own sake* and the only proper response to them is love. In this view, at the heart of liberty is the freedom to choose the good, not to create it. True freedom is liberation not from the *external* "constraint" that calls me to good, but from the *internal* constraint that hinders my choice of the good. True liberty is not freedom to indulge one's compulsions, but freedom from the compulsion to indulge. The truth sets us free. And the truth is that the Son of God took on flesh and died and rose again to free us from all that hinders our capacity to love as he loves.

Turn to Christ

This is the message of salvation proclaimed with authority by Christ's body, the Church. Indeed, the Church herself, as the Bride of Christ, is the sign of this salvation. Furthermore, this message of God's love and salvation is written in human flesh right from the beginning— in the "great mystery" of our creation as male and female and our call to become "one flesh." As John Paul observes, "The Church cannot therefore be understood as the mystical body of Christ, as the sign of man's covenant with God in Christ, or as the universal sacrament of salvation, unless we keep in mind the 'great mystery' involved in the creation of man as male and female and the vocation of both to conjugal love, to fatherhood and to motherhood."[31]

With modern rationalism, however, man loses sight of the "great mystery" of his being—he loses sight of the ultimate Mystery that is Being. As John Paul wrote:

> Modern rationalism *does not tolerate mystery*. It does not accept the mystery of man as male and female, nor is it willing to admit that the

---

31. *Letter to Families*, 19.

full truth about man has been revealed in Jesus Christ. In particular, it does not accept the "great mystery" proclaimed in the *Letter to the Ephesians* but radically opposes it. It may well acknowledge, in the context of a vague deism, the possibility or even the need for a supreme or divine Being. But it firmly rejects the idea of a God who became man in order to save man. For rationalism, it is unthinkable that God should be the Redeemer, much less that *he should be "the bridegroom,"* the primordial and unique source of the human love between spouses. Rationalism provides a radically different way of looking at creation and the meaning of human existence. But once man begins to lose sight of a God who loves him, a God who calls man through Christ to live in him and with him, and once the family no longer has the possibility of sharing in the "great mystery," what is left except the mere *temporal dimension of life?* Earthly life becomes nothing more than the scenario of a battle for existence, a desperate search for gain, and financial gain before all else.[32]

Rationalism does not tolerate mystery because "mystery," by definition, lies beyond rational categories. Those who subscribe to rationalism remain locked within the boundaries of their own finite ability to comprehend. Mystery, paradox, beauty—the transcendent meaning of birth, life, suffering, and death become lost. They make no "sense." The God-given dignity of every human being becomes lost. Love becomes lost. Even if man has made great progress in understanding his own biology and psychology, "with regard to his deepest, metaphysical dimension contemporary man remains a being unknown to himself."[33]

The Church responds to just such a man with the bold declaration: *Christ reveals man to himself and makes his supreme calling clear.* Man cannot live without love—and *Christ is that love.* Man cannot find himself except by making a sincere gift of himself—and *Christ alone can inspire that gift.* In other words, to you who think you are the measure of reality, turn to Christ, who is the center of the universe and of history. To you who, with Descartes, would say, "I think, therefore I am," turn to him who says, "I am because I am" (see Jn 8:58). To you who have lost the meaning of birth, life, suffering, and death, turn to him who was born, lived, suffered, died—*and rose again!* To you who think life is a battle to gain more and more, sell all you have and give the

---

32. Ibid.
33. Ibid.

money to the poor (see Mt 19:21). To you who think freedom comes from rejecting any claim to truth, turn to him who is the Truth and he will set you free. To you who do not know love, turn to him who is Love and receive the gift he gives—his own divine life. Abandon yourself entirely to him and you will find yourself.

This is the drama of human existence. This is the Gospel. And, we shall say it again, God stamped an image of it right from the beginning in human flesh—in the "great mystery" of masculinity and femininity and the call to communion. But, as John Paul observes, the "deep-seated roots of the 'great mystery'...have been lost in the modern way of looking at things. The 'great mystery' is threatened in us and all around us."[34] From various points of view, we live in "'a *society which is sick* [because it] has broken away from the full truth about man, from the truth about what man and woman really are as persons. Thus it cannot adequately comprehend the real meaning of the gift of persons in marriage, responsible love at the service of fatherhood and motherhood, and the true grandeur of procreation."[35] As a result we "are facing an immense threat to life: not only to the life of individuals but also to that of civilization itself."[36] John Paul II's TOB will prove so pivotal in the new evangelization because it reunites modern man with the "great mystery" of what and who man and woman really are as persons made in the divine image.

Knowing the true grandeur of God's plan for sexuality is, of course, one thing. Living it is another. In all truth, it is impossible to live the sublime vision of the body and sexuality that John Paul upheld...*unless* there is some way of subjecting our sexual bodies and the deep impulses of our hearts to a profound and lasting transformation, to an efficacious redemption. I would propose that John Paul's proclamation of the *real power* of Christ's death and resurrection to effect just such a redemption is the greatest contribution of his TOB, the great "*pearl*" of his catechesis. Many are tempted to hold "the form of religion" while "denying the power of it" (2 Tim 3:5). This, according to the Holy Father "is the cry of the new evangelization."[37] This also, I would add, is the cry of John Paul II's TOB.

---

34. Ibid.
35. Ibid., 20.
36. Ibid., 21.
37. *Orientale Lumen*, 3.

3. In Conclusion...

John Paul II does not mince words when he asserts that "the challenge facing us is an arduous one: only the concerted efforts of all those who believe in the value of life can prevent a setback of unforeseeable consequences for civilization."[38] In the concluding paragraphs of *Crossing the Threshold of Hope*, the Holy Father affirmed that "Andre Malraux was certainly right when he said that the twenty-first century would be the century of religion or it would not be at all."[39]

At the beginning of the third Christian millennium, it is time for the Church and the world to "cross the threshold of hope" into a new springtime. It is time to make our "passover" from a culture of death to a culture of life. "We are certainly not seduced," the Pope writes, "by the naive expectation that, faced with the great challenges of our time, we shall find some magic formula. No, we shall not be saved by a formula, but by a Person, and the assurance which he gives us: *I am with you!*"[40]

Christ the Bridegroom is with us! In the midst of the dramatic clash between good and evil that we are witnessing in our day, Christ makes a continual gift of himself to us—a gift of his body in the power of the Holy Spirit. With confidence in this gift, John Paul II seemed to believe that with the celebration of the Great Jubilee "a new time of advent" is upon us, "at the end of which, like two thousand years ago, 'every man will see the salvation of God.'" In journeying to that end, a collision between the forces of good and evil "may in many cases be of a tragic nature and may perhaps lead to fresh defeats for humanity. But," John Paul continued, "the Church firmly believes that on God's part there is always a salvific self-giving."[41] Man and woman's call to life-giving communion is placed at the center of this great struggle between good and evil, between life and death, between love and all that is opposed to love.[42] When John Paul asked, "Who will win?" he immediately responded: "The one who welcomes the gift."[43]

---

38. *Evangelium Vitae*, 91.
39. *Crossing the Threshold of Hope*, p. 229.
40. *Novo Millennio Inuente*, 29.
41. *Dominum et Vivificantem*, 55.
42. See *Letter to Families*, 23.
43. *Dominum et Vivificantem*, 55.

Mary, Mother of God...
Mary, bride without spot or wrinkle or any such thing...
Mary, one who welcomes the gift...
Pray for us that we might welcome the gift,
now and at the hour of our death. Amen.

EPILOGUE—IN REVIEW

1. If the future of humanity passes by way of marriage and the family, the future of marriage and the family passes by way of John Paul II's TOB. There will be no renewal of the Church and of the world without a renewal of marriage and the family. And there will be no renewal of marriage and the family without a fresh theological proposal that compellingly demonstrates to the modern world how the Christian sexual ethic is a liberating, redeeming ethos that corresponds perfectly with the most noble aspirations of the human heart.

2. Understanding the human body as a theology must not be relegated to the level of an obscure interest of a few specialized theologians. It has ramifications for all of theology and all of anthropology. Understanding our bodies theologically must be the interest of everyone who desires to understand the true meaning of human existence.

3. As the centuries pass, the Church is always advancing toward the fullness of divine truth. John Paul's TOB represents a crucial step in this advancement. While it is the fruit of two thousand years of reflection on the word of God, it has also been forged under the particular pressures and trials of this historical moment. In the Easter Vigil liturgy we exult in the "happy fault of Adam which won for us so great a Redeemer." We might also exult in the "happy fault" of the sexual revolution, which won for us so great a theology of the body.

4. The urgency of the "new evangelization" stems not only from the fact that the number of those not yet reached by the Gospel is still immense, but also because entire groups of the baptized are without a living relationship with Christ and his Church. The new evangelization is not a matter of inventing a new program. The program is the same as ever. What is needed is a proclamation of the Gospel that is new in ardor, methods, and expression.

5. In the new evangelization we must come to a deeper understanding of the mysteries of faith and find meaningful language with which to convey these mysteries to others. We must share with modern men and women the "unsearchable riches of Christ" and make known "the plan of the mystery hidden for ages in God." This is *precisely* what John Paul II's TOB provides: a deeper understanding of the mysteries of faith and a meaningful way to share them with men and women today.

6. "God comes to us in the things we know best and can verify most easily, the things of our everyday life, apart from which we cannot understand ourselves." What do we know better, what can we verify more easily, what is more "everyday" than the experience of embodiment? This experience puts us directly in touch with the question of solitude. And if solitude is the *human question*, communion is the *divine answer*.

7. If the spirit of the Gospel is not incarnated with the basic human experiences—with the "ache" of solitude and the longing for communion—it will remain detached from what is essentially human. "To make the Church *the home and school of communion*: that is the great challenge facing us in the millennium which is now beginning, if we wish to be faithful to God's plan and respond to the world's deepest yearnings."

8. When we view the Gospel message through the interpretive key of man and woman's call to incarnate communion, not only does the Gospel take on flesh, but even the most controversial teachings of the Church begin to make sense. Through the spousal analogy we become attentive to the coherence of the truths of faith among themselves and within the whole plan of revelation. Conversely, Christianity's "inner logic" collapses and virtually everything it

teaches becomes contested as soon as we divorce ourselves from the spousal mystery.

9. "Christ fully reveals man to himself." This serves in a certain sense as the Church's reply to modern rationalism. Here the religion of the God who became man meets the religion of man who makes himself God. There need not be a contest of wills between man and God. For God is not jealous of his own rule and leery of the freedom he has given his creature. Christ fully reveals that God is Love. He fully reveals that man is destined to be a "partner of the Absolute." Christ thus fully reveals man to himself and makes his supreme calling clear.

10. With *Gaudium et Spes* 22 as a reply to rationalism, the Church says: To you who, with Descartes, would say, "I think, therefore I am," turn to him who says, "I am because I am." To you who think life is a battle to gain more and more, sell all you have and give the money to the poor. To you who think freedom comes from rejecting any claim to truth, turn to him who is the Truth and he will set you free. Abandon yourself entirely to Christ and you will find yourself.

11. We are facing an immense threat to civilization because we cannot see the "great mystery" revealed through the body and the true grandeur of sexuality and procreation. How can we reclaim the true dignity of man and woman's relationship and build a true culture of life? Only if there is the possibility of experiencing an efficacious redemption of our bodies and a transformation of the deep impulses of our hearts.

12. Faced with the great challenges of our time, it is naive to think we shall find some magic formula to save us. We shall not be saved by a formula, but by Christ and his cross. *Do not empty the Cross of its power!* This is the cry of the new evangelization. And this is the cry of John Paul II's TOB.

13. In the midst of the dramatic clash between good and evil that we are witnessing in our day, Christ makes a continual gift of himself to us. Man and woman's call to life-giving communion is placed at the center of this great struggle between good and evil, between life and death, between love and all that is opposed to love. Who will win? The one who welcomes the gift.

Bibliography

———⟨∞⟩———

Works by Karol Wojtyla

The Acting Person. Trans. Andrzej Potocki. Ed. A. Tymieniecka. *Analecta Husserliana* 10. Dordrecht, Holland: Reidel, 1979.

The Collected Plays and Writings on Theater. Trans. Boleslaw Taborski. Berkeley: University of California Press, 1987.

Faith According to St. John of the Cross. San Francisco: Ignatius Press, 1981.

Fruitful and Responsible Love. New York: Seabury Press, 1978.

Love and Responsibility. Trans. H.T. Willetts. San Francisco: Ignatius Press, 1993.

Max Scheler y la etica cristiana. Madrid: Biblioteca de Autores Cristianos, 1982.

Person and Community: Selected Essays. Trans. Theresa Sandok. Ed. A. N. Woznicki. Catholic Thought From Lublin. New York: Peter Lang, 1993.

Sign of Contradiction. New York: Seabury Press, 1979.

Sources of Renewal. San Francisco: Harper & Row, 1979.

The Word Made Flesh: The Meaning of the Christmas Season. New York: HarperCollins, 1994.

Works by Pope John Paul II

"Address to the Pontifical Biblical Commission." April 11, 1997

Blessed are the Pure of Heart. Boston, MA: Pauline Books & Media, 1983.

Catechesi Tradendae. Boston, MA: Pauline Books & Media, 1979.

Centesimus Annus. Boston, MA: Pauline Books & Media, 1991.

Christifideles Laici. Boston, MA: Pauline Books & Media, 1988.

Crossing the Threshold of Hope. New York: Knopf, 1994.

Dives in Misericordia. Boston, MA: Pauline Books & Media, 1980.

Dominum et Vivificantem. Boston, MA: Pauline Books & Media, 1986.

Ecclesia in America. Boston, MA: Pauline Books & Media, 1999.

Evangelium Vitae. Boston, MA: Pauline Books & Media, 1995.

Familiaris Consortio. Boston, MA: Pauline Books & Media, 1981.

Fides et Ratio. Boston, MA: Pauline Books & Media, 1998.

"Homily on the Mount of Beatitudes, Galilee." March 24, 2000.

"Homily at the Mass Celebrating the Restored Sistine Chapel." April 8, 1994.

Laborem Exercens. Boston, MA: Pauline Books & Media, 1981.

Man and Woman He Created Them: A Theology of the Body. Boston, MA: Pauline Books & Media, 2006.

Memory and Identity: Conversations at the Dawn of a Millennium. New York: Rizzoli, 2005.

Mulieris Dignitatem. Boston, MA: Pauline Books & Media, 1988.

Novo Millennio Ineunte. Boston, MA: Pauline Books & Media, 2001.

Orientale Lumen. Boston, MA: Pauline Books & Media, 1995.

Original Unity of Man and Woman. Boston, MA: Pauline Books & Media, 1981.

Redemptoris Custos. Boston, MA: Pauline Books & Media, 1989.

Redemptor Hominis. Boston, MA: Pauline Books & Media, 1979.

Redemptoris Mater. Boston, MA: Pauline Books & Media, 1987.

Redemptoris Missio. Boston, MA: Pauline Books & Media, 1990.

Reflections on Humanae Vitae. Boston, MA: Pauline Books & Media, 1984.

Rise, Let Us Be on Our Way. New York: Warner Books, 2004.

Sollicitudo Rei Socialis. Boston, MA: Pauline Books & Media, 1987.

Springtime of Evangelization: The Complete Texts of the Holy Father's 1998 ad Limina Addresses to the Bishops of the United States. San Diego/San Francisco: Basilica, Ignatius Press, 1999.

Tertio Millennio Adveniente. Boston, MA: Pauline Books & Media, 1994.

The Theology of the Body: Human Love in the Divine Plan. Boston, MA: Pauline Books & Media, 1997.

The Theology of Marriage and Celibacy. Boston, MA: Pauline Books & Media, 1986.

"Truth Cannot Contradict Truth." Address to the Pontifical Academy of Sciences, October 22, 1996.

Ut Unum Sint. Boston, MA: Pauline Books & Media, 1995.

Veritatis Splendor. Boston, MA: Pauline Books & Media, 1993.

Other Magisterial Documents

Benedict XVI. *Deus Caritas Est*. Boston, MA: Pauline Books & Media, 2006.

Catechism of the Catholic Church, 2nd ed. Washington, DC: Libreria Editrice Vaticana, 1997.

Code of Canon Law. Washington, DC: Canon Law Society of America, 1983.

Congregation for the Doctrine of the Faith. *Declaration on Certain Questions Concerning Sexual Ethics*. Boston, MA: Pauline Books & Media, 1975.

———. *Donum Vitae*. Boston, MA: Pauline Books & Media, 1987.

Leo XIII. *Arcanum*, in *The Papal Encyclicals 1878–1903*. Ed. Claudia Carlen. Wilmington, NC: McGrath, 1986, 29–40.

Paul VI. *Evangelii Nuntiandi*. Boston, MA: Pauline Books & Media, 1975.

———. *Humanae Vitae*. Boston, MA: Pauline Books & Media, 1968.

Pius XI. *Casti Connubii*. Boston, MA: Pauline Books & Media, 1930.

Pontifical Biblical Commission. *The Interpretation of the Bible in the Church*. Boston, MA: Pauline Books & Media, 1993.

———. *The Jewish People and Their Sacred Scriptures in the Christian Bible*. Boston, MA: Pauline Books & Media, 2002.

Pontifical Council for the Family. *Preparation for the Sacrament of Marriage*. Boston, MA: Pauline Books & Media, 1996.

———. *The Truth and Meaning of Human Sexuality*. Boston, MA: Pauline Books & Media, 1996.

———. *Vademecum for Confessors Concerning Some Aspects of the Morality of Conjugal Life*. Boston, MA: Pauline Books & Media, 1997.

Sacred Congregation for Catholic Education. *Educational Guidance in Human Love*. Boston, MA: Pauline Books & Media, 1983.

Second Vatican Council. *Closing Speeches*. Boston, MA: Pauline Books & Media, 1965.

———. *Dignitatis Humanae*. Boston, MA: Pauline Books & Media, 1965.

———. *Gaudium et Spes*. Boston, MA: Pauline Books & Media, 1965.

———. *Lumen Gentium*. Boston, MA: Pauline Books & Media, 1964.

Vatican Commission for Religious Relations with the Jews. *Notes on the Correct Way to Present the Jews and Judaism in Preaching and Catechesis in the Roman Catholic Church*. June 24, 1985.

Other Sources

Albacete, Lorenzo. *God at the Ritz: A Priest-Scientist Talks about Science, Sex, Politics, and Religion*. New York: Crossroads, 2002.

Allen, Sr. Prudence. "Integral Sex Complementarity and the Theology of Communion." *Communio* (Winter 1990): 523–44.

———. *The Concept of Woman: The Aristotelian Revolution 750 B.C.–A.D. 1250*. Grand Rapids, MI: Eerdmans, 1997.

———. *The Concept of Woman: The Humanist Reformation 1250–1500*. Grand Rapids, MI: Eerdmans, 2002.

Aquinas, Thomas. *Summa Theologica*, in *Basic Writings of St. Thomas Aquinas*. Ed. Anton C. Pegis. New York: Random House, 1945.

Augustine. Sermon LXIX, c. 2, 3, *Patrologia Latina*, 38, 441.

Baput, Jean-Pierre. "The Chastity of Jesus and the Refusal to Grasp." *Communio* (Spring 1997): 5–13.

Beigel, Gerard. *Faith and Social Justice in the Teaching of Pope John Paul II*. New York: Peter Lang, 1997.

Buttiglione, Rocco. *Karol Wojtyla: The Thought of the Man Who Became Pope John Paul II*. Grand Rapids, MI: Eerdmans, 1997.

Catholic Truth Society. *The Wisdom of John Paul II*. London: CTS Publications, 2001.

De Haro, Ramon Garcia. *Marriage and the Family in the Documents of the Magisterium*. Trans. William E. May. San Francisco: Ignatius Press, 1993.

De la Potterie, Ignace. *Mary in the Mystery of the Covenant*. New York: Alba House, 1992.

De Lubac, Henri. *The Drama of Atheistic Humanism*. San Francisco: Ignatius Press, 1995.

――――. *The Mystery of the Supernatural*. New York: Crossroad Herder, 1998.

De Montfort, Louis. *True Devotion to the Blessed Virgin*. Bay Shore, NY: Montfort Publications, 1993.

――――. *The Secret of Mary*. Bay Shore, NY: Montfort Publications, 1998.

Derrick, Christopher. *Sex and Sacredness*. San Francisco: Ignatius Press, 1982.

Dooley, David, ed. *The Collected Works of G. K. Chesterton*. Vol. 1. San Francisco: Ignatius Press, 1986.

Elliot, Peter J. *What God Has Joined*. Homebush, Australia: St. Paul/Alba House, 1990.

Fagan, Patrick. "A Culture of Inverted Sexuality." *Catholic World Report* (November 1998): 57.

Freud, Sigmund. *Introductory Lectures in Psychoanalysis*. New York: W. W. Norton & Company, 1966.

Gneuhs, Geoffrey, ed. *The Legacy of Pope John Paul II: His Contribution to Catholic Thought*. New York: Herder & Herder, 2000.

Giussani, Luigi. *The Religious Sense*. Montreal, Quebec: McGill-Queen's University Press, 1997.

Hogan, Richard M., and John M. LeVoir. *Covenant of Love: Pope John Paul II on Sexuality, Marriage, and Family in the Modern World*. San Francisco: Ignatius Press, 1992.

Kreeft, Peter. *Everything You Ever Wanted to Know about Heaven*. San Francisco: Ignatius Press, 1990.

Kupczak, Jaroslaw. *Destined for Liberty*. Washington, DC: Catholic University of America Press, 2000.

Lawler, Boyle, and May. *Catholic Sexual Ethics*, 2nd ed. Huntington, IN: Our Sunday Visitor, 1998.

Lawler, Philip. "The Price of Virtue." *Catholic World Report* (July 1997): 58.

Mann, Judy. "A Lesson on Lust for the Vatican." *Washington Post*, October 10, 1980: B1 and B2.

Martin, Ralph and Peter, Williamson, ed. *Pope John Paul II and the New Evangelization: How You Can Bring the Good News to Others*. San Francisco: Ignatius Press, 1995.

May, William E. *Marriage: The Rock on which the Family Is Built*. San Francisco: Ignatius Press, 1995.

Newman, Cathy. "The Enigma of Beauty." *National Geographic*, (January 2000), 95–121.

Poupard, Cardinal Paul. "Galileo: Report on Papal Commission Findings." *Origins*, November 12, 1992.

Prokes, Mary Timothy, FSE. *Toward a Theology of the Body*. Grand Rapids, MI: Eerdmans, 1996.

Ratzinger, Joseph. *The Spirit of the Liturgy*. San Francisco: Ignatius Pess, 2000.

Rousseau, Mary. "Eucharist and Gender." *Catholic Dossier*, September/October 1996, 19–23.

Schmitz, Kenneth. *At the Center of the Human Drama: The Philosophical Anthropology of Karol Wojtyla/Pope John Paul II*. Washington, DC: Catholic University of America Press, 1993.

Scola, Angelo. "The Nuptial Mystery at the Heart of the Church." *Communio* (Winter 1998): 631–62.

————. *The Nuptial Mystery*. Grand Rapids, MI: Eerdmans, 2005.

Shivanandan, Mary. *Crossing the Threshold of Love: A New Vision of Marriage in the Light of John Paul II's Anthropology*. Washington, DC: Catholic University of America Press, 1999.

Stein, Edith. *The Collected Works*. Vol. 2. *Essays on Woman*. Washington, DC: ICS Publications, 1987.

Steinberg, Leo. *The Sexuality of Christ in Renaissance Art and in Modern Oblivion*. Chicago, IL: University of Chicago Press, 1996.

Von Balthasar, Hans Urs. *The Theology of Karl Barth*. San Francisco: Ignatius Press/Communio Books, 1992.

Von Hildebrand, Dietrich. *Marriage: The Mystery of Faithful Love*. Manchester, NH: Sophia Institute Press, 1991.

Waddell, Helen. *The Desert Fathers*. Ann Arbor: University of Michigan Press, 1957.

Weigel, George. *Witness to Hope: The Biography of Pope John Paul II*. New York: Harper Collins, 1999.

Waldstein, Michael. "Pope John Paul II's Personalist Teaching and St. Thomas Aquinas: Disagreement or Development of Doctrine?" Lecture presented at Thomas Aquinas College, January 12, 2001.

————. "John Paul II and St. Thomas on Love and the Trinity." *Anthropotes* 18 (2002): 113–38, 269–86.

————. Introduction. *Man and Woman He Created Them: A Theology of the Body*. Boston, MA: Pauline Books & Media, 2006.

West, Christopher. *Theology of the Body I: Head and Heart Immersion Course Study Guide*. West Chester, PA: Ascension Press, 2007.

————. *Good News About Sex and Marriage: Answers to Your Honest Questions About Catholic Teaching*. Rev. ed. Ann Arbor, MI: Servant Publications, 2006.

————. *The Love That Satisfies: Reflections on Eros and Agape*. West Chester, PA: Ascension Press, 2007.

————. *Theology of the Body for Beginners: A Basic Introduction to John Paul II's Sexual Revolution*. West Chester, PA: Ascension Press, 2004.

Index

A

abortion, 41, 327, 533, 568, 587
  Supreme Court ruling on, 608
Absolute, man as, 607–10
abstinence, 342, 550. *See also* periodic
  abstinence
  as essential to conjugal love, 360–61,
    541, 545–46
  and natural regulation of births, 521,
    534, 540–46
  as permanent moral attitude, 564–66
accomplishment of mystery, sacrament
  as, 407–8
acquiring self-mastery, 266, 566–69
The Acting Person (Wojtyla), 65, 151
activity versus passivity, 65, 203, 388
Adam, 12, 14, 24, 26, 61, 92, 96–100,
  102, 104, 106, 116, 127, 134, 136, 153,
  160, 178, 182, 186, 241, 254–55, 263,
  269, 306, 315, 328–30, 397, 408,
  424–26, 429, 477, 503, 507, 600, 605
  versus Christ, 255, 329–30
  dream of, 104–5
  foreshadowing of Christ in, 98
  love for Eve, 106
  naming of animals, 97–98, 102, 155,
    159
  original solitude of, 96–99
  rib of, 104–5
  sleep of, 104–5

tilling the earth, 97
understanding of death, 100–101
"adequate anthropology," 69, 75, 87, 169,
  178, 278–79, 290, 332, 437, 580, 584
adultery, 75, 206, 207–11, 437, 469
  compromise about, 206–7
  immorality of, 171
  Israel compared to, 209–10, 469
  and lust, 189
  and marriage, 209–10
adultery in the heart, xxx, 75, 120, 154,
  169, 171, 174, 176–77, 189, 206, 211,
  278, 282
  and lustful looks, 217–19
  within marriage, 222–27
affairs of the Lord, devotion to, 357–58
affirmation
  of the goodness of life, 160–61
  of marriage, celibacy as, 348–49
  need for, 578–79
  of the person, 137
agape, 392, 514
  integration with eros, 247, 447,
    493–98, 502, 509, 550
alienation from God, 39, 159, 182, 188,
  383, 426
  death as, 100–101
  loneliness of, 100–101
"alone," understanding gift of God in,
  129–30

analogy of euthanasia and contraception, 550–51

analogy of belonging, 205–6

analogy of faith and spousal analogy, 606–7

angelism, 332
    versus animalism, 39–41, 48, 175, 248

animals versus man, 13, 38, 39, 97–100, 102, 136, 155, 159, 193, 218, 543–45
    celibacy, 351–52
    freedom of choice, 97, 119, 134, 184
    loss of unity, 184
    original unity, 107–8
    self-mastery, 184, 545
    shame, 138, 184
    unrepeatability of the person, 134, 153–54

anonymity, danger in art, 285–87

anthropological hermeneutics, 364

anthropological realism, 258–59

anthropology, 41, 48, 51, 96–97, 129, 135, 324, 352, 361, 378–79
    biblical, 120–23, 262, 530
    and ethics, 63, 91, 145, 171, 176–78, 206, 237, 257, 435, 530, 586
    link with theology, 11, 21–22, 35, 39, 59, 60–63, 99, 109–12, 171, 200, 223, 304, 328, 435, 470–72, 608
    of redemption, 436–37
    of the resurrection, 304, 327, 340
    sexual ethics and, 68, 130–33, 206, 210–11, 225, 340, 435, 543, 547, 564
    as theology of the body, 69, 75, 93, 169, 251, 277–80, 290, 332, 437, 580, 584, 585

anti-procreative versus non-procreative, 542

anti-Word, Satan as, 36–41, 48, 181, 379, 423, 506, 529, 539, 581, 608

"appropriation" versus "gift," 141, 196, 203–5

Aquinas, St. Thomas, xxviii, 51–56, 59, 65, 109, 175, 267, 304, 404, 431, 565–66

art
    naked body in, xxx, 283–86

versus pornography, 287–90

"atheistic humanism," 42–43, 47

Augustine, St., 56, 100, 109, 126, 404, 567–68, 598

authentic freedom, 265–66, 546, 572–73
    in self-mastery, 569–71

authentic love, 155, 201, 203, 412, 443, 445, 487–91, 494, 497, 556, 562–64
    harmony with respect for life, 530–35
    rejoicing with the truth, 560–61

authentic conjugal spirituality, 360, 551–84
    contraception as antithesis of, 581–83

B

Babylon versus the Church, 539–40

balance
    arousal and emotion, 573–74
    of gift of God, 203–5, 382–86
    within marriage, 119
    in morality, 229–30
    need for, 43

Baptism, xxxiv, 117, 255, 306, 404, 408
    spousal character of, 394–95, 434, 511

"be fruitful and multiply," 45, 49, 91, 120, 581

beautiful, eros as, 242–47, 482, 493

beauty. See also physical beauty
    concept of, 201
    desire for, 243–46, 250–51, 260, 390, 397–98, 479, 493
    experience of, 276
    of God's original plan, 89, 93, 352, 603
    of the human body, masculinity and femininity, sexual difference, xxx, xxxi, 13, 20–21, 107, 135, 137, 152, 199, 212–15, 220, 234, 247, 284, 287, 289, 317, 322–23, 387, 478–79, 514–15, 579
    as image of holiness, 395–97
    love as recognition of, 400–402
    of Mary, 400–401
    and spousal love, 18, 59, 243, 266, 348, 397, 403, 435, 480, 482
    standards of, 401–2

of woman, appreciation for, 134,
157–58, 213, 398–401, 490
belonging
between lovers, 390, 392, 484–85,
488–90, 492
to God/Christ, 118, 206, 321, 484,
489
versus possession, 205–6, 497
betrayal versus holiness, 547, 554–558
biblical anthropology, key to, 121–23
biblical aspects of marriage and procreation, 584–86
biology, 16, 30, 44, 68, 91, 154, 157–58,
268, 281, 379, 528, 542–44, 547–49,
576, 583, 585, 611
birth control. *See* contraception; natural
regulation of births
birth control pills, 531–32
birth regulation. *See* contraception; natural regulation of births
"Blessed Virgin," Mary as, 117
blindness of impurity, 276–77
blood, sacrifice of, 27, 50
bodily experience, original unity as,
115–16
body. *See also* language of the body; living
the body; spousal meaning of the body;
prophetism of the body; redemption of
the body; resurrection of the body
Christianity's view on, 22–23
cult of, 396
decency of, 217, 232–33
epiphany of, 20–21, 49, 247
experience of, 126, 128
fascination with, 477–78
glory of God in, 149, 275–76
God's plan of salvation in, 24,
378–81
goodness of, 127–28
harmony in, 36, 39, 61, 98–99,
126–27, 131–33, 269–70, 307,
385, 437, 484, 544, 579–80
holiness of, 124, 153, 267–69,
272–73, 281, 397, 400–402, 419,
436, 513–14
honor for, 22, 158, 267–72
as image of God, 61, 99, 103,
109–10, 112, 121, 125, 127, 134,
138, 149, 152–53, 156–57, 161,

182–85, 198, 210, 278, 318, 330,
333, 398, 418, 450, 484, 515
pedagogy of, 279–80, 534, 550–52
as perennial object of culture,
284–85
pervaded by grace, 420–21
portrayals of, 268–69, 283–91
as proclamation of God's covenant
love, 467–68
redemptive meaning of, 450–51
revelation of mystery of God,
109–10
as revelation of personhood, 102–3
as sacramental sign, 231–32, 416
sacramentality of, 15–17, 37, 66,
213, 548
sacredness of, 22, 393–94, 439, 515
as sacrifice to God, 50
self-mastery of, 201–3
separation of soul from, 303–4,
542–44
as sign of mystery of God, 17–21,
109–10, 152, 471
as spiritual body, 331–32
spirituality of, 280–81
spiritualization of, 307–8
spousal significance of, 450–51
suspicion toward, 22–23
as theology, 422–71
transcendence of, 187
unity with spirit, 102–3
viewed as "dirty," 232
as witness to love, 313–14
body and soul, harmony of, 39–40,
303–5, 307–8
body of Christ. *See* Christ's body
bondage
to decay, 328–29, 361
liberation from, 125, 170, 228–29
of lust, 265–66, 274–75
bride as sister, 481–84
Bride of Christ versus Babylon, 539–40
burning bush imagery, 247

C

call of Christ within human hearts, 242
call to glory as gift of God, 148–49
call to holiness
celibacy as, 358–59
marriage as, 358–59

call to liberation, *Humanae Vitae* as, 535

capacity to love, effect of concupiscence
on, 199–201

catechesis
definition of theology of the body,
7–9
structure of theology of the body,
73–77

celibacy. *See also* virginity
as affirmation of marriage, 348–49
as "better" than marriage, 341–43,
357–58
as call to holiness, 358–59
as communion between God and
man, 113–14
and communion of persons, 343–44
as completion of marriage, 345–49
and concupiscence, 343
and conjugal love, 346–47
as devotion to affairs of the Lord,
357–58
ethos of, 339–41
eunuchs, 334–36
as exception to the rule, 335, 343
as exceptional calling, 341–43
as expression of spousal love, 339–41
as fulfillment of sexuality, 343–44
as gift of God, 358–59
interior integration of, 357–58
for the kingdom, 332–61
as liberation from concupiscence,
351–52
spousal meaning of the body
revealed in, 346–48
and spousal union, 350–51
and original solitude, 343–44
Paul's teaching on, 352–61
and redemption, 337–41
as renunciation, 117–18, 336,
349–50
as sacrifice, 342–44, 349–51
as sign, 335–37
and spiritual fruitfulness, 337–41
as "superior" to marriage, 341–43,
357–58
as supernatural, 335–37
as transformation, 352
as voluntary, 335–37
centrality of Christ, 408–9

chapel analogy (epiphany), 20–21

charity, perfection measured by, 345–46

chastity
and conjugal spirituality, 552–54
and interior harmony of marriage,
579–80
and internal problem of every marriage, 505, 574–75

children, parents' relationship with,
264–65

choice
freedom of, 146–47, 489–90, 557–58
and original nakedness, 424–25
and original solitude, 424–25
as part of freedom of the gift,
134–35
and sexual attraction, 119–20

chosen by eternal love, 136–37

Christ. *See also* Incarnate Christ; Word of
God
versus Adam, 255, 329–30
call within human hearts, 242
centrality of, 408–9
communion with, 64–65
as continuity, 74, 123, 248, 298
conversion to, 201–2, 215, 251, 265
discussion with Pharisees, 87–90, 92
ethic and ethos, 171–73
foreshadowing in Adam, 98
freedom in, 202–3, 212–13, 274–75
fulfillment of *proto-evangelium*, 362
happiness in, 140
love for the Church, 430–31
message of salvation, 610
mystery of divine love revealed in,
408–9
and Old Testament ethos, 207–13
perennail election in, 150
power of resurrection, 240
reconciliation offered by, 87–88
as Redeemer, 46, 50, 184, 240, 252,
276, 346, 411–13, 416, 418, 434,
523, 534–35, 584, 600, 611
redemption through, 2, 61, 88, 118,
126, 133, 138–41, 169–70, 184,
203–4, 240, 390, 394–96, 406,
409, 414, 418, 499, 534–35, 612
resurrection of, 327–29
revelation of gift of God, 610

reverence for, 385–86
union with the Church, 378,
  386–87, 389–92, 405–6
unity with, 132, 276, 302, 500, 556
whole mission of, 249, 598
Christian humanism
  and contraception, 609
  freedom in, 607–10
Christian morality, 408, 523
  elements of sacrifice and victory
    in, 523
Christian realism, 552–54
Christianity, 16, 48, 50
  versus modern world, 51–53
  view on the body, 22–23, 231
"Christo-centrism," 46
Christ's body. *See also* Incarnate Christ
  mercy revealed in, 126
  mystery of God revealed in, 16
Church
  versus Babylon, 539–40
  Christ's love for, 430–31
  evangelization of, 600–607
  versus modern world, 68–69
  sexual ethic of, 67, 111, 186
  teaching on sexual morality, 210–11,
    239–40
  union with Christ, 378, 386–87,
    389–92, 405–6
circumcision, 26–27
civilization, conjugal union as core of,
  43–44
clothing
  in heaven, 305–6
  and modesty, 270–72
common experience of lust, 217
communication
  as communion of persons, 125
  and marriage, 125
  and original nakedness, 124–26
communion between God and man,
  316–18
  call to, 99–100
  celibacy as, 113–14
  original solitude as preparation for,
    99–103
  spousal mystery as, 405
  Trinity as model of, 112

as virginal communion, 321–22
communion of persons, 106, 109. *See also*
  gift of self
  and analogy of belonging, 205–6
  and celibacy, 343–44
  communication as, 125
  conjugal union as, 574–75
  contraception, effect on, 537–38
  fundamental nature of, 325
  and gift of self, 107, 136–37, 143,
    440–41
  image of Trinity in, 108–9
  and incarnate love, 131–32
  in Joseph and Mary's marriage,
    338–39
  longing for, 603–4
  lust, effect on, 193–97
  marriage as, 113
  in original conjugal act, 114–15
  original unity as, 107–8
  perfection of, 320–21
  and procreation, 120
  and resurrection of the body, 302–5
  sexual communion, 110–11
  sexuality separated from, 193–94
  Trinity as model of, 108–9
  union of communion, 320–21
  virginal communion, 321–22,
    336–37
communion with Christ, 64–65
Communism, 42, 264
complementarity
  dimension of love, 30
  of marriage and celibacy, 345–49
  of sexual difference, 387
completion
  of husband by wife, 430–31
  of spousal meaning of the body,
    136–37
compromise
  with concupiscence, 172, 208
  in law (in Israel), 207–8
concept of beauty, effect of lust on, 201
Conception. *See* procreation
concupiscence, 117. *See also* lust
  and celibacy, 343
  compromise with, 172, 208
  effect on capacity to love, 199–201
  interior constriction of, 578–79

liberation from, 351–52
versus love, 562–64
and marriage, 341
marriage as outlet for, 225, 341,
  355–56, 442–43
overcoming, 441–42
and redemption of the body, 361
struggle with, 212–16, 438–39
and Wisdom literature, 211–12, 216
conjugal chastity. *See* self-mastery
conjugal love
  abstinence as essential to, 360–61,
    541, 545–46
  and contraception, 523
  as fulfillment of ends of marriage,
    561–62
  role in life of spouses, 558–62
conjugal spirituality
  authentic, 360, 551–84
  and chastity, 552–54
  contraception as antithesis of,
    580–83
  infallible means of living, 554–56
conjugal union. *See also* language of the
  body; original conjugal act; sexual
  union
  and celibacy, 346–48
  celibacy as affirmation of, 348–49
  closing off Holy Spirit from, 582–83
  as communion of persons, 574–75
  as consummation of marriage,
    463–65
  and contraception, 526–29
  as core of family and civilization,
    44–45
  culture of love in, 393
  and Incarnate Christ, 415–16
  interior order of, 574
  as liturgical, 140–43, 360–61
  periodic abstinence from, 550
  and procreation, 445–46, 524–26
  salvific fear of violating, 576–77
  significance of, 577–79
  in the Spirit, 444
  unitive and procreative meanings of,
    445–46, 524–26
conquering. *See* victory
conscious experience. *See* experience
consent in marriage, 462–65, 470

consequences of sin, 87, 329
consummation
  of marriage, 462–65
  as sign of marriage, 461–67
  through the Eucharist, 25–27
continence. *See* abstinence; celibacy; self-
  mastery
continuity
  Christ as, 74–75, 123, 248, 298
  of God's plan, 419–20
  between original innocence and sin-
    fulness, 143, 238, 298
  between original man and historical
    man, 153, 157, 248–49
  principle of, 298, 311
  of spousal analogy, 410–13
  and redemption of the body, 92–94
contraception. *See also* Humanae Vitae
  and analogy of euthanasia, 550–1
  as antithesis of authentic conjugal
    spirituality, 580–83
  as betrayal of humanity, 547, 557
  and conjugal love, 523
  and conjugal union, 526–29
  as contradiction, 540, 562–64
  effect on communion of persons,
    532–33, 537–38
  evil of, 538–40
  immorality of, 68–70, 528–33
  language of, 528–29
  versus natural regulation of births,
    540–42
  and progress of civilization, 586–87
  reason for invention of, 545–46
  and secular versus Christian human-
    ism, 609
contractual moment of marriage, 462
contradiction
  contraception as, 540, 562–64
  signs of, 66–67
control, gaining over men, 197
conversion to Christ, 201–2, 215, 251,
  265
coping mechanisms for sin, 212, 214
cosmic dimension of redemption of the
  body, 361
cosmic shame, 187
counter-signs of mystery of God, 526–29

covenant of God
    revealed in naked Christ, 27
    revealed in spousal mystery, 26
covenant of life, 301
covenants
    call to communion with God,
        99–100
    signs of, 26–27
created relations, 318
creation. *See also* mystery of creation;
    sacrament of creation; sign of creation
    accounts of, 90–92
    dominion over, 97–98
    effect of original sin on, 185–86
    gift of God in, 128–29
    as myth, 95
    original solitude, 96–98
    reasons for, 112, 128–29, 135
    spousal mystery of, 128–29
    through Word of God, 36
    unity with redemption, 452
    of woman, 104–6
cult of the body, 396
culture and ethics, 42–46
culture of death, 9, 40–41, 67, 81, 132,
    228, 327, 596
    theology of the body as antidote to,
        597–606, 613
culture of life, theology of the body as
    foundation of, 597–606, 613
culture of love in conjugal union, 393
culture of lust, 228

D

danger of anonymity in art, 285–87
death. *See also* culture of death
    Adam's understanding of, 100–101
    as alienation from God, 100–101
    versus immortality, 100–101
    versus life, 501–4, 563, 613
    life overcoming, 160–61
    of the Spirit, 261–62
    victory over, 327–29, 363
decay versus hope, 328, 361
decency of the body, 233
democracy, 52, 264
denial

of Fatherhood of God, 37, 41, 80,
    101, 180–82, 446, 540
of gift of God, 178–80
of God, 41–42
dependence on God, 101
depravity, utter, 200
Derrick, Christopher, *Sex and Sacredness
    (A Catholic Homage to Venus)*, 528
Descartes, René, 12, 51, 81, 332, 543,
    611, 616
devotion to affairs of the Lord, 357–58
diabolic versus symbolic, 38
dignity. *See* human dignity
"dirty," view of body and sex as, 232–33
discernment of the heart, 244–46
distortion
    of primordial sacrament, 159
    of sexual desire, 189–90, 197
distraction from temptation, 251–52
divine answer and human question,
    602–6
divine-human communion, 316–20
divine love, experience of, 43–44
divine mystery. *See* mystery of God
divine Subject, God as, 146
divinizing spiritualization of the body,
    307–9
divorce, Christ's response to Pharisees,
    88–92
divorce culture, love in, 206
dominion over creation, 98
    versus self-mastery, 544–45
double alienation, 443
double solitude, 107, 443
double unity, 103, 105, 107
doubt on the gift, 178, 180, 314, 447, 491
dream of Adam, 105
dress. *See* clothing
duty and values, 55, 173

E

earthly marriage as foreshadowing of
    heavenly marriage, 447–48
ecstasy, 104–5, 364, 482
election in Christ and marriage, 150

elimination of shame, 139

Elohist creation account, 90–92, 98–99, 163

emotion versus arousal, 571–74

ends of marriage, fulfillment of, 561–62

epiclesis, 582–83

epiphany of the body, 20–21, 49, 247

eros
    and ethos, 243–44, 247, 294, 443, 505
    fullness of, 246
    integration with agape, 247, 447, 493–98, 502, 509, 550
    limitations of, 494–7
    versus lust, 170, 242–44
    Plato's definition of, 243
    as true, good, and beautiful, 243

erotic love
    and senses, 491
    in Song of Songs, 410, 474–75, 493

erotic phenomena, definition of, 243

error of Manichaeism. See Manichaeism

eschatological experience, 310, 312–13, 318, 320

eschatological hope and redemption, 446–49

eschatological man, continuity with original man, 143, 298

eternal communion, 312, 315, 317, 320, 342, 433, 581

eternal election in Christ and original unity, 418–20

eternal life, hope of, 448

eternal love, chosen by, 136–37

eternal plan of love, interpretation of, 557

eternal sexuality versus lust, 221–22

ethic and ethos, 171–73

ethical content of sexual union, 583–84

ethical dimension of sexual communion, 111

ethical realism, 258–59

ethical system of Max Scheler, 55–56

ethics
    and anthropology, 91, 210, 237
    and culture, 42–46
    and personalism, 71, 586

and progress of civilization, 586–88
    rooted in anthropology, 145
    sexual ethics, 210, 225
    and technology, 586–88

ethics of pure duty (Immanuel Kant), 55

ethos
    of celibacy, 339–41
    and eros, 243–44, 247, 294, 443, 505
    and ethic, 171–73
    fulfillment of the law, 173–76
    of human practice, 229–30
    of marriage, 339–41, 443
    Old Testament ethos, 206–11
    and praxis, 229–30
    of redemption, 190, 199, 202, 215, 234, 236–38, 244, 248–52, 255, 260, 263, 287, 315, 339–41, 355–56, 383, 437–39, 458, 471, 473, 505, 508, 515, 530, 553, 566, 569, 572–73

ethos of the gift and subjectivity, 144–48

Eucharist, 255
    consummation through, 25–27
    as nourishment, 403
    and spousal love, 403

eunuchs, 334–36

euthanasia and contraception, analogy of, 550–51

evangelization, 595–616
    and the Church, 600–607
    and theology of the body, 50, 282, 596–97

Eve, love of Adam for, 106

evil
    assignment of, 230–33
    of contraception, 538–40
    definition of, 91
    versus good, 469, 501–3, 506, 613
    root of, 43–44

existence
    and spousal meaning of the body, 138–39

experience
    Adam's understanding of death, 100–101
    of beauty, 478–80
    of the body, 127
    of divine love, 46

of grace, 309, 314
of human dignity, 250–51
of the incarnate person, 378–80
of lust, 198–99, 217–19
of original nakedness, 121–28, 134, 425
of original solitude, 425–26
of original unity, 425–26
primary experience of man, 96–97
and revelation, 94–96
of salvation from lust, 212–15
of shame, 124–26, 184–92
of spousal meaning of the body, 133
experiential reality, faith as, 55
exploitation, 12, 134, 196
exterior nakedness, 127
external modesty and lust, 217

F
faith, 239–41
analogy of faith, 606–7
definition of, 258, 553
as experiential reality, 55
and intellect, 55
justification by, 257–59
role in reconciliation, 47
veils of faith, 409–10
family
as anchor of society, 44–45
conjugal union as core of, 44–45
fascination with the body, 477–78
fatherhood, 156–57
of Joseph, 338–39
Fatherhood of God, denial of, 37, 41, 80, 101, 180–82, 446, 540
fear
and nakedness, 185–87
and relative shame, 187–88
and shame, 185–87
"fear of the Lord," 277, 386, 570
femininity
eulogy of, 157–58
and masculinity, 105–6, 194–96
meaning of, 43–44
feminist movement, 196
fertility. See contraception; natural regulation of births; procreation

fidelity to the gift, 141–42
first Adam versus last Adam, 329–30
first feast of humanity, spousal meaning of the body as, 148–49
flat-tire analogy, relationship between the sexes, 88
flesh
and death of the Spirit, 261–62
sacrifice of, 26–27
versus Spirit, 256–57
works of, 259–61
foreshadowing
of Christ in Adam, 98
of heavenly marriage by earthly marriage, 447–48
mystery of Christ, 15
forgiveness of God, 420
form, interplay with matter, 465–67
fraternal love as basis for spousal love, 481–83
free will of man. See freedom of choice
freedom. See also liberation
authentic freedom, 265–66, 546, 572–73
versus bondage to lust, 265–66, 274–75
of choice, 146–47, 489–90, 557–58
in Christ, 202–3, 212–13, 274–75
definition of, 101
from the law, 260–61
of man, 36
and purity, 262–65
in secular versus Christian humanism, 608–9
and sexual counter-revolution, 72–73
true freedom, 203, 441, 535, 553, 570, 610
and truth, 52–53, 57–58
freedom from sin and purity of heart, 212–13
freedom of the gift, 125, 133–35, 136, 141, 146–48, 185, 188, 201–3, 228, 238, 246, 250, 262–63, 265–66, 274–75, 341, 364, 425, 441, 485, 487, 515, 548–49, 569–71, 578–79, 605, 610
perfection of, 322–24
and self-mastery, 544–46
source of, 322

Freud, 68, 104, 237, 282

fruit of the Spirit, 259–60

fruitfulness, dimension of love, 28

fruits of self-mastery, 569–70

fulfillment
    of ends of marriage, 561–62
    of law, 173–75
    of man, 350–51
    of marriage, 302–3
    of *proto-evangelium* by Christ, 362
    of sacrament of creation, 427–28
    seeking in marriage, 162–63
    of sexuality, celibacy as, 343–44
    of spousal meaning of the body,
        309–10, 320

future of the human ethos, 144–45

G

Gaudium et Spes, gift of self and com-
    munion of persons, 440–41

gender difference. *See also* sexual differen-
    tiation
    and shame, 182–83

gift, 18. *See also* freedom of the gift
    versus "appropriation," 141, 196,
        203–4
    of salvation, 93–94

gift of God, 49, 112–13
    call to glory as, 148–49
    celibacy and marriage as, 358–59
    in creation, 128–29
    denial of, 178–79
    eschatological experience of, 313
    grace as, 139–40
    grasping versus receiving, 174,
        179–80, 397, 490, 584
    living of, 129–30, 313–14, 384–85
    maintaining balance of, 204–5
    to man, 139, 263, 414
    in original nakedness, 129–30
    in original solitude, 129–30
    in original unity, 129–30
    questioning of, 178–79
    for reconciliation, 47–48
    in resurrection of the body, 309–10
    revelation of, 610
    in sexuality, 128–29
    and veils of faith, 409–10

gift of self, 111–14, 136–38, 445–46. *See
    also* communion of persons; ethos of
    the gift
    chosen by eternal love, 135–36
    and communion of persons, 107,
        136, 137, 143, 440–41
    fidelity to, 141–42
    giving and receiving, 387–88
    interpenetration of giving and
        receiving, 142–43, 387–88
    and personalism, 34–35
    and spousal meaning of the body,
        131–32
    as submission, 385

giving and receiving
    gift of self, 387–88
    interpenetration of, 142–43

glory of God
    in the body, 275–76
    versus veils of faith, 409–10

God
    as divine Subject, 146
    knowledge of, 318

God of life, 301

God's bounty, maximum fullness of,
    350–51

God's covenant love, proclamation of,
    467–68

God's glory. *See* glory of God

God's love. *See* love of God

God's plan
    continuity of, 419–20
    of salvation, 382

good
    definition of, 91
    eros as, 242–43
    versus evil, 469, 501–3, 506, 613

goodness of life, affirming, 49, 161

goodness of the body, 127–28

"Gospel of the body," 14–15, 499,
    567–77, 588, 595–96

grace, 239–42
    body pervaded by, 420–21
    experience of, 314
    as gift of God, 139
    of God, 93
    of mystery of creation, 419
    of mystery of redemption, 419

and nature, 431–35
of original happiness, 139–43
of original innocence, 139–40, 419
and purity of heart, 147–48
radical character of, 413–15
restoration of, 188, 231, 240–41, 432–33
in sacraments of creation and redemption, 427–29
of salvation, 389–90
for victory over sin, 438–39
grasping versus receiving, 179, 219
growing in holiness, 250–51

H

happiness. *See also* original happiness
in Christ, 139–40
and spousal meaning of the body, 137–38
harmony
between authentic love and respect for life, 530–40
in the body, 269–70
of body and soul, 39, 303–6, 307–10
interior harmony of marriage, 579–80
of sexuality and spirituality, 39
of subjective experience with objective reality, 60
head-body analogy of marriage, 391–92
healing
rift from original sin, 46–50
of sexuality, 189–90
heart, 176–78. *See also* adultery in the heart
call of Christ within, 242
discernment of, 243–46
of layman in John Paul II, 345
living the body from, 197–203
heaven, clothing in, 305–6
heavenly marriage, earthly marriage as foreshadowing of, 447–48
heavenly mysteries, theology of the body as explanation of, 601–2
"helper," understanding gift of God in, 129–30
heritage of the human heart, 242
historical man

versus original man, 238–39
spousal meaning of the body for, 147–48
historical sinfulness, 92–94
history versus prehistory, 94–96
holiness, 232. *See also* purity of heart
beauty as image of, 395–97
versus betrayal, 547, 554–58
of the body, 266–68
celibacy as call to, 358–59
definition of, 358, 421
growing in, 250–51
as inner transformation, 244–47
marriage as call to, 358–59
and original nakedness, 152
Holy Spirit
closing off from, 581–83
conjugal union in, 443–48
death of the Spirit, 261–62
divinizing spiritualization of the body, 308
versus flesh, 256–57
fruit of, 259–60
restoration of grace through, 240–41
sensitivity from, 575–76
work in Pope John Paul II, 67
honor for the body, 22, 158, 267–72
hope
versus decay, 328
of eternal life, 447–48
of every day, 361, 436–37
of redemption, 445–47
human body. *See* body
human dignity, 438
experience of, 250–51
importance in marriage, 224
and nakedness, 124
of woman, 235
human ethos, future of, 144–47
human experience. *See* experience
human life, questions of, 162–63
human love, debate over meaning of, 562–66
human question and divine answer, 602–6
Humanae Vitae, 76, 77, 82, 120, 159, 161, 162, 282, 283, 403, 423, 430, 506, 515, 521, 522, 536, 541, 542, 544, 546, 561, 564, 574, 577, 580, 589, 592–94

and authentic conjugal spirituality, 551–58
as call to liberation and responsible parenthood, 562, 590–91
commentary on, 521–35
debate over meaning of human love, 562–66
elements of sacrifice and victory in, 523–30
and integral vision of man, 547–51
moral norm taught by, 530–35
pastoral concern of, 533–35
questions raised by, 584–88
Humanae Vitae crisis, 67–70
humanization and evangelization, 588
husbands
appreciation for wife's beauty, 397–400
completion by wives, 430–31

I
icon, marriage as, 326–27
idol, marriage as, 326–27
image of God
body as, 182
communion of persons as, 108–11
man created in, 90–92
original nakedness as witness of, 182
and procreation, 156–57
image of holiness, physical beauty as, 395–97
image of Trinity in communion of persons, 156–57
immanent shame, 187–89
immodesty, 270–72
immorality. *See also* morality
of adultery, 171
of contraception, 67–70, 527, 530–34
immortality versus death, 100–101
impurity
and death of the Spirit, 261–62
versus purity, 676–77
Incarnate Christ, 14. *See also* Christ's body
and conjugal union, 415–16
healing rift from original sin, 46–49
mystery of God revealed in, 21–22
and original unity, 417–20

revelation of love in, 49–50
as ultimate reality, 73
incarnate communion, 97, 110, 115, 143, 302, 316–17, 321, 378, 419, 422, 427, 606
incarnate love and communion of persons, 130–31
incarnate person, experience of, 378–81
incarnational love, 451
incontinent act of intercourse, 573
indissolubility of marriage, 89–90
individualism, 135–36
initiation of the gift, 203–5
inner transformation, 244–46
innocence. *See* original innocence
integral vision of man, 547–48
and *Humanae Vitae*, 547–51
integral vision of natural regulation of births, 547–51
intellect and faith, 55
intensification of marital affection, self-mastery as, 266
intercourse. *See* conjugal union
interior constriction of concupiscence, 578
interior dimension of the gift, 421
interior experience of God, 57
interior harmony of marriage and chastity, 578
interior integration of celibacy, 357–58
interior nakedness, 127
purity of love for, 136–38
interior order of conjugal life, 574
internal problem of every marriage and chastity, 574–75
interpenetration of giving and receiving, 142–43
interplay of form and matter, 465–67
interpretation
of eternal plan of love, 557
of Song of Songs, 475–76
intimacy and experience of original nakedness, 126–27
intimacy with God and unrepeatability of the person, 309–10
Israel as adulterous wife, 209–10, 469

J

Jesus. *See* Christ

John of the Cross, 31, 34, 46, 54–55, 62, 64, 71, 80, 146, 311, 440, 488, 599

John Paul II (Pope). *See also* Wojtyla, Karol
   background of, 42
   heart of layman in, 345
   Holy Spirit's work in, 67
   priority in theology of the body catechesis, 584–85

Joseph
   fatherhood of, 339
   role in mystery of the Incarnation, 338–39
   virginal marriage to Mary, 338–39

joys of purity, 278

justification by faith, 257–59, 262

K

Kant, Immanuel, ethics of pure duty, 55

kingdom, celibacy for. *See* celibacy

knowledge
   versus consciousness, 57–58
   of God, 318–19
   meaning of, 154–56
   scientific versus biblical, 161–62
   and sexual union, 153–56
   and unity, 155

knowledge-generation cycle, 159–61

L

language of contraception, 539

language of the body, 467
   liturgical language, 512–14
   and lust, 470–72
   man as author of, 468–69
   mystical language, 512
   and sacramental sign, 512–14
   speaking in truth, 469–70, 472–73

last Adam versus first Adam, 255

law
   compromise in, 207–8
   freedom from, 260–61
   fulfillment of, 173–75
   versus justification by faith, 257–59

legalism, 172, 211

liberation. *See also* freedom
   from concupiscence, 229, 351–52
   Humanae Vitae as call to, 535
   from lust, 227–33

life. *See also* culture of life
   affirming goodness of, 160–61
   versus death, 501–4, 536, 613
   God of, 301
   offered to God, 49
   overcoming death, 160–61

life-giving meaning of Christ's love for the Church, 430–31

life of spouses, role of conjugal love in, 558–62

light in revelation, 306

liturgical language of the body, 509–12

lived morality, 175, 228–33

living of gift of God, 313–14, 383–86

living the body, 197–203

logos, 16, 62, 259

loneliness of alienation from God, 100

longing for communion of persons, 603–4

look, purity of, 477–78

looking lustfully, 217–19

Lord's Prayer, 181

loss
   of purity, 147, 189–91
   of supernatural efficacy, 425–26
   of unity, 185

Louis de Montfort, 487

love. *See also* agape; authentic love; conjugal love; eros; eternal love; spousal love
   of Adam for Eve, 106
   body as witness to, 313–14
   Christ's love for the Church, 430–31
   directed toward a person, 351–52
   in divorce culture, 206
   and experience of beauty, 478–80
   as incarnational, 451
   versus lust, 182–84, 200–201, 445–47, 488–89
   man and woman as subjects of, 148–53
   man's need for, 49–50
   and spousal meaning of the body, 130–32
   spousal mystery as dimension of, 29–31

paternal love, 412
proclamation of God's covenant love,
    467–68
as reason for creation, 128–29
as recognition of beauty, 400–402
revelation in Incarnate Christ, 49–50
sexual union for, 131
and shame, 124, 138
test of, 155
Trinity as prototype of, 30–31
and true beauty, 397
unity in, 392–93
and unrepeatability of the person,
    154
victory over death, 501–7
Love and Responsibility (Wojtyla), 45, 64,
    71, 82, 114, 122, 190, 270, 361, 393,
    504, 572
love of God, 46–47, 49, 112, 139–40
restoration through, 410–12
lovers, belonging between, 488–90
loving versus using, 72
Lublin School of Philosophy, 63, 82, 532
lust. *See also* concupiscence; shame
    and adultery, 189
    adultery in the heart, 207, 222–23
    bondage to, 265
    burning bush imagery, 247
    common experience of, 217
    communion of persons, effect on,
        193–97
    concept of beauty, effect on, 202
    culture of, 228
    as distortion of sexual desire, 192
    as effect of shame, 182–84
    versus eros, 169–70
    versus eternal sexuality, 221–22
    experience of, 198–99
    and experience of shame, 189,
        269–70
    and external modesty, 217
    importance of overcoming, 125
    and language of the body, 470–72
    liberation from, 227–33
    and living the body, 197–203
    and loss of virginity, 117
    versus love, 182–84, 200–201,
        445–47, 488–89

within marriage, 222–27
and masters of suspicion, 236–38
and original sin, 177–88
original solitude/unity/nakedness,
    188
overcoming, 250–51, 470–72,
    566–69
phenomenon of, 216
psychological understanding of,
    220–21
redemption from, 226, 237, 265
redemption versus repression,
    251–52
as reduction, 219–22, 226
salvation from, 212–14
versus spousal meaning of the body,
    220–21
subjection to, 196–97
threefold concupiscence, 177
tragedy of, 194
"turn away your eyes," 214–16
victory over, 118, 214, 232, 233–35,
    236, 238
lustful looks, 189, 217–19

M

male domination, 194–96
man
    as Absolute, 607–10
    as author of language of the body,
        468–69
    blaming woman for lust, 235
    created in image of God, 90–92
    dominion over creation, 98
    double unity of, 103, 105, 107
    freedom of, 36
    fulfillment of, 350–51
    gaining control over, 197
    gift of God to, 139, 269, 414
    initiation of the gift, 203–5
    integral vision of, 547–48
    need for affirmation, 578–79
    original solitude. *See* original solitude
    original unity. *See* original unity
    as partner of the Absolute, 607–10
    possibilities of, 239–40, 535
    relationship with God, 102
    responsibility toward woman, 203–5
    self-consciousness of, 54, 97–98

self-determination of, 97, 102,
106–7, 119, 128, 154–55, 188,
201, 203, 218–19, 250, 264, 333,
468–69, 563
solitude of, 603–4
spiritualization of, 139
as subject of truth and love, 148–53
subjection to lust, 196–97
supreme vocation of, 364
as unity of spirit and body, 102–3
man versus animals
celibacy, 351–52
freedom of choice, 97, 119, 134, 184
loss of unity, 184
original unity, 107–8
self-mastery, 184, 545
shame, 138, 184
unrepeatability of the person, 134,
153–54
Manichaeism, error of, 230–34, 290,
512–13
Mann, Judy, "A Lesson on Lust for the
Vatican," 226–27
man's need for love, 49–50
man's view of God, paradigm shift in,
48–49
marital affection, authentication and
intensification of, 569–71
marital spirituality. See conjugal spirituality
marriage. See also conjugal union; spousal
mystery
and adultery, 209–10
adultery in the heart within, xxx, 75,
154, 169, 171, 174, 176–77, 189,
206, 211, 278, 282
balance within, 119
as basic structure for salvation,
433–35
biblical and personalist aspects of,
585–86
as call to holiness, 358–59
celibacy as affirmation of, 348–49
celibacy as "superior" to, 341–43,
357–58
celibacy's completion of, 345–49
Christ's response to Pharisees,
87–90, 92
and communication, 125

as communion of persons, 113
and concupiscence, 341
consent in, 462–65, 470
consummation and words of consent
as signs of, 462–65, 470
consummation of, 462–65
contractual moment of, 462
and election in Christ, 150
as embracing the universe, 451–52
essence of, 153
as essential part of sacramental economy, 432–34
ethos of, 339–41, 443
expectations of, 326
fulfillment of, 302–3
as fundamental to mystery of creation, 324–25
as gift of God, 358–59
head-body analogy of, 391–92
human dignity within, 224
as icon or idol, 326–27
importance of prayer and the sacraments, 554–56
interior harmony of, 578
lust in, 222–27
mutual submission in, 385
as mystery, 512–15
and mystery of Christ, 389–90
and mystery of Ephesians, 377–81
mystery of God in, 378–80
nakedness in, 191
original spirituality of, 427–28,
575–77
as outlet for concupiscence, 225, 341,
355–56, 442–43
Paul's teaching on, 353–55
perfection of communion in, 315
periodic abstinence in, 360–61, 550
and personalism, 203
and perspective of life, 301
as primordial sacrament, 302, 311,
417–23
as prototype for sacraments, 431–35
reconciliation offered by Christ,
87–88
and resurrection of the body, 302–6
as revelation of mystery of God, 404,
407, 416–17
revelation of salvific will of God,
439–41

reverence for Christ within, 385–86
role of conjugal love in, 463–65
as sacrament of redemption, 432–34, 442, 451
as sacramental sign, 461–67
sacramentality of, 162, 280, 333, 346, 348–49, 375–515, 575, 584–85
seeking fulfillment in, 162–63
sexual union in, 210–11
shamelessness in, 192
as sign of mystery of God, 406–7
significance in Old Testament, 334–35
speaking in truth, 472–73
spousal meaning of the body revealed in, 346–48
union of Christ and the Church, 377–78, 405–7
unity and indissolubility of, 89–90
unity in love, 392–93
and unrepeatability of the person, 154
marriage, sacrament of, 152, 375–520
body as sign of mystery of God, 151–52
celibacy as affirmation of, 348–49
communion with Christ, 405, 582, 604
covenant of life, 301
incarnate communion, 110, 316–18
meaning of sacraments, 302–3
sexual communion in, 111
conjugal spirituality, 554–58
Marx, 237
Mary
beauty of, 400–401
as "Blessed Virgin," 117
as model of the Church, 309
virginal marriage to Joseph, 117, 338–39
masculinity
and femininity, 105–6, 194–96
meaning of, 43–44
master-slave relationship paradigm, 48–49
masters of suspicion, 236–38
matter, interplay with form, 465–67
mature spontaneity and noble gratification, 244–47

meaning of human existence. See meaning of life
meaning of life, 238–39, 132–33
and resurrection of the body, 315–16
and sexuality, 132–33
and spousal-redemptive significance of the body, 450–51
mercy of God, 126, 214, 504, 556, 557
mercy, revealed in Christ's body, 126
message of salvation, 534, 610–12
Michelangelo, Sistine Chapel painting, 284, 288–89
misogyny, 195
model of the Church, Mary as, 309
modern rationalism, 12–15, 51–52, 61–62, 68
Church's response to, 606–12
modern world
versus Christianity, 51–53
versus Church, 68–69
modesty, 122, 217
authentic modesty, 270–72
and clothing, 270–72
monogamy and polygamy in Old Testament, 207–9
moral law, personalist understanding of, 531–32
moral life, purpose of, xxxiv, 145, 172
moral norm taught by Humanae Vitae, 524–26, 529, 530–35
moral purity versus physical purity, 254–56
moral relativism, 53, 60
moralism, 172, 290
morality. See also Christian morality; immorality; sexual morality
balance in, 229–30
basis of, 144–45
ethic and ethos, 145
fulfillment of the law, 173–75
mortal sin, 261
motherhood, 156–57
eulogy of, 258
mutual self-giving, dimension of love, 30, 59, 146, 537
mutual submission in marriage, 383–86

mysteries of faith and theology of the body, 601–2

mystery
  marriage as, 512–15
  sacrament as, 404–5
  sacrament as accomplishment of, 407–8

mystery of Christ
  foreshadowing, 98
  and marriage, 389–90

mystery of creation, 120
  grace of, 240–41
  marriage and procreation as fundamental to, 324–25
  procreation as part of, 445–46

mystery of divine love, revelation in Christ, 408–9

mystery of Ephesians and marriage, 377–78

mystery of God
  body as sign of, 23, 152, 471
  in marriage, 378–80
  marriage as revelation of, 404, 407, 416–17
  marriage as sign of, 406–7
  and primordial sacrament, 149–53
  revealed in Christ's body, 16–17, 27, 133, 408, 449
  revealed in the body, 17–21, 109–10, 152, 471
  signs and counter-signs of, 20, 23–24, 526–30
  in spousal mystery, 23–28
  in union of Christ and the Church, 378

mystery of man, 14, 51, 62, 109, 180, 278, 287

mystery of redemption
  grace of, 419
  procreation as part of, 445–46

mystery of the Father, revelation of, 14–15, 27, 79, 181, 188

mystery of the Incarnation, Joseph's role in, 338–39

mystery of the person, 486, 488

mystical language of the body, 379

mysticism, spousal mysticism, 23, 311, 599–600

myth, creation accounts as, 95–96

N

naked Christ, covenant revealed in, 27

nakedness. *See also* original nakedness
  after resurrection of the body, 305–6
  effect of original sin on, 122–23
  and fear, 185–87
  and human dignity, 124–25
  in marriage, 191
  portrayals of, 283–91
  and shame, 182–84
  and sin, 36–37

natural family planning (NFP), 550–51, 582–83

natural law, 173
  personalist interpretation of, 282, 530–31, 548–49

natural regulation of births, 536–46
  and abstinence, 521, 534, 540–46
  versus contraception, 540–42
  integral vision of, 547–51

nature and grace, 431–35

Nazis, effect on John Paul II, 42

new Adam. *See* last Adam

New Covenant related to Old Covenant, 175–76

new evangelization. *See* evangelization

New Testament, continuity of spousal analogy in, 410–13

NFP. *See* natural family planning

Nietzsche, 237

noble gratification and mature spontaneity, 246–47

non-procreative versus anti-procreative, 542

nourishment, Eucharist as, 403

nude. *See* nakedness

O

objective reality, 51–53
  harmony with subjective experience, 53, 61–62, 71–72

objectivity, marriage with subjectivity, 60

objectivity versus subjectivity, 65–66, 71–72
  balance between, 173
  in creation accounts, 91–92
  ethic and ethos, 171–72

fulfillment of the law, 173–75
original nakedness, 123–24
revelation and experience, 94–95
sexuality separated from communion
of persons, 193–94
Old Covenant versus New Covenant,
175–76
Old Testament
continuity of spousal analogy in,
410–13
significance of marriage in, 334–35
Old Testament ethos, 206–11
ongoing conversion to Christ, 200
original conjugal act, communion of persons in, 114–15
original happiness, grace of, 139–40
original human experience, 94–96
original innocence, 92–93
continuity with sinfulness, 92–94
conjugal unity in, 114–17
definition of, 92
echoes of, 72, 90, 92–93
and the exchange of the gift, 141–42
grace of, 139–40
of knowledge, 125–26
as purity of heart, 92–94, 141
original man
continuity with eschatological man,
143
versus historical man, 239
original nakedness, 36, 96, 120–26, 129,
269–70
and choice, 424–25
and communication, 124–26
experience of, 121–28, 134, 425
freedom of the gift, 134
gift of God in, 129–30
and holiness, 152
as interior and exterior nakedness,
127
and intimacy, 126–27
lack of shame in, 121–23
lust, effect on, 188
man looking at, 217–19
purity in, 125–26
and purity of heart, 147–48
versus relative shame, 187–88
understanding experience of, 123–24

witness of image of God, 182
original sin, 36–42, 127, 132–33
and concupiscence, 177–78
denial of Fatherhood of God, 37, 41,
80, 101, 180–82, 446, 540
fear in nakedness, 185–87
flesh versus Spirit, 256–57
healing rift from, 46–50
and loss of supernatural efficacy,
425–26
nakedness, effect on, 123–23
original virginal value of man, effect
on, 116–17
plagiarizing of sacraments, 36–38
and spousal imagery, 180
original solitude, 96–98, 129
of Adam, 96–99
affirmed by original unity, 107–8
and celibacy, 343–44
and choice, 424–25
experience of, 425–26
gift of God in, 129–30
versus immanent shame, 187–89
link with original unity, 103, 119
lust, effect on, 188
of man, 96–103
as preparation for communion with
God, 99–103
as revealed in the body, 102–3
original spirituality of marriage, 427–28,
575–77
original unity, 96, 103, 106–111, 129
as bodily and spiritual experience,
115–16
with Christ, 308–10
as communion of persons, 107–8
and eternal election in Christ,
418–19
experience of, 424–26
gift of God in, 129–30
and Incarnate Christ, 417–20
lust, effect on, 188
original solitude affirmed by, 107–8
original solitude as part of, 103, 119
versus relative shame, 187–88
sexual union in, 114–17
original virginal value of man, 116–17
"otherness." See complementarity
"Our Father" prayer, 181

overcoming
    death with life, 160–61
    lust, 250–51, 471–72, 566–69
ownership, right of, 209

P
paradigm shift in man's view of God,
    48–49
parents. *See also* responsible parenthood
    relationship with children, 264–65
participation, definition of, 151
partner of the Absolute, man as, 607–10
partnership with God, 101
passivity versus activity, 65, 203, 388
passover, 9, 346, 487, 495, 596, 613
pastoral concern of *Humanae Vitae*,
    533–35
fatherly love, 412–13
Paul
    teaching on celibacy and marriage,
        352–61
peace of the interior gaze, 126, 189, 398,
    484, 579
pedagogy of the body, 279–80, 534,
    550–52
Penance, sacrament of, 554–55, 557, 571
perennial object of culture, body as,
    284–85
perfect freedom of the gift, 322–23
perfection
    of communion of persons, 320–21
    measured by charity, 345–46
    of subjectivity, 314–15
    of union, 321
periodic abstinence, 360–61, 550. *See also*
    natural regulation of births
permanent moral attitude, abstinence as,
    564–66
personal content of sexual union, 512
personalism
    and ethics, 71, 586
    and gift of self, 34–35
    in *Humanae Vitae*, 157
    and marriage, 203
    Thomistic personalism, 54–56
personalist aspects of marriage and pro-
    creation, 585–86

personalist ethic, 223, 225
personalist interpretation of natural law,
    282, 530–31, 548–49
personalist understanding of the moral
    law, 531–32
personalistic norm, 72–73
perversion, 188
Pharisees, discussion with, 87–90, 92
phenomenology, 34, 55–59, 173
phenomenon of lust, 216
philosophical anthropology, 92, 112, 586
philosophical project of Karol Wojtyla,
    51–62
philosophy
    objectivity versus subjectivity, 65–66,
        71–72
    phenomenology, 34, 55–59, 173
photography, danger of anonymity in,
    285–87
physical beauty as image of holiness,
    395–97
physical fruitfulness and spiritual fruitful-
    ness, 349
physical purity versus moral purity,
    254–56
piety, 272–73, 295, 385, 570, 576
plagiarizing of sacraments, 36–38
Plato, definition of eros, 243
polygamy and monogamy in Old
    Testament, 207–9
pornography, 30, 232–33, 322–23
    versus art, 283–86
possession versus belonging, 205–6, 497
power of Christ's resurrection, 327–29
power of God, 382
    in the Scriptures, 299–301
praxis and ethos, 229–30
prayer, importance in marriage, 554–56
pregnancy, avoiding. *See* contraception;
    natural regulation of births
prehistory versus history, 94–96
primary experience of man, 97
primordial sacrament, 148–53
    distortion of, 159
    marriage as, 302, 311, 417–23
    and mystery of God, 149–53

plagiarizing, 36–38
renewal of, 432–33, 449
Satan's attacks on, 423
principle of continuity, 298–311
procreation. *See also* fatherhood; motherhood
avoiding selfishness in, 546–47
biblical and personalist aspects of,
585–86
and communion of persons, 120
and conjugal union, 445–46, 524–26
and eschatological hope, 446–48
as fundamental to mystery of creation, 324–26
and image of God, 156–57
and knowledge-generation cycle,
159–61
link with sex, 68
as part of mystery of creation and
redemption, 445–46
physical and spiritual fruitfulness,
337–39
sexual union for, 132
and suffering, 445–46
procreative attitude in responsible parenthood, 549–51
procreative meaning of conjugal union,
445–46, 524–26
progress of civilization
and contraception, 586–87
and ethics, 586–88
prophetism of the body, 467–69
proto-evangelium, fulfillment by Christ,
362
prototype for sacraments, marriage as,
431–35
archetype of spousal love, Trinity as, 32
psychological understanding of lust,
220–21
pure and simple guiding thread of existence, 228
purity. *See also* purity of heart
authentic purity, 270–72
and freedom, 262–65
glorifying God in the body, 275–76
versus impurity, 276–77
joys of, 278
of look, 477–78

loss of, 147, 189–91
in original nakedness, 125–26
and self-control, 266–68
symbols of, 306
victory over lust, 233–35
and wisdom, 276–77
purity of heart, 61, 226–28, 253–56,
262–65, 289, 399–400. *See also* holiness; purity
coping mechanisms for sin, 212, 214
and freedom from sin, 212–13
and grace, 147–48
original innocence as, 92–94, 141
and original nakedness, 125–26
and spiritual life, 253–56
and subjectivity, 147–48
purity of love
for exterior and interior nakedness,
136–37

Q
questioning of gift of God, 178–79
questions raised by *Humanae Vitae*,
584–88

R
radical character of grace and spousal
analogy, 414–15
radical exploitation, 188
radical individualism, 112, 136, 188
radical perversion, 188
rationalism. *See* modern rationalism
receiving and giving
gift of self, 387–88
interpenetration of, 142–43
receiving versus grasping, 179–219
receptivity of the gift, 180, 204
recognition of beauty, love as, 400–402
reconciliation, 46–48
gift of God for, 47–48
offered by Christ, 87–88
role of faith in, 47
of truth, 51–53
Redeemer, Christ as, xxx, 46, 50, 184,
240, 252, 276, 346, 411–13, 416, 418,
434, 524, 534–35, 584, 600, 611

redemption, 47, 117, 158–59, 214, 226, 238, 242, 246–47, 257, 266, 269–70, 272–73, 279, 283, 290, 309, 397, 400, 401, 408, 413, 426, 431, 470, 478, 490, 512, 527, 529, 551, 572. *See also* mystery of redemption; sacrament of redemption; sign of redemption
  anthropological and ethical realism of, 258–59
  anthropology of, 436–37
  and celibacy, 337–41
  ethos of, 190, 199, 202, 215, 234, 236–38, 244, 248–52, 255, 260, 263, 287, 315, 339–41, 355–56, 383, 437–39, 458, 471, 473, 505, 508, 515, 530, 553, 566, 569, 572–73
  hope of, 446–48
  from lust, 226, 237, 265
  versus repression, 251–52
  and resurrection, 170, 329–30
  through Christ, 2, 61, 88, 118, 126, 133, 138–41, 169–70, 184, 203–4, 240, 390, 394–96, 406, 409, 414, 418, 499, 534–35, 612
  unity with creation, 314, 452
  unity with spousal love, 448, 450
redemption of the body, 23, 46, 92–94, 133, 138, 250–52, 276, 289, 307, 313, 318, 323, 329, 340–41, 356, 361–65, 385, 390, 435, 462, 471, 472, 523, 560, 563–64, 584, 596
  authentic modesty and authentic purity, 270–73
  celibacy as sign, 335–37
  and concupiscence, 363
  cosmic dimension of, 261–65
  grace of God, 93
  lust versus eros, 169–70
  marriage and personalism, 202–3
  marriage as outlet for concupiscence, 224–25
  seeking fulfillment in marriage, 162–63
  victory over lust, 233–35
  as whole mission of Christ, 248–49
redemptive meaning of the body, 450–51
redemptive meaning of love, 448–52
reduction, lust as, 219–22, 226
regulation of births. *See* contraception

relationality, 111–14
relative shame, 187–89
relativism. *See* moral relativism
religion, rift with science, 51–53
religious content of sexual union, 583–84
renewal
  of the covenant with God, 301, 428
  of the family, 283, 597
  of primordial sacrament, 432–33, 449
  sources of, 65–66
renunciation, celibacy as, 117–18, 336, 349–51
repression versus redemption, 251–52
respect for life, harmony with authentic love, 530–35
responsibility of man toward woman, 203–5
responsible parenthood, 536, 544, 547, 562, 612
  Humanae Vitae as call to, 535–37, 549–50, 574
  procreative attitude in, 549–51
restlessness as part of eros, 494
restoration
  of God's plan, 88, 200, 249
  of grace, 188, 241
  of spousal meaning of the body, 362
  through love of God, 412
resurrection
  of Christ, 46, 133, 143, 163, 175, 206, 214, 227, 237–40, 248, 297, 300–301, 355, 362–63, 402, 408, 419, 445, 447, 449, 497, 499, 552, 555, 576, 612
  power of, 261, 266, 612
  and redemption, 170, 329–30
resurrection of the body, 249, 297–98, 329–32
  and communion of persons, 302–5
  gift of God in, 309–10
  and marriage, 302–6
  and meaning of life, 315–16
  nakedness after, 305–6
  Sadducees' question about, 299–302
  and sexual differentiation, 303–5
  and theological anthropology, 304
  as union of soul and body, 303–40

revelation, 89, 110, 147, 150, 177, 189,
208, 220, 223, 229, 282, 315, 327–28,
334, 440, 476, 490, 530, 539, 585, 606
    biblical, 7, 24, 243, 585, 599
    covenant of God in spousal mystery,
        26
    and experience, 94–96, 138, 184, 248
    of gift of God, 610
    in light, 306
    of love in Incarnate Christ, 49–50
    of mercy in Christ's body, 126, 420
    of mystery of divine love, 26–27, 49,
        73, 181, 188, 407, 410, 451
    of mystery of God in Christ's body,
        16–17, 27, 408, 449
    of mystery of God in marriage, 404,
        407, 416
    of mystery of God in the body,
        109–11, 189, 213, 280, 288, 333,
        375
    of mystery of the Father, 181, 188
    new aspects of, 412–13
    of personhood in the body, 13, 69,
        102–3, 120–22, 129, 143, 161,
        182, 189, 193, 335, 346, 350, 411
    of salvific will of God, 389, 405–6,
        439–41
    of spousal meaning of the body, 130,
        132–33, 135, 160, 522, 547, 557
reverence for Christ within marriage,
    385–86
rib of Adam, 104–5
right of ownership, 209
rights and duties of spouses, 359–61
root of evil, 43–44

S
sacrament of creation, 421–23, 432–35,
    451
    fulfillment in sacrament of redemp-
        tion, 427–31
    grace in, 427–30
sacrament of marriage, 23, 149–50, 162,
    280, 375, 389, 407, 434, 440–41, 444,
    449, 451, 462, 465–66, 475, 493, 510,
    512, 538, 552, 571
    body as sign of mystery of God,
        151–52
    celibacy as affirmation of, 333,
        348–49

communion with Christ, 18–19
covenant of life, 301–2
incarnate communion, 97, 110, 115,
    143, 302, 316–17, 321, 378, 419,
    422, 427, 606
meaning of sacraments, 302–3
sexual communion in, 111
sacrament of redemption
    fulfillment of sacrament of creation
        in, 427–33
    grace in, 427–28
    marriage as, 432–34, 442, 451
sacramental dimension of sexual com-
    munion, 110–11
sacramental economy, marriage as essen-
    tial part of, 432–34
sacramental order, foundation of, 23,
    416–17, 433–34
sacramental sign, 409, 429–30, 527
    body as, 231–32, 416
    celibacy as, 335–37
    and language of the body, 463–67,
        510, 512–13
    marriage as, 333, 376, 390, 461–67,
        470–72, 480, 499, 500, 526, 529,
        536
    sexual communion as, 111, 502, 508,
        540, 563
sacramentality
    of the body, 15–17, 37, 66, 213, 548
    of creation, 152
    of marriage, 162, 280, 333, 346,
        348–49, 375–515, 577, 584–85
sacraments. See also primordial sacrament
    as accomplishment of mystery, 404–8
    definition of, 403–4
    importance in marriage, 554–56
    marriage as prototype for, 433–35
    meaning of, 302
    as mystery, 150, 403–6
    plagiarizing of, 37
    sexual communion as, 111
sacred and sensual in Song of Songs,
    476–77
sacredness
    of the body, 438–39
    of sex, 528
sacrifice
    celibacy as, 342–44, 349–51

elements in *Humanae Vitae*, 523–30
of flesh and blood, 27, 50
sacrifice to God, body as, 50
sacrificial love, victory over death, 500–509
Sadducees, question about resurrection of the body, 299–302
salvation
    gift of, 93–94
    God's plan in the body, 378–82
    grace of, 389
    from lust, 212–14
    marriage as basic structure for, 433–35
    message of, 534, 610–12
salvific fear of violating the sign, 577
salvific will of God, revelation of, 439–41
same-sex attractions, 190
Satan
    as anti-Word, 36–41, 48, 181, 379, 423, 506, 529, 539, 581, 608
    attacks on primordial sacrament, 423
    attraction of, 426
    distortion of primordial sacrament, 159
    plagiarizing of sacraments, 36–37
    stages of attack, 41–42
    symbolic versus diabolic, 38–39
Scheler, Max, 34, 55–56, 62, 65, 71, 173
science of the body versus theology of the body, 161–63
science, rift with religion, 51–53
Scriptures
    power of God in, 299–301
    spousal mystery in, 23–28
second discovery of sex, 193–94
Second Vatican Council, 10, 14, 21, 34, 36, 64, 65, 98, 107, 109, 112, 131, 265, 345, 364, 378, 405, 424, 500, 524, 531, 535, 601, 607–8
secular humanism, 135–36
    and contraception, 609
    freedom in, 607–10
self-communication of God, 241, 258, 309, 312, 409, 553
self-consciousness of man, 54, 97–98
self-control, 134–35, 203, 247, 259–60, 355–56, 442, 545, 567, 569

and purity, 266–68
self-determination of man, 97, 102, 106–7, 119, 128, 154–55, 188, 201, 203, 218–19, 250, 264, 333, 468–69, 563
self-donation, 29, 48, 55, 59, 71, 379, 387, 406, 409, 538, 539, 572
self-experience, reflection on, 56, 57
self-giving. *See* gift of self
self-gratification, 48, 183, 206, 379, 423
self-mastery, 119–20, 184, 192, 202, 238, 247, 266, 273, 398, 563
    acquiring, 266, 566–69
    authentic freedom in, 187
    as authentication and intensification of marital affection, 566–71
    of the body, 200–203
    versus dominion over creation, 541–44
    and freedom of the gift, 134, 544–46
    fruits of, 569–71
    as permanent moral attitude, 564–68
selfishness, avoiding in procreation, 546
senses and erotic love, 487
sensitivity from Holy Spirit, 575–77
eros and agape in Song of Songs, 493–98
sensuality
    and sexuality, 488–90
    versus spirituality, 332
separation of soul and body, 303, 542–44
sex
    definition of, 106
    link with procreation, 68
    second discovery of, 193–94
Sex and Sacredness (A Catholic Homage to Venus) (Derrick), 528
sex education, 280–81
sexual attraction
    and choice, 119
    spiritual maturity in, 449, 514–15
sexual behavior and effect on society, 186
sexual communion, 110
    as sacrament, 111
sexual complementarity, 142
sexual revolution and freedom, 72
sexual desire. *See also* eros

burning bush imagery, 247
distortion of, 189–92, 197
self-mastery of, 119–20
and shame, 141–42
spontaneity of, 244–47
sexual differentiation. *See also* gender
difference
complementarity of, 387
importance of, 205
relationality revealed by, 112–14
and resurrection of the body, 303–5
sexual ethics, 71–72, 111
anthropology and, 68, 130–33, 206,
210–11, 225, 340, 435, 543, 547,
564
of Church, 70
sexual intercourse. *See* conjugal union
sexual morality, 44–45, 438
Church's teaching on, 281–83
confusion about, 45
and shame, 122
and social justice, 186
sexual revolution, 9, 14, 67–68, 72, 326,
600
sexual union. *See also* communion of persons; conjugal union
as affirmation of the person, 137
ethical content of, 583–84
as experience of being chosen by
eternal love, 135–36
as expression of original virginal
value of man, 118–19
as icon or idol, 326–27
and knowledge, 153–56
for love and procreation, 132
in marriage, 210–11
in original unity, 114–20
personal content of, 583–84
religious content of, 583–84
and sacramentality of creation, 152
sexual utilitarianism, 72
sexuality
celibacy as fulfillment of, 343–44
eternal sexuality, 221–22
excitement versus emotion, 571–73
gift of God in, 128–29
harmony with spirituality, 39
healing of, 189–90

living the body, 197–203
and Manichaeism, 230–31
and meaning of life, 132–33
meaning of masculinity and femininity, 43–44
reconciliation offered by Christ,
87–88
sacredness of, 528
and sensuality, 487
separated from communion of persons, 193–94
and shame, 188–89
as temporal response of communion,
114
viewed as "dirty," 233–34
shame. *See also* lust; relative shame
beginning of, 182–84
dimensions of, 184–85
effect on spousal meaning of the
body, 190–91
elimination of, 139
experience of, 269–70
and fear, 185–87
and gender difference, 182–84
immanent and relative shame, 187–89
lack of in original nakedness, 121–23
as loss of purity of heart, 147–48
and love, 122, 138
and lust, 189
and naked body in art, 284–87
and nakedness, 182–84
phenomenon of, 124–26
and sexual morality, 122
and sexuality, 141–42, 188–89
twofold meaning of, 189–92
shamelessness, 122, 188
in marriage, 192
Sign of Contradiction (Wojtyla), 66
sign of creation, 428–30
sign of marriage
consummation as, 463–67
words of consent as, 463–67
sign of mystery of God
body as, 151–52, 393–94
marriage as, 406–7
sign of redemption, 428–30
sign of the covenant, sexual union in
marriage, 210–11

signs
  as communication, 19–20
  of contradiction, 66
  of covenants, 26–27
  of mystery of God, 526–30
"signs of the times," 9, 42, 66
sin. *See also* original sin
  consequences of, 87–88
  coping mechanisms for, 214–16
  definition of, 183–84
  distortion of primordial sacrament,
    158–59
  effect on woman, 194–96
  forgiveness of, 420, 428, 555
  grace for victory over, 438–39
  and loss of supernatural efficacy,
    425–26
  loss of unity, 184
  and nakedness, 36–37
  and original innocence, 92–98
  victory over, 238
sinfulness. *See also* historical sinfulness
  continuity with original innocence,
    92–94
single people and spousal meaning of the
  body, 347–48
Sistine Chapel painting (Michelangelo),
  284, 288–89
sleep of Adam, 104–5
social justice and sexual morality, 186
society
  effect of sexual behavior on, 228
  false standard of beauty in, 398
  family as anchor of, 44–45
solitude. *See also* original solitude
  of man, 603–4
Song of Songs
  erotic love in, 474–78
  interpretation of, 475
  sensual and sacred in, 476–77
soul and body, harmony of, 39, 303–6,
  307–10
soul, separation from the body, 303–4,
  542–44
Sources of Renewal (Wojtyla), 65
Spirit. *See* Holy Spirit
spirit, unity with body, 102–3

spiritual battle, 381
spiritual body, 331–32
spiritual experience, original unity as,
  115–16
spiritual fruitfulness
  and celibacy, 337–41
  and physical fruitfulness, 349
spiritual life and purity of heart, 254–61
spiritual mystery, body as sign of, 15
spirituality. *See also* conjugal spirituality
  of the body, 280–81
  harmony with sexuality, 39
  in marriage, 551–58
  original spirituality of marriage,
    575–77
  versus sensuality, 331
spiritualization
  of the body, 307–8
  of man, 139
spiritually mature sexual attraction,
  514–15
spontaneity of sexual desire, 244–47
spousal analogy, 23–31. *See also* spousal
  mystery
  and analogy of faith, 606–7
  of Christ and the Church, 386–90
  continuity between Old and New
    Testaments, 410–15
  keystone of, 405–7
  and radical character of grace,
    414–15
  unity with Christ, 308–10
spousal character of Baptism, 394–95,
  434, 511
spousal imagery
  and male domination, 195–96
  and original sin, 179–80
spousal love
  celibacy as expression of, 339–41
  and Eucharist, 403
  fraternal love as basis for, 481–83
  and true beauty, 397–402
  unity with redemption, 448–50
spousal meaning of the body, 130–33
  in art, 285
  completion of, 136–38
  effect of shame on, 191

and existence, 138–39
as first feast of humanity, 148–49
fulfillment of, 309–10, 320
and future of the human ethos,
144–45
giving and receiving the gift of self,
387–88
and happiness, 137–38
for historical man, 147–48
versus lust, 220–21
pervaded by grace, 420–21
revealed in marriage and celibacy,
346–48
rooted in love, 138–39
and single people, 347–48
spousal mystery, 29–31
as communion between God and
man, 412–13
covenant of God revealed in, 26
of creation, 128–29
as dimension of love, 30
in Scriptures, 412–13
spousal mysticism, 599–600
spousal significance of the body, 450–51
spousal theology. See spousal mystery
spousal union
and celibacy, 350–51
as theology, 422
spouses, rights and duties of, 359–61
standards of beauty, 401–2
struggle with concupiscence, 438–39
submission. See also mutual submission
definition of, 385
to concupiscence, 196–97
subjective experience, harmony with
objective reality, 61
subjectivity
and ethos of the gift, 144–47
marriage with objectivity, 60–62
perfection of, 314–15
and purity of heart, 147–48
subjectivity versus objectivity, 56, 65,
71–72
balance between, 173
in creation accounts, 91–92, 98–99
ethic and ethos, 171–73
fulfillment of the law, 173–76
original nakedness, 123

revelation and experience, 94–96
sexuality separated from communion
of persons, 193–94
suffering and procreation, 445–47
supernatural, celibacy as, 335–37
supernatural efficacy, loss of, 425–26
Supreme Court of the United States, 608
supreme vocation of man, 364
suspicion
masters of suspicion, 236–38
toward body, 22–23
symbolic and the diabolic, 38–39
symbolism in wedding feast of Cana,
254–55
symbols of purity, 306

T

tardemah, 104–5
task of the body and sexuality, 280
technology and ethics, 586–88
temperance, 565
temporal response of communion, sexuality as, 114
temptation
distraction from, 251–52
as questioning gift of God, 178–82
Tertullian, 37, 380, 404
theological anthropology, 61, 69, 75, 93,
111, 278, 435, 470–71
and resurrection of the body, 304
theology
and anthropology, marriage of,
21–23
body as, 422, 471
spousal union as, 421–23
ramifications of theology of the body
for, 597–98
theology of the body, 7
as antidote to culture of death,
597–606
defined, 7–9
and evangelization, 281–83
fundamental nature of, 364–65
as pedagogy, 279–80, 534, 550–51
ramifications for theology, 597–98
versus science of the body, 161–63
structure of, 73–77

as understanding of mysteries of faith, 601–2
theology of the family, 551
Thomistic personalism, 54–56
threefold concupiscence, 177
tilling the earth, 97
torpor, 104–5
total vision of man and standards of beauty, 67–70, 161, 162, 241, 315, 375, 401–2, 522
tragedy of concupiscence, 194
transcendence of the body, 147
transformation
    from within, 245
    celibacy as, 352
tree of the knowledge of good and evil, 92
trinitarian life, 151, 153, 155, 322, 473, 527, 575
trinitarian mystery of love and gift, 313
trinitarian order, 320–21
trinitarian relations, 318
Trinity
    as archetype of spousal love, 32
    in communion of persons, 318
    inspiration for communion between God and man, 312–13
    as model of communion of persons, 108–9
true beauty and spousal love, 397–403
true, eros as, 242–46
true freedom, definition of, 610
trust of God, 557
truth
    and freedom, 52, 62
    and language of the body, 469–70, 470–74
    man and woman as subjects of, 148–53
    rejoicing with, 560–61
truth about man, development of, 324–27
"turn away your eyes," 214–16
twentieth century, turbulence of, 3

U
ultimate reality, Christ as, 73
uncreated relations, 318

union
    with Christ's body, 14–15
    of communion, 319–22
    perfection of, 321
union of Christ and the Church, 406–7
    great mystery of, 378
    spousal analogy of, 386–87, 389–90
unitive meaning
    of Christ's love for the Church, 430–31
    of conjugal union, 524–26
unity. See also original unity
    between creation and redemption, 451–52
    double unity of man, 103–6
    of eternal communion, 314–15
    and knowledge, 153–54
    loss of, 184
    in love, 392–93
    man as unity of spirit and body, 102–3
    of marriage, 89–90
    in original innocence, 115–16
    original unity with Christ, 308–10
    of soul and body, 303–6, 307–10
    of spousal love and redemption, 448–50
unity-in-duality, 119
unrepeatability of the person, 154
    and intimacy with God, 309–10
using versus loving, 72

V
values and duty, 55, 173
Vatican, nude artwork in, 289
veils of faith versus glory of God, 409–10
Veritatis Splendor, xxxiv, 170
victory
    elements of in Humanae Vitae, 523
    of good, 506, 564
    of love, 505
    of spirit over body, 307
    over concupiscence, 170, 202, 279, 364, 470–74, 523
    over death, 327–29, 363
    over lust, 118, 214, 232, 233–35, 236, 238
    over sin, 159, 239, 363

violating the sign, salvific fear of, 577

virginal communion, 321–22, 335–37

virginal experience of spousal communion, 310

virginal marriage of Joseph and Mary, 338–39, 462

virginity. *See also* celibacy; original virginal value of man
loss of, 117
of Mary, 15, 28, 117, 306, 329, 337–38
vocation, celibacy as, 334–38
voluntary, celibacy as, 335–37

vows. *See* words of consent

W

Waldstein, Michael, 3, 4, 10, 26, 33, 34, 69, 73, 74, 289, 474, 522, 527

wedding feast of Cana, symbolism in, 254–55

wedding vows. *See* words of consent

Weigel, George (*Witness to Hope: The Biography of Pope John Paul II*), 2, 9, 64, 67, 73, 136, 146, 264, 345, 524, 598

whole mission of Christ, 598
redemption of the body as, 248–49

wisdom and purity, 276–77

Wisdom literature and concupiscence, 212–16

witness to love, body as, 313–14

wives
completion of husbands, 430–31
husband's appreciation for beauty of, 397–400

Wojtyla, Karol. *See also* John Paul II (Pope)

The Acting Person, 65
background of, 42–43
criticism of, 57
linking work with Pope John Paul II's work, 67
Love and Responsibility, 45, 64, 71, 82, 114, 122, 190, 270, 361, 393, 504, 572
philosophical project of, 51–62
shaping of thought of, 63–67
Sign of Contradiction, 66
Sources of Renewal, 65

woman
appreciation for beauty of, 389–99
creation of, 104–5
dignity within marriage, 224–25
effect of sin on, 193–96
eulogy of, 157–58
gaining control over man, 197
man blaming for lust, 235
need for affirmation, 578
original unity. *See* original unity
receptivity of the gift, 180
responsibility of man toward, 204
as subject of truth and love, 148–53
subjection to lust, 196–97

women's liberation movement, 196

Word of God. *See also* Incarnate Christ
creation through, 36

words of consent as sign of marriage, 463–67

works of the flesh, 259–61

Y

Yahwist creation account, 90–92
subjectivity in, 98–99

"your maker is your husband," 410–12

youthfulness, desire for, 396–97

If you would like to attend one of Christopher West's week-long courses on the Theology of the Body, visit tobinstitute.org

BOOKS & MEDIA

The Daughters of St. Paul operate book and media centers at the following addresses. Visit, call or write the one nearest you today, or find us on the World Wide Web, www.pauline.org.

CALIFORNIA

3908 Sepulveda Blvd, Culver City, CA 90230	310-397-8676
935 Brewster Avenue, Redwood City, CA 94063	650-369-4230
5945 Balboa Avenue, San Diego, CA 92111	858-565-9181

FLORIDA

145 S.W. 107th Avenue, Miami, FL 33174	305-559-6715

HAWAII

1143 Bishop Street, Honolulu, HI 96813	808-521-2731
Neighbor Islands call:	866-521-2731

ILLINOIS

172 North Michigan Avenue, Chicago, IL 60601	312-346-4228

LOUISIANA

4403 Veterans Memorial Blvd, Metairie, LA 70006	504-887-7631

MASSACHUSETTS

885 Providence Hwy, Dedham, MA 02026	781-326-5385

MISSOURI

9804 Watson Road, St. Louis, MO 63126	314-965-3512

NEW YORK

64 W. 38th Street, New York, NY 10018	212-754-1110

PENNSYLVANIA

Philadelphia—relocating	215-676-9494

SOUTH CAROLINA

243 King Street, Charleston, SC 29401	843-577-0175

VIRGINIA

1025 King Street, Alexandria, VA 22314	703-549-3806

CANADA

3022 Dufferin Street, Toronto, ON M6B 3T5	416-781-9131

¡También somos su fuente para libros, videos y música en español!